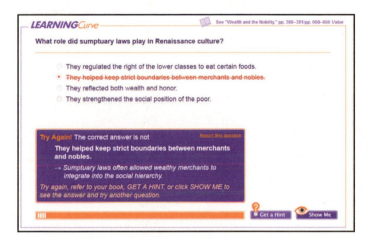

Understanding
Western Society

A HISTORY   SECOND EDITION

VOLUME 2 **From the Age of Exploration to the Present**

John P. McKay
University of Illinois at Urbana-Champaign

Clare Haru Crowston
University of Illinois at Urbana-Champaign

Merry E. Wiesner-Hanks
University of Wisconsin–Milwaukee

Joe Perry
Georgia State University

Bedford / St. Martin's
Boston • New York

For Bedford/St. Martin's

Vice President, Editorial, Macmillan Higher Education Humanities: Edwin Hill
Publisher for History: Michael Rosenberg
Senior Executive Editor for History and Technology: William J. Lombardo
Director of Development for History: Jane Knetzger
Developmental Editor: Kathryn Abbott
Production Editor: Annette Pagliaro Sweeney
Senior Production Supervisor: Dennis Conroy
Executive Marketing Manager: Sandra McGuire
Project Manager: John Shannon, Jouve
Editorial Assistant: Emily DiPietro
Cartography: Mapping Specialists, Ltd.
Photo Researcher: Carole Frohlich and Elisa Gallagher, The Visual Connection Image Research, Inc.
Director of Rights and Permissions: Hilary Newman
Senior Art Director: Anna Palchik
Cover Design: William Boardman
Cover Art: A Venetian al Fresco, 1885 (oil on canvas), Logsdail, William (1859–1944) / Private Collection / Christie's Images / Bridgeman Images.
Composition: Jouve
Printing and Binding: RR Donnelley and Sons

Manufactured in the United States of America.

9 8 7 6 5
f e d c b

For information, write: Bedford/St. Martin's, 75 Arlington Street, Boston, MA 02116 (617-399-4000)

ISBN: 978-1-4576-8675-7 (Combined Edition)
ISBN: 978-1-4576-9490-5 (Volume I)
ISBN: 978-1-4576-9491-2 (Volume II)

Understanding
Western Society

A HISTORY

VOLUME 2

How to use this book to figure out what's really important

The **chapter title** tells you the subject of the chapter and identifies the time span that will be covered.

The **opening question** and **chapter introduction** identify the most important themes, events, and people that will be explored in the chapter.

15
ABSOLUTISM AND CONSTITUTIONALISM
CA. 1589–1725

> **What were the most important political trends in seventeenth-century Europe?** Chapter 15 examines seventeenth-century political developments. The seventeenth century was a period of crisis and transformation in Europe. Agricultural and manufacturing slumps led to food shortages and shrinking population rates. Religious and dynastic conflicts led to almost constant war, visiting violence and destruction on ordinary people and reshaping European states. While absolutism emerged as the solution to these challenges in many European states, a small minority, most notably England and the Dutch Republic, adopted a different path, placing sovereignty in the hands of privileged groups rather than the Crown.

 **LearningCurve**
After reading the chapter, use LearningCurve to retain what you've read.

444

Memorizing facts and dates for a history class won't get you very far. That's because history isn't just about "facts." This textbook is designed to help you focus on what's truly significant in the history of Western societies and to give you practice thinking like a historian.

Life at the French Royal Court. King Louis XIV receives foreign ambassadors to celebrate a peace treaty. (Erich Lessing/Art Resource, NY)

> What made the seventeenth century an "age of crisis"?

> Why did France rise and Spain fall during this period?

> What explains the rise of absolutism in Prussia and Austria?

> What were the distinctive features of Russian and Ottoman absolutism?

> How and why did the constitutional state triumph in the Dutch Republic and England?

> What was the baroque style in art and music, and where was it popular?

The **chapter-opening questions** are also the questions that open each new section of the chapters and will be addressed in turn on the following pages. You should think about answers to these as you read.

Each section has tools that help you focus on what's important.

The **question in red** asks about the specific topic being discussed in this section. Pause to answer each one after you read the section.

> ## What were the distinctive features of Russian and Ottoman absolutism?

Peter the Great This compelling portrait by Grigory Musikiysky captures the strength and determination of the warrior-tsar in 1723, after more than three decades of personal rule. In his hand Peter holds the scepter, symbol of royal sovereignty, and across his breastplate is draped an ermine fur, a mark of honor. In the background are the battleships of Russia's new Baltic fleet and the famous St. Peter and St. Paul Fortress that Peter built in St. Petersburg. (Hermitage/St. Petersburg, Russia/ Bridgeman Art Library)

A FAVORITE PARLOR GAME of nineteenth-century intellectuals was debating whether Russia was a Western (European) or non-Western (Asian) society. This question was particularly fascinating because it was unanswerable. To this day, Russia differs from the West in some fundamental ways, though its history has paralleled that of the West in other aspects.

There was no question in the minds of Europeans, however, that the Ottomans were outsiders. Even absolutist rulers disdained Ottoman sultans as cruel and tyrannical despots. Despite stereotypes, however, the Ottoman Empire was in many ways more tolerant than its Western counterparts, providing protection and security to other religions while steadfastly maintaining the Muslim faith. Flexibility and openness to other ideas and practices were sources of strength for the empire.

The Mongol Yoke and the Rise of Moscow

The two-hundred-year period of rule by the Mongol khan (king) set the stage for the rise of absolutist Russia. The Mongols, a group of nomadic tribes from present-day Mongolia, established an empire that, at its height, stretched from Korea to

CHAPTER LOCATOR | What made the seventeenth century an "age of crisis"? | Why did France rise and Spain fall during this period?

The Ottomans also employed a distinctive form of government administration. The top ranks of the bureaucracy were staffed by the sultan's slave corps. Because Muslim law prohibited enslaving other Muslims, the sultan's agents purchased slaves along the borders of the empire. Within the realm, the sultan levied a "tax" of one thousand to three thousand male children on the conquered Christian populations in the Balkans every year. These young slaves were raised in Turkey as Muslims and were trained to fight and to administer. The most talented Ottoman slaves rose to the top of the bureaucracy, where they might acquire wealth and power. The less fortunate formed the core of the sultan's army, the janissary corps. These highly organized and efficient troops gave the Ottomans a formidable advantage in war with western Europeans. By 1683, service in the janissary corps had become so prestigious that the sultan ceased recruitment by force, and it became a volunteer army open to Christians and Muslims.

The Ottomans divided their subjects into religious communities, and each *millet*, or "nation," enjoyed autonomous self-government under its religious leaders. The Ottoman Empire recognized Orthodox Christians, Jews, Armenian Christians, and Muslims as distinct millets. The millet system created a powerful bond between the Ottoman ruling class and religious leaders, who supported the sultan's rule in return for extensive authority over their own communities.

Istanbul (known outside the empire by its original name, Constantinople) was the capital of the empire. The "old palace" was for the sultan's female family members. The newer Topkapi palace was where officials worked and young slaves trained for future administrative or military careers. Sultans married women of the highest social standing while keeping many concubines of low rank. To prevent the elite families into which they married from acquiring influence over the government, sultans procreated only with their concubines and not with official wives. They also adopted a policy of allowing each concubine to produce only one male heir. At a young age, each son went to govern a province of the empire accompanied by his mother. These practices were intended to stabilize power and prevent a recurrence of the civil wars of the late fourteenth and early fifteenth centuries.

Sultan Suleiman undid these policies when he boldly married his concubine, a former slave of Polish origin named Hürrem, and had several children with her. (See "Individuals in Society: Hürrem," page 472.) Starting with Suleiman, imperial wives began to take on more power. Marriages were arranged between sultans' daughters and high-ranking servants, creating powerful new members of the imperial household. Over time, the sultan's exclusive authority waned in favor of a more bureaucratic administration.

janissary corps
▶ The core of the sultan's army, composed of slave conscripts from non-Muslim parts of the empire; after 1683, it became a volunteer force.

millet system
▶ A system used by the Ottomans whereby subjects were divided into religious communities, with each millet (nation) enjoying autonomous self-government under its religious leaders.

Key terms in the margins give you background on important people, ideas, and events. Use these for reference while you read, but also think about which terms are emphasized and why they matter.

QUICK REVIEW <

What were the commonalities and differences between the development of absolutism in the Russian and Ottoman Empires?

The **quick review** helps you check your recall of the section before you resume reading.

| What explains the rise of absolutism in Prussia and Austria? | What were the distinctive features of Russian and Ottoman absolutism? | How and why did the constitutional state triumph in the Dutch Republic and England? | What was the baroque style in art and music, and where was it popular? | ☑ LearningCurve Check what you know. |

471

The **chapter locator** at the bottom of the page puts this section in the context of the chapter as a whole, so you can see how this section relates to what's coming next.

The Chapter Study Guide provides a process that will build your understanding and your historical skills.

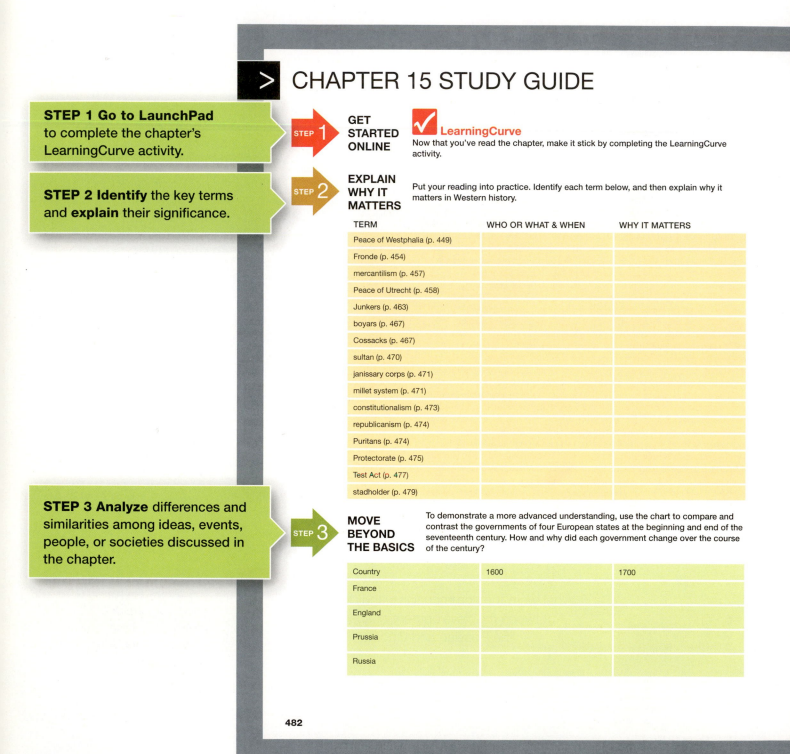

CHAPTER 15 STUDY GUIDE

STEP 1 Go to LaunchPad to complete the chapter's LearningCurve activity.

STEP 1

GET STARTED ONLINE

✓ **LearningCurve**

Now that you've read the chapter, make it stick by completing the LearningCurve activity.

STEP 2 Identify the key terms and **explain** their significance.

STEP 2

EXPLAIN WHY IT MATTERS

Put your reading into practice. Identify each term below, and then explain why it matters in Western history.

TERM	WHO OR WHAT & WHEN	WHY IT MATTERS
Peace of Westphalia (p. 449)		
Fronde (p. 454)		
mercantilism (p. 457)		
Peace of Utrecht (p. 458)		
Junkers (p. 463)		
boyars (p. 467)		
Cossacks (p. 467)		
sultan (p. 470)		
janissary corps (p. 471)		
millet system (p. 471)		
constitutionalism (p. 473)		
republicanism (p. 474)		
Puritans (p. 474)		
Protectorate (p. 475)		
Test Act (p. 477)		
stadholder (p. 479)		

STEP 3 Analyze differences and similarities among ideas, events, people, or societies discussed in the chapter.

STEP 3

MOVE BEYOND THE BASICS

To demonstrate a more advanced understanding, use the chart to compare and contrast the governments of four European states at the beginning and end of the seventeenth century. How and why did each government change over the course of the century?

Country	1600	1700
France		
England		
Prussia		
Russia		

STEP 4 **PUT IT ALL TOGETHER**   Now, take a step back and try to explain the big picture. Remember to use specific examples from the chapter in your answers.

ABSOLUTISM

▸ What common challenges were faced by absolutist monarchs? How did the rulers of France, Austria, and Prussia respond to these challenges?

▸ What social and economic trends accompanied the rise of absolutism in eastern Europe?

CONSTITUTIONALISM

▸ Why did the efforts of English monarchs to build an absolutist state fail?

▸ In what ways was the Dutch Republic unique among seventeenth-century states?

RUSSIA AND THE OTTOMAN EMPIRE

▸ How did the Russian tsars gain control over Russia's landowning elite?

▸ How did the Ottoman absolutist state differ from its European counterparts?

MAKE CONNECTIONS

▸ How did the conflicts and tensions unleashed by the Reformation shape seventeenth-century political developments?

▸ What steps were taken during the seventeenth century toward the emergence of the modern nation-state?

> IN YOUR OWN WORDS

Imagine that you must give an oral report to the class answering the following question: **What were the most important political trends in seventeenth-century Europe?** What would be the most important points and why?

STEP 4 Answer the big-picture questions using specific examples or evidence from the chapter.

ACTIVE RECITATION Explain how you would answer the chapter-opening question in your own words to make sure you have a firm grasp of the most important themes and events of the chapter.

483

PREFACE: Why This Book This Way

U*nderstanding Western Society* grew out of many conversations we have had among ourselves and with other instructors about the teaching and learning of history. We knew that instructors wanted a Western Civilization text that introduced students to the broad sweep of history but that also re-created the lives of ordinary men and women in appealing human terms. We knew that instructors wanted a text that presented cutting-edge scholarship in new fields of historical inquiry. We also knew that many instructors wanted a text that would help students focus as they read, keep their interest in the material, and encourage them to learn historical thinking skills. It is our hope that *Understanding Western Society* addresses all of these concerns.

New Tools for Teaching and Measuring Outcomes

With requests for clear and transparent learning outcomes coming from all quarters and with students who bring increasingly diverse levels of skills to class, even veteran teachers can find preparing for today's courses a trying matter. The introduction of **LaunchPad** to the second edition offers a breakthrough for instructors. With LaunchPad we have reconceived the textbook as a suite of tools in multiple formats that allows each format do what it does best to capture students' interest and help instructors create meaningful lessons. But one of the best benefits is that instructors using LaunchPad will find they have a number of assessment tools that allow them to see what their students do and don't know and to measure student achievement all in one convenient space. For example, LaunchPad comes with **LearningCurve**—an adaptive learning tool that garners over a 90 percent student satisfaction rate and helps students master book content. When LearningCurve is assigned, the grade book results show instructors where the entire class or individual students may be struggling, which in turn allows instructors to adjust lectures and course activities accordingly—a benefit not only for traditional classes but invaluable for hybrid, online, and newer "flipped" classes as well. In addition, not only can instructors assign all of the questions that appear in the print book and view the responses in the grade book, they have the option to assign automatically graded multiple-choice questions for all of the book features. Plus many more prebuilt **activities to foster critical reading and chronological reading skills** are available in LaunchPad, along with a **test building tool and additional primary sources** that all can be used for customized assignments than will report into the grade book for **simplified assessment**. With LaunchPad for *Understanding Western Society*, we make the tough job of teaching simpler by providing everything an instructor needs in one convenient space so instructors can set and achieve the learning outcomes they desire. To learn more about the benefits of LearningCurve and LaunchPad, see the "Versions and Supplements" section.

Understanding Western Society: Bringing the Past to Life for Students

At the point when the parent text, *A History of Western Society*, was first conceptualized, social history was dramatically changing the ways we understood the past, and the original authors decided to create a book that would re-create the lives of ordinary people in appealing human terms, while also giving major economic, political, cultural, and intellectual developments the attention they unquestionably deserve. We three new authors remain committed to advancing this vision for today's classroom, with a broader definition of social history that brings the original idea into the twenty-first century.

History as a discipline never stands still, and over the last several decades, cultural history has joined social history as a source of dynamism. The focus on cultural history has been heightened in the second edition in a way that highlights the interplay between men's and women's lived experiences and the ways men and women reflect on these experiences to create meaning. We know that engaging students' interest in the past is often a challenge, but we also know that the text's hallmark approach—the emphasis on daily life and individual experience in its social and cultural dimensions—connects with students and makes the past vivid and accessible.

Additional "Life" Chapters

Although social and cultural history can be found in every chapter, they are particularly emphasized in the acclaimed "Life" chapters that have always distinguished this book. In response to popular demand by reviewers of the previous edition, these have been increased to five in this edition and now include Chapter 4: Life in the Hellenistic World, 336–30 B.C.E. and Chapter 30: Life in an Age of Globalization, 1990 to the Present, which join Chapter 10: Life in Villages and Cities of the High Middle Ages, 1000–1300; Chapter 18: Life in the Era of Expansion, 1650–1800; and Chapter 22: Life in the Emerging Urban Society, 1840–1914.

An Inquiry-based Model Designed for Understanding

By employing innovative pedagogy, we believe that *Understanding Western Society* helps students not only understand the book's major developments but also begin to grasp the question-driven methodology that is at the heart of the historian's craft. Each chapter opens with a **NEW chapter-opening question** that drives students toward the overarching themes of the chapter, followed by a **brief chapter introduction** that identifies the most important events and people to be discussed. **Section-opening headings** expressed as questions and **section-ending quick review questions** further model the kinds of questions historians ask and help students engage in inquiry-based reading and understanding.

Chapter Study Guides Designed for Active Learning

At the core of *Understanding Western Society's* unique pedagogical features are the revised **Chapter Study Guides** that provide a carefully structured four-step process to help students build deep understanding of the chapter material. In **Step 1**, students go to LaunchPad to complete the LearningCurve activity, to ensure that they have a grasp of the basic content and concepts of the chapter. In **Step 2**, students not only identify the chapter's key terms but also explain why each matters. In **Step 3**, they begin to apply their understanding of the chapter material through activities that ask them to consider comparison, change over time, or cause and effect. In **Step 4**, analytical and synthetic questions require students to engage in higher-order historical thinking. And, finally, in an active recitation exercise, students **answer the chapter-opening question** to realize their understanding of the chapter fully. In LaunchPad, instructors can assign the **NEW Guided Reading Exercise** for each chapter, which prompts students to read actively to collect information that answers a broad analytic question central to the chapter as a whole.

Primary Sources for Teaching Critical Thinking and Analysis

New assignable **Online Document Projects** in LaunchPad are tied closely to each chapter of *Understanding Western Society*. Each assignment, based on either the "Individuals in Society" feature described below or on key developments from the "Life" chapters (Chapters 4, 10, 18, 22, and 30), prompts students to explore a key question through analysis of multiple sources. Chapter 14, for example, asks students to analyze documents on the complexities of race, identity, and slavery in the early modern era to shed light on the conditions that made the story of Juan de Pareja, a mixed-race man who went from a life in slavery to a free artist, possible. The assignments feature a wealth of textual and visual sources as well as video and audio. Assignments based on the "Individuals and Society" feature include three to four documents in each assignment, while those based on the "Life" chapters include six to eight documents. These Online Document Projects provide instructors with a rich variety of assignment options that encourage students to draw their own conclusions, with the help of short-answer questions, multiple-choice questions that provide instant feedback, and a final essay assignment that asks students to use the sources in creative ways.

We have also revised our **primary source documents collection**, *Sources for Western Society*, to add more visual sources and to align the readings closely with the chapter topics and themes. Each chapter of the reader also includes a set of related documents called "Sources in Conversation." The documents are now available in a fully assignable and assessable electronic format within each LaunchPad unit, and the accompanying multiple-choice questions measure comprehension and hold students accountable for their reading.

Student Engagement with Biography

In addition to the primary source program, we are proud of the unique boxed essay feature in each chapter—**Individuals in Society**—that personalizes larger developments and makes them tangible. These popular biographical essays offer brief studies of individuals or groups, informing students about the societies in which they lived. We have found that readers empathize with these human beings as they themselves seek to define their own identities. The spotlighting of individuals, both famous and obscure, perpetuates the book's continued attention to cultural and intellectual developments, highlights human agency, and reflects changing interests within the historical profession as well as the development of "micro-history." **NEW** features include essays on Anna Jansz of Rotterdam, an Anabaptist martyr; Hürrem, a concubine who became a powerful figure in the Ottoman Empire during the sixteenth century; and Rebecca Protten, a former slave and leader in the Moravian missionary movement. As mentioned previously, the majority of these features are tied to **NEW Online Document Projects**, available in LaunchPad, that allow students to explore further the historical conditions in which these individuals lived.

Geographic and Visual Literacy

We recognize students' difficulties with geography and visual analysis, and the new edition retains our **Mapping the Past map activities** and **Picturing the Past visual activities**. Included in each chapter, these activities ask students to analyze the map or visual and make connections to the larger processes discussed in the narrative, giving them valuable practice in reading and interpreting maps and images. In LaunchPad, they are assignable, and students can submit their work. Throughout the textbook and online in LaunchPad, more than **75 full-size maps** illustrate major developments in the chapter. In addition, **50 spot maps** are embedded in the narrative to show specific areas under discussion.

Chronological Reasoning

To help students make comparisons, understand change over time, and see relationships among contemporaneous events, each chapter begins with a **chapter chronology** that reviews major developments discussed in the chapter. This chronology, available from every page in LaunchPad, allows students to compare developments over the centuries.

Better-Prepared Students

To help students fully understand their reading and come to class prepared, instructors who adopt LaunchPad for *Understanding Western Society* can assign the **LearningCurve** formative assessment activities. This online learning tool is popular with students because it helps them rehearse content at their own pace in a nonthreatening, game-like environment. LearningCurve is also popular with instructors because the reporting features allow them to track overall class trends and spot topics that are giving students trouble so they can adjust their lectures and class activities. When LearningCurve is assigned, students come to class better prepared and instructors can better evaluate and adjust their classes.

To further encourage students to read and assimilate the text fully as well as measure how well they do this, instructors can assign the **new multiple-choice summative quizzes** in LaunchPad, where they are automatically graded. These secure tests not only encourage students to study the book, they can be assigned at specific intervals as high-stakes testing and thus provide another means for analyzing class performance.

Updated Organization and Coverage

To meet the demands of the evolving course, we took a close and critical look at the book's structure and have made changes in the organization of chapters to reflect the way the course is taught today. Most notably, in addition to consolidating some coverage in the two new "Life" chapters described above, we have combined the three chapters on the High Middle Ages in the previous edition into two (Chapters 9 and 10), restructuring and in some cases shortening sections but retaining all key concepts and topics, resulting in one fewer chapter overall. Chapter 9 now focuses more tightly on political, legal, and institutional developments in church and state, and Chapter 10 on the life of both villagers and city folk.

This edition is also enhanced by the incorporation of a wealth of new scholarship and subject areas that immerse students in the dynamic and ongoing work of history. Chapters 1 through 6 have been revised intensively to incorporate the exciting cross-disciplinary scholarship that has emerged over the last several decades on the Paleolithic and Neolithic, river-valley civilizations, and the ancient Mediterranean. For example, archaeologists working at Göbekli Tepe in present-day Turkey have unearthed rings of massive, multi-ton, elaborately carved limestone pillars built around 9000 B.C.E. by groups of foragers, which has led to a rethinking of the links among culture, religion, and the initial development of agriculture. Similarly, new research on the peoples of Mesopotamia, based on cuneiform writing along with other sources, has led scholars to revise the view that they were fatalistic, and instead to emphasize that Mesopotamians generally anticipated being well treated by the gods if they behaved morally. Throughout these chapters, new material on cross-cultural connections, the impact of technologies, and changing social relationships has been added, particularly in Chapter 4, which has been recast as "Life in the Hellenistic World." Other additions include an expanded discussion of the historiography of the fall of the Roman Empire (Chapter 7); new material on the reconquista (Chapter 9); recent ideas on the impact of empire on the Scientific Revolution (Chapter 16); more on the experiences of African Americans, Native Americans, and women in the revolutionary era (Chapter 19); significant updates to the Industrial Revolution coverage, including increased attention to the global context (Chapter 20); revised treatment of ideologies and Romanticism (Chapter 21); new coverage of the popular appeal of nationalism (Chapter 23); new material on orientalism and European imperialism (Chapter 24); extensive updates on the Cold War (Chapter 28); up-to-date coverage of contemporary events in the final chapter, now called "Life in the Age of Globalization, 1990 to the Present," including the Euro crisis, issues surrounding immigration and Muslims in Europe, and the Arab Spring (Chapter 30).

Acknowledgments

It is a pleasure to thank the many instructors who critiqued the parent textbook, *A History of Western Society*, Eleventh Edition. Their feedback helped inform the shape this book has taken.

William M. Abbott, Fairfield University
Joseph Avitable, Quinnipiac University
Dudley Belcher, Tri-County Technical College

Amy Bix, Iowa State University

Nancy Bjorklund, Fullerton College

Robert Blackey, California State University, San Bernardino

Stephen Blumm, Montgomery County Community College

Robert Brennan, Cape Fear Community College

Daniel Bubb, Gonzaga University

Jeff Burson, Georgia Southern University

George Carson, Central Bible College

Michael Cavey, Northern Virginia Community College

Marie Therese Champagne, University of West Florida

Mark W. Chavalas, University of Wisconsin-LaCrosse

David Cherry, Montana State University, Bozeman

Benzion Chinn, Ohio State University

Thomas Colbert, Marshalltown Community College

Elizabeth Collins, Triton College

Amy Colon, Sullivan County Community College

Kristen Cornelis, Community Colleges of Spokane, Institute for Extended Learning

Michael H. Creswell, Florida State University

Andrea DeKoter, State University of New York at Cortland

Donna Donald, Liberty University

Kurt J. Eberly, Tidewater Community College

John Ebley, Anne Arundel Community College

Christopher Ferguson, Auburn University

Robert Figueira, Lander University

Paula Findlen, Stanford University

Jennifer Foray, Purdue University

Laura Gathagan, State University of New York at Cortland

Stephen Gibson, Allegany College of Maryland

Gregory Golden, Rhode Island College

Jack Goldstone, George Mason University

Chuck Goodwin, Illinois Valley Community College

Dolores Grapsas, New River Community College

Robert Grasso, Monmouth University

Robert H. Greene, University of Montana

Edward Gutierrez, University of Hartford

David Halahmy, Cypress College

Michael Harkins, Harper College

David M. Head, John Tyler Community College

Jeff Horn, Manhattan College

Barry Jordan, Cape Fear Community College

Cheryl L. Kajs, Pellissippi State Community College

Michael Kennedy, High Point University

Michele Kinney, Strayer University

Willem Klooster, Clark University

Pamela Koenig, Seminole State College

Roy G. Koepp, University of Nebraska at Kearney

James Krapfl, McGill University

Andrew E. Larsen, Marquette University

Kenneth Loiselle, Rice University

Susan Mattern, University of Georgia

Maureen A. McCormick, Florida State College at Jacksonville

James McIntyre, Moraine Valley Community College

Deena McKinney, East Georgia College

Linda A. McMillin, Susquehanna University

Jennifer McNabb, Western Illinois University

Michael Meng, Clemson University

Scott Merriman, Troy University

Ryan Messenger, Monroe Community College/Genesee Community College

Byron J. Nakamura, Southern Connecticut State University

Jeannine Olson, Rhode Island College

Lisa Ossian, Des Moines Area Community College

Jotham Parsons, Duquesne University

Margaret Peacock, The University of Alabama

Kathy L. Pearson, Old Dominion University

Amanda Podany, California State Polytechnic University, Pomona

Ann Pond, Bishop State Community College

Matthew Restall, Pennsylvania State University

Michael D. Richards, Northern Virginia Community College

Jason Ripper, Everett Community College

Russell J. Rockefeller, Anne Arundel Community College

Leonard N. Rosenband, Utah State University

Mark Edward Ruff, Saint Louis University

Ernest Rugenstein, Hudson Valley Community College

Anne Ruszkiewicz, Sullivan County Community College

Wendy A. Sarti, Oakton Community College

Linda Scherr, Mercer County Community College

Elise Shelton, Trident Technical College

Chris Shepard, Trident Technical College

Robert Shipley, Widener University

Sherri Singer, Alamance Community College

Daniel Snell, University of Oklahoma

Steven Soper, The University of Georgia

Susan Souza-Mort, Bristol Community College

James Taw, Valdosta State University

Alfred T. Terrell, Yuba College

Timothy Thibodeau, Nazareth College

Karl Valois, University of Connecticut, Torrington

Liana Vardi, University at Buffalo, The State University of New York

Joseph Villano, Indian River State College

Gregory Vitarbo, Meredith College

David Weiland, Collin County Community College

Scott White, Scottsdale Community College

Pamela Wolfe, Yeshiva of Greater Washington

James Wright, Triton College

Sergei Zhuk, Ball State University.

It is also a pleasure to thank the many people who have assisted us over the years, first at Houghton Mifflin and now at Bedford/St. Martin's and Macmillan

Education. At Bedford/St. Martin's and Macmillan Education, these include developmental editors Kathryn Abbott and Annette Fantasia, associate editor Emily DiPietro, executive editor Traci Crowell, director of development Jane Knetzger, publisher for history Mary Dougherty, photo researcher Carole Frohlich, production editor Annette Pagliaro Sweeney, cover designer Billy Boardman, market development manager Katherine Bates, executive marketing manager Sandi McGuire, and marketing assistant Alex Kaufman. We would like to thank the staff at Jouve North America for composition and production services.

Many of our colleagues at the University of Illinois, the University of Wisconsin–Milwaukee, and Georgia State University continue to provide information and stimulation, often without even knowing it. We thank them for it. We also thank the many students over the years with whom we have used earlier editions of this book. Their reactions and opinions helped shape the revisions to this edition, and we hope it remains worthy of the ultimate praise that they bestowed on it, that it's "not boring like most textbooks." Merry Wiesner-Hanks would, as always, also like to thank her husband Neil, without whom work on this project would not be possible. Clare Haru Crowston thanks her husband Ali and her children Lili, Reza, and Kian, who are joyous reminders of the vitality of life that we try to showcase in this book. Joe Perry thanks his colleagues and students at Georgia State for their intellectual stimulation and is grateful to Joyce de Vries for her unstinting support and encouragement.

Each of us has benefited from the criticism of our coauthors, although each of us assumes responsibility for what he or she has written. Merry Wiesner-Hanks has intensively reworked and revised John Buckler's Chapters 1 through 6 and has revised Chapters 7 through 13; Clare Crowston has written and revised Chapters 14 through 19 and took responsibility for John McKay's Chapter 20; and Joe Perry took responsibility for John McKay's Chapters 21 through 24 and has written and revised Chapters 25 through 30.

We'd especially like to thank the founding authors, John P. McKay, Bennett D. Hill, and John Buckler, for their enduring contributions and for their faith in each of us to carry on their legacy.

Clare Haru Crowston
Merry E. Wiesner-Hanks
Joe Perry

VERSIONS AND SUPPLEMENTS

Adopters of *Understanding Western Society* and their students have access to abundant print and digital resources and tools, including documents, assessment and presentation materials, the acclaimed Bedford Series in History and Culture volumes, and much more. And for the first time, the full-featured LaunchPad course space provides access to the narrative with all assignment and assessment opportunities at the ready. See below for more information, visit the book's catalog site at **bedfordstmartins.com/mckaywestunderstanding/catalog**, or contact your local Bedford/St. Martin's sales representative.

Get the Right Version for Your Class

To accommodate different course lengths and course budgets, *Understanding Western Society* is available in several different formats, including three-hole-punched, loose-leaf Budget Books versions and low-priced PDF e-books, which include the *Bedford e-Book to Go* from our Web site and other PDF e-books from other commercial sources. And for the best value of all, package a new print book with LaunchPad at no additional charge to get the best each format offers—a print version for easy portability and reading with a LaunchPad interactive e-book and course space with loads of additional assignment and assessment options.

- **Combined Volume** (Chapters 1–30): available in paperback, loose-leaf, and e-book formats and in LaunchPad
- **Volume 1, From Antiquity to the Enlightenment** (Chapters 1–16): available in paperback, loose-leaf, and e-book formats and in LaunchPad
- **Volume 2, From the Age of Exploration to the Present** (Chapters 14–30): available in paperback, loose-leaf, and e-book formats and in LaunchPad

As noted below, any of these volumes can be packaged with additional titles for a discount. To get ISBNs for discount packages, see the online catalog at **bedfordstmartins.com/mckaywestunderstanding/catalog** or contact your Bedford/St. Martin's representative.

NEW Assign LaunchPad — A Content-rich and Assessment-ready Interactive e-Book and Course Space

Available for discount purchase on its own or for packaging with new books at no additional charge, LaunchPad is a breakthrough solution for today's courses. Intuitive and easy to use for students and instructors alike, LaunchPad is ready to use as is, but it can be edited, customized with your own material, and assigned in seconds. *LaunchPad for Understanding Western Society* includes Bedford/St. Martin's high-quality content all in one place, including the full interactive e-book and the *Sources for Western Society* documents collection, plus LearningCurve formative quizzing, guided reading activities designed to help students read actively for key concepts, additional primary sources, images, videos, chapter summative quizzes, and more.

Through a wealth of formative and summative assessments, including short answer, essay questions, multiple-choice quizzing, and the adaptive learning program of LearningCurve (see the full description ahead), students gain confidence and get into their reading *before* class. Map and visual activities engage students with visual analysis and critical thinking as they work through each unit, while special boxed features become more meaningful through automatically graded multiple-choice exercises and short-answer questions that prompt students to analyze their reading.

LaunchPad integrates easily with course management systems, and with fast ways to build assignments; rearrange chapters; and add new pages, sections, and links, it lets teachers build the courses they want to teach and hold students accountable. For more information, visit **launchpadworks.com** or, to arrange a demo, contact us at **history@bedfordstmartins.com**.

✅ NEW Assign LearningCurve So Your Students Come to Class Prepared

Students using LaunchPad receive access to LearningCurve for *Understanding Western Society*. Assigning LearningCurve in place of reading quizzes is easy for instructors, and the reporting features help instructors track overall class trends and spot topics that are giving students trouble so they can adjust their lectures and class activities. This online learning tool is popular with students because it was designed to help them rehearse content at their own pace in a nonthreatening, game-like environment. The feedback for wrong answers provides instructional coaching and sends students back to the book for review. Students answer as many questions as necessary to reach a target score, with repeated chances to revisit material they haven't mastered. When LearningCurve is assigned, students come to class better prepared.

Take Advantage of Instructor Resources

Bedford/St. Martin's has developed a rich array of teaching resources for this book and for this course. They range from lecture and presentation materials and assessment tools to course management options. Most can be found in LaunchPad or can be downloaded or ordered at **bedfordstmartins.com/mckaywestunderstanding /catalog**.

▶ **Instructor's Resource Manual.** The instructor's resource manual offers both experienced and first-time instructors tools for preparing lectures and running discussions. It includes chapter content learning objectives, annotated chapter outlines, teaching strategies, and a guide to chapter-specific supplements available for the text, plus suggestions on how to get the most out of LearningCurve and a survival guide for first-time teaching assistants.

▶ **Guide to Changing Editions.** Designed to facilitate an instructor's transition from the previous edition of *Understanding Western Society* to the current edition, this guide presents an overview of major changes as well as of changes in each chapter.

▶ **Computerized Test Bank.** The test bank includes a mix of fresh, carefully crafted multiple-choice, short-answer, and essay questions for each chapter. It also contains volume-wide essay questions. All questions appear in Microsoft Word format and in easy-to-use test bank software that allows instructors to add, edit, re-sequence, and print questions and answers. Instructors can also export questions into a variety of formats, including Blackboard, Desire2Learn, and Moodle.

▶ *The Bedford Lecture Kit:* **PowerPoint Maps and Images.** Look good and save time with *The Bedford Lecture Kit*. These presentation materials are download-able individually from the Instructor Resources tab at **bedfordstmartins.com /mckaywestunderstanding/catalog**. They include all maps, figures, and select images from the textbook in JPEG and PowerPoint formats.

Package and Save Your Students Money

For information on free packages and discounts worth up to 50%, visit **bedfordstmartins.com/mckaywestunderstanding/catalog**, or contact your local Bedford/St. Martin's sales representative. The products that follow all qualify for discount packaging.

▶ *Sources for Western Society,* **Third Edition.** This primary-source collection— available in Volume 1 and Volume 2 versions—provides a revised and expanded selection of sources to accompany *Understanding Western Society*, Second Edition. Each chapter features five or six written and visual sources by well-known figures and ordinary individuals alike. With over fifty new selections—including a dozen new visual sources—and enhanced pedagogy throughout, students are given the tools to engage critically with canonical and lesser-known sources and prominent and ordinary voices. Each chapter includes a "Sources in Conversation" feature that presents differing views on key topics. This companion reader is an exceptional value for students and offers plenty of assignment options for instructors. Available free when packaged with the print text and included in the LaunchPad e-book. Also available on its own as a downloadable PDF e-book.

▶ **The Bedford Series in History and Culture.** More than 100 titles in this highly praised series combine first-rate scholarship, historical narrative, and important primary documents for undergraduate courses. Each book is brief, inexpensive, and focused on a specific topic or period. For a complete list of titles, visit **bedfordstmartins.com/history/series**.

▶ *Rand McNally Atlas of Western Civilization.* This collection of over fifty full-color maps highlights social, political, and cross-cultural change and interaction from classical Greece and Rome to the postindustrial Western world. Each map is thoroughly indexed for fast reference.

▶ *The Bedford Glossary for European History.* This handy supplement for the survey course gives students historically contextualized definitions for hundreds of terms—from *Abbasids* to *Zionism*—that they will encounter in lectures, reading, and exams.

▶ **Trade Books.** Titles published by sister companies Hill and Wang; Farrar, Straus and Giroux; Henry Holt and Company; St. Martin's Press; Picador; and Palgrave Macmillan are available at a 50% discount when packaged with Bedford/St. Martin's textbooks. For more information, visit **bedfordstmartins.com/tradeup**.

▶ *A Pocket Guide to Writing in History.* This portable and affordable reference tool by Mary Lynn Rampolla provides reading, writing, and research advice useful to students in all history courses. Concise yet comprehensive advice on approaching typical history assignments, developing critical reading skills, writing effective history papers, conducting research, using and documenting sources, and avoiding plagiarism—enhanced with practical tips and examples throughout—have made this slim reference a bestseller.

▶ *A Student's Guide to History.* This complete guide to success in any history course provides the practical help students need to be successful. In addition to introducing students to the nature of the discipline, author Jules Benjamin teaches a wide range of skills, from preparing for exams to approaching common writing assignments, and explains the research and documentation process with plentiful examples.

▶ *The Social Dimension of Western Civilization.* Combining current scholarship with classic pieces, this reader's forty-eight secondary sources, compiled by Richard M. Golden, hook students with the fascinating and often surprising details of how everyday Western people worked, ate, played, celebrated, worshiped, married, procreated, fought, persecuted, and died.

BRIEF CONTENTS

CONTENTS

14

EUROPEAN EXPLORATION AND CONQUEST

1450–1650 *410*

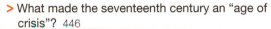

17

THE EXPANSION OF EUROPE

1650–1800 *516*

18

LIFE IN THE ERA OF EXPANSION

1650–1800 *546*

19
REVOLUTIONS IN POLITICS

1775–1815   *576*

20
THE REVOLUTION IN ENERGY AND INDUSTRY

CA. 1780–1850   *610*

23
THE AGE OF NATIONALISM

1850–1914   *706*

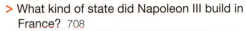

24
THE WEST AND THE WORLD

1815–1914   *740*

27

DICTATORSHIPS AND THE SECOND WORLD WAR

1919–1945   *840*

28

COLD WAR CONFLICT AND CONSENSUS

1945–1965   *878*

MAPS, FIGURES, AND TABLES

SPECIAL FEATURES

INTRODUCTION: The Origins of Modern Western Society

The notion of "the West" has ancient origins. Greek civilization grew up in the shadow of earlier civilizations to the south and east of Greece, especially Egypt and Mesopotamia. Greeks defined themselves in relation to these more advanced cultures, which they lumped together as "the East." They passed this conceptualization on to the Romans, who in turn transmitted it to the peoples of western and northern Europe. When Europeans established overseas colonies in the late fifteenth century, they believed they were taking Western culture with them, even though many of its elements, such as Christianity, had originated in what Europeans by that point regarded as the East. Throughout its long history, the meaning of "the West" has shifted, but in every era it has meant more than a geographical location.

The Ancient World

The ancient world provided several cultural elements that the modern world has inherited. First came the traditions of the Hebrews, especially their religion, Judaism, with its belief in one god and in themselves as a chosen people. The Hebrews developed their religious ideas in books that were later brought together in the Hebrew Bible, which Christians term the Old Testament. Second, Greek architectural, philosophical, and scientific ideas have exercised a profound influence on Western thought. Third, Rome provided the Latin language, the instrument of verbal and written communication for more than a thousand years, and concepts of law and government that molded Western ideas of political organization. Finally, Christianity, the spiritual faith and ecclesiastical organization that derived from the life and teachings of a Jewish man, Jesus of Nazareth, also came to condition Western religious, social, and moral values and systems.

The Hebrews

The Hebrews were nomadic pastoralists who may have migrated into the Nile Delta from the east, seeking good land for their herds of sheep and goats. According to the Hebrew Bible, they were enslaved by the Egyptians but were led out of Egypt by a charismatic leader named Moses. The Hebrews settled in the area between the Mediterranean and the Jordan River known as Canaan. They were organized into tribes, each tribe consisting of numerous families who thought of themselves as all related to one another and having a common ancestor.

In Canaan, the nomadic Hebrews encountered a variety of other peoples, whom they both learned from and fought. The Bible reports that the inspired

A Golden Calf

According to the Hebrew Bible, Moses descended from Mount Sinai, where he had received the Ten Commandments, to find the Hebrews worshiping a golden calf, which was against Yahweh's laws. In July 1990, an American archaeological team found this model of a gilded calf inside a pot. The figurine, which dates to about 1550 B.C.E., is strong evidence for the existence in Canaan of religious traditions that involved animals as divine symbols. (Courtesy of the Leon Levy Expedition to Ashkelon. Photo: Carl Andrews)

leader Saul established a monarchy over the twelve Hebrew tribes and that the kingdom grew under the leadership of King David. David's successor Solomon (ca. 965–925 B.C.E.) launched a building program including cities; palaces; fortresses; roads; and a temple at Jerusalem, which became the symbol of Hebrew unity. This unity did not last long, however; at Solomon's death, his kingdom broke into two separate states, Israel and Judah.

In their migration, the Hebrews had come in contact with many peoples, such as the Mesopotamians and the Egyptians, who had many gods. The Hebrews came to believe in a single god, Yahweh, who had created all things and who took a strong personal interest in the individual. According to the Bible, Yahweh made a covenant with the Hebrews: if they worshipped Yahweh as their only god, he would consider them his chosen people and protect them from their enemies. This covenant was to prove a constant force in the Hebrews' religion, Judaism, a word taken from the kingdom of Judah.

Worship was embodied in a series of rules of behavior, the Ten Commandments, which Yahweh gave to Moses. These required certain kinds of religious observances and forbade the Hebrews to steal, lie, murder, or commit adultery, thus creating a system of ethical absolutes. From the Ten Commandments, a complex system of rules of conduct was created and later written down as Hebrew law, beginning with the Torah—the first five books of the Hebrew Bible. Hebrew Scripture, a group of books written over many centuries, also contained history, hymns of praise, prophecy, traditions, advice, and other sorts of writings. Jews today revere these texts, as do many Christians, and Muslims respect them, all of which gives them particular importance.

The Greeks

The people of ancient Greece built on the traditions and ideas of earlier societies to develop a culture that fundamentally shaped Western civilization. Drawing on their day-by-day experiences as well as logic and empirical observation, the Greeks developed ways of understanding and explaining the world around them, which grew into modern philosophy and science. They also created new political forms, including the small independent city-state known as the *polis*. Scholars label the period dating from around 1100 B.C.E. to 323 B.C.E., in which the polis predominated, the Hellenic Age. Two poleis were especially powerful: Sparta, which created a military state in which men remained in the army most of their lives, and Athens, which created a democracy in which male citizens had a direct voice.

Athens created a brilliant culture, with magnificent art and architecture whose grace and beauty still speak to people. In their comedies and tragedies,

Athenians Aeschylus, Sophocles, and Euripides were the first playwrights to treat eternal problems of the human condition. Athens also experimented with the political system we call democracy. Greek democracy meant the rule of citizens, not "the people" as a whole, and citizenship was generally limited to free adult men whose parents were citizens. Women were citizens for religious and reproductive purposes, but their citizenship did not give them the right to participate in government. Free men who were not children of a citizen, resident foreigners, and slaves were not citizens and had no political voice. Thus ancient Greek democracy did not reflect the modern concept that all people are created equal, but it did permit male citizens to share in determining the diplomatic and military policies of the polis.

Classical Greece of the fifth and fourth centuries B.C.E. also witnessed an incredible flowering of philosophical ideas. Some Greeks began to question their old beliefs and myths, and they sought rational rather than supernatural explanations for natural phenomena. They began an intellectual revolution with the idea that nature was predictable, creating what we now call philosophy and science. These ideas also emerged in medicine: Hippocrates, the most prominent physician and teacher of medicine of his time, sought natural explanations for diseases and natural means to treat them.

The Sophists, a group of thinkers in fifth century B.C.E. Athens, applied philosophical speculation to politics and language, and questioned the beliefs and laws of the polis to understand their origin. They believed that excellence in both politics and language could be taught, and they provided lessons for the young men of Athens who wished to learn how to persuade others in the often tumultuous Athenian democracy.

Socrates (ca. 470–399 B.C.E.), whose ideas are known only through the works of others, also applied philosophy to politics and to people. Because he posed questions rather than giving answers, it is difficult to say exactly what Socrates thought about many things, although he does seem to have felt that, through knowledge, people could approach the supreme good and thus find happiness. Most of what we know about Socrates comes from his student Plato (427–347 B.C.E.), who wrote dialogues in which Socrates asks questions and who also founded the Academy, a school dedicated to philosophy. Plato developed the theory that there are two worlds: the impermanent, changing world that we know through our senses, and the eternal, unchanging realm of "forms" that constitute the essence of true reality. According to Plato, true knowledge and the possibility of living a virtuous life come from contemplating ideals forms. Plato's student Aristotle (384–322 B.C.E.) also thought that true knowledge was possible, but he believed that such knowledge came from observation of the world, analysis of natural phenomena, and logical reasoning, not contemplation. He investigated the nature of government, ideas of matter and motion, outer space, ethics, and language and literature, among other subjects. Aristotle's ideas later profoundly shaped both Muslim and Western philosophy and theology.

Echoing the broader culture, Plato and Aristotle viewed philosophy as an exchange between men in which women had no part. The ideal for Athenian citizen women was a secluded life, although how far this ideal was actually a reality is impossible to know. Women in citizen families probably spent most of their time at home, leaving the house only to attend religious festivals, and perhaps occasionally plays.

Greek political and intellectual advances took place against a background of constant warfare. The long and bitter struggle between the cities of Athens and Sparta, called the Peloponnesian War (439–404 B.C.E.), ended in Athens's defeat. Shortly afterward, Sparta, Athens, and Thebes contested for hegemony in Greece, but no single state was strong enough to dominate the others. Taking advantage of the situation, Philip II (359–336 B.C.E.) of Macedonia, a small kingdom encompassing part of modern Greece and parts of the Balkans, defeated a combined Theban-Athenian army in 338 B.C.E. Unable to resolve their domestic quarrels, the Greeks lost their freedom to the Macedonian invader.

Philip was assassinated just two years after he had conquered Greece, and his throne was inherited by his son, Alexander. In twelve years, Alexander conquered an empire stretching from Macedonia across the Middle East into Asia as far as India. He established cities and military colonies in strategic spots as he advanced eastward. but he died at the age of thirty-two while planning his next campaign.

Alexander left behind an empire that quickly broke into smaller kingdoms, but more important, his death ushered in an era, the Hellenistic, in which Greek culture, the Greek language, and Greek thought spread widely, blending with local traditions. The Hellenistic period stretches from Alexander's death in 323 B.C.E. to the Roman conquest in 30 B.C.E. of the kingdom established in Egypt by Alexander's successors. Greek immigrants moved to the cities and colonies established by Alexander and his successors, spreading the Greek language, ideas, and traditions in a process scholars later called Hellenization. Local people who wanted to rise in wealth or status learned Greek. The economic and cultural connections of the Hellenistic world later proved valuable to the Romans, allowing them to trade products and ideas more easily over a broad area.

The mixing of peoples in the Hellenistic era influenced religion, philosophy, and science. The Hellenistic kings built temples to the old Greek gods and promoted rituals and ceremonies that honored them, but new deities, such as Tyche—the goddess and personification of luck, fate, chance, and fortune—also gained prominence. More people turned to mystery religions, which blended Greek and non-Greek elements and offered their adherents secret knowledge, unification with a deity, and sometimes life after death. Others turned to practical philosophies that provided advice on how to live a good life. These included Epicureanism, which advocated moderation to achieve a life of contentment, and Stoicism, which advocated living in accordance with nature. In the scholarly realm, Hellenistic thinkers made advances in mathematics, astronomy, and mechanical design. Additionally, physicians used observation and dissection to better understand the way the human body works.

Despite the new ideas, the Hellenistic period did not see widespread improvements in the way most people lived and worked. Cities flourished, but many people who

Hellenistic Married Life

This small terra-cotta figurine from Myrina in what is now Turkey, made in the second century B.C.E., shows a newly married couple sitting on a bridal bed. The groom is drawing back the bride's veil, and she is exhibiting the modesty that was a desired quality in young women. Figurines representing every stage of life became popular in the Hellenistic period and were used for religious offerings in temples and sacred places. This one was found in a tomb. (Erich Lessing/Art Resource, NY)

lived in rural areas were actually worse off than they had been before because of higher rents and taxes. Technology was applied to military needs but not to the production of food or other goods.

The Greek world was largely conquered by the Romans, and the various Hellenistic monarchies became part of the Roman Empire. In cultural terms, the lines of conquest were reversed, however, as the Romans were tremendously influenced by Greek art, philosophy, and ideas, all of which have had a lasting impact on the modern world as well.

Rome: From Republic to Empire

The city of Rome, situated near the center of the boot-shaped peninsula of Italy, conquered all of Italy, then the western Mediterranean basin, and then areas in the east that had been part of Alexander's empire. Rome thus created an empire that, at its largest, stretched from England to Egypt and from Portugal to Persia. The Romans spread the Latin language throughout much of their empire, providing a common language for verbal and written communication for more than a thousand years. They also established concepts of law and government that molded Western legal systems, ideas of political organization, and administrative practices.

The city of Rome developed from small villages and was influenced by the Etruscans who lived to the north. Sometime in the sixth century B.C.E. a group of aristocrats revolted against the ruling king and established a republican form of government in which the main institution of power was the Senate, an assembly of aristocrats, rather than a single monarch. According to tradition, this happened in 509 B.C.E., so scholars customarily divide Roman history into two primary stages: the republic, from 509 to 27 B.C.E., in which Rome was ruled by the Senate, and the empire, from 27 B.C.E. to 476 C.E., in which Roman territories were ruled by an emperor.

In the years following the establishment of the republic, the Romans fought numerous wars with their neighbors on the Italian peninsula. Their superior military institutions, organization, and manpower allowed them to conquer or take into their influence most of Italy by about 265 B.C.E. Once they had conquered an area, the Romans built roads and often shared Roman citizenship. Roman expansion continued. In a series of wars, they conquered lands all around the Mediterranean, creating an overseas empire that brought them unheard of power and wealth. First they defeated the Carthaginians in the Punic Wars, and then they turned east. Declaring the Mediterranean *mare nostrum*, "our sea," the Romans began to create a political and administrative machinery to hold the Mediterranean together under a mutually shared cultural and political system of provinces ruled by governors sent from Rome.

The Romans created several assemblies through which men elected high officials and passed ordinances. The most important of these was the Senate, a political assembly—initially only of hereditary aristocrats called patricians—that advised officials and handled government finances. The common people of Rome, known as plebeians, were initially excluded from holding offices or sitting in the Senate, but a long political and social struggle led to a broadening of the base of political power to include male plebeians. The basis of Roman society for both patricians and plebeians was the family, headed by the paterfamilias, who held authority over his wife, children, and servants. Households often included slaves, who also provided labor for fields and mines.

A lasting achievement of the Romans was their development of law. Roman civil law consisted of statutes, customs, and forms of procedure that regulated the lives of citizens. As the Romans came into more frequent contact with foreigners, Roman officials applied a broader "law of the peoples" to matters such as peace treaties, the treatment of prisoners of war, and the exchange of diplomats. All sides were to be treated the same regardless of their nationality. By the late republic, Roman jurists had widened this still further into the concept of natural law based in part on Stoic ideas they had learned from Greek thinkers. Natural law, according to these thinkers, is made up of rules that govern human behavior and that come from applying reason rather than customs or traditions, and so apply to all societies. In reality, Roman officials generally interpreted the law to the advantage of Rome, of course, at least to the extent that the strength of Roman armies allowed them to enforce it. But Roman law came to be seen as one of the most important contributions Rome made to the development of Western civilization.

Law was not the only facet of Hellenistic Greek culture to influence the Romans. The Roman conquest of the Hellenistic East led to the wholesale confiscation of Greek sculpture and paintings to adorn Roman temples and homes. Greek literary and historical classics were translated into Latin; Greek philosophy was studied in the Roman schools; educated people learned Greek as well as Latin as a matter of course. Public baths based on the Greek model—with exercise rooms, swimming pools, and reading rooms—served not only as centers for recreation and exercise but also as centers of Roman public life.

The wars of conquest eventually created serious political problems for the Romans, which surfaced toward the end of the second century B.C.E. Overseas warfare required huge armies for long periods of time. A few army officers gained fabulous wealth, but most soldiers did not and returned home to find their farms in ruins. Those with cash to invest bought up small farms, creating vast estates called *latifundia*. Landless veterans migrated to Rome seeking work. Unable to compete with the tens of thousands of slaves in Rome, they formed a huge unemployed urban population. Rome divided into political factions, each of which named a supreme military commander, who led Roman troops against external enemies but also against each other. Civil war erupted.

Out of the violence and disorder emerged Julius Caesar (100–44 B.C.E.), a victorious general, shrewd politician, and highly popular figure. He took practical steps to end the civil war, such as expanding citizenship and sending large numbers of the urban poor to found colonies and spread Roman culture in Gaul, Spain, and North Africa. Fearful that Caesar's popularity and ambition would turn Rome into a monarchy, a group of aristocratic conspirators assassinated him in 44 B.C.E. Civil war was renewed. In 31 B.C.E., Caesar's grandnephew and adopted son Octavian defeated his rivals and became master of Rome. For his success, the Senate in 27 B.C.E. gave Octavian the name Augustus, meaning "revered one." Although the Senate did not mean this to be a decisive break, that date is generally used to mark the end of the Roman Republic and the start of the Roman Empire.

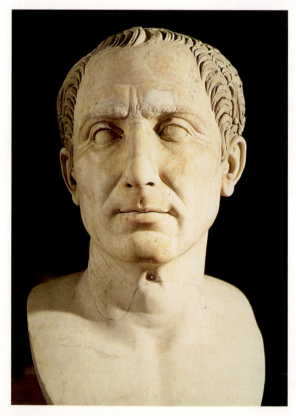

Julius Caesar

In this bust from the first century B.C.E., the sculptor portrays Caesar as a man of power and intensity. Showing individuals as representing certain virtues was common in Roman portraiture. (Museo Archeologico Nazionale Naples/Scala/Art Resource, NY)

Augustus rebuilt effective government. Although he claimed that he was restoring the republic, he actually transformed the government into one in which all power was held by a single ruler, gradually taking over many of the offices that traditionally had been held by separate people. Without specifically saying so, Augustus created the office of emperor. The English word *emperor* is derived from the Latin word *imperator*, an origin that reflects the fact that Augustus's command of the army was the main source of his power.

Augustus ended domestic turmoil and secured the provinces. He founded new colonies, mainly in the western Mediterranean basin, which promoted the spread of Greco-Roman culture and the Latin language to the West. Magistrates exercised authority in their regions as representatives of Rome. Augustus broke some of the barriers between Italy and the provinces by extending citizenship to many of the provincials who had supported him. Later emperors added more territory, and a system of Roman roads and sea-lanes united the empire, with trade connections extending to India and China. For two hundred years the Mediterranean world experienced what later historians called the *pax Romana*—a period of prosperity, order, and relative peace.

In the third century c.e., this prosperity and stability gave way to a period of domestic upheaval and foreign invasion. Rival generals backed by their troops contested the imperial throne in civil wars. Groups labeled by the Romans as barbarians, such as the Visigoths, Ostrogoths, Gauls, and others, migrated to and invaded the Roman Empire from the north and east. Civil war and invasions devastated towns and farms, causing severe economic depression. The emperors Diocletian (285–305 c.e.) and Constantine (306–337 c.e.) tried to halt the general disintegration by reorganizing the empire, expanding the state bureaucracy, building more defensive works, and imposing heavier taxes. For administrative purposes, Diocletian divided the empire into a western half and an eastern half, and Constantine established the new capital city of Constantinople in the east. Their attempts to solve the empire's problems failed, however. The emperors ruling from Constantinople could not provide enough military assistance to repel invaders in the western half of the Roman Empire. In 476, a Germanic chieftain, Odoacer, deposed the Roman emperor in the west and did not take on the title of emperor, calling himself instead the king of Italy. This date thus marks the official end of the Roman Empire in the west, although the Roman Empire in the east, later called the Byzantine Empire, would last for nearly another thousand years.

After the Western Roman Empire's decline, the rich legacy of Greco-Roman culture was absorbed by the medieval world. The Latin language remained the basic medium of communication among educated people in central and western Europe for the next thousand years; for almost two thousand years, Latin literature formed the core of all Western education. Roman roads, buildings, and aqueducts remained in use. Rome left its mark on the legal and political systems of most European countries. Rome had preserved the best of ancient culture for later times.

The Spread of Christianity

The ancient world also left behind a powerful religious legacy, Christianity. Christianity derives from the teachings of a Jewish man, Jesus of Nazareth (ca. 3 b.c.e.–29 c.e.). According to the accounts of his life written down and preserved by his followers, Jesus preached of a heavenly kingdom of eternal happiness in a life after death and of the importance of devotion to God and love of others. His teachings were based on Hebrew Scripture and reflected a conception of God and morality that came from Jewish tradition, but he deviated from traditional Jewish teachings in insisting that he taught in his own name, not simply in the name of Yahweh. He came to establish a spiritual kingdom, he said, not an earthly one, and he urged his followers and listeners to concentrate on the world to come, not on material goods or earthly relationships. Some Jews believed that Jesus was the long-awaited savior who would bring prosperity and happiness, while others thought he was religiously dangerous. The Roman official of Judaea, Pontius Pilate, feared that the popular agitation surrounding Jesus could lead to revolt against Rome. He arrested Jesus, met with him, and sentenced him to death by crucifixion—the usual method for common criminals. Jesus's followers maintained that he rose from the dead three days later.

Those followers might have remained a small Jewish sect but for the preaching of a Hellenized Jew, Paul of Tarsus (ca. 5–67 C.E.). Paul traveled widely and wrote letters of advice, many of which were copied and circulated, transforming Jesus's ideas into more specific moral teachings. Paul urged that Jews and non-Jews be accepted on an equal basis, and the earliest converts included men and women from all social classes. People were attracted to Christian teachings for a variety of reasons: it offered a message of divine forgiveness and eternal life, taught that every individual has a role to play in building the kingdom of God, and fostered a deep sense of community and identity in the often highly mobile Roman world.

Some Roman officials and emperors opposed Christianity and attempted to stamp it out, but most did not, and by the second century, Christianity began to establish more permanent institutions, including a hierarchy of officials. It attracted more highly educated individuals, and it modified teachings that seemed upsetting to Romans. In 313, the emperor Constantine legalized Christianity, and in 380, the emperor Theodosius made it the official religion of the empire. Carried by settlers, missionaries, and merchants to Gaul, Spain, North Africa, and Britain, Christianity formed a basic element of Western civilization.

Christian writers also played a powerful role in the conservation of Greco-Roman thought. They used Latin as their medium of communication, thereby preserving it. They copied and transmitted classical texts. Writers such as Saint Augustine of Hippo (354–430) used Roman rhetoric and Roman history to defend Christian theology. In so doing, they assimilated classical culture to Christian teaching.

The Middle Ages

Fifteenth-century scholars believed that they were living in a period of rebirth that had recaptured the spirit of ancient Greece and Rome. What separated their time from classical antiquity, in their opinion, was a long period of darkness to which a seventeenth-century professor gave the name "Middle Ages." In this conceptualization, Western history was divided into three periods—ancient, medieval, and modern—an organization that is still in use today. Recent scholars have demonstrated, however, that the thousand-year period between roughly the fifth and fourteenth centuries was not one of stagnation but witnessed great changes in every realm of life: social, political, intellectual, economic, and religious. The men and women of the Middle Ages built on the cultural heritage of the Greco-Roman world and on the traditions of barbarian groups to create new ways of doing things.

The Early Middle Ages

The time period that historians mark off as the early Middle Ages, extending from about the fifth to the tenth centuries, saw the emergence of a distinctly Western society and culture. The geographical center of that society shifted northward from the Mediterranean basin to western Europe. Whereas a rich urban life and flourishing trade had characterized the ancient world, the barbarian invasions led to the decline of cities and the destruction of commerce. Early medieval society was rural and local, with the village serving as the characteristic social unit.

Several processes were responsible for the development of European culture. First, Europe became Christian. Missionaries traveled throughout Europe instructing Germanic, Celtic, and Slavic peoples in the basic tenets of the Christian faith. Seeking to gain more converts, the Christian Church incorporated pagan beliefs and holidays, creating new rituals and practices that were meaningful to people, and creating a sense of community through parish churches and the veneration of saints.

Second, as barbarian groups migrated into the Western Roman Empire, they often intermarried with the old Roman aristocracy. The elite class that emerged held the dominant political, social, and economic power in early — and later — medieval Europe. Barbarian customs and tradition, such as ideals of military prowess and bravery in battle, became part of the mental furniture of Europeans.

Third, in the seventh and eighth centuries, Muslim military conquests carried Islam, the religion inspired by the prophet Muhammad (ca. 571–632), from the Arab lands across North Africa, the Mediterranean basin, and Spain into southern France. The Arabs eventually translated many Greek texts. Beginning in the ninth century, when those texts were translated from Arabic into Latin, they came to play a role in the formation of European scientific and philosophical thought.

Monasticism, an ascetic form of Christian life first practiced in Egypt and characterized by isolation from the broader society, simplicity of living, and abstention from sexual activity, flourished and expanded in both the Byzantine East and the Latin West. Medieval people believed that the communities of monks and nuns provided an important service: prayer on behalf of the broader society. In a world lacking career opportunities, monasteries also offered education for the children of the upper classes. Men trained in monastery schools served royal and baronial governments as advisers, secretaries, diplomats, and treasurers; monks in the West also pioneered the clearing of wasteland and forestland.

One of the barbarian groups that settled within the Roman Empire and allied with the Romans were the Franks, and after the Roman Empire collapsed they expanded their holdings, basing some of their government on Roman principles. In the eighth century, the dynamic warrior-king of the Franks, Charles the Great, or Charlemagne (768–814), came to control most of central and western continental Europe except Muslim Spain, and western Europe achieved a degree of political unity. Charlemagne supported Christian missionary efforts and encouraged both classical and Christian scholarship. His coronation in 800 by the pope at Rome in a ceremony filled with Latin anthems represented a fusion of classical, Christian, and barbarian elements, as did Carolingian culture more generally. In the ninth century, Vikings, Muslims, and Magyars (early Hungarians) raided and migrated into Europe, leading to the collapse of centralized power. Charlemagne's empire was divided, and real authority passed into the hands of local strongmen. Out of this vulnerable society, which was constantly threatened by outside invasions, a new political form involving mutual obligations, later called feudalism, developed. The power of the local nobles in the feudal structure rested on landed estates worked by peasants in another system of mutual obligation termed manorialism, in which the majority of peasants were serfs, required to stay on the land where they were born and pay obligations to a lord in labor and products.

The High and Later Middle Ages

By the beginning of the eleventh century, the European world showed distinct signs of recovery, vitality, and creativity. Over the next two centuries, a period called the High Middle Ages, that recovery and creativity manifested itself in every facet of culture—economic, social, political, intellectual, and artistic. A greater degree of peace paved the way for these achievements.

The Viking, Muslim, and Magyar invasions gradually ended. Warring knights supported ecclesiastical pressure against violence, and disorder declined. A warming climate, along with technological improvements such as water mills and horse-drawn plows, increased the available food supply. Most people remained serfs, living in simple houses in small villages, but a slow increase in population led to new areas being cultivated, and some serfs were able to buy their freedom.

Relative security and the increasing food supply allowed for the growth and development of towns in the High Middle Ages. Towns gained legal and political rights, merchant and craft guilds grew more powerful, and towns became centers of production as well as trading centers. In medieval social thinking, three classes existed: the clergy, who prayed; the nobility, who fought; and the peasantry, who tilled the land. The merchant class, which engaged in manufacturing and trade, sought freedom from the jurisdiction of feudal lords, and pursued wealth with a fiercely competitive spirit, fit none of the standard categories. Townspeople represented a radical force for change. Trade brought in new ideas as well as merchandise, and towns developed into intellectual and cultural centers.

The growth of towns and cities went hand in hand with a revival of regional and international trade. For example, Italian merchants traveled to the regional fairs of France and Flanders to exchange silk from China and slaves from the Crimea for English woolens, French wines, and Flemish textiles. Merchants adopted new business techniques and a new attitude toward making money. They were eager to invest surplus capital to make more money. These developments added up to what scholars have termed a commercial revolution, a major turning point in the economic and social life of the West. The development of towns and commerce was to lay the foundations for Europe's transformation, centuries later, from a rural agricultural society into an urban industrial society—a change with global implications.

The High Middle Ages also saw the birth of the modern centralized state. The concept of the state had been one of Rome's great legacies to Western civilization, but for almost five hundred years after the disintegration of the Roman Empire in the West, political authority was weak.

Medieval Childhood

In this illustration from the margins of a fourteenth-century French book of poetry, a mother carries her infant in a cradle. The baby is tightly swaddled in cloth, a common practice that came from medieval ideas about how children's limbs developed and from concerns about an infant's safety in households with open fires, where domestic animals walked freely, and where parents and older siblings had work to do. (Pierpont Morgan Library/Art Resource, NY)

Charlemagne had far less control of what went on in his kingdom than had Roman emperors, and after the Carolingian empire broke apart, political authority was completely decentralized, with power spread among many feudal lords. Beginning in the last half of the tenth century, however, feudal rulers began to develop new institutions of law and government that enabled them to assert their power over lesser lords and the general population. Centralized states slowly crystallized, first in France and England, and then in Spain and northern Europe. In Italy and Germany, however, strong independent local authorities predominated.

Medieval rulers required more officials, larger armies, and more money with which to pay for them. They developed financial bureaucracies, of which the most effective were those in England. They also sought to transform a hodgepodge of oral and written customs and rules into a uniform system of laws acceptable and applicable to all their peoples. In France, local laws and procedures were maintained, but the king also established a royal court that published laws and heard appeals. In England, the king's court regularized procedures, and the idea of a common law that applied to the whole country developed. Fiscal and legal measures enacted by King John led to opposition from the high nobles of England, who in 1215 forced him to sign the Magna Carta, agreeing to observe the law. English kings following John recognized this common law, a law that their judges applied throughout the country. Exercise of common law often involved juries of local people to answer questions of fact. The common law and jury system of the Middle Ages have become integral features of Anglo-American jurisprudence. In the fourteenth century, kings also summoned meetings of the leading classes in their kingdoms, and thus were born representative assemblies, most notably the English Parliament.

In their work of consolidation and centralization, kings increasingly used the knowledge of university-trained officials. Universities first emerged in western Europe in the twelfth century. Medieval universities were educational institutions for men that produced trained officials for the new bureaucratic states. The universities at Bologna in Italy and Montpellier in France, for example, were centers for the study of Roman law. Paris became the leading university for the study of philosophy and theology. Medieval Scholastics (philosophers and theologians) sought to harmonize Greek philosophy, especially the works of Aristotle, with Christian teaching. They wanted to use reason to deepen the understanding of what was believed on faith. At the University of Paris, Thomas Aquinas (1225–1274) wrote an important synthesis of Christian revelation and Aristotelian philosophy in his *Summa Theologica*. Medieval universities developed the basic structures familiar to modern students: colleges, universities, examinations, and degrees. Colleges and universities are another major legacy of the Middle Ages to the modern world.

At the same time that states developed, energetic popes built their power within the Western Christian Church and asserted their superiority over kings and emperors. A papal call to retake the holy city of Jerusalem led to nearly two centuries of warfare between Christians and Muslims. Christian warriors, clergy, and settlers moved out from western and central Europe in all directions so that, through conquest and colonization, border regions were gradually incorporated into a more uniform European culture

Most people in medieval Europe were Christian, and the village or city church was the center of community life, where people attended services, honored the

saints, and received the sacraments. The village priest blessed the fields before the spring planting and the fall harvesting. In everyday life, people engaged in rituals heavy with religious symbolism, and every life transition was marked by a ceremony with religious elements. Guilds of merchants sought the protection of patron saints and held elaborate public celebrations on the saints' feast days. Indeed, the veneration of saints — men and women whose lives contemporaries perceived as outstanding in holiness — and an increasingly sophisticated sacramental system became central features of popular religion. University lectures and meetings of parliaments began with prayers. Kings relied on the services of bishops and abbots in the work of the government. Gothic cathedrals, where people saw beautiful stained-glass windows and listened to complex music, manifested medieval people's deep Christian faith and their pride in their own cities.

The high level of energy and creativity that characterized the twelfth and thirteenth centuries could not be sustained indefinitely. In the fourteenth century, every conceivable disaster struck western Europe. The climate turned colder and wetter, leading to poor harvests and widespread famine. People weakened by hunger were more susceptible to disease, and in the middle of the fourteenth century, the bubonic plague (or Black Death) swept across the continent, taking a terrible toll on population. England and France became deadlocked in a long and bitter struggle known as the Hundred Years' War (1337–1453). War devastated the countryside, especially in France, leading to widespread discontent and peasant revolts. Workers in cities also revolted against dismal working conditions, and violent crime and ethnic tensions increased. Many urban residents were increasingly dissatisfied with the Christian Church and turned to heretical movements that challenged church power. Schism in the Catholic Church resulted in the simultaneous claim by two popes of jurisdiction. In spite of the pessimism and crises, however, important institutions and cultural forms, including representative assemblies and national literatures, emerged.

Early Modern Europe

While war gripped northern Europe, a new culture emerged in southern Europe. The fourteenth century witnessed the beginning of remarkable changes in many aspects of Italian intellectual, artistic, and cultural life. Artists and writers thought they were living in a new golden age, but not until the sixteenth century was this change given the label we use today — the Renaissance, from the French version of a word meaning "rebirth." The term was first used by the artist and art historian Giorgio Vasari (1511–1574) to describe the art of "rare men of genius" such as his contemporary Michelangelo. Through their works, Vasari judged, the glory of the classical past had been reborn after centuries of darkness or had perhaps even been surpassed. Vasari used the word *Renaissance* to describe painting, sculpture, and architecture, what he termed the Major Arts. Gradually, however, *Renaissance* was used to refer to many aspects of life at this time, first in Italy and then in the rest of Europe. This new attitude had a slow diffusion out of Italy, with the result that the Renaissance happened at different times in different parts of Europe. Italian art of the fourteenth through the early sixteenth century is described as "Renaissance," as is English literature of the late sixteenth century (including Shakespeare).

About a century after Vasari coined the word *Renaissance*, scholars began to view the cultural and political changes of the Renaissance, along with the religious changes of the Reformation and the European voyages of exploration, as ushering in the "modern" world. Since then, some historians have chosen to view the Renaissance as a bridge between the medieval and modern eras because it corresponded chronologically with the late medieval period and because there was much continuity along with the changes. Others have questioned whether the word *Renaissance* should be used at all to describe an era in which many social groups saw decline rather than advance. These debates remind us that the labels *medieval, Renaissance*, and *modern* are intellectual constructs devised after the fact. They all contain value judgments, as do other chronological designations, such as the golden age of Athens and the Roaring Twenties.

The Renaissance

In the commercial revival of the Middle Ages, ambitious merchants amassed great wealth, especially in the city-states of northern Italy. These city-states were communes in which all citizens shared power, but political instability often led to their transformation into city-states ruled by single individuals. As their riches and power grew, rulers and merchants displayed their wealth in great public buildings as well as magnificent courts — palaces where they lived and conducted business. Political rulers, popes, and powerful families hired writers, artists, musicians, and architects through the system of patronage, which allowed for a great outpouring of culture.

The Renaissance was characterized by self-conscious awareness among fourteenth- and fifteenth-century Italians — particularly scholars and writers known as humanists — that they were living in a new era. Key to this attitude was a serious interest in the Latin classics, a belief in individual potential, and a more secular attitude toward life. All of these are evident in the political theory developed in the Renaissance, particularly that of Machiavelli. Humanists opened schools for boys and young men to train them for active lives of public service, but they had doubts about whether humanist education was appropriate for women. As humanism spread to northern Europe, religious concerns became more pronounced, and Christian humanists set out plans for the reform of church and society. Their ideas reached a much wider audience than did those of early humanists because of the development of the printing press with movable metal type, which revolutionized communication.

Botticelli, *Primavera* (Spring), ca. 1482 Framed by a grove of orange trees, Venus, goddess of love, is flanked on her right by Flora, goddess of flowers and fertility, and on her left by the Three Graces, goddesses of banquets, dance, and social occasions. Above, Venus's son Cupid, the god of love, shoots darts of desire, while at the far right the wind god Zephyrus chases the nymph Chloris. The entire scene rests on classical mythology, though some art historians claim that Venus is an allegory for the Virgin Mary. Botticelli captured the ideal of female beauty in the Renaissance: slender, with pale skin, a high forehead, red-blond hair, and sloping shoulders. (Digital image © The Museum of Modern Art/Licensed by Scala/Art Resource, NY)

Interest in the classical past and in the individual also shaped Renaissance art in terms of style and subject matter. Painting became more naturalistic, and the individual portrait emerged as a distinct artistic genre. Wealthy merchants, cultured rulers, and powerful popes all hired painters, sculptors, and architects to design and ornament public and private buildings. Art in Italy became more secular and classical, while that in northern Europe retained a more religious tone. Artists began to understand themselves as having a special creative genius, though they continued to produce works on order for patrons, who often determined the content and form.

Social hierarchies in the Renaissance built on those of the Middle Ages, with the addition of new features that evolved into the modern social hierarchies of race, class, and gender. In the fifteenth century, black slaves entered Europe in sizable numbers for the first time since the collapse of the Roman Empire, and Europeans fit them into changing understandings of ethnicity and race. The medieval hierarchy of orders based on function in society intermingled with a new hierarchy based on wealth, with new types of elites becoming more powerful. The Renaissance debate about women led many to discuss women's nature and proper role in society, a discussion sharpened by the presence of a number of ruling queens in this era.

Beginning in the fifteenth century, rulers utilized aggressive methods to rebuild their governments. First in the regional states of Italy, then in the expanding monarchies of France, England, and Spain, rulers began the work of reducing violence, curbing unruly nobles, and establishing domestic order. They attempted to secure their borders and enhanced methods of raising revenue. The monarchs of western Europe emphasized royal majesty and royal sovereignty and insisted on the respect and loyalty of all subjects, including the nobility. In central Europe the Holy Roman emperors attempted to do the same, but they were not able to overcome the power of local interests to create a unified state.

The Reformation

Calls for reform of the Christian Church began very early in its history. When Christianity became the official religion of the Roman Empire in the fourth century, many believers thought that it had abandoned its original mission, and they called for a return to a church that was not linked to the state. Throughout the Middle Ages, individuals and groups argued that the church had become too wealthy and powerful, and urged monasteries, convents, bishoprics, and the papacy to give up their property and focus on service to the poor. Some asserted that basic teachings of the church were not truly Christian and that changes were needed in theology as well as in institutional structures and practices. The Christian humanists of the late fifteenth and early sixteenth centuries urged reform, primarily through educational and social change. Throughout the centuries, men and women believed that the early Christian Church represented a golden age akin to the golden age of the classical past celebrated by Renaissance humanists.

Thus sixteenth-century cries for reformation were hardly new. What was new, however, was the breadth with which they were accepted and their ultimate impact. In 1500, there was one Christian Church in western Europe to which all Christians at least nominally belonged. Fifty years later there were many, a situation that continues today. Thus, along with the Renaissance, the Reformation is often seen as a key element in the creation of the "modern" world.

In 1517, Martin Luther (1483–1546), a priest and professor of theology at a small German university, launched an attack on clerical abuses. The Catholic Church in the early sixteenth century had serious problems, and many individuals and groups had long called for reform. This background of discontent helps explain why Martin Luther's ideas found such a ready audience. Luther and other Protestants developed a new understanding of Christian doctrine that emphasized faith, the power of God's grace, and the centrality of the Bible. Protestant ideas were attractive to educated people and urban residents, and they spread rapidly through preaching, hymns, and the printing press. By 1530, many parts of the Holy Roman Empire and Scandinavia had broken with the Catholic Church.

Some reformers developed more radical ideas about infant baptism, ownership of property, and the separation between church and state. Both Protestants and Catholics regarded these as dangerous, and radicals were banished or executed. The German Peasants' War, in which Luther's ideas were linked to calls for social and economic reform, was similarly put down harshly. The Protestant reformers did not break with medieval ideas about the proper gender hierarchy, though they did elevate the status of marriage and viewed orderly households as the key building blocks of society.

The progress of the Reformation was shaped by the political situation in the Holy Roman Empire. The Habsburg emperor, Charles V, ruled almost half of Europe along with Spain's overseas colonies. Within the empire his authority was limited, however, and local princes, nobles, and cities actually held the most power. This decentralization allowed the Reformation to spread. Charles remained firmly Catholic, and in the 1530s religious wars began in Germany. These were brought to an end with the Peace of Augsburg in 1555, which allowed rulers to choose whether their territory would be Catholic or Lutheran.

In England the political issue of the royal succession triggered that country's break with Rome, and a Protestant church was established. Protestant ideas also spread into France and eastern Europe. In all these areas, a second generation of reformers built on Lutheran and Zwinglian ideas to develop their own theology and plans for institutional change. The most important of the second-generation reformers was John Calvin, whose ideas would come to shape Christianity over a much wider area than did Luther's. The Roman Catholic Church responded slowly to the Protestant challenge, but by the 1530s, the papacy was leading a movement for reform within the church instead of blocking it. Catholic doctrine was reaffirmed at the Council of Trent, and reform measures, such as the opening of seminaries for priests and a ban on holding multiple church offices, were introduced. New religious orders such as the Jesuits and the Ursulines spread Catholic ideas through teaching, and in the case of the Jesuits through missionary work.

Religious differences led to riots, civil wars, and international conflicts in the later sixteenth century. In France and the Netherlands, Calvinist Protestants and Catholics used violence against each other, and religious differences became mixed with political and economic grievances. Long civil wars resulted; one in the Netherlands became an international conflict. War ended in France with the Edict of Nantes in which Protestants were given some civil rights, and in the Netherlands with a division of the country into a Protestant north and Catholic south. The era of religious wars was also the time of the most extensive witch persecutions in European history, as both Protestants and Catholics tried to rid their cities and states of people they regarded as linked to the Devil.

The Renaissance and the Reformation are often seen as two of the key elements in the creation of the "modern" world. The radical changes brought by the Reformation contained many aspects of continuity, however. Sixteenth-century reformers looked back to the early Christian Church for their inspiration, and many of their reforming ideas had been advocated for centuries. Most Protestant reformers worked with political leaders to make religious changes, just as early church officials had worked with Emperor Constantine and his successors as Christianity became the official religion of the Roman Empire in the fourth century. The spread of Christianity and the spread of Protestantism were accomplished not only by preaching, persuasion, and teaching, but also by force and violence. The Catholic Reformation was carried out by activist popes, a church council, and new religious orders, like earlier reforms of the church had been.

Just as they linked with earlier developments, the events of the Reformation were also closely connected with what is often seen as the third element in the "modern" world, discussed in Chapter 1 of this book: European exploration and colonization. Only a week after Martin Luther stood in front of Emperor Charles V at the Diet of Worms declaring his independence in matters of religion, Ferdinand Magellan, a Portuguese sea captain with Spanish ships, was killed in a group of islands off the coast of Southeast Asia. Charles V had provided the backing for Magellan's voyage, the first to circumnavigate the globe. Magellan viewed the spread of Christianity as one of the purposes of his trip, and later, in the sixteenth century, institutions created as part of the Catholic Reformation, including the Jesuit order and the Inquisition, would operate in European colonies overseas as well as in Europe itself. The islands where Magellan was killed were later named the Philippines, in honor of Charles's son Philip, who sent an ill-fated expedition, the Spanish Armada, against Protestant England. Philip's opponent Queen Elizabeth was similarly honored when English explorers named a huge chunk of territory in North America Virginia as a tribute to their Virgin Queen. The desire for wealth and power was an important motivation in the European voyages and colonial ventures, but so was religious zeal.

Understanding Western Society

A HISTORY

VOLUME 2

14

EUROPEAN EXPLORATION AND CONQUEST

1450–1650

> **What were the motives behind European overseas expansion, and what were the consequences for Europe, the Americas, and Africa?** Chapter 14 examines European overseas expansion in the early modern era. Before 1450, Europeans were relatively marginal players in a centuries-old trading system that linked Africa, Asia, and Europe. Europeans' search for better access to Asian trade led to a new empire in the Indian Ocean and the accidental discovery of the Western Hemisphere. Within a few decades, European colonies in South and North America would join this worldwide web of commerce. Capitalizing on the goods and riches they found in the Americas, Europeans came to dominate trading networks and built political empires of truly global proportions. The era of globalization had begun, bringing with it new forms of cultural exchange, assimilation, conversion, and resistance.

 **LearningCurve**

After reading the chapter, use LearningCurve to retain what you've read.

> What was the Afroeurasian trading world before Columbus?

> How and why did Europeans undertake ambitious voyages of expansion?

> What was the impact of European conquest on the New World?

> How did Europe and the world change after Columbus?

> How did expansion change European attitudes and beliefs?

Life in the Age of Discovery. The arrival of the Portuguese in Japan in 1453 inspired a series of artworks depicting the *namban-jin* or southern barbarians, as they were known. (akg-images/ De Agostini Picture Library)

What was the Afroeurasian trading world before Columbus?

COLUMBUS DID NOT SAIL WEST ON A WHIM. To understand his and other Europeans' explorations, we must first understand late medieval trade networks. Historians now recognize that a type of world economy, known as the Afroeurasian trade world, linked the products and people of Asia, Africa, and Europe in the fifteenth century. The West was not the dominant player before Columbus, and the European voyages derived from a desire to share in and control the wealth coming from the Indian Ocean.

The Trade World of the Indian Ocean

The Indian Ocean was the center of the Afroeurasian trade world. Its location made it a crossroads for exchange among China, India, the Middle East, Africa, and Europe (**Map 14.1**). From the seventh through the fourteenth centuries, the

CHAPTER LOCATOR | **What was the Afroeurasian trading world before Columbus?**

1271–1295
– Marco Polo travels to China

1443
– Portuguese establish first African trading post at Arguin

1492
– Columbus lands in the Americas

1511
– Portuguese capture Malacca from Muslims

1518
– Spanish king authorizes slave trade to New World colonies

1519–1522
– Magellan's expedition circumnavigates the world

1521
– Cortés conquers the Mexica Empire

1533
– Pizarro conquers the Inca Empire

1602
– Dutch East India Company established

volume of this trade steadily increased, declining only during the years of the Black Death.

Merchants congregated in a series of cosmopolitan port cities strung around the Indian Ocean. The most developed area of this commercial web was in the South China Sea. In the fifteenth century, the port of Malacca became a great commercial entrepôt (AHN-truh-poh), a trading post to which goods were shipped for storage while awaiting redistribution.

The Mongol emperors opened the doors of China to the West, encouraging Europeans, like the Venetian trader and explorer Marco Polo, to do business there. Marco Polo's tales of his travels from 1271 to 1295 and his encounter with the Great Khan fueled Western fantasies about the exotic Orient. After the Mongols fell to the Ming Dynasty in 1368, China entered a period of economic expansion, population growth, and urbanization. By the end of the dynasty in 1644, the Chinese population had tripled to between 150 million and 200 million. Historians agree that China had the most advanced economy in the world until at least the start of the eighteenth century.

China also took the lead in exploration, sending Admiral Zheng He's fleet along the trade web as far west as Egypt. From 1405 to 1433, each of his seven expeditions involved hundreds of ships and tens of thousands of men.[1] Court conflicts and the need to defend against renewed Mongol encroachment led to the abandonment of the maritime expeditions after the deaths of Zheng He and the emperor. China's turning away from external trade opened new opportunities for European states to claim a decisive role in world trade.

Another center of trade in the Indian Ocean was India. The subcontinent had ancient links with its neighbors to the northwest: trade between South Asia and Mesopotamia dates back to the origins of human civilization. Romans had acquired cotton textiles, exotic animals, and other luxury goods from India. Arab merchants who circumnavigated India on their way to trade in the South China Sea established trading posts along the southern coast of India. India was an important contributor of goods to the world trading system; much of the world's pepper was grown there, and Indian cotton textiles were highly prized.

How and why did Europeans undertake ambitious voyages of expansion?	What was the impact of European conquest on the New World?	How did Europe and the world change after Columbus?	How did expansion change European attitudes and beliefs?	✓ LearningCurve Check what you know.

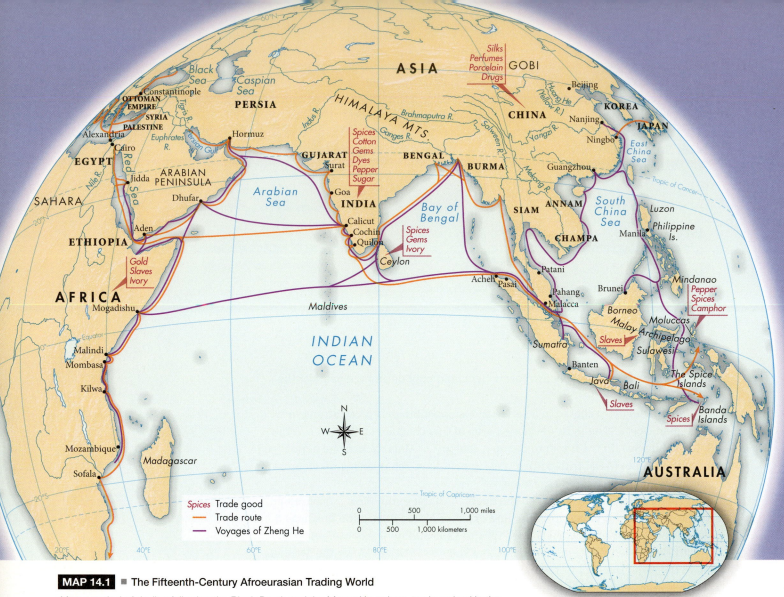

MAP 14.1 ■ The Fifteenth-Century Afroeurasian Trading World

After a period of decline following the Black Death and the Mongol invasions, trade revived in the fifteenth century. Muslim merchants dominated trade, linking ports in East Africa and the Red Sea with those in India and the Malay Archipelago. Chinese admiral Zheng He's voyages (1405–1433) followed the most important Indian Ocean trade routes in the hope of imposing Ming dominance of trade and tribute.

The Trading States of Africa

In the fifteenth century, most of the gold that reached Europe came from the western part of the Sudan region in West Africa and from the Akan (AH-kahn) peoples living near present-day Ghana. Transported across the Sahara by Arab and African traders on camels, the gold was sold in the ports of North Africa. Other trading routes led to the Egyptian cities of Alexandria and Cairo, where the Venetians held commercial privileges.

Nations inland that sat astride the north-south caravan routes grew wealthy from this trade. In the mid-thirteenth century the kingdom of Mali emerged as an important player on the overland trade route, gaining prestige from its ruler Mansa Musa's fabulous pilgrimage to Mecca from 1324–1325. In later centuries,

CHAPTER LOCATOR | **What was the Afroeurasian trading world before Columbus?**

the diversion of gold away from the trans-Sahara routes would weaken the inland states of Africa politically and economically.

Gold was one important object of trade; slaves were another. Slavery was practiced in Africa, as it was virtually everywhere else in the world, before the arrival of Europeans. Arabic and African merchants took West African slaves to the Mediterranean to be sold in European, Egyptian, and Middle Eastern markets and also brought eastern Europeans—a major element of European slavery—to West Africa as slaves. In addition, Indian and Arabic merchants traded slaves in the coastal regions of East Africa.

Legends about Africa played an important role in Europeans' imagination of the outside world. They long cherished the belief in a Christian nation in Africa ruled by a mythical king, Prester John, who was believed to be a descendant of one of the three kings who visited Jesus after his birth.

> **Africa and the Afroeurasian Trading World, ca. 1450**

- **North Africa:** Cairo, the capital of the Mamluk Egyptian empire, was a center of Islamic learning and religious authority as well as a hub for Indian Ocean trade goods

- **West Africa:** Connected to Islamic trading networks, West Africa was an important source of slaves, salt, and gold

- **East Africa:** Swahili-speaking city-states engaged in the Indian Ocean trade, exchanging ivory, rhinoceros horn, tortoise shells, and slaves for textiles, spices, cowrie shells, porcelain, and other goods

The Ottoman and Persian Empires

The Middle East served as an intermediary for trade among Asia, Africa, and Europe and was also an important supplier of goods, especially silk and cotton, for foreign exchange. Two great rival empires, the Persian Safavids (sah-FAH-vidz) and the Turkish Ottomans, dominated the region. Persian merchants could be found in trading communities as far away as the Indian Ocean. Persia was also a major producer and exporter of silk.

Under Sultan Mohammed II (r. 1451–1481), the Ottomans captured Europe's largest city, Constantinople, in May 1453. Renamed Istanbul, the city became the capital of the Ottoman Empire. By the mid-sixteenth century, the Ottomans controlled the sea trade in the eastern Mediterranean, Syria, Palestine, Egypt, and the rest of North Africa, and their power extended into Europe as far west as Vienna.

Ottoman expansion frightened Europeans. The Ottoman armies seemed invincible and the empire's desire for expansion limitless. The strength of the Ottomans helps explain some of the missionary fervor Christians brought to new territories. It also raised economic concerns. With trade routes to the East dominated by the Ottomans, Europeans wished to find new trade routes free of Ottoman control.

Genoese and Venetian Middlemen

In the late Middle Ages, the Italian city-states of Venice and Genoa controlled the European luxury trade with the East. In 1304, Venice established formal relations with the sultan of Mamluk Egypt, opening operations in Cairo, the gateway to

| How and why did Europeans undertake ambitious voyages of expansion? | What was the impact of European conquest on the New World? | How did Europe and the world change after Columbus? | How did expansion change European attitudes and beliefs? | ✓ LearningCurve Check what you know. |

415

Asian trade. Venetian merchants specialized in luxury goods which they obtained from middlemen in the eastern Mediterranean and Asia Minor.[2]

Venice's ancient rival was Genoa. In the wake of the Crusades, Genoa dominated the northern route to Asia through the Black Sea. Expansion in the thirteenth and fourteenth centuries took the Genoese as far as Persia and the Far East. In 1291, they sponsored an expedition into the Atlantic in search of India. The ships were lost, and their exact destination and motivations remain unknown. This voyage reveals the long roots of Genoese interest in Atlantic exploration.

In the fifteenth century, with Venice claiming victory in the spice trade, the Genoese shifted focus from trade to finance and from the Black Sea to the western Mediterranean. When Spanish and Portuguese voyages began to explore the western Atlantic (see pages 419–421), Genoese merchants, navigators, and financiers provided their skills to the Iberian monarchs, whose own subjects had much less commercial experience. Genoese merchants would eventually help finance Spanish colonization of the New World.

A major element of Italian trade was slavery. Merchants purchased slaves, many of whom were fellow Christians, in the Balkans. The men were sold to Egypt for the sultan's army or sent to work as agricultural laborers in the Mediterranean. Young girls, who constituted the majority of the trade, were sold in western Mediterranean ports as servants or concubines. After the loss of the Black Sea — and thus the source of slaves — to the Ottomans, the Genoese sought new supplies of slaves in the West, taking the Guanches (indigenous peoples from the Canary Islands), Muslim prisoners and Jewish refugees from Spain, and by the early 1500s both black and Berber Africans. With the growth of Spanish colonies in the New World, Genoese and Venetian merchants would become important players in the Atlantic slave trade.

Italian experience in colonial administration, slaving, and international trade served as a model for the Iberian states as they pushed European expansion to new heights. Mariners, merchants, and financiers from Venice and Genoa — most notably Christopher Columbus — played a crucial role in bringing the fruits of this experience to the Iberian Peninsula and to the New World.

> **QUICK REVIEW**

What role did Europe play in the Afroeurasian trading world prior to 1492?

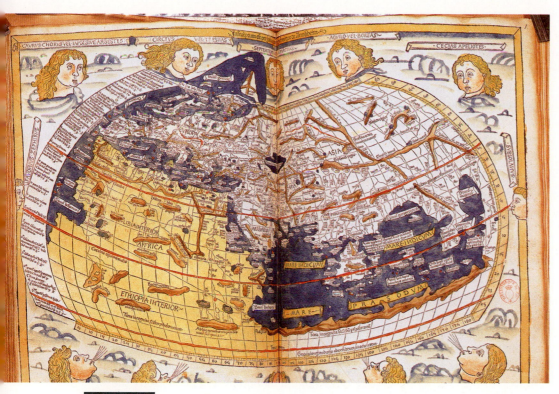

How and why did Europeans undertake ambitious voyages of expansion?

Ptolemy's Geography The recovery of Ptolemy's *Geography* in the early fifteenth century gave Europeans new access to ancient geographical knowledge. This 1486 world map, based on Ptolemy, is a great advance over medieval maps but contains errors with significant consequences for future exploration. It shows a single continent watered by a single ocean, with land covering three-quarters of the world's surface. Africa and Asia are joined with Europe, making the Indian Ocean a landlocked sea and rendering the circumnavigation of Africa impossible. Australia and the Americas are nonexistent, and the continent of Asia is stretched far to the east, greatly shortening the distance from Europe to Asia via the Atlantic. (Bibliothèque nationale de France/Giraudon/The Bridgeman Art Library)

AS WE HAVE SEEN, Europe was by no means isolated before the voyages of exploration and its "discovery" of the New World. But because they did not produce many products desired by Eastern elites, Europeans played only a small role in the Indian Ocean trading world. As Europe recovered after the Black Death, new European players entered the scene with novel technology, eager to spread Christianity and to undo Italian and Ottoman domination of trade with the East. A century after the plague, Iberian explorers began the overseas voyages that helped create the modern world.

Causes of European Expansion

European expansion had multiple causes. By the middle of the fifteenth century, Europe was experiencing a revival of population and economic activity after the lows of the Black Death. This revival created demand for luxuries, especially

How and why did Europeans undertake ambitious voyages of expansion?	What was the impact of European conquest on the New World?	How did Europe and the world change after Columbus?	How did expansion change European attitudes and beliefs?	✓ **LearningCurve** Check what you know.

spices, from the East. The fall of Constantinople and subsequent Ottoman control of trade routes created obstacles to fulfilling these demands. Europeans needed to find new sources of precious metal to trade with the Ottomans or find trade routes that bypassed the Ottomans.

Religious fervor was another important catalyst for expansion. The passion and energy ignited by the Christian reconquista (reconquest) of the Iberian Peninsula encouraged the Portuguese and Spanish to continue the Christian crusade. Overseas exploration was in some ways a transfer of the crusading spirit to new non-Christian territories. Because the remaining Muslim states, such as the mighty Ottoman Empire, were too strong to defeat, Iberians turned their attention elsewhere.

Combined with eagerness to earn profits and to spread Christianity was the desire for glory and the urge to chart new waters. Scholars have frequently described the European discoveries as a manifestation of Renaissance curiosity about the physical universe. The detailed journals many voyagers kept attest to their wonder and fascination with the new peoples and places they visited. Eagerness for exploration was heightened by a lack of opportunity at home. After the reconquista, young men of the Spanish upper classes found their economic and political opportunities greatly limited. The ambitious turned to the sea to seek their fortunes.

Their voyages were made possible by the growth of government power. The Spanish monarchy was stronger than before and in a position to support foreign ventures. In Portugal, explorers also looked to the monarchy, to Prince Henry the Navigator in particular (page 419), for financial support and encouragement. Like voyagers, monarchs shared a mix of motivations, from the desire to please God to the desire to win glory and profit from trade. Competition among European monarchs and between Protestant and Catholic states was an important factor in encouraging the steady stream of expeditions that began in the late fifteenth century.

The people who stayed at home had a powerful impact on the process. Royal ministers and factions at court influenced monarchs to provide or deny support for exploration. The small number of people who could read served as a rapt audience for tales of fantastic places and unknown peoples. Cosmography, natural history, and geography aroused enormous interest among educated people in the fifteenth and sixteenth centuries. One of the most popular books of the time was the fourteenth-century text *The Travels of Sir John Mandeville*, which purported to be a firsthand account of the author's travels in the Holy Land, Egypt, Ethiopia, the Middle East, and India and his service to the Mamluk sultan of Egypt and the Mongol Great Khan of China. Although we now know the stories were fictional, these fantastic tales of cannibals, one-eyed giants, men with the heads of dogs, and other marvels convinced audiences through their vividly and persuasively described details. Christopher Columbus took a copy of Mandeville and the equally popular and more reliable *The Travels of Marco Polo* on his voyage in 1492.

Technology and the Rise of Exploration

Technological developments in shipbuilding, weaponry, and navigation also paved the way for European expansion. Since ancient times, most seagoing vessels had been narrow, open boats called galleys, propelled largely by slaves or convicts manning the oars. Though well suited to the placid waters of the Mediterranean, galleys could not withstand the rough winds and uncharted shoals of

CHAPTER LOCATOR | What was the
Afroeurasian trading
world before Columbus?

418 CHAPTER 14 EUROPEAN EXPLORATION AND CONQUEST

the Atlantic. The need for sturdier craft, as well as population losses caused by the Black Death, forced the development of a new style of ship that would not require much labor to sail. In the course of the fifteenth century, the Portuguese developed the **caravel**, a small, light, three-mast sailing ship. Though somewhat slower than the galley, the caravel held more cargo. Its triangular lateen sails and sternpost rudder also made the caravel a much more maneuverable vessel. When fitted with cannon, it could dominate larger vessels.

Great strides in cartography and navigational aids were also made during this period. Around 1410, Arab scholars reintroduced Europeans to **Ptolemy's *Geography***. Written in the second century C.E., the work synthesized the geographical knowledge of the classical world. Ptolemy's work provided significant improvements over medieval cartography, but it also contained crucial errors. Unaware of the Americas, Ptolemy showed the world as much smaller than it is, so that Asia appeared not very distant from Europe to the west. Based on this work, cartographers fashioned new maps that combined classical knowledge with the latest information from mariners. First the Genoese and Venetians, and then the Portuguese and Spanish, took the lead in these advances.

The magnetic compass enabled sailors to determine their direction and position at sea. The astrolabe, an instrument invented by the ancient Greeks and perfected by Muslim navigators, was used to determine the altitude of the sun and other celestial bodies. It permitted mariners to plot their latitude, that is, their precise position north or south of the equator.

Like the astrolabe, much of the new technology that Europeans used on their voyages was borrowed from the East. Gunpowder, the compass, and the sternpost rudder were Chinese inventions. The lateen sail, which allowed European ships to tack against the wind, was a product of the Indian Ocean trade world. Advances in cartography drew on the rich tradition of Judeo-Arabic mathematical and astronomical learning in Iberia. In exploring new territories, European sailors thus called on techniques and knowledge developed over centuries in China, the Muslim world, and during travels on the Indian Ocean.

The Portuguese Overseas Empire

For centuries, Portugal was a small, poor nation on the margins of European life. The principal activities of its inhabitants were fishing and subsistence farming. Yet Portugal had a long history of seafaring and navigation. Blocked from access to western Europe by Spain, the Portuguese turned to the Atlantic and North Africa, whose waters they knew better than other Europeans. Nature favored the Portuguese: winds blowing along their coast offered passage to Africa, its Atlantic islands, and ultimately Brazil.

In the early phases of Portuguese exploration, Prince Henry (1394–1460), a younger son of the king, played a leading role. A nineteenth-century scholar dubbed Henry "the Navigator" because of his support for the study of geography and navigation and for the annual expeditions he sponsored down the western coast of Africa.

The objectives of Portuguese exploration policy included military glory; the conversion of Muslims; and a quest to find gold, slaves, and an overseas route to the spice markets of India. Portugal's conquest of Ceuta, an Arab city in northern Morocco, in 1415 marked the beginning of European overseas expansion. In the

caravel
► A small, maneuverable, three-mast sailing ship developed by the Portuguese in the fifteenth century that gave the Portuguese a distinct advantage in exploration and trade.

Ptolemy's *Geography*
► A second-century-C.E. work that synthesized the classical knowledge of geography and introduced the concepts of longitude and latitude. Reintroduced to Europeans about 1410 by Arab scholars, its ideas allowed cartographers to create more accurate maps.

How and why did Europeans undertake ambitious voyages of expansion?

What was the impact of European conquest on the New World?

How did Europe and the world change after Columbus?

How did expansion change European attitudes and beliefs?

☑ LearningCurve
Check what you know.

419

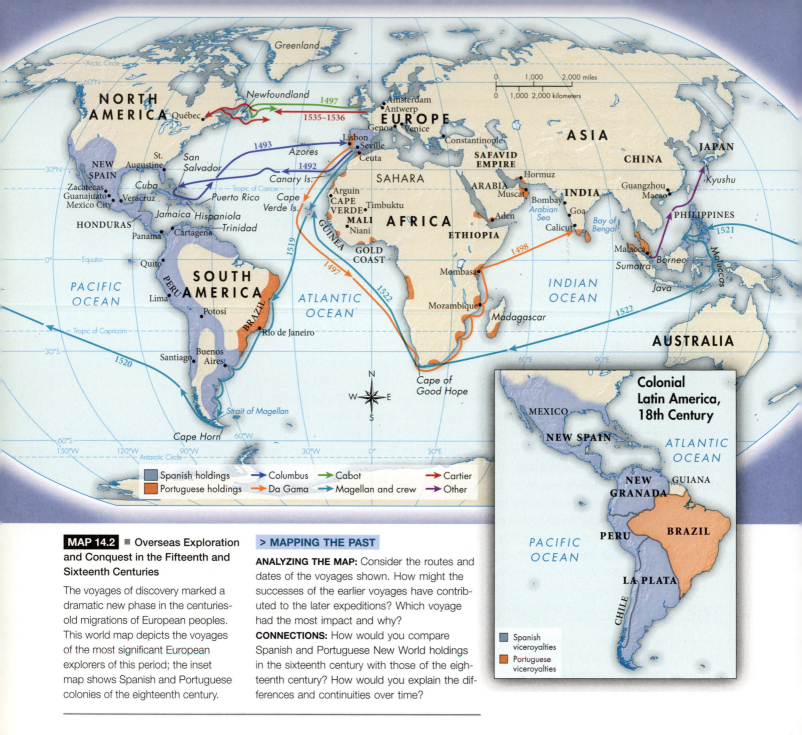

MAP 14.2 ■ Overseas Exploration and Conquest in the Fifteenth and Sixteenth Centuries

The voyages of discovery marked a dramatic new phase in the centuries-old migrations of European peoples. This world map depicts the voyages of the most significant European explorers of this period; the inset map shows Spanish and Portuguese colonies of the eighteenth century.

> MAPPING THE PAST

ANALYZING THE MAP: Consider the routes and dates of the voyages shown. How might the successes of the earlier voyages have contributed to the later expeditions? Which voyage had the most impact and why?

CONNECTIONS: How would you compare Spanish and Portuguese New World holdings in the sixteenth century with those of the eighteenth century? How would you explain the differences and continuities over time?

1420s, under Henry's direction, the Portuguese began to settle the Atlantic islands of Madeira (ca. 1420) and the Azores (1427). In 1443, they founded their first African commercial settlement at Arguin in North Africa. By the time of Henry's death in 1460, his support for exploration was vindicated by thriving sugar plantations on the Atlantic islands, the first arrival of enslaved Africans in Portugal (see page 431), and new access to African gold.

The Portuguese next established trading posts and forts on the gold-rich Guinea coast and penetrated into the African continent all the way to Timbuktu (**Map 14.2**). By 1500, Portugal controlled the flow of African gold to Europe. The golden century of Portuguese prosperity had begun.

The Portuguese then pushed farther south down the west coast of Africa. In 1487, Bartholomew Diaz rounded the Cape of Good Hope at the southern tip, but storms and a threatened mutiny forced him to turn back. A decade later, Vasco da Gama succeeded in rounding the Cape, and, with the help of an Indian guide, he reached the port of Calicut in India. Overcoming local hostility, he returned to Lisbon loaded with spices and samples of Indian cloth. Thereafter, a Portuguese convoy set out for passage around the Cape every March.

Lisbon became the entrance port for Asian goods into Europe, but this was not accomplished without a fight. Muslim-controlled port city-states had long controlled the rich spice trade of the Indian Ocean, and they did not surrender their dominance willingly. From 1500 to 1511, the Portuguese used a combination of bombardment and diplomatic treaties to establish trading forts at Calicut, Malacca, Hormus, and Goa, thereby laying the foundation for Portuguese imperialism in the sixteenth and seventeenth centuries.

In March 1493, between the voyages of Diaz and da Gama, Spanish ships under a Genoese mariner named Christopher Columbus (1451–1506), in the service of the Spanish crown, entered Lisbon harbor. Spain had also begun the quest for an empire.

The Problem of Christopher Columbus

Christopher Columbus is a controversial figure in history—glorified by some as a courageous explorer, vilified by others as a cruel exploiter of Native Americans. Rather than judging Columbus by debates and standards of our time, it is more important to understand him in the context of his own time. First, what kind of man was Columbus, and what forces or influences shaped him? Second, in sailing westward from Europe, what were his goals? Third, did he achieve his goals, and what did he make of his discoveries?

In his dream of a westward passage to the Indies, Columbus embodied a long-standing Genoese ambition to circumvent Venetian domination of eastward trade, which was now being claimed by the Portuguese. Columbus was very knowledgeable about the sea. He had worked as a mapmaker, and he was familiar with fifteenth-century Portuguese navigational developments and the use of the compass as a nautical instrument. Columbus was also a deeply religious man. Like the Spanish rulers and most Europeans of his age, Columbus understood Christianity as a missionary religion that should be carried to all places of the earth. He viewed himself as a divine agent, fated to spread Christianity beyond Europe.

What was the object of this first voyage? Columbus gave the answer in the very title of the expedition, "The Enterprise of the Indies." He wanted to find a direct ocean trading route to Asia. Rejected for funding by the Portuguese in 1483 and by Ferdinand and Isabella in 1486, the project finally won the backing of the Spanish monarchy in 1492. Inspired by the stories of Mandeville and Marco Polo, Columbus dreamed of reaching the court of the Mongol emperor, the Great Khan (not realizing that the Ming Dynasty had overthrown the Mongols in 1368). Based on Ptolemy's *Geography* and other texts, he expected to pass the islands of Japan and then land on the east coast of China.

How did Columbus interpret what he had found, and in his mind did he achieve what he had set out to do? Columbus's small fleet left Spain on August 3,

| How and why did Europeans undertake ambitious voyages of expansion? | What was the impact of European conquest on the New World? | How did Europe and the world change after Columbus? | How did expansion change European attitudes and beliefs? | ✓ LearningCurve Check what you know. |

421

1492. He landed in the Bahamas, which he christened San Salvador, on October 12, 1492. Columbus believed he had found some small islands off the east coast of Japan. On encountering natives of the islands, he gave them some beads and "many other trifles of small value," pronouncing them delighted with these gifts and eager to trade. Believing he was in the Indies, he called them "Indians," a name later applied to all inhabitants of the Americas.

Scholars have identified the inhabitants of the islands as the Taino people, speakers of the Arawak language, who inhabited Hispaniola (modern-day Haiti and Dominican Republic) and other islands in the Caribbean. Columbus received reassuring reports from Taino villagers of the presence of gold and of a great king in the vicinity. From San Salvador, Columbus sailed southwest, believing that this course would take him to Japan or the coast of China. He landed instead on Cuba on October 28. Deciding that he must be on the mainland near the coastal city of Quinsay (now Hangzhou), he sent a small embassy inland with letters from Ferdinand and Isabella and instructions to locate the grand city.

The landing party found only small villages. Confronted with this disappointment, Columbus apparently gave up on his aim to meet the Great Khan. Instead, he focused on trying to find gold or other valuables among the peoples he had discovered. The sight of Taino people wearing gold ornaments on Hispaniola seemed to prove that gold was available in the region. In January, confident that its source would soon be found, he headed back to Spain to report on his discovery. News of his voyage spread rapidly across Europe.[3]

Over the next decades, the Spanish would follow a policy of conquest and colonization in the New World rather than one of exchange with equals. On his second voyage, Columbus forcibly subjugated the island of Hispaniola and enslaved its indigenous peoples. On this and subsequent voyages, Columbus brought with him settlers for the new Spanish territories, along with agricultural seed and livestock. Columbus himself, however, had limited skills in governing. Revolt soon broke out against him and his brother on Hispaniola. A royal expedition sent to investigate returned the brothers to Spain in chains. Columbus was cleared of wrongdoing, but the territories remained under royal control.

Columbus was very much a man of his times. To the end of his life in 1506, he believed that he had found small islands off the coast of Asia. He could not know that the scale of his discoveries would revolutionize world power, raising issues of trade, settlement, government bureaucracy, and the rights of native and African peoples.

Columbus's First Voyage to the New World, 1492–1493

Later Explorers

The Florentine navigator Amerigo Vespucci (veh-SPOO-chee) (1454–1512) realized what Columbus had not. Writing about his discoveries on the coast of modern-day Venezuela, Vespucci stated: "Those new regions which we found and explored with the fleet . . . we may rightly call a New World." In recognition of Amerigo's bold claim, the continent was named for him.

To settle competing claims to the Atlantic discoveries, Spain and Portugal turned to Pope Alexander VI. The resulting **Treaty of Tordesillas** (tor-duh-SEE-yuhs) in 1494 gave Spain everything to the west of an imaginary line drawn down the Atlantic and Portugal everything to the east. This arbitrary division worked in

Treaty of Tordesillas

▶ The 1494 agreement giving Spain everything to the west of an imaginary line drawn down the Atlantic and giving Portugal everything to the east.

CHAPTER LOCATOR | What was the Afroeurasian trading world before Columbus?

422 CHAPTER 14 EUROPEAN EXPLORATION AND CONQUEST

Portugal's favor when in 1500 an expedition led by Pedro Alvares Cabral, en route to India, landed on the coast of Brazil, which Cabral claimed as Portuguese territory.

The search for profits determined the direction of Spanish exploration. With insignificant profits from the Caribbean compared to the enormous riches that the Portuguese were reaping in Asia, Spain renewed the search for a western passage to Asia. In 1519, with this goal in mind, Ferdinand Magellan (1480–1521) sailed southwest across the Atlantic to Brazil, and after a long search along the coast, he located the treacherous straits that now bear his name, passing through them into the Pacific (see Map 14.2, page 420). From there, his fleet sailed north up the west coast of South America and then headed west into the immense expanse of the Pacific toward the Malay Archipelago.

Terrible storms, disease, starvation, and violence devastated the expedition. Magellan had set out with a fleet of five ships and around 270 men. Sailors on two of the ships attempted mutiny on the South American coast; one ship was lost, and another ship deserted and returned to Spain before even traversing the straits. The trip across the Pacific took ninety-eight days, and the men survived on rats and sawdust. Magellan himself died in a skirmish in the islands known today as the Philippines. Only one ship, with eighteen men aboard, returned to Spain from the east by way of the Indian Ocean, the Cape of Good Hope, and the Atlantic in 1522. The voyage—the first to circumnavigate the globe—had taken close to three years.

This voyage revolutionized Europeans' understanding of the world by demonstrating the vastness of the Pacific. The earth was clearly much larger than Columbus had believed. Although the voyage made a small profit in spices, it also demonstrated that the westward passage to the Indies was too long and dangerous for commercial purposes. Spain soon abandoned the attempt to oust Portugal from the Eastern spice trade and concentrated on exploiting her New World territories.

Spain's European rivals also set sail across the Atlantic during the early days of exploration in search of a northwest passage to the Indies. In 1497, John Cabot, a Genoese merchant living in London, undertook a voyage to Brazil but discovered Newfoundland instead. The next year he returned and reconnoitered the New England coast. These forays proved futile. Between 1576 and 1578, Martin Frobisher made three voyages in and around the Canadian bay that now bears his name. Frobisher brought a quantity of ore back to England with him, but it proved to be worthless.

Early French exploration of the Atlantic was equally frustrating. Between 1534 and 1541, Frenchman Jacques Cartier made several voyages and explored the St. Lawrence region of Canada, searching for a passage to the wealth of Asia. When this hope proved vain, the French turned to a new source of profit within Canada itself: trade in beavers and other furs. As had the Portuguese in Asia, French traders bartered with local peoples, who maintained control over their trade goods. French fishermen also competed with Spanish and English ships for the teeming schools of cod they found in the Atlantic waters around Newfoundland.

Spanish Conquest in the New World

In 1519, the year Magellan departed on his worldwide expedition, the Spanish sent an exploratory expedition from their post in Cuba to the mainland under the command of the **conquistador** (kahn-KEES-tuh-dor) Hernando Cortés (1485–1547).

conquistador

▶ Spanish for "conqueror"; Spanish soldier-explorers, such as Hernando Cortés and Francisco Pizarro, who sought to conquer the New World for the Spanish crown.

How and why did Europeans undertake ambitious voyages of expansion?

What was the impact of European conquest on the New World?

How did Europe and the world change after Columbus?

How did expansion change European attitudes and beliefs?

✓ LearningCurve
Check what you know.

423

Invasion of Tenochtitlán, 1519–1521

→ Cortés's original route, 1519
→ Cortés's retreat, 1520
→ Cortés's return route, 1520–1521

Cortés was to launch the conquest of the **Mexica Empire**. Its people were later called the Aztecs, but now most scholars prefer to use the term *Mexica* to refer to them and their empire.

The Mexica Empire was ruled by Montezuma II (r. 1502–1520) from his capital at Tenochtitlán (tay-nawch-teet-LAHN), now Mexico City. Larger than any European city of the time, it was the heart of a sophisticated civilization with advanced mathematics, astronomy, and engineering; a complex social system; and oral poetry and historical traditions.

Cortés landed on the coast of the Gulf of Mexico on April 21, 1519. The Spanish camp was soon visited by delegations of unarmed Mexica leaders bearing lavish gifts and news of their great emperor. (See "Picturing the Past: Doña Marina Translating for Hernando Cortés During His Meeting with Montezuma," page 425.) Impressed with the wealth of the local people, Cortés soon began to exploit internal dissension within the empire to his own advantage.

Cortés quickly forged an alliance with the Tlaxcalas (Tlah-scalas) and other subject kingdoms, which chafed under Mexica rule. In October, a combined Spanish-Tlaxcalan force occupied the city of Cholula, the second largest in the empire and its religious capital, and massacred many thousands of inhabitants. Strengthened by this display of power, Cortés made alliances with other native kingdoms. In November 1519, with a few hundred Spanish men and some six thousand indigenous warriors, Cortés marched on Tenochtitlán.

Uncertain of how he should respond, Montezuma refrained from attacking the Spaniards as they advanced toward his capital and welcomed Cortés and his men into Tenochtitlán. His hesitation proved disastrous. When Cortés took Montezuma hostage and tried to rule the Mexica through the emperor's authority, Montezuma's influence over his people crumbled.

In May 1520, Spanish forces massacred Mexica warriors dancing at an indigenous festival. This act provoked an uprising within Tenochtitlán, during which Montezuma was killed. The Spaniards and their allies escaped from the city and began gathering forces against the Mexica. One year later, in May 1521, Cortés laid siege to Tenochtitlán at the head of an army of approximately 1,000 Spanish and 75,000 native warriors.[4] Spanish victory in August 1521 resulted from Spain's superior technology and the effects of the siege and smallpox. After the defeat of Tenochtitlán, Cortés and other conquistadors began the systematic conquest of Mexico.

More surprising than the defeat of the Mexica was the fall of the remote **Inca Empire**. Like the Mexica, the Incas had created a civilization that rivaled that of the Europeans in population and complexity. To unite their vast and well-fortified empire, the Incas built an extensive network of roads, along which traveled a highly efficient postal service. The imperial government, with its capital in the city of Cuzco, taxed, fed, and protected its subjects.

At the time of the Spanish invasion, the Inca Empire had been weakened by an epidemic of disease, possibly smallpox. Even worse, the empire had been embroiled in a civil war over succession. Francisco Pizarro (ca. 1475–1541), a conquistador of modest Spanish origins, landed on the northern coast of Peru on May 13, 1532, the very day Atahualpa (ah-tuh-WAHL-puh) won control of the empire after five years of fighting. As Pizarro advanced across the steep Andes toward Cuzco, Atahualpa was proceeding to the capital for his coronation.

Like Montezuma in Mexico, Atahualpa was aware of the Spaniards' move-

CHAPTER LOCATOR | What was the Afroeurasian trading world before Columbus?

CHAPTER 14

424 EUROPEAN EXPLORATION AND CONQUEST

Doña Marina Translating for Hernando Cortés

In April 1519, Doña Marina (or Malintzin as she is known in Nahuatl [NAH-wah-tuhl]) was among twenty women given to the Spanish as slaves. Fluent in Nahuatl and Yucatec Mayan (spoken by a Spanish priest accompanying Cortés), she acted as an interpreter and diplomatic guide for the Spanish. She had a close relationship with Cortés and bore his son, Don Martín Cortés, in 1522. This image, which shows her translating during a meeting between Cortés and Montezuma, was created by Tlaxcalan artists shortly after the conquest of Mexico and represents one indigenous perspective on the events. (The Granger Collection, New York)

> PICTURING THE PAST

ANALYZING THE IMAGE: What role does Doña Marina (far right) appear to be playing in this image? Does she appear to be subservient or equal to Cortés (right, seated)? How did the painter indicate her identity as non-Spanish?
CONNECTIONS: How do you think the native rulers negotiating with Cortés might have viewed her? What about a Spanish viewer of this image? What does the absence of other women here suggest about the role of women in these societies?

ments. He sent envoys to invite the Spanish to meet him in the provincial town of Cajamarca. His plan was to lure the Spanish into a trap. With an army of some forty thousand men stationed nearby, Atahualpa felt he had little to fear. Instead, the Spaniards ambushed and captured him, collected an enormous ransom in gold, and then executed him in 1533. The Spanish now marched on the capital of the empire itself, profiting once again from internal conflicts to form alliances with local peoples. When Cuzco fell in 1533, the Spanish plundered immense riches in gold and silver.

How and why did Europeans undertake ambitious voyages of expansion? | What was the impact of European conquest on the New World? | How did Europe and the world change after Columbus? | How did expansion change European attitudes and beliefs? | ✓LearningCurve Check what you know.

425

Early French and English Settlement in the New World

For over a hundred years, the Spanish and the Portuguese dominated settlement in the New World. The first English colony was founded at Roanoke (in what is now North Carolina) in 1585. After a three-year loss of contact with England, the settlers were found to have disappeared; their fate remains a mystery. The colony of Virginia, founded by a private company of investors at Jamestown in 1607, also struggled in its first years and relied on food from the Powhatan Confederacy. Over time, the colony gained a steady hold by producing tobacco for a growing European market.

Settlement on the coast of New England was undertaken for different reasons. There, radical Protestants sought to escape Anglican repression in England and begin new lives. The small and struggling outpost of Plymouth (1620), founded by the Pilgrims who arrived on the *Mayflower*, was followed by Massachusetts (1630), a colony of Puritans that grew into a prosperous settlement.

Whereas the Spanish conquered indigenous empires and established large-scale dominance over Mexico and Peru, English settlements merely hugged the Atlantic coastline. This did not prevent conflict with the indigenous inhabitants over land and resources, however. At Jamestown, for example, English expansion undermined prior cooperation with the Powhatan Confederacy; disease and warfare with the English led to drastic population losses among the Powhatans.

French navigator and explorer Samuel de Champlain founded the first permanent French settlement, at Quebec, in 1608. Ville-Marie, latter-day Montreal, was founded in 1642. Following the waterways of the St. Lawrence, the Great Lakes, and the Mississippi, the French ventured into much of modern-day Canada and at least thirty-five of the fifty states of the United States. French traders forged relations with the Huron Confederacy, a league of four indigenous nations that dominated a large region north of Lake Erie, as a means of gaining access to hunting grounds and trade routes for beaver and other animals. In 1682, French explorer René-Robert Cavelier LaSalle descended the Mississippi to the Gulf of Mexico, opening the way for French occupation of Louisiana.

While establishing their foothold in the north, the French slowly acquired new territories in the West Indies, including Cayenne (1604), St. Christophe (1625), Martinique, Guadeloupe, and Saint-Domingue (1697) on the western side of the island of Hispaniola. These islands became centers of tobacco and then sugar production. French ambitions on the mainland and in the Caribbean sparked a century-long competition with the English.

European involvement in the Americas led to the profound transformation of pre-existing indigenous societies and the rise of a transatlantic slave trade. It also led to an acceleration of global trade and cultural exchange. Over time, the combination of indigenous, European, and African cultures gave birth to new societies in the New World. In turn, the profits of trade and the impact of cultural exchange greatly influenced European society.

> QUICK REVIEW

What role did technology play in initiating the European Age of Discovery? What role did ideas and beliefs play?

CHAPTER LOCATOR | What was the Afroeurasian trading world before Columbus?

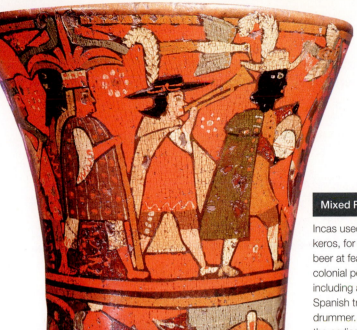

Mixed Race Procession

Incas used drinking vessels, known as keros, for the ritual consumption of maize beer at feasts. This kero from the early colonial period shows a procession including an Incan leader preceded by a Spanish trumpet player and an African drummer. This is believed to be one of the earliest representations of an African in the Americas. (akg-images/Werner Forman)

What was the impact of European conquest on the New World?

THE GROWING EUROPEAN PRESENCE in the New World transformed its land and its peoples forever. Violence and disease wrought devastating losses, while surviving peoples encountered new political, social, and economic organizations imposed by Europeans. The Columbian exchange brought infectious diseases to the Americas, but it also gave new crops to the Old World that altered consumption patterns in Europe and across the globe (see page 430).

Colonial Administration

Spanish conquistadors had claimed the lands they had "discovered" for the Spanish crown. As the wealth of the new territories became apparent, the Spanish government acted to impose its authority and remove that of the original conquerors. The House of Trade, located in Seville, controlled the flow of goods and people to and from the colonies, while the Council of the Indies guided royal policy and served as the highest court for colonial affairs.

The crown divided its New World possessions into two **viceroyalties,** or administrative divisions: New Spain, with the capital at Mexico City, and Peru, with the capital at Lima. Two new viceroyalties added in the eighteenth century were New Granada, with Bogotá as its administrative center, and La Plata, with Buenos Aires as the capital (see Map 14.2, page 420).

The Portuguese adopted similar patterns of rule. India House in Lisbon functioned much like the Spanish House of Trade, and royal representatives oversaw its possessions in West Africa and Asia. To secure the vast expanse of Brazil, the Portuguese implemented the system of captaincies, hereditary grants of land given to nobles and loyal officials who bore the costs of settling and administering their territories. Over time, the Crown secured greater power over the captaincies, appointing royal governors to act as administrators.

viceroyalties
▶ The name for the four administrative units of Spanish possessions in the Americas: New Spain, Peru, New Granada, and La Plata.

How and why did Europeans undertake ambitious voyages of expansion?	**What was the impact of European conquest on the New World?**	How did Europe and the world change after Columbus?	How did expansion change European attitudes and beliefs?	✓ LearningCurve Check what you know.

Like their European neighbors, France and England initially entrusted their overseas colonies to individual explorers and monopoly trading companies. By the end of the seventeenth century, the French crown had successfully imposed direct rule over New France and other colonies. The king appointed military governors to rule alongside intendants, royal officials possessed of broad administrative and financial authority within their intendancies.

England's colonies followed a distinctive path. Drawing on English traditions of representative government (see Chapter 15, page 477), English colonists established their own autonomous assemblies to regulate local affairs. Wealthy merchants and landowners dominated the assemblies, although even common men had more say in politics than was the case in England.

Impact of European Settlement on the Lives of Indigenous Peoples

Before Columbus's arrival, the Americas were inhabited by thousands of groups of indigenous peoples, each with distinct cultures and languages. Their patterns of life varied widely, from hunter-gatherer tribes organized into tribal confederations on the North American plains to the large-scale agriculture-based empires of the Mexica and the Inca. Although historians continue to debate the numbers, the best estimate is that in 1492 the peoples of the Americas numbered around 50 million.

Their lives were radically transformed by the arrival of Europeans. In the sixteenth century, perhaps two hundred thousand Spaniards immigrated to the New World. After assisting in the conquest of the Mexica and the Incas, these men carved out vast estates called haciendas in temperate grazing areas and imported Spanish livestock. In coastal tropical areas, the Spanish erected huge plantations to supply sugar to the European market. Around 1550, silver was discovered in present-day Bolivia and Mexico. To work the cattle ranches, sugar plantations, and silver mines, the conquistadors first turned to the indigenous peoples.

encomienda system

▶ A system whereby the Spanish crown granted the conquerors the right to employ groups of Indians forcibly in exchange for providing food, shelter, and Christian teaching.

The Spanish quickly established the **encomienda system**, in which the Crown granted the conquerors the right to employ groups of Native Americans as laborers or to demand tribute from them in exchange for providing food and shelter. Theoretically, the Spanish were supposed to care for the indigenous people under their command and teach them Christianity; in actuality, the system was a brutal form of exploitation only one level removed from slavery.

The new conditions and hardships imposed by conquest and colonization resulted in enormous native population losses. The major cause of death was disease. Having little or no resistance to diseases brought from the Old World, the inhabitants of the New World fell victim to smallpox, typhus, influenza, and other illnesses. Another factor was overwork, from which native workers died in staggering numbers. Forced labor diverted local people from agricultural work, leading to malnutrition, reduced fertility rates, and starvation. Malnutrition and hunger in turn lowered resistance to disease. Many indigenous peoples also died through outright violence in warfare.[5]

The Franciscan Bartolomé de Las Casas (1474–1566) was one of the most outspoken critics of Spanish brutality against indigenous peoples. Las Casas and other missionaries asserted that the Indians had human rights, and through their persistent pressure, the Spanish emperor Charles V abolished the worst abuses of the encomienda system in 1531.

CHAPTER LOCATOR | What was the Afroeurasian trading world before Columbus?

Franciscan, Dominican, and Jesuit missionaries who accompanied the conquistadors and other European settlers played an important role in converting indigenous peoples to Christianity, teaching them European methods of agriculture, and instilling loyalty to their colonial masters. In areas with small Spanish populations, the friars set up missions for a period of ten years, after which established churches and priests would take over and they could move on to new areas. Jesuits in New France also established missions far distant from the centers of French settlement.

Missionaries' success in conversion varied over time and space. In Central and South America, large-scale conversion forged enduring Catholic cultures in Portuguese and Spanish colonies. Galvanized by their opposition to Catholicism and fueled by their own religious fervor, English colonizers also made efforts to convert indigenous peoples. On the whole, however, these attempts were less successful, in part because the English did not establish wholesale dominance over large native populations as did the Spanish.

Rather than a straightforward imposition of Christianity, conversion entailed a complex process of cultural exchange. Catholic friars were among the first Europeans to seek understanding of native cultures and languages as part of their effort to render Christianity comprehensible to indigenous people. In turn, Christian ideas and practices in the New World took on a distinctive character.

The pattern of devastating disease and population loss occurred everywhere Europeans settled. The best estimate of native population loss is a decline from roughly 50 million people in 1492 to around 9 million by 1700. It is important to note, however, that native populations and cultures did survive the conquest period, sometimes by blending with European incomers and sometimes by maintaining cultural autonomy.

For colonial administrators, the main problem posed by the astronomically high death rate was the loss of a subjugated labor force to work the mines and sugar plantations. As early as 1511, King Ferdinand of Spain observed that the Indians seemed to be "very frail" and that "one black could do the work of four Indians."[6] Thus was born an absurd myth, and the new tragedy of the transatlantic slave trade would soon follow (see page 431).

Life in the Colonies

Many factors helped to shape life in European colonies, including geographical location, religion, indigenous cultures and practices, patterns of European settlement, and the cultural attitudes and official policies of the European nations that claimed them as empire. Throughout the New World, colonial settlements were hedged by immense borderlands where European power was weak and Europeans and non-Europeans interacted on a more equal basis.

Women played a crucial role in the creation of new identities and the continuation of old ones. The first explorers formed unions with native women, through coercion or choice, and relied on them as translators and guides and to form alliances with indigenous powers. As settlement developed, the character of each colony was influenced by the presence or absence of European women. Where women and children accompanied men, as in the British colonies and the Spanish mainland colonies, new settlements took on European languages, religion, and ways of life. Where European women did not accompany men, as on the west

How and why did Europeans undertake ambitious voyages of expansion?

What was the impact of European conquest on the New World?

How did Europe and the world change after Columbus?

How did expansion change European attitudes and beliefs?

☑ LearningCurve
Check what you know.

429

coast of Africa and most European outposts in Asia, local populations largely retained their own cultures, to which male Europeans acclimatized themselves.

Most women who crossed the Atlantic were Africans, constituting four-fifths of the female newcomers before 1800.[7] Wherever slavery existed, masters profited from their power to engage in sexual relations with enslaved women. One important difference among European colonies was in the status of children born from such unions. In some colonies, mostly those dominated by the Portuguese, Spanish, or French, substantial populations of free people of color descended from the freed children of such unions. In English colonies, masters were less likely to free children they fathered with female slaves.

The mixing of indigenous peoples with Europeans and Africans created whole new populations and ethnicities and complex self-identities. In Spanish America, the word *mestizo*— *métis* in French—described people of mixed Native American and European descent. The blanket terms "mulatto" and "people of color" were used for those of mixed African and European origin. With its immense slave-based plantation agriculture system, large indigenous population, and relatively low Portuguese immigration, Brazil developed a particularly complex racial and ethnic mosaic.

The Columbian Exchange

Columbian exchange

▶ The exchange of animals, plants, and diseases between the Old and the New Worlds.

The migration of peoples to the New World led to an exchange of animals, plants, and disease, a complex process known as the **Columbian exchange**. Columbus had brought sugar plants on his second voyage; Spaniards also introduced rice and bananas from the Canary Islands, and the Portuguese carried these items to Brazil. Everywhere they settled, the Spanish and Portuguese brought and raised wheat. Grapes and olives brought over from Spain did well in parts of Peru and Chile.

Apart from wild turkeys and game, Native Americans had no animals for food. They did not domesticate animals for travel or use as beasts of burden, except for alpacas and llamas in the Inca Empire. On his second voyage in 1493, Columbus introduced horses, cattle, sheep, dogs, pigs, chickens, and goats. The horse enabled the Spanish conquerors and native populations to travel faster and farther and to transport heavy loads. In turn, Europeans returned home with many food crops that became central elements of their diet.

Disease brought by European people and animals was perhaps the most important form of exchange. The wave of catastrophic epidemic disease that swept the Western Hemisphere after 1492 can be seen as an extension of the swath of devastation wreaked by the Black Death in the 1300s, first in Asia and then in Europe. The world after Columbus was thus unified by disease as well as by trade and colonization.

> **QUICK REVIEW**

What policies and institutions did the Spanish and Portuguese develop to facilitate the exploitation of Indian labor and the natural resources of the Americas?

CHAPTER LOCATOR | What was the Afroeurasian trading world before Columbus?

Silver Coin from Potosí After the discovery of the Americas, a wave of new items entered European markets, silver foremost among them. The incredibly rich silver mines at Potosí (in modern-day Bolivia) were the source of this eight-reale coin struck at the mine during the reign of Charles II. Such coins were the original "pieces of eight" prized by pirates and adventurers. (Hoberman Collection/SuperStock)

THE CENTURIES-OLD AFROEURASIAN TRADE WORLD was forever changed by the European voyages of discovery and their aftermath. For the first time, a truly global economy emerged in the sixteenth and seventeenth centuries. The ancient civilizations of Europe, Africa, the Americas, and Asia confronted one another in new and rapidly evolving ways. Those confrontations often led to conquest and exploitation, but they also contributed to cultural exchange and renewal.

Sugar and Slavery

Throughout the Middle Ages, slavery was deeply entrenched in the Mediterranean, but it was not based on race; many slaves were white. How, then, did black African slavery enter the European picture and take root in the Americas? In 1453, the Ottoman capture of Constantinople halted the flow of white slaves from the eastern Mediterranean to western Europe. The successes of the Iberian reconquista also meant that the supply of Muslim captives had drastically diminished. Cut off from its traditional sources of slaves, Mediterranean Europe then turned to sub-Saharan Africa, which had a long history of internal slave trading. (See "Individuals in Society: Juan de Pareja," page 432.) As Portuguese explorers began

| How and why did Europeans undertake ambitious voyages of expansion? | What was the impact of European conquest on the New World? | **How did Europe and the world change after Columbus?** | How did expansion change European attitudes and beliefs? | ☑ LearningCurve Check what you know. |

431

During the long wars of the reconquista, Muslims and Christians captured each other in battle and used the defeated as slaves. As the Muslims were gradually eliminated from Iberia in the fifteenth and sixteenth centuries, the Spanish and Portuguese turned to the west coast of Africa for a new supply of slaves. Most slaves worked as domestic servants rather than in the fields. Some received specialized training as artisans.

Not all people of African descent were slaves, and some experienced both freedom and slavery in a single lifetime. The life and career of Juan de Pareja (pah-REH-huh) illustrates the complexities of the Iberian slave system and the heights of achievement possible for those who gained freedom.

Pareja was born in Antequera, an agricultural region and the old center of Muslim culture near Seville in southern Spain. Of his parents we know nothing. Because a rare surviving document calls him a "mulatto," one of his parents must have been white and the other must have had some African blood. In 1630, Pareja applied to the mayor of Seville

for permission to travel to Madrid to visit his brother and "to perfect his art." The document lists his occupation as "a painter in Seville." Because it mentions no other name, it is reasonable to assume that Pareja arrived in Madrid a free man. Sometime between 1630 and 1648, however, he came into the possession of the artist Diego Velázquez (1599–1660); Pareja became a slave.

How did Velázquez acquire Pareja? By purchase? As a gift? Had Pareja fallen into debt or committed some crime and thereby lost his freedom? We do not know. Velázquez, the greatest Spanish painter of the seventeenth century, had a large studio with many assistants. Pareja was set to grinding powders to make colors and to preparing canvases. He must have demonstrated ability because when Velázquez went to Rome in 1648, he chose Pareja to accompany him.

In 1650, as practice for a portrait of Pope Innocent X, Velázquez painted Pareja. The portrait shows Pareja dressed in fine clothing and gazing self-confidently at the viewer. Displayed in Rome in a public exhibition of Velázquez's work, the painting won acclaim from his contemporaries. That same year, Velázquez signed the document that gave Pareja his freedom, to become effective in 1654. Pareja lived out the rest of his life as an independent painter.

What does the public career of Pareja tell us about the man and his world? Pareja's career suggests that a person of African descent might fall into slavery and yet still acquire professional training and work alongside his master in a position of confidence. If lucky enough to be freed, a former slave could exercise a profession and live his own life in Madrid. Pareja's experience was far from typical for a slave in the seventeenth century, but it reminds us of the myriad forms that slavery took in this period.

Velázquez, *Juan de Pareja*, 1650. (Private Collection/Photo © Christie's Images/The Bridgeman Art Library)

QUESTIONS FOR ANALYSIS

1. Slavery was an established institution in Spain. Speculate on Velázquez's possible reasons for giving Pareja his freedom.
2. In what ways does Pareja represent Europe's increasing participation in global commerce and exploration?

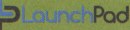

ONLINE DOCUMENT PROJECT

How could an individual like Pareja experience both slavery and freedom in a single lifetime? Keeping the question above in mind, analyze sources from Pareja's contemporaries that reflect changing ideas about racial identity and slavery, and then complete a writing assignment based on the evidence and details from this chapter. *See inside the front cover to learn more.*

Sources: Jonathan Brown, *Velázquez: Painter and Courtier* (New Haven, Conn.: Yale University Press, 1986); *Grove Dictionary of Art* (New York: Macmillan, 2000); Sister Wendy Beckett, *Sister Wendy's American Collection* (New York: Harper Collins Publishers, 2000), p. 15.

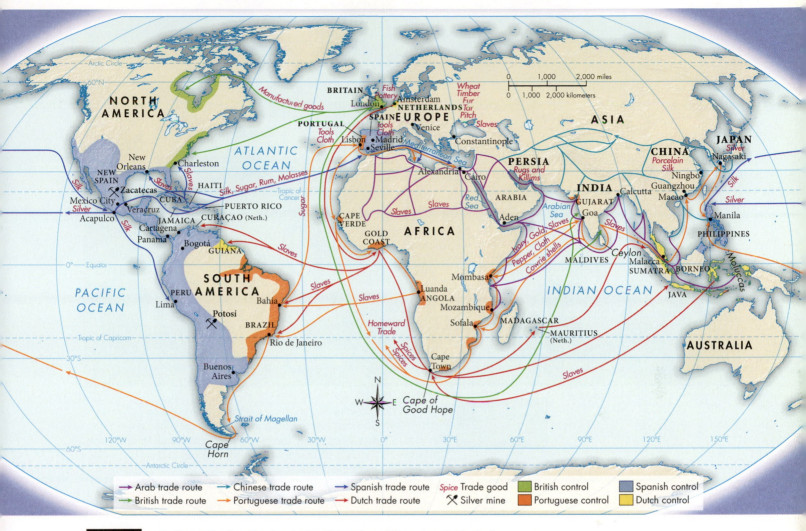

MAP 14.3 ■ **Seaborne Trading Empires in the Sixteenth and Seventeenth Centuries**

By the mid-seventeenth century, trade linked all parts of the world except for Australia. Notice that trade in slaves was not confined to the Atlantic but involved almost all parts of the world.

their voyages along the western coast of Africa, one of the first commodities they sought was slaves. In 1444, the first ship returned to Lisbon with a cargo of enslaved Africans. From 1490 to 1530, Portuguese traders brought hundreds of enslaved Africans to Lisbon each year (**Map 14.3**), where they eventually constituted 10 percent of the city's population.

In this stage of European expansion, the history of slavery became intertwined with the history of sugar. Originally sugar was an expensive luxury that only the very affluent could afford, but population increases and monetary expansion in the fifteenth century led to increasing demand. Native to the South Pacific, sugar was taken in ancient times to India. From there, sugar crops traveled to China and the Mediterranean. When Genoese and other Italians colonized the Canary Islands and the Portuguese settled on the Madeira Islands, sugar plantations came to the Atlantic.

How and why did Europeans undertake ambitious voyages of expansion?

What was the impact of European conquest on the New World?

How did Europe and the world change after Columbus?

How did expansion change European attitudes and beliefs?

✓ **LearningCurve** Check what you know.

A New World Sugar Refinery, Brazil Sugar was the most important and most profitable plantation crop in the New World. This image shows the processing and refinement of sugar on a Brazilian plantation. Sugarcane was grown, harvested, and processed by African slaves, who labored under brutal and ruthless conditions to generate enormous profits for plantation owners. (French School/Getty Images)

Sugar was a particularly difficult and demanding crop to produce for profit. The demands of sugar production only increased with the invention of roller mills to crush the cane more efficiently. Yields could be augmented, but only if a sufficient labor force was found to work the mills. Europeans solved the labor problem by forcing first native islanders and then enslaved Africans to provide the backbreaking work.

Sugar gave New World slavery its distinctive characteristics. Columbus himself brought the first sugar plants to the New World. The transatlantic slave trade began in 1518 when the Spanish emperor Charles V authorized traders to bring enslaved Africans to the Americas. The Portuguese brought slaves to Brazil around 1550; by 1600, four thousand were being imported annually. After its founding in 1621, the Dutch West India Company transported thousands of Africans to Brazil and the Caribbean, mostly to work on sugar plantations. In the mid-seventeenth century the English got involved.

Conditions for enslaved Africans on the Atlantic passage were often lethal. Before 1700, when slavers decided it was better business to improve conditions, some 20 percent of slaves died on the voyage.[8] To increase profits, slave traders

CHAPTER LOCATOR | What was the Afroeurasian trading world before Columbus?

packed several hundred captives on each ship. On sugar plantations, death rates from the brutal pace of labor were extremely high, leading to a constant stream of new shipments of slaves from Africa.

In total, scholars estimate that European traders shipped over 10 million enslaved Africans across the Atlantic from 1518 to 1800 (of whom roughly 8.5 million disembarked), with the peak of the trade occurring in the eighteenth century.[9] By comparison, only 2 to 2.5 million Europeans migrated to the New World during the same period.

Spanish Silver and Its Economic Effects

The sixteenth century has often been called Spain's golden century, but silver mined in the Americas was the true source of Spain's wealth. In 1545, the Spanish discovered an extraordinary source of silver at Potosí (poh-toh-SEE) (in present-day Bolivia) in territory conquered from the Inca Empire. By 1550, Potosí yielded perhaps 60 percent of all the silver mined in the world. From Potosí and the mines at Zacatecas (za-kuh-TAY-kuhhs) and Guanajuato (gwah-nah-HWAH-toh) in Mexico, huge quantities of precious metals poured forth. Between 1503 and 1650, 35 million pounds of silver and over 600,000 pounds of gold entered Seville's port. Spanish predominance, however, proved temporary.

In the sixteenth century, Spain experienced a steady population increase, creating a sharp rise in the demand for food and goods. Spanish colonies in the Americas also demanded consumer goods, such as cloth and luxury goods. Spain had expelled some of its best farmers and businessmen—the Muslims and Jews—in the fifteenth century; as a result, the Spanish economy was suffering and could not meet the new demands. The excess of demand over supply led to widespread inflation. The result was a rise in production costs and a further decline in Spain's productive capacity.

Did the flood of silver bullion from the Americas cause the inflation? Prices rose most steeply before

 Philip II, ca. 1533

This portrait of Philip II as a young man and crown prince of Spain is by the celebrated artist Titian, court painter to Philip's father, Charles V. After taking the throne, Philip became another great patron of the artist. (Palazzo Pitti, Florence, Italy/The Bridgeman Art Library)

How and why did Europeans undertake ambitious voyages of expansion?

What was the impact of European conquest on the New World?

How did Europe and the world change after Columbus?

How did expansion change European attitudes and beliefs?

☑ LearningCurve
Check what you know.

435

1565, but bullion imports reached their peak between 1580 and 1620. Thus, silver did not cause the initial inflation. It did, however, exacerbate the situation, and, along with the ensuing rise in population, the influx of silver significantly contributed to the upward spiral of prices. Inflation severely strained government budgets. Several times between 1557 and 1647, Spain's King Philip II and his successors wrote off the state debt, thereby undermining confidence in the government and leaving the economy in shambles.

Philip II paid his armies and foreign debts with silver bullion, and Spanish inflation was thus transmitted to the rest of Europe. Between 1560 and 1600, much of Europe experienced large price increases. Spain suffered most severely, but all European countries were affected. Because money bought less, people who lived on fixed incomes, such as nobles, were badly hurt. Those who owed fixed sums of money, such as the middle class, prospered because in a time of rising prices, debts lessened in value each year. Food costs rose most sharply, and the poor fared worst of all.

In many ways, though, it was not Spain but China that controlled the world trade in silver. The Chinese demanded silver for their products and for the payment of imperial taxes. China was thus the main buyer of world silver, absorbing half the world's production. The silver market drove world trade, with New Spain and Japan being mainstays on the supply side and China dominating the demand side. The world trade in silver is one of the best examples of the new global economy that emerged in this period.

The Birth of the Global Economy

With the Europeans' discovery of the Americas and their exploration of the Pacific, the entire world was linked for the first time in history by seaborne trade. The opening of that trade created three successive commercial empires: the Portuguese, the Spanish, and the Dutch.

The Portuguese were the first worldwide traders. In the sixteenth century, they controlled the sea route to India (see Map 14.3, page 433). From their fortified bases at Goa on the Arabian Sea and at Malacca on the Malay Peninsula, ships carried goods to the Portuguese settlement at Macao in the South China Sea. From Macao, Portuguese ships loaded with Chinese silk and porcelain sailed to Japan and the Philippines, where Chinese goods were exchanged for Spanish silver from New Spain. Throughout Asia, the Portuguese traded in slaves. The Portuguese exported horses from Mesopotamia and copper from Arabia to India; from India they exported hawks and peacocks for the Chinese and Japanese markets. They brought back to Portugal Asian spices that had been purchased with textiles produced in India and with gold and ivory from East Africa. They also shipped back sugar from their colony in Brazil, produced by enslaved Africans whom they had transported across the Atlantic.

Coming to empire a few decades later than the Portuguese, the Spanish were determined to claim their place in world trade. The Spanish Empire in the New World was basically a land empire, but across the Pacific the Spaniards built a seaborne empire centered at Manila in the Philippines. The city of Manila served as the transpacific bridge between Spanish America and China. In Manila, Spanish traders used silver from American mines to purchase Chinese silk for European markets. After 1640, the Spanish silk trade declined in the face of stiff competition from Dutch imports.

The Dutch Empire was initially built on spices. In 1599, a Dutch fleet returned to Amsterdam carrying 600,000 pounds of pepper and 250,000 pounds of cloves and nutmeg. Those who had invested in the expedition received a 100 percent profit. The voyage led to the establishment in 1602 of the Dutch East India Company, founded with the stated intention of capturing the spice trade from the Portuguese.

The Dutch set their sights on gaining direct access to and control of the Indonesian sources of spices. In return for assisting Indonesian princes in local squabbles and disputes with the Portuguese, the Dutch won broad commercial concessions. Through agreements, seizures, and outright military aggression, they gained control of the western access to the Indonesian archipelago in the first half of the seventeenth century. Gradually, they acquired political domination over the archipelago itself. By the 1660s, the Dutch had managed to expel the Portuguese from Ceylon and other East Indian islands, thereby establishing control of the lucrative spice trade.

Not content with challenging the Portuguese in the Indian Ocean, the Dutch also aspired to a role in the Americas. Founded in 1621, when the Dutch were at war with the Spanish, the Dutch West India Company aggressively sought to open trade with North and South America and capture Spanish territories there. The company captured or destroyed hundreds of Spanish ships, seized the Spanish silver fleet in 1628, and captured portions of Brazil and the Caribbean. The Dutch also interceded successfully in the transatlantic slave trade, establishing a large number of trading stations on the west coast of Africa.

QUICK REVIEW <

How was the era of global contact shaped by new commodities, commercial empires, and forced migrations?

How and why did Europeans undertake ambitious voyages of expansion?

What was the impact of European conquest on the New World?

How did Europe and the world change after Columbus?

How did expansion change European attitudes and beliefs?

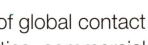 LearningCurve
Check what you know.

437

How did expansion change European attitudes and beliefs?

Titus Andronicus With classical allusions, fifteen murders and executions, a Gothic queen who takes a black lover, and incredible violence, this early Shakespearean tragedy (1594) was a melodramatic thriller that enjoyed enormous popularity with the London audience. The shock value of a dark-skinned character on the English stage is clearly shown in this illustration. (Bibliothèque Nationale, Paris, France/ Giraudon/The Bridgeman Art Library)

THE AGE OF OVERSEAS EXPANSION heightened Europeans' contacts with the rest of the world. These contacts gave birth to new ideas about the inherent superiority or inferiority of different races, in part to justify European participation in the slave trade. Cultural encounters also inspired more positive views. The essays of Michel de Montaigne epitomized a new spirit of skepticism and cultural relativism, while the plays of William Shakespeare reflected the efforts of one great writer to come to terms with the cultural complexity of his day.

CHAPTER LOCATOR | What was the Afroeurasian trading world before Columbus?

New Ideas About Race

At the beginning of the transatlantic slave trade, most Europeans grouped Africans into the despised categories of pagan heathens and Muslim infidels. Africans were certainly not the only peoples subject to such dehumanizing attitudes. Jews were also viewed as alien people who, like Africans, were naturally sinful and depraved. More generally, elite Europeans were accustomed to viewing the peasant masses as a lower form of humanity.[10]

As Europeans turned to Africa for new sources of slaves, they drew on and developed ideas about Africans' primitiveness and barbarity to defend slavery and even argue that enslavement benefited Africans by bringing the light of Christianity to heathen peoples. Over time, the institution of slavery fostered a new level of racial inequality. In contrast to peasants and Jews, Africans gradually became seen as utterly distinct from and wholly inferior to Europeans. Black skin became equated with slavery itself as Europeans at home and in the colonies convinced themselves that blacks were destined by God to serve them as slaves in perpetuity.

After 1700, the emergence of new methods of observing and describing nature led to the use of science to define race. Although the term originally referred to a nation or an ethnic group, henceforth "race" would mean biologically distinct groups of people, whose physical differences produced differences in culture, character, and intelligence.

Michel de Montaigne and Cultural Curiosity

Racism was not the only possible reaction to the new worlds emerging in the sixteenth century. Decades of religious fanaticism, bringing civil anarchy and war, led some Catholics and Protestants to doubt that any one faith contained absolute truth. Added to these doubts was the discovery of peoples in the New World who had radically different ways of life. These shocks helped produce ideas of skepticism and cultural relativism. Skepticism is a school of thought founded on doubt that total certainty or definitive knowledge is ever attainable. Cultural relativism suggests that one culture is not necessarily superior to another, just different. Both notions found expression in the work of Frenchman Michel de Montaigne (mahn-TAYN) (1533–1592).

Montaigne developed a new literary genre, the essay, to express his ideas. Published in 1580, Montaigne's *Essays* consisted of short reflections. Intending his works to be accessible to ordinary people, Montaigne wrote in French rather than Latin and in an engaging conversational style. His essays were quickly translated into other European languages and became some of the most widely read texts of the early modern period.

Montaigne's essay "Of Cannibals" reveals the impact of overseas discoveries on one thoughtful European. In contrast to the prevailing views of his day, he rejected the notion that one culture is superior to another. Speaking of native Brazilians, he wrote, "I find that there is nothing barbarous and savage in this nation [Brazil], . . . except, that everyone gives the title of barbarism to everything that is not according to his usage."[11]

| How and why did Europeans undertake ambitious voyages of expansion? | What was the impact of European conquest on the New World? | How did Europe and the world change after Columbus? | **How did expansion change European attitudes and beliefs?** | ✓ LearningCurve Check what you know. |

439

In his own time, few would have agreed with Montaigne's challenge to ideas of European superiority or his even more radical questioning of the superiority of humans over animals. Nevertheless, his popular essays contributed to a basic shift in attitudes. "Wonder," he said, "is the foundation of all philosophy, research is the means of all learning, and ignorance is the end."[12] Montaigne thus inaugurated an era of doubt.

William Shakespeare and His Influence

In addition to the essay as a literary genre, the period fostered remarkable creativity in other branches of literature. England—especially in the latter part of Queen Elizabeth I's reign and in the first years of her successor, James I (r. 1603–1625)—witnessed remarkable literary expression. The undisputed master of the period was the dramatist William Shakespeare. Born in 1564 to a successful glove manufacturer in Stratford-upon-Avon, Shakespeare grew into a Renaissance man with a deep appreciation of classical culture, individualism, and humanism.

Like Montaigne's essays, Shakespeare's work reveals the impact of the new discoveries and contacts of his day. The title character of *Othello* is described as a "Moor of Venice." In Shakespeare's day, the term "Moor" referred to Muslims of North African origin, including those who had migrated to the Iberian Peninsula. It could also be applied, though, to natives of the Iberian Peninsula who converted to Islam or to non-Muslim Berbers in North Africa. To complicate things even more, references in the play to Othello as "black" in skin color have led many to believe that Shakespeare intended him to be a sub-Saharan African. This confusion in the play aptly reflects the uncertainty in Shakespeare's own time about racial and religious classifications. In contrast to the prevailing view of Moors as inferior, Shakespeare presents Othello as a complex human figure, whose only crime is to have "loved [his wife] not wisely, but too well."

> ## QUICK REVIEW

How did European expansion change the way Europeans saw themselves and their relationships with the other peoples of the world?

CHAPTER LOCATOR | What was the Afroeurasian trading world before Columbus?

440 CHAPTER 14 EUROPEAN EXPLORATION AND CONQUEST

LOOKING BACK LOOKING AHEAD

In 1517, Martin Luther issued his "Ninety-five Theses," launching the Protestant Reformation; just five years later, Ferdinand Magellan's expedition sailed around the globe, shattering European notions of terrestrial geography. Within a few short years, old medieval certainties about Heaven and earth began to collapse. In the ensuing decades, Europeans struggled to come to terms with religious difference at home and the multitudes of new peoples and places they encountered abroad. While some Europeans were fascinated and inspired by this new diversity, too often the result was violence. Europeans endured decades of civil war between Protestants and Catholics, and indigenous peoples suffered massive population losses as a result of European warfare, disease, and exploitation. Both Catholic and Protestant religious leaders condoned the African slave trade that was to bring suffering and death to millions of Africans.

Even as the voyages of discovery coincided with the fragmentation of European culture, they also belonged to longer-term processes of state centralization and consolidation. The new monarchies of the Renaissance produced stronger and wealthier governments capable of financing the huge expenses of exploration and colonization. Competition to gain overseas colonies became an integral part of European politics. The path from medieval Christendom to the modern nation-state led the world through religious warfare and global encounter.

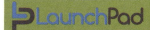

ONLINE DOCUMENT PROJECT
Juan de Pareja

How could an individual like Pareja experience both slavery and freedom in a single lifetime?

You encountered Juan de Pareja's story on page 432. Keeping the question above in mind, examine primary sources from Pareja's time. *See inside the front cover to learn more.*

How and why did Europeans undertake ambitious voyages of expansion?	What was the impact of European conquest on the New World?	How did Europe and the world change after Columbus?	How did expansion change European attitudes and beliefs?	✓ LearningCurve Check what you know.

CHAPTER 14 STUDY GUIDE

STEP 1 GET STARTED ONLINE

 **LearningCurve**

Now that you've read the chapter, make it stick by completing the LearningCurve activity.

STEP 2 EXPLAIN WHY IT MATTERS

Put your reading into practice. Identify each term below, and then explain why it matters in Western history.

TERM	WHO OR WHAT & WHEN	WHY IT MATTERS
caravel (p. 419)		
Ptolemy's *Geography* (p. 419)		
Treaty of Tordesillas (p. 422)		
conquistador (p. 423)		
Mexica Empire (p. 424)		
Inca Empire (p. 424)		
viceroyalties (p. 427)		
encomienda system (p. 428)		
Columbian exchange (p. 430)		

STEP 3 MOVE BEYOND THE BASICS

To demonstrate a more advanced understanding, use the table below to identify the motives behind Spanish expansion across the Atlantic, and describe the motives, actions, and subsequent institutions of the Spanish conquest in the Americas.

Motives	Conquests	Institutions

STEP 4 PUT IT ALL TOGETHER

Now, take a step back and try to explain the big picture. Remember to use specific examples from the chapter in your answers.

THE EUROPEAN VOYAGES OF DISCOVERY

▶ What role did Europe play in world trade prior to 1492?

▶ What role did governments play in European expansion? What role did technology play?

THE IMPACT OF CONQUEST IN THE AMERICAS

▶ What explains the dramatic decline in native populations after the arrival of Europeans in the New World?

▶ How did the Columbian Exchange transform the Americas?

THE IMPACT OF CONQUEST IN EUROPE AND AROUND THE WORLD

▶ What role did increasing demand for sugar play in shaping the economy and society of the New World?

▶ How did European expansion give rise to new ideas about race?

MAKE CONNECTIONS

▶ How did the developments of the Late Middle Ages create the conditions that made European expansion in the fifteenth and sixteenth centuries possible?

▶ Defend or refute the following statement: "The era of global trade began in the sixteenth century and was initiated by European conquests in the Americas."

> IN YOUR OWN WORDS

Imagine that you must give an oral report to the class answering the following question: **What were the motives behind European overseas expansion, and what were the consequences for Europe, the Americas, and Africa?** What would be the most important points and why?

15

ABSOLUTISM AND CONSTITUTIONALISM

CA. 1589–1725

> **What were the most important political trends in seventeenth-century Europe?** Chapter 15 examines seventeenth-century political developments. The seventeenth century was a period of crisis and transformation in Europe. Agricultural and manufacturing slumps led to food shortages and shrinking population rates. Religious and dynastic conflicts led to almost constant war, visiting violence and destruction on ordinary people and reshaping European states. While absolutism emerged as the solution to these challenges in many European states, a small minority, most notably England and the Dutch Republic, adopted a different path, placing sovereignty in the hands of privileged groups rather than the Crown.

LearningCurve

After reading the chapter, use LearningCurve to retain what you've read.

> What made the seventeenth century an "age of crisis"?

> Why did France rise and Spain fall during this period?

> What explains the rise of absolutism in Prussia and Austria?

> What were the distinctive features of Russian and Ottoman absolutism?

> How and why did the constitutional state triumph in the Dutch Republic and England?

> What was the baroque style in art and music, and where was it popular?

Life at the French Royal Court. King Louis XIV receives foreign ambassadors to celebrate a peace treaty. (Erich Lessing/Art Resource, NY)

> What made the seventeenth century an "age of crisis"?

Estonian Serfs in the 1660s

The Estonians were conquered by German military nobility in the Middle Ages and reduced to serfdom. The German-speaking nobles ruled the Estonian peasants with an iron hand, and Peter the Great reaffirmed their domination when Russia annexed Estonia. (Getty Images)

HISTORIANS OFTEN REFER TO THE SEVENTEENTH CENTURY as an age of crisis. After the economic and demographic growth of the sixteenth century, Europe faltered into stagnation and retrenchment. This was partially due to climate changes beyond anyone's control, but it also resulted from bitter religious divides, increased governmental pressures, and war. In the long run, however, governments proved increasingly able to impose their will on the populace, and the period witnessed spectacular growth in army size as well as new forms of taxation, government bureaucracies, and increased state sovereignty.

The Social Order and Peasant Life

Peasants occupied the lower tiers of a society organized in hierarchical levels. At the top, the monarch was celebrated as a semidivine being, chosen by God to embody the state. In Catholic countries, the clergy occupied the second level. Next came nobles, whose privileged status derived from their ancient bloodlines and military service. Prosperous mercantile families had bought their way into the

CHAPTER LOCATOR | **What made the seventeenth century an "age of crisis"?** | Why did France rise and Spain fall during this period?

446   **CHAPTER 15**   ABSOLUTISM AND CONSTITUTIONALISM

ca. 1500–1650
– Consolidation of serfdom in eastern Europe

1533–1584
– Reign of Ivan the Terrible in Russia

1589–1610
– Reign of Henry IV in France

1598–1613
– Time of Troubles in Russia

1620–1740
– Growth of absolutism in Austria and Prussia

1642–1649
– English civil war, which ends with execution of Charles I

1643–1715
– Reign of Louis XIV in France

1653–1658
– Military rule in England under Oliver Cromwell (the Protectorate)

1660
– Restoration of English monarchy under Charles II

1665–1683
– Jean-Baptiste Colbert applies mercantilism to France

1670
– Charles II agrees to re-Catholicize England in secret agreement with Louis XIV

ca. 1680–1750
– Construction of absolutist palaces

1682
– Louis XIV moves court to Versailles

1682–1725
– Reign of Peter the Great in Russia

1683–1718
– Habsburgs push the Ottoman Turks from Hungary

1685
– Edict of Nantes revoked in France

1688–1689
– Glorious Revolution in England

1701–1713
– War of the Spanish Succession

nobility through service to the rising monarchies of the fifteenth and sixteenth centuries and constituted a second tier of nobles. Those lower on the social scale, the peasants and artisans who constituted the vast majority of the population, were expected to defer to their betters with humble obedience. This was the so-called Great Chain of Being that linked God to his creation in a series of ranked social groups.

In addition to being rigidly hierarchical, European societies were patriarchal in nature, with men assuming authority over women as a God-given prerogative. The family thus represented a microcosm of this social order. The father ruled his family like a king ruled his domains. Fathers did not possess the power of life and death, but they were entitled to use physical violence, imprisonment, and other forceful measures to impose their authority. These powers were balanced by expectations that a good father would provide and care for his dependents.

In the seventeenth century, most Europeans lived in the countryside. The hub of the rural world was the small peasant village centered on a church and a manor. In western Europe, a small number of peasants in each village owned enough land to feed themselves and had the livestock and plows necessary to work their land. These independent farmers were leaders of the peasant village. They employed the landless poor, rented out livestock and tools, and served as agents for the noble lord. Below them were small landowners and tenant farmers who did not have enough land to be self-sufficient. At the bottom were villagers

What explains the rise of absolutism in Prussia and Austria?	What were the distinctive features of Russian and Ottoman absolutism?	How and why did the constitutional state triumph in the Dutch Republic and England?	What was the baroque style in art and music, and where was it popular?	LearningCurve Check what you know.

who worked as dependent laborers and servants. In eastern Europe, the vast majority of peasants toiled as serfs for noble landowners and did not own land in their own right (see page 462).

Famine and Economic Crisis

European rural society lived on the edge of subsistence. Because of the crude technology and low crop yield, peasants were constantly threatened by scarcity and famine. In the seventeenth century a period of colder and wetter climate throughout Europe, dubbed the "little ice age" by historians, meant a shorter farming season with lower yields. A bad harvest created food shortages; a series of bad harvests could lead to famine. Recurrent famines significantly reduced the population of early modern Europe. Most people did not die of outright starvation but through the spread of diseases like smallpox and typhoid, which were facilitated by malnutrition and exhaustion. Outbreaks of bubonic plague continued in Europe until the 1720s.

Given the harsh conditions of life, industry also suffered. The output of woolen textiles, one of the most important European manufactures, declined sharply in the first half of the seventeenth century. Food prices were high, wages stagnated, and unemployment soared. This economic crisis was not universal: it struck various regions at different times and to different degrees. In the middle decades of the century, for example, Spain, France, Germany, and England all experienced great economic difficulties, but these years were the golden age of the Netherlands.

The urban poor and peasants were the hardest hit. When the price of bread rose beyond their capacity to pay, they frequently expressed their anger by rioting, with women often taking the lead. In towns they invaded bakers' shops to seize bread and resell it at a "just price." In rural areas they attacked convoys taking grain to the cities. Historians have used the term "moral economy" for this vision of a world in which community needs predominate over competition and profit.

The Thirty Years' War

In the first half of the seventeenth century, the fragile balance of life was violently upturned by the ravages of the Thirty Years' War (1618–1648). The Holy Roman Empire was a confederation of hundreds of principalities, independent cities, duchies, and other polities loosely united under an elected emperor. The uneasy truce between Catholics and Protestants created by the Peace of Augsburg in 1555 deteriorated as the faiths of various areas shifted. Lutheran princes felt compelled to form the Protestant Union (1608), and Catholics retaliated with the Catholic League (1609). Each alliance was determined that the other should make no religious or territorial advance. Dynastic interests were also involved; the Spanish Habsburgs strongly supported the goals of their Austrian relatives: the unity of the empire and the preservation of Catholicism within it.

The war began in 1618 with the outbreak of civil war in Bohemia between the Catholic League and the Protestant Union. It would continue for three decades, involve an ever-shifting array of alliances, and draw every major European power into the fighting.

CHAPTER LOCATOR | **What made the seventeenth century an "age of crisis"?** | Why did France rise and Spain fall during this period?

CHAPTER 15
448 ABSOLUTISM AND CONSTITUTIONALISM

- **Bohemian Phase (1618–1625)** Civil war in Bohemia between the Catholic League and the Protestant Union; Catholic forces defeated Protestants at the Battle of the White Mountain (1620)

- **Danish Phase (1625–1629)** So called because of the leadership of the Protestant king Christian IV of Denmark (r. 1588–1648); witnessed additional Catholic victories; the Catholic imperial army swept through Silesia, north to the Baltic, and east into Pomerania

- **Swedish Phase (1630–1635)** Began with the arrival in Germany of the Swedish king Gustavus Adolphus (r. 1594–1632) and his army in support of the empire's Protestants; France subsidized the Swedes, hoping to weaken Habsburg power in Europe; Gustavus Adolphus won two important battles but was fatally wounded in combat

- **French Phase (1635–1648)** Prompted by French fears of Habsburg resurgence; France declared war on Spain and sent military as well as financial assistance; peace was finally achieved in October 1648

The 1648 **Peace of Westphalia** that ended the Thirty Years' War marked a turning point in European history. For the most part, conflicts fought over religious faith receded. The treaties recognized the independent authority of more than three hundred German princes (**Map 15.1**), reconfirming the emperor's severely limited authority. The Augsburg agreement of 1555 became permanent, adding Calvinism to Catholicism and Lutheranism as legally permissible creeds. The north German states remained Protestant, the south German states Catholic.

The Thirty Years' War was the most destructive event for the central European economy and society prior to the world wars of the twentieth century. Perhaps one-third of urban residents and two-fifths of the rural population died, leaving entire areas depopulated. Trade in southern German cities was virtually destroyed. Agricultural areas suffered catastrophically. Many small farmers lost their land, allowing nobles to enlarge their estates and consolidate their control.[1]

Peace of Westphalia

▶ The name of a series of treaties that concluded the Thirty Years' War in 1648 and marked the end of large-scale religious violence in Europe.

Achievements in State-Building

In the context of war and economic depression, seventeenth-century monarchs began to make new demands on their people. Across Europe, states sought to protect and expand their frontiers, raise new taxes, consolidate central control, and compete for new colonies in the New and Old Worlds.

Rulers encountered formidable obstacles in achieving these goals. Some were purely material. Without paved roads, telephones, or other modern technology, it took weeks to convey orders from the central government to the provinces. Rulers also suffered from lack of information about their realms, making it impossible to police and tax the population effectively. Local power structures presented another serious obstacle. Nobles, the church, provincial and national assemblies, town councils, guilds, and other bodies held legal privileges, which could not easily be rescinded. In some kingdoms many people spoke a language different from that of the Crown, further diminishing their willingness to obey its commands.

| What explains the rise of absolutism in Prussia and Austria? | What were the distinctive features of Russian and Ottoman absolutism? | How and why did the constitutional state triumph in the Dutch Republic and England? | What was the baroque style in art and music, and where was it popular? | ✓ **LearningCurve** Check what you know. |

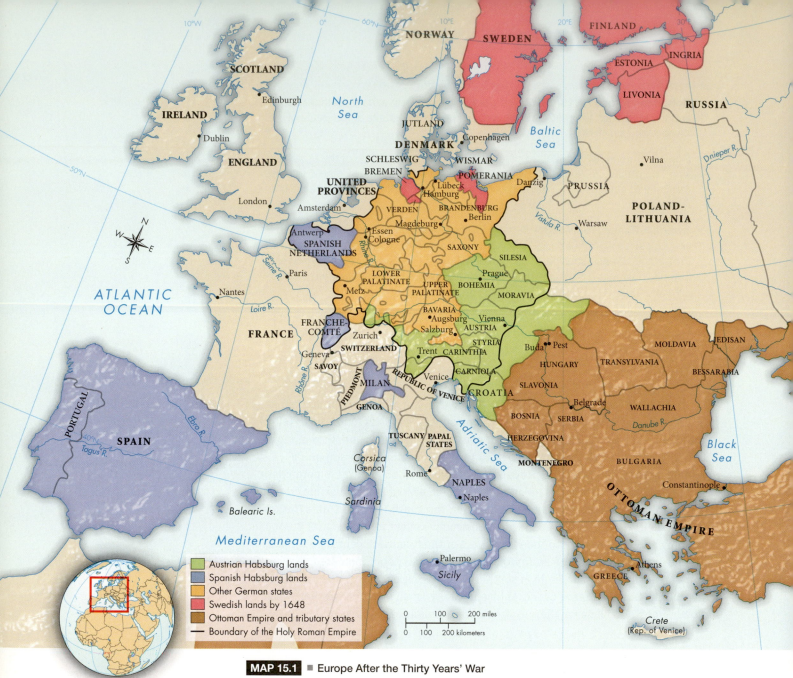

MAP 15.1 ■ Europe After the Thirty Years' War

This map shows the political division of Europe after the Treaty of Westphalia (1648) ended the war. France emerged as the strongest power in Europe at the end of the Thirty Years' War. Based on this map, what challenges did the French state still face in dominating Europe after 1648? How does the map represent Swedish gains and Spanish losses in the Treaty of Westphalia?

Nonetheless, over the course of the seventeenth century, governments achieved new levels of central control. This increased authority focused on four areas in particular: greater taxation, growth in armed forces, larger and more efficient bureaucracies, and the increased ability to compel obedience from subjects. Over time, centralized power added up to something close to sovereignty. A state may be termed sovereign when it possesses a monopoly over the instruments of

CHAPTER LOCATOR | **What made the seventeenth century an "age of crisis"?** | Why did France rise and Spain fall during this period?

450 **CHAPTER 15** ABSOLUTISM AND CONSTITUTIONALISM

justice and the use of force within clearly defined boundaries. In a sovereign state, no system of courts, such as church tribunals, competes with state courts in the dispensation of justice, and private armies, such as those of feudal lords, present no threat to central authority. While seventeenth-century states did not acquire total sovereignty, they made important strides toward that goal.

Warfare and the Growth of Army Size

The driving force of seventeenth-century state-building was warfare. In medieval times, feudal lords had raised armies only for particular wars or campaigns; now monarchs began to recruit their own forces and maintain permanent standing armies. Instead of serving their own interests, army officers were required to be loyal and obedient to those who commanded them. New techniques for training and deploying soldiers meant a rise in the professional standards of the army.

Along with professionalization came an explosive growth in army size. The French took the lead, with the army growing from roughly 125,000 men in the Thirty Years' War to 340,000 at the end of the seventeenth century.[2] Other European powers were quick to follow the French example. The rise of absolutism in central and eastern Europe led to a vast expansion in the size of armies. Great Britain followed a similar, albeit distinctive pattern. Instead of building a land army, the British focused on naval forces and eventually built the largest navy in the world.

Popular Political Action

As governments continuously raised taxes to meet the costs of war, neighborhood riots over the cost of bread turned into armed uprisings. Popular revolts were extremely common in England, France, Spain, Portugal, and Italy during the Thirty Years' War. In 1640, Philip IV of Spain faced revolt in Catalonia, the economic center of his realm. At the same time he struggled to put down uprisings in Portugal and in the northern provinces of the

The Professionalization of the Swedish Army

Swedish king Gustavus Adolphus, surrounded by his generals, gives thanks to God for the safe arrival of his troops in Germany during the Thirty Years' War. (Military Academy of Karlberg)

| What explains the rise of absolutism in Prussia and Austria? | What were the distinctive features of Russian and Ottoman absolutism? | How and why did the constitutional state triumph in the Dutch Republic and England? | What was the baroque style in art and music, and where was it popular? | ✓ LearningCurve Check what you know. |

451

Netherlands. In 1647, the city of Palermo, in Spanish-occupied Sicily, exploded in protest over food shortages caused by a series of bad harvests. From there, insurgency spread to the rest of the island and eventually to Naples on the mainland. Apart from affordable food, rebels demanded the suppression of extraordinary taxes and participation in municipal government. Some dreamed of a republic that would abolish noble tax exemptions. Despite initial successes, the revolt lacked unity and strong leadership, and it could not withstand the forces of the state.

In France, urban uprisings became a frequent aspect of the social and political landscape. Beginning in 1630 and continuing on and off through the early 1700s, major insurrections occurred at Dijon, Bordeaux (bor-DOH), Montpellier, Lyons, and Amiens. All were characterized by deep popular anger and violence directed at outside officials sent to collect taxes.

Municipal and royal authorities often struggled to overcome popular revolt. They feared that stern repressive measures, such as sending in troops to fire on crowds, would create martyrs and further inflame the situation; full-scale occupation of a city would be very expensive and would detract from military efforts elsewhere. The limitations of royal authority gave some leverage to rebels. To quell riots, royal edicts were sometimes suspended, prisoners released, and discussions initiated.

By the beginning of the eighteenth century, this leverage had largely disappeared. Municipal governments were better integrated into the national structure, and local authorities had prompt military support from the central government. People who publicly opposed royal policies and taxes received swift and severe punishment.

> **QUICK REVIEW**

What were the common crises and achievements of seventeenth-century European states?

CHAPTER LOCATOR | What made the seventeenth century an "age of crisis"?

Why did France rise and Spain fall during this period?

CHAPTER 15
452 ABSOLUTISM AND CONSTITUTIONALISM

Spanish Troops The long wars that Spain fought over Dutch independence, in support of Habsburg interests in Germany, and against France left the country militarily exhausted and financially drained by the mid-seventeenth century. In this detail from a painting by Peeter Snayers, Spanish troops — thin, emaciated, and probably unpaid — straggle away from battle. (Prado, Madrid, Spain/Index/The Bridgeman Art Library)

KINGS IN ABSOLUTIST STATES asserted that they were responsible to God alone. They claimed exclusive power to make and enforce laws, denying any other institution or group the authority to check their power. France's Louis XIV is often seen as the epitome of an absolute monarch. In truth, his success relied on collaboration with nobles, and thus his example illustrates both the achievements and the compromises of absolutist rule.

As French power rose in the seventeenth century, the glory of Spain faded. Once the fabulous revenue from American silver declined, Spain's economic stagnation could no longer be disguised, and the country faltered under weak leadership.

The Foundations of Absolutism

Louis XIV's absolutism had long roots. In 1589, his grandfather Henry IV (r. 1589–1610), the founder of the Bourbon dynasty, acquired a devastated country. Civil wars between Protestants and Catholics had wracked France since 1561. Poor harvests had reduced peasants to starvation, and commercial activity had declined drastically. Henri le Grand (Henry the Great), as the king was called, inaugurated a remarkable recovery.

| What explains the rise of absolutism in Prussia and Austria? | What were the distinctive features of Russian and Ottoman absolutism? | How and why did the constitutional state triumph in the Dutch Republic and England? | What was the baroque style in art and music, and where was it popular? | ✓ **LearningCurve** Check what you know. |

He did so by keeping France at peace during most of his reign. Although he had converted to Catholicism, he issued the Edict of Nantes, allowing Protestants the right to worship in 150 traditionally Protestant towns throughout France. He sharply lowered taxes and instead charged royal officials an annual fee to guarantee the right to pass their positions down to their heirs. He also improved the infrastructure of the country, building new roads and canals and repairing the ravages of years of civil war. Despite his efforts at peace, Henry was murdered in 1610 by a Catholic zealot, setting off a national crisis.

After the death of Henry IV, his wife, the queen-regent Marie de' Medici, headed the government for the nine-year-old Louis XIII (r. 1610–1643). In 1628 Armand Jean du Plessis — Cardinal Richelieu (1585–1642) — became first minister of the French crown. Richelieu's maneuvers allowed the monarchy to maintain power within Europe and within its own borders despite the turmoil of the Thirty Years' War.

Cardinal Richelieu's political genius is best reflected in the administrative system he established to strengthen royal control. He extended the use of intendants, commissioners for each of France's thirty-two districts who were appointed directly by the monarch, to whom they were solely responsible. As the intendants' power increased under Richelieu, so did the power of the centralized French state.

Under Richelieu, the French monarchy also acted to repress Protestantism. Louis personally supervised the siege of La Rochelle, an important port city and a major commercial center with strong ties to Protestant Holland and England. The fall of La Rochelle in 1628 was one step in the removal of Protestantism as a strong force in French life.

Richelieu did not aim to wipe out Protestantism in the rest of Europe, however. His main foreign policy goal was to destroy the Catholic Habsburgs' grip on territories that surrounded France. Consequently, Richelieu supported Habsburg enemies, including Protestants. For the French cardinal, interests of state outweighed religious considerations.

Richelieu's successor as chief minister for the next child-king, the four-year-old Louis XIV, was Cardinal Jules Mazarin (1602–1661). Along with the regent, Queen Mother Anne of Austria, Mazarin continued Richelieu's centralizing policies. His struggle to increase royal revenues to meet the costs of war led to the uprisings of 1648–1653 known as the **Fronde**. In Paris, magistrates of the Parlement of Paris, the nation's most important court, were outraged by the Crown's autocratic measures. These so-called robe nobles (named for the robes they wore in court) encouraged violent protest by the common people. During the first of several riots, the queen mother fled Paris with Louis XIV. As rebellion spread outside Paris and to the sword nobles (the traditional warrior nobility), civil order broke down completely. In 1651, Anne's regency ended with the declaration of Louis as king in his own right. Much of the rebellion died away, and its leaders came to terms with the government.

The violence of the Fronde had significant results for the future. The twin evils of noble rebellion and popular riots left the French wishing for peace and for a strong monarch to impose order. This was the legacy that Louis XIV inherited in 1661 when he assumed personal rule. Humiliated by his flight from Paris, he was determined to avoid any recurrence of rebellion.

Fronde

▶ A series of violent uprisings during the early reign of Louis XIV triggered by growing royal control and increased taxation.

CHAPTER LOCATOR | What made the seventeenth century an "age of crisis"? | **Why did France rise and Spain fall during this period?**

454 CHAPTER 15 ABSOLUTISM AND CONSTITUTIONALISM

Louis XIV and Absolutism

In the reign of Louis XIV (r. 1643–1715), the longest in European history, the French monarchy reached the peak of absolutist development. In the magnificence of his court and the brilliance of the culture that he presided over, Louis dominated his age. Religion, Anne, and Mazarin all taught Louis the doctrine of the divine right of kings: God had established kings as his rulers on earth, and they were answerable ultimately to him alone. To symbolize his central role in the divine order, when he was fifteen years old Louis danced at a court ballet dressed as the sun, thereby acquiring the title of the Sun King. (See "Picturing the Past: *Louis XIV, King of France and Navarre*, 1701.")

In addition to parading his power before the court, Louis worked very hard at the business of governing. He ruled his realm through several councils of state

Louis XIV, King of France and Navarre, 1701

This was one of Louis XIV's favorite portraits of himself. He liked it so much that he had many copies of the portrait made, in full and half-size format. (Louvre, Paris, France/Giraudon/The Bridgeman Art Library)

> **PICTURING THE PAST**

ANALYZING THE IMAGE: Why do you think the king liked the portrait so much? What image of the king does it present to the viewer? What details does the painter include, and what impression do they convey?

CONNECTIONS: How does this representation of royal power compare with the images of Peter the Great (page 466) and Charles I (page 473)? Which do you find the most impressive, and why?

| What explains the rise of absolutism in Prussia and Austria? | What were the distinctive features of Russian and Ottoman absolutism? | How and why did the constitutional state triumph in the Dutch Republic and England? | What was the baroque style in art and music, and where was it popular? | ☑ LearningCurve Check what you know. |

455

and insisted on taking a personal role in many of their decisions. He selected councilors from the recently ennobled or the upper middle class because he believed "that the public should know, from the rank of those whom I chose to serve me, that I had no intention of sharing power with them."[3]

Although personally tolerant, Louis hated division within the realm and insisted that religious unity was essential to his royal dignity and to the security of the state. He thus pursued the policy of Protestant repression launched by Richelieu. In 1685, Louis revoked the Edict of Nantes.

Despite his claims to absolute authority, multiple constraints existed on Louis's power. As a representative of divine power, he was obliged to rule in a manner consistent with virtue and benevolence. He had to uphold the laws issued by his royal predecessors. He also relied on the collaboration of nobles. Without their cooperation, it would have been impossible to extend his power throughout France or wage his many foreign wars. Louis's need to elicit noble cooperation led him to revolutionize court life at his spectacular palace at Versailles.

Life at Versailles

Throughout most of the seventeenth century, the French court had no fixed home, following the monarch to his numerous palaces and country residences. In 1682, Louis moved his court and government to the newly renovated palace at Versailles. The palace quickly became the center of political, social, and cultural life. The king required all great nobles to spend at least part of the year in attendance on him there, so he could keep an eye on their activities. Because he controlled the distribution of state power and wealth, nobles had no choice but to obey and compete with each other for his favor at Versailles. The glorious palace, with its sumptuous interiors and extensive formal gardens, was a mirror to the world of French glory, soon copied by would-be absolutist monarchs across Europe.

Louis further revolutionized court life by establishing an elaborate set of etiquette rituals to mark every moment of his day, from waking up and dressing in the morning to removing his clothing and retiring at night. Courtiers vied for the honor of participating in these ceremonies, with the highest in rank claiming the privilege of handing the king his shirt.

These rituals may seem absurd, but they were far from trivial. The king controlled immense resources and privileges; access to him meant favored treatment for government offices, military and religious posts, state pensions, honorary titles, and a host of other benefits. Courtiers sought these rewards for themselves and their family members and followers. A system of patronage—in which a higher-ranked individual protected a lower-ranked one in return for loyalty and services—flowed from the court to the provinces. Through this mechanism, Louis gained cooperation from powerful nobles.

Although they could not hold public offices or posts, women played a central role in the patronage system. At court, the king's wife, mistresses, and other female relatives recommended individuals for honors, advocated policy decisions, and brokered alliances between factions. Noblewomen played a similar role, bringing their family connections to marriage and thus forming powerful social networks.

Louis XIV was also an enthusiastic patron of the arts, commissioning many sculptures and paintings for Versailles as well as performances of dance and music. Louis XIV also loved the stage, and in the plays of Molière and Racine his

CHAPTER LOCATOR | What made the seventeenth century an "age of crisis"? | **Why did France rise and Spain fall during this period?**

456 CHAPTER 15 ABSOLUTISM AND CONSTITUTIONALISM

court witnessed the finest achievements in the history of the French theater. In this period, aristocratic ladies wrote many genres of literature and held salons in their Parisian mansions where they engaged in witty and cultured discussions of poetry, art, theater, and the latest worldly events.

With Versailles as the center of European politics, French culture grew in international prestige. French became the language of polite society and international diplomacy, gradually replacing Latin as the language of scholarship and learning. Royal courts across Europe spoke French, and the great aristocrats of Russia, Sweden, Germany, and elsewhere were often more fluent in French than in the tongues of their homelands. France inspired a cosmopolitan European culture in the late seventeenth century that looked to Versailles as its center.

French Financial Management Under Colbert

France's ability to build armies and fight wars depended on a strong economy. Fortunately for Louis, his controller general, Jean-Baptiste Colbert (1619–1683), proved to be a financial genius. Colbert's central principle was that the wealth and the economy of France should serve the state. To this end, from 1665 to his death in 1683, Colbert rigorously applied mercantilist policies to France.

Mercantilism is a collection of governmental policies for the regulation of economic activities by and for the state. It derives from the idea that a nation's international power is based on its wealth, specifically its supply of gold and silver. To accumulate wealth, a country always had to sell more goods abroad than it bought. To decrease the purchase of goods outside France, Colbert insisted that French industry should produce everything needed by the French people.

To increase exports, Colbert supported old industries and created new ones, focusing especially on textiles, which were the most important sector of the economy. Colbert enacted new production regulations, created guilds to boost quality standards, and encouraged foreign craftsmen to emigrate to France. To encourage the purchase of French goods, he abolished many domestic tariffs and raised tariffs on foreign products. In 1664, Colbert founded the Company of the East Indies with (unfulfilled) hopes of competing with the Dutch for Asian trade. He also hoped to make Canada—rich in untapped minerals and some of the best agricultural land in the world—part of a vast French empire. With this in mind, he sent four thousand colonists to Quebec.

During Colbert's tenure as controller general, Louis was able to pursue his goals without massive tax increases and without creating a stream of new offices. The constant pressure of warfare after Colbert's death, however, undid many of his economic achievements.

mercantilism

▶ A system of economic regulations aimed at increasing the power of the state based on the belief that a nation's international power was based on its wealth, specifically its supply of gold and silver.

Louis XIV's Wars

Louis XIV kept France at war for thirty-three of the fifty-four years of his personal rule. François le Tellier, marquis de Louvois, Louis's secretary of state for war, created a professional army in which the French state, rather than private nobles, employed the soldiers. Uniforms and weapons were standardized, and a rational system of training and promotion was devised. As in so many other matters, his model was followed across Europe.

| What explains the rise of absolutism in Prussia and Austria? | What were the distinctive features of Russian and Ottoman absolutism? | How and why did the constitutional state triumph in the Dutch Republic and England? | What was the baroque style in art and music, and where was it popular? | ✓ LearningCurve Check what you know. |

457

The Acquisitions of Louis XIV, 1668–1713

Territory gained
- 1668
- 1678
- 1713

Louis's goal was to expand France to what he considered its natural borders. His armies managed to extend French borders to include important commercial centers in the Spanish Netherlands and Flanders as well as the entire province of Franche-Comté between 1667 and 1678. In 1681, Louis seized the city of Strasbourg, and three years later he sent his armies into the province of Lorraine. At that moment the king seemed invincible. In fact, Louis had reached the limit of his expansion. The wars of the 1680s and 1690s brought no additional territories but placed unbearable strains on French resources. Colbert's successors resorted to desperate measures to finance these wars, including devaluation of the currency and new taxes.

Louis's last war was endured by a French people suffering high taxes, crop failure, and widespread malnutrition and death. In 1700, the childless Spanish king Charles II (r. 1665–1700) died, opening a struggle for control of Spain and its colonies. His will bequeathed the Spanish crown and its empire to Philip of Anjou, Louis XIV's grandson (Louis's wife, Maria-Theresa, was Charles's sister). The will violated a prior treaty by which the European powers had agreed to divide the Spanish possessions between the king of France and the Holy Roman emperor, both brothers-in-law of Charles II. Claiming that he was following both Spanish and French interests, Louis broke with the treaty and accepted the will, thereby triggering the War of the Spanish Succession (1701–1713).

In 1701, the English, Dutch, Austrians, and Prussians formed the Grand Alliance against Louis XIV. War dragged on until 1713. The **Peace of Utrecht**, which ended the war, allowed Louis's grandson Philip to remain king of Spain on the understanding that the French and Spanish crowns would never be united. France surrendered Newfoundland, Nova Scotia, and the Hudson Bay territory to England, which also acquired Gibraltar, Minorca, and control of the African slave trade from Spain (**Map 15.2**).

The Peace of Utrecht represented the balance-of-power principle in operation, setting limits on the extent to which any one power—in this case, France—could expand. It also marked the end of French expansion. Thirty-five years of war had given France the rights to all of Alsace and some commercial centers in the north. But at what price? In 1714, an exhausted France hovered on the brink of bankruptcy. It is no wonder that, when Louis XIV died on September 1, 1715, many subjects felt as much relief as they did sorrow.

The Decline of Absolutist Spain in the Seventeenth Century

By the early seventeenth century, the seeds of Spanish disaster were sprouting. Between 1610 and 1650, Spanish trade with the colonies in the New World fell 60 percent due to competition from local industries in the colonies and from Dutch and English traders. At the same time, the native Indian and African slaves who toiled in the South American silver mines suffered frightful epidemics of disease. Ultimately, the mines that filled the empire's treasury started to run dry, and the quantity of metal produced steadily declined after 1620.

In Madrid, however, royal expenditures constantly exceeded income. To meet mountainous state debt, the Crown repeatedly devalued the coinage and declared bankruptcy, which resulted in the collapse of national credit. Meanwhile, manu-

CHAPTER LOCATOR | What made the seventeenth century an "age of crisis"? | **Why did France rise and Spain fall during this period?**

458 **CHAPTER 15** ABSOLUTISM AND CONSTITUTIONALISM

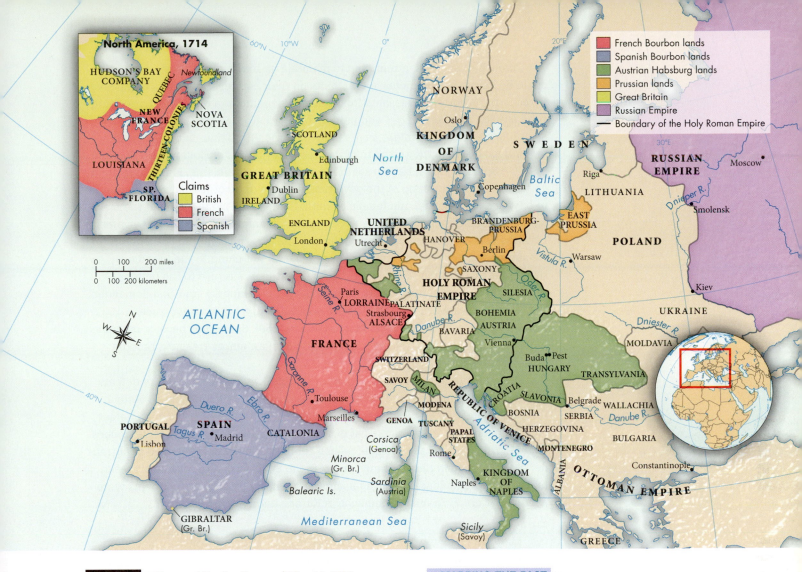

North America, 1714

HUDSON'S BAY COMPANY
QUEBEC
Newfoundland
NEW FRANCE
NOVA SCOTIA
THIRTEEN COLONIES
LOUISIANA
SP. FLORIDA

Claims
- British
- French
- Spanish

Legend:
- French Bourbon lands
- Spanish Bourbon lands
- Austrian Habsburg lands
- Prussian lands
- Great Britain
- Russian Empire
- Boundary of the Holy Roman Empire

MAP 15.2 ■ Europe After the Peace of Utrecht, 1715

The series of treaties commonly called the Peace of Utrecht ended the War of the Spanish Succession and redrew the map of Europe. A French Bourbon king succeeded to the Spanish throne. France surrendered the Spanish Netherlands (later Belgium), then in French hands, to Austria, and recognized the Hohenzollern rulers of Prussia. Spain ceded Gibraltar to Great Britain, for which it has been a strategic naval station ever since. Spain also granted Britain the *asiento*, the contract for supplying African slaves to the Americas.

> MAPPING THE PAST

ANALYZING THE MAP: Identify the areas on the map that changed hands as a result of the Peace of Utrecht. How did these changes affect the balance of power in Europe?

CONNECTIONS: How and why did so many European countries possess scattered or noncontiguous territories? What does this suggest about European politics in this period? Does this map suggest potential for future conflict?

facturing and commerce shrank. In contrast to the other countries of western Europe, Spain had a tiny middle class. To make matters worse, the Crown expelled some three hundred thousand *Moriscos*, or former Muslims, in 1609, significantly reducing the pool of skilled workers and merchants. Those working in the textile industry were forced out of business by steep inflation that pushed their production costs to the point where they could not compete in colonial and international markets.[4]

| What explains the rise of absolutism in Prussia and Austria? | What were the distinctive features of Russian and Ottoman absolutism? | How and why did the constitutional state triumph in the Dutch Republic and England? | What was the baroque style in art and music, and where was it popular? | ✓ LearningCurve Check what you know. |

Spanish aristocrats, attempting to maintain an extravagant lifestyle they could no longer afford, increased the rents on their estates. High rents and heavy taxes in turn drove the peasants from the land, leading to a decline in agricultural productivity. In cities, wages and production stagnated. Spain also ignored new scientific methods that might have improved agricultural and manufacturing techniques because they came from the heretical nations of Holland and England.

The Spanish crown had no solutions to these dire problems. Philip III (r. 1598–1621) handed the running of the government to the duke of Lerma, who used it to advance his personal and familial wealth. Philip IV (r. 1621–1665) left the management of his several kingdoms to Gaspar de Guzmán, Count-Duke of Olivares. Olivares was an able administrator who has often been compared to Richelieu. He succeeded in devising new sources of revenue but clung to the grandiose belief that the solution to Spain's difficulties rested in a return to the imperial tradition of the sixteenth century. Unfortunately, the imperial tradition demanded the revival of war with the Dutch at the expiration of a twelve-year truce in 1622 and a long war with France over Mantua (1628–1659). Spain thus became embroiled in the Thirty Years' War. These conflicts, on top of an empty treasury, brought disaster.

Spain's situation worsened with internal conflicts and fresh military defeats through the remainder of the seventeenth century. In 1640, Spain faced serious revolts in Catalonia and Portugal. In 1643, the French inflicted a crushing defeat on a Spanish army at Rocroi in what is now Belgium. By the Treaty of the Pyrénées of 1659, which ended the French-Spanish conflict, Spain was compelled to surrender extensive territories to France. In 1688, the Spanish crown reluctantly recognized the independence of Portugal, almost a century after the two crowns were joined. The era of Spanish dominance in Europe had ended.

> **QUICK REVIEW**

What factors led to the rise of the French absolutist state under Louis XIV, and why did absolutist Spain experience decline in the same period?

CHAPTER LOCATOR | What made the seventeenth century an "age of crisis"? | Why did France rise and Spain fall during this period?

460 CHAPTER 15 ABSOLUTISM AND CONSTITUTIONALISM

What explains the rise of absolutism in Prussia and Austria?

A Prussian Giant Grenadier

Frederick William I wanted tall, handsome soldiers. He dressed them in tight, bright uniforms to distinguish them from the peasant population from which most soldiers came. He also ordered several portraits of his favorites, such as this one, from his court painter, J. C. Merk. Grenadiers (greh-nuh-DEERZ) wore the miter cap instead of an ordinary hat so that they could hurl their heavy grenades unimpeded by a broad brim. (Portrait of Grenadier James Kirkland, Irish member of the Potsdamer Riesengarde (giant guards of Potsdam), c.1718, Merk, Johann Christof (fl.1714) / Deutsches Historisches Museum, Berlin, Germany/© DHM/The Bridgeman Art Library)

THE RULERS OF EASTERN EUROPE also labored to build strong absolutist states in the seventeenth century. But they built on social and economic foundations far different from those in western Europe, namely, serfdom and the strong nobility who benefited from it. The most successful states were Austria and Prussia, which witnessed the rise of absolutism between 1620 and 1740.

What explains the rise of absolutism in Prussia and Austria?	What were the distinctive features of Russian and Ottoman absolutism?	How and why did the constitutional state triumph in the Dutch Republic and England?	What was the baroque style in art and music, and where was it popular?	✓ LearningCurve Check what you know.

The Return of Serfdom in the East

While economic and social hardship was common across Europe, important differences existed between east and west. In the west, the demographic losses of the Black Death allowed peasants to escape from serfdom as they acquired enough land to feed themselves. In eastern Europe, seventeenth-century peasants had largely lost their ability to own land independently. Eastern lords dealt with the labor shortages caused by the Black Death by restricting the right of their peasants to move and thus take advantage of better opportunities elsewhere. Lords steadily took more and more of their peasants' land and arbitrarily imposed heavier labor obligations.

The gradual erosion of the peasantry's economic position was bound up with manipulation of the legal system. The local lord was also the local prosecutor, judge, and jailer. There were no independent royal officials to provide justice or uphold the common law. The power of the lord reached far into serfs' everyday lives. Not only was their freedom of movement restricted but they were also required permission to marry or could be forced to marry. Lords could reallocate the lands worked by their serfs at will or sell serfs apart from their families.

Between 1500 and 1650, the consolidation of serfdom in eastern Europe was accompanied by the growth of commercial agriculture, particularly in Poland and eastern Germany. As economic expansion and population growth resumed after 1500, eastern lords increased the production of their estates by squeezing sizable surpluses out of the impoverished peasants. They then sold these surpluses to foreign merchants, who exported them to the growing cities of wealthier western Europe.

It was not only the peasants who suffered in eastern Europe. With the approval of kings, landlords systematically undermined the medieval privileges of the towns and the power of the urban classes. Instead of selling products to local merchants, landlords sold directly to foreigners, bypassing local towns. The population of the towns and the urban middle classes declined greatly. This development both reflected and promoted the supremacy of noble landlords in most of eastern Europe in the sixteenth century.

The Austrian Habsburgs

Like all of central Europe, the Habsburgs emerged from the Thirty Years' War impoverished and exhausted. Their efforts to destroy Protestantism in the German lands and to turn the weak Holy Roman Empire into a real state had failed. Although the Habsburgs remained the hereditary emperors, real power lay in the hands of a bewildering variety of separate political jurisdictions. Defeat in central Europe encouraged the Habsburgs to turn away from a quest for imperial dominance and to focus inward and eastward in an attempt to unify their diverse holdings.

Habsburg victory over Bohemia during the Thirty Years' War was an important step in this direction. Ferdinand II (r. 1619–1637) drastically reduced the power of the Bohemian Estates, the largely Protestant representative assembly. He also confiscated the landholdings of Protestant nobles and gave them to loyal Catholic nobles and to the foreign aristocratic mercenaries who led his armies. After 1650, a large portion of the Bohemian nobility was of recent origin and owed its success to the Habsburgs.

CHAPTER LOCATOR | What made the seventeenth century an "age of crisis"? | Why did France rise and Spain fall during this period?

462 CHAPTER 15
ABSOLUTISM AND CONSTITUTIONALISM

With the support of this new nobility, the Habsburgs established direct rule over Bohemia. Under their rule, the condition of the enserfed peasantry worsened substantially. Protestantism was also stamped out. These changes were important steps in creating absolutist rule in Bohemia.

Ferdinand III (r. 1637–1657) continued to build state power. He centralized the government in the empire's German-speaking provinces, which formed the core Habsburg holdings. For the first time, a permanent standing army was ready to put down any internal opposition. The Habsburg monarchy then turned east toward the plains of Hungary, which had been divided between the Ottomans and the Habsburgs in the early sixteenth century. Between 1683 and 1699, the Habsburgs pushed the Ottomans from most of Hungary and Transylvania. The recovery of all the former kingdom of Hungary was completed in 1718.

The Hungarian nobility, despite its reduced strength, effectively thwarted the full development of Habsburg absolutism. Throughout the seventeenth century, Hungarian nobles rose in revolt against attempts to impose absolute rule. They never triumphed decisively but neither were they crushed the way the nobility in Bohemia had been in 1620. In 1703, with the Habsburgs bogged down in the War of the Spanish Succession, the Hungarians rose in one last patriotic rebellion under Prince Francis Rákóczy. The prince and his forces were eventually defeated, but the Habsburgs agreed to restore many of the traditional privileges of the aristocracy in return for Hungarian acceptance of hereditary Habsburg rule. Thus Hungary, unlike Austria and Bohemia, was never fully integrated into a centralized, absolute Habsburg state.

Despite checks on their ambitions in Hungary, the Habsburgs made significant achievements in state-building elsewhere by forging consensus with the church and the nobility. A sense of common identity and loyalty to the monarchy grew among elites in Habsburg lands, even to a certain extent in Hungary. German became the language of the state, and Catholicism helped fuse a collective identity.

Prussia in the Seventeenth Century

In the fifteenth and sixteenth centuries, the Hohenzollern family had ruled parts of eastern Germany as the imperial electors of Brandenburg and the dukes of Prussia. When he came to power in 1640, twenty-year-old Frederick William, later known as the Great Elector, was determined to unify his three provinces and enlarge his holdings. These provinces were Brandenburg; Prussia, inherited in 1618; and scattered territories along the Rhine inherited in 1614 (**Map 15.3**). Each had its own estates. Although the estates had not met regularly during the chaotic Thirty Years' War, taxes could not be levied without their consent. The estates of Brandenburg and Prussia were dominated by the nobility and the landowning classes, known as the **Junkers**.

Frederick William profited from ongoing European war and the threat of invasion from Russia when he argued for the need for a permanent standing army. In 1660, he persuaded Junkers in the estates to accept taxation without consent in order to fund an army. They agreed to do so in exchange for reconfirmation of their own privileges, including authority over the serfs. Having won over the Junkers, the king crushed potential opposition to his power from the towns. One

Junkers
▶ The nobility of Brandenburg and Prussia, they were reluctant allies of Frederick William in his consolidation of the Prussian state.

What explains the rise of absolutism in Prussia and Austria? | What were the distinctive features of Russian and Ottoman absolutism? | How and why did the constitutional state triumph in the Dutch Republic and England? | What was the baroque style in art and music, and where was it popular? | ✓ LearningCurve Check what you know.

463

MAP 15.3 ■ The Growth of Austria and Brandenburg-Prussia to 1748

Austria expanded to the southwest into Hungary and Transylvania at the expense of the Ottoman Empire. It was unable to hold the rich German province of Silesia, however, which was conquered by Brandenburg-Prussia.

by one, Prussian cities were eliminated from the estates and subjected to new taxes on goods and services. Thereafter, the estates' power declined rapidly because the Great Elector had both financial independence and superior force.

During his reign, Frederick William tripled state revenue and expanded the army drastically. In 1688, a population of 1 million supported a peacetime standing army of 30,000. In 1701, the elector's son, Frederick I, received the elevated title of king of Prussia (instead of elector) as a reward for aiding the Holy Roman emperor in the War of the Spanish Succession.

The Consolidation of Prussian Absolutism

Frederick William I, the Soldiers' King (r. 1713–1740), completed his grandfather's work, eliminating the last traces of parliamentary estates and local self-government. He established true Prussian absolutism and transformed Prussia into a military

CHAPTER LOCATOR | What made the seventeenth century an "age of crisis"? | Why did France rise and Spain fall during this period?

state. Frederick William was intensely attached to military life. He always wore an army uniform, and he lived the highly disciplined life of the professional soldier.

Penny-pinching and hard-working, Frederick William achieved results. The king and his ministers built an exceptionally honest and conscientious bureaucracy to administer the country and foster economic development. Twelfth in Europe in population, Prussia had the fourth-largest army by 1740. The Prussian army was the best in Europe, astonishing foreign observers with its precision, skill, and discipline.

Nevertheless, Prussians paid a heavy and lasting price for the obsessions of their royal drillmaster. Army expansion was achieved in part through forced conscription, which was declared lifelong in 1713. Desperate draftees fled the country or injured themselves to avoid service. Finally, in 1733, Frederick William I ordered that all Prussian men would undergo military training and serve as reservists in the army, allowing him to preserve both agricultural production and army size. To appease the Junkers, the king enlisted them to lead his growing army. The proud nobility thus commanded the peasantry in the army as well as on the estates.

With all men harnessed to the war machine, Prussian civil society became rigid and highly disciplined. As a Prussian minister later summed up, "To keep quiet is the first civic duty."[5] Thus the policies of Frederick William I, combined with harsh peasant bondage and Junker tyranny, laid the foundations for a highly militaristic country.

QUICK REVIEW

What were the social conditions of eastern Europe, and how did the rulers of Austria and Prussia transform their nations into powerful absolutist monarchies?

What explains the rise of absolutism in Prussia and Austria?

What were the distinctive features of Russian and Ottoman absolutism?

How and why did the constitutional state triumph in the Dutch Republic and England?

What was the baroque style in art and music, and where was it popular?

✔ LearningCurve
Check what you know.

What were the distinctive features of Russian and Ottoman absolutism?

Peter the Great This compelling portrait by Grigory Musikiysky captures the strength and determination of the warrior-tsar in 1723, after more than three decades of personal rule. In his hand Peter holds the scepter, symbol of royal sovereignty, and across his breastplate is draped an ermine fur, a mark of honor. In the background are the battleships of Russia's new Baltic fleet and the famous St. Peter and St. Paul Fortress that Peter built in St. Petersburg. (Hermitage/St. Petersburg, Russia/ Bridgeman Art Library)

A FAVORITE PARLOR GAME of nineteenth-century intellectuals was debating whether Russia was a Western (European) or non-Western (Asian) society. This question was particularly fascinating because it was unanswerable. To this day, Russia differs from the West in some fundamental ways, though its history has paralleled that of the West in other aspects.

There was no question in the minds of Europeans, however, that the Ottomans were outsiders. Even absolutist rulers disdained Ottoman sultans as cruel and tyrannical despots. Despite stereotypes, however, the Ottoman Empire was in many ways more tolerant than its Western counterparts, providing protection and security to other religions while steadfastly maintaining the Muslim faith. Flexibility and openness to other ideas and practices were sources of strength for the empire.

The Mongol Yoke and the Rise of Moscow

The two-hundred-year period of rule by the Mongol khan (king) set the stage for the rise of absolutist Russia. The Mongols, a group of nomadic tribes from present-day Mongolia, established an empire that, at its height, stretched from Korea to

CHAPTER LOCATOR | What made the seventeenth century an "age of crisis"? | Why did France rise and Spain fall during this period?

CHAPTER 15
466 ABSOLUTISM AND CONSTITUTIONALISM

eastern Europe. In the thirteenth century the Mongols conquered the Slavic princes and forced them to pay tribute. The princes of Moscow became particularly adept at serving the Mongols. Ivan III (r. 1462–1505), known as Ivan the Great, successfully expanded the principality of Moscow toward the Baltic Sea.

By 1480, Ivan III was strong enough to defy Mongol control and declare the autonomy of Moscow. To legitimize their new position, the princes of Moscow modeled themselves on the Mongol khans. Like the khans, the Muscovite state forced weaker Slavic principalities to render tribute previously paid to Mongols and borrowed Mongol institutions such as the tax system, postal routes, and census. Loyalty from the highest-ranking nobles, or **boyars**, helped the Muscovite princes consolidate their power.

Another source of legitimacy for Moscow was its claim to the political and religious legacy of the Byzantine Empire. After the fall of Constantinople to the Turks in 1453, the princes of Moscow saw themselves as the heirs of both the caesars (or emperors) and Orthodox Christianity.

The Tsar and His People

Developments in Russia took a chaotic turn with the reign of Ivan IV (r. 1533–1584), the famous Ivan the Terrible. Ivan's reign was successful in defeating the remnants of Mongol power; adding vast new territories to the realm; and laying the foundations for the huge, multiethnic Russian empire. After the sudden death of his wife, however, Ivan began a campaign of persecution against those he suspected of opposing him. He executed members of leading boyar families, along with their families, friends, servants, and peasants. To replace them, Ivan created a new service nobility, whose loyalty was guaranteed by their dependence on the state for land and titles.

As landlords demanded more from the serfs who survived the persecutions, growing numbers of peasants fled toward wild, recently conquered territories to the east and south. There they joined free groups and warrior bands known as **Cossacks**. Ivan responded by tying peasants more firmly to the land and to noble landholders. Simultaneously, he ordered that urban dwellers be bound to their towns and jobs so that he could tax them more heavily. These restrictions checked the growth of the Russian middle classes and stood in sharp contrast to economic and social developments in western Europe.

After the death of Ivan and his successor, Russia entered a chaotic period known as the Time of Troubles (1598–1613). While Ivan's relatives struggled for power, ordinary people suffered drought, crop failure, and plague. The Cossacks and peasants rebelled against nobles and officials, demanding fair treatment. This social explosion from below brought the nobles, big and small, together. They crushed the Cossack rebellion and brought Ivan's sixteen-year-old grandnephew, Michael Romanov, to the throne (r. 1613–1645).

Although the new tsar successfully reconsolidated central authority, he and his successors did not improve the lot of the common people. In 1649, a law extended serfdom to all peasants in the realm, giving lords unrestricted rights over their serfs and establishing penalties for harboring runaways. Social and religious uprisings among the poor and oppressed continued through the seventeenth century.

boyars

▶ The highest-ranking members of the Russian nobility.

The Expansion of Russia to 1725

Cossacks

▶ Free groups and outlaw armies originally comprising runaway peasants living on the borders of Russian territory from the fourteenth century onward. By the end of the sixteenth century, they had formed an alliance with the Russian state.

What explains the rise of absolutism in Prussia and Austria?

What were the distinctive features of Russian and Ottoman absolutism?

How and why did the constitutional state triumph in the Dutch Republic and England?

What was the baroque style in art and music, and where was it popular?

☑ LearningCurve
Check what you know.

Despite the turbulence of the period, the Romanov tsars, like their Western counterparts, made several important achievements during the second half of the seventeenth century. After a long war, Russia gained land in Ukraine from Poland in 1667 and completed the conquest of Siberia by the end of the century. Territorial expansion was accompanied by growth of the bureaucracy and the army. The tsars employed foreign experts to reform the Russian army, and they enlisted Cossack warriors to fight Siberian campaigns. Russian imperialist expansion to the east paralleled the Western powers' exploration and conquest of the Atlantic world in the same period.

The Reforms of Peter the Great

Heir to Romanov efforts at state-building, Peter the Great (r. 1682–1725) embarked on a tremendous campaign to accelerate and complete these processes. Fascinated by weapons and foreign technology and eager to gain support against the Ottoman Empire, the tsar led a group of 250 Russian officials and young nobles on a tour of western European capitals. Peter met with foreign kings, toured the sites, and learned shipbuilding and other technical skills from local artisans and experts. He was particularly impressed with the growing economic power of the Dutch and the English, and he considered how Russia could profit from their example.

Returning to Russia, Peter entered into a secret alliance with Denmark and Poland to wage a sudden war of aggression against Sweden, with the goal of securing access to the Baltic Sea and opportunities for westward expansion. Eighteen-year-old Charles XII of Sweden (1697–1718), however, surprised Peter. He defeated Denmark quickly in 1700, then turned on Russia. His well-trained professional army attacked and routed unsuspecting Russians besieging the Swedish fortress of Narva on the Baltic coast. It was, for the Russians, a grim beginning to the long and brutal Great Northern War, which lasted from 1700 to 1721.

Peter responded to this defeat with measures designed to increase state power, strengthen his armies, and gain victory. He required all nobles to serve in the army or in the civil administration—for life. A more modern army and government required skilled experts, so Peter created new schools and universities and required every young nobleman to spend five years in education away from home. Peter established an interlocking military-civilian bureaucracy with fourteen ranks, and he decreed that all had to start at the bottom and work toward the top. Drawing on his experience abroad, Peter sought talented foreigners and placed them in his service. These measures gradually combined to make the army and government more powerful and efficient.

Peter also greatly increased the service requirements of commoners. In the wake of the Narva disaster, he established a regular standing army of more than two hundred thousand peasant-soldiers, drafted for life and commanded by noble officers. He added an additional hundred thousand men in special regiments of Cossacks and foreign mercenaries. To fund the army, taxes on peasants increased threefold during Peter's reign. Serfs were also arbitrarily assigned to work in the growing number of factories and mines that supplied the military.

Peter's new war machine was able to crush the small army of Sweden in Ukraine at Poltava in 1709, one of the most significant battles in Russian history.

CHAPTER LOCATOR | What made the seventeenth century an "age of crisis"? | Why did France rise and Spain fall during this period?

468 CHAPTER 15
ABSOLUTISM AND CONSTITUTIONALISM

Saint Basil's Cathedral, Moscow

With its sloping roofs and colorful onion-shaped domes, Saint Basil's is a striking example of powerful Byzantine influences on Russian culture. According to tradition, an enchanted Ivan the Terrible blinded the cathedral's architects to ensure that they would never duplicate their fantastic achievement, which still dazzles the beholder in today's Red Square. (George Holton/Photo Researchers)

Russia's victory against Sweden was conclusive in 1721, and Estonia and present-day Latvia came under Russian rule for the first time. After his victory at Poltava, Peter channeled enormous resources into building St. Petersburg, a new Western-style capital on the Baltic to rival the great cities of Europe.

The government drafted twenty-five thousand to forty thousand men each summer to labor in St. Petersburg. Many of these laborers died from hunger, sickness, and accidents. Nobles were ordered to build costly palaces in St. Petersburg and to live in them most of the year. Merchants and artisans were required to settle and build in the new capital. The building of St. Petersburg was, in truth, an enormous direct tax levied on the wealthy, with the peasantry forced to do the manual labor.

There were other important consequences of Peter's reign. For Peter, modernization meant westernization, and both Westerners and Western ideas flowed into Russia for the first time. He required nobles to shave their heavy beards, wear Western clothing, and attend parties where young men and women would mix

| What explains the rise of absolutism in Prussia and Austria? | **What were the distinctive features of Russian and Ottoman absolutism?** | How and why did the constitutional state triumph in the Dutch Republic and England? | What was the baroque style in art and music, and where was it popular? | ☑ LearningCurve Check what you know. |

469

MAP 15.4 ■ The Ottoman Empire at Its Height, 1566

The Ottomans, like their great rivals the Habsburgs, rose to rule a vast dynastic empire encompassing many different peoples and ethnic groups. The army and the bureaucracy served to unite the disparate territories into a single state under an absolutist ruler.

Map legend:
- Ottoman state, ca. 1300
- Ottoman Empire under Suleiman, 1566
- Tributary states of the Sultan, 1566

together and freely choose their own spouses. From these efforts, a new elite class of Western-oriented Russians began to emerge.

Peter's reforms were unpopular with many Russians, nobles and serfs alike. Nonetheless, his modernizing and westernizing of Russia paved the way for it to move somewhat closer to the European mainstream in its thought and institutions during the Enlightenment, especially under Catherine the Great.

The Growth of the Ottoman Empire

The Ottomans came out of Central Asia as conquering warriors, settled in Anatolia (present-day Turkey), and, at their peak in the mid-sixteenth century, ruled one of the most powerful empires in the world (see Chapter 14). Their possessions stretched from western Persia across North Africa and into the heart of central Europe (**Map 15.4**).

The Ottoman Empire was built on a unique model of state and society. Agricultural land was the personal hereditary property of the **sultan**, and peasants paid taxes to use the land. Thus, there was an almost complete absence of private landed property and no hereditary nobility.

sultan

▶ The ruler of the Ottoman Empire; he owned all the agricultural land of the empire and was served by an army and bureaucracy composed of highly trained slaves.

CHAPTER LOCATOR | What made the seventeenth century an "age of crisis"? | Why did France rise and Spain fall during this period?

The Ottomans also employed a distinctive form of government administration. The top ranks of the bureaucracy were staffed by the sultan's slave corps. Because Muslim law prohibited enslaving other Muslims, the sultan's agents purchased slaves along the borders of the empire. Within the realm, the sultan levied a "tax" of one thousand to three thousand male children on the conquered Christian populations in the Balkans every year. These young slaves were raised in Turkey as Muslims and were trained to fight and to administer. The most talented Ottoman slaves rose to the top of the bureaucracy, where they might acquire wealth and power. The less fortunate formed the core of the sultan's army, the **janissary corps**. These highly organized and efficient troops gave the Ottomans a formidable advantage in war with western Europeans. By 1683, service in the janissary corps had become so prestigious that the sultan ceased recruitment by force, and it became a volunteer army open to Christians and Muslims.

The Ottomans divided their subjects into religious communities, and each *millet*, or "nation," enjoyed autonomous self-government under its religious leaders. The Ottoman Empire recognized Orthodox Christians, Jews, Armenian Christians, and Muslims as distinct millets. The **millet system** created a powerful bond between the Ottoman ruling class and religious leaders, who supported the sultan's rule in return for extensive authority over their own communities.

Istanbul (known outside the empire by its original name, Constantinople) was the capital of the empire. The "old palace" was for the sultan's female family members. The newer Topkapi palace was where officials worked and young slaves trained for future administrative or military careers. Sultans married women of the highest social standing while keeping many concubines of low rank. To prevent the elite families into which they married from acquiring influence over the government, sultans procreated only with their concubines and not with official wives. They also adopted a policy of allowing each concubine to produce only one male heir. At a young age, each son went to govern a province of the empire accompanied by his mother. These practices were intended to stabilize power and prevent a recurrence of the civil wars of the late fourteenth and early fifteenth centuries.

Sultan Suleiman undid these policies when he boldly married his concubine, a former slave of Polish origin named Hürrem, and had several children with her. (See "Individuals in Society: Hürrem," page 472.) Starting with Suleiman, imperial wives began to take on more power. Marriages were arranged between sultans' daughters and high-ranking servants, creating powerful new members of the imperial household. Over time, the sultan's exclusive authority waned in favor of a more bureaucratic administration.

janissary corps
▶ The core of the sultan's army, composed of slave conscripts from non-Muslim parts of the empire; after 1683, it became a volunteer force.

millet system
▶ A system used by the Ottomans whereby subjects were divided into religious communities, with each millet (nation) enjoying autonomous self-government under its religious leaders.

QUICK REVIEW <

What were the commonalities and differences between the development of absolutism in the Russian and Ottoman Empires?

| What explains the rise of absolutism in Prussia and Austria? | **What were the distinctive features of Russian and Ottoman absolutism?** | How and why did the constitutional state triumph in the Dutch Republic and England? | What was the baroque style in art and music, and where was it popular? | ☑ LearningCurve Check what you know. |

471

INDIVIDUALS IN SOCIETY
Hürrem

Hürrem and her ladies in the harem. (Bibliothèque nationale de France)

In Muslim culture, *harem* means a sacred place or a sanctuary. The term was applied to the part of the household occupied by women and children and forbidden to men outside the family. The most famous harem member in the history of Ottoman sultans was Hürrem, wife of Suleiman the Magnificent.

Like many of the sultan's concubines, Hürrem (1505?–1558) was of foreign birth. Tradition holds that she was born Aleksandra Lisowska in the kingdom of Poland (present-day Ukraine). Captured during a Tartar raid and enslaved, she entered the imperial harem between 1517 and 1520, when she was about fifteen years old. Reports from Venetian visitors claimed that she was not outstandingly beautiful but was possessed of wonderful grace, charm, and good humor, earning her the Turkish nickname Hürrem, or "joyful one." Soon after her arrival, Hürrem became the imperial favorite.

Suleiman's love for Hürrem led him to set aside all precedents for the role of a concubine, including the rule that concubines must cease having children once they gave birth to a male heir. By 1531, Hürrem had given Suleiman one daughter and five sons. In 1533 or 1534, Suleiman entered formal marriage with his consort — an unprecedented and scandalous honor for a concubine. Suleiman reportedly lavished attention on his wife and defied convention by allowing her to remain in the palace throughout her life instead of accompanying her son to a provincial governorship.

Contemporaries were shocked by Hürrem's influence over the sultan and resentful of the apparent role she played in politics and diplomacy. The Venetian ambassador Bassano wrote that "the Janissaries and the entire court hate her and her children likewise, but because the Sultan loves her, no one dares to speak."* Court rumors circulated that Hürrem used witchcraft to control the sultan and ordered the sultan's execution of his first-born son by another mother.

The correspondence between Suleiman and Hürrem, unavailable until the nineteenth century, along with Suleiman's own diaries, confirms her status as the sultan's most trusted confidant and adviser. During his frequent absences, the pair exchanged passionate love letters. Hürrem included political information and warned of potential uprisings. She also intervened in affairs between the empire and her former home, apparently helping Poland attain its privileged diplomatic status. She brought a feminine touch to diplomatic relations, sending personally embroidered articles to foreign leaders.

Hürrem used her enormous pension to contribute a mosque, two schools, a hospital, a fountain, and two public baths to Istanbul. In Jerusalem, Mecca, and Istanbul, she provided soup kitchens and hospices for pilgrims and the poor. She died in 1558, eight years before her husband. Her son Selim II (r. 1566–1574) inherited the throne.

Relying on Western observers' reports, historians traditionally depicted Hürrem as a manipulative and power-hungry social climber. They portrayed her career as the beginning of a "sultanate of women" in which strong imperial leadership gave way to court intrigue and debauchery. More recent historians have emphasized the intelligence and courage Hürrem demonstrated in navigating the ruthlessly competitive world of the harem.

Hürrem's journey from Ukrainian maiden to concubine to sultan's wife captured enormous public attention. She is the subject of numerous paintings, plays, and novels, as well as an opera, a ballet, and a symphony by the composer Haydn. Interest in and suspicion of Hürrem continues. In 2003, a Turkish miniseries once more depicted her as a scheming intriguer.

QUESTIONS FOR ANALYSIS

1. What types of power did Hürrem exercise during her lifetime? How did her gender enable her to attain certain kinds of power and also constrain her ability to exercise it?
2. What can an exceptional woman like Hürrem reveal about the broader political and social world in which she lived?

Source: Leslie P. Pierce, *The Imperial Harem: Women and Sovereignty in the Ottoman Empire* (New York: Oxford University Press, 1993).

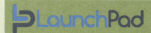 LaunchPad

ONLINE DOCUMENT PROJECT

What forces shaped Western views of Hürrem? Keeping the question above in mind, examine characterizations of Hürrem as seen through the eyes of a Habsburg diplomat, and then complete a writing assignment based on the evidence and details from this chapter. *See inside the front cover to learn more.*

* Quoted in Galina Yermolenko, "Roxolana: The Greatest Empress of the East," *The Muslim World* 95 (2005): 235.

How and why did the constitutional state triumph in the Dutch Republic and England?

Van Dyck, *Charles I at the Hunt*, ca. 1635

Anthony Van Dyck was the greatest of Rubens's many students. In 1633, he became court painter to Charles I. This portrait of Charles just dismounted from a horse emphasizes the aristocratic bearing, elegance, and innate authority of the king. Van Dyck had a profound influence on portraiture in England and beyond; some scholars believe that this portrait influenced Rigaud's 1701 portrayal of Louis XIV (see page 455). (Louvre, Paris, France/Giraudon/The Bridgeman Art Library)

WHILE FRANCE, PRUSSIA, RUSSIA, AND AUSTRIA developed absolutist states, England and the Netherlands evolved toward **constitutionalism**, which is the limitation of government by law. Constitutionalism also implies a balance between the authority and power of the government, on the one hand, and the rights and liberties of the subjects, on the other. By definition, all constitutionalist governments have a constitution, be it written or unwritten.

Despite their common commitment to constitutional government, England and the Dutch Republic represented significantly different alternatives to absolute

constitutionalism
▶ A form of government in which power is limited by law and balanced between the authority and power of the government, on the one hand, and the rights and liberties of the subjects or citizens on the other hand; could include constitutional monarchies or republics.

| What explains the rise of absolutism in Prussia and Austria? | What were the distinctive features of Russian and Ottoman absolutism? | **How and why did the constitutional state triumph in the Dutch Republic and England?** | What was the baroque style in art and music, and where was it popular? | ☑ LearningCurve Check what you know. |

republicanism

▶ A form of government in which there is no monarch and power rests in the hands of the people as exercised through elected representatives.

rule. After decades of civil war and an experiment with **republicanism**, the English opted for a constitutional monarchy in 1688. This settlement retained a monarch as the titular head of government but vested sovereignty in an elected parliament. Upon gaining independence from Spain in 1648, the Dutch rejected monarchical rule, adopting a republican form of government in which elected estates held supreme power.

Absolutist Claims in England

In 1603, Queen Elizabeth's Scottish cousin James Stuart succeeded her as James I (r. 1603–1625). James was a firm believer in the divine right of kings. He went so far as to lecture the House of Commons: "There are no privileges and immunities which can stand against a divinely appointed King."[6] Such a view ran directly counter to English traditions that a person's property could not be taken away without due process of law. James I and his son Charles I (r. 1625–1649) considered such constraints intolerable and a threat to their divine-right prerogative. Consequently, bitter squabbles erupted between the Crown and the House of Commons. The expenses of England's intervention in the Thirty Years' War only exacerbated tensions. Charles I's response was to refuse to summon Parliament from 1629 onward.

Religious Divides and the English Civil War

Relations between the king and the House of Commons were also embittered by religious issues. In the early seventeenth century, growing numbers of English people felt dissatisfied with the Church of England established by Henry VIII (r. 1509–1547). Many **Puritans** believed that the Protestant Reformation of the sixteenth century had not gone far enough. They wanted to "purify" the Anglican Church of lingering Roman Catholic elements.

Puritans

▶ Members of a sixteenth- and seventeenth-century reform movement within the Church of England that advocated purifying it of Roman Catholic elements.

James I responded to such ideas by declaring, "No bishop, no king." For James, bishops were among the chief supporters of the throne. His son and successor, Charles I, further antagonized religious sentiments. Not only did he marry a Catholic princess, but he also supported the heavy-handed policies of the archbishop of Canterbury William Laud (1573–1645). In 1637, Laud attempted to impose two new elements on church organization in Scotland: a new prayer book, modeled on the Anglican *Book of Common Prayer*, and bishoprics. The Presbyterian Scots rejected these elements and revolted. To finance an army to put down the Scots, King Charles was compelled to call a meeting of Parliament in November 1640.

Charles had ruled from 1629 to 1640 without Parliament, financing his government through extraordinary stopgap levies considered illegal by most English people. Most members of Parliament were not willing to trust such a despotic king with an army. Many supported the Scots' resistance to Charles's religious innovations. Accordingly, this Parliament, called the "Long Parliament" because it sat from 1640 to 1660, enacted legislation that limited the power of the monarch and made government without Parliament impossible.

In 1641, the Commons passed the Triennial Act, which compelled the king to summon Parliament every three years. The Commons impeached Archbishop

CHAPTER LOCATOR | What made the seventeenth century an "age of crisis"? | Why did France rise and Spain fall during this period?

474 CHAPTER 15 ABSOLUTISM AND CONSTITUTIONALISM

Laud and then threatened to abolish bishops. King Charles, fearful of a Scottish invasion, reluctantly accepted these measures.

The next act in the conflict was precipitated by the outbreak of rebellion in Ireland, where English governors and landlords had long exploited the people. In 1641, the Catholic gentry of Ireland led an uprising in response to a feared invasion by anti-Catholic forces of the British Long Parliament.

Without an army, Charles I could neither come to terms with the Scots nor respond to the Irish rebellion. After a failed attempt to arrest parliamentary leaders, Charles left London for the north of England. There, he recruited an army drawn from the nobility and its cavalry staff, the rural gentry, and mercenaries. In response, Parliament formed its own army, the New Model Army, composed of the militia of the city of London and country squires with business connections.

The English civil war (1642–1649) pitted the king against Parliament. After three years of fighting, Parliament's New Model Army defeated the king's armies at the Battles of Naseby and Langport in the summer of 1645. Charles, though, refused to concede defeat. Both sides jockeyed for position, waiting for a decisive event, which arrived in the form of the army under the leadership of Oliver Cromwell, a member of the House of Commons and a devout Puritan. In 1647, Cromwell's forces captured the king and dismissed anti-Cromwell members of the Parliament. In 1649, the remaining representatives, known as the "Rump Parliament," put Charles on trial for high treason. Charles was found guilty and beheaded on January 30, 1649.

The English Civil War, 1642–1649

Parliamentarians
Royalists
Major battle

Cromwell and Puritanical Absolutism in England

With the execution of Charles, kingship was abolished. In its place, Oliver Cromwell and his supporters enshrined a commonwealth, or republican government, known as the **Protectorate**. Theoretically, legislative power rested in the surviving members of Parliament, and executive power was lodged in a council of state. In fact, the army controlled the government, and Oliver Cromwell controlled the army, ruling what was essentially a military dictatorship.

The fiction of republican government was maintained until 1655 when, after repeated disputes, Cromwell dismissed Parliament. Cromwell continued the standing army and proclaimed quasi-martial law. Reflecting Puritan ideas of morality, Cromwell's state forbade sports, closed the theaters, and rigorously censored the press.

Cromwell had long associated Catholicism in Ireland with sedition and heresy, and led an army there to reconquer the country in August 1649. In the wake of Cromwell's invasion, the English banned Catholicism in Ireland, executed priests, and confiscated land from Catholics for English and Scottish settlers. These brutal acts left a legacy of Irish hatred for England.

Cromwell adopted mercantilist policies similar to those of absolutist France. He enforced a Navigation Act (1651) requiring that English goods be transported on English ships. The act sparked a short but successful war with the commercially threatened Dutch. While mercantilist legislation ultimately benefited English commerce, for ordinary people, the turmoil of foreign war only added to the harsh conditions of life induced by years of civil war.

Protectorate

▶ The English military dictatorship (1653–1658) established by Oliver Cromwell following the execution of Charles I.

What explains the rise of absolutism in Prussia and Austria?

What were the distinctive features of Russian and Ottoman absolutism?

How and why did the constitutional state triumph in the Dutch Republic and England?

What was the baroque style in art and music, and where was it popular?

✓ LearningCurve
Check what you know.

"The Royall Oake of Brittayne"

The chopping down of this tree, as shown in a cartoon from 1649, signifies the end of royal authority, stability, and the rule of law. As pigs graze (representing the unconcerned common people), being fattened for slaughter, Oliver Cromwell, with his feet in Hell, quotes Scripture. This is a royalist view of the collapse of Charles I's government and the rule of Cromwell. (© The British Library Board, E.1052)

The Protectorate collapsed when Cromwell died in 1658 and his ineffectual son succeeded him. Fed up with military rule, the English longed for a return to civilian government and, with it, common law and social stability. By 1660, they were ready to restore the monarchy.

The Restoration of the English Monarchy

The Restoration of 1660 brought to the throne Charles II (r. 1660–1685). Both houses of Parliament were also restored, together with the established Anglican Church. The Restoration failed to resolve two serious problems, however. What was to be the attitude of the state toward Puritans, Catholics, and dissenters from the established church? And what was to be the relationship between the king and Parliament?

CHAPTER LOCATOR | What made the seventeenth century an "age of crisis"? | Why did France rise and Spain fall during this period?

To answer the first question, Parliament enacted the **Test Act** of 1673 against those outside the Church of England, denying them the right to vote, hold public office, preach, teach, attend the universities, or even assemble for meetings. But these restrictions could not be enforced.

In politics, Charles II's initial determination to work well with Parliament did not last long. Finding that Parliament did not grant him an adequate income, Charles entered into a secret agreement with his cousin Louis XIV in 1670. The French king would give Charles £200,000 annually, and in return Charles would relax the laws against Catholics, gradually re-Catholicize England, and convert to Catholicism himself. When the details of this treaty leaked out, a great wave of anti-Catholic sentiment swept England.

When Charles died and his Catholic brother James became king, the worst English anti-Catholic fears were realized. As king, James II (r. 1685–1688) was an active promoter of Catholicism and made no effort to hide his religious agenda. Attempting to broaden his base of support with Protestant dissenters and non-conformists, James granted religious freedom to all.

James's opponents, a powerful coalition of eminent persons in Parliament and the Church of England, offered the English throne to James's heir, his Protestant daughter Mary, and her Dutch husband, Prince William of Orange. In December 1688, James II, his queen, and their infant son fled to France. Early in 1689, William and Mary were crowned king and queen of England.

Constitutional Monarchy and Cabinet Government

The "Glorious Revolution" of 1688–1689 represented the final destruction of the idea of divine-right monarchy. The men who instigated the revolution framed their intentions in the Bill of Rights, which was formulated in direct response to Stuart absolutism. Law was to be made in Parliament; once made, it could not be suspended by the Crown. Parliament had to be called at least once every three years. The independence of the judiciary was established, and there was to be no standing army in peacetime. Significant legal restrictions were imposed on Catholics. William and Mary accepted these principles when they took the throne, and the House of Parliament passed the Bill of Rights in December 1689.

The Glorious Revolution and the concept of representative government found its best defense in political philosopher John Locke's *Second Treatise of Civil Government* (1690). Locke (1632–1704) maintained that a government that oversteps its proper function—protecting the natural rights of life, liberty, and property—becomes a tyranny. Under a tyrannical government, the people have the natural right to rebellion.

During the course of the eighteenth century, the cabinet system of government evolved. In a cabinet system, the leading ministers, who must have seats in and the support of a majority of the House of Commons, formulate common policy and conduct the business of the country. During the administration of one royal minister, Sir Robert Walpole, who led the cabinet from 1721 to 1742, the idea developed that the cabinet was responsible to the House of Commons. In the English cabinet system, both legislative power and executive power are held by the leading ministers, who form the government.

What explains the rise of absolutism in Prussia and Austria?

What were the distinctive features of Russian and Ottoman absolutism?

How and why did the constitutional state triumph in the Dutch Republic and England?

What was the baroque style in art and music, and where was it popular?

✓ LearningCurve
Check what you know.

477

The Dutch Republic in the Seventeenth Century

In the late sixteenth century, the seven northern provinces of the Netherlands fought for and won their independence from Spain. The independence of the Republic of the United Provinces of the Netherlands was recognized in 1648 in the treaty that ended the Thirty Years' War. In this period, often called the "golden age of the Netherlands," Dutch ideas and attitudes played a profound role in shaping a new and modern worldview. At the same time, the United Provinces developed its own distinctive model of a constitutional state.

Jan Steen, *The Merry Family*, 1668

In this painting from the Dutch golden age, a happy family enjoys a boisterous song while seated around the dining table. Despite its carefree appearance, the painting was intended to teach a moral lesson. The children are shown drinking wine and smoking, bad habits they have learned from their parents. The inscription hanging over the mantelpiece (upper right) spells out the message clearly: "As the Old Sing, so Pipe the Young." (Album/Art Resource, NY)

CHAPTER LOCATOR | What made the seventeenth century an "age of crisis"? | Why did France rise and Spain fall during this period?

The Dutch established a republic, a state in which power rested in the hands of the people and was exercised through elected representatives. An oligarchy of wealthy businessmen called regents handled domestic affairs in each province's Estates (assemblies). The provincial Estates held almost all the power. A federal assembly, or States General, handled foreign affairs and war, but it did not possess sovereign authority. Holland, the province with the largest navy and the most wealth, usually dominated the republic and the States General.

In each province, the Estates appointed an executive officer, known as the **stadholder**. In theory, the stadholder was freely chosen by the Estates and answerable to them: in practice, however, the strong and influential House of Orange usually held the office of stadholder in several of the seven provinces of the republic. This meant that tensions always lingered between supporters of the House of Orange and those of the staunchly republican Estates, who suspected that the princes of Orange harbored monarchical ambitions.

The political success of the Dutch rested on their phenomenal commercial prosperity. The Dutch came to dominate the shipping business. They boasted the lowest shipping rates and largest merchant marine in Europe, allowing them to undersell foreign competitors (see Chapter 14). Trade and commerce brought the Dutch the highest standard of living in Europe, perhaps in the world. Salaries were high, and all classes of society ate well.

The moral and ethical bases of that commercial wealth were thrift, frugality, and religious toleration. Jews enjoyed a level of acceptance and assimilation in Dutch business and general culture unique in early modern Europe. In the Dutch Republic, toleration paid off: it attracted a great deal of foreign capital and investment.

stadholder
▶ The executive officer in each of the United Provinces of the Netherlands, a position often held by the princes of Orange.

QUICK REVIEW <

What explains the differences between the establishment of constitutionalism in England and the Dutch Republic?

What explains the rise of absolutism in Prussia and Austria?

What were the distinctive features of Russian and Ottoman absolutism?

How and why did the constitutional state triumph in the Dutch Republic and England?

What was the baroque style in art and music, and where was it popular?

☑ LearningCurve
Check what you know.

> What was the baroque style in art and music, and where was it popular?

Rubens, *Garden of Love*, 1633–1634

This painting is an outstanding example of the lavishness and richness of baroque art. Born and raised in northern Europe, Peter Paul Rubens trained as a painter in Italy. Upon his return to the Spanish Netherlands, he became a renowned and amazingly prolific artist, patronized by rulers across Europe. Rubens was a devout Catholic, and his work conveys the emotional fervor of the Catholic Reformation. (Prado, Madrid, Spain/Giraudon/The Bridgeman Art Library)

ROME AND THE REVITALIZED CATHOLIC CHURCH of the late sixteenth century spurred the early development of the baroque style. The papacy and the Jesuits encouraged the growth of an intensely emotional, exuberant art. They wanted artists to appeal to the senses and thereby touch the souls and kindle the faith of ordinary churchgoers while proclaiming the power and confidence of the reformed Catholic Church. In addition to this underlying religious emotionalism, the baroque drew its sense of drama, motion, and ceaseless striving from the Catholic Reformation. The baroque style developed with exceptional vigor in Catholic countries, but it had broad appeal and Protestants accounted for some of the finest examples of baroque style, especially in music.

In painting, the baroque reached maturity early with Peter Paul Rubens (1577–1640), the most outstanding and most representative of baroque painters. Studying in his native Flanders and in Italy, where he was influenced by masters of the High Renaissance such as Michelangelo, Rubens developed his own rich, sensuous, colorful style, which was characterized by animated figures, melodramatic contrasts, and monumental size.

CHAPTER LOCATOR | What made the seventeenth century an "age of crisis"? | Why did France rise and Spain fall during this period?

CHAPTER 15
480 ABSOLUTISM AND CONSTITUTIONALISM

In music, the baroque style reached its culmination almost a century later in the music of Johann Sebastian Bach (1685–1750). Organist and choirmaster of several Lutheran churches across Germany, Bach was equally at home writing secular concertos and sublime religious cantatas. Bach's organ music combined the baroque spirit of invention, tension, and emotion in an unforgettable striving toward the infinite. Unlike Rubens, Bach was not fully appreciated in his lifetime, but since the early nineteenth century his reputation has grown steadily.

QUICK REVIEW

Why did the Catholic Church promote the baroque style?

LOOKING BACK LOOKING AHEAD The first half of the seventeenth century was marked by the spread of religious and dynastic warfare across Europe, resulting in the death and dislocation of many millions. This catastrophe was compounded by recurrent episodes of crop failure, famine, and epidemic disease, all of which contributed to a stagnant economy and population loss. In the middle decades of the seventeenth century, the very survival of the European monarchies established in the Renaissance appeared in doubt.

With the re-establishment of order in the second half of the century, maintaining political and social stability was of paramount importance to European rulers and elites. In western and eastern Europe, a host of monarchs proclaimed their God-given and "absolute" authority to rule in the name of peace, unity, and good order. Rulers' ability to impose such claims in reality depended a great deal on compromise with local elites, who acquiesced to state power in exchange for privileges and payoffs. In this way, absolutism and constitutionalism did not always differ as much as they claimed. Both systems relied on political compromises forged from decades of strife.

The eighteenth century was to see this status quo thrown into question by new Enlightenment aspirations for human society, which themselves derived from the inquisitive and self-confident spirit of the Scientific Revolution. By the end of the century, demands for real popular sovereignty would challenge the foundations of the political order so painfully achieved in the seventeenth century.

LaunchPad

ONLINE DOCUMENT PROJECT
Hürrem

What forces shaped Western views of Hürrem?

You encountered Hürrem's story on page 472. Keeping the question above in mind, examine characterizations of Hürrem as seen through the eyes of a Habsburg diplomat. *See inside the front cover to learn more.*

| What explains the rise of absolutism in Prussia and Austria? | What were the distinctive features of Russian and Ottoman absolutism? | How and why did the constitutional state triumph in the Dutch Republic and England? | What was the baroque style in art and music, and where was it popular? | ✓ **LearningCurve** Check what you know. |

CHAPTER 15 STUDY GUIDE

 STEP 1

GET STARTED ONLINE

 **LearningCurve**

Now that you've read the chapter, make it stick by completing the LearningCurve activity.

 STEP 2

EXPLAIN WHY IT MATTERS

Put your reading into practice. Identify each term below, and then explain why it matters in Western history.

TERM	WHO OR WHAT & WHEN	WHY IT MATTERS
Peace of Westphalia (p. 449)		
Fronde (p. 454)		
mercantilism (p. 457)		
Peace of Utrecht (p. 458)		
Junkers (p. 463)		
boyars (p. 467)		
Cossacks (p. 467)		
sultan (p. 470)		
janissary corps (p. 471)		
millet system (p. 471)		
constitutionalism (p. 473)		
republicanism (p. 474)		
Puritans (p. 474)		
Protectorate (p. 475)		
Test Act (p. 477)		
stadholder (p. 479)		

 STEP 3

MOVE BEYOND THE BASICS

To demonstrate a more advanced understanding, use the chart to compare and contrast the governments of four European states at the beginning and end of the seventeenth century. How and why did each government change over the course of the century?

Country	1600	1700
France		
England		
Prussia		
Russia		

ABSOLUTISM

▶ What common challenges were faced by absolutist monarchs? How did the rulers of France, Austria, and Prussia respond to these challenges?

▶ What social and economic trends accompanied the rise of absolutism in eastern Europe?

CONSTITUTIONALISM

▶ Why did the efforts of English monarchs to build an absolutist state fail?

▶ In what ways was the Dutch Republic unique among seventeenth-century states?

RUSSIA AND THE OTTOMAN EMPIRE

▶ How did the Russian tsars gain control over Russia's landowning elite?

▶ How did the Ottoman absolutist state differ from its European counterparts?

MAKE CONNECTIONS

▶ How did the conflicts and tensions unleashed by the Reformation shape seventeenth-century political developments?

▶ What steps were taken during the seventeenth century toward the emergence of the modern nation-state?

> **IN YOUR OWN WORDS**

Imagine that you must give an oral report to the class answering the following question: **What were the most important political trends in seventeenth-century Europe?** What would be the most important points and why?

16

TOWARD A NEW WORLDVIEW

1540–1789

> **What new ways of looking at nature, society, and government emerged in the Early Modern period?** Chapter 16 examines the Scientific Revolution and the Enlightenment. In the sixteenth and seventeenth centuries, fundamentally new ways of understanding the natural world emerged. The new science entailed the search for precise knowledge of the physical world based on the union of experimental observations with sophisticated mathematics. In the eighteenth century, philosophers extended the use of reason from the study of nature to human society. While the Scientific Revolution ushered in modern science, the Enlightenment created concepts of human rights, equality, progress, universalism, and tolerance that still guide Western societies today. At the same time, some people used their new understanding of nature and reason to proclaim their own superiority, thus rationalizing attitudes such as racism and male chauvinism.

LearningCurve

After reading the chapter, use LearningCurve to retain what you've read.

> What revolutionary discoveries were made in the sixteenth and seventeenth centuries?

> What intellectual and social changes occurred as a result of the Scientific Revolution?

> What new ideas about society and human relations emerged in the Enlightenment?

> What impact did new ways of thinking have on politics?

Life During the Scientific Revolution. This 1768 painting by Joseph Wright captures the popularization of science and experimentation during the Enlightenment. (National Gallery, London/The Bridgeman Art Library)

What revolutionary discoveries were made in the sixteenth and seventeenth centuries?

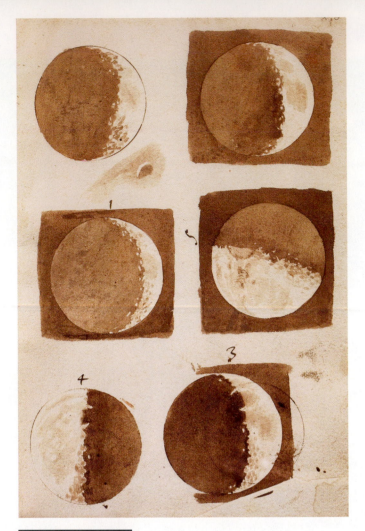

Galileo's Telescopic Observations of the Moon

Among the many mechanical devices Galileo invented was a telescope that could magnify objects thirty times (other contemporary telescopes could magnify objects only three times). Using this telescope, he obtained the empirical evidence that proved the Copernican system and sketched many illustrations of his observations, including the six phases of the moon shown here. (akg-images/Rabatti–Domingie)

UNTIL THE MIDDLE OF THE SIXTEENTH CENTURY, Europeans relied on an understanding of motion and matter drawn from the ancient Greek philosopher Aristotle and adapted to Christian theology. The rise of the university, along with the intellectual vitality of the Renaissance and technological advancements, inspired scholars to make closer observations and seek better explanations. From the sun-centered universe proposed by the Polish astronomer Nicolaus Copernicus to the great synthesis of physics and astronomy accomplished by the English scientist Isaac Newton, a revolutionary new understanding of the universe had emerged by the end of the seventeenth century.

CHAPTER LOCATOR | **What revolutionary discoveries were made in the sixteenth and seventeenth centuries?**

ca. 1540–1700 – Scientific Revolution	**ca. 1740–1789** – Salons led by Parisian elites
ca. 1690–1789 – Enlightenment	**1751–1772** – Philosophes publish *Encyclopedia: The Rational Dictionary of the Sciences, the Arts, and the Crafts*
ca. 1700–1800 – Growth of book publishing	**1756–1763** – Seven Years' War
1720–1780 – Rococo style in art and decoration	**1762–1796** – Reign of Catherine the Great of Russia
1740–1748 – War of the Austrian Succession	**1780–1790** – Reign of Joseph II of Austria
1740–1780 – Reign of the empress Maria Theresa of Austria	**1791** – Establishment of the Pale of Settlement
1740–1786 – Reign of Frederick the Great of Prussia	

Scientific Thought in 1500

The term *science* as we use it today came into use only in the nineteenth century. Prior to the Scientific Revolution, many different scholars and practitioners were involved in aspects of what came together to form science. One of the most important disciplines was **natural philosophy**, which focused on fundamental questions about the nature of the universe, its purpose, and how it functioned. In the early 1500s, natural philosophy was still based primarily on the ideas of Aristotle, the great Greek philosopher of the fourth century B.C.E. Medieval theologians brought Aristotelian philosophy into harmony with Christian doctrines. According to the revised Aristotelian view, a motionless earth was fixed at the center of the universe and was encompassed by ten separate concentric crystal spheres that revolved around it. Beyond the tenth sphere was Heaven, with the throne of God and the souls of the saved. Angels kept the spheres moving in perfect circles.

Aristotle's cosmology made intellectual sense, but it could not account for the observed motions of the stars and planets and, in particular, provided no explanation for the apparent backward motion of the planets. The great second-century scholar Ptolemy (see Chapter 14) offered a cunning solution to this dilemma. According to Ptolemy, the planets moved in small circles, called epicycles, each of which moved in turn along a larger circle, or deferent. Ptolemaic astronomy was less elegant than Aristotle's neat nested circles and required complex calculations, but it provided a surprisingly accurate model for predicting planetary motion.

Aristotle's views, revised by medieval philosophers, also dominated thinking about physics and motion on earth. Aristotle had distinguished sharply between the world of the celestial spheres and that of the earth—the sublunar world. The

natural philosophy

▶ An early modern term for the study of the nature of the universe, its purpose, and how it functioned; it encompassed what we call science today.

What intellectual and social changes occurred as a result of the Scientific Revolution?	What new ideas about society and human relations emerged in the Enlightenment?	What impact did new ways of thinking have on politics?	✓ LearningCurve Check what you know.

spheres consisted of a perfect, incorruptible "quintessence." The sublunar world, however, was made up of four imperfect, changeable elements: air, fire, water, and earth. Aristotle and his followers also believed that a uniform force moved an object at a constant speed and that the object would stop as soon as that force was removed.

Origins of the Scientific Revolution

Why did Aristotelian teachings give way to new views about the universe? The Scientific Revolution drew on long-term developments in European culture, as well as borrowings from Arabic scholars. The first important development was the medieval university. By the thirteenth century, permanent universities had been established in western Europe to train the lawyers, doctors, and church leaders society required. By 1300, philosophy had taken its place alongside law, medicine, and theology. Medieval philosophers acquired a limited but real independence from theologians and a sense of free inquiry.

Medieval universities drew on rich traditions of Islamic learning. With the expansion of Islam into lands of the Byzantine Empire in the seventh and eighth centuries, the Muslim world had inherited ancient Greek learning, to which Islamic scholars added their own commentaries and new discoveries. Many Greek texts, which were lost to the West after the fall of the Western Roman Empire in the fifth century, re-entered circulation through translation from Arabic in the twelfth century; these became the basis for the curriculum of the medieval universities. In the fourteenth and fifteenth centuries, leading universities established new professorships of mathematics, astronomy, and optics within their faculties of philosophy. Thus, the stage was set for the union of mathematics with natural philosophy that was to be a hallmark of the Scientific Revolution.

The Renaissance also stimulated scientific progress. Renaissance patrons played a role in funding scientific investigations, as they did for art and literature. Renaissance artists' turn toward realism and their use of geometry to convey three-dimensional perspective encouraged scholars to practice close observation and to use mathematics to describe the natural world. The quest to restore the glories of the ancient past led to the rediscovery of even more classical texts. The fall of Constantinople to the Muslim Ottomans in 1453 resulted in a great influx of little-known Greek works as Christian scholars fled to Italy with their precious texts.

Developments in technology also encouraged the emergence of the Scientific Revolution. The rise of printing in the mid-fifteenth century provided a faster and less expensive way to circulate knowledge across Europe. Fascination with the new discoveries being made in Asia and the Americas greatly increased the demand for printed material. Publishers found an eager audience for the books and images they issued about unknown peoples, plants, animals, and other new findings.

The navigational problems of long sea voyages in the age of overseas expansion, along with the rise of trade and colonization, led to their own series of technological innovations. Navigation and cartography were critical in the development of many new scientific instruments, such as the telescope, barometer, thermometer, pendulum clock, microscope, and air pump. Better instruments, which permitted

CHAPTER LOCATOR | **What revolutionary discoveries were made in the sixteenth and seventeenth centuries?**

more accurate observations, enabled the rise of experimentation as a crucial method of the Scientific Revolution.

Recent historical research has also focused on the contribution to the Scientific Revolution of practices that no longer belong to the realm of science, such as astrology. Many of the most celebrated astronomers were also astrologers and spent much time devising horoscopes for their patrons. Used as a diagnostic tool in medicine, astrology formed a regular part of the curriculum of medical schools.

Centuries-old practices of magic and alchemy also remained important traditions for natural philosophers. Unlike modern-day conjurers, the practitioners of magic strove to understand and control hidden connections they perceived among different elements of the natural world, such as that between a magnet and iron. The idea that objects possessed invisible or "occult" qualities that allowed them to affect other objects through their innate "sympathy" with each other was a particularly important legacy of the magical tradition.

The Copernican Hypothesis

As a young man, the Polish cleric Nicolaus Copernicus (1473–1543) was drawn to the vitality of the Italian Renaissance. After studies at the University of Kraków, he departed for Italy, where he studied astronomy, medicine, and church law. Copernicus noted that astronomers still depended on the work of Ptolemy for their most accurate calculations, but he felt that Ptolemy's cumbersome and occasionally inaccurate rules detracted from the majesty of a perfect creator. He preferred an alternative ancient Greek idea: that the sun, rather than the earth, was at the center of the universe.

Finishing his university studies and returning to a position in church administration in East Prussia, Copernicus worked on his hypothesis from 1506 to 1530. Without questioning the Aristotelian belief in crystal spheres or the idea that circular motion was divine, Copernicus theorized that the stars and planets, including the earth, revolved around a fixed sun.

The **Copernican hypothesis** had enormous scientific and religious implications, many of which the conservative Copernicus did not anticipate. First, it put the stars at rest, their apparent nightly movement simply a result of the earth's rotation. Thus, his hypothesis destroyed the main reason for believing in crystal spheres capable of moving the stars around the earth. Second, Copernicus's theory suggested a universe of staggering size. If, in the course of a year, the earth moved around the sun and yet the stars appeared to remain in the same place, then the universe was unthinkably large. Third, by using mathematics instead of philosophy to justify his theories, he challenged the traditional hierarchy of the disciplines. And by characterizing the earth as just another planet, Copernicus destroyed the basic idea of Aristotelian physics—that the earthly sphere was quite different from the heavenly one.

Other events were almost as influential as the Copernican hypothesis in creating doubts about traditional astronomy. In 1572, a new star appeared and shone very brightly for almost two years. The new star, which was actually a distant exploding star, made an enormous impression on people. It seemed to contradict the idea that the heavenly spheres were unchanging and therefore perfect. In

Copernican hypothesis
▶ The idea that the sun, not the earth, was the center of the universe.

What intellectual and social changes occurred as a result of the Scientific Revolution?

What new ideas about society and human relations emerged in the Enlightenment?

What impact did new ways of thinking have on politics?

☑ LearningCurve
Check what you know.

489

1577, a new comet suddenly moved through the sky, cutting a straight path across the supposedly impenetrable crystal spheres. It was time, as a sixteenth-century scientific writer put it, for "the radical renovation of astronomy."[1]

Brahe, Kepler, and Galileo: Proving Copernicus Right

Born into a Danish noble family, Tycho Brahe (TEE-koh BRAH-hee) (1546–1601) established himself as Europe's leading astronomer with his detailed observations of the new star of 1572. Aided by generous grants from the king of Denmark, Brahe built the most sophisticated observatory of his day.

Upon the king's death, Brahe acquired a new patron in the Holy Roman emperor Rudolph II and built a new observatory in Prague. For twenty years, Brahe meticulously observed the stars and planets with the naked eye, compiling much more complete and accurate data than ever before. His limited understanding of mathematics and his sudden death in 1601, however, prevented him from making much sense out of his mass of data.

It was left to Brahe's assistant, Johannes Kepler (1571–1630), to rework Brahe's mountain of observations. Kepler's examination of his predecessor's meticulously recorded findings convinced him that Ptolemy's astronomy could not explain them. Abandoning the notion of epicycles and deferents—which even Copernicus had retained in part—Kepler developed three new and revolutionary laws of planetary motion. First, he demonstrated that the orbits of the planets around the sun are elliptical rather than circular. Second, he demonstrated that the planets do not move at a uniform speed in their orbits. When a planet is close to the sun it moves more rapidly, and it slows as it moves farther away from the sun. He also proved that the time a planet takes to make its complete orbit is precisely related to its distance from the sun.

Kepler's contribution was monumental. Whereas Copernicus had used mathematics to

Hevelius and His Wife

Portable sextants were used to chart a ship's position at sea by measuring the altitude of celestial bodies above the horizon. Astronomers used much larger sextants to measure the angular distances between two bodies. Here, Johannes Hevelius uses the great brass sextant at the Danzig observatory, with the help of his wife, Elisabetha. Six feet in radius, this instrument was closely modeled on the one used by Tycho Brahe. (f Typ 620.73.451, Houghton Library, Harvard University)

CHAPTER LOCATOR | **What revolutionary discoveries were made in the sixteenth and seventeenth centuries?**

describe planetary movement, Kepler proved mathematically the precise relations of a sun-centered (solar) system. He thus united for the first time the theoretical cosmology of natural philosophy with mathematics. His work demolished the old system of Aristotle and Ptolemy, and with his third law he came close to formulating the idea of universal gravitation (see page 492).

Beyond his great contribution to astronomy, Kepler pioneered the field of optics. He was the first to explain the role of refraction within the eye in creating vision, and he invented an improved telescope. He was also a great mathematician whose work furnished the basis for integral calculus and advances in geometry.

Kepler was not, however, the consummate modern scientist that these achievements suggest. His duties as court mathematician included casting horoscopes, and he based his own daily life on astrological principles. He also wrote at length on cosmic harmonies and explained, for example, elliptical motion through ideas about the beautiful music created by the combined motion of the planets. His career exemplifies the complex interweaving of ideas and beliefs in the emerging science of his day.

While Kepler was unraveling planetary motion, a young Florentine professor of mathematics named Galileo Galilei (1564–1642) was challenging all the old ideas about motion. His great achievement was the elaboration and consolidation of the **experimental method**. That is, rather than speculate about what might or should happen, Galileo conducted controlled experiments to find out what actually did happen.

In his early experiments, Galileo focused on deficiencies in Aristotle's theories of motion. He measured the movement of a rolling ball across a surface, repeating the action again and again to verify his results. In his famous acceleration experiment, he showed that a uniform force—in this case, gravity—produced a uniform acceleration. Through another experiment, he formulated the **law of inertia**. He found that rest was not the natural state of objects. Rather, an object continues in motion forever unless stopped by some external force. His discoveries proved Aristotelian physics wrong.

Galileo then applied the experimental method to astronomy. On hearing details about the invention of the telescope in Holland, Galileo made one for himself and trained it on the heavens. He quickly discovered the first four moons of Jupiter, which clearly suggested that Jupiter could not possibly be embedded in any impenetrable crystal sphere as Aristotle and Ptolemy maintained. This discovery provided new evidence for the Copernican theory, in which Galileo already believed. Galileo then pointed his telescope at the moon. He wrote in 1610 in *The Sidereal Messenger:* "By the aid of a telescope anyone may behold [the Milky Way] in a manner which so distinctly appeals to the senses that all the disputes which have tormented philosophers through so many ages are exploded by the irrefutable evidence of our eyes, and we are freed from wordy disputes upon the subject."[2]

In 1597, when Johannes Kepler sent Galileo an early publication defending Copernicus, Galileo replied that it was too dangerous to express his support for heliocentrism publicly. The rising fervor of the Catholic Reformation increased the church's hostility to such radical ideas, and in 1616, the Holy Office placed the works of Copernicus and his supporters, including Kepler, on a list of books Catholics were forbidden to read.

Galileo was a devout Catholic who sincerely believed that his theories did not

experimental method
▶ The approach, pioneered by Galileo, that the proper way to explore the workings of the universe was through repeatable experiments rather than speculation.

law of inertia
▶ A law formulated by Galileo that states that motion, not rest, is the natural state of an object, and that an object continues in motion forever unless stopped by some external force.

What intellectual and social changes occurred as a result of the Scientific Revolution? | What new ideas about society and human relations emerged in the Enlightenment? | What impact did new ways of thinking have on politics? | ✓ LearningCurve Check what you know.

491

detract from the perfection of God. Out of caution he silenced his beliefs for several years, until in 1623 he saw new hope with the ascension of Pope Urban VIII, a man sympathetic to developments in the new science. However, Galileo's 1632 *Dialogue on the Two Chief Systems of the World* went too far. Published in Italian and widely read, this work openly lampooned the traditional views of Aristotle and Ptolemy and defended those of Copernicus. The papal Inquisition placed Galileo on trial for heresy. Imprisoned and threatened with torture, the aging Galileo recanted.

Newton's Synthesis

By about 1640, despite the efforts of the church, the work of Brahe, Kepler, and Galileo had been largely accepted by the scientific community. But the new findings failed to explain what forces controlled the movement of the planets and objects on earth. That challenge was taken up by English scientist Isaac Newton (1642–1727).

Newton was born into the lower English gentry in 1642, and he enrolled at Cambridge University in 1661. A genius who spectacularly united the experimental and theoretical-mathematical sides of modern science, Newton was an intensely devout, albeit non-orthodox Christian. Newton was also fascinated by alchemy. He viewed alchemy as one path, alongside mathematics and astronomy, to the truth of God's creation. Like Kepler and other practitioners of the Scientific Revolution, he studied the natural world not for its own sake, but to understand the divine plan.

Newton's towering accomplishment was a single explanatory system that could integrate the astronomy of Copernicus, as corrected by Kepler's laws, with the physics of Galileo and his predecessors. *Philosophicae Naturalis Principia Mathematica* (1687) laid down Newton's three laws of motion, using a set of mathematical laws that explain motion and mechanics. The key feature of the Newtonian synthesis was the **law of universal gravitation**. According to this law, every body in the universe attracts every other body in the universe in a precise mathematical relationship, whereby the force of attraction is proportional to the quantity of matter of the objects and inversely proportional to the square of the distance between them. The whole universe was unified in one coherent system. The German mathematician and philosopher Gottfried von Leibniz, with whom Newton contested the invention of calculus, was outraged by Newton's claim that the "occult" force of gravity could allow bodies to affect one another at great distances. Newton's religious faith, as well as his alchemical belief in the innate powers of certain objects, allowed him to dismiss such criticism.

law of universal gravitation
▶ Newton's law that all objects are attracted to one another and that the force of attraction is proportional to the objects' quantity of matter and inversely proportional to the square of the distance between them.

> **QUICK REVIEW**

In what ways do Newton's breakthroughs represent the culmination of the Scientific Revolution?

What intellectual and social changes occurred as a result of the Scientific Revolution?

Metamorphoses of the Caterpillar and Moth Maria Sibylla Merian (1647–1717), the stepdaughter of a Dutch painter, became a celebrated scientific illustrator in her own right. Her finely observed pictures of insects in the South American colony of Suriname introduced many new species. For Merian, science was intimately tied with art: she not only painted but also bred caterpillars and performed experiments on them. Her two-year stay in Suriname, accompanied by a teenage daughter, was a daring feat for a seventeenth-century woman. (akg-images)

THE CREATION OF A NEW SCIENCE was not accomplished by a handful of brilliant astronomers working alone. Scholars in many fields—medicine, chemistry, and botany, among others—used new methods to seek answers to long-standing problems, sharing their results in a community that spanned Europe. At the same time, monarchs and entrepreneurs launched explorations to uncover and understand the natural riches of newly conquered empires around the globe.

What intellectual and social changes occurred as a result of the Scientific Revolution?	What new ideas about society and human relations emerged in the Enlightenment?	What impact did new ways of thinking have on politics?	☑ **LearningCurve** Check what you know.

Bacon, Descartes, and the Scientific Method

One of the keys to the achievement of a new worldview in the seventeenth century was the development of better ways of obtaining knowledge about the world. Two important thinkers, Francis Bacon (1561–1626) and René Descartes (day-KAHRT) (1596–1650), were influential in describing and advocating for improved scientific methods based on experimentation and mathematical reasoning, respectively.

Rejecting the Aristotelian and medieval method of using speculative reasoning to build general theories, the English politician and writer Francis Bacon formalized the empirical method, which had already been used by Brahe and Galileo, into the general theory of inductive reasoning known as **empiricism**. In Bacon's view, the researcher who wants to learn more about leaves or rocks, for example, should not speculate about the subject but should rather collect a multitude of specimens and then compare and analyze them to derive general principles. Bacon's work, and his prestige as lord chancellor under James I, led to the widespread adoption of what was called experimental philosophy in England after his death.

On the continent, more speculative methods retained support. Accepting Galileo's claim that all elements of the universe are composed of the same matter and drawing on ancient Greek atomist philosophies, the French philosopher René Descartes developed the idea that matter was made up of identical "corpuscles" that collided together in an endless series of motions. All occurrences in nature could be analyzed as matter in motion and, according to Descartes, the total "quantity of motion" in the universe was constant. Descartes's mechanistic view of the universe depended on the idea that a vacuum was impossible, which meant that every action had an equal reaction, continuing in an eternal chain reaction.

Although Descartes's hypothesis about the vacuum was proved wrong, his notion of a mechanistic universe intelligible through the physics of motion proved inspirational. Decades later, Newton rejected Descartes's idea of a full universe and several of his other ideas, but retained the notion of a mechanistic universe as a key element of his own system.

Descartes's greatest achievement was to develop his initial vision into a whole philosophy of knowledge and science. The Aristotelian cosmos was appealing in part because it corresponded with the evidence of the human senses. When the senses were proven to be wrong, Descartes decided it was necessary to doubt them and everything that could reasonably be doubted, and then, as in geometry, to use deductive reasoning from self-evident truths, which he called "first principles," to ascertain scientific laws. Descartes's reasoning ultimately reduced all substances to "matter" and "mind" — that is, to the physical and the spiritual. His view of the world as consisting of two fundamental entities is known as **Cartesian dualism**. Descartes's thought was highly influential in France and the Netherlands, but less so in England, where experimental philosophy won the day.

Both Bacon's inductive experimentalism and Descartes's deductive mathematical reasoning had their faults. Bacon's inability to appreciate the importance of mathematics and his obsession with practical results clearly showed the limitations of antitheoretical empiricism. Likewise, some of Descartes's positions demonstrated the inadequacy of rigid, dogmatic rationalism. For example, he believed that it was possible to deduce the whole science of medicine from first principles.

empiricism

▶ A theory of inductive reasoning that calls for acquiring evidence through observation and experimentation rather than deductive reason and speculation.

Cartesian dualism

▶ Descartes's view that all of reality could ultimately be reduced to mind and matter.

CHAPTER LOCATOR | What revolutionary discoveries were made in the sixteenth and seventeenth centuries?

494 CHAPTER 16
TOWARD A NEW WORLDVIEW

Although insufficient on their own, Bacon's and Descartes's extreme approaches are combined in the modern scientific method, which began to crystallize in the late seventeenth century.

Medicine, the Body, and Chemistry

The Scientific Revolution soon inspired renewed study of the microcosm of the human body. For many centuries, the ancient Greek physician Galen's explanation of the body carried the same authority as Aristotle's account of the universe. According to Galen, the body contained four humors. Illness was believed to result from an imbalance of humors, which is why doctors frequently prescribed bloodletting to expel "excess" blood.

Swiss physician and alchemist Paracelsus (1493–1541) was an early proponent of the experimental method in medicine and pioneered the use of chemicals and drugs to address what he saw as chemical, rather than humoral, imbalances. Another experimentalist, Flemish physician Andreas Vesalius (1516–1564), studied anatomy by dissecting human bodies. The experimental approach also led English royal physician William Harvey (1578–1657) to discover the circulation of blood through the veins and arteries in 1628. Harvey was the first to explain that the heart worked like a pump and to explain the function of its muscles and valves.

Some decades later, Irishman Robert Boyle (1627–1691) helped found the modern science of chemistry. Following Paracelsus's lead, he undertook experiments to discover the basic elements of nature, which he believed was composed of infinitely small atoms. Boyle was the first to create a vacuum, thus disproving Descartes's belief that a vacuum could not exist in nature, and he discovered Boyle's law (1662), which states that the pressure of a gas varies inversely with volume.

Empire and Natural History

While the traditional story of the Scientific Revolution focuses exclusively on developments within Europe itself, and in particular on achievements in mathematical astronomy, more recently scholars have emphasized the impact of Europe's overseas empires on the accumulation and transmission of knowledge about the natural world. Building on the rediscovery of classical texts, early modern scholars published new works cataloguing forms of life in northern Europe, Asia, and the Americas that were unknown to the ancients. These encyclopedias of natural history included realistic drawings and descriptions that emphasized the usefulness of animal and plant species for trade, medicine, food, and other practical concerns. Much of the new knowledge contained in such works resulted from scientific expeditions, often sponsored by European governments eager to learn about and profit from their imperial holdings.

MAJOR CONTRIBUTORS TO THE SCIENTIFIC REVOLUTION

■ **Nicolaus Copernicus (1473–1543)**
On the Revolutions of the Heavenly Spheres (1543); theorized that the sun, rather than the earth, was the center of the galaxy

■ **Paracelsus (1493–1541)**
Swiss physician and alchemist who pioneered the use of chemicals and drugs to address illness

■ **Andreas Vesalius (1514–1564)**
On the Structure of the Human Body (1543)

■ **Tycho Brahe (1546–1601)**
Built observatory and compiled data for the *Rudolphine Tables*, a new table of planetary data

■ **Francis Bacon (1561–1626)**
Advocated experimental method, formalizing theory of inductive reasoning known as empiricism

■ **Galileo Galilei (1564–1642)**
Used telescopic observation to provide evidence for Copernican hypothesis; experimented to formulate laws of physics, such as inertia

■ **Johannes Kepler (1571–1630)**
Used Brahe's data to prove the Copernican hypothesis mathematically; his new laws of planetary motion united for the first time natural philosophy and mathematics; completed the *Rudolphine Tables* in 1627

■ **William Harvey (1578–1657)**
Discovery of circulation of blood (1628)

■ **René Descartes (1596–1650)**
Used deductive reasoning to formulate the theory of Cartesian dualism

■ **Robert Boyle (1627–1691)**
Boyle's law (1662) governing the pressure of gases

■ **Isaac Newton (1642–1727)**
Principia Mathematica (1687); set forth the law of universal gravitation, which synthesized previous findings of motion and matter

What intellectual and social changes occurred as a result of the Scientific Revolution?

What new ideas about society and human relations emerged in the Enlightenment?

What impact did new ways of thinking have on politics?

✓ LearningCurve
Check what you know.

Science and Society

The rise of modern science had many consequences, some of which are still unfolding. First, it went hand in hand with the rise of a new social group—the international scientific community. Members of this community were linked together by common interests and shared values as well as by journals and the learned scientific societies founded in many countries in the late seventeenth and eighteenth centuries. Second, as governments intervened to support and sometimes direct research, the new scientific community became closely tied to the state and its agendas. At the same time, scientists developed a critical attitude toward established authority that would inspire thinkers to question traditions in other domains as well.

In recent years, historians have emphasized the crossover between the work of artisans and the rise of science, particularly in the development of the experimental method. Many craftsmen developed a strong interest in emerging scientific ideas and, in turn, the practice of science in the seventeenth century often relied on artisans' expertise in making instruments and conducting precise experiments.

Some things did not change in the Scientific Revolution. Scholars have noted that nature was often depicted as a female, whose veil of secrecy needed to be stripped away and penetrated by male experts. New "rational" methods for approaching nature did not question traditional inequalities between the sexes— and may have worsened them in some ways. For example, the rise of universities and other professional institutions for science raised new barriers because most of these organizations did not accept women.

A number of noteworthy exceptions existed, however. In Italy, universities and academies did offer posts to women. Women across Europe worked as makers of wax anatomical models and as botanical and zoological illustrators, like Maria Sibylla Merian. They were also very much involved in informal scientific communities, attending salons (see page 502), participating in scientific experiments, and writing learned treatises. Some female intellectuals became full-fledged members of the philosophical dialogue. In England, Margaret Cavendish, Anne Conway, and Mary Astell all contributed to debates about Descartes's mind-body dualism, among other issues.

By the time Louis XIV died in 1715, many of the scientific ideas that would eventually coalesce into a new worldview had been assembled. Yet Christian Europe was still strongly attached to its established political and social structures and its traditional spiritual beliefs. By 1775, however, a large portion of western Europe's educated elite had embraced the new ideas. This was the work of many men and women across Europe who participated in the Enlightenment, either as publishers, writers, and distributors of texts or as members of the eager public that consumed them.

> **QUICK REVIEW**

How did the ideas of Bacon and Descartes contribute to the development of the scientific method?

CHAPTER LOCATOR | What revolutionary discoveries were made in the sixteenth and seventeenth centuries?

What new ideas about society and human relations emerged in the Enlightenment?

Enlightenment Culture

An actor performs the first reading of a new play by Voltaire at the salon of Madame Geoffrin. Voltaire, then in exile, is represented by a bust statue. (Académie des Sciences, Belles-Lettres, Rouen, France/Giraudon/ The Bridgeman Art Library)

> **PICTURING THE PAST**

ANALYZE THE IMAGE: Which of these people do you think is the hostess, Madame Geoffrin, and why? Using details from the painting to support your answer, how would you describe the status of the people shown?

MAKE CONNECTIONS: What does this image suggest about the reach of Enlightenment ideas to common people? To women? Does the painting of the bookstore on page 503 suggest a broader reach? Why?

THE SCIENTIFIC REVOLUTION was a crucial factor in the creation of the new worldview of the eighteenth-century **Enlightenment**. This worldview grew out of a rich mix of diverse and often conflicting ideas. Nonetheless, three central concepts stand at the core of Enlightenment thinking. The first and foremost idea was that the methods of natural science could and should be used to examine and understand all aspects of life. Nothing was to be accepted on faith; everything was to be submitted to **rationalism**, a secular, critical way of thinking. A second important Enlightenment concept was that the scientific method was capable of discovering the laws of human society as well as those of nature. These tenets led to the third key idea, that of progress. Armed with the proper method of discovering the laws of human existence, Enlightenment thinkers believed, it was at least possible for human beings to create better societies and better people.

Enlightenment
▶ The influential intellectual and cultural movement of the late seventeenth and eighteenth centuries that introduced a new worldview based on the use of reason, the scientific method, and progress.

rationalism
▶ A secular, critical way of thinking in which nothing was to be accepted on faith and everything was to be submitted to reason.

The Emergence of the Enlightenment

The generation that came of age between the publication of Newton's *Principia* in 1687 and the death of Louis XIV in 1715 tied the crucial knot between the Scientific Revolution and a new outlook on life. Whereas medieval and Reformation

---

What intellectual and social changes occurred as a result of the Scientific Revolution?

What new ideas about society and human relations emerged in the Enlightenment?

What impact did new ways of thinking have on politics?

 LearningCurve
Check what you know.

thinkers had been concerned primarily with abstract concepts of sin and salvation, and Renaissance humanists had drawn their inspiration from the classical past, Enlightenment thinkers believed that their era had gone far beyond antiquity and that intellectual progress was very possible. Talented writers of that generation popularized hard-to-understand scientific achievements and set an agenda of human problems to be addressed through the methods of science.

Like the Scientific Revolution, the Enlightenment was also fueled by Europe's increased contacts with the wider world. In the wake of the great discoveries of the fifteenth and sixteenth centuries, the rapidly growing travel literature taught Europeans that the peoples of China, India, Africa, and the Americas all had their own very different beliefs and customs. Some Europeans began to look at truth and morality in relative, rather than absolute, terms. If anything was possible, who could say what was right or wrong?

The excitement of the Scientific Revolution also generated doubt and uncertainty, contributing to a widespread crisis in late-seventeenth-century European thought. In the wake of the devastation wrought by the Thirty Years' War, some people asked whether ideological conformity in religious matters was really necessary. Others skeptically asked if religious truth could ever be known with absolute certainty and concluded that it could not. The atmosphere of doubt spread from religious to political issues. This was a natural extension, since many rulers viewed religious dissent as a form of political opposition and took harsh measures to stifle unorthodox forms of worship. Thus, questioning religion inevitably led to confrontations with the state.

These concerns combined spectacularly in the career of Pierre Bayle (1647–1706), a French Protestant, or Huguenot, who took refuge from government persecution in the tolerant Dutch Republic. Bayle critically examined the religious beliefs and persecutions of the past in his *Historical and Critical Dictionary* (1697). Demonstrating that human beliefs had been extremely varied and very often mistaken, he concluded that nothing can ever be known beyond all doubt, a view known as skepticism. His very influential *Dictionary* was found in more private libraries of eighteenth-century France than any other book.

Like Bayle, many Huguenots fled France for the Dutch Republic, a center of early Enlightenment thought for people of many faiths. The Dutch Jewish philosopher Baruch Spinoza (1632–1677) borrowed Descartes's emphasis on rationalism and his methods of deductive reasoning, but he rejected the French thinker's mind-body dualism. Instead, Spinoza came to believe that mind and body are united in one substance and that God and nature were merely two names for the same thing. He envisioned a deterministic universe in which good and evil were merely relative values and our actions were shaped by outside circumstances, not free will. Spinoza was excommunicated by the relatively large Jewish community of Amsterdam for his controversial religious ideas, but he was heralded by his Enlightenment successors as a model of personal virtue and courageous intellectual autonomy.

Out of this period of intellectual turmoil came John Locke's *Essay Concerning Human Understanding* (1690). In this work, Locke (1632–1704), a physician and member of the Royal Society, brilliantly set forth a new theory about how human beings learn and form their ideas. Locke insisted that all ideas are derived from experience. The human mind at birth is like a blank tablet, or tabula rasa, on which the environment writes the individual's understanding and beliefs. Human development is therefore determined by education and social institutions. Locke's essay contributed to the theory of sensationalism, the idea that all human ideas and thoughts are produced as a result of sensory impressions. With his emphasis on the role of perception in the acquisition of knowledge, Locke provided a systematic justification of Bacon's emphasis on the importance of observation and experimentation. The *Essay Concerning Human Understanding* passed through many editions and translations and, along with Newton's *Principia*, was one of the dominant intellectual inspirations of the Enlightenment.

The Influence of the Philosophes

The spread of the Enlightenment spirit of inquiry and debate owed a great deal to the work of the **philosophes** (fee-luh-SZOFZ), a group of intellectuals who proudly proclaimed that they, at long last, were bringing the light of reason to their ignorant fellow humans. *Philosophe* is the French word for "philosopher," and in the mid-eighteenth century France became a hub of Enlightenment thought.

philosophes

▶ A group of French intellectuals who proclaimed that they were bringing the light of knowledge to their fellow humans in the Age of Enlightenment.

> Reasons Why France Became a Major Hub of Enlightenment Thought	
French power and prestige	France was the wealthiest and most populous country in Europe; French was the international language of the elite
Political discontent in France	Rising political discontent in France led to calls for reform among educated elite
Ambitions of French philosophes	French philosophes were determined to spread their ideas throughout the international Republic of Letters

One of the greatest philosophes, the baron de Montesquieu (mahn-tuhs-KYOO) (1689–1755), pioneered this approach in *The Persian Letters*, a brilliant and extremely influential social satire published in 1721 and considered the first major work of the French Enlightenment. It consisted of amusing letters supposedly written by two Persian travelers who, as outsiders, saw European customs in unique ways, thereby allowing Montesquieu a vantage point for criticizing existing practices and beliefs.

Having gained fame by using wit as a weapon against cruelty and superstition, Montesquieu set out to apply the critical method to the problem of government in *The Spirit of Laws* (1748). The result was a complex, comparative study of republics, monarchies, and despotisms. Showing that forms of government were shaped by history and geography, Montesquieu focused on the conditions that would promote liberty and prevent tyranny. He argued for a separation of powers, with political power divided and shared by a variety of classes and legal estates.

The most famous and perhaps most representative philosophe was François Marie Arouet, who was known by the pen name Voltaire (vohl-TAIR) (1694–1778). Early in his career, he was arrested on two occasions for insulting noblemen. Voltaire moved to England for three years in order to avoid a longer prison term in France, and in England he came to share Montesquieu's enthusiasm for English liberties and institutions.

Returning to France, Voltaire had the great fortune of meeting Gabrielle-Emilie Le Tonnelier de Breteuil, marquise du Châtelet (SHAH-tuh-lay) (1706–1749),

What intellectual and social changes occurred as a result of the Scientific Revolution?

What new ideas about society and human relations emerged in the Enlightenment?

What impact did new ways of thinking have on politics?

☑ LearningCurve
Check what you know.

499

a noblewoman with a passion for science. Inviting Voltaire to live in her country house at Cirey in Lorraine and becoming his long-time companion (under the eyes of her tolerant husband), Madame du Châtelet studied physics and mathematics and published scientific articles and translations, including the first—and only—translation of Newton's *Principia* into French.)

While living at Cirey, Voltaire wrote works praising England and popularizing English science. He lauded Newton as history's greatest man because he had used his genius for the benefit of humanity. In the true style of the Enlightenment, Voltaire mixed the glorification of science and reason with an appeal for better individuals and institutions.

Like almost all of the philosophes, however, Voltaire was a reformer, not a revolutionary, in politics. He pessimistically concluded that the best one could hope for in the way of government was a good monarch because human beings "are very rarely worthy to govern themselves." Nor did Voltaire believe in social and economic equality, insisting that the idea of making servants equal to their masters was "absurd and impossible." The only realizable equality, Voltaire thought, was that "by which the citizen only depends on the laws which protect the freedom of the feeble against the ambitions of the strong."[3]

Voltaire's philosophical and religious positions were much more radical than his social and political beliefs. In the tradition of Bayle, his writings challenged the Catholic Church and Christian theology at almost every point. Like many eighteenth-century Enlightenment thinkers, Voltaire was a deist, envisioning God as akin to a clockmaker who set the universe in motion and then ceased to intervene in human affairs. Above all, Voltaire and most of the philosophes hated all forms of religious intolerance, which they believed led to fanaticism.

The ultimate strength of the philosophes lay in their dedication and organization. The philosophes felt keenly that they were engaged in a common undertaking that transcended individuals. Their greatest and most representative intellectual achievement was, quite fittingly, a group effort—the seventeen-volume *Encyclopedia: The Rational Dictionary of the Sciences, the Arts, and the Crafts*, edited by Denis Diderot (DEE-duh-roh) (1713–1784) and Jean le Rond d'Alembert (dah-luhm-BEHR) (1717–1783). Published between 1751 and 1772, it contained seventy-two thousand articles by leading scientists, writers, skilled workers, and progressive priests, and it treated every aspect of life and knowledge. Not every article was daring or original, but the overall effect was little short of revolutionary. Science and the industrial arts were exalted, religion and immortality questioned. Intolerance, legal injustice, and out-of-date social institutions were openly criticized. The encyclopedists were convinced that greater knowledge would result in greater human happiness because knowledge was useful and made possible economic, social, and political progress. Summing up the new worldview of the Enlightenment, the *Encyclopedia* was widely read, especially in less-expensive reprint editions, and it was extremely influential.

Jean-Jacques Rousseau

In the early 1740s, Jean-Jacques Rousseau (1712–1778), the son of a poor Swiss watchmaker, made his way into the Parisian Enlightenment through his brilliant intellect. Like other Enlightenment thinkers, Rousseau was passionately committed to individual freedom. Unlike them, however, he attacked rationalism and civilization as destroying, rather than liberating, the individual. Warm, spontaneous feeling had to complement and correct cold intellect. The basic goodness of the individual and the unspoiled child had to be protected from the cruel refinements of civilization. Rousseau's ideals greatly influenced the early romantic movement, which rebelled against the culture of the Enlightenment in the late eighteenth century.

Rousseau also called for a rigid division of gender roles. According to Rousseau, women and men were radically different beings. Destined by nature to assume a passive role in sexual relations, women should also be subordinate in social life. Women's love for displaying themselves in public, attending social gatherings, and pulling the strings of power was unnatural and had a corrupting effect on both politics and society. Rousseau thus rejected the sophisticated way of life of Parisian elite women. His criticism led to calls for privileged women to renounce their frivolous ways and stay at home to care for their children.

Rousseau's contribution to political theory in *The Social Contract* (1762) was based on two fundamental concepts: the general will and popular sovereignty. According to Rousseau, the general will is sacred and absolute, reflecting the common interests of all the people, who have displaced the monarch as the holder of sovereign power. The general will is not necessarily the will of the majority, however. At times, the general will may be the authentic, long-term needs of the people as correctly interpreted by a farsighted minority. Little noticed in its day, Rousseau's concept of the general will had a great impact on the political aspirations of the American and French Revolutions.

The International Enlightenment

The Enlightenment was a movement of international dimensions, with thinkers traversing borders in a constant exchange of visits, letters, and printed materials. The Republic of Letters was a truly cosmopolitan set of networks stretching from western Europe to its colonies in the Americas, to Russia and eastern Europe, and along the routes of trade and empire to Africa and Asia. Within this broad international conversation, scholars have identified regional and national particularities.

The Scottish Enlightenment, which was centered in Edinburgh, was marked

MAJOR FIGURES OF THE ENLIGHTENMENT

■ **Baruch Spinoza (1632–1677)**
Early Enlightenment thinker excommunicated from the Jewish religion for his concept of a deterministic universe

■ **John Locke (1632–1704)**
Essay Concerning Human Understanding (1690)

■ **Gottfried Wilhelm von Leibniz (1646–1716)**
German philosopher and mathematician known for his optimistic view of the universe

■ **Pierre Bayle (1647–1706)**
Historical and Critical Dictionary (1697)

■ **Montesquieu (1689–1755)**
The Persian Letters (1721); *The Spirit of Laws* (1748)

■ **Voltaire (1694–1778)**
Renowned French philosopher and author of more than seventy works

■ **David Hume (1711–1776)**
Central figure of the Scottish Enlightenment; *Of Natural Characters* (1748)

■ **Jean-Jacques Rousseau (1712–1778)**
The Social Contract (1762)

■ **Denis Diderot (1713–1784) and Jean le Rond d'Alembert (1717–1783)**
Editors of *Encyclopedia: The Rational Dictionary of the Sciences, the Arts, and the Crafts* (1751–1772)

■ **Adam Smith (1723–1790)**
The Theory of Moral Sentiments (1759); *An Inquiry into the Nature and Causes of the Wealth of Nations* (1776)

■ **Immanuel Kant (1724–1804)**
What Is Enlightenment? (1784); *On the Different Races of Man* (1775)

■ **Moses Mendelssohn (1729–1786)**
Major philosopher of the Haskalah, or Jewish Enlightenment

■ **Cesare Beccaria (1738–1794)**
On Crimes and Punishments (1764)

What intellectual and social changes occurred as a result of the Scientific Revolution?

What new ideas about society and human relations emerged in the Enlightenment?

What impact did new ways of thinking have on politics?

✓ LearningCurve
Check what you know.

501

by an emphasis on common sense and scientific reasoning. A central figure in Edinburgh was David Hume (1711–1776), whose emphasis on civic morality and religious skepticism had a powerful impact at home and abroad. Building on Locke's teachings on learning, Hume argued that the human mind is really nothing but a bundle of impressions. These impressions originate only in sensory experiences and our habits of joining these experiences together. Because our ideas ultimately reflect only our sensory experiences, our reason cannot tell us anything about questions that cannot be verified by sensory experience (in the form of controlled experiments or mathematics), such as the origin of the universe or the existence of God. Paradoxically, Hume's rationalistic inquiry ended up undermining the Enlightenment's faith in the power of reason.

Another major figure of the Scottish Enlightenment was Adam Smith. In *An Inquiry into the Nature and Causes of the Wealth of Nations* (1776), Smith attacked the laws and regulations that, he argued, prevented commerce from reaching its full capacity (see Chapter 17).

The Enlightenment in British North America was heavily influenced by English and Scottish thinkers, especially John Locke, and by Montesquieu's arguments for checks and balances in government. Leaders of the American Enlightenment, including Benjamin Franklin and Thomas Jefferson, would play a leading role in the American Revolution (see Chapter 19).

After 1760, Enlightenment ideas were hotly debated in the German-speaking states, often in dialogue with Christian theology. Immanuel Kant (1724–1804) was the greatest German philosopher of his day. Kant posed the question of the age when he published a pamphlet in 1784 entitled *What Is Enlightenment?* He answered, "*Sapere Aude* [dare to know]! 'Have the courage to use your own understanding' is therefore the motto of enlightenment." He argued that if intellectuals were granted the freedom to exercise their reason publicly in print, enlightenment would almost surely follow.

Northern Europeans often regarded the Italian states as culturally backward, yet important developments in Enlightenment thought took place in the Italian peninsula. In northern Italy, a central figure was Cesare Beccaria (1738–1794), a nobleman educated at Jesuit schools and the University of Pavia. His *On Crimes and Punishments* (1764) was a passionate plea for reform of the penal system that decried the use of torture, arbitrary imprisonment, and capital punishment, and advocated the prevention of crime over the reliance on punishment.

Urban Culture and Life in the Public Sphere

A series of new institutions and practices encouraged the spread of enlightened ideas in the late seventeenth and eighteenth centuries. First, the European production and consumption of books grew significantly. The types of books people read changed dramatically. The proportion of religious and devotional books published in Paris declined after 1750; history and law held constant; the arts and sciences surged.

Reading more books on many more subjects, the educated public approached reading in a new way. The result was what some scholars have called a **reading revolution**. The old style of reading in Europe had been centered on a core of sacred texts that taught earthly duty and obedience to God. Reading had been patriarchal and communal, with the father slowly reading the text aloud to his

reading revolution

▶ The transition in Europe from a society where literacy consisted of patriarchal and communal reading of religious texts to a society where literacy was commonplace and reading material was broad and diverse.

CHAPTER LOCATOR | What revolutionary discoveries were made in the sixteenth and seventeenth centuries?

502   CHAPTER 16
TOWARD A NEW WORLDVIEW

The French Book Trade Book consumption surged in the eighteenth century and, along with it, new bookstores. This appealing bookshop in France, with its intriguing ads for the latest works, offers to put customers "Under the Protection of Minerva," the Roman goddess of wisdom. Large packets of books sit ready for shipment to foreign countries. (akg-images/De Agostini Picture Library)

assembled family. Now reading involved a broader field of books that constantly changed. Reading became individual and silent, and texts could be questioned. Subtle but profound, the reading revolution ushered in new ways of relating to the written word.

Conversation, discussion, and debate also played a critical role in the Enlightenment. Evolving from the gatherings presided over by the *précieuses* in the late seventeenth century (see Chapter 15), the **salon** was a regular meeting held in the elegant private drawing rooms (or salons) of talented, wealthy men and women. There they encouraged the exchange of witty observations on literature, science, and philosophy among great aristocrats, wealthy middle-class financiers, high-ranking officials, and noteworthy foreigners. Many of the most celebrated salons were hosted by women, known as *salonnières* (sah-lahn-YEHRZ). Invitations to salons were highly coveted; introductions to the rich and powerful could make the career of an ambitious writer, and, in turn, the social elite found amusement and cultural prestige in their ties to up-and-coming artists and men of letters. (See "Picturing the Past: Enlightenment Culture," page 497.)

The salon thus represented an accommodation between the ruling classes and the leaders of Enlightenment thought. Salons were sites in which the philosophes,

salon

▶ Regular social gathering held by talented and rich Parisians in their homes, where philosophes and their followers met to discuss literature, science, and philosophy.

| What intellectual and social changes occurred as a result of the Scientific Revolution? | **What new ideas about society and human relations emerged in the Enlightenment?** | What impact did new ways of thinking have on politics? | ✓ LearningCurve Check what you know. |

503

the French nobility, and the prosperous middle classes intermingled and influenced one another while maintaining due deference to social rank. Critical thought about almost any question became fashionable and flourished alongside hopes for human progress through greater knowledge and enlightened public opinion.

Elite women also exercised great influence on artistic taste. Soft pastels, ornate interiors, sentimental portraits, and starry-eyed lovers protected by hovering cupids were all hallmarks of the style they favored. This style, known as **rococo** (ruh-KOH-koh), was popular throughout Europe in the period from 1720 to 1780.

While membership at the salons was restricted to the wellborn, the well connected, and the exceptionally talented, a number of institutions provided the rest of society with access to Enlightenment ideas. Lending libraries served an important function for people who could not afford their own books. The coffeehouses that first appeared in the late seventeenth century became meccas of philosophical discussion. In addition to these institutions, book clubs, debating societies, Masonic lodges (groups of Freemasons, a secret society that accepted craftsmen and shopkeepers as well as middle-class men and nobles), and newspapers all played roles in the creation of a new **public sphere** that celebrated open debate informed by critical reason. The public sphere was an idealized space where members of society came together as individuals to discuss issues relevant to the society, economics, and politics of the day.

What of the common people? Did they participate in the Enlightenment? Enlightenment philosophes did not direct their message to peasants or urban laborers. They believed that the masses had no time or talent for philosophical speculation and that elevating them would be a long and potentially dangerous process. Despite these prejudices, the ideas of the philosophes did find an audience among some members of the common people. At a time of rising literacy, book prices were dropping and many philosophical ideas were popularized in cheap pamphlets and through public reading. Although they were barred from salons and academies, ordinary people were not immune to the new ideas in circulation.

Race and the Enlightenment

If philosophers did not believe the lower classes qualified for enlightenment, how did they regard individuals of different races? In recent years, historians have found in the Scientific Revolution and the Enlightenment a crucial turning point in European ideas about race. A primary catalyst for new ideas about race was the urge to classify nature, an urge unleashed by the Scientific Revolution's insistence on careful empirical observation. As scientists developed taxonomies of plant and animal species, they also began to classify humans into hierarchically ordered "races."

Using the word *race* to designate biologically distinct groups of humans, akin to distinct animal species, was new. Previously, Europeans grouped other peoples into "nations" based on their historical, political, and cultural affiliations, rather than on supposedly innate physical differences. When European thinkers drew up a hierarchical classification of human species, their own "race" was placed, of course, at the top. Europeans had long believed they were culturally superior. Now emerging ideas about racial difference told them they were biologically superior as well. In turn, scientific racism helped legitimate and justify the tremendous growth of slavery that occurred during the eighteenth century.

Racist ideas did not go unchallenged. The abbé Raynal's *History of the Two Indies* (1770) fiercely attacked slavery and the abuses of European colonization.

Encyclopedia Image of the Cotton Industry

This romanticized image of slavery in the West Indies cotton industry was published in Diderot and d'Alembert's *Encyclopedia*. It shows enslaved men, at right, gathering and picking over cotton bolls, while the woman at left mills the bolls to remove their seeds. The *Encyclopedia* presented mixed views on slavery; one article described it as "indispensable" to economic development, while others argued passionately for the natural right to freedom of all mankind. (Courtesy, Dover Publications. From Denis Diderot, *Pictorial Encyclopedia of Trades and Industry*, edited by Charles C. Gillispie (Dover Publications, 1959).)

Encyclopedia editor Denis Diderot adopted Montesquieu's technique of criticizing European attitudes through the voice of outsiders in his dialogue between Tahitian villagers and their European visitors. Scottish philosopher James Beattie (1735–1803) responded directly to claims of white superiority by pointing out that Europeans had started out as savage as nonwhites supposedly were and that many non-European peoples in the Americas, Asia, and Africa had achieved high levels of civilization. Former slaves, like Olaudah Equiano (see Chapter 17) and Ottobah Cugoana published eloquent memoirs testifying to the horrors of slavery and the innate equality of all humans. These challenges to racism, however, were in the minority. Many other Enlightenment voices supporting racial inequality—Thomas Jefferson among them—may be found.

QUICK REVIEW

How did Enlightenment thinkers challenge the social, political, and cultural status quo? In what ways did they reinforce it?

What intellectual and social changes occurred as a result of the Scientific Revolution?

What new ideas about society and human relations emerged in the Enlightenment?

What impact did new ways of thinking have on politics?

☑ **LearningCurve** Check what you know.

What impact did new ways of thinking have on politics?

Catherine the Great Strongly influenced by the Enlightenment, Catherine the Great cultivated the French philosophes and instituted moderate reforms, only to reverse them in the aftermath of Pugachev's rebellion. This equestrian portrait now hangs above her throne in the palace throne room in St. Petersburg. (Musée des Beaux-Arts, Chartres/The Bridgeman Art Library)

M**ANY GOVERNMENT OFFICIALS** were interested in philosophical ideas. They were among the best-educated members of society, and their daily involvement in complex affairs of state made them naturally attracted to ideas for improving human society. Encouraged and instructed by these officials, some absolutist rulers tried to reform their governments in accordance with Enlightenment ideals — what historians have called the **enlightened absolutism** of the later eighteenth century. The most influential of the new-style monarchs were in Prussia, Russia, and Austria, and their example illustrates both the achievements and the great limitations of enlightened absolutism. France experienced its own brand of enlightened absolutism in the contentious decades prior to the French Revolution (see Chapter 19).

enlightened absolutism
▶ Term coined by historians to describe the rule of eighteenth-century monarchs who, without renouncing their own absolute authority, adopted Enlightenment ideals of rationalism, progress, and tolerance.

CHAPTER LOCATOR | What revolutionary discoveries were made in the sixteenth and seventeenth centuries?

Frederick the Great of Prussia

Frederick II (r. 1740–1786), commonly known as Frederick the Great, built masterfully on the work of his father, Frederick William I (see Chapter 15). When the young empress Maria Theresa of Austria inherited the Habsburg dominions upon the death of her father Charles VI, Frederick pounced. He invaded her rich province of Silesia (sigh-LEE-zhuh), defying Prussian promises to respect the Pragmatic Sanction, a diplomatic agreement that had guaranteed Maria Theresa's succession. In 1742, as other greedy powers vied for her lands in the European War of the Austrian Succession (1740–1748), Maria Theresa was forced to cede almost all of Silesia to Prussia. In one stroke, Prussia had doubled its population to 6 million people. Now Prussia unquestionably stood as a European Great Power.

Though successful in 1742, Frederick had to fight against great odds to save Prussia from total destruction after the ongoing competition between Britain and France for colonial empire brought another great conflict in 1756. Maria Theresa, seeking to regain Silesia, formed an alliance with the leaders of France and Russia. The aim of the alliance during the resulting Seven Years' War (1756–1763) was to conquer Prussia and divide its territory. Despite invasions from all sides, Frederick fought on with stoic courage. In the end he was miraculously saved: Peter III came to the Russian throne in 1762 and called off the attack against Frederick, whom he greatly admired.

The terrible struggle of the Seven Years' War tempered Frederick's interest in territorial expansion and brought him to consider how more humane policies for his subjects might also strengthen the state. Thus, Frederick went beyond a superficial commitment to Enlightenment culture for himself and his circle. He allowed his subjects to believe as they wished in religious and philosophical matters. He promoted the advancement of knowledge, improving his country's schools and permitting scholars to publish their findings. Frederick tried to improve the lives of his subjects more directly, promoting legal reform and economic growth.

The legal system and the bureaucracy were Frederick's primary tools. Prussia's laws were simplified, torture was abolished, and judges decided cases quickly and impartially. Prussian officials became famous for their hard work and honesty. After the Seven Years' War ended in 1763, Frederick's government energetically promoted the reconstruction of agriculture and industry.

Frederick's dedication to high-minded government went only so far, however. While he condemned serfdom in the abstract, he accepted it in practice and did not free the serfs on his own estates. He accepted and extended the privileges of the nobility, who remained the backbone of the army and the entire Prussian state.

In reforming Prussia's bureaucracy, Frederick drew on the principles of **cameralism**, the German science of public administration that emerged in the decades following the Thirty Years' War. Influential throughout the German lands, cameralism held that monarchy was the best of all forms of government; all elements of society should be placed at the service of the state; and, in turn, the state should make use of its resources and authority to improve society. Predating the Enlightenment, cameralist interest in the public good was usually inspired by the needs of war. Cameralism shared with the Enlightenment an emphasis on rationality, progress, and utilitarianism.

Prussia, 1740
Prussian gains, 1742
Austria, 1740
Boundary of the Holy Roman Empire

Königsberg

Berlin

POLAND

SILESIA

Prague

Vienna

AUSTRIA

HUNGARY

The War of the Austrian Succession, 1740–1748

cameralism

► View that monarchy was the best form of government; all elements of society should serve the monarch; and, in turn, the state should use its resources and authority to increase the public good.

What intellectual and social changes occurred as a result of the Scientific Revolution?

What new ideas about society and human relations emerged in the Enlightenment?

What impact did new ways of thinking have on politics?

☑ LearningCurve
Check what you know.

507

Catherine the Great of Russia

Catherine the Great of Russia (r. 1762–1796) was one of the most remarkable rulers of her age, and the French philosophes adored her. Catherine had drunk deeply at the Enlightenment well. Never questioning that absolute monarchy was the best form of government, she set out to rule in an enlightened manner. She had three main goals. First, she worked hard to continue Peter the Great's effort to bring the culture of western Europe to Russia (see Chapter 15). To do so, she imported Western architects, musicians, and intellectuals. She bought masterpieces of Western art and patronized the philosophes. With these actions, Catherine won good press in the West for herself and for her country. This intellectual ruler, who wrote plays and loved good talk, set the tone for the entire Russian nobility. Peter the Great westernized Russian armies, but it was Catherine who westernized the imagination of the Russian nobility.

Catherine's second goal was domestic reform, and she began her reign with sincere and ambitious projects. In 1767, she appointed a legislative commission to prepare a new law code. This project was never completed, but Catherine did restrict the practice of torture and allowed limited religious toleration. She also tried to improve education and strengthen local government. The philosophes applauded these measures and hoped more would follow.

Such was not the case. In 1773, a Cossack soldier named Emelian Pugachev sparked a gigantic uprising of thousands of serfs. Proclaiming himself the true tsar, Pugachev issued orders abolishing serfdom, taxes, and army service. Pugachev's army proved no match for Catherine's noble-led army, and Pugachev was captured and executed. Pugachev's rebellion put an end to any intentions Catherine had about reforming the system. In 1785, she freed nobles forever from taxes and state service. Under Catherine, the Russian nobility attained its most exalted position, and serfdom entered its most oppressive phase.

Catherine's third goal was territorial expansion, and in this respect she was extremely successful. Her armies subjugated the last descendants of the Mongols and the Crimean Tartars, and began the conquest of the Caucasus (KAW-kuh-suhs). Her greatest coup by far was the partition of Poland (**Map 16.1**). When, between 1768 and 1772, Catherine's armies scored unprecedented victories against the Ottomans and thereby threatened to disturb the balance of power between Russia and Austria in eastern Europe, Frederick of Prussia obligingly came forward with a deal. He proposed that Turkey be let off easily and that Prussia, Austria, and Russia each compensate itself by taking a gigantic slice of the weakly ruled Polish territory. The first partition of Poland took place in 1772. Subsequent partitions in 1793 and 1795 gave away the rest of Polish territory, and the ancient republic of Poland vanished from the map.

The Austrian Habsburgs

Another female monarch, Maria Theresa (r. 1740–1780) of Austria, set out to reform her nation, although traditional power politics was a more important motivation for her than were Enlightenment teachings. Maria Theresa was a remark-

CHAPTER LOCATOR | What revolutionary discoveries were made in the sixteenth and seventeenth centuries?

508 CHAPTER 16 TOWARD A NEW WORLDVIEW

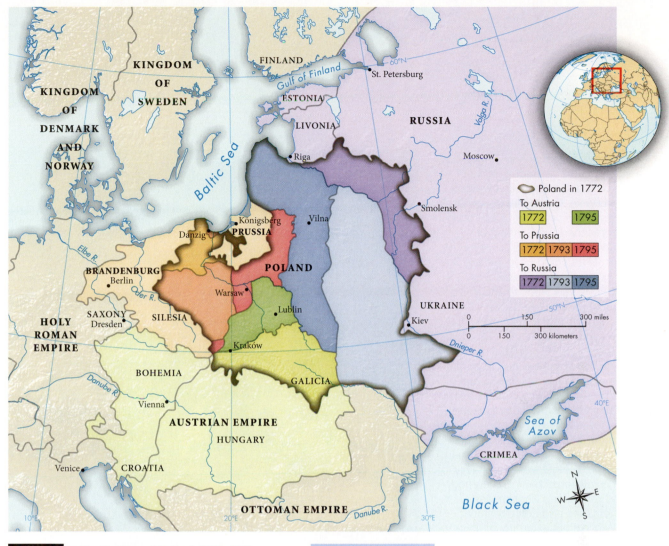

MAP 16.1 ■ The Partition of Poland, 1772–1795

In 1772, war between Russia and Austria threatened over Russian gains from the Ottoman Empire. To satisfy desires for expansion without fighting, Prussia's Frederick the Great proposed that parts of Poland be divided among Austria, Prussia, and Russia. In 1793 and 1795, the three powers partitioned the remainder, and the republic of Poland ceased to exist.

> MAPPING THE PAST

ANALYZING THE MAP: Of the three powers that divided the kingdom of Poland, which gained the most territory? How did the partition affect the geographical boundaries of each state, and what was the significance? What border with the former Poland remained unchanged? Why do you think this was the case?

CONNECTIONS: What does it say about European politics at the time that a country could simply cease to exist on the map? Could that happen today?

---

able but old-fashioned absolutist. Her more radical son, Joseph II (r. 1780–1790), drew on Enlightenment ideals, earning the title of "revolutionary emperor."

Emerging from the long War of the Austrian Succession in 1748 with the serious loss of Silesia, Maria Theresa was determined to introduce reforms that would make the state stronger and more efficient. First, she initiated church reform, with measures aimed at limiting the papacy's influence, eliminating many religious

| What intellectual and social changes occurred as a result of the Scientific Revolution? | What new ideas about society and human relations emerged in the Enlightenment? | **What impact did new ways of thinking have on politics?** | ✓ LearningCurve Check what you know. |

INDIVIDUALS IN SOCIETY
Moses Mendelssohn and the Jewish Enlightenment

In 1743, a small, humpbacked Jewish boy with a stammer left his poor parents in Dessau in central Germany and walked eighty miles to Berlin, the capital of Frederick the Great's Prussia. According to one story, when the boy reached the Rosenthaler (ROH-zuhn-taw-lehr) Gate, the only one through which Jews could pass, he told the inquiring watchman that his name was Moses and that he had come to Berlin "to learn." The watchman laughed and waved him through. "Go Moses, the sea has opened before you."*

In Berlin, the young Mendelssohn studied Jewish law and eked out a living copying Hebrew manuscripts in a beautiful hand. But he was soon fascinated by an intellectual world that had been closed to him in the Dessau ghetto, where, like most Jews throughout central Europe, he had spoken Yiddish — a mixture of German, Polish, and Hebrew. Now, working mainly on his own, he mastered German; learned Latin, Greek, French, and English; and studied mathematics and Enlightenment philosophy. Word of his exceptional abilities spread in Berlin's Jewish community (the dwelling of 1,500 of the city's 100,000 inhabitants). He began tutoring the children of a wealthy Jewish silk merchant, and he soon became the merchant's clerk and later his partner. But his great passion remained the life of the mind and the spirit, which he avidly pursued in his off-hours.

Gentle and unassuming in his personal life, Mendelssohn was a bold thinker. Reading eagerly in Western philosophy since antiquity, he was, as a pious Jew, soon convinced that Enlightenment teachings need not be opposed to Jewish thought and religion. He concluded that reason could complement and strengthen religion, although each would retain its integrity as a separate sphere.[†] Developing his idea in his first great work, *On the Immortality of the Soul* (1767), Mendelssohn used the neutral setting of a philosophical dialogue between Socrates and his followers

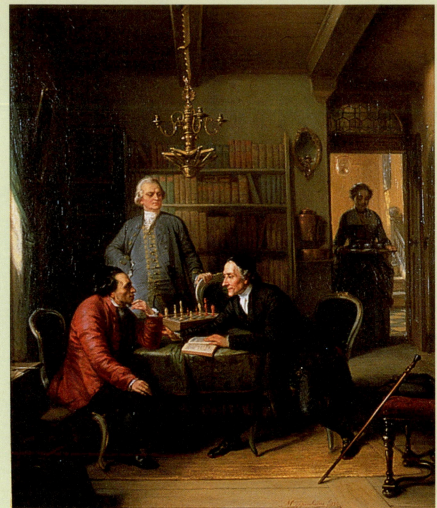

Lavater (right) attempts to convert Mendelssohn, in a painting by Moritz Oppenheim of an imaginary encounter. (akg-images)

LaunchPad

ONLINE DOCUMENT PROJECT

How did Moses Mendelssohn fit into the larger Enlightenment debate about religious tolerance? Examine primary sources written by Mendelssohn and his contemporaries, and then complete a writing assignment based on the evidence and details from this chapter. *See inside the front cover to learn more.*

*H. Kupferberg, *The Mendelssohns: Three Generations of Genius* (New York: Charles Scribner's Sons, 1972), p. 3.
[†]David Sorkin, *Moses Mendelssohn and the Religious Enlightenment* (Berkeley: University of California Press, 1996), pp. 8ff.

in ancient Greece to argue that the human soul lived forever. In refusing to bring religion and critical thinking into conflict, he was strongly influenced by contemporary German philosophers who argued similarly on behalf of Christianity. He reflected the way the German Enlightenment generally supported established religion, in contrast to the French Enlightenment, which attacked it.

Mendelssohn's treatise on the human soul captivated the educated German public, which marveled that a Jew could have written a philosophical masterpiece. In the excitement, a Christian zealot named Lavater challenged Mendelssohn in a pamphlet to accept Christianity or to demonstrate how the Christian faith was not "reasonable." Replying politely but passionately, the Jewish philosopher affirmed that his studies had only strengthened him in his faith, although he did not seek to convert anyone not born into Judaism. Rather, he urged toleration in religious matters and spoke up courageously against Jewish oppression.

Orthodox Jew and German philosophe, Moses Mendelssohn serenely combined two very different worlds. He built a bridge from the ghetto to the dominant culture over which many Jews would pass, including his novelist daughter Dorothea and his famous grandson, the composer Felix Mendelssohn.

QUESTIONS FOR ANALYSIS

1. How did Mendelssohn seek to influence Jewish religious thought in his time?
2. How do Mendelssohn's ideas compare with those of the French Enlightenment?

holidays, and reducing the number of monasteries. Second, a whole series of administrative renovations strengthened the central bureaucracy, smoothed out some provincial differences, and revamped the tax system, taxing even the lands of nobles, who were previously exempt from taxation. Third, the government sought to improve the lot of the agricultural population, cautiously reducing the power of lords over their hereditary serfs and their partially free peasant tenants.

Coregent with his mother from 1765 onward, Joseph II moved forward rapidly with further reforms when he came to the throne in 1780. Most notably, Joseph abolished serfdom in 1781, and in 1789, he decreed that peasants could pay landlords in cash rather than through labor on their land. This measure was violently rejected not only by the nobility but also by the peasants it was intended to help because they lacked the necessary cash. When a disillusioned Joseph died prematurely at forty-nine, the entire Habsburg empire was in turmoil. His brother Leopold II (r. 1790–1792) canceled Joseph's radical edicts in order to re-establish order.

Despite differences in their policies, Joseph II and the other absolutists of the later eighteenth century combined old-fashioned state-building with the culture and critical thinking of the Enlightenment. In doing so, they succeeded in expanding the role of the state in the life of society. Their failure to implement policies we would recognize as humane and enlightened—such as abolishing serfdom—may reveal inherent limitations in Enlightenment thinking about equality and social justice, rather than deficiencies in their execution of Enlightenment programs.

Jewish Life and the Limits of Enlightened Absolutism

Perhaps the best example of the limitations of enlightened absolutism are the debates surrounding the emancipation of the Jews. Europe's small Jewish populations lived under highly discriminatory laws. For the most part, Jews were confined to tiny, overcrowded ghettos, were excluded by law from most professions, and could be ordered out of a kingdom at a moment's notice.

Haskalah

▶ The Jewish Enlightenment of the second half of the eighteenth century, led by the Prussian philosopher Moses Mendelssohn.

The Pale of Settlement, 1791

In the eighteenth century, an Enlightenment movement known as the Haskalah emerged from within the European Jewish community; it was led by the Prussian philosopher Moses Mendelssohn (1729–1786). (See "Individuals in Society: Moses Mendelssohn and the Jewish Enlightenment," page 510.) Christian and Jewish Enlightenment philosophers, including Mendelssohn, began to advocate for freedom and civil rights for European Jews. In an era of reason and progress, they argued, restrictions on religious grounds could not stand.

Arguments for tolerance won some ground. The British Parliament passed a law allowing naturalization of Jews in 1753 but later repealed the law due to public outrage. The most progressive reforms took place under Austrian emperor Joseph II. Among his liberal edicts of the 1780s were measures intended to integrate Jews more fully into society, including eligibility for military service, admission to higher education and artisanal trades, and removal of requirements for special clothing or emblems.

Many monarchs rejected all ideas of emancipation. Although he permitted freedom of religion to his Christian subjects, Frederick the Great of Prussia firmly opposed any general emancipation for the Jews, as he did for the serfs. Catherine the Great, who acquired most of Poland's large Jewish population when she annexed part of that country in the late eighteenth century, similarly refused. In 1791, she established the Pale of Settlement, a territory including parts of modern-day Poland, Latvia, Lithuania, Ukraine, and Belarus, in which most Jews were required to live. Jewish habitation was restricted to the Pale until the Russian Revolution in 1917.

> QUICK REVIEW

What aspects of their states did enlightened monarchs attempt to reform? What aspects did they generally leave untouched?

CHAPTER LOCATOR | What revolutionary discoveries were made in the sixteenth and seventeenth centuries?

LOOKING BACK LOOKING AHEAD

Hailed as the origin of modern thought, the Scientific Revolution must also be seen as a product of its past. Medieval universities gave rise to important new scholarship, and the ambition and wealth of Renaissance patrons nurtured intellectual curiosity. Religious faith also influenced the Scientific Revolution, inspiring thinkers to understand the glory of God's creation while bringing censure and personal tragedy to others. Natural philosophers following Copernicus pioneered new methods of observing and explaining nature while drawing on centuries-old traditions of mysticism, astrology, alchemy, and magic.

The Enlightenment ideas of the eighteenth century were a similar blend of past and present; they could serve as much to bolster absolutist monarchical regimes as to inspire revolutionaries to fight for individual rights and liberties. Although the Enlightenment fostered critical thinking about everything from science to religion, the majority of Europeans, including many prominent thinkers, remained devout Christians.

The achievements of the Scientific Revolution and the Enlightenment are undeniable. Key Western values of rationalism, human rights, and open-mindedness were born from these movements. With their new notions of progress and social improvement, Europeans would embark on important revolutions in industry and politics in the centuries that followed. Nonetheless, others have seen a darker side. For these critics, the mastery over nature permitted by the Scientific Revolution now threatens to overwhelm the earth's fragile equilibrium, and the Enlightenment belief in the universal application of reason can lead to arrogance and intolerance of other people's spiritual, cultural, and political values. Such vivid debates about the legacy of these intellectual and scientific developments testify to their continuing importance in today's world.

LaunchPad

ONLINE DOCUMENT PROJECT

Moses Mendelssohn

How did Moses Mendelssohn fit into the larger Enlightenment debate about religious tolerance?

You encountered Moses Mendelssohn's story on page 510. Keeping the question above in mind, examine primary sources from Mendelssohn's time—including a letter to a contemporary, an excerpt from a play, and a philosophical treatise—to draw your own conclusions. *See inside the front cover to learn more.*

What intellectual and social changes occurred as a result of the Scientific Revolution?

What new ideas about society and human relations emerged in the Enlightenment?

What impact did new ways of thinking have on politics?

✓ LearningCurve
Check what you know.

513

CHAPTER 16 STUDY GUIDE

STEP 1 **GET STARTED ONLINE**

 **LearningCurve**

Now that you've read the chapter, make it stick by completing the LearningCurve activity.

STEP 2 **EXPLAIN WHY IT MATTERS**

Put your reading into practice. Identify each term below, and then explain why it matters in Western history.

TERM	WHO OR WHAT & WHEN	WHY IT MATTERS
natural philosophy (p. 487)		
Copernican hypothesis (p. 489)		
experimental method (p. 491)		
law of inertia (p. 491)		
law of universal gravitation (p. 492)		
empiricism (p. 494)		
Cartesian dualism (p. 494)		
Enlightenment (p. 497)		
rationalism (p. 497)		
philosophes (p. 499)		
reading revolution (p. 502)		
salon (p. 503)		
rococo (p. 504)		
public sphere (p. 504)		
enlightened absolutism (p. 506)		
cameralism (p. 507)		
Haskalah (p. 512)		

STEP 3 **MOVE BEYOND THE BASICS**

To demonstrate a more advanced understanding of the Scientific Revolution, fill in the chart included below with descriptions of the major contributions of the figures listed in the chart. Be sure to include both concrete discoveries and contributions to the development of the scientific method.

	Discoveries and contributions
Nicolaus Copernicus	
Tycho Brahe	
Johannes Kepler	
Francis Bacon	
René Descartes	
Galileo Galilei	
Isaac Newton	

STEP 4 **PUT IT ALL TOGETHER** Now, take a step back and try to explain the big picture. Remember to use specific examples from the chapter in your answers.

THE SCIENTIFIC REVOLUTION

▶ What was revolutionary about the Scientific Revolution?

▶ What role did religion play in the Scientific Revolution? How did religious belief both stimulate and hinder scientific inquiry?

THE ENLIGHTENMENT

▶ How did the Scientific Revolution contribute to the emergence of the Enlightenment?

▶ How did Enlightenment thinkers deal with issues of gender and race?

ENLIGHTENED ABSOLUTISM

▶ Why did many Enlightenment thinkers see absolute monarchy as a potential force for good?

▶ How did Enlightenment ideas contribute to the expansion of the role of the state in central and eastern European society?

MAKE CONNECTIONS

▶ Compare and contrast medieval and early modern approaches to the study of nature.

▶ Is it accurate to describe the worldview that emerged out of the Scientific Revolution and the Enlightenment as "modern"? Why or why not?

> **IN YOUR OWN WORDS**

Imagine that you must give an oral report to the class answering the following question: **What new ways of looking at nature, society, and government emerged in the Early Modern period?** What would be the most important points and why?

17
THE EXPANSION OF EUROPE

1650–1800

> How and why did the society and economy of Europe change in the eighteenth century?

Chapter 17 examines European demographic and economic changes in the eighteenth century. In 1700, peasants on the land and artisans in their shops lived little better than had their ancestors in the Middle Ages. Yet the economic basis of European life was beginning to change. In the course of the eighteenth century, the European economy emerged from the long crisis of the seventeenth century, responded to challenges, and began to expand once again. Population resumed its growth, while colonial empires extended and developed. This expansion of agriculture, industry, trade, and population led toward one of the most influential developments in human history, the Industrial Revolution, a topic considered in Chapter 20.

LearningCurve

After reading the chapter, use LearningCurve to retain what you've read.

> How did European agriculture change between 1650 and 1800?

> Why did the European population rise dramatically in the eighteenth century?

> How and why did rural industry intensify in the eighteenth century?

> What were guilds, and why did they become controversial in the eighteenth century?

> What role did colonial markets play in Europe's development?

Life in the Expanding Europe of the Eighteenth Century. The activities of the bustling cosmopolitan port of Marseilles were common to ports across Europe in the eighteenth century. (Gianni Dagli Orti/The Art Archive at Art Resource, NY)

How did European agriculture change between 1650 and 1800?

The Vegetable Market, 1662

The wealth and well-being of the industrious, capitalistic Dutch shine forth in this winsome market scene by Dutch artist Hendrick Sorgh. The market woman's baskets are filled with delicious fresh produce that ordinary citizens can afford — eloquent testimony to the responsive, enterprising character of Dutch agriculture. (Rijksmuseum, Amsterdam)

AT THE END OF THE SEVENTEENTH CENTURY, the economy of Europe was agrarian. With the exception of the Dutch Republic and England, at least 80 percent of the people of western Europe drew their livelihoods from agriculture. In eastern Europe, the percentage was considerably higher. Yet even in a rich agricultural region such as the Po Valley in northern Italy, every bushel of wheat seed sown yielded on average only five or six bushels of grain at harvest. By modern standards, output was distressingly low.

In most regions of Europe, climatic conditions produced poor or disastrous harvests every eight or nine years. In famine years the number of deaths soared far above normal. A third of a village's population might disappear in a year or two. But new developments in agricultural technology and methods gradually brought an end to the ravages of hunger in western Europe.

CHAPTER LOCATOR | **How did European agriculture change between 1650 and 1800?**

The Legacy of the Open-Field System

Why, in the late seventeenth century, did many areas of Europe produce barely enough food to survive? The answer lies in the pattern of farming that had developed in the Middle Ages, which sustained fairly large numbers of people but did not produce material abundance. From the Middle Ages up to the seventeenth century, much of Europe was farmed through the open-field system. The land to be cultivated was divided into several large fields, which were in turn cut up into long, narrow strips. The fields were open, and the strips were not enclosed into small plots by fences or hedges. The whole peasant village followed the same pattern of plowing, sowing, and harvesting in accordance with long-standing traditions.

The ever-present problem was soil exhaustion. Wheat planted year after year in a field will deplete nitrogen in the soil. Because the supply of manure for fertilizer was limited, the only way for the land to recover was to lie fallow for a period of time. In the early Middle Ages, a year of fallow was alternated with a year of cropping; then three-year rotations were introduced.

Traditional village rights reinforced communal patterns of farming. In addition to rotating field crops in a uniform way, villages maintained open meadows for hay and natural pasture. After the harvest, villagers also pastured their animals on the wheat or rye stubble. In many places such pasturing followed a brief period, also established by tradition, for the gleaning of grain. In this process, poor women would go through the fields picking up the few single grains that

Why did the European population rise dramatically in the eighteenth century?	How and why did rural industry intensify in the eighteenth century?	What were guilds, and why did they become controversial in the eighteenth century?	What role did colonial markets play in Europe's development?	☑ LearningCurve Check what you know.

had fallen to the ground in the course of the harvest. Many villages were surrounded by woodlands, also held in common, which provided essential firewood, building materials, and nutritional roots and berries.

The state and landlords continued to levy heavy taxes and high rents, thereby stripping peasants of much of their meager earnings. The level of exploitation varied. Generally speaking, the peasants of eastern Europe were worst off. As we saw in Chapter 15, they were serfs bound to their lords in hereditary service. Well into the nineteenth century, individual Russian serfs and serf families were regularly bought and sold.

Social conditions were better in western Europe, where peasants were generally free from serfdom. In France, western Germany, England, and the Low Countries (modern-day Belgium and the Netherlands), peasants could own land and could pass it on to their children. Even in these regions, however, life in the village was hard, and poverty was the reality for most people.

New Methods of Agriculture

The seventeenth century saw important gains in productivity in some regions that would slowly extend to the rest of Europe. By 1700, less than half of the population of Britain and the Dutch Republic worked in agriculture, producing enough to feed the remainder of the population. Many elements combined in this production growth, but the key was new ways of rotating crops that allowed farmers to forgo the unproductive fallow period altogether and maintain their land in continuous cultivation. The secret to eliminating the fallow lay in deliberately alternating grain with crops that restored nutrients to the soil, such as peas and beans, root crops such as turnips and potatoes, and clover and other grasses.

Over time, crop rotation spread to other parts of Europe, and farmers developed increasingly sophisticated patterns of crop rotation to suit different kinds of soils. Ongoing experimentation, fueled by developments in the Scientific Revolution (see Chapter 16), led to more methodical farming.

Advocates of the new crop rotations, who included an emerging group of experimental scientists, some government officials, and a few big landowners, believed that new methods were scarcely possible within the traditional framework of open fields and common rights. Advocates of improvement argued that innovating agriculturalists needed to enclose and consolidate their scattered holdings into compact, fenced-in fields in order to farm more effectively. In doing so, the innovators also needed to enclose the village's natural pastureland, or common, into individual shares. According to proponents of this movement, known as **enclosure**, the upheaval of village life was the necessary price of technical progress.

That price seemed too high to many rural people who had small, inadequate holdings or very little land at all. Traditional rights were precious to these poor peasants, who used commonly held pastureland to graze livestock, and marshlands or forest outside the village as a source for foraged goods. Thus, when the small landholders and the village poor could effectively oppose the enclosure of the open fields and the common lands, they did so. In many countries they found

enclosure

▶ The movement to fence in fields in order to farm more effectively, which came at the expense of poor peasants who relied on common fields for farming and pasture.

allies among the larger, predominantly noble landowners who were also wary of enclosure because it required large investments in purchasing and fencing land and thus posed risks for them as well.

The old system of unenclosed open fields and the new system of continuous rotation coexisted in Europe for a long time. Throughout the end of the eighteenth century, the new system of enclosure was extensively adopted only in the Low Countries and England.

The Leadership of the Low Countries and England

The seventeenth-century Dutch Republic, already the most advanced country in Europe in many areas of human endeavor (see Chapter 15), pioneered advancements in agriculture. By the middle of the seventeenth century, intensive farming was well established, and the innovations discussed above were all present. Agriculture was highly specialized and commercialized, especially in the province of Holland.

One reason for early Dutch leadership in farming was that the area was one of the most densely populated in Europe. To feed themselves and provide employment, the Dutch were forced at an early date to seek maximum yields from their land and to increase the cultivated area through the steady draining of marshes and swamps. The pressure of population was connected with the second cause: the growth of towns and cities. Stimulated by commerce and overseas trade, Amsterdam grew from thirty thousand to two hundred thousand inhabitants in its golden seventeenth century. The growing urban population provided Dutch peasants with markets for all they could produce and allowed each region to specialize in what it did best.

The English were among the best students of Dutch farming. In the mid-seventeenth century, English farmers borrowed the system of continuous crop rotation from the Dutch. They also drew on Dutch expertise in drainage and water control. Large parts of seventeenth-century Holland had once been sea and sea marsh, and the efforts of centuries had made the Dutch the world's leaders in drainage. In the first half of the seventeenth century, Dutch experts made a great contribution to draining the extensive marshes, or fens, of wet and rainy England. Swampy wilderness was converted into thousands of acres of some of the best land in England.

Based on seventeenth-century achievements, English agriculture continued to progress during the eighteenth century, growing enough food to satisfy a rapidly growing population. Jethro Tull (1674–1741) was an important English innovator. A true son of the early Enlightenment, Tull adopted a critical attitude toward accepted ideas about farming and tried to develop better methods through empirical research. He was especially enthusiastic about using horses, rather than slower-moving oxen, for plowing. He also advocated sowing seed with drilling equipment rather than scattering it by hand. Drilling distributed seed in an even manner and at the proper depth.

One of the most important—and bitterly contested—aspects of agricultural development was the enclosure of open fields and commons. More than half the

Why did the European population rise dramatically in the eighteenth century?

How and why did rural industry intensify in the eighteenth century?

What were guilds, and why did they become controversial in the eighteenth century?

What role did colonial markets play in Europe's development?

☑ LearningCurve
Check what you know.

521

farmland in England was enclosed through private initiatives prior to 1700; Parliament completed this work in the eighteenth century. From the 1760s to 1815, a series of acts of Parliament enclosed most of the remaining common land. Arthur Young, another agricultural experimentalist, celebrated large-scale enclosure as a necessary means to achieve progress. Many of his contemporaries, as well as the historians that followed him, echoed that conviction. More recent research, however, has shown that regions that maintained open-field farming were still able to adopt crop rotation and other innovations, suggesting that enclosures were not a prerequisite for increased production.

By eliminating common rights and greatly reducing the access of poor men and women to the land, the eighteenth-century enclosure movement marked the completion of two major historical developments in England—the rise of market-oriented estate agriculture and the emergence of a landless rural proletariat. By the early nineteenth century, a tiny minority of wealthy English and Scottish landowners held most of the land and pursued profits aggressively, leasing their holdings through agents at competitive prices to middle-size farmers, who relied on landless laborers for their workforce. Not only was the small landholder deprived of his land, but improvements in technology meant that fewer laborers were needed to work the large farms, and unemployment spread throughout the countryside. In no other European country had this **proletarianization**—this transformation of large numbers of small peasant farmers into landless rural wage earners—gone so far. England's village poor found the cost of change heavy and unjust.

proletarianization
▶ The transformation of large numbers of small peasant farmers into landless rural wage earners.

> **QUICK REVIEW**

What important developments led to increased agricultural production, and how did these changes affect peasants?

CHAPTER LOCATOR | How did European agriculture change between 1650 and 1800?

CHAPTER 17
522 THE EXPANSION OF EUROPE

Why did the European population rise dramatically in the eighteenth century?

The Plague at Marseilles The bishop of Marseilles blesses victims of the plague that overwhelmed Marseilles in 1720. Some one hundred thousand people died in the outbreak, which was the last great episode of plague in western Europe. (© RMN-Grand Palais/Art Resource, NY)

ANOTHER FACTOR THAT AFFECTED THE EXISTING ORDER OF LIFE and forced economic changes in the eighteenth century was the beginning of the population explosion. Explosive growth continued in Europe until the twentieth century, by which time it was affecting non-Western areas of the globe. In this section we examine the background and causes of the population growth; the following section considers how the challenge of more mouths to feed and more hands to employ affected the European economy.

Long-Standing Obstacles to Population Growth

Until 1700, the total population of Europe grew slowly much of the time, and it followed an irregular cyclical pattern (**Figure 17.1**). This cyclical pattern had a great influence on many aspects of social and economic life. The terrible ravages of the Black Death of 1348–1350 caused a sharp drop in population and food prices after 1350 and also created a labor shortage throughout Europe.

By the mid-sixteenth century, much of Europe had returned to its pre-plague population levels. In this buoyant period, farmers brought new land into cultivation

| **Why did the European population rise dramatically in the eighteenth century?** | How and why did rural industry intensify in the eighteenth century? | What were guilds, and why did they become controversial in the eighteenth century? | What role did colonial markets play in Europe's development? | ☑ **LearningCurve** Check what you know. |

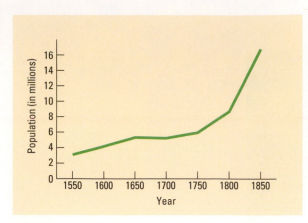

FIGURE 17.1 ■ The Growth of Population in England, 1550–1850

England is a good example of both the uneven increase of European population before 1700 and the third great surge of growth that began in the eighteenth century. Source: Data from E. A. Wrigley et al., *English Population History from Family Reconstitution, 1580–1837* (Cambridge: Cambridge University Press, 1997), p. 614.

and urban settlements grew significantly. But this well-being eroded in the course of the sixteenth century. The second great surge of population growth outstripped the growth of agricultural production after about 1500. There was less food per person, and food prices rose more rapidly than wages, a development intensified by the inflow of precious metals from the Americas (see Chapter 14, page 435) and a general, if uneven, European price revolution. The result was a substantial decline in living standards throughout Europe. By 1600, the pressure of population on resources was severe in much of Europe, and widespread poverty was an undeniable reality.

Births and deaths, fertility and mortality, were in a crude but effective balance. The population grew modestly in normal years at a rate of perhaps 0.5 to 1 percent. Although population growth of even 1 percent per year seems fairly modest, it will produce a very large increase over a long period: in three hundred years it will result in sixteen times as many people. Yet such significant increases did not occur in agrarian Europe. In certain abnormal years and tragic periods—the Black Death was only the most extreme example—many more people died than were born, and total population fell sharply, even catastrophically. A number of years of modest growth would then be necessary to make up for those who had died in an abnormal year. Such savage increases in deaths occurred periodically in the seventeenth century on a local and regional scale, and these demographic crises combined to check the growth of population until after 1700.

The grim reapers of demographic crisis were famine, epidemic disease, and war. Episodes of famine were inevitable in all eras of premodern Europe, given low crop yields and unpredictable climatic conditions. In the seventeenth century, much of Europe experienced unusually cold and wet weather, which produced even more severe harvest failures and food shortages than usual. Contagious diseases also continued to ravage Europe's population on a periodic basis. War was another scourge, and its indirect effects were even more harmful than the purposeful killing during military campaigns. Soldiers and camp followers passed all manner of contagious diseases throughout the countryside. Armies requisitioned scarce food supplies and disrupted the agricultural cycle, while battles destroyed precious crops, livestock, and farmlands.

The New Pattern of the Eighteenth Century

In the eighteenth century, the population of Europe began to grow markedly. Europeans grew in numbers steadily from 1720 to 1789, with especially dramatic increases after about 1750 (**Figure 17.2**). Between 1700 and 1835, the population of Europe doubled in size.

The basic cause of European population increase as a whole was a decline in mortality—fewer deaths. One of the primary reasons behind this decline was the mysterious disappearance of the bubonic plague after the early 1720s. Following the Black Death in the fourteenth century, plagues had remained part of the European experience, striking again and again with savage force, particularly in towns. Exactly why plague disappeared is unknown. Stricter measures of quarantine in

CHAPTER LOCATOR | How did European agriculture change between 1650 and 1800?

CHAPTER 17

524 THE EXPANSION OF EUROPE

Mediterranean ports and along the Austrian border with the Ottoman Empire helped by carefully isolating human carriers of plague. Chance and plain good luck were probably just as important.

Advances in medical knowledge did not contribute much to reducing the death rate in the eighteenth century. However, improvements in the water supply and sewage, which were frequently promoted by strong absolutist monarchies, resulted in somewhat better public health and helped reduce diseases such as typhoid and typhus in some urban areas of western Europe. Improvements in water supply and the drainage of swamps also reduced Europe's large insect population. Thus early public health measures helped the decline in mortality that began with the disappearance of plague and continued into the early nineteenth century.

Human beings also became more successful in their efforts to safeguard the supply of food. The eighteenth century was a time of considerable canal and road building in western Europe. These advances in transportation, which were also among the more positive aspects of strong absolutist states, lessened the impact of local crop failure and famine. Emergency supplies could be brought in, and localized starvation became less frequent. Wars became less destructive than in the seventeenth century and spread fewer epidemics. None of the population growth would have been possible if not for the advances in agricultural production in the seventeenth and eighteenth centuries, which increased the food supply and contributed nutritious new foods. In short, population grew in the eighteenth century primarily because years of higher-than-average death rates were less catastrophic. Famines, epidemics, and wars continued to occur and to affect population growth, but their severity moderated.

Population growth intensified the imbalance between the number of people and the economic opportunities available to them. Deprived of land by the enclosure movement, the rural poor were forced to look for new ways to make a living.

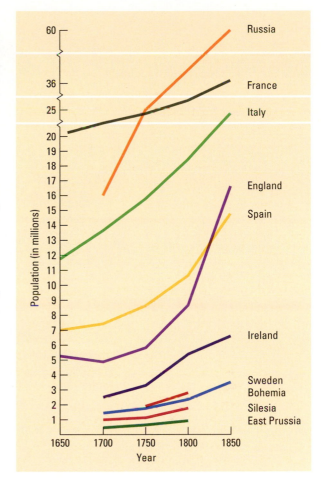

FIGURE 17.2 ■ The Increase of Population in Europe, 1650–1850

Population grew across Europe in the eighteenth century, though the most dramatic increases occurred after 1750. Russia experienced the largest increase and emerged as Europe's most populous state, as natural increase was complemented by growth from territorial expansion. Source: Data from Massimo Livi Bacci, *The Population of Europe* (Wiley-Blackwell, 2000), p. 8.

> **Factors Contributing to the Eighteenth-Century Decline in Mortality Rates**

- The disappearance of the bubonic plague after the early 1720s
- Improvements in the water supply and sewage reduced incidence of certain diseases
- Advances in transportation lessened the impact of local crop failure and famine
- Wars became less destructive and spread fewer epidemics

QUICK REVIEW <

Why did mortality rates start to drop after 1700?

| Why did the European population rise dramatically in the eighteenth century? | How and why did rural industry intensify in the eighteenth century? | What were guilds, and why did they become controversial in the eighteenth century? | What role did colonial markets play in Europe's development? | ☑ LearningCurve Check what you know. |

How and why did rural industry intensify in the eighteenth century?

The Linen Industry in Ireland Many steps went into making textiles. Here the women are beating away the woody part of the flax plant so that the man can comb out the soft part. The combed fibers will then be spun into thread and woven into cloth by this family enterprise. The increased labor of women and girls from the late seventeenth century helped produce a significant expansion in the production of textiles in western Europe. (Private Collection/The Stapleton Collection/The Bridgeman Art Library)

THE GROWTH OF POPULATION increased the number of rural workers with little or no land, and this in turn contributed to the development of industry in rural areas. The poor in the countryside increasingly needed to supplement their agricultural earnings with other types of work, and urban capitalists were eager to employ them, often at lower wages than urban workers received. **Cottage industry**, which consisted of manufacturing with hand tools in peasant cottages and work sheds, grew markedly in the eighteenth century and became a crucial feature of the European economy.

The Putting-Out System

Cottage industry was often organized through the **putting-out system**. The two main participants in the putting-out system were the merchant capitalist and the rural worker. In this system, the merchant loaned, or "put out," raw materials to cottage workers, who processed the raw materials in their own homes and returned the finished products to the merchant. The relative importance of earnings from the land and from industry varied greatly for handicraft workers, although industrial wages usually became more important for a given family with time.

The putting-out system grew because it had competitive advantages. Underemployed labor was abundant, and poor peasants and landless laborers would

cottage industry
▶ A stage of industrial development in which rural workers used hand tools in their homes to manufacture goods on a large scale for sale in a market.

putting-out system
▶ The eighteenth-century system of rural industry in which a merchant loaned raw materials to cottage workers, who processed them and returned the finished products to the merchant.

CHAPTER LOCATOR | How did European agriculture change between 1650 and 1800?

work for low wages. Because production in the countryside was unregulated, workers and merchants could change procedures and experiment as they saw fit. Because workers did not need to meet rigid guild standards, cottage industry became capable of producing many kinds of goods. Although luxury goods for the rich demanded special training, close supervision, and centralized workshops, the limited skills of rural industry proved sufficient for everyday articles.

Rural manufacturing developed most successfully in England, particularly for the spinning and weaving of woolen cloth. By 1700, English industry was generally more rural than urban and heavily reliant on the putting-out system. Most continental countries, with the exception of Flanders and the Dutch Republic, developed rural industry more slowly. The latter part of the eighteenth century witnessed a remarkable expansion of rural industry in certain densely populated regions of continental Europe (**Map 17.1**).

The Lives of Rural Textile Workers

Until the nineteenth century, the industry that employed the most people in Europe was textiles. The making of linen, woolen, and eventually cotton cloth was the typical activity of cottage workers engaged in the putting-out system. A look inside the cottage of the English weaver illustrates a way of life as well as an economic system. The rural worker lived in a small, often single-room cottage with tiny windows and little space. There were only a few pieces of furniture, of which the weaver's loom was by far the largest and most important.

Handloom weaving was a family enterprise. All members of the family helped in the work. Operating the loom was usually considered a man's job, reserved for the male head of the family. Women and children worked at auxiliary tasks; they prepared the warp (vertical) threads and mounted them on the loom, wound threads

The Weaver's Repose

This painting by Decker Cornelis Gerritz (1594–1637) captures the pleasure of release from long hours of toil in cottage industry. The loom realistically dominates the cramped living space and the family's modest possessions. (© Royal Museums of Fine Arts of Belgium, Brussels/photo: J. Geleyns/Ro scan)

Why did the European population rise dramatically in the eighteenth century?

How and why did rural industry intensify in the eighteenth century?

What were guilds, and why did they become controversial in the eighteenth century?

What role did colonial markets play in Europe's development?

☑ LearningCurve
Check what you know.

MAP 17.1 ■ Industry and Population in Eighteenth-Century Europe

The growth of cottage manufacturing in rural areas helped country people increase their income and contributed to population growth. The putting-out system began in England, and much of the work was in the textile industry. Cottage industry was also strong in the Low Countries — modern-day Belgium and the Netherlands.

> MAPPING THE PAST

ANALYZING THE MAP: What does this map suggest about the relationship between population density and the growth of textile production? What geographical characteristics seem to have played a role in encouraging this industry?

CONNECTIONS: How would you account for the distribution of each type of cloth across Europe? Did metal production draw on different demographic and geographical conditions? Why do you think this was the case?

on bobbins for the weft (horizontal) threads, and sometimes operated the warp frame while the father passed the shuttle.

The work of four or five spinners was needed to keep one weaver steadily employed. Since the weaver's family usually could not produce enough thread, merchants hired the wives and daughters of agricultural workers, who took on spinning work in their spare time. In England, many widows and single women also became "spinsters," so many in fact that the word became a synonym for an unmarried woman.

Relations between workers and employers were often marked by sharp conflict. There were constant disputes over the weights of materials and the quality of finished work. Merchants accused workers of stealing raw materials, and weavers complained that merchants delivered underweight bales. Suspicion abounded.

Conditions were particularly hard for female workers. While men could earn

CHAPTER LOCATOR | How did European agriculture change between 1650 and 1800?

decent wages through long hours of arduous labor, women's wages were usually much lower because they were not considered the family's primary wage earner. In England's Yorkshire wool industry, a male wool comber earned a good wage of 12 shillings or more a week, while a female spinner could hope for only 3½ shillings.[1] A single or widowed spinner faced a desperate struggle with poverty. Any period of illness or unemployment could spell disaster for her and any children she might have.

From the merchant capitalist's point of view, the problem was not low wages but maintaining control over the labor force. Cottage workers were scattered across the countryside, and their availability for work varied with the agricultural calendar. Merchants bitterly resented their lack of control over rural labor because their own livelihood depended on their ability to meet orders on time. They accused workers—especially female spinners—of laziness, drunkenness, and immorality. If workers failed to produce enough thread, they reasoned, it must be because their wages were too high and they had little incentive to work.

Merchants thus insisted on maintaining the lowest possible wages to force the "idle" poor into productive labor. They also lobbied for, and obtained, new police powers over workers. Imprisonment and public whipping became common punishments for pilfering small amounts of yarn or cloth. For poor workers, their right to hold on to the bits and pieces left over in the production process was akin to the traditional peasant right of gleaning in common lands. With progress came the loss of traditional safeguards for the poor.

The Industrious Revolution

One scholar has used the term **industrious revolution** to summarize the social and economic changes taking place in northwestern Europe in the late seventeenth and early eighteenth centuries.[2] This occurred as households reduced leisure time; stepped up the pace of work; and, most important, redirected the labor of women and children away from the production of goods for household consumption and toward wage work. In the countryside, the spread of cottage industry can be seen as one manifestation of the industrious revolution, while in the cities there was a rise in female employment outside the home. By working harder and increasing the number of wageworkers, rural and urban households could purchase more goods, even in a time of stagnant or falling wages.

These new sources and patterns of labor established important foundations for the Industrial Revolution of the late eighteenth and nineteenth centuries (see Chapter 20). They created households in which all members worked for wages rather than in a family business and in which consumption relied on market-produced rather than homemade goods. It was not until the mid-nineteenth century, with rising industrial wages, that a new model emerged in which the male "breadwinner" was expected to earn enough to support the whole family, and women and children were relegated back to the domestic sphere. With women estimated to compose 40 percent of the global workforce, today's world is experiencing a second industrious revolution in a similar climate of stagnant wages and increased demand for consumer goods.[3]

industrious revolution
▶ The shift that occurred as families in northwestern Europe focused on earning wages instead of producing goods for household consumption; this reduced their economic self-sufficiency but increased their ability to purchase consumer goods.

QUICK REVIEW

What role did the family play in eighteenth-century rural industry?

Why did the European population rise dramatically in the eighteenth century?

How and why did rural industry intensify in the eighteenth century?

What were guilds, and why did they become controversial in the eighteenth century?

What role did colonial markets play in Europe's development?

✓ LearningCurve
Check what you know.

529

> What were guilds, and why did they become controversial in the eighteenth century?

Guild Procession in Seventeenth-Century Brussels Guilds played an important role in the civic life of the early modern city. They collected taxes from their members, imposed quality standards and order on the trades, and represented the interests of commerce and industry to the government. In return, they claimed exclusive monopolies over their trades and the right to govern their own affairs. Guilds marched in processions, like the one shown here, at important city events, proudly displaying their corporate insignia. (V&A Images, London/Art Resource, NY)

guild system
▶ The organization of artisanal production into trade-based associations, or guilds, each of which received a monopoly over its trade and the right to train apprentices and hire workers.

ONE CONSEQUENCE OF THE GROWTH OF RURAL INDUSTRY was an undermining of the traditional **guild system** that protected urban artisans. Guilds continued to dominate production in towns and cities, providing their masters with economic privileges as well as a proud social identity, but they increasingly struggled against competition from rural workers. Meanwhile, those excluded

CHAPTER LOCATOR | How did European agriculture change between 1650 and 1800?

from guild membership—women, day laborers, Jews, and foreigners—worked on the margins of the urban economy.

In the second half of the eighteenth century, critics attacked the guilds as outmoded institutions that obstructed technical progress and innovation. Until recently, most historians repeated that view. An ongoing reassessment of guilds now emphasizes their ability to adapt to changing economic circumstances.

Urban Guilds

Originating around 1200 during the economic boom of the Middle Ages, the guild system reached its peak in most of Europe in the seventeenth and eighteenth centuries. During this period, urban guilds increased dramatically in cities and towns across Europe.

Guild masters occupied the summit of the world of work. Each guild possessed a detailed set of privileges, including exclusive rights to produce and sell certain goods; access to restricted markets in raw materials; and the rights to train apprentices, hire workers, and open shops. Any individual who violated these monopolies could be prosecuted. Guilds also served social and religious functions, providing a locus of sociability and group identity to the middling classes of European cities.

To ensure there was enough work to go around, guilds jealously restricted their membership. Most urban men and women worked in non-guild trades as domestic servants; as manual laborers; and as vendors of food, used clothing, and other goods.

While most were hostile to women, a small number of guilds did accept women. Most involved needlework and textile production, occupations that were considered appropriate for women. In 1675, seamstresses gained a new all-female guild in Paris, and soon seamstresses joined tailors' guilds in parts of France, England, and the Dutch Republic. By the mid-eighteenth century, male masters began to hire more female workers, often in defiance of their own guild statutes.

Adam Smith and Economic Liberalism

At the same time that cottage industry began to infringe on the livelihoods of urban artisans, new Enlightenment ideals called into question the very existence of the guild system. Eighteenth-century critics derided guilds as outmoded and exclusionary institutions that obstructed technical innovation and progress. One of the best-known critics of government regulation of trade and industry was Adam Smith (1723–1790), a leading figure of the Scottish Enlightenment (see Chapter 16, page 501). Smith criticized guilds for their stifling and outmoded restrictions, a critique he extended to all state monopolies and privileged companies. Far preferable was free competition, which would best protect consumers from price gouging and give all citizens a fair and equal right to do what they did best. Smith advocated a more highly developed "division of labor," which entailed separating craft production into individual tasks to increase workers' speed and efficiency.

Why did the European population rise dramatically in the eighteenth century?

How and why did rural industry intensify in the eighteenth century?

What were guilds, and why did they become controversial in the eighteenth century?

What role did colonial markets play in Europe's development?

✓ LearningCurve
Check what you know.

531

trians, and British victory on all colonial fronts was ratified in the **Treaty of Paris**. Britain had realized its goal of monopolizing a vast trading and colonial empire.

The Atlantic Economy

As the volume of transatlantic trade increased, the regions bordering the ocean were increasingly drawn into an integrated economic system. Commercial exchange in the Atlantic has traditionally been referred to as the "triangle trade," designating a three-way transport of goods: European commodities, like guns and textiles, to Africa; enslaved Africans to the colonies; and colonial goods, such as cotton, tobacco, and sugar, back to Europe (see Map 17.2, page 535).

Throughout the eighteenth century, the economies of European nations bordering the Atlantic Ocean, especially England, relied more and more on colonial exports. By 1800, sales to European countries—England's traditional trading partners—represented only half of exports, down from three-quarters a century earlier. England also benefited from importing colonial products (**Figure 17.3**). Colonial monopolies allowed the English to obtain a steady supply of such goods at beneficial prices and to re-export them to other nations at high profits. Many colonial goods, like sugar and tobacco, required processing before consumption and thus contributed new manufacturing jobs in England. In the eighteenth century, stimulated by trade and empire building, England's capital city, London, grew into the West's largest and richest city. Thus the mercantilist system achieved remarkable success for England, and by the 1770s, the country stood on the threshold of the epoch-making changes that would become known as the Industrial Revolution (see Chapter 20).

Although they lost many possessions to the English in the Seven Years' War, the French still profited enormously from colonial trade. The colonies of Saint-Domingue (modern-day Haiti), Martinique, and Guadeloupe remained in French hands and provided immense fortunes in plantation agriculture and slave trading during the second half of the eighteenth century. The wealth generated from colonial trade fostered the confidence of the merchant classes in Paris, Bordeaux, and other large cities, and merchants soon joined other elite groups clamoring for political reforms.

The third major player in the Atlantic economy, Spain, also saw its colonial fortunes improve during the eighteenth century. Not only did it gain Louisiana from France in 1763 but its influence expanded westward all the way to northern California through the efforts of Spanish missionaries and ranchers. Its mercantilist goals were boosted by a recovery in silver production, which had dropped significantly in the seventeenth century.

Silver mining also stimulated food production for the mining camps, and wealthy Spanish landowners developed a system of **debt peonage** to keep indigenous workers on their estates. Under this system, which was similar to serfdom, a

FIGURE 17.3 ■ Exports of English Manufactured Goods, 1700–1774

While trade between England and Europe stagnated after 1700, English exports to Africa and the Americas boomed and greatly stimulated English economic development. (Source: Data from R. Davis, "English Foreign Trade, 1700–1774," *Economic History Review*, 2d ser., 15 [1962]: 302–303.)

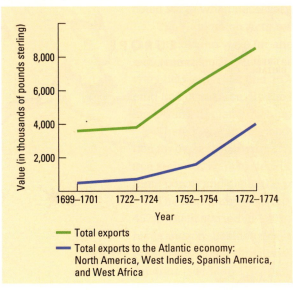

— Total exports

— Total exports to the Atlantic economy: North America, West Indies, Spanish America, and West Africa

debt peonage

▶ A form of serfdom that allowed a planter or rancher to keep his workers or slaves in perpetual debt bondage by periodically advancing food, shelter, and a little money.

CHAPTER LOCATOR | How did European agriculture change between 1650 and 1800?

planter or rancher would keep workers in perpetual debt bondage by advancing them food, shelter, and a little money.

Although the triangle trade model highlights some of the most important flows of commerce across the Atlantic, it significantly oversimplifies the picture. For example, a brisk intercolonial trade also existed, with the Caribbean slave colonies importing food in the form of fish, flour, and livestock from the northern colonies and rice from the south, in exchange for sugar and slaves (see Map 17.2, page 535). Many colonial traders violated imperial monopolies to trade with the most profitable partners, regardless of nationality. Moreover, the Atlantic economy was inextricably linked to trade with the Indian and Pacific Oceans (see page 541).

The Atlantic Slave Trade

At the core of the Atlantic world were the misery and profit of the **Atlantic slave trade**. The forced migration of millions of Africans was a key element in the Atlantic system and western European economic expansion throughout the eighteenth century. The brutal practice intensified dramatically after 1700 and especially after 1750 with the growth of trade and demand for slave-produced goods like sugar and cotton. According to the most authoritative source, European traders purchased and shipped 6.5 million enslaved Africans across the Atlantic between 1701 and 1800—more than half of the estimated total of 12.5 million Africans transported between 1450 and 1900, of whom 15 percent died in procurement and transit.[4]

The rise of plantation agriculture was responsible for the tremendous growth of the slave trade. Among all European colonies, the plantations of Portuguese Brazil received by far the largest number of enslaved Africans over the entire period of the slave trade—45 percent of the total. Another 45 percent were divided among the many Caribbean colonies. The colonies of mainland North America took only 3 percent of slaves arriving from Africa.

Some African merchants and rulers who controlled exports profited from the greater demand for slaves. With their newfound wealth, some Africans gained access to European and colonial goods, including firearms. But generally such economic returns did not spread very far, and the negative consequences of the expanding slave trade predominated. Wars among African states to obtain salable captives increased, and leaders used slave profits to purchase more arms than textiles and consumer goods. While the populations of Europe and Asia grew substantially in the eighteenth century, the population of Africa stagnated or possibly declined.

Most Europeans did not personally witness the horrors of the slave trade between Africa and the Americas, and until the early part of the eighteenth century they considered the African slave trade a legitimate business. But as details of the plight of enslaved people became known, a campaign to abolish slavery developed in Britain. In the late 1780s, the abolition campaign grew into a mass movement of public opinion, the first in British history. British women were prominent in this movement, denouncing the immorality of human bondage and stressing the cruel and sadistic treatment of enslaved women and families. These attacks put the defenders of slavery on the defensive. In 1807, Parliament abolished the British slave trade, although slavery continued in British colonies and the Americas for decades.

Atlantic slave trade

▶ The forced migration of Africans across the Atlantic for slave labor on plantations and in other industries; the trade reached its peak in the eighteenth century and ultimately involved more than 12 million Africans.

Plantation Zones, ca. 1700

Why did the European population rise dramatically in the eighteenth century?

How and why did rural industry intensify in the eighteenth century?

What were guilds, and why did they become controversial in the eighteenth century?

What role did colonial markets play in Europe's development?

✓ LearningCurve
Check what you know.

Identities and Communities of the Atlantic World

Not only slaves and commodities but also cultural ideas and values—as well as free people of European, African, and American descent—circulated through the eighteenth-century Atlantic world. As contacts between the Atlantic coasts of the Americas, Africa, and Europe became more frequent, and as European settlements grew into well-established colonies, new identities and communities emerged.

The term *Creole* referred to people of Spanish ancestry born in the Americas. Wealthy Creoles and their counterparts throughout the Atlantic colonies prided themselves on following European ways of life. Over time, however, the colonial elite came to feel that their circumstances gave them different interests and characteristics from those of their home population. Creole traders and planters increasingly resented the regulations and taxes imposed by colonial bureaucrats, and such resentment would eventually lead to revolution against colonial powers.

Not all Europeans in the colonies were wealthy. Numerous poor or middling whites worked as clerks, shopkeepers, craftsmen, and plantation managers. With the exception of British North America, white Europeans made up a minority of the population. Since European migrants were disproportionately male, much of the population of the Atlantic world descended from unions—forced or through choice—of European men and indigenous or African women. (See "Picturing the Past: Mulatto Painting," page 539).

Mixed-race populations sometimes rose to the colonial elite. The Spanish conquistadors often consolidated their power through marriage to the daughters of local rulers, and their descendants were among the most powerful inhabitants of Spanish America. In the Spanish and French Caribbean, as in Brazil, many masters acknowledged and freed their mixed-race children, leading to sizable populations of free people of color. Given advantages because of their fathers, some became wealthy land and slave owners in their own right.

British colonies followed a distinctive pattern. There, whole families, rather than individual men, migrated, resulting in a rapid increase in the white population. This development was favored by British colonial law, which forbade marriage between English men and women and Africans or Native Americans. In the British colonies of the Caribbean and the southern mainland, masters tended to leave their mixed-race progeny in slavery rather than freeing them, maintaining a stark discrepancy between free whites and enslaved people of color.[5]

Converting indigenous people to Christianity was a key ambition for all European powers in the New World. Galvanized by the Protestant Reformation and the perceived need to protect and spread Catholicism, Catholic powers actively sponsored missionary efforts. Catholic religious orders established missions throughout Spanish, Portuguese, and French colonies (see Chapter 14, page 428). In Central and South America, large-scale conversion forged enduring Catholic cultures in Portuguese and Spanish colonies. Conversion efforts in North America were less effective because indigenous settlements were more scattered and native people were less integrated into colonial communities. On the whole, Protestants were less active as missionaries in this period, although some dissenters, like Moravians, Quakers, and Methodists, did seek converts among indigenous and enslaved people. (See "Individuals in Society: Rebecca Protten," page 540.)

CHAPTER LOCATOR | How did European agriculture change between 1650 and 1800?

Mulatto Painting

The caption in the upper left-hand corner of this mid-eighteenth-century painting identifies the family as being composed of a Spanish father and a black mother, whose child is described as "mulatto." The painting was number six in a series of sixteen images by the painter Jose de Alcibar, each showing a different racial and ethnic combination. The series belonged to a popular genre in the Spanish Americas known as *castas* paintings, which commonly depicted sixteen different forms of racial mixing.

(Francisco Clapera, De Espanol, y Negra, Mulato, c. 1785. Denver Art Museum Collection. Gift of Frederick and Jan Mayer, 2011.428.4. © Denver Art Museum.)

> **PICTURING THE PAST**

ANALYZING THE IMAGE: How would you characterize the relations among mother, father, and child as shown in this painting? Does the painter suggest power relations within the family? What attitude does the painter seem to have toward the family?

CONNECTIONS: Why do you think such paintings were so popular? Who do you think the audience might have been, and why would viewers be fascinated by such images?

The practice of slavery reveals important limitations on efforts to spread Christianity. Slave owners often refused to baptize their slaves, fearing that enslaved people would use their Christian status to claim additional rights. In some areas, particularly among the mostly African-born slaves of the Caribbean, elements of African religious belief and practice endured, often incorporated with Christian traditions.

The Colonial Enlightenment

Enlightenment ideas thrived in the colonies, although with as much diversity and disagreement as in Europe (see Chapter 16). The colonies of British North America were deeply influenced by the Scottish Enlightenment, with its emphasis on

| Why did the European population rise dramatically in the eighteenth century? | How and why did rural industry intensify in the eighteenth century? | What were guilds, and why did they become controversial in the eighteenth century? | **What role did colonial markets play in Europe's development?** | ✓ LearningCurve Check what you know. |

539

INDIVIDUALS IN SOCIETY
Rebecca Protten

In the mid-1720s, a young English-speaking girl who came to be known as Rebecca traveled by ship from Antigua to the small Danish sugar colony of St. Thomas, today part of the U.S. Virgin Islands. Eighty-five percent of St. Thomas's four thousand inhabitants were of African descent, almost all enslaved. Sugar plantations demanded backbreaking work, and slave owners used extremely brutal methods to maintain control, including amputations and beheadings for runaways.

Surviving documents refer to Rebecca as a "mulatto," indicating a mixed European and African ancestry. A wealthy Dutch-speaking planter named van Beverhout purchased the girl for his household staff, sparing her a position in the grueling and deadly sugar fields. Rebecca won the family's favor, and they taught her to read, write, and speak Dutch. They also shared with her their Protestant faith and took the unusual step of freeing her.

As a free woman, she continued to work as a servant for the van Beverhouts and to study the Bible and spread its message of spiritual freedom. In 1736, she met some missionaries for the Moravian Church, a German Protestant sect that emphasized emotion and communal worship, and devoted its mission work to the enslaved peoples of the Caribbean. The missionaries were struck by Rebecca's piety and her potential to assist their work. As one wrote: "She researches diligently in the Scriptures, loves the Savior, and does much good for other Negro women because she does not simply walk alone with her good ways but instructs them in the Scriptures as well." A letter Rebecca sent to Moravian women in Germany declared: "Oh how good is the Lord. My heart melts when I think of it. His name is wonderful. Oh! Help me to praise him, who has pulled me out of the darkness. I will take up his cross with all my heart and follow the example of his poor life."*

Rebecca soon took charge of the Moravians' female missionary work. Every Sunday and every evening after work, she would walk for miles to lead meetings with enslaved and free black women. The meetings consisted of reading and writing lessons, prayers, hymns, a sermon, and individual discussions in which she encouraged her new sisters in their spiritual growth.

*Quotations from Jon F. Sensbach, *Rebecca's Revival: Creating Black Christianity in the Atlantic World* (Cambridge, Mass.: Harvard University Press, 2006), pp. 61; 63.

A portrait of Rebecca Protten with her second husband and their daughter, Anna-Maria. (Courtesy of Jon F. Sensbach. Used by permission of the Moravian Archives Herrnhut, GS-393.)

In 1738. Rebecca married a German Moravian missionary, Matthaus Freundlich, a rare but not illegal case of mixed marriage. The same year, her husband bought a plantation, with slaves, to serve as the headquarters of their mission work. The Moravians — and presumably Rebecca herself — wished to spread Christian faith among slaves and improve their treatment but did not oppose the institution of slavery itself.

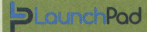 LaunchPad

ONLINE DOCUMENT PROJECT
What does Rebecca Protten's story reveal about the complex relationship among slavery, race, and religion in the eighteenth century? Examine primary sources concerning these interconnected issues, and then complete a writing assignment based on the evidence and details from this chapter. *See inside the front cover to learn more.*

Authorities nonetheless feared that baptized and literate slaves would agitate for freedom, and they imprisoned Rebecca and Matthaus and tried to shut down the mission. Only the unexpected arrival on St. Thomas of German aristocrat and Moravian leader Count Zinzendorf saved the couple. Exhausted by their ordeal, they left for Germany in 1741 accompanied by their small daughter, but both father and daughter died soon after their arrival.

In Marienborn, a German center of the Moravian faith, Rebecca encountered other black Moravians, who lived in equality alongside their European brethren. In 1746, she married another missionary, Christian Jacob Protten, son of a Danish sailor and, on his mother's side, grandson of a West African king. She and another female missionary from St. Thomas were ordained as deaconesses, probably making them the first women of color to be ordained in the Western Christian Church.

In 1763, Rebecca and her husband set out for her husband's birthplace, the Danish slave fort at Christiansborg (in what is now Accra, Ghana) to establish a school for mixed-race children. Her husband died in 1769, leaving Rebecca a widow once more. After declining the offer of passage back to the West Indies in 1776, she died in obscurity near Christiansborg in 1780.

QUESTIONS FOR ANALYSIS

1. Why did Moravian missionaries assign such an important leadership role to Rebecca? What particular attributes did she offer?
2. Why did Moravians, including Rebecca, accept the institution of slavery instead of fighting to end it?
3. What does Rebecca's story teach us about the Atlantic world of the mid-eighteenth century?

pragmatic approaches to the problems of life. Following the Scottish model, leaders in the colonies adopted a moderate, commonsense version of the Enlightenment that emphasized self-improvement and ethical conduct.

Some thinkers went even further in their admiration for Enlightenment ideas. Benjamin Franklin's writings and political career provide an outstanding example of the combination of the pragmatism and economic interests of the Scottish Enlightenment with the constitutional theories of John Locke, Jean-Jacques Rousseau, and the baron de Montesquieu.

Northern Enlightenment thinkers often depicted the Spanish American colonies as the epitome of the superstition and barbarity they contested. The Catholic Church strictly controlled the publication of books there, just as it did on the Iberian Peninsula. Nonetheless, educated elites were well aware of the new currents of thought, and the universities, newspapers, and salons of Spanish America produced their own reform ideas. In all European colonies, one effect of Enlightenment thought was to encourage colonists to criticize the policies of the mother country and aspire toward greater autonomy.

Trade and Empire in Asia and the Pacific

As the Atlantic economy took shape, Europeans continued to vie for dominance in the Asian trade. Between 1500 and 1600, the Portuguese had become major players in the Indian Ocean trading world, eliminating Venice as Europe's chief supplier of spices and other Asian luxury goods. The Portuguese dominated but did not fundamentally alter the age-old pattern of Indian Ocean trade, which involved merchants from many areas as more or less autonomous players. This situation changed radically with the intervention of the Dutch and then the English (see Chapter 14).

Formed in 1602, the Dutch East India Company had taken control of the Portuguese spice trade in the Indian Ocean, with the port of Batavia (Jakarta) in Java as its center of operations. Unlike the Portuguese, the Dutch transformed the Indian Ocean trading world. Whereas East Indian states and peoples maintained independence under the Portuguese,

This Indian miniature shows the wife (center) of a British officer attended by many Indian servants. A British merchant (left) awaits her attention. The picture reflects the luxurious lifestyle of the British elite in India, many members of which returned home with colossal fortunes. (Werner Forman/Art Resource, NY)

who treated them as autonomous business partners, the Dutch established outright control and reduced them to dependents.

After these successes, the Dutch hold in Asia faltered in the eighteenth century due to the company's failure to diversify to meet changing consumption patterns. Spices continued to compose much of its shipping, despite their declining importance in the European diet. Fierce competition from its main rival, the English East India Company (established in 1600), also severely undercut Dutch trade.

Britain initially struggled for a foothold in Asia. With the Dutch monopolizing the Indian Ocean, the British turned to India. Throughout the seventeenth century, the English East India Company relied on trade concessions from the powerful Mughal emperor, who granted only piecemeal access to the subcontinent. Finally, in 1716, the Mughals conceded empire-wide trading privileges. As Mughal power waned, British East India Company agents increasingly intervened in local affairs and made alliances or waged war against Indian princes.

Britain's great rival for influence in India was France. During the War of the Austrian Succession, British and French forces in India supported opposing rulers in local power struggles. In 1757, East India Company forces under Robert Clive conquered the rich northeastern province of Bengal at the Battle of Plassey. French-English rivalry was finally resolved by the Treaty of Paris, which granted all of France's possessions in India to the British—with the exception of Pondicherry, an Indian Ocean port city. With the elimination of their rival, British ascendancy in India accelerated, and by the early nineteenth century, the company had overcome vigorous Indian resistance to gain economic and political dominance of much of the subcontinent; direct administration by the British government replaced East India Company rule after a large-scale rebellion in 1857.

The rising economic and political power of Europeans in this period drew on the connections they established between the Asian and Atlantic trade worlds. An outstanding example is the trade in cowrie shells. These seashells, originating in the Maldive Islands in the Indian Ocean, were used as a form of currency in West Africa. European traders obtained them in Asia, and then traded them for slaves in West Africa. Indian textiles were also prized in Africa and played a similar role in exchange. Thus the trade of the Atlantic was inseparable from Asian commerce, and Europeans were increasingly found dominating commerce in both worlds.

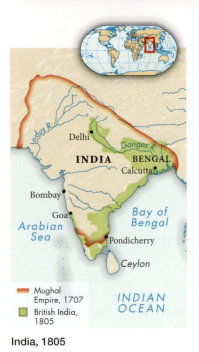

India, 1805

> **QUICK REVIEW**

What role did trade and empire play in shaping European colonial policies in the seventeenth and eighteenth centuries?

CHAPTER LOCATOR | How did European agriculture change between 1650 and 1800?

LOOKING BACK LOOKING AHEAD

By the turn of the eighteenth century, western Europe had begun to shake off the effects of long decades of famine, disease, warfare, economic depression, and demographic stagnation. The eighteenth century witnessed a breakthrough in agricultural production that, along with improved infrastructure and the retreat of epidemic disease, contributed to a substantial increase in population. One crucial catalyst for agricultural innovation was the Scientific Revolution, which provided new tools of empirical observation and experimentation. The Enlightenment as well, with its emphasis on progress and public welfare, convinced government officials, scientists, and informed landowners to seek better solutions to old problems. By the end of the century, industry and trade had also attracted enlightened commentators who advocated free markets and less government control. Modern ideas of political economy thus constitute one more legacy of the Enlightenment.

As the era of European exploration and conquest gave way to colonial empire building, the eighteenth century witnessed increased consolidation of global markets and bitter competition among Europeans for the spoils of empire. From its slow inception in the mid-fifteenth century, the African slave trade reached brutal heights in the second half of the eighteenth century. The eighteenth-century Atlantic world thus tied the shores of Europe, the Americas, and Africa in a web of commercial and human exchange that also had strong ties with the Pacific and the Indian Oceans.

The new dynamics of the eighteenth century prepared the way for world-shaking changes. Population growth and rural industry began to undermine long-standing traditions of daily life in western Europe. The transformed families of the industrious revolution developed not only new habits of work but also a new sense of confidence in their abilities. By the 1770s, England was approaching an economic transformation fully as significant as the great political upheaval destined to develop shortly in neighboring France. In the same period, the first wave of resistance to European domination rose up in the colonies. The great revolutions of the late eighteenth century would change the world forever.

ONLINE DOCUMENT PROJECT

Rebecca Protten

What does Rebecca Protten's story reveal about the complex relationship among slavery, race, and religion in the eighteenth century?

You encountered Rebecca Protten's story on page 540. Keeping the question above in mind, examine primary sources concerning these interconnected issues—including an account of early Moravian missionary activity in the West Indies, an essay on the conversion of slaves, and a pamphlet on the same topic. *See inside the front cover to learn more.*

Why did the European population rise dramatically in the eighteenth century?

How and why did rural industry intensify in the eighteenth century?

What were guilds, and why did they become controversial in the eighteenth century?

What role did colonial markets play in Europe's development?

✓ LearningCurve
Check what you know.

CHAPTER 17 STUDY GUIDE

STEP 1 GET STARTED ONLINE

LearningCurve

Now that you've read the chapter, make it stick by completing the LearningCurve activity.

STEP 2 EXPLAIN WHY IT MATTERS

Put your reading into practice. Identify each term below, and then explain why it matters in Western history.

TERM	WHO OR WHAT & WHEN	WHY IT MATTERS
enclosure (p. 520)		
proletarianization (p. 522)		
cottage industry (p. 526)		
putting-out system (p. 526)		
industrious revolution (p. 529)		
guild system (p. 530)		
economic liberalism (p. 532)		
Navigation Acts (p. 534)		
Treaty of Paris (p. 536)		
debt peonage (p. 536)		
Atlantic slave trade (p. 537)		

STEP 3 MOVE BEYOND THE BASICS

To demonstrate a more advanced understanding of the major social and economic developments of the eighteenth century, fill in the chart below by describing the causes and consequences of the agricultural revolution, the eighteenth-century population explosion, and the growth of rural industry.

	Causes	Consequences
Agricultural revolution		
Population growth		
Growth of rural industry		

PUT IT ALL TOGETHER

Now, take a step back and try to explain the big picture. Remember to use specific examples from the chapter in your answers.

THE AGRICULTURAL REVOLUTION AND POPULATION GROWTH

▶ What was revolutionary about the agricultural revolution?

▶ Why did European population growth begin to accelerate from 1700 on?

RURAL INDUSTRY

▶ How and why did the nature and importance of rural industry change over the course of the eighteenth century?

▶ What developments does this term "industrial revolution" aim to summarize?

THE ATLANTIC WORLD AND GLOBAL TRADE

▶ How did European nations define their economic interests and what role did such definitions play in European policies and actions overseas?

▶ What role did slavery play in the Atlantic economy and in emerging colonial communities?

MAKE CONNECTIONS

▶ Compare and contrast the eighteenth century and the High Middle Ages.

  ▶ Compare and contrast the eighteenth century with the current era.

> ## IN YOUR OWN WORDS

Imagine that you must give an oral report to the class answering the following question: **How and why did the society and economy of Europe change in the eighteenth century?** What would be the most important points and why?

18

LIFE IN THE ERA OF EXPANSION

1650–1800

> **How and why did daily life in Europe change in the eighteenth century?** Chapter 18 examines everyday life in the era of expansion. The discussion of agriculture and industry in the last chapter showed the common people at work, straining to make ends meet within the larger context of population growth, gradual economic expansion, and ferocious political competition at home and overseas. This chapter shows us how that world of work was embedded in a rich complex of family organization, community practices, everyday experiences, and collective attitudes. As with the economy, traditional habits and practices of daily life changed considerably over the eighteenth century. Change was particularly dramatic in the growing cities of northwestern Europe, where traditional social controls were undermined by the anonymity and increased social interaction of the urban setting.

After reading the chapter, use LearningCurve to retain what you've read.

Life in the Eighteenth Century. The huge fresh-food market known as Les Halles was the pulsing heart of eighteenth-century Paris. Here, peddlers offer food and drink to the men and women of the market. (akg-images)

> How did marriage and family life change in the eighteenth century?

> What was life like for children, and how did attitudes toward childhood evolve?

> How did increasing literacy and new patterns of consumption affect people's lives?

> What role did religion play in eighteenth-century society?

> How did the practice of medicine evolve in the eighteenth century?

How did marriage and family life change in the eighteenth century?

The Village Wedding

The spirited merrymaking of a peasant wedding was a popular theme of European artists in the eighteenth century. Given the harsh conditions of life, a wedding provided a treasured moment of feasting, dancing, and revelry. With the future of the village at stake, the celebration of marriage was a public event. (Private Collection/The Bridgeman Art Library)

THE BASIC UNIT OF SOCIAL ORGANIZATION is and has always been the family. Within the structure of the family, human beings love, mate, and reproduce. It is primarily the family that teaches the child, imparting values and customs that condition an individual's behavior for a lifetime. The family is also an institution woven into the web of history, but that does not mean that the family is static. It evolves and changes, assuming different forms in different times and places. The eighteenth century witnessed such an evolution: patterns of marriage shifted and individuals adapted and conformed to the new and changing realities of the family unit.

Late Marriage and Nuclear Families

The three-generation extended family was a rarity in western and central Europe. When young European couples married, they normally established their own households and lived apart from their parents, much like the nuclear families (a family group consisting of parents and their children with no other relatives) common in America today. If a three-generation household came into existence, it was usually because a widowed parent moved into the home of a married child.

The average person married many years after reaching adulthood and many more after beginning to work. Studies of western Europe in the seventeenth and

CHAPTER LOCATOR | **How did marriage and family life change in the eighteenth century?**

eighteenth centuries show that both men and women married for the first time at an average age of twenty-five to twenty-seven. Furthermore, 10 to 20 percent of men and women in western Europe never married at all. Matters were different in eastern Europe, where the multigeneration household was the norm, marriage occurred around age twenty, and permanent celibacy was much less common.

Why did young people in western Europe delay marriage? The main reason was that couples normally did not marry until they could start an independent household and support themselves and their future children. Peasants often needed to wait until their father's death to inherit land and marry. In the towns, men and women worked to accumulate enough savings to start a small business and establish their own home.

Laws and tradition also discouraged early marriage. In some areas, couples needed permission from the local lord or landowner to marry. Poor couples had particular difficulty securing the approval of local officials, who believed that freedom to marry for the lower classes would result in more landless paupers, more abandoned children, and more money for welfare. Village elders often agreed.

The custom of late marriage combined with the nuclear-family household distinguished western European society from other areas of the world. Historians have argued that this late-marriage pattern was responsible for at least part of the economic advantage western Europeans acquired relative to other world regions. Late marriage joined a mature man and a mature woman—two adults who had already accumulated social and economic capital and could transmit self-reliance and skills to the next generation. This marriage pattern also favored a greater degree of equality between husband and wife.

Work away from Home

Many young people worked within their families until they could start their own households. Many others left home to work elsewhere. In the trades, a lad would enter apprenticeship around age fifteen and finish in his late teens or early twenties. During that time, he would not be permitted to marry. An apprentice from a

What was life like for children, and how did attitudes toward childhood evolve? | How did increasing literacy and new patterns of consumption affect people's lives? | What role did religion play in eighteenth-century society? | How did the practice of medicine evolve in the eighteenth century? | ✓ LearningCurve Check what you know.

549

rural village would typically move to a city or town to learn a trade. If he was lucky and had connections, he might eventually be admitted to a guild and establish his economic independence. Many poor families could not afford apprenticeships for their sons. Without craft skills, these youths drifted from one tough job to another.

Many adolescent girls also left their families to work. The range of opportunities open to them was more limited, however. Apprenticeship was sometimes available with mistresses in traditionally female occupations like seamstress, linen draper, or midwife. With the growth in production of finished goods for the emerging consumer economy during the eighteenth century (see Chapter 17), demand rose for skilled female labor and, with it, greater opportunities for women.

Service in another family's household was by far the most common job for girls, and even middle-class families often sent their daughters into service. The legions of young servant girls worked hard but had little independence. Constantly under the eye of her mistress, the servant girl had many tasks. Often the work was endless, for there were few laws to limit exploitation. Court records are full of servant girls' complaints of physical mistreatment by their mistresses.

Male apprentices told similar tales of abuse and they shared the legal status of "servant" with housemaids, but they were far less vulnerable to the sexual exploitation that threatened young girls. In theory, domestic service offered a girl protection and security in a new family. But in practice she was often the easy prey of a lecherous master or his sons or friends. If the girl became pregnant, she could be fired and thrown out in disgrace. Many families could not or would not accept such a girl back into the home. Forced to make their own way, these girls had no choice but to turn to a harsh life of prostitution (see page 553) and petty thievery.

Young Serving Girl

Increased migration to urban areas in the eighteenth century contributed to a loosening of traditional morals and soaring illegitimacy rates. Young women who worked as servants or shopgirls could not be supervised as closely as those who lived at home. The themes of seduction, fallen virtue, and familial conflict were popular in eighteenth-century art, such as in this painting by Pietro Longhi (1702–1785). (akg-images/Cameraphoto)

CHAPTER LOCATOR | **How did marriage and family life change in the eighteenth century?**

Premarital Sex and Community Controls

Ten years between puberty and marriage was a long time for sexually mature young people to wait. Many unmarried couples satisfied their sexual desires with fondling and petting. Others went further and engaged in premarital intercourse. Those who did so risked pregnancy and the stigma of illegitimate birth. Birth control was not unknown in Europe before the nineteenth century, but it was primitive and unreliable.

Despite the lack of reliable contraception, premarital sex did not result in a large proportion of illegitimate births in most parts of Europe until 1750. Where collective control over sexual behavior among youths failed, community pressure to marry often prevailed. A study of seven representative parishes in seventeenth-century England shows that around 20 percent of children were conceived before the couple was married, while only 2 percent were born out of wedlock.[1]

The combination of low rates of illegitimate birth with large numbers of pregnant brides reflects the powerful **community controls** of the traditional village, particularly the open-field village, with its pattern of cooperation and common action. An unwed mother with an illegitimate child was inevitably viewed as a grave threat to the economic, social, and moral stability of the community. Irate parents, anxious village elders, indignant priests, and stern landlords all combined to pressure young people who wavered about marriage in the face of unexpected pregnancies. In the countryside, these controls meant that premarital sex was not entered into lightly and that it was generally limited to those contemplating marriage.

The concerns of the village and the family weighed heavily on couples' lives after marriage as well. Whereas uninvolved individuals today try to stay out of the domestic disputes of their neighbors, the people in peasant communities gave such affairs loud and unfavorable publicity either at the time or during the carnival season (see page 560). Relying on degrading public rituals, known as **charivari**, the young men of the village would typically gang up on their victim and force him or her to sit astride a donkey facing backward and holding up the donkey's tail. They would parade the overly brutal spouse-beater or the adulterous couple around the village, loudly proclaiming the offenders' misdeeds.

community controls
▶ A pattern of cooperation and common action in a traditional village that sought to uphold the economic, social, and moral stability of the closely knit community.

charivari
▶ Degrading public rituals used by village communities to police personal behavior and maintain moral standards.

New Patterns of Marriage and Illegitimacy

In the second half of the eighteenth century, long-standing patterns of marriage and illegitimacy shifted dramatically. One important change was an increased ability for young people to choose partners for themselves rather than following the interests of their families. This change occurred because social and economic transformations made it harder for families and communities to supervise young people's behavior. More youths in the countryside worked for their own wages rather than on a family farm, and their economic autonomy translated into increased freedom of action. Moreover, many youths joined the flood of migrants to the cities, either with their families or in search of work on their own. Urban life provided young people with more social contacts and less social control.

A less positive outcome of loosening social control was an **illegitimacy explosion**, concentrated in England, France, Germany, and Scandinavia. In Frankfurt,

illegitimacy explosion
▶ The sharp increase in out-of-wedlock births that occurred in Europe between 1750 and 1850, caused by low wages and the breakdown of community controls.

| What was life like for children, and how did attitudes toward childhood evolve? | How did increasing literacy and new patterns of consumption affect people's lives? | What role did religion play in eighteenth-century society? | How did the practice of medicine evolve in the eighteenth century? | ✓ LearningCurve Check what you know. |

Germany, for example, births out of wedlock rose steadily from about 2 percent of all births in the early 1700s to a peak of about 25 percent around 1850. In Bordeaux, France, 36 percent of all babies were born out of wedlock by 1840. The rise in numbers did not alter social disapproval of single mothers and their offspring, leaving them in desperate circumstances.

> ### > The Illegitimacy Explosion

- Concentrated in England, France, Germany, and Scandinavia
- Frankfurt, Germany: Births out of wedlock rise from 2 percent in the early 1700s to 25 percent around 1850
- Bordeaux, France: 36 percent of all babies born out of wedlock by 1840
- In small towns and villages, the 1 to 3 percent illegitimacy rate in 1750 rose to 10 to 20 percent by 1850

Why did the number of illegitimate births skyrocket? One reason was a rise in sexual activity among young people. The loosened social controls that gave young people more choice in marriage also provided them with more opportunities to yield to the attraction of the opposite sex. As in previous generations, many of the young couples who engaged in sexual activity intended to marry.

The problem for young women who became pregnant was that fewer men followed through on their promises. The second half of the eighteenth century witnessed sharply rising prices for food, homes, and other necessities of life. Many soldiers, day laborers, and male servants were no doubt sincere in their proposals, but their lives were insecure, and they hesitated to take on the burden of a wife and child.

Thus, while some happy couples benefited from matches of love rather than convenience, in many cases the intended marriage did not take place. The romantic yet practical dreams and aspirations of young people were frustrated by low wages, inequality, and changing economic and social conditions. Old patterns of marriage and family were breaking down. Only in the late nineteenth century would more stable patterns reappear.

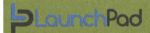

ONLINE DOCUMENT PROJECT

The Inner Life of the Individual

How did the increasing emphasis on the inner life and development of the individual in the eighteenth century find expression in the art of the period?

Keeping the question above in mind, analyze a series of paintings by Jean-Baptiste-Siméon Chardin that depict various aspects of daily life and reveal the era's increased attention to individual emotion and development. *See inside the front cover to learn more.*

CHAPTER LOCATOR | How did marriage and family life change in the eighteenth century?

Sex on the Margins of Society

Not all sex acts took place between men and women hopeful of marriage. Prostitution offered both single and married men an outlet for sexual desire. After a long period of relative tolerance, prostitutes encountered increasingly harsh and repressive laws in the sixteenth and early seventeenth centuries as officials across Europe closed licensed brothels and declared prostitution illegal.

Despite this repression, prostitution continued to flourish in the eighteenth century. Most prostitutes were working women who turned to the sex trade when confronted with unemployment. Such women did not become social pariahs; they retained ties with the communities of laboring poor to which they belonged. If caught by the police, however, they were liable to imprisonment or banishment. Venereal disease was also a constant threat.

Relations between individuals of the same sex attracted even more condemnation than did prostitution because they defied the Bible's limitation of sex to the purposes of procreation. Male same-sex relations were prohibited by law in most European states, under pain of death. Such laws were enforced unevenly, however, most strictly in Spain and far less so in the Scandinavian countries and Russia.[2]

Protected by their status, nobles and royals sometimes openly indulged their same-sex passions, which were accepted as long as they married and produced legitimate heirs. It was common knowledge that King James I, sponsor of the first translation of the Bible into English, had male lovers, but such relations did not prevent him from having seven children with his wife, Anne of Denmark.

In the late seventeenth century, new homosexual subcultures began to emerge in Paris, Amsterdam, and London, with their own slang, meeting places, and styles of dress. Unlike the relations described above, which involved men who took both wives and male lovers, these groups included men exclusively oriented toward other men. A new self-identity began to form among homosexual men: a belief that their same-sex desire made them fundamentally different from other men.

Same-sex relations existed among women as well, but they attracted less anxiety and condemnation than those among men. Some women were prosecuted for "unnatural" relations; others attempted to escape the narrow confines imposed on them by dressing as men. The beginnings of a distinctive lesbian subculture appeared in London at the end of the eighteenth century.

Across the early modern period, traditional tolerance for sexual activities outside heterosexual marriage faded. This process accelerated in the eighteenth century as Enlightenment critics attacked court immorality and preached virtue and morality for middle-class men, who were expected to prove their worthiness to claim the reins of political power.

QUICK REVIEW

What changes occurred in marriage and the family during the eighteenth century?

What was life like for children, and how did attitudes toward childhood evolve?	How did increasing literacy and new patterns of consumption affect people's lives?	What role did religion play in eighteenth-century society?	How did the practice of medicine evolve in the eighteenth century?	✓ LearningCurve Check what you know.

What was life like for children, and how did attitudes toward childhood evolve?

The First Step of Childhood This tender picture of a baby's first steps toward an adoring mother exemplifies new attitudes toward children and raising them that were ushered in by the Enlightenment. Authors like Jean-Jacques Rousseau encouraged elite mothers like the one pictured here to take a more personal interest in raising their children instead of leaving them in the hands of indifferent wet nurses and nannies. Many women responded eagerly to this call, and the period saw a more sentimentalized view of childhood and family life. (Erich Lessing/Art Resource, NY)

ON THE WHOLE, western European women married late but then began bearing children rapidly. If a woman married before she was thirty, and if both she and her husband lived to fifty, she would most likely give birth to six or more children. Infant mortality varied across Europe but was very high by modern standards, and many women died in childbirth due to limited medical knowledge.

For those children who did survive, new Enlightenment ideals in the latter half of the century stressed the importance of parental nurturing. New world-views also led to an increase in elementary schools throughout Europe, but formal education reached only a minority of ordinary children.

Child Care and Nursing

Newborns entered a dangerous world. They were vulnerable to infectious diseases, and many babies died of dehydration brought about by bad bouts of ordinary diarrhea. Of those who survived infancy, many more died in childhood. Even

CHAPTER LOCATOR | How did marriage and family life change in the eighteenth century?

in a rich family, little could be done for an ailing child. Childbirth was also dangerous. Women who bore six children faced a cumulative risk of dying in childbirth of 5 to 10 percent, a thousand times as great as the risk in Europe today.[3]

In the countryside, women of the lower classes generally breast-fed their infants for two years or more. Although not a foolproof means of birth control, breast-feeding decreases the likelihood of pregnancy by delaying the resumption of ovulation. By nursing their babies, women limited their fertility and spaced their children two or three years apart. Nursing also saved lives: breast-fed infants received precious immunity-producing substances and were more likely to survive than those who were fed other food.

Across Europe, women of the aristocracy and upper middle class seldom nursed their own children because they found breast-feeding undignified and it interfered with their social responsibilities. Wealthy women hired live-in wet nurses to suckle their babies. Working women in the cities also relied on wet nurses because they needed to earn a living. Unable to afford live-in wet nurses, they often turned to the cheaper services of women in the countryside. Rural **wet-nursing** was a widespread business in the eighteenth century.

In the second half of the eighteenth century, critics mounted a harsh attack against wet-nursing. Enlightenment thinkers proclaimed that wet-nursing was robbing European society of reaching its full potential. They were convinced, incorrectly, that the population was declining (in fact it was rising, but they lacked accurate population data) and blamed this decline on women's failure to nurture their children properly. Some also railed against practices of contraception and masturbation, which they believed were robbing their nations of potential children. Despite these complaints, many women continued to rely on wet nurses for convenience or from necessity.

wet-nursing
▶ A widespread and flourishing business in the eighteenth century in which women were paid to breast-feed other women's babies.

Foundlings and Infanticide

The young woman who could not provide for an unwanted child had few choices, especially if she had no prospect of marriage. Abortions were illegal, dangerous, and apparently rare. In desperation, some women, particularly in the countryside, hid unwanted pregnancies, delivered in secret, and smothered their newborn infants. If discovered, infanticide was punishable by death.

Women in cities had more choices for disposing of babies they could not support. Foundling homes (orphanages) first took hold in Italy, Spain, and Portugal in the sixteenth century, spreading to France in 1670 and the rest of Europe thereafter. By the end of the eighteenth century, European foundling hospitals were admitting annually about one hundred thousand abandoned children, nearly all of them infants.

At their best, foundling homes were a good example of Christian charity and social concern in an age of great poverty and inequality. Yet the foundling home was no panacea. Millions of babies entered foundling homes, but few left. Even in the best of these homes, 50 percent of the babies normally died within a year. In the worst, fully 90 percent did not survive, falling victim to infectious disease, malnutrition, and neglect.[4] There appears to have been no differentiation by sex in the numbers of children sent to foundling hospitals.

| What was life like for children, and how did attitudes toward childhood evolve? | How did increasing literacy and new patterns of consumption affect people's lives? | What role did religion play in eighteenth-century society? | How did the practice of medicine evolve in the eighteenth century? | ✓ LearningCurve Check what you know. |

555

Attitudes Toward Children

What were the typical circumstances of children's lives? Some scholars have claimed that high mortality rates prevented parents from forming emotional attachments to young children. With a reasonable expectation that a child might die, some scholars believe, parents maintained an attitude of indifference, if not downright negligence. Most historians now believe, however, that seventeenth- and eighteenth-century parents did love their children, suffered anxiously when they fell ill, and experienced extreme anguish when they died.

In a society characterized by much violence and brutality, discipline of children was often severe. The axiom "Spare the rod and spoil the child" seems to have been coined in the mid-seventeenth century. Susannah Wesley (1669–1742), mother of John Wesley, the founder of Methodism (see page 567), agreed. According to her, the first task of a parent toward her children was "to conquer the will, and bring them to an obedient temper." She reported that her babies were "taught to fear the rod, and to cry softly."[5] They were beaten for lying, stealing, disobeying, and quarreling, and forbidden from playing with other neighbor children. Susannah's methods of disciplining her children were probably extreme even in her own day, but they do reflect a broad consensus that children were born with an innately sinful will that parents must overcome.

The Enlightenment produced an enthusiastic new discourse about childhood and child rearing. Starting around 1760, critics called for greater tenderness toward children and proposed imaginative new teaching methods. In addition to supporting foundling homes and urging women to nurse their babies, these new voices ridiculed the practice of swaddling babies and using whaleboned corsets to mold children's bones. Instead of dressing children in miniature versions of adult clothing, critics called for comfortable clothing to allow freedom of movement. Rather than emphasizing original sin, these enlightened voices celebrated the child as an innocent product of nature. They viewed nature as inherently positive, so Enlightenment educators advocated safeguarding and developing children's innate qualities rather than thwarting and suppressing them. Accordingly, they believed the best hopes for a new society, untrammeled by the prejudices of the past, lay in a radical reform of child-rearing techniques.

One of the century's most influential works on child rearing was Jean-Jacques Rousseau's *Emile, or On Education* (1762). Rousseau argued that boys' education should include plenty of fresh air and exercise and that they should be taught practical craft skills in addition to rote book learning. Reacting to what he perceived as the vanity and frivolity of upper-class Parisian women, Rousseau insisted that girls' education focus on their future domestic responsibilities. For Rousseau, women's "nature" destined them solely for a life of marriage and child rearing.

The Spread of Elementary Schools

The availability of education outside the home gradually increased over the early modern period. The wealthy led the way in the sixteenth century with special colleges, often run by Jesuits in Catholic areas. Schools charged specifically with educating children of the common people began to appear in the second half of the seventeenth century. They taught six- to twelve-year-old children basic literacy, religion, and perhaps some arithmetic for the boys and needlework for the girls. The number of such schools expanded in the eighteenth century, although they were never sufficient to educate the majority of the population.

Religion played an important role in the spread of education. From the middle of the seventeenth century, Presbyterian Scotland was convinced that the path to salvation lay in careful study of the Scriptures, and it established an effective network of parish schools for rich and poor alike. The Church of England and the dissenting congregations—Puritans, Presbyterians, Quakers, and so on—established "charity schools" to instruct poor children. The first proponents of universal education, in Prussia, were inspired by the Protestant idea that every believer should be able to read the Bible and by the new idea of raising a population capable of effectively serving the state.

Catholic states pursued their own programs of popular education. In the 1660s, France began setting up charity schools to teach poor children their catechism and prayers as well as reading and writing. These were run by parish priests or by new teaching orders created for this purpose. Enthusiasm for popular education was even greater in the Habsburg empire. Inspired by the expansion of schools in rival Protestant German states, Maria Theresa issued her own compulsory education edict in 1774, imposing five hours of school, five days a week, for all children aged six to twelve.[6] Across Europe some elementary education was becoming a reality, and schools became increasingly significant in the life of the child.

QUICK REVIEW

How did Enlightenment ideas shape attitudes toward childhood and education in the eighteenth century?

| What was life like for children, and how did attitudes toward childhood evolve? | How did increasing literacy and new patterns of consumption affect people's lives? | What role did religion play in eighteenth-century society? | How did the practice of medicine evolve in the eighteenth century? | ✓ LearningCurve Check what you know. |

557

How did increasing literacy and new patterns of consumption affect people's lives?

Chocolate Drinking These Spanish tiles from 1710 illustrate the new practice of preparing and drinking hot chocolate. Originating in the New World, chocolate was one of the many new foods imported to Europe in the wake of the voyages of discovery. The first Spanish chocolate mills opened in the mid-seventeenth century, and consumption of chocolate rapidly increased. The inclusion of these tiles in the decoration of a nobleman's house testifies to public interest in the new drink. (Courtesy, Museu de Ceramica. Photo: Guillem Fernandez-Huerta)

BECAUSE OF THE NEW EFFORTS IN EDUCATION, basic literacy was expanding among the popular classes, whose reading habits centered primarily on religious material but who also began to incorporate more practical and entertaining literature. In addition to reading, people of all classes enjoyed a range of leisure activities including storytelling, fairs, festivals, and sports.

One of the most important developments in European society in the eighteenth century was the emergence of a fledgling consumer culture. Much of the expansion took place among the upper and upper-middle classes, but a boom in cheap reproductions of luxury items also opened doors for people of modest means. This "consumer revolution," as it has been called, created new expectations for comfort, hygiene, and self-expression, thus dramatically changing European daily life in the eighteenth century.

CHAPTER LOCATOR | How did marriage and family life change in the eighteenth century?

Popular Literature

The surge in childhood education in the eighteenth century led to a remarkable growth in literacy between 1600 and 1800. Whereas in 1600 only one male in six was barely literate in France and Scotland, and one in four in England, by 1800 almost nine out of ten Scottish males, two out of three French males (**Map 18.1**), and more than half of English males were literate. In all three countries, the bulk of the jump occurred in the eighteenth century. Women were also increasingly literate, although they lagged behind men.

The growth in literacy promoted growth in reading, and historians have carefully examined what the common people read. While the Bible remained the overwhelming favorite, especially in Protestant countries, short pamphlets known as chapbooks were the staple of popular literature. Printed on the cheapest paper, many chapbooks featured Bible stories, prayers, and the lives of saints and exemplary Christians.

Entertaining, often humorous stories formed a second element of popular literature. Fairy tales, medieval romances, true crime stories, and fantastic adventures were some of the delights that filled the peddler's pack as he approached a village. Some popular literature was highly practical, dealing with rural crafts, household repairs, useful plants, and similar matters. Much lore was stored in almanacs, where calendars listing secular, religious, and astrological events were mixed with agricultural schedules, arcane facts, and jokes. The almanac was highly appreciated even by many in the comfortable classes. In this way, elites still shared some elements of a common culture with the masses.

While it is safe to say that the vast majority of ordinary people did not read the great works of the Enlightenment, they were not immune from the new ideas. Urban working people were exposed to Enlightenment thought through the rumors and gossip that spread through city streets, workshops, markets, and taverns. They also had access to cheap pamphlets that helped translate Enlightenment critiques into ordinary language. Servants, who usually came from rural areas and traveled home periodically, were well situated to transmit ideas from educated employers to the village.

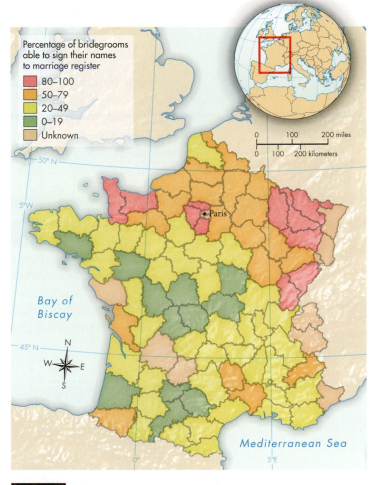

MAP 18.1 ■ Literacy in France, ca. 1789

Literacy rates increased but still varied widely between and within states in eighteenth-century Europe.

> **MAPPING THE PAST**

ANALYZING THE MAP: What trends in French literacy rates does this map reveal? Which regions seem to be ahead? How would you explain the regional variations?

CONNECTIONS: Note the highly variable nature of literacy rates across the country. Why might the rate of literacy be higher closer to the capital city of Paris? Why would some areas have low rates?

| What was life like for children, and how did attitudes toward childhood evolve? | **How did increasing literacy and new patterns of consumption affect people's lives?** | What role did religion play in eighteenth-century society? | How did the practice of medicine evolve in the eighteenth century? | ✔ LearningCurve Check what you know. |

559

Leisure and Recreation

Despite the spread of literacy, the culture of the village remained largely oral rather than written. In the cold, dark winter months, peasant families gathered around the fireplace to sing, tell stories, do craftwork, and keep warm. In some parts of Europe, women would gather together in someone's cottage to chat, sew, spin, and laugh. A favorite recreation of men was drinking and talking with buddies in public places, and it was a sorry village that had no tavern.

Towns and cities offered a wider range of amusements, including fairs, pleasure gardens, theaters, and lending libraries. Leisure activities were another form of consumption marked by growing commercialization. For example, commercial, profit-making spectator sports, including horse races, boxing matches, and bullfights, emerged in this period.

Blood sports, such as bullbaiting and cockfighting, also remained popular with the masses. In bullbaiting, the bull, usually staked on a chain in the courtyard of an inn, was attacked by ferocious dogs for the amusement of the innkeeper's clients. Eventually the maimed and tortured animal was slaughtered by a butcher and sold as meat. In cockfighting, two roosters slashed and clawed each other in a small ring until the victor won—and the loser died.

Popular recreation merged with religious celebration in a variety of festivals and processions throughout the year. The most striking display of these religiously inspired events was **carnival**, a time of reveling and excess in Catholic Europe, especially in Mediterranean countries. Carnival preceded Lent—the forty days of fasting and penitence before Easter—and for a few exceptional days in February or March, a wild release of drinking, masquerading, and dancing

blood sports
▶ Events such as bullbaiting and cockfighting that involved inflicting violence and bloodshed on animals and that were popular with the eighteenth-century European masses.

carnival
▶ The few days of revelry in Catholic countries that preceded Lent and that included drinking, masquerading, dancing, and rowdy spectacles that turned the established order upside down.

A Boxing Match

In this early-eighteenth-century painting, two men spar in a boxing match staged in London for the entertainment of the gathered crowd. (bpk, Berlin/Gemaeldegalerie Alte Meiser, Museumslandschaft Hessen Kassel/Art Resource, NY)

CHAPTER LOCATOR | How did marriage and family life change in the eighteenth century?

reigned. In addition, a combination of plays, processions, and raucous spectacles turned the established order upside down. Peasants dressed as nobles and men as women, and rich masters waited on their servants at the table. This annual holiday gave people a chance to release their pent-up frustrations and aggressions before life returned to the usual pattern of hierarchy and hard work.

In trying to place the vibrant popular culture of the common people in broad perspective, historians have stressed the growing criticism levied against it by the educated elites in the second half of the eighteenth century. These elites, who had previously shared the popular enthusiasm for religious festivals, carnival, drinking in taverns, blood sports, and the like, now tended to see superstition, sin, disorder, and vulgarity in these activities.[7] The resulting attack on popular culture, which was tied to the clergy's efforts to eliminate paganism and superstition, was intensified as an educated public embraced the critical worldview of the Enlightenment.

New Foods and Appetites

At the beginning of the eighteenth century, ordinary men and women depended on grain as fully as they had in the past. Even peasants normally needed to buy some grain for food, and, in full accord with landless laborers and urban workers, they believed in the moral economy and the **just price**. That is, they believed that prices should be "fair," protecting both consumers and producers, and that just prices should be imposed by government decree if necessary. When prices rose above this level, they often took action in the form of bread riots (see Chapter 15, page 448).

The rural poor also ate a quantity of vegetables. Peas and beans were probably the most common. In most regions other vegetables appeared on the tables of the poor in season, primarily cabbages, carrots, and wild greens. Fruit was mostly limited to the summer months. Too precious to drink, milk was used to make cheese and butter, which peasants sold in the market to earn cash for taxes and land rents.

The common people of Europe ate less meat in 1700 than in 1500 because their general standard of living had declined and meat was more expensive. Harsh laws in most European countries reserved the right to hunt and eat game to nobles and large landowners. Few laws were more bitterly resented — or more frequently broken — by ordinary people than those governing hunting.

The diet of small traders and artisans — the people of the towns and cities — was less monotonous than that of the peasantry. Bustling markets provided a substantial variety of meats, vegetables, and fruits, although bread and beans still formed the bulk of such families' diets. Not surprisingly, the diet of the rich was quite different from that of the poor. A truly elegant upper-class dinner consisted of an abundance of rich meat and fish dishes laced with piquant sauces and complemented with sweets, cheeses, and wine in great quantities.

Patterns of food consumption changed markedly as the century progressed. Because of a growth of market gardening, a greater variety of vegetables appeared in towns and cities. This was particularly the case in the Low Countries and England, which pioneered new methods of farming. Introduced into Europe from the Americas, the humble potato provided an excellent new food source, and, after initial resistance, the potato became an important dietary supplement in much of Europe by the end of the century.

just price
▶ The idea that prices should be fair, protecting both consumers and producers, and that they should be imposed by government decree if necessary.

What was life like for children, and how did attitudes toward childhood evolve?

How did increasing literacy and new patterns of consumption affect people's lives?

What role did religion play in eighteenth-century society?

How did the practice of medicine evolve in the eighteenth century?

☑ LearningCurve
Check what you know.

561

The most remarkable dietary change in the eighteenth century was in the consumption of commodities imported from abroad. Originally expensive and rare luxury items, goods like tea, sugar, coffee, chocolate, and tobacco became dietary staples for people of all social classes. Most of the new consumables were produced in European colonies in the Americas. In many cases, the labor of enslaved peoples enabled the expansion in production and drop in prices that allowed such items to spread to the masses.

Why were colonial products so popular? Part of the motivation for consuming these products was a desire to emulate the luxurious lifestyles of the elite. The quickened pace of work in the eighteenth century created new needs for stimulants among working people. With the widespread adoption of these products (which turned out to be mildly to extremely addictive), working people in Europe became increasingly dependent on faraway colonial economies and enslaved labor. Their understanding of daily necessities and how to procure those necessities shifted definitively, linking them to global trade networks they could not comprehend or control.

Toward a Consumer Society

Along with foodstuffs, all manner of other goods increased in variety and number in the eighteenth century. This proliferation led to a growth in consumption and new attitudes toward consumer goods so wide-ranging that some historians have referred to an eighteenth-century **consumer revolution**.[8] The result of this revolution was the birth of a new type of society in which people derived their self-identity as much from their consuming practices as from their working lives and place in the production process. As people gained the opportunity to pick and choose among a new variety of consumer goods, new notions of individuality and self-expression developed. The full emergence of a consumer society did not take place until much later, but its roots lie in the eighteenth century.

Increased demand for consumer goods was not merely an innate response to increased supply. Eighteenth-century merchants cleverly pioneered new techniques to incite demand: they initiated marketing campaigns, opened fancy boutiques with large windows, and advertised the patronage of royal princes and princesses. (See "Picturing the Past: The Fashion Merchant," page 563.) By diversifying their product lines and greatly accelerating the turnover of styles, they seized the reins of fashion from the courtiers who had earlier controlled it. Instead of setting new styles, duchesses and marquises now bowed to the dictates of fashion merchants. (See "Individuals in Society: Rose Bertin, 'Minister of Fashion,'" page 564.) Fashion also extended beyond court circles to touch many more items and social groups.

Clothing was one of the chief indicators of the growth of consumerism. Shrewd entrepreneurs made fashionable clothing seem more desirable, while legions of women entering the textile and needle trades made it ever cheaper. As a result, eighteenth-century western Europe witnessed a dramatic rise in the consumption of clothing, particularly in large cities. Colonial economies again played an important role in lowering the cost of materials, such as cotton and vegetable dyes, largely due to the unpaid toil of enslaved Africans.

Cheaper copies of elite styles made it possible for working people to aspire to follow fashion for the first time. The spread of fashion challenged the traditional

consumer revolution

▶ The wide-ranging growth in consumption and new attitudes toward consumer goods that emerged in the cities of northwestern Europe in the second half of the eighteenth century.

The Fashion Merchant

Well-to-do women spent their mornings preparing their toilettes and receiving visits from close friends and purveyors of various goods and services. In this 1746 painting by François Boucher, a leisured lady has just been coiffed by her hairdresser. Wearing the cape she donned to protect her clothing from the hair powder, she receives a fashion merchant, who displays an array of ribbons and other finery. (Photo12/ARJ)

> PICTURING THE PAST

ANALYZING THE IMAGE: In this painting, which woman is the fashion merchant and which is her client? What are they doing at the moment the picture is painted? How would you characterize the relationship between the two women in this painting?

CONNECTIONS: In what ways does the fashion merchant's attire provide evidence of the consumer revolution of the eighteenth century? Compare this image to the painting of the serving girl (page 550). What contrasting images of the working woman do these two images present?

social order of Europe by blurring the boundaries between social groups and making it harder to distinguish between noble and commoner on the bustling city streets.

Women took the lead in the spread of fashion. Parisian women significantly out-consumed men, acquiring larger and more expensive wardrobes than those of their male counterparts. This was true across the social spectrum; in ribbons,

| What was life like for children, and how did attitudes toward childhood evolve? | How did increasing literacy and new patterns of consumption affect people's lives? | What role did religion play in eighteenth-century society? | How did the practice of medicine evolve in the eighteenth century? | ☑ LearningCurve Check what you know. |

563

One day in 1779, as the French royal family rode in a carriage through the streets of Paris, Queen Marie Antoinette noticed her fashion merchant, Rose Bertin, observing the royal procession. "Ah! There is mademoiselle Bertin," the queen exclaimed, waving her hand. Bertin responded with a curtsy. The king then stood and greeted Bertin, followed by the royal family and their entourage.* The incident shocked the public, for no common merchant had ever received such homage from royalty.

Bertin had come a long way from her humble beginnings. Born in 1747 to a poor family in northern France, she moved to Paris in the 1760s to work as a shop assistant. Bertin eventually opened her own boutique on the fashionable rue Saint-Honoré. In 1775, Bertin received the highest honor of her profession when she was selected by Marie Antoinette as one of her official purveyors.

Based on the queen's patronage and riding the wave of the new consumer revolution, Bertin became one of the most successful entrepreneurs in Europe. Bertin established not only a large clientele but also a reputation for pride and arrogance. She refused to work for non-noble customers, claiming that the orders of the queen and the court required all her attention. She astounded courtiers by referring to her "work" with the queen, as though the two were collaborators rather than absolute monarch and lowly subject. Bertin's close relationship with Marie Antoinette and the fortune the queen spent on her wardrobe hurt the royal family's image. One journalist derided Bertin as a "minister of fashion," whose influence outstripped that of all the others in royal government.

In January 1787, rumors spread through Paris that Bertin had filed for bankruptcy with debts of 2 to 3 million livres (a garment worker's annual salary was around 200 livres). Despite her notoriously high prices and rich clients, this news did not shock Parisians because the nobility's reluctance to pay its debts was equally well known. Bertin somehow held on to her business. Some said she had spread the bankruptcy rumors herself to shame the court into paying her bills.

Bertin remained loyal to the Crown during the tumult of the French Revolution (see Chapter 19) and sent dresses to the queen even after the arrest of the royal family. Fearing for her life, she left France for Germany in 1792 and continued to ply her profession in exile. She returned to France in 1800 and died in 1813, one year before the restoration of the Bourbon monarchy might have renewed her acclaim.†

*Mémoires secrets pour servir à l'histoire de la république des lettres en France, vol. 13, 299, 5 mars 1779 (London: John Adamson, 1785).
†On Rose Bertin, see Clare Haru Crowston, "The Queen and Her 'Minister of Fashion': Gender, Credit and Politics in Pre-Revolutionary France," Gender and History 14, 1 (April 2002): 92–116.

This portrait of Rose Bertin was painted at the height of her popularity in 1780. (Image copyright © The Metropolitan Museum of Art. Image source: Art Resource, NY)

Rose Bertin scandalized public opinion with her self-aggrandizement and ambition, yet history was on her side. She was the first celebrity fashion stylist and one of the first self-made career women to rise from obscurity to fame and fortune based on her talent, taste, and hard work. Her legacy remains in the exalted status of today's top fashion designers and in the dreams of small-town girls hoping to make it in the big city.

QUESTIONS FOR ANALYSIS

1. Why was the relationship between Queen Marie Antoinette and Rose Bertin so troubling for the general public? Why would relations between a queen and a fashion merchant have political implications?
2. Why would someone who sold fashionable clothing and accessories rise to such a prominent position in business and society? What makes fashion so important in the social world?

shoes, gloves, and lace, European working women reaped in the consumer revolution what they had sown in the industrious revolution (see Chapter 17, page 529). There were also new gender distinctions in dress. Previously, noblemen had vied with noblewomen in the magnificence of their apparel; by the end of the eighteenth century men were wearing early versions of the plain dark suit that remains standard male formal wear in the West. This was one more aspect of the increasingly rigid differences drawn between appropriate male and female behavior.

Changes in outward appearances were reflected in inner spaces as new attitudes about privacy and intimate life also emerged. Historians have used notaries' probate inventories to peer into ordinary people's homes. In 1700, the cramped home of a modest family consisted of a few rooms, each of which had multiple functions. In the eighteenth century, families began attributing specific functions to specific rooms. They also began to erect inner barriers within the home to provide small niches in which individuals could seek privacy.

New levels of comfort and convenience accompanied this trend toward more individualized ways of life. In 1700, a meal might be served in a common dish, with each person dipping his or her spoon into the pot. By the end of the eighteenth century, even humble households contained a much greater variety of cutlery and dishes, making it possible for each person to eat from his or her own plate. More books and prints, which also proliferated at lower prices, decorated the shelves and walls. Improvements in glassmaking provided more transparent glass, which allowed daylight to penetrate into gloomy rooms. Cold and smoky hearths were increasingly replaced by more efficient and cleaner coal stoves. Rooms were warmer, better lit, more comfortable, and more personalized, and the spread of street lighting made it safer to travel in cities at night.

Standards of bodily and public hygiene also improved. Public bathhouses, popular across Europe in the Middle Ages, had gradually closed in the early modern period due to concerns over sexual promiscuity and infectious disease. Many Europeans came to fear that immersing the body in hot water would allow harmful elements to enter the skin. From the mid-eighteenth century on, enlightened doctors revised their views and began to urge more frequent bathing. Officials also took measures to improve the cleaning of city streets in which trash, human soil, and animal carcasses were often left to rot.

The scope of the new consumer economy should not be exaggerated. These developments were concentrated in large cities in northwestern Europe and North America. Even in these centers, the elite benefited the most from new modes of life. This was not yet the society of mass consumption that emerged toward the end of the nineteenth century with the full expansion of the Industrial Revolution. The eighteenth century did, however, lay the foundations for one of the most distinctive features of modern Western life: societies based on the consumption of goods and services obtained through the market in which individuals form their identities and self-worth through the goods they consume.

QUICK REVIEW <

What connections existed between European overseas colonies and the emergence of the new European consumer economy?

What was life like for children, and how did attitudes toward childhood evolve?

How did increasing literacy and new patterns of consumption affect people's lives?

What role did religion play in eighteenth-century society?

How did the practice of medicine evolve in the eighteenth century?

 LearningCurve
Check what you know.

What role did religion play in eighteenth-century society?

Hogarth's Satirical View of the Church William Hogarth (1697–1764) was one of the foremost satirical artists of his day. This image mocks a London Methodist meeting, where the congregation swoons in enthusiasm over the preacher's sermon. The woman in the foreground giving birth to rabbits refers to a hoax perpetrated in 1726 by a servant named Mary Tofts; the gullibility of those who believed Tofts is likened to that of the Methodist congregation. (The Israel Museum, Jerusalem, Israel/Vera & Arturo Schwarz Collection of Dada and Surrealist Art/The Bridgeman Art Library)

THOUGH THE CRITICAL SPIRIT of the Enlightenment made great inroads in the eighteenth century, the majority of ordinary men and women, especially those in rural areas, retained strong religious faith. The church promised salvation, and it gave comfort in the face of sorrow and death. Religion also remained strong because it was embedded in local traditions and everyday social experience.

Yet the popular religion of village Europe was also enmeshed in a larger world of church hierarchies and state power. These powerful outside forces sought to regulate religious life at the local level. Their efforts created tensions that helped set the scene for vigorous religious revivals in Protestant Germany and England as well as in Catholic France.

CHAPTER LOCATOR | How did marriage and family life change in the eighteenth century?

Church Hierarchy

In the eighteenth century, religious faith not only endured but grew in many parts of Europe. The local parish church remained the focal point of religious devotion and community cohesion. Neighbors came together in church for baptisms, marriages, funerals, and special events. Priests and parsons kept the community records, distributed charity, looked after orphans, and provided primary education to the common people. Thus the parish church was woven into the very fabric of community life.

While the parish church remained central to the community, it was also subject to greater control from the state. In Protestant areas, princes and monarchs headed the official church, selecting personnel and imposing detailed rules. Clergy of the official church dominated education, and followers of other faiths suffered religious and civil discrimination.

Catholic monarchs in this period also took greater control of religious matters in their kingdoms, weakening papal authority. In both Spain and Portugal, the Catholic Church was closely associated with the state, a legacy of the long internal reconquista and sixteenth-century imperial conquests overseas. In the eighteenth century, the Spanish crown took firm control of ecclesiastical appointments.

France went even further in establishing a national Catholic Church, known as the Gallican Church. Louis XIV's expulsion of Protestants in 1685 was accompanied by an insistence on the king's prerogative to choose and control bishops and issue laws regarding church affairs. Catholicism gained new ground in the Holy Roman Empire with the conversion of a number of Protestant princes and with successful missionary work by Catholic orders among the populace. While it could not eradicate Protestantism altogether, the Habsburg monarchy successfully consolidated Catholicism as a pillar of its political control.

Protestant Revival

Official efforts to reform state churches in the eighteenth century were confronted by a wave of religious enthusiasm from below. By the late seventeenth century, the vast transformations of the Protestant Reformation were complete and had been widely adopted in most Protestant churches. Medieval practices of idolatry, saint worship, and pageantry were abolished; stained-glass windows were smashed and murals whitewashed. Yet many official Protestant churches had settled into a smug complacency. This, along with the growth of state power and bureaucracy in local parishes, threatened to eclipse one of the Reformation's main goals—to bring all believers closer to God.

In the Reformation heartland, one concerned German minister wrote that the Lutheran Church "had become paralyzed in forms of dead doctrinal conformity" and badly needed a return to its original inspiration.[9] His voice was one of many that prepared and then guided a Protestant revival that succeeded because it answered the intense but increasingly unsatisfied needs of common people.

The Protestant revival began in Germany in the late seventeenth century. It was known as **Pietism** (PIE-uh-tih-zum), and three aspects helped explain its powerful appeal. First, Pietism called for a warm, emotional religion that everyone could experience. Enthusiasm—in prayer, in worship, in preaching, in life itself—was the key concept.

Pietism
► A Protestant revival movement in early-eighteenth-century Germany and Scandinavia that emphasized a warm and emotional religion, the priesthood of all believers, and the power of Christian rebirth in everyday affairs.

| What was life like for children, and how did attitudes toward childhood evolve? | How did increasing literacy and new patterns of consumption affect people's lives? | **What role did religion play in eighteenth-century society?** | How did the practice of medicine evolve in the eighteenth century? | ✓ LearningCurve Check what you know. |

567

Second, Pietism reasserted the earlier radical stress on the priesthood of all believers, thereby reducing the gulf between official clergy and Lutheran laity. Pietists also believed in the practical power of Christian rebirth in everyday affairs. Reborn Christians were expected to lead good, moral lives and to come from all social classes.

Pietism soon spread through the German-speaking lands and to Scandinavia. It also had a major impact on John Wesley (1703–1791), who served as the catalyst for popular religious revival in England. When Wesley went to Oxford University to prepare for the clergy, he mapped a fanatically earnest "scheme of religion." At Oxford, he organized a Holy Club for similarly minded students, who were soon known contemptuously as **Methodists** because they were so methodical in their devotion. Yet like the young Martin Luther, Wesley remained intensely troubled about his own salvation even after his ordination as an Anglican priest in 1728.

Wesley's anxieties related to grave problems of the faith in England. The government shamelessly used the Church of England to provide favorites with high-paying jobs. Both church and state officials failed to respond to the spiritual needs of the people, and services and sermons had settled into an uninspiring routine. Enlightenment skepticism was making inroads among the educated classes, and deism—a belief in God but not in organized religion—was becoming popular.

Wesley's inner search in the 1730s was deeply affected by his encounter with Moravian Pietists, whose inspirational example and spiritual counseling led to a mystical, emotional "conversion" in 1738. This emotional experience resolved Wesley's intellectual doubts about the possibility of his own salvation. He was convinced that any person, no matter how poor or uneducated, might have a similarly heartfelt conversion and gain the same blessed assurance. He took the good news to the people, traveling some 225,000 miles by horseback and preaching more than forty thousand sermons between 1750 and 1790. Because existing churches were often overcrowded and the church-state establishment was hostile, Wesley preached in open fields. People came in large numbers. Of critical importance was Wesley's rejection of Calvinist predestination—the doctrine of salvation granted to only a select few. Instead, he preached that all men and women who earnestly sought salvation might be saved. It was a message of hope and joy, of free will and universal salvation.

Wesley's ministry eventually resulted in a new denomination. And just as Wesley had been inspired by the Pietist revival in Germany, so evangelicals in the Church of England and the old dissenting groups now followed Wesley's example of preaching to all people, giving impetus to an even broader awakening among the lower classes. Thus, in Protestant countries, religion continued to be a vital force in the lives of the people.

Catholic Piety

Religion also flourished in Catholic Europe around 1700, but there were important differences from Protestant practice. First, the visual contrast was striking; baroque art still lavished rich and emotionally exhilarating figures and images on Catholic churches, just as most Protestants had removed theirs during the Reformation. People in Catholic Europe on the whole participated more actively in formal worship than did Protestants.

The tremendous popular strength of religion in Catholic countries can in part be explained by the church's integral role in community life and popular culture.

Methodists

▶ Members of a Protestant revival movement started by John Wesley, so called because they were so methodical in their devotion.

CHAPTER LOCATOR | How did marriage and family life change in the eighteenth century?

In addition to the great processional days—such as Palm Sunday, the joyful re-enactment of Jesus's triumphal entry into Jerusalem—each parish had its own saints' days, processions, and pilgrimages. Millions of Catholic men and women also joined religious associations, known as confraternities, where they participated in prayer and religious services and collected funds for poor relief and members' funerals. The Reformation had largely eliminated such festivities in Protestant areas.

Catholicism had its own version of the Pietist revivals that shook Protestant Europe. **Jansenism** originated with Cornelius Jansen (1585–1638), bishop of Ypres in the Spanish Netherlands, who called for a return to the austere early Christianity of Saint Augustine. In contrast to the worldly Jesuits, Jansen emphasized the heavy weight of original sin and accepted the doctrine of predestination. Although outlawed by papal and royal edicts as Calvinist heresy, Jansenism attracted Catholic followers eager for religious renewal, particularly among the French. Many members of France's urban elite, especially judicial nobles and some parish priests, became known for their Jansenist piety and spiritual devotion. Such stern religious values encouraged the judiciary's increasing opposition to the French monarchy in the second half of the eighteenth century. Among the urban poor, a different strain of Jansenism took hold. Prayer meetings brought men and women together in ecstatic worship, and some participants fell into convulsions and spoke in tongues.

Jansenism
▶ A sect of Catholicism originating with Cornelius Jansen that emphasized the heavy weight of original sin and accepted the doctrine of predestination; it was outlawed as heresy by the pope.

Marginal Beliefs and Practices

In the countryside, many peasants continued to hold religious beliefs that were marginal to the Christian faith altogether, often of obscure or even pagan origin. The ordinary person combined strong Christian faith with a wealth of time-honored superstitions.

Inspired initially by the fervor of the Reformation era, then by the critical rationalism of the Enlightenment, religious and secular authorities sought increasingly to "purify" popular spirituality. The severity of the attack on popular belief varied widely by country and region. Where authorities pursued purification vigorously, as in Austria under Joseph II, pious peasants saw only an incomprehensible attack on age-old faith and drew back in anger. Their reaction dramatized the growing tension between the attitudes of educated elites and the common people.

It was in this era of growing intellectual disdain for popular beliefs that the persecution of witches slowly came to an end across Europe. Common people in the countryside continued to fear the Devil and his helpers, but the elite increasingly dismissed such fears and refused to prosecute suspected witches. The last witch was executed in England in 1682, the same year France prohibited witchcraft trials. By the late eighteenth century, most European states and their colonies had followed suit.

QUICK REVIEW ◀

What were the patterns of popular religion, and how did they interact with the worldview of the educated public and their Enlightenment ideals?

What was life like for children, and how did attitudes toward childhood evolve?

How did increasing literacy and new patterns of consumption affect people's lives?

What role did religion play in eighteenth-century society?

How did the practice of medicine evolve in the eighteenth century?

☑ LearningCurve
Check what you know.

How did the practice of medicine evolve in the eighteenth century?

The Wonderful Effects of the New Inoculation! The talented caricaturist James Gillray satirized widespread anxieties about the smallpox vaccination in this lively image. The discoveries of Edward Jenner a few years prior to Gillray's caricature had led to the adoption of a safer vaccine derived from cowpox. The artist mocks this breakthrough by showing cows bursting from the boils supposedly brought on by the vaccine. (Private Collection/The Bridgeman Art Library)

ALTHOUGH SIGNIFICANT BREAKTHROUGHS IN MEDICAL SCIENCE would not come until the middle and late nineteenth century, the Enlightenment inspired a great deal of research and experimentation in the 1700s. Medical practitioners greatly increased in number, although their techniques did not differ much from those of previous generations. Care of the sick in this era was the domain of several competing groups: traditional healers, apothecaries (pharmacists), physicians, surgeons, and midwives. From the Middle Ages through the seventeenth century, both men and women were medical practitioners. Because women were generally denied admission to medical colleges, however, the range of medical activities open to them was restricted. In the eighteenth century, women's traditional roles as midwives and healers eroded even further.

Faith Healing and General Practice

During the course of the eighteenth century, traditional healers remained active, drawing on folk knowledge about the curative properties of roots, herbs, and other plants. Faith healing also remained popular, especially in the countryside. In

CHAPTER LOCATOR | How did marriage and family life change in the eighteenth century?

570 CHAPTER 18 LIFE IN THE ERA OF EXPANSION

the larger towns and cities, apothecaries sold a vast number of herbs, drugs, and patent medicines.

Physicians, who were invariably men, were apprenticed in their teens to practicing physicians for several years of on-the-job training. This training was then rounded out with hospital work or some university courses. Because their training was expensive, physicians came mainly from prosperous families and they usually concentrated on urban patients from similar social backgrounds. Nevertheless, even poor people spent hard-won resources to seek treatment for their loved ones. Physicians in the eighteenth century were increasingly willing to experiment with new methods, but time-honored practices lay heavily on them.

Improvements in Surgery

Long considered to be craftsmen comparable to butchers and barbers, surgeons began studying anatomy seriously and improved their art in the eighteenth century. With endless opportunities to practice, army surgeons on gory battlefields led the way.

The eighteenth-century surgeon (and patient) labored in the face of incredible difficulties. Almost all operations were performed without painkillers. Many patients died from the agony and shock of such operations. Surgery was also performed in utterly unsanitary conditions because there was no knowledge of bacteriology and the nature of infection. The simplest wound treated by a surgeon could fester and lead to death.

Midwifery

Midwives continued to deliver the overwhelming majority of babies throughout the eighteenth century. Trained initially by another woman practitioner—and regulated by a guild in many cities—the midwife primarily assisted in labor and delivering babies. She also treated female problems, such as irregular menstrual cycles, breast-feeding difficulties, infertility, and venereal disease, and ministered to small children.

The midwife orchestrated labor and birth in a woman's world, where friends and relatives assisted the pregnant woman in the familiar surroundings of her own home. The male surgeon rarely entered this female world because most births, then as now, were normal and spontaneous. After the invention of forceps became publicized in 1734, surgeon-physicians used their monopoly over this and other instruments to seek lucrative new business. Attacking midwives as ignorant and dangerous, they sought to undermine faith in midwives and persuaded growing numbers of wealthy women of the superiority of their services.

Research suggests that women practitioners successfully defended much but not all of their practice in the eighteenth century. One enterprising French midwife, Madame du Coudray, wrote a widely used textbook, *Manual on the Art of Childbirth* (1757), in order to address complaints about incompetent midwives. She then secured royal financing for her campaign to teach birthing techniques. Du Coudray traveled all over France using a life-size model of the female torso and fetus to help teach illiterate women.

Women also continued to perform almost all nursing. Female religious orders ran many hospitals, and at-home nursing was almost exclusively the province of

What was life like for children, and how did attitudes toward childhood evolve?

How did increasing literacy and new patterns of consumption affect people's lives?

What role did religion play in eighteenth-century society?

How did the practice of medicine evolve in the eighteenth century?

LearningCurve
Check what you know.

571

French midwife Madame du Coudray used this life-size model of a female torso and fetus to teach illiterate women about childbirth. (Musée Flaubert d'histoire de la médecine, Rouen)

women. Although they were excluded from the growing ranks of formally trained and authorized practitioners, women continued to perform the bulk of informal medical care.

The Conquest of Smallpox

Experimentation and the intensified search for solutions to human problems led to some real advances in medicine after 1750. The eighteenth century's greatest medical triumph was the eradication of smallpox. With the progressive decline of bubonic plague, smallpox became the most terrible of the infectious diseases, and it is estimated that 60 million Europeans died of it in the eighteenth century.

The first step in the conquest of this killer in Europe came in the early eighteenth century. An English aristocrat, Lady Mary Wortley Montagu, learned about the long-established practice of smallpox inoculation in the Muslim lands of western Asia while her husband was serving as British ambassador to the Ottoman Empire. She had her own son successfully inoculated with the pus from a smallpox victim and was instrumental in spreading the practice in England after her return in 1722. But inoculation was risky and was widely condemned because about one person in fifty died from it. In addition, people who had been inoculated were infectious and often spread the disease.

While the practice of inoculation with the smallpox virus was refined over the century, the crucial breakthrough was made by Edward Jenner (1749–1823), a talented country doctor. His starting point was the countryside belief that dairymaids who had contracted cowpox did not get smallpox. Cowpox produces sores that resemble those of smallpox, but the disease is mild and is not contagious.

For eighteen years, Jenner practiced a kind of Baconian science, carefully collecting data. Finally, in 1796, he performed his first vaccination on a young boy using matter taken from a milkmaid with cowpox. After performing more success-

CHAPTER LOCATOR | How did marriage and family life change in the eighteenth century?

ful vaccinations, Jenner published his findings in 1798. The new method of treatment spread rapidly, and smallpox soon declined to the point of disappearance in Europe and then throughout the world.

What were the most significant changes in the practice of medicine during the eighteenth century?

 **LOOKING BACK LOOKING AHEAD** The fundamental patterns of life in early modern Europe remained very much the same up to the eighteenth century. The vast majority of people lived in the countryside and followed age-old rhythms of seasonal labor in the fields and farmyard. The daily life of a peasant in 1700 would have been familiar to his ancestors in the 1400s.

And yet, the economic changes inaugurated in the late seventeenth century—intensive agriculture, cottage industry, the industrious revolution, and colonial expansion—contributed to the profound social and cultural transformation of daily life in eighteenth-century Europe. Men and women of the laboring classes, especially in the cities, experienced change in many facets of their daily lives: in loosened community controls over sex and marriage, rising literacy rates, new goods and ways of utilizing space, and a wave of religious piety that challenged traditional orthodoxies. Both their age-old cultural practices and new religious fervor were met with mounting disbelief and ridicule by the educated classes in a period of increased distance between popular and elite culture.

Economic, social, and cultural change would culminate in the late eighteenth century with the outbreak of revolution in the Americas and Europe. Initially led by the elite, political upheavals relied on the enthusiastic participation of the poor and their desire for greater inclusion in the life of the nation. Such movements also encountered resistance from the common people when revolutionaries trampled on their religious faith. For many observers, contemporaries and historians alike, the transformations of the eighteenth century constituted a fulcrum between the old world of hierarchy and tradition and the modern world with its claims to equality and freedom.

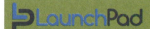

ONLINE DOCUMENT PROJECT

The Inner Life of the Individual

How did the increasing emphasis on the inner life and development of the individual in the eighteenth century find expression in the art of the period?

Keeping the question above in mind, analyze a series of paintings by Jean-Baptiste-Siméon Chardin that depict various aspects of daily life and reveal the era's increased attention to individual emotion and development. *See inside the front cover to learn more.*

| What was life like for children, and how did attitudes toward childhood evolve? | How did increasing literacy and new patterns of consumption affect people's lives? | What role did religion play in eighteenth-century society? | How did the practice of medicine evolve in the eighteenth century? | ✓ **LearningCurve** Check what you know. |

CHAPTER 18 STUDY GUIDE

STEP 1 — GET STARTED ONLINE

✓ **LearningCurve**

Now that you've read the chapter, make it stick by completing the LearningCurve activity.

STEP 2 — EXPLAIN WHY IT MATTERS

Put your reading into practice. Identify each term below, and then explain why it matters in Western history.

TERM	WHO OR WHAT & WHEN	WHY IT MATTERS
community controls (p. 551)		
charivari (p. 551)		
illegitimacy explosion (p. 551)		
wet-nursing (p. 555)		
blood sports (p. 560)		
carnival (p. 560)		
just price (p. 561)		
consumer revolution (p. 562)		
Pietism (p. 567)		
Methodists (p. 568)		
Jansenism (p. 569)		

STEP 3 — MOVE BEYOND THE BASICS

To demonstrate a more advanced understanding of the major trends in European social and cultural life in the Age of Expansion, fill in the chart below with descriptions of social and cultural developments in four key areas: marriage and family life, childhood and education, popular culture and consumerism, and religious life. How did the demographic and economic developments you studied in Chapter 17 shape the social and cultural developments you learned about in this chapter?

	Developments
Marriage and family life	
Childhood and education	
Popular culture and consumerism	
Religious life	

STEP 4 PUT IT ALL TOGETHER Now, take a step back and try to explain the big picture. Remember to use specific examples from the chapter in your answers.

MARRIAGE, FAMILY, AND CHILDHOOD

▶ How did social and economic changes contribute to new patterns of marriage and illegitimacy in the eighteenth century?

▶ Why did states become more involved in education in the eighteenth century?

POPULAR CULTURE AND CONSUMERISM

▶ How did the growth of literacy alter popular culture?

▶ How did the emergence of a culture of consumption change notions of individuality and self-expression?

RELIGIOUS AUTHORITY AND BELIEFS

▶ What role did the state play in eighteenth-century religion?

▶ What explains the emergence of eighteenth-century religious revival movements? What kinds of changes in European religious life did revivalists hope to spark?

MAKE CONNECTIONS

▶ Compare and contrast European family life in 1600 and 1800. What had changed? What had stayed the same?

▶ What connections can you make between contemporary social and cultural norms and the social and cultural developments and trends outlined in this chapter?

> **IN YOUR OWN WORDS**

Imagine that you must give an oral report to the class answering the following question: **How and why did daily life in Europe change in the eighteenth century?** What would be the most important points and why?

19
REVOLUTIONS IN POLITICS

1775–1815

> **What led to the great revolutions of the late eighteenth and early nineteenth centuries, and how did these revolutions change over time?**

Chapter 19 examines the great wave of revolution that rocked both sides of the Atlantic Ocean in the last decades of the eighteenth century. The revolutionary era began in North America in 1775. Then, in 1789, France became the leading revolutionary nation. It established first a constitutional monarchy, then a radical republic, and finally a new empire under Napoleon that would last until 1815. Inspired both by the ideals of the Revolution on the continent and by their own experiences and desires, the slaves of Saint-Domingue rose up in 1791. Their rebellion would eventually lead to the creation of the new independent nation of Haiti in 1804. In Europe and its colonies abroad, the age of modern politics was born.

LearningCurve
After reading the chapter, use LearningCurve to retain what you've read.

Life in Revolutionary France. On the eve of the French Revolution, angry crowds like this one gathered in Paris to protest the high-handed actions of the royal government. (Musée de la Ville de Paris, Musée Carnavalet, Paris, France/Giraudon/The Bridgeman Art Library)

> What were the factors behind the revolutions of the late eighteenth century?

> Why and how did American colonists forge a new, independent nation?

> How did the events of 1789 result in a constitutional monarchy in France?

> Why and how did the French Revolution take a radical turn?

> Why did Napoleon Bonaparte assume control of France and much of Europe?

> How did slave revolt on colonial Saint-Domingue lead to the independent nation of Haiti?

What were the factors behind the revolutions of the late eighteenth century?

THE ORIGINS OF THE LATE-EIGHTEENTH-CENTURY REVOLUTIONS in British North America, France, and Haiti were complex. No one cause lay behind them, nor was revolution inevitable or foreordained. However, certain important factors helped set the stage for reform. Among them were fundamental social and economic changes and political crises that eroded state authority. Another significant cause of revolutionary fervor was the impact of political ideas derived from the Enlightenment. Perhaps most important, financial crises generated by war expenses brought European states to their knees and allowed abstract discussions of reform to become pressing realities.

Social Change

Eighteenth-century European society was legally divided into groups with special privileges, such as the nobility and the clergy, and groups with special burdens, such as the peasantry. Nobles, the largest landowners, enjoyed exemption from direct taxation as well as exclusive rights to hunt game, carry swords, and wear gold ribbon in their clothing. In most countries, various middle-class groups enjoyed privileges that allowed them to monopolize all sorts of economic activity. Poor peasants and urban laborers, who constituted the vast majority of the population, bore the brunt of taxation and were excluded from the world of privilege.

Traditional prerogatives for elite groups persisted in societies undergoing dramatic and destabilizing change. Europe's population rose rapidly after 1750, and its cities and towns swelled in size. Inflation kept pace with population growth, making it ever more difficult to find affordable food and living space. While the poor struggled with rising prices, investors grew rich from the spread of manufacture in the countryside and overseas trade. Old distinctions between landed aristocracy and city merchants began to fade as enterprising nobles put money into trade and as rising middle-class bureaucrats and merchants purchased landed estates and noble titles. Marriages between proud nobles and wealthy, educated commoners (called the *bourgeoisie* [boor-ZJWAH-zee] in France) served both groups' interests, and a mixed-caste elite began to take shape. In the context of these changes, ancient privileges seemed to pose an intolerable burden to many observers.

Another social change involved the racial regimes established in European colonies to legitimize and protect slavery. By the late eighteenth century, European law accepted that only Africans and people of African descent were subject to slavery. Even free people of color—a term for nonslaves of African or mixed African-European descent—were subject to special laws restricting their rights.

CHAPTER LOCATOR | **What were the factors behind the revolutions of the late eighteenth century?** | Why and how did American colonists forge a new, independent nation?

1775–1783 – American Revolution	**1793–1794** – Robespierre's Reign of Terror
1786–1789 – Height of French monarchy's financial crisis	**1794** – Robespierre deposed and executed; France abolishes slavery in all territories
1789 – Ratification of U.S. Constitution; storming of the Bastille; feudalism abolished in France	**1794–1799** – Thermidorian reaction
1789–1799 – French Revolution	**1799–1815** – Napoleonic era
1790 – Burke publishes *Reflections on the Revolution in France*	**1804** – Haitian republic declares independence
1791 – Slave insurrection in Saint-Domingue	**1812** – Napoleon invades Russia
1792 – Wollstonecraft publishes *A Vindication of the Rights of Woman*	**1814–1815** – Napoleon defeated and exiled
1793 – Execution of Louis XVI	

Racial privilege conferred a new dimension of entitlement on Europeans in the colonies. The contradiction between slavery and the Enlightenment ideals of liberty and equality was all too evident to the enslaved and free people of color.

Growing Demands for Liberty and Equality

In addition to destabilizing social changes, the ideals of liberty and equality helped fuel revolutions in the Atlantic world. What did these concepts mean to eighteenth-century people, and why were they so radical and revolutionary in their day?

The call for liberty was first of all a call for individual human rights. Before the revolutionary period, even the most enlightened monarchs believed they needed to regulate what people wrote and believed. Opposing this long-standing practice, supporters of the cause of individual liberty (who became known as "liberals" in the early nineteenth century) demanded freedom to worship according to the dictates of their consciences, an end to censorship, and freedom from arbitrary laws and from judges who simply obeyed orders from the government.

The call for liberty was also a call for a new kind of government. Reformers believed that the people had sovereignty—that is, that the people alone had the authority to make laws limiting an individual's freedom of action. In practice, this system of government meant choosing legislators who represented the people and were accountable to them. Monarchs might retain their thrones, but their rule should be constrained by the will of the people.

Equality was a more ambiguous idea. Eighteenth-century liberals argued that, in theory, all citizens should have identical rights and liberties and that the

| How did the events of 1789 result in a constitutional monarchy in France? | Why and how did the French Revolution take a radical turn? | Why did Napoleon Bonaparte assume control of France and much of Europe? | How did slave revolt on colonial Saint-Domingue lead to the independent nation of Haiti? | ✓ **LearningCurve**
Check what you know. |

579

nobility had no right to special privileges based on birth. However, they accepted a number of distinctions. First, they generally believed that equality between men and women was neither practical nor desirable. Second, few questioned the inequality between blacks and whites.

Finally, liberals never believed that everyone should be equal economically. Great differences in fortune between rich and poor were perfectly acceptable. The essential point was that every free white male should have a legally equal chance at economic gain. However limited they appear to modern eyes, these demands for liberty and equality were revolutionary given that a privileged elite had long existed with little opposition.

The two most important Enlightenment references for late-eighteenth-century liberals were John Locke and the baron de Montesquieu (see Chapter 16). Locke maintained that England's long political tradition rested on "the rights of Englishmen" and on representative government through Parliament. He argued that if a government oversteps its proper function of protecting the natural rights of life, liberty, and private property, it becomes a tyranny. Montesquieu was also inspired by English constitutional history and the Glorious Revolution, which placed sovereignty in Parliament (see Chapter 15, page 477). He, too, believed that powerful "intermediary groups" offered the best defense of liberty against despotism.

Revolutions thus began with aspirations for equality and liberty among the social elite. Soon, however, dissenting voices emerged as some revolutionaries became frustrated with the limitations of liberal notions of equality and liberty and clamored for a more complete realization of these concepts. Depending on location, their demands included political rights for women and free people of color, the emancipation of slaves, and government regulations to reduce economic inequality. The age of revolution was thus marked by sharp conflicts over how far reform should go once it was initiated.

The Seven Years' War

The roots of revolutionary ideas could be found in the writings of Locke or Montesquieu, but it was by no means inevitable that their ideas would result in revolution. Instead, events—political, economic, and military—created crises that opened the door for radical action. One of the most important was the global conflict known as the Seven Years' War (1756–1763).

The war's battlefields stretched from central Europe to India to North America, pitting a new alliance of England and Prussia against the French and Austrians. Its origins were in conflicts left unresolved at the end of the War of the Austrian Succession in 1748 (see Chapter 16, page 507). In central Europe, Austria's Maria Theresa vowed to win back Silesia, which Prussia took in the war of succession, and to crush Prussia, thereby re-establishing the Habsburgs' traditional leadership in German affairs. By the end of the Seven Years' War, Maria Theresa had almost succeeded, but Prussia survived with its boundaries intact.

Unresolved tensions also lingered in North America, particularly regarding the border between the French and British colonies. The encroachment of English settlers into territory claimed by the French in the Ohio Valley resulted in skirmishes that soon became war. French forces achieved major victories until 1758, but the tide of the conflict turned when the British diverted resources from the war in Europe.

CHAPTER LOCATOR | **What were the factors behind the revolutions of the late eighteenth century?** | Why and how did American colonists forge a new, independent nation?

North America, 1763

Territorial claims
- British, 1755
- Additional British, 1763
- French, 1763
- Spanish, 1763
- Russian, 1763

ALASKA

ROCKY MOUNTAINS

HUDSON'S BAY COMPANY

Hudson Bay

QUEBEC

French fishing rights

THIRTEEN COLONIES

New York

Proclamation Line of 1763

LOUISIANA

NEW SPAIN

New Orleans

ATLANTIC OCEAN

PACIFIC OCEAN

Gulf of Mexico

CUBA

SAINT-DOMINGUE

GUADELOUPE (Fr.)

JAMAICA

MARTINIQUE (Fr.)

Caribbean Sea

BELIZE

MOSQUITO COAST

NEW GRANADA

0 400 800 mi.
0 400 800 km

India, 1767

- British claims, 1767

INDIA

BENGAL
Calcutta

Arabian Sea

Bay of Bengal

Madras

Pondicherry (Fr.)

0 250 500 mi.
0 250 500 km

ATLANTIC OCEAN

0 250 500 miles
0 250 500 kilometers

Europe, 1763

- Allies: Austria, France, Russia, Saxony, Spain, Sweden
- Allies: Great Britain, Portugal, Prussia

SWEDEN

RUSSIA

GREAT BRITAIN

London

North Sea

Baltic Sea

Danzig

PRUSSIA

PRUSSIA

Berlin

SAXONY

POLAND-LITHUANIA

Paris

Prague

FRANCE

Buda Pest

AUSTRIAN EMPIRE

PORTUGAL

Madrid

SPAIN

Lisbon

Rome

Adriatic Sea

OTTOMAN EMPIRE

Mediterranean Sea

The Seven Years' War, 1756–1763

- Main areas of conflict

MAP 19.1 ■ European Claims in North America and India Before and After the Seven Years' War, 1755–1763

As a result of the war, France lost its territories in North America and India. In an effort to avoid conflicts with Native Americans living in the newly conquered territory, the British government in 1763 prohibited colonists from settling west of the Appalachian Mountains. One of the few remaining French colonies in the Americas, Saint-Domingue was the most profitable plantation colony in the New World.

British victory on all colonial fronts was ratified in the 1763 Treaty of Paris. Canada and all French territory east of the Mississippi River passed to Britain, and France ceded Louisiana to Spain as compensation for Spain's loss of Florida to Britain. France also gave up most of its holdings in India, opening the way to British dominance on the Indian subcontinent (**Map 19.1**).

By 1763, Britain had become the leading European power in both trade and empire, but such power came at a tremendous cost in war debt. France emerged from the conflict humiliated and broke, but with its profitable Caribbean colonies intact. In the aftermath of war, both British and French governments had to raise taxes to repay loans, raising a storm of protest and demands for fundamental reform. The seeds of revolutionary conflict in the Atlantic world were thus sown.

QUICK REVIEW

How did eighteenth-century social and intellectual developments help set the stage for the revolutionary era?

| How did the events of 1789 result in a constitutional monarchy in France? | Why and how did the French Revolution take a radical turn? | Why did Napoleon Bonaparte assume control of France and much of Europe? | How did slave revolt on colonial Saint-Domingue lead to the independent nation of Haiti? | ☑ **LearningCurve** Check what you know. |

> Why and how did American colonists forge a new, independent nation?

Commemorative Teapot Manufacturers were quick to bring products to the market celebrating weighty political events, like this British teapot heralding "Stamp Act Repeal'd." By purchasing such items, ordinary people could champion political causes of the day and bring public affairs into their private lives. (Courtesy of the Peabody Essex Museum, Salem, Massachusetts)

INCREASED TAXES WERE A CRUCIAL FACTOR behind colonial protests in the New World, where the era of liberal political revolution began. After revolting against their home country, the thirteen mainland colonies of British North America succeeded in establishing a new unified government. In founding a government based on liberal principles, the Americans set an example that would have a forceful impact on France and its colonies.

The Origins of the Revolution

The high cost of the Seven Years' War doubled the British national debt. Anticipating further expenses to defend newly conquered territories, the government in London broke with a tradition of loose colonial oversight and announced that they would maintain a large army in North America and tax the colonies directly. In 1765, Parliament passed the Stamp Act, which levied taxes on a long list of commercial and legal documents, diplomas, newspapers, almanacs, and playing cards.

These measures seemed perfectly reasonable to the British: a much heavier stamp tax already existed in Britain, and proceeds from the tax were to fund the defense of the colonies. Nonetheless, the colonists vigorously protested the Stamp Act by rioting and by boycotting British goods. Thus Parliament reluctantly repealed it.

This dispute raised important political questions. To what extent could the British government reassert its power while limiting the authority of elected colonial bodies? Who had the right to make laws for Americans? The British government replied that Americans were represented in Parliament, albeit indirectly (like most British people), and that Parliament ruled throughout the empire. Many

CHAPTER LOCATOR

What were the factors behind the revolutions of the late eighteenth century?

Why and how did American colonists forge a new, independent nation?

582 CHAPTER 19
REVOLUTIONS IN POLITICS

Americans felt otherwise. Thus British colonial administration and parliamentary supremacy came to appear as unacceptable threats to existing American liberties.

Americans' resistance to these threats was fed by the great degree of independence they had long enjoyed. In British North America, unlike in England and Europe, no powerful established church existed, and religious freedom was taken for granted. Colonial assemblies made the important laws. Also, the right to vote was much more widespread than in England. Moreover, greater political equality was matched by greater social and economic equality, at least for the free white population.

In 1773, disputes over taxes and representation flared up again. Under the Tea Act of that year, the British government permitted the East India Company to ship tea from China directly to its agents in the colonies rather than through London middlemen, who sold to independent merchants in the colonies. Thus the company secured a profitable monopoly on the tea trade, and colonial merchants were excluded.

In protest, Boston men disguised as Native Americans staged a rowdy protest (later called the Boston Tea Party) by boarding East India Company ships and throwing tea from them into the harbor. In response, the so-called Coercive Acts of 1774 closed the port of Boston, curtailed local elections, and expanded the royal governor's power. County conventions in Massachusetts urged that such measures be "rejected as the attempts of a wicked administration to enslave America." Other colonial assemblies joined in the denunciations. In September 1774, the First Continental Congress met in Philadelphia. The more radical members of this assembly argued successfully against concessions to the English crown. The British Parliament also rejected compromise, and in April 1775, fighting between colonial and British troops began at Lexington and Concord.

Independence from Britain

As fighting spread, the colonists moved slowly toward open calls for independence. The uncompromising attitude of the British government and its use of German mercenaries did much to dissolve loyalties to the home country and to unite the separate colonies. *Common Sense* (1775), a brilliant attack by the recently arrived English radical Thomas Paine (1737–1809), also mobilized public opinion in favor of independence.

On July 4, 1776, the Second Continental Congress adopted the Declaration of Independence. Written by Thomas Jefferson and others, this document boldly listed the tyrannical acts committed by George III (r. 1760–1820) and confidently proclaimed the natural rights of mankind and the sovereignty of the American states. The Declaration of Independence in effect universalized the traditional rights of English people and made them the rights of all mankind.

On the international scene, the French wanted revenge against the British for the humiliating defeats of the Seven Years' War. Thus they sympathized with the rebels and supplied guns and gunpowder from the beginning of the conflict. In 1778, the French government offered a formal alliance to the American ambassador in Paris, Benjamin Franklin, and in 1779 and 1780, the Spanish and Dutch declared war on Britain. Catherine the Great of Russia helped organize the League of Armed Neutrality to protect neutral shipping rights and succeeded in hampering Britain's naval power.

| How did the events of 1789 result in a constitutional monarchy in France? | Why and how did the French Revolution take a radical turn? | Why did Napoleon Bonaparte assume control of France and much of Europe? | How did slave revolt on colonial Saint-Domingue lead to the independent nation of Haiti? | ✓ LearningCurve Check what you know. |

THE AMERICAN REVOLUTION

1765	Britain passes the Stamp Act.
1773	Britain passes the Tea Act.
1774	Britain passes the Coercive Acts in response to the Boston Tea Party in the colonies; the First Continental Congress refuses concessions to the English crown.
April 1775	Fighting begins between colonial and British troops.
July 4, 1776	Second Continental Congress adopts the Declaration of Independence.
1777–1780	The French, Spanish, and Dutch side with the colonists against Britain.
1783	Treaty of Paris recognizes the independence of the American colonies.
1787	U.S. Constitution is signed.
1791	The first ten amendments to the Constitution (the Bill of Rights) are ratified.

Thus, by 1780, Britain was engaged in a war against most of Europe as well as the thirteen colonies. In these circumstances, and in the face of severe reverses in India, in the West Indies, and at Yorktown in Virginia, a new British government decided to cut its losses and end the war. Under the Treaty of Paris of 1783, Britain recognized the independence of the thirteen colonies and ceded all its territory between the Allegheny Mountains and the Mississippi River to the Americans.

Framing the Constitution

The American Revolution was consolidated by the Constitution, the Bill of Rights, and the creation of a national republic. Assembling in Philadelphia in 1787, the delegates to the Constitutional Convention were determined to end the period of economic depression, social uncertainty, and leadership under a weak central government. The delegates decided to grant the federal, or central, government important powers: regulation of domestic and foreign trade, the right to tax, and the means to enforce its laws.

When the results of the secret deliberations of the Constitutional Convention were presented to the states for ratification, a great public debate began. The opponents of the proposed Constitution—the Antifederalists—charged that the framers of the new document had taken too much power from the individual states and made the federal government too strong. Many Antifederalists feared for the individual freedoms for which they had fought. To overcome these objections, the Federalists promised to spell out these basic freedoms as soon as the new Constitution was adopted. The result was the first ten amendments to the Constitution, which the first Congress passed shortly after it met in New York in March 1789. These amendments, ratified in 1791, formed an effective Bill of Rights to safeguard the individual.

Limitations of Liberty and Equality

The American Constitution and the Bill of Rights exemplified the strengths and the limits of what came to be called classical liberalism. Liberty meant individual freedoms and political safeguards. Liberty also meant representative government, but it did not mean democracy, with its principle of one person, one vote. Equality meant equality before the law, not equality of political participation or wealth. It did not mean equal rights for slaves, indigenous peoples, or women.

> ## QUICK REVIEW

Why did tensions between North American colonists and the British government grow in the years following the Seven Years' War?

CHAPTER LOCATOR | What were the factors behind the revolutions of the late eighteenth century? | Why and how did American colonists forge a new, independent nation?

584 CHAPTER 19
REVOLUTIONS IN POLITICS

How did the events of 1789 result in a constitutional monarchy in France?

The Three Estates

In this political cartoon from 1789, a peasant of the third estate struggles under the weight of a happy clergyman and a plumed nobleman. The caption — "Let's hope this game ends soon" — sets forth a program of reform that any peasant could understand. (© RMN-Grand Palais/Art Resource, NY)

NO COUNTRY FELT THE CONSEQUENCES of the American Revolution more deeply than France. The American Revolution undeniably fueled dissatisfaction with the old monarchical order in France. Yet the French Revolution did not mirror the American example. It was more radical and more complex, more influential and more controversial, more loved and more hated. For Europeans and most of the rest of the world, it was the great revolution of the eighteenth century, the revolution that opened the modern era in politics.

Breakdown of the Old Order

As did the American Revolution, the French Revolution had its immediate origins in the government's financial difficulties. The efforts of the ministers of King Louis XV (r. 1715–1774) to raise taxes to meet the expenses of the War of the Austrian Succession and the Seven Years' War were thwarted by the high courts,

| How did the events of 1789 result in a constitutional monarchy in France? | Why and how did the French Revolution take a radical turn? | Why did Napoleon Bonaparte assume control of France and much of Europe? | How did slave revolt on colonial Saint-Domingue lead to the independent nation of Haiti? | ✓ LearningCurve Check what you know. |

known as the parlements. The noble judges of the parlements resented the Crown's threat to their exemption from taxation and decried the government's actions as a form of royal despotism.

When renewed efforts to reform the tax system met a similar fate in 1776, the government was forced to finance its enormous expenditures during the American war with borrowed money. As a result, the national debt soared. In 1786, the finance minister informed the timid king Louis XVI (r. 1774–1792) that the nation was on the verge of bankruptcy.

> **Annual Expenditures by the French Monarchy Under Louis XVI**

- Interest payments on the national debt: 50 percent
- Maintenance of the military: 25 percent
- Maintenance of the royal family and the court at Versailles: 6 percent
- Productive functions of the state (transportation, general administration, etc.): less than 20 percent

The Formation of the National Assembly

Spurred by a depressed economy and falling tax receipts, Louis XVI's minister of finance revived old proposals to impose a general tax on all landed property as well as to form provincial assemblies to help administer the tax, and he convinced the king to call an assembly of notables in 1787 to gain support for the idea. The assembled notables, mainly aristocrats and high-ranking clergy, declared that such sweeping tax changes required the approval of the **Estates General**, the representative body of all three estates, which had not met since 1614. As its name indicates, the Estates General was a legislative body with representatives from the three orders, or **estates**, of society: the clergy, nobility, and everyone else.

Facing imminent bankruptcy, the king tried to reassert his authority. He dismissed the notables and established new taxes by decree. The judges of the Parlement of Paris promptly declared the royal initiative null and void. When the king tried to exile the judges, a tremendous wave of protest swept the country. Finally, in July 1788, a beaten Louis XVI bowed to public opinion and called for the Estates General. Absolute monarchy was collapsing.

Following centuries-old tradition, each estate met separately to elect delegates, first at local assemblies and then at a regional level. The petitions for change drafted by the assemblies showed a surprising degree of consensus about the key issues confronting the realm. In all three estates, voices spoke in favor of replacing absolutism with a constitutional monarchy in which laws and taxes would require the consent of the Estates General in regular meetings. There was also the strong feeling that individual liberties would have to be guaranteed by law and that economic regulations should be loosened.

On May 5, 1789, the twelve hundred delegates of the three estates gathered in Versailles for the opening session of the Estates General. Despite widespread hopes for serious reform, the Estates General quickly deadlocked over the issue of voting procedures. Controversy had begun during the electoral process itself, when the government confirmed that, following precedent, each estate should meet and vote separately. During the lead-up to the Estates General, critics had

Estates General

▶ A legislative body in prerevolutionary France made up of representatives of each of the three classes, or estates. It was called into session in 1789 for the first time since 1614.

estates

▶ The three legal categories, or orders, of France's inhabitants: the clergy, the nobility, and everyone else.

CHAPTER LOCATOR | What were the factors behind the revolutions of the late eighteenth century? | Why and how did American colonists forge a new, independent nation?

586
CHAPTER 19
REVOLUTIONS IN POLITICS

The Tennis Court Oath, June 20, 1789 Painted two years after the event shown, this dramatic painting by Jacques-Louis David depicts a crucial turning point in the early days of the Revolution. On June 20, delegates of the third estate arrived at their meeting hall in the Versailles palace to find the doors closed and guarded. Fearing the king was about to dissolve their meeting by force, the deputies reassembled at a nearby indoor tennis court and swore a solemn oath not to disperse until they had been recognized as the National Assembly. (Musée de la Ville de Paris, Musée Carnavalet, Paris/Giraudon/The Bridgeman Art Library)

demanded a single assembly dominated by the third estate. The government conceded that the third estate should have as many delegates as the clergy and the nobility combined, but then upheld a system granting one vote per estate instead of one vote per person. This meant that the two privileged estates could always outvote the third.

In angry response, delegates of the third estate refused in June 1789 to meet until the king ordered the clergy and nobility to sit with them in a single body. On June 17, the third estate voted to call itself the **National Assembly**. On June 20, excluded from their hall because of "repairs," the delegates moved to a large indoor tennis court where they swore the famous Tennis Court Oath, pledging

National Assembly
▶ The first French revolutionary legislature, made up primarily of representatives of the third estate and a few from the nobility and clergy, in session from 1789 to 1791.

| How did the events of 1789 result in a constitutional monarchy in France? | Why and how did the French Revolution take a radical turn? | Why did Napoleon Bonaparte assume control of France and much of Europe? | How did slave revolt on colonial Saint-Domingue lead to the independent nation of Haiti? | ✔ LearningCurve Check what you know. |

not to disband until they had been recognized as a national assembly and had written a new constitution.

The king's response was disastrously ambivalent. On June 23, he made a conciliatory speech urging reforms, and four days later he ordered the three estates to meet together. At the same time, Louis apparently followed the advice of relatives and court nobles who urged him to dissolve the Assembly by force. The king called an army of eighteen thousand troops toward the capital to bring the delegates under control, and on July 11, he dismissed his finance minister and other more liberal ministers. It appeared that the monarchy was prepared to use violence to restore its control.

Popular Uprising and the Rights of Man

While delegates at Versailles were pressing for political rights, economic hardship gripped the common people. Conditions were already tough due to the disastrous financial situation of the Crown. A poor grain harvest in 1788 caused the price of bread to soar, and inflation spread quickly throughout the economy. As a result, demand for manufactured goods collapsed, and many artisans and small traders lost work.

Against this background of poverty and political crisis, the people of Paris entered decisively onto the revolutionary stage. They believed that, to survive, they should have steady work and enough bread at fair prices. They also feared that the dismissal of the king's liberal finance minister would put them at the mercy of aristocratic landowners and grain speculators. At the beginning of July, knowledge spread of the massing of troops near Paris. On July 14, 1789, several hundred people stormed the Bastille (ba-STEEL), a royal prison, to obtain weapons for the city's defense. Faced with popular violence, Louis soon announced the reinstatement of his finance minister and the withdrawal of troops from Paris. The National Assembly was now free to continue its work.

Just as the laboring poor of Paris had been roused to a revolutionary fervor, the struggling French peasantry had also reached a boiling point. In the summer of 1789, peasants throughout France began to rise in insurrection against their lords. In some areas, peasants reoccupied common lands enclosed by landowners and seized forests. Fear of marauders and vagabonds hired by vengeful landlords—called the **Great Fear** by contemporaries—seized the rural poor and fanned the flames of rebellion.

Faced with chaos, the National Assembly responded to peasant demands with a surprise maneuver on the night of August 4, 1789. By a decree of the Assembly, all the old noble privileges were abolished along with the tithes paid to the church. From this point on, French peasants would seek mainly to protect and consolidate this victory.

Having granted new rights to the peasantry, the National Assembly moved forward with its reforms. On August 27, 1789, it issued the Declaration of the Rights of Man and of the Citizen. This clarion call of the liberal revolutionary ideal guaranteed equality before the law, representative government for a sovereign people, and individual freedom.

The National Assembly's declaration had little practical effect for the poor and hungry people of Paris. The economic crisis worsened after the fall of the Bastille. Aristocrats fled the country, and the luxury market collapsed. Foreign markets

The Great Fear, 1789

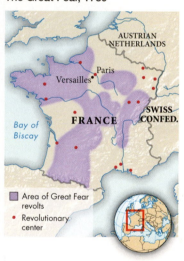

Great Fear
▶ The fear of noble reprisals against peasant uprisings that seized the French countryside and led to further revolt.

CHAPTER LOCATOR | What were the factors behind the revolutions of the late eighteenth century? | Why and how did American colonists forge a new, independent nation?

588 CHAPTER 19 REVOLUTIONS IN POLITICS

The Women of Paris March to Versailles On October 5, 1789, a large group of poor Parisian women marched to Versailles to protest the high price of bread. For the people of Paris, the king was the baker of last resort, responsible for feeding his people during times of scarcity. The angry women forced the royal family to return with them and to live in Paris rather than remain isolated from their subjects at court. (Musée de la Ville de Paris, Musée Carnavalet, Paris, France/Giraudon/The Bridgeman Art Library)

also shrank, and unemployment among the working classes grew. In addition, women—the traditional managers of food and resources in poor homes—could no longer look to the church, which had been stripped of its tithes, for aid.

On October 5, some seven thousand women marched the twelve miles from Paris to Versailles to demand action. This great crowd, "armed with scythes, sticks and pikes," invaded the National Assembly; forced their way into the royal apartments; killed some of the royal bodyguards; and searched for the queen, Marie Antoinette, who was widely despised for her frivolous and supposedly immoral behavior. The only way to calm the disorder was for the king to live closer to his people in Paris, as the crowd demanded.

Liberal elites brought the Revolution into being and continued to lead politics. Yet the people of France were now roused. They would henceforth play a crucial role in the unfolding of events.

A Constitutional Monarchy and Its Challenges

The day after the women's march on Versailles, the National Assembly followed the king to Paris, and the next two years, until September 1791, saw the consolidation of the liberal revolution. In June 1790, the National Assembly abolished the

| **How did the events of 1789 result in a constitutional monarchy in France?** | Why and how did the French Revolution take a radical turn? | Why did Napoleon Bonaparte assume control of France and much of Europe? | How did slave revolt on colonial Saint-Domingue lead to the independent nation of Haiti? | ✓ LearningCurve Check what you know. |

nobility, and in July, the king swore to uphold the as-yet-unwritten constitution, effectively enshrining a constitutional monarchy. The king remained the head of state, but all lawmaking power now resided in the National Assembly, elected by the wealthiest half of French males. The constitution passed in September 1791 broadened women's rights to seek divorce, to inherit property, and to obtain financial support for illegitimate children from fathers, but it excluded women from political office and voting.

This decision was attacked by a small number of men and women who believed that the rights of man should be extended to all French citizens. Olympe de Gouges (1748–1793), a self-taught writer and woman of the people, protested the evils of slavery as well as the injustices done to women. In September 1791, she published her *Declaration of the Rights of Woman*, proclaiming, "Woman is born free and remains equal to man in rights." De Gouges's position found little sympathy among leaders of the Revolution, however.

In addition to ruling on women's rights, the National Assembly replaced the complicated patchwork of historic provinces with eighty-three departments of approximately equal size, a move toward more rational and systematic methods of administration. Guilds, workers' associations, and internal customs fees were abolished in the name of economic liberty. Thus the National Assembly applied the spirit of the Enlightenment in a thorough reform of France's laws and institutions.

The National Assembly also imposed a radical reorganization on religious life. The Assembly granted religious freedom to the small minority of French Protestants and Jews. In November 1789, it nationalized the Catholic Church's property and abolished monasteries. The government used all former church property as collateral to guarantee a new paper currency, the assignat (A-sihg-nat), and then sold the property in an attempt to put the state's finances on a solid footing.

In July 1790, with the Civil Constitution of the Clergy, the National Assembly established a national church with priests chosen by voters. It then forced the Catholic clergy to take an oath of loyalty to the new government. Many sincere Christians, especially those in the countryside, were appalled by these changes in the religious order. The attempt to remake the Catholic Church, like the abolition of guilds and workers' associations, sharpened the conflict between the educated classes and the common people that had been emerging in the eighteenth century.

> **QUICK REVIEW**

What role did ordinary French people play in shaping the course of the first phase of the French Revolution?

CHAPTER LOCATOR | What were the factors behind the revolutions of the late eighteenth century? | Why and how did American colonists forge a new, independent nation?

590 CHAPTER 19 REVOLUTIONS IN POLITICS

Why and how did the French Revolution take a radical turn?

The Figure of Liberty

In this painting, the figure of Liberty bears a copy of the Declaration of the Rights of Man and of the Citizen in one hand and a pike to defend them in the other. The painting, by female artist and ardent revolutionary Nanine Vallain, hung in the Jacobin Club until its fall from power. (Musée de la Revolution Française, Vizille/The Bridgeman Art Library)

WHEN LOUIS XVI ACCEPTED THE NATIONAL ASSEMBLY'S CONSTITUTION in September 1791, a young provincial lawyer and delegate named Maximilien Robespierre (1758–1794) concluded that "the Revolution is over." Robespierre was right in the sense that the most constructive and lasting reforms were in place. Yet he was wrong in suggesting that turmoil had ended: a much more radical stage lay ahead.

The International Response

The outbreak of revolution in France produced great excitement and a sharp division of opinion in Europe and the United States. On the one hand, liberals and radicals saw a mighty triumph of liberty over despotism. On the other hand,

How did the events of 1789 result in a constitutional monarchy in France?

Why and how did the French Revolution take a radical turn?

Why did Napoleon Bonaparte assume control of France and much of Europe?

How did slave revolt on colonial Saint-Domingue lead to the independent nation of Haiti?

☑ **LearningCurve** Check what you know.

conservative leaders such as British statesman Edmund Burke (1729–1797) were intensely troubled. In 1790, Burke published *Reflections on the Revolution in France*, in which he defended inherited privileges. He predicted that reform like that occurring in France would lead only to chaos and tyranny.

One passionate rebuttal came from a young writer in London, Mary Wollstonecraft (1759–1797). Incensed by Burke's book, Wollstonecraft (WOOL-stuhn-kraft) wrote a blistering attack, *A Vindication of the Rights of Man* (1790). Two years later, she published her masterpiece, *A Vindication of the Rights of Woman* (1792). Like de Gouges in France, Wollstonecraft demanded equal rights for women.

The kings and nobles of continental Europe, who had at first welcomed the Revolution in France as weakening a competing power, now feared its impact. In June 1791, the royal family was arrested and returned to Paris after trying to slip out of France. To the monarchs of Austria and Prussia, the arrest of a crowned monarch was unacceptable. Two months later, they issued the Declaration of Pillnitz, which professed their willingness to intervene in France to restore Louis XVI's rule if necessary. It was expected to have a sobering effect on revolutionary France without causing war.

But the crowned heads of Europe misjudged the situation. The new French representative body, called the Legislative Assembly, that convened in October 1791 had new delegates and a different character. Although the delegates were still prosperous, well-educated middle-class men, they were younger and less cautious than their predecessors. Many of them belonged to the political **Jacobin Club**.

Jacobins and other deputies reacted with patriotic fury to the Declaration of Pillnitz. They said that if the kings of Europe were attempting to incite war against France, then "we will incite a war of people against kings."[1] In April 1792, France declared war on Francis II, the Habsburg monarch.

France's crusade against tyranny went poorly at first. Prussia joined Austria against the French, who broke and fled at their first military encounter with this First Coalition of foreign powers united against the Revolution. The Legislative Assembly declared the country in danger, and volunteers rallied to the capital. In this wartime atmosphere, rumors of treason by the king and queen spread in Paris. On August 10, 1792, a revolutionary crowd attacked the royal palace at the Tuileries (TWEE-luh-reez), while the royal family fled to the Legislative Assembly. Rather than offering refuge, the Assembly suspended the king from all his functions, imprisoned him, and called for a constitutional assembly to be elected by universal male suffrage.

Jacobin Club
▶ A political club in revolutionary France whose members were well-educated radical republicans.

The Second Revolution and the New Republic

The fall of the monarchy marked a radicalization of the Revolution, a phase that historians often call the **second revolution**. Louis's imprisonment was followed by the September Massacres. Fearing invasion by the Prussians and riled up by rumors that counter-revolutionaries would aid the invaders, angry crowds stormed the prisons and killed jailed priests and aristocrats. In late September 1792, the new, popularly elected National Convention, which replaced the Legislative Assembly, proclaimed France a republic, a nation in which the people, instead of a monarch, held sovereign power.

second revolution
▶ The second phase of the French Revolution, from 1792 to 1795, during which the fall of the French monarchy introduced a rapid radicalization of politics.

CHAPTER LOCATOR | What were the factors behind the revolutions of the late eighteenth century? | Why and how did American colonists forge a new, independent nation?

As with the Legislative Assembly, many members of the new National Convention belonged to the Jacobin Club of Paris. But the Jacobins themselves were increasingly divided into two bitterly opposed groups—the **Girondists** (juh-RAHN-dihsts) and **the Mountain**, led by Robespierre and another young lawyer, Georges Jacques Danton.

This division emerged clearly after the National Convention overwhelmingly convicted Louis XVI of treason. The Girondists accepted his guilt but did not wish to put the king to death. By a narrow majority, the Mountain carried the day, and Louis was executed on January 21, 1793. Marie Antoinette suffered the same fate later that year. But both the Girondists and the Mountain were determined to continue the "war against tyranny." The Prussians had been stopped at the Battle of Valmy on September 20, 1792, one day before the republic was proclaimed. French armies then invaded Savoy and captured Nice, moved into the German Rhineland, and by November 1792 were occupying the entire Austrian Netherlands (modern Belgium). In February 1793, the National Convention, already at war with Austria and Prussia, declared war on Britain, the Dutch Republic, and Spain as well. Republican France was now at war with almost all of Europe.

Groups within France added to the turmoil. Peasants in western France revolted against being drafted into the army, with the Vendée region of Brittany emerging as the epicenter of revolt. Devout Catholics, royalists, and foreign agents encouraged their rebellion, and the counter-revolutionaries recruited veritable armies to fight for their cause.

In March 1793, the National Convention was locked in a life-and-death political struggle between members of the Mountain and the more moderate Girondists. With the middle-class delegates so bitterly divided, the people of Paris once again emerged as the decisive political factor. The laboring poor and the petty traders were often known as the **sans-culottes**. (See "Picturing the Past: Contrasting Visions of the Sans-Culottes," page 594.) They demanded radical political action to defend the Revolution. The Mountain, sensing an opportunity to outmaneuver the Girondists, joined with sans-culottes activists to engineer a popular uprising. On June 2, 1793, armed sans-culottes invaded the National Convention and forced its deputies to arrest twenty-nine Girondist deputies for treason. All power passed to the Mountain.

The Convention also formed the Committee of Public Safety in April 1793 to deal with threats from within and outside France. The committee, led by Robespierre, held dictatorial power, allowing it to use whatever force necessary to defend the Revolution. Moderates in leading provincial cities revolted against the committee's power and demanded a decentralized government. Counter-revolutionary forces in the Vendée won significant victories, and the republic's armies were driven back on all fronts. By July 1793, only the areas around Paris and on the eastern frontier were firmly held by the central government. Defeat seemed imminent.

Total War and the Terror

A year later, in July 1794, the central government had reasserted control over the provinces, and the Austrian Netherlands and the Rhineland were once again in French hands. This remarkable change of fortune was due to the revolutionary

Girondists
▶ A moderate group that fought for control of the French National Convention in 1793.

the Mountain
▶ Led by Robespierre, the French National Convention's radical faction, which seized legislative power in 1793.

Areas of Insurrection, 1793

Vendée Rebellion
Counter-revolutionary insurrections

sans-culottes
▶ The laboring poor of Paris, so called because the men wore trousers instead of the knee breeches of the aristocracy and middle class; the word came to refer to the militant radicals of the city.

How did the events of 1789 result in a constitutional monarchy in France?

Why and how did the French Revolution take a radical turn?

Why did Napoleon Bonaparte assume control of France and much of Europe?

How did slave revolt on colonial Saint-Domingue lead to the independent nation of Haiti?

✔ LearningCurve
Check what you know.

593

Des Tetes ! _ du Sang ! _ la Mort ! _ à la Lanterne ! à la Guillotine . _ point de Reine ! _ Je suis la Deesse de la Liberté ! _ l'egalité ! _ que Londres soit brulé ! _ que Paris soit Libre ! _ Vive la Guillotine ! _

A PARIS BELLE.

Contrasting Visions of the Sans-Culottes

These two images offer profoundly different representations of a sans-culotte woman. The image on the left was created by a French artist, while the image on the right is English. The French words above the image on the right read in part, "Heads! Blood! Death! . . . I am the Goddess of Liberty! . . . Long Live the Guillotine!" (Bibliothèque nationale de France)

> PICTURING THE PAST

ANALYZING THE IMAGES: How would you describe the woman on the left? What qualities does the artist seem to ascribe to her, and how do you think these qualities relate to the sans-culottes and the Revolution? How would you characterize the facial expression and attire of the woman on the right? How does the inclusion of the text contribute to your impressions of her?

CONNECTIONS: What does the contrast between these two images suggest about differences between French and English perceptions of the sans-culottes and of the French Revolution? Why do you think the artists have chosen to depict women?

government's success in harnessing the explosive forces of a planned economy, revolutionary terror, and modern nationalism in a total war effort.

Robespierre and the Committee of Public Safety advanced on several fronts in 1793 and 1794, seeking to impose republican unity across the nation. First, they collaborated with the sans-culottes, who continued pressing the common people's case for fair prices and a moral economic order. Rather than let supply and demand determine prices, the government set maximum prices for key products. Though the state was too weak to enforce all its price regulations, it did fix the price of bread in Paris at levels the poor could afford.

The people were also put to work, mainly producing arms and munitions for the war effort. The government told craftsmen what to produce, nationalized many small workshops, and requisitioned raw materials and grain. Through these economic reforms the second revolution produced an emergency form of socialism.

CHAPTER LOCATOR | What were the factors behind the revolutions of the late eighteenth century? | Why and how did American colonists forge a new, independent nation?

594 CHAPTER 19
REVOLUTIONS IN POLITICS

Second, while radical economic measures supplied the poor with bread and the armies with weapons, the **Reign of Terror** (1793–1794) enforced compliance with republican beliefs and practices. Special revolutionary courts responsible only to Robespierre's Committee of Public Safety tried "enemies of the nation" for political crimes. Some forty thousand French men and women were executed or died in prison, making Robespierre's Reign of Terror one of the most controversial phases of the Revolution. Presented as a necessary measure to save the republic, the Terror was a weapon directed against all suspected of opposing the revolutionary government.

The Terror also sought to bring the Revolution into all aspects of everyday life. The government sponsored revolutionary art and songs as well as a new series of secular festivals. The government attempted to rationalize French daily life by adopting the decimal system for weights and measures and a new calendar based on ten-day weeks. Another important element of this cultural revolution was the campaign of de-Christianization, which aimed to eliminate Catholic symbols and beliefs. Fearful of the hostility aroused in rural France, however, Robespierre called for a halt to de-Christianization measures in mid-1794.

The third and perhaps most decisive element in the French republic's victory over the First Coalition was its ability to draw on the power of dedication to a national state and a national mission. An essential part of modern nationalism, which would fully emerge throughout Europe in the nineteenth century, this commitment was something new in history. With a common language and a common tradition newly reinforced by the ideas of popular sovereignty and democracy, large numbers of French people were stirred by a common loyalty.

The all-out mobilization of French resources under the Terror combined with the fervor of nationalism to create an awesome fighting machine. After August 1793, all unmarried young men were subject to the draft, and by January 1794, French armed forces outnumbered those of their enemies almost four to one.[2] By spring 1794, French armies were victorious on all fronts. The republic was saved.

Reign of Terror

▶ The period from 1793 to 1794 during which Robespierre's Committee of Public Safety tried and executed thousands suspected of treason and a new revolutionary culture was imposed.

THE FRENCH REVOLUTION

■ National Assembly (1789–1791)

May 5, 1789	Estates General meets at Versailles
June 17, 1789	Third estate declares itself the National Assembly
June 20, 1789	Tennis Court Oath
July 14, 1789	Storming of the Bastille
July–August 1789	Great Fear
August 4, 1789	Abolishment of feudal privileges
August 27, 1789	Declaration of the Rights of Man and of the Citizen
October 5, 1789	Women march on Versailles; royal family returns to Paris
November 1789	National Assembly confiscates church land
July 1790	Civil Constitution of the Clergy establishes a national church; Louis XVI agrees to constitutional monarchy
June 1791	Royal family arrested while fleeing France
August 1791	Declaration of Pillnitz

■ Legislative Assembly (1791–1792)

April 1792	France declares war on Austria
August 1792	Mob attacks the palace, and Legislative Assembly takes Louis XVI prisoner

■ National Convention (1792–1795)

September 1792	September Massacres; National Convention abolishes monarchy and declares France a republic
January 1793	Louis XVI executed
February 1793	France declares war on Britain, the Dutch Republic, and Spain; revolts take place in some provinces
March 1793	Struggle between Girondists and the Mountain
April 1793	Creation of the Committee of Public Safety
June 1793	Arrest of Girondist leaders
September 1793	Price controls instituted
October 1793	National Convention bans women's political societies
1793–1794	Reign of Terror
Spring 1794	French armies victorious on all fronts
July 1794	Robespierre executed; Thermidorian reaction begins

■ The Directory (1795–1799)

1795	Economic controls abolished; suppression of the sans-culottes begins
1799	Napoleon seizes power

How did the events of 1789 result in a constitutional monarchy in France?

Why and how did the French Revolution take a radical turn?

Why did Napoleon Bonaparte assume control of France and much of Europe?

How did slave revolt on colonial Saint-Domingue lead to the independent nation of Haiti?

✓ LearningCurve Check what you know.

The Thermidorian Reaction and the Directory

The success of the French armies led Robespierre and the Committee of Public Safety to relax the emergency economic controls, but they extended the political Reign of Terror. In March 1794, Robespierre's Terror wiped out many of his critics. Two weeks later, Robespierre sent long-standing collaborators whom he believed had turned against him, including Danton, to the guillotine. A group of radicals and moderates in the Convention, knowing that they might be next, organized a conspiracy. They howled down Robespierre when he tried to speak to the National Convention on July 27, 1794—a date known as 9 Thermidor according to France's newly adopted republican calendar. The next day it was Robespierre's turn to be guillotined.

As Robespierre's closest supporters followed their leader to the guillotine, the respectable middle-class lawyers and professionals who had led the liberal revolution of 1789 reasserted their authority. This period of **Thermidorian reaction**, as it was called, hearkened back to the beginnings of the Revolution; the middle class rejected the radicalism of the sans-culottes in favor of moderate policies that favored property owners.

In 1795, the middle-class members of the National Convention wrote yet another constitution to guarantee their economic position and political supremacy. As in previous elections, the mass of the population could vote only for electors who would in turn elect the legislators, but the new constitution greatly reduced the number of men eligible to become electors by including a substantial property requirement. To prevent a new Robespierre from monopolizing power, the new Assembly granted executive power to a five-man body, called the Directory.

The Directory continued to support French military expansion abroad. War was no longer so much a crusade as a response to economic problems. Large, victorious French armies reduced unemployment at home. However, the French people quickly grew weary of the corruption and ineffectiveness that characterized the Directory. In 1799, Napoleon Bonaparte ended the Directory in a coup d'état (koo day-TAH) and substituted a strong dictatorship for a weak one.

Thermidorian reaction

▶ A reaction to the violence of the Reign of Terror in 1794, resulting in the execution of Robespierre and the loosening of economic controls.

> **QUICK REVIEW**

Why and how did the French Revolution take such a radical turn, entailing terror at home and war with European powers?

CHAPTER LOCATOR | What were the factors behind the revolutions of the late eighteenth century? | Why and how did American colonists forge a new, independent nation?

596 CHAPTER 19
REVOLUTIONS IN POLITICS

The Coronation of Napoleon, 1804 In this detail from a grandiose painting by Jacques-Louis David, Napoleon, instead of the pope, prepares to crown his wife, Josephine, in an elaborate ceremony in Notre Dame Cathedral. Napoleon, the ultimate upstart, also crowned himself. Pope Pius VII, seated glumly behind the emperor, is reduced to being a spectator. (Louvre, Paris, France/The Bridgeman Art Library)

NAPOLEON BONAPARTE (1769–1821) realized that he needed to put an end to civil strife in France in order to create unity and consolidate his rule. And he did. But Napoleon saw himself as a man of destiny, and the glory of war and the dream of universal empire proved irresistible. For years, he went from victory to victory, but in the end he was destroyed by a mighty coalition united in fear of his restless ambition.

Napoleon's Rule of France

Born in Corsica into an impoverished noble family in 1769, Napoleon left home and became a lieutenant in the French artillery in 1785. Rising rapidly in the new army, Napoleon was placed in command of French forces in Italy and won brilliant victories there in 1796 and 1797. His next campaign, in Egypt, was a failure, but Napoleon returned to France before the fiasco was generally known, and his reputation remained intact.

Napoleon soon learned that some prominent members of the legislature were plotting against the Directory. The plotters' dissatisfaction stemmed not so much from the Directory's ruling dictatorially as from the fact that it was a weak dictatorship. Ten years of upheaval and uncertainty had made firm rule much more appealing than liberty and popular politics to these disillusioned revolutionaries.

How did the events of 1789 result in a constitutional monarchy in France?

Why and how did the French Revolution take a radical turn?

Why did Napoleon Bonaparte assume control of France and much of Europe?

How did slave revolt on colonial Saint-Domingue lead to the independent nation of Haiti?

☑ **LearningCurve** Check what you know.

The flamboyant thirty-year-old Napoleon, nationally revered for his heroism, was an ideal figure of authority. On November 9, 1799, Napoleon and his conspirators ousted the Directors, and the following day soldiers disbanded the legislature. Napoleon was named first consul of the republic, and a new constitution consolidating his position was overwhelmingly approved by a nationwide vote in December 1799. Republican appearances were maintained, but Napoleon became the real ruler of France.

Napoleon's domestic policy centered on using his popularity and charisma to maintain order and end civil strife. He did so by appeasing powerful groups in France, according them favors in return for loyal service. Napoleon's bargain with the solid middle class was codified in the famous Civil Code of March 1804, also known as the **Napoleonic Code**, which reasserted two of the fundamental principles of the Revolution of 1789: equality of all male citizens before the law, and security of wealth and private property. Napoleon won over peasants by defending the gains in land and status they had won during the Revolution.

At the same time, Napoleon consolidated his rule by recruiting disillusioned revolutionaries to form a network of ministers, prefects, and centrally appointed mayors. Nor were members of the old nobility slighted. In 1800 and again in 1802, Napoleon granted amnesty to one hundred thousand émigrés on the condition that they return to France and take a loyalty oath. Members of this returning elite soon ably occupied many high posts in the expanding centralized state.

Napoleon applied his diplomatic skills to healing the Catholic Church in France so that it could serve as a bulwark of social stability. After arduous negotiations, Napoleon and Pope Pius VII (pontificate 1800–1823) signed the Concordat (kuhn-KOHR-dat) of 1801. The pope obtained the right for French Catholics to practice their religion freely, but Napoleon gained political power: his government now nominated bishops, paid the clergy, and exerted great influence over the church.

The domestic reforms of Napoleon's early years were his greatest achievement, but order and unity had a price: authoritarian rule. Women lost many of the gains they had made in the 1790s. Under the Napoleonic Code, women were dependents of either their fathers or their husbands, and they could not make contracts or have bank accounts in their own names. Napoleon also curtailed free speech and freedom of the press and manipulated voting in the occasional elections. After 1810, political suspects were held in state prisons, as they had been during the Terror.

Napoleon's Expansion in Europe

Napoleon was above all a great military man. After coming to power in 1799, he sent peace feelers to Austria and Great Britain, the two remaining members of the Second Coalition that had been formed against France in 1798. When they rejected his overtures, Napoleon's armies decisively defeated the Austrians. In the Treaty of Lunéville (1801), Austria accepted the loss of almost all its Italian possessions, and German territory on the west bank of the Rhine was incorporated into France. The British agreed to the Treaty of Amiens in 1802, allowing France to control the former Dutch Republic, the Austrian Netherlands, the west bank of the Rhine, and most of the Italian peninsula.

In 1802, Napoleon was secure but driven to expand his power. Aggressively redrawing the map of Germany to weaken Austria and encourage the secondary states of southwestern Germany to side with France, Napoleon tried to restrict

Napoleonic Code

▶ French civil code promulgated in 1804 that reasserted the 1789 principles of the equality of all male citizens before the law and the absolute security of wealth and private property, as well as restricting rights accorded to women by previous revolutionary laws.

German Confederation of the Rhine, 1806

CHAPTER LOCATOR | What were the factors behind the revolutions of the late eighteenth century? | Why and how did American colonists forge a new, independent nation?

British trade with all of Europe. He then plotted to attack Great Britain, but his Mediterranean fleet was destroyed by Lord Nelson at the Battle of Trafalgar on October 21, 1805. Invasion of England was henceforth impossible. Renewed fighting had its advantages, however, for the first consul used the wartime atmosphere to have himself proclaimed emperor in late 1804.

Austria, Russia, and Sweden joined with Britain to form the Third Coalition against France shortly before the Battle of Trafalgar. Actions such as Napoleon's assumption of the Italian crown had convinced both Alexander I of Russia and Francis II of Austria that Napoleon was a threat to the European balance of power. Yet they were no match for Napoleon, who scored a brilliant victory over them at the Battle of Austerlitz in December 1805. Alexander I decided to pull back, and Austria accepted large territorial losses in return for peace as the Third Coalition collapsed.

Napoleon then proceeded to reorganize the German states. In 1806, he abolished many of the tiny German states as well as the ancient Holy Roman Empire. He established by decree the German Confederation of the Rhine, a union of fifteen German states minus Austria, Prussia, and Saxony. Naming himself "protector" of the confederation, Napoleon firmly controlled western Germany.

Napoleon's intervention in German affairs alarmed the Prussians, who mobilized their armies after more than a decade of peace with France. Napoleon attacked and won two more brilliant victories in October 1806 at Jena and Auerstädt. The war with Prussia, now joined by Russia, continued into the following spring. After Napoleon's larger armies won another victory, Alexander I of Russia was ready to negotiate the peace. In the subsequent treaties of Tilsit in 1807, Prussia lost half of its population, while Russia accepted Napoleon's reorganization of western and central Europe and promised to enforce Napoleon's economic blockade against British goods.

The Grand Empire and Its End

Napoleon saw himself increasingly as the emperor of Europe, not just of France. The so-called **Grand Empire** he built had three parts. The core, or first part, was an ever-expanding France. The second part consisted of a number of dependent satellite kingdoms, on the thrones of which Napoleon placed members of his large family. The third part comprised the independent but allied states of Austria, Prussia,

THE NAPOLEONIC ERA

November 1799	Napoleon overthrows the Directory
December 1799	Napoleon's new constitution approved
1800	Foundation of the Bank of France
1801	France defeats Austria and acquires Italian and German territories in the Treaty of Lunéville; Napoleon signs papal Concordat
1802	Treaty of Amiens
March 1804	Napoleonic Code
December 1804	Napoleon crowned emperor
October 1805	Britain defeats the French fleet at the Battle of Trafalgar
December 1805	Napoleon defeats Austria and Russia at the Battle of Austerlitz
1807	Napoleon redraws map of Europe in the treaties of Tilsit
1808	Spanish revolt against French occupation
1810	Height of the Grand Empire
June 1812	Napoleon invades Russia
Fall–Winter 1812	Napoleon makes a disastrous retreat from Russia
March 1814	Russia, Prussia, Austria, and Britain sign the Treaty of Chaumont, pledging alliance to defeat Napoleon
April 1814	Napoleon abdicates and is exiled to Elba; Louis XVIII restored to constitutional monarchy
February–June 1815	Napoleon escapes from Elba but is defeated at the Battle of Waterloo; Louis XVIII restored to throne for second time

Grand Empire

▶ The empire over which Napoleon and his allies ruled, encompassing nearly all of Europe except Great Britain and Russia.

How did the events of 1789 result in a constitutional monarchy in France?

Why and how did the French Revolution take a radical turn?

Why did Napoleon Bonaparte assume control of France and much of Europe?

How did slave revolt on colonial Saint-Domingue lead to the independent nation of Haiti?

☑ LearningCurve
Check what you know.

Continental System

▶ A blockade imposed by Napoleon to halt all trade between continental Europe and Britain, thereby weakening the British economy and military.

and Russia. After 1806, Napoleon expected both satellites and allies to support his **Continental System**, a blockade in which no ship coming from Britain or her colonies could dock at a port controlled by the French. It was intended to halt all trade between Britain and continental Europe, thereby destroying the British economy and its military force.

The impact of the Grand Empire on the peoples of Europe was considerable. In the areas incorporated into France and in the satellites (**Map 19.2**), Napoleon abolished feudal dues and serfdom to the benefit of the peasants and middle class. Yet Napoleon had to put the prosperity and special interests of France first in order to safeguard his power base. Levying heavy taxes in money and men for his armies, he came to be regarded more as a conquering tyrant than as an enlightened liberator.

The first great revolt occurred in Spain. In 1808, a coalition of Catholics, monarchists, and patriots rebelled against Napoleon's attempts to make Spain a French satellite. French armies occupied Madrid, but the foes of Napoleon fled to the hills and waged uncompromising guerrilla warfare. Spain was a clear warning: resistance to French imperialism was growing.

Yet Napoleon pushed on. In 1810, when the Grand Empire was at its height, Britain still remained at war with France, helping the guerrillas in Spain and Portugal. The Continental System was a failure. Instead of harming Britain, the system provoked the British to set up a counter-blockade, which created hard times in France. Perhaps looking for a scapegoat, Napoleon turned on Alexander I of Russia, who in 1811 openly repudiated Napoleon's war of prohibitions against British goods.

Napoleon's invasion of Russia began in June 1812. Originally planning to winter in the Russian city of Smolensk, Napoleon recklessly pressed on toward Moscow. The great Battle of Borodino that followed was a draw. Alexander ordered the evacuation of Moscow, which the Russians then burned in part, and he refused to negotiate. Finally, after five weeks in the scorched and abandoned city, Napoleon ordered a retreat, one of the greatest military disasters in history. When the frozen remnants of his army staggered into Poland and Prussia in December, 370,000 men had died and another 200,000 had been taken prisoner.[3]

Leaving his troops to their fate, Napoleon raced to Paris to raise yet another army. Possibly he might still have saved his throne if he had been willing to accept a France reduced to its historical size. But Napoleon refused. Austria and Prussia deserted Napoleon and joined Russia and Great Britain in the Treaty of Chaumont in March 1814, by which the four powers pledged allegiance to defeat the French emperor.

Less than a month later, on April 4, 1814, a defeated Napoleon abdicated his throne. After this unconditional abdication, the victorious allies granted Napoleon the island of Elba off the coast of Italy as his own tiny state. Napoleon was allowed to keep his imperial title, and France was required to pay him a yearly income of 2 million francs. The allies also agreed to the restoration of the Bourbon dynasty under Louis XVIII (r. 1814–1824) and promised to treat France with leniency in a peace settlement.

Napoleon staged a daring escape from Elba in February 1815 and marched on Paris with a small band of followers. French officers and soldiers who had fought so long for their emperor responded to the call. Louis XVIII fled, and once more Napoleon took command. But Napoleon's gamble was a desperate long shot because the allies were united against him. At the end of a frantic period known

CHAPTER LOCATOR | What were the factors behind the revolutions of the late eighteenth century? | Why and how did American colonists forge a new, independent nation?

600 CHAPTER 19 REVOLUTIONS IN POLITICS

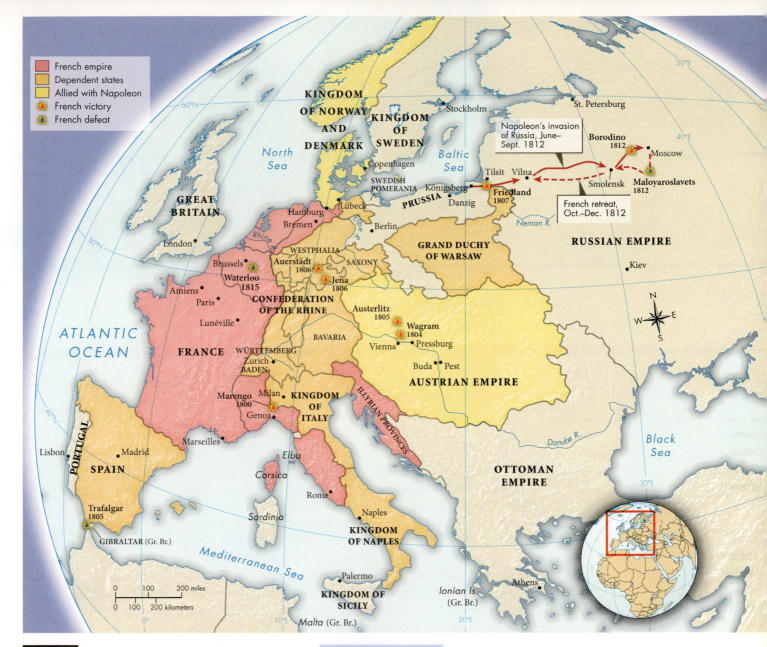

MAP 19.2 ■ Napoleonic Europe in 1812

At the height of the Grand Empire in 1810, Napoleon had conquered or allied with every major European power except Britain. But in 1812, angered by Russian repudiation of his ban on trade with Britain, Napoleon invaded Russia — with disastrous results. Compare this map with Map 15.2 (page 459), which shows the division of Europe in 1715.

> MAPPING THE PAST

ANALYZING THE MAP: How had the balance of power shifted in Europe from 1715 to 1812? What changed, and what remained the same? What was the impact of Napoleon's wars on Germany and the Italian peninsula?
CONNECTIONS: Why did Napoleon succeed in achieving vast territorial gains where Louis XIV did not?

---

as the Hundred Days, they crushed his forces at Waterloo on June 18, 1815. Louis XVIII returned to the throne, and the allies dealt more harshly with the French.

QUICK REVIEW

How did Napoleon gain and consolidate dictatorial power, and what were the reasons for his downfall?

| How did the events of 1789 result in a constitutional monarchy in France? | Why and how did the French Revolution take a radical turn? | **Why did Napoleon Bonaparte assume control of France and much of Europe?** | How did slave revolt on colonial Saint-Domingue lead to the independent nation of Haiti? | ☑ LearningCurve Check what you know. |

How did slave revolt on colonial Saint-Domingue lead to the independent nation of Haiti?

Slave Revolt on Saint-Domingue

This illustration, from the proslavery perspective, emphasizes the violence and destructiveness of the slave rebellion in Saint-Domingue. Many white settlers fled to the United States and other Caribbean islands with as much of their property, including slaves, as they could take with them. (The Library Company of Philadelphia)

THE EVENTS THAT LED TO THE CREATION of the independent nation of Haiti constitute the third, and perhaps most extraordinary, chapter of the revolutionary era in the late eighteenth century. Prior to 1789, Saint-Domingue, the French colony that was to become Haiti, reaped huge profits through a ruthless system of slave-based plantation agriculture. News of revolution in France lit a powder keg of contradictory aspirations among white planters, free people of color, and slaves. While revolutionary authorities debated how far to extend the rights of man on Saint-Domingue, first free people of color and then enslaved people took matters into their own hands, rising up to claim their freedom. A massive slave revolt in 1791 ultimately succeeded in ending slavery and winning independence from France. In 1804, Haiti became the first nation in history to claim its freedom through slave revolt.

Revolutionary Aspirations in Saint-Domingue

On the eve of the French Revolution, Saint-Domingue was inhabited by a variety of social groups who resented and mistrusted one another. The European population included French colonial officials, wealthy plantation owners and merchants, and poor immigrants. Individuals of French or European descent born in the colonies were called Creoles. Vastly outnumbering the white population were the colony's five hundred thousand enslaved people alongside a sizable population of some forty thousand free people of African and mixed African and European descent. Members of this last group referred to themselves as free people of color.

Most of the island's enslaved population performed grueling toil in the island's sugar plantations. The highly outnumbered planters used extremely brutal methods,

CHAPTER LOCATOR | What were the factors behind the revolutions of the late eighteenth century? | Why and how did American colonists forge a new, independent nation?

such as beating, maiming, and executing slaves, to maintain their control. The 1685 Code Noir (Black Code) that set the parameters of slavery was intended to provide minimal standards of humane treatment, but its tenets were rarely enforced.

Despite their brutality, slaveholders on Saint-Domingue freed a surprising number of their slaves, mostly their own mixed-race children. The Code Noir had originally granted free people of color the same legal status as whites. From the 1760s on, however, the rising prosperity and visibility of this group provoked resentment from the white population. Colonial administrators began rescinding the rights of free people of color.

The political and intellectual turmoil of the 1780s raised new challenges and possibilities for each of Saint-Domingue's social groups. For enslaved people, news of abolitionist movements in France led to hopes that the mother country might grant them freedom. Free people of color looked to reforms in Paris as a means of gaining political enfranchisement and reasserting equal status with whites. The Creole elite, not surprisingly, saw matters very differently. Determined to defend slavery and to protect their way of life, they looked to revolutionary ideals of representative government for the chance to gain control of their own affairs.

The National Assembly frustrated the hopes of all these groups. Cowed by colonial representatives who claimed that support for free people of color would result in slave insurrection and independence, the Assembly refused to extend French constitutional safeguards to the colonies. At the same time, however, the Assembly also reaffirmed French monopolies over colonial trade, thereby angering Creole planters as well.

In July 1790, Vincent Ogé (aw-JHZAY) (ca. 1750–1791), a free man of color, raised an army of several hundred and sent letters to the new Provincial Assembly of Saint-Domingue demanding political rights for all free citizens. But Ogé's demands were refused, so he and his followers turned to armed insurrection. After initial victories, his army was defeated, and Ogé was tortured and executed by colonial officials. Revolutionary leaders in Paris were more sympathetic to Ogé's cause. In May 1791, responding to what it perceived as partly justified grievances, the National Assembly granted political rights to free people of color born to two free parents who possessed sufficient property. When news of this legislation arrived in Saint-Domingue, the white elite was furious, and the colonial governor refused to enact it. Violence now erupted between groups of whites and free people of color in parts of the colony.

The Outbreak of Revolt

In August 1791, slaves, who had witnessed the confrontation between whites and free people of color for over a year, took events into their own hands. Revolts began on a few plantations on the night of August 22. Within a few days, the uprising had swept much of the northern plain, creating a growing slave army. During the next month, enslaved combatants attacked and destroyed hundreds of sugar and coffee plantations.

On April 4, 1792, as war loomed with the European states, the National Assembly issued a decree extending full citizenship rights to free people of color, including the right to vote for men. The Assembly hoped this measure would win the loyalty of free people of color and their aid in defeating the slave rebellion.

| How did the events of 1789 result in a constitutional monarchy in France? | Why and how did the French Revolution take a radical turn? | Why did Napoleon Bonaparte assume control of France and much of Europe? | **How did slave revolt on colonial Saint-Domingue lead to the independent nation of Haiti?** | ☑ LearningCurve Check what you know. |

603

Warfare in Europe soon spread to Saint-Domingue (**Map 19.3**). Since the beginning of the slave insurrection, the Spanish colony of Santo Domingo, just to the east of Saint-Domingue, had supported rebel slaves. In early 1793, the Spanish began to bring slave leaders and their soldiers into the Spanish army. Toussaint L'Ouverture (TOO-sahn LOO-vehr-toor) (1743–1803), a freed slave who had joined the revolt, was named a Spanish officer. In September, the British navy blockaded the colony, and invading British troops captured French territory on the island. For the Spanish and British, revolutionary chaos provided a tempting opportunity to capture a profitable colony.

Desperate for forces to oppose France's enemies, commissioners sent by the newly elected National Convention promised to emancipate all those who fought for France. By October 1793, they had abolished slavery throughout the colony. On February 4, 1794, the Convention ratified the abolition of slavery and extended it to all French territories.

The tide of battle began to turn when Toussaint L'Ouverture switched sides, bringing his military and political skills, along with four thousand well-trained soldiers, to support the French war effort. By 1796, the French had regained control of the colony, and L'Ouverture had emerged as a key military leader. (See "Individuals in Society: Toussaint L'Ouverture," page 605.) In May 1796, he was named commander of the western province of Saint-Domingue. The increasingly conservative nature of the French government during the Thermidorian reaction, however, threatened to undo the gains made by former slaves and free people of color.

The War of Haitian Independence

With Toussaint L'Ouverture acting increasingly as an independent ruler of the western province of Saint-Domingue, another general, André Rigaud (1761–1811), set up his own government in the southern peninsula. Civil war broke out between the two sides in 1799, when L'Ouverture's forces, led by his lieutenant, Jean Jacques Dessalines (1758–1806), invaded the south. Victory over Rigaud in 1800 gave L'Ouverture control of the entire colony.

This victory was soon challenged by Napoleon, who had his own plans for re-establishing slavery and using the profits as a basis for expanding French power. Napoleon ordered his brother-in-law, General Charles-Victor-Emmanuel Leclerc (1772–1802), to lead an expedition to the island to crush the new regime. In 1802, Leclerc landed in Saint-Domingue and ordered the arrest of Toussaint L'Ouverture. The rebel leader, along with his family, was deported to France, where he died in 1803.

It was left to L'Ouverture's lieutenant, Jean Jacques Dessalines, to unite the resistance, and he led it to a crushing victory over French forces. On January 1, 1804, Dessalines formally declared the independence of Saint-Domingue and the creation of the new sovereign nation of Haiti, the name used by the pre-Columbian inhabitants of the island. The Haitian constitution was ratified in 1805.

THE HAITIAN REVOLUTION

May 1791	French National Assembly enfranchises free men of color born of two free parents
August 1791	Slave insurrections in Saint-Domingue
April 1792	French National Assembly grants full citizenship rights to free people of color, including the right to vote for men
September 1793	British troops invade Saint-Domingue
February 1794	Abolition of slavery in all French territories
1796	France regains control of Saint-Domingue under Toussaint L'Ouverture
1803	Death of Toussaint L'Ouverture in France
January 1804	Declaration of Haitian independence
May 1805	First Haitian constitution

INDIVIDUALS IN SOCIETY
Toussaint L'Ouverture

Little is known of the early life of Saint-Domingue's brilliant military and political leader Toussaint L'Ouverture. He was born in 1743 on a plantation outside Le Cap owned by the Count de Bréda. According to tradition, L'Ouverture was the eldest son of a captured African prince from modern-day Benin. Toussaint Bréda, as he was then called, occupied a privileged position among slaves. Instead of performing backbreaking labor in the fields, he served his master as a coachman and livestock keeper. He also learned to read and write French and some Latin, but he was always more comfortable with the Creole dialect.

During the 1770s, the plantation manager emancipated L'Ouverture, who subsequently leased his own small coffee plantation and slaves. He married Suzanne Simone, who already had one son, and the couple had another son during their marriage. In 1791, he joined the slave uprisings that swept Saint-Domingue, and he took on the *nom de guerre* ("war name") L'Ouverture, meaning "the opening." L'Ouverture rose to prominence among rebel slaves allied with Spain and by early 1794 controlled his own army. A devout Catholic who led a frugal and ascetic life, L'Ouverture impressed others with his enormous physical energy, intellectual acumen, and air of mystery. In 1794, he defected to the French side and led his troops to a series of victories against the Spanish. In 1795, the National Convention promoted L'Ouverture to brigadier general.

Over the next three years, L'Ouverture successively eliminated rivals for authority on the island. First he freed himself of the French commissioners sent to govern the colony. With a firm grip on power in the northern province, L'Ouverture defeated General André Rigaud in 1800 to gain control in the south. His army then marched on the capital of Spanish Santo Domingo on the eastern half of the island, meeting little resistance. The entire island of Hispaniola was now under his command.

With control of Saint-Domingue in his hands, L'Ouverture was confronted with the challenge of building a post-emancipation society, the first of its kind. The task was made even more difficult by the chaos wreaked by war, the destruction of plantations, and bitter social and racial tensions. For L'Ouverture, the most pressing concern was to re-establish the plantation economy. Without revenue to pay his army, the gains of the rebellion could be lost. He therefore encouraged white planters to return to reclaim their property. He also adopted harsh policies toward former slaves, forcing them back to their plantations and restricting their ability to acquire land. When they resisted, he sent troops across the island to enforce submission. L'Ouverture's 1801 constitution reaffirmed his draconian labor policies and named L'Ouverture governor for life, leaving Saint-Domingue as a colony in name alone. In June 1802, French forces arrested L'Ouverture and jailed him at Fort de Joux in France's Jura Mountains near the Swiss border. L'Ouverture died of pneumonia on April 7, 1803. It was left to his lieuten-

Equestrian portrait of Toussaint L'Ouverture. (Photos 12/Alamy)

ant, Jean Jacques Dessalines, to win independence for the new Haitian nation.

QUESTIONS FOR ANALYSIS

1. Toussaint L'Ouverture was both slave and slave owner. How did each experience shape his life and actions?
2. What did Toussaint L'Ouverture and Napoleon Bonaparte have in common? How did they differ?

LaunchPad

ONLINE DOCUMENT PROJECT

How did slaves and free people of color from France's Caribbean colonies respond to the French Revolution? Keeping the above question in mind, explore documents that reveal how slaves and free people of color in the colonies and in Paris made their concerns part of the revolutionary dialogue, and then complete a writing assignment based on the evidence and details from this chapter. *See inside the front cover to learn more.*

MAP 19.3 ■ The War of Haitian Independence, 1791–1804

Neighbored by the Spanish colony of Santo Domingo, Saint-Domingue was the most profitable European colony in the Caribbean. In 1770, the French transferred the capital from Le Cap to Port-au-Prince. Slave revolts erupted in the north near Le Cap in 1791. Port-au-Prince became the capital of the newly independent Haiti in 1804.

Haiti was born from the first successful large-scale slave revolt in history. This event spread shock and fear through slaveholding societies in the Caribbean and the United States. Fearing the spread of rebellion to the United States, President Thomas Jefferson refused to recognize Haiti as an independent nation. The liberal proponents of American Revolution thus chose to protect slavery at the expense of revolutionary ideals of universal human rights. The French government imposed crushing indemnity charges on Haiti to recompense the loss of French property, dealing a harsh blow to the fledgling nation's economy.

Yet Haitian independence had fundamental repercussions for world history, helping spread the idea that liberty, equality, and fraternity must apply to all people. The next phase of Atlantic revolution soon opened in the Spanish American colonies.

> QUICK REVIEW

How did the various social groups on Saint-Domingue respond to the challenges and opportunities created by the French Revolution?

CHAPTER LOCATOR | What were the factors behind the revolutions of the late eighteenth century? | Why and how did American colonists forge a new, independent nation?

LOOKING BACK LOOKING AHEAD

A great revolutionary wave swept both sides of the Atlantic Ocean in the late eighteenth century. The revolutions in British North America, France, and Haiti were individual and unique, but they shared common origins and consequences for Western and, indeed, world history. The eighteenth century inaugurated monumental changes: population grew, urbanization spread, and literacy increased. Enlightenment ideals influenced all orders of society and reformers increasingly championed limitations on monarchical authority in the name of popular sovereignty.

The Atlantic world was an essential context for this age of revolutions. The movement of peoples, commodities, and ideas across the Atlantic Ocean in the eighteenth century created a world of common debates, conflicts, and aspirations. The high stakes of colonial empire heightened competition among European states, leading to a series of wars that generated crushing costs for overburdened treasuries. For both the British in their North American colonies and the French at home, the desperate need for new taxes weakened government authority and opened the door to revolution. In turn, the ideals of the French Revolution inspired slaves and free people of color in Saint-Domingue, thus opening the promise of liberty, equality, and fraternity to people of all races.

The chain reaction did not end with the birth of an independent Haiti in 1804. On the European continent throughout the nineteenth and early twentieth centuries, periodic convulsions occurred as successive generations struggled over political rights first proclaimed by the generation of 1789. Meanwhile, as dramatic political events unfolded, a parallel economic revolution was gathering steam. This was the Industrial Revolution, originating around 1780 and accelerating through the end of the eighteenth century (see Chapter 20). After 1815, the twin forces of industrialization and democratization would combine to transform Europe and the world.

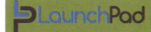

ONLINE DOCUMENT PROJECT
Toussaint L'Ouverture

How did slaves and free people of color from France's Caribbean colonies respond to the French Revolution?

You encountered Toussaint L'Ouverture's story on page 606. Keeping the question above in mind, explore documents that reveal how slaves and free people of color in the colonies and in Paris made their concerns part of the revolutionary dialogue. *See inside the front cover to learn more.*

| How did the events of 1789 result in a constitutional monarchy in France? | Why and how did the French Revolution take a radical turn? | Why did Napoleon Bonaparte assume control of France and much of Europe? | How did slave revolt on colonial Saint-Domingue lead to the independent nation of Haiti? | ✓ LearningCurve Check what you know. |

CHAPTER 19 STUDY GUIDE

GET STARTED ONLINE

 **LearningCurve**

Now that you've read the chapter, make it stick by completing the LearningCurve activity.

EXPLAIN WHY IT MATTERS

Put your reading into practice. Identify each term below, and then explain why it matters in Western history.

TERM	WHO OR WHAT & WHEN	WHY IT MATTERS
Estates General (p. 586)		
estates (p. 586)		
National Assembly (p. 587)		
Great Fear (p. 588)		
Jacobin Club (p. 592)		
second revolution (p. 592)		
Girondists (p. 593)		
the Mountain (p. 593)		
sans-culottes (p. 593)		
Reign of Terror (p. 595)		
Thermidorian reaction (p. 596)		
Napoleonic Code (p. 598)		
Grand Empire (p. 599)		
Continental System (p. 600)		

MOVE BEYOND THE BASICS

To demonstrate a more advanced understanding of the four main phases of the French Revolution, fill out the chart below. How did the nature of the Revolution change between 1789 and 1799?

	Leaders and key groups	Policies and reforms	Winners and losers
The first revolution: 1789–1791			
The second revolution: 1791–1794			
The Directory: 1794–1799			
Napoleonic France: 1799–1815			

PUT IT ALL TOGETHER

Now, take a step back and try to explain the big picture. Remember to use specific examples from the chapter in your answers.

THE OUTBREAK OF REVOLUTION IN BRITISH NORTH AMERICA AND FRANCE

▶ Is it fair to say that problems with government finances *caused* the French Revolution? Why or why not?

▶ What are the most important similarities and differences between the American and French Revolutions?

WORLD WAR AND REPUBLICAN FRANCE

▶ What justifications were offered for the use of violence as a political tool during the second phase of the French Revolution? In your opinion, how valid were these justifications?

▶ How did war and the threat of war shape the course of the Revolution between 1791 and 1799?

THE NAPOLEONIC ERA AND THE HAITIAN REVOLUTION

▶ Should Napoleon be considered a "revolutionary"? Why or why not?

▶ How did the people of Saint-Domingue react to the news of revolution in France? How would you explain their reaction?

MAKE CONNECTIONS

▶ What connections can you make between the revolutions of the late eighteenth century and long-term early modern social and economic trends?

▶ In what ways did the French Revolution mark the beginning of a new era in European politics?

> IN YOUR OWN WORDS

Imagine that you must give an oral report to the class answering the following question: **What led to the great revolutions of the late eighteenth and early nineteenth centuries, and how did these revolutions change over time?** What would be the most important points and why?

20

THE REVOLUTION IN ENERGY AND INDUSTRY

CA. 1780–1850

> **How did the Industrial Revolution transform the society and economy of Europe?** Chapter 20 examines the causes and consequences of the Industrial Revolution, which took off around 1780 in Great Britain and soon began to influence continental Europe and the United States. Industrialization profoundly modified much of the human experience. It changed patterns of work, transformed the social class structure and the way people thought about class, and eventually altered the international balance of political power. It is quite possible that only the development of agriculture during Neolithic times had a comparable impact and significance.

LearningCurve

After reading the chapter, use LearningCurve to retain what you've read.

> What were the
  origins of the
  Industrial
  Revolution in
  Britain?

> How did countries
  outside Britain
  respond to the
  challenge of
  industrialization?

> How did work and
  daily life evolve
  during the
  Industrial
  Revolution?

> What were
  the social
  consequences of
  industrialization?

Life in the Industrial Revolution. Daily life for industrial workers was harsh, especially for the many child laborers who worked in the new factories and in other industries, like the glassworks pictured here. (Heritage/The Image Works)

What were the origins of the Industrial Revolution in Britain?

James Nasmyth's Mighty Steam Hammer

Nasmyth's invention was the forerunner of the modern pile driver, and its successful introduction in 1832 epitomized the rapid development of steam-power technology in Britain. In this painting by the inventor himself, workers manipulate a massive iron shaft being hammered into shape at Nasmyth's foundry near Manchester. (Science & Society Picture Library, London)

THE INDUSTRIAL REVOLUTION BEGAN IN GREAT BRITAIN, the nation created in 1707 by the formal union of Scotland, Wales, and England. Just as France was a trailblazer in political change, Britain was the leader in economic development, and it must therefore command special attention.

Origins of the British Industrial Revolution

Although many aspects of the origins of the British Industrial Revolution are still matters for scholarly debate, it is generally agreed that industrial changes grew out of a long process of development. The Scientific Revolution and Enlightenment fostered a new worldview that embraced progress and the role of research and experimentation in understanding and mastering the natural world. Britain's vibrant scientific and Enlightenment culture allowed British industrialists to exploit the latest findings of scientists and technicians from other countries.

In the economic realm, the seventeenth-century expansion of English woolen cloth exports throughout Europe brought commercial profits and high wages—to

ca. 1765
– Hargreaves invents spinning jenny; Arkwright creates water frame

1769
– Watt patents modern steam engine

1775–1783
– American Revolution

ca. 1780–1850
– Industrial Revolution; population boom in Britain

1799
– Combination Acts passed

1802–1833
– Series of Factory Acts passed by British government to limit the workday of child laborers and set minimum hygiene and safety requirements

1810
– Strike of Manchester cotton spinners

ca. 1815
– Industrial gap between continental Europe and Britain widens

1824
– Combination Acts repealed

1829
– Stephenson introduces the *Rocket,* an early locomotive

1830s
– Industrial banks in Belgium

1834
– *Zollverein* erected among most German states

1842
– Mines Act passed in Britain

1844
– Engels publishes *The Condition of the Working Class in England*

1850s
– Japan begins to adopt Western technologies; industrial gap widens between the West and the rest of the world

1851
– Great Exhibition held at Crystal Palace in London

1860s
– Germany and the United States begin to industrialize rapidly

the detriment of traditional producers in Flanders and Italy. By the eighteenth century, the expanding Atlantic economy and trade with India and China were also serving Britain well. The mercantilist colonial empire that Britain aggressively built, augmented by a strong position in Latin America and in the African slave trade, provided raw materials like cotton and a growing market for British goods (see Chapter 17, page 536). Strong demand for British manufacturing meant that British workers earned high wages compared to the rest of Europe.

Agriculture also played an important role in bringing about the Industrial Revolution in Britain. English farmers were second only to the Dutch in productivity in 1700, and they were continually adopting new methods of farming. Because of increasing efficiency, landowners were able to produce more food with a smaller workforce. By the mid-eighteenth century, on the eve of the Industrial Revolution, less than half of Britain's population worked in agriculture. The enclosure movement had deprived many small landowners of their land, leaving the landless poor to work as hired agricultural laborers or in cottage industry. These groups created a large pool of potential laborers for the new factories.

Abundant food and high wages meant that the ordinary English family no longer had to spend almost everything it earned just to buy bread. Thus the family could spend more on manufactured goods. They could also pay to send their children to school. Britain's populace enjoyed high levels of literacy and numeracy

| How did countries outside Britain respond to the challenge of industrialization? | How did work and daily life evolve during the Industrial Revolution? | What were the social consequences of industrialization? | ✓ LearningCurve Check what you know. |

Industrial areas
- ■ Coal deposit
- ○ Metal goods
- ■ Woolen cloth
- — Canals, 1800
- — Navigable rivers

Cottage Industry and Transportation in Eighteenth-Century Great Britain

Industrial Revolution

▶ A term first coined in 1799 to describe the burst of major inventions and economic expansion that began in Britain in the late eighteenth century.

(knowledge of mathematics) compared to the rest of Europe. Moreover, in the eighteenth century, the members of the average British family were redirecting their labor away from unpaid work for household consumption and toward work for wages that they could spend on goods, a trend reflecting the increasing commercialization of the entire European economy.

Britain also benefited from rich natural resources and a well-developed infrastructure. In an age when it was much cheaper to ship goods by water than by land, no part of England was more than fifty miles from navigable water. Beginning in the 1770s, a canal-building boom enhanced this advantage. Rivers and canals provided easy movement of England's and Wales's enormous deposits of iron and coal, resources that would be critical raw materials in Europe's early industrial age. The abundance of coal combined with high wages in manufacturing placed Britain in a unique position among European nations: its manufacturers had extremely strong incentives to develop technologies to draw on the power of coal to increase workmen's productivity.

A final factor favoring British industrialization was the heavy hand of the British state and its policies, especially in the formative decades of industrial change. The British government taxed its population aggressively and spent the money on a navy to protect imperial commerce and on an army that could be used to quell uprisings by disgruntled workers. Starting with the Navigation Acts under Oliver Cromwell (see Chapter 15), the British state also adopted aggressive tariffs, or duties, on imported goods to protect its industries.

All these factors combined to initiate the **Industrial Revolution**, a term first coined in 1799 to describe the burst of major inventions and technical changes under way. This technical revolution went hand in hand with an impressive quickening in the annual rate of industrial growth in Britain. Whereas industry had grown at only 0.7 percent between 1700 and 1760 (before the Industrial Revolution), it grew at the much higher rate of 3 percent between 1801 and 1831 (when industrial transformation was in full swing).[1]

Technological Innovations and Early Factories

The pressure to produce more goods for a growing market and to reduce the labor costs of manufacturing was directly related to the first decisive breakthrough of the Industrial Revolution: the creation of the world's first machine-powered factories in the British cotton textile industry. Technological innovations in the manufacture of cotton cloth led to a new system of production and social relationships.

The putting-out system that developed in the seventeenth-century textile industry involved a merchant who loaned, or "put out," raw materials to cottage workers who processed the raw materials in their own homes and returned the finished products to the merchant. There was always a serious imbalance in textile production based on cottage industry: the work of four or five spinners was needed to keep one weaver steadily employed. Cloth weavers constantly had to find more thread and more spinners.

Given this situation, many a tinkering worker knew that a better spinning wheel promised rich rewards. It proved hard to spin the traditional raw materials—wool and flax—with improved machines, but cotton was different. Cotton textiles had first been imported into Britain from India by the East India Company. In the

Woman Working a Spinning Jenny

The loose cotton strands on the slanted bobbins shown in this illustration of Hargreaves's spinning jenny passed up to the sliding carriage and then on to the spindles (inset) in back for fine spinning. The worker, almost always a woman, regulated the sliding carriage with one hand, and with the other she turned the crank on the wheel to supply power. By 1783, one woman could spin by hand a hundred threads at a time. (spinning jenny: Mary Evans Picture Library/The Image Works)

eighteenth century, a lively market for cotton cloth emerged in West Africa, where the English and other Europeans traded it in exchange for slaves. By 1760, a tiny domestic cotton industry had emerged in northern England, but it could not compete with cloth produced by low-paid workers in India and other parts of Asia. International competition thus drove English entrepreneurs to invent new technologies to bring down labor costs.

After many experiments over a generation, a gifted carpenter, James Hargreaves, invented his cotton-spinning jenny about 1765. At almost the same moment, a barber-turned-manufacturer named Richard Arkwright invented (or possibly pirated) another kind of spinning machine, the water frame. These breakthroughs produced an explosion in the infant cotton textile industry in the 1780s. By 1790, the new machines were producing ten times as much cotton yarn as had been made in 1770.

Hargreaves's **spinning jenny** was simple, inexpensive, and powered by hand. In early models, from six to twenty-four spindles were mounted on a

spinning jenny

▶ A simple, inexpensive, hand-powered spinning machine created by James Hargreaves in 1765.

How did countries outside Britain respond to the challenge of industrialization?   How did work and daily life evolve during the Industrial Revolution?   What were the social consequences of industrialization?   ☑ LearningCurve Check what you know.

615

sliding carriage, and each spindle spun a fine, slender thread. Now it was the male weaver who could not keep up with the vastly more efficient female spinner.

Arkwright's **water frame** employed a different principle. It quickly acquired a capacity of several hundred spindles and demanded much more power than a single operator could provide. A solution was found in waterpower. The water frame required large specialized mills to take advantage of the rushing currents of streams and rivers. The factories they powered employed as many as one thousand workers from the very beginning. Gradually, all cotton spinning was concentrated in large-scale water-powered factories.

Despite the significant increases in productivity, the working conditions in the early cotton factories were atrocious. Adult weavers and spinners were reluctant to leave the safety and freedom of work in their own homes to labor in noisy and dangerous factories where the air was filled with cotton fibers. Therefore, factory owners often turned to young orphans and children who had been abandoned by their parents and put in the care of local parishes. Parish officers often "apprenticed" such unfortunate foundlings to factory owners. Such child workers were forced by law to labor for their "masters" for as many as fourteen years. Housed, fed, and locked up nightly in factory dormitories, the young workers labored thirteen or fourteen hours a day for little or no pay. Harsh physical punishment maintained brutal discipline.

The creation of the world's first machine-powered factories in the British cotton textile industry in the 1770s and 1780s, which grew out of the putting-out system of cottage production, was a major historical development. Both symbolically and substantially, the big new cotton mills marked the beginning of the Industrial Revolution in Britain. By 1831, the largely mechanized cotton textile industry accounted for fully 22 percent of the country's entire industrial production.

The Steam Engine Breakthrough

Eighteenth-century Europe, like other areas of the world, relied mainly on wood for energy, and human beings and animals continued to perform most work. This dependence meant that Europe and the rest of the world remained poor in energy and power. By the eighteenth century, wood was in ever-shorter supply. Processed wood (charcoal) was the fuel that was mixed with iron ore in the blast furnace to produce pig iron. The iron industry's appetite for wood was enormous, and by 1740, the British iron industry was stagnating. Vast forests enabled Russia in the eighteenth century to become the world's leading producer of iron, much of which was exported to Britain. As wood became ever more scarce, the British looked to coal as an alternative.

To produce more coal, mines had to be dug deeper and deeper and were constantly filling with water. Mechanical pumps, usually powered by animals walking in circles at the surface, had to be installed. At one mine, fully five hundred horses were used in pumping. Such power was expensive and bothersome. In an attempt to overcome these disadvantages, Thomas Savery in 1698 and Thomas Newcomen in 1705 invented the first primitive **steam engines**. Both engines burned coal to produce steam, which was then used to operate a pump. By the early 1770s, many of the Savery engines and hundreds of the Newcomen engines were operating successfully in English and Scottish mines.

water frame
▶ A spinning machine created by Richard Arkwright that had a capacity of several hundred spindles and used waterpower; it therefore required a larger and more specialized mill — a factory.

steam engines
▶ A breakthrough invention by Thomas Savery in 1698 and Thomas Newcomen in 1705 that burned coal to produce steam, which was then used to operate a pump; the early models were superseded by James Watt's more efficient steam engine, patented in 1769.

In 1763, a gifted young Scot named James Watt (1736–1819) was drawn to a critical study of the steam engine. Watt was employed at the time by the University of Glasgow as a skilled craftsman making scientific instruments. In 1763, Watt was called on to repair a Newcomen engine being used in a physics course. After a series of observations, Watt saw that the Newcomen engine's waste of energy could be reduced by adding a separate condenser. This splendid invention, patented in 1769, greatly increased the efficiency of the steam engine.

To invent something is one thing; to make it a practical success is quite another. Watt needed skilled workers, precision parts, and capital, and the relatively advanced nature of the British economy proved essential. A partnership in 1775 with Matthew Boulton, a wealthy English industrialist, provided Watt with adequate capital and exceptional skills in salesmanship that equaled those of the renowned pottery king, Josiah Wedgwood. (See "Individuals in Society: Josiah Wedgwood," page 618.) Among Britain's highly skilled locksmiths, tinsmiths, and millwrights, Watt found mechanics who could install, regulate, and repair his sophisticated engines. From ingenious manufacturers such as the cannonmaker John Wilkinson, Watt was gradually able to purchase precision parts. By the late 1780s, the firm of Boulton and Watt had made the steam engine a practical and commercial success in Britain.

The steam engine was quickly put to use in several industries in Britain. It drained mines and made possible the production of ever more coal to feed steam engines elsewhere. The steam-power plant began to replace waterpower in cotton-spinning factories during the 1780s, contributing greatly to that industry's phenomenal rise. Steam also took the place of waterpower in flour mills, in the malt mills used in breweries, in the flint mills supplying the pottery industry, and in the mills exported by Britain to the West Indies to crush sugarcane.

Coal and steam power promoted important breakthroughs in other industries. The British iron industry was radically transformed. Originally, the smoke and fumes resulting from coal burning meant that coal could not be used as a cheap substitute for expensive charcoal in smelting iron. Starting around 1710, ironmakers began to use coke—a smokeless and hot-burning fuel produced by heating coal to rid it of water and other impurities—to smelt pig iron. After 1770, the adoption of steam-driven bellows in blast furnaces allowed for great increases in the quantity of pig iron produced by British ironmakers. In the 1780s, Henry Cort developed the puddling furnace, which allowed pig iron to be refined in turn with coke. Cort also developed steam-powered rolling mills, which were capable of turning out finished iron in every shape and form.

The economic consequence of these technical innovations was a great boom in the British iron industry. In 1740, annual British iron production was only 17,000 tons. With the spread of coke smelting and the impact of Cort's inventions, production had reached 260,000 tons by 1806. In 1844, Britain produced 3 million tons of iron. Once expensive, iron became the cheap, basic, indispensable building block of the economy.

The Coming of the Railroads

The first steam locomotive was built by Richard Trevithick after much experimentation. George Stephenson acquired glory for his locomotive named *Rocket*, which sped down the track of the just-completed Liverpool and Manchester

Rocket

▶ The name given to George Stephenson's effective locomotive that was first tested in 1829 on the Liverpool and Manchester Railway at 24 miles per hour.

How did countries outside Britain respond to the challenge of industrialization?

How did work and daily life evolve during the Industrial Revolution?

What were the social consequences of industrialization?

☑ LearningCurve
Check what you know.

As the making of cloth and iron was revolutionized by technical change and factory organization, so too were the production and consumption of pottery. Acquiring beautiful tableware became a craze for eighteenth-century consumers, and continental monarchs often sought prestige in building royal china works. But the grand prize went to Josiah Wedgwood, who wanted to "astonish the world."

The twelfth child of a poor potter, Josiah Wedgwood (1730–1795) grew up in the pottery district of Staffordshire in the English Midlands, where many tiny potteries made simple earthenware utensils for sale in local markets. Growing up as an apprentice in the family business inherited by his oldest brother, Wedgwood struck off on his own in 1752. Soon manager of a small pottery, Wedgwood learned that new products recharged lagging sales. Studying chemistry and determined to succeed, Wedgwood spent his evenings experimenting with different chemicals and firing conditions.

In 1759, after five years of tireless efforts, Wedgwood perfected a beautiful new green glaze. Now established as a master potter, he opened his own factory and began manufacturing teapots and tableware finished in his green and other unique glazes, or adorned with printed scenes far superior to those being produced by competitors. Wedgwood's products caused a sensation among consumers, and his business quickly earned substantial profits. Subsequent breakthroughs, including ornamental vases imitating classical Greek models and jasperware for jewelry, contributed greatly to Wedgwood's success.

Competitors were quick to copy Wedgwood's new products and sell them at lower prices. Thus Wedgwood and his partner Thomas Bentley sought to cultivate an image of superior fashion, taste, and quality in order to develop and maintain a dominant market position. They did this by first capturing the business of the trendsetting elite. In one brilliant coup, the partners first sold a very large cream-colored dinner set to Britain's queen, which they quickly christened "Queen's ware" and sold as a very expensive, must-have luxury to English aristocrats. Equally brilliant was Bentley's suave expertise in the elegant London showroom selling Wedgwood's imitation Greek vases, which became the rage after the rediscovery of the Roman towns Pompeii and Herculaneum in the mid-eighteenth century.

Above all, once Wedgwood had secured his position as the luxury market leader, he was able to successfully extend his famous brand to the growing middle class, capturing an enormous mass market for his "useful ware." Thus when sales of a luxury good grew "stale," Wedgwood made tasteful modifications and sold it to the middling classes for twice the price his competitors could charge. This unbeatable combination of mass appeal and high prices all across Europe brought Wedgwood great fame and enormous wealth.

A workaholic with an authoritarian streak, Wedgwood contributed substantially to the development of the factory system. In 1769, he opened a model factory on a new canal he had promoted. With two hundred workers in several departments, Wedgwood exercised tremendous control over his workforce, imposing fines for many infractions, such as being late, drinking on the job, or wasting material. He wanted, he said, to create men who would be

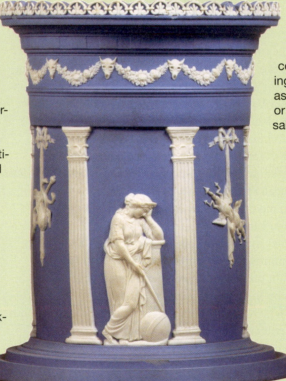

Typical Wedgwood jasperware, this elegant cylindrical vase, decorated in the form of a miniature Roman household altar, was destined for the luxury market. (Image copyright © The Metropolitan Museum of Art. Image source: Art Resource, NY)

LaunchPad

ONLINE DOCUMENT PROJECT

How did observers of early industrialization imagine the relationship between workers and their work, and between workers and their employers? Explore different views on the impact of industrial production on individual workers in light of Wedgwood's approach to industrial labor. Then complete a writing assignment based on the evidence and details from this chapter. *See inside the front cover to learn more.*

Josiah Wedgwood, who perfected jasperware, a fine-grained pottery usually made in "Wedgwood blue" with white decoration. (Down House, Downe, Kent, UK/© English Heritage Photo Library/The Bridgeman Art Library)

like "machines" that "cannot err." Yet Wedgwood also recognized the value in treating workers well. He championed a division of labor that made most workers specialists who received ongoing training. He also encouraged employment of family groups, who were housed in company row houses with long, narrow backyards suitable for raising vegetables and chickens. Paying relatively high wages and providing pensions and some benefits, Wedgwood developed a high-quality labor force that learned to accept his rigorous discipline and carried out his ambitious plans.

QUESTIONS FOR ANALYSIS

1. How and why did Wedgwood succeed?
2. Was Wedgwood a good boss or a bad one? Why?
3. How did Wedgwood exemplify the new class of factory owners?

Railway at a maximum speed of 24 miles per hour in 1829. The line from Liverpool to Manchester was a financial as well as a technical success, and many private companies quickly emerged to build more rail lines. Within twenty years they had completed the main trunk lines of Great Britain (**Map 20.1**). Other countries were quick to follow, with the first steam-powered trains operating in the United States in the 1830s and in Brazil, Chile, Argentina, and the British colonies of Canada, Australia, and India in the 1850s.

The significance of the railroad was tremendous. It dramatically reduced the cost and uncertainty of shipping freight over land. This advance had many economic consequences. Previously, markets had tended to be small and local; as the barrier of high transportation costs was lowered, markets became larger and even nationwide. Larger markets encouraged larger factories with more sophisticated machinery in a growing number of industries. Such factories could make goods more cheaply and gradually subjected most cottage workers and many urban artisans to severe competitive pressures. In all countries, the construction of railroads created a strong demand for unskilled labor and contributed to the growth of a class of urban workers.

Water travel was also transformed by the steam engine. French engineers completed the first steamships in the 1770s, and the first commercial steamships came into use in North America several decades later.

Industry and Population

In 1851, London hosted an industrial fair called the Great Exhibition in the newly built **Crystal Palace**. The building was made entirely of glass and iron, both of which were now cheap and abundant. Sponsored by the British royal family, the exhibition celebrated the new era of industrial technology and the kingdom's role as world economic leader.

Crystal Palace

▶ The location of the Great Exhibition in 1851 in London; an architectural masterpiece made entirely of glass and iron.

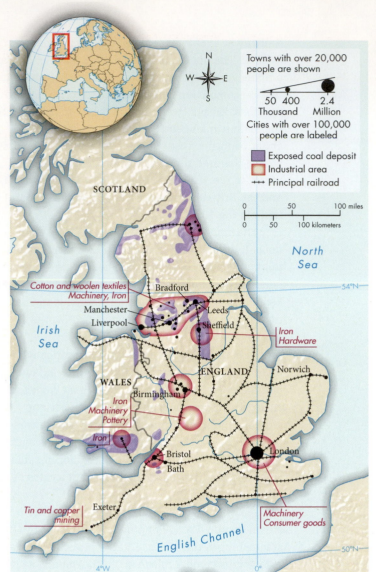

MAP 20.1 ■ The Industrial Revolution in Great Britain, ca. 1850

Industry concentrated in the rapidly growing cities of the north and the center of England, where rich coal and iron deposits were close to one another.

Map labels:

Towns with over 20,000 people are shown

50   400   2.4
Thousand   Million

Cities with over 100,000 people are labeled

■ Exposed coal deposit
□ Industrial area
┼┼┼ Principal railroad

0   50   100 miles
0 50 100 kilometers

SCOTLAND

North Sea

54°N

Irish Sea

Cotton and woolen textiles Machinery, Iron

Bradford
Manchester
Liverpool
Leeds
Sheffield

Iron Hardware

WALES

ENGLAND

Norwich

Birmingham

Iron Machinery Pottery

Iron

Bristol
Bath

London

Exeter

Tin and copper mining

Machinery Consumer goods

English Channel

50°N

4°W   0°

Britain's claim to be the "workshop of the world" was no idle boast because it produced two-thirds of the world's coal and more than half of all iron and cotton cloth. More generally, in 1860, Britain produced a remarkable 20 percent of the entire world's output of industrial goods, whereas it had produced only about 2 percent of the total in 1750.[2] As the British economy significantly increased its production of manufactured goods, the gross national product (GNP) rose roughly fourfold at constant prices between 1780 and 1851. At the same time, the population of Britain boomed, growing from about 9 million in 1780 to almost 21 million in 1851. Thus growing numbers consumed much of the increase in total production.

Based on the lessons of history, many contemporaries feared that the rapid growth in population would inevitably lead to disaster. In his *Essay on the Principle of Population* (1798), Thomas Malthus (1766–1834) concluded that the only hope of warding off "positive checks" to population growth such as famine and disease was "prudential restraint." That is, young men and women had to limit the growth of population by marrying late in life. But Malthus was not optimistic about this possibility. The powerful attraction of the sexes, he feared, would cause most people to marry early and have many children.

Economist David Ricardo (1772–1823) spelled out the pessimistic implications of Malthus's thought. Ricardo's depressing **iron law of wages** posited that, because of the pressure of population growth, wages would always sink to subsistence level over an extended period of time. That is, wages would be just high enough to keep workers from starving.

Malthus, Ricardo, and their followers were proved wrong in the long run, largely because industrialization improved productivity beyond what they could imagine. However, until the 1820s or even the 1840s, contemporary observers might reasonably have concluded that the economy and the total population were racing neck and neck, with the outcome very much in doubt. There was another problem as well. Perhaps workers, farmers, and ordinary people did not get their

iron law of wages

► Theory proposed by English economist David Ricardo suggesting that the pressure of population growth prevents wages from rising above the subsistence level.

CHAPTER LOCATOR | What were the origins of the Industrial Revolution in Britain?

rightful share of the new wealth. Perhaps only the rich got richer, while the poor
got poorer or made no progress. We will turn to this great issue after looking at
the process of industrialization beyond the British Isles.

QUICK REVIEW

How did the Industrial Revolution in Britain
develop between 1780 and 1850?

How did countries outside Britain respond to the challenge of industrialization?	How did work and daily life evolve during the Industrial Revolution?	What were the social consequences of industrialization?	☑ LearningCurve Check what you know.

How did countries outside Britain respond to the challenge of industrialization?

A German Ironworks, 1845 The Borsig ironworks in Berlin mastered the new British method of smelting iron ore with coke. Germany, and especially the state of Prussia, was well endowed with both iron and coal, and the rapid exploitation of these resources after 1840 transformed a poor agricultural country into an industrial powerhouse. (akg-images)

AS NEW TECHNOLOGIES and new ways of employing labor began to revolutionize production in Britain, other countries took notice and began to emulate its example. With the end of the Napoleonic Wars, the countries of the European continent quickly adopted British inventions and achieved their own pattern of technological innovation and economic growth. By the last decades of the nineteenth century, western European countries as well as the United States and Japan had industrialized their economies to a considerable, albeit variable, degree. Outside western Europe, industrialization proceeded more gradually, with uneven jerks and national and regional variations.

National and International Variations

Comparative data on industrial production in different countries over time help give us an overview of what happened. One set of data, the work of a Swiss scholar, compares the level of industrialization on a per capita basis in several countries from 1750 to 1913. These data are far from perfect, but they reflect basic trends and are presented in **Table 20.1** for closer study.

Table 20.1 presents a comparison of how much industrial product was produced, on average, for each person in a given country in a given year. All the numbers are expressed in terms of a single index number of 100, which equals the per

CHAPTER LOCATOR | What were the origins of the Industrial Revolution in Britain?

TABLE 20.1 ■ Per Capita Levels of Industrialization, 1750–1913

	1750	1800	1830	1860	1880	1900	1913
Great Britain	10	16	25	64	87	100	115
Belgium	9	10	14	28	43	56	88
United States	4	9	14	21	38	69	126
France	9	9	12	20	28	39	59
Germany	8	8	9	15	25	52	85
Austria-Hungary	7	7	8	11	15	23	32
Italy	8	8	8	10	12	17	26
Russia	6	6	7	8	10	15	20
China	8	6	6	4	4	3	3
India	7	6	6	3	2	1	2

Note: All entries are based on an index value of 100, equal to the per capita level of industrialization in Great Britain in 1900. Data for Great Britain include Ireland, England, Wales, and Scotland.

Source: P. Bairoch, "International Industrialization Levels from 1750 to 1980," *Journal of European Economic History* 11 (Spring 1982): 294, U.S. Journals at Cambridge University Press.

capita level of industrial goods in Great Britain in 1900. Every number in the table is thus a percentage of the 1900 level in Britain and is directly comparable with other numbers. The countries are listed in roughly the order that they began to use large-scale, power-driven technology.

What does this overview tell us? First, one sees in the first column that in 1750 all countries were fairly close together, including non-Western nations such as China and India. Both China and India had been extremely important players in early modern world trade, earning high profits from exporting their luxury goods (see Chapter 14). However, the column headed 1800 shows that Britain had opened up a noticeable lead over all countries by 1800, and that gap progressively widened as the Industrial Revolution accelerated through 1830 and reached full maturity by 1860.

Second, the table shows that Western countries began to emulate the British model successfully over the course of the nineteenth century, with significant variations in the timing and in the extent of industrialization. Belgium, achieving independence from the Netherlands in 1831 and rich in iron and coal, led in adopting Britain's new technology, and it experienced a truly revolutionary surge between 1830 and 1860. France developed factory production more gradually, and most historians now detect no burst in French mechanization and no acceleration in the growth of overall industrial output that may accurately be called revolutionary. Its slow but steady growth—and continued dominance of the market in luxury goods using traditional artisanal techniques—was overshadowed by the spectacular rise of the German lands and the United States after 1860 in what has been termed the "second industrial revolution."

Finally, the late but substantial industrialization in eastern and southern Europe meant that all European states as well as the United States managed

How did countries outside Britain respond to the challenge of industrialization?

How did work and daily life evolve during the Industrial Revolution?

What were the social consequences of industrialization?

✓ LearningCurve
Check what you know.

623

to raise per capita industrial levels in the nineteenth century. These increases stood in stark contrast to the decreases that occurred at the same time in many non-Western countries, most notably in China and India, as Table 20.1 shows. European countries industrialized to a greater or lesser extent even as most of the non-Western world stagnated. Japan, which is not included in this table, stands out as an exceptional area of non-Western industrial growth in the second half of the nineteenth century. After the forced opening of the country to the West in the 1850s, Japanese entrepreneurs began to adopt Western technology and manufacturing methods, resulting in a production boom by the late nineteenth century. Different rates of wealth- and power-creating industrial development, which heightened disparities within Europe, also greatly magnified existing inequalities between Europe and the rest of the world.

Industrialization in Continental Europe

When the pace of British industry began to accelerate in the 1780s, continental businesses began to adopt the new methods as they proved their profitability. British industry enjoyed clear superiority, but the European continent was close behind. During the period of the revolutionary and Napoleonic Wars, from 1793 to 1815, however, western Europe experienced tremendous political and social upheaval that temporarily halted economic development. With the return of peace in 1815, however, western European countries again began to play catch-up.

They faced significant challenges. In the newly mechanized industries, British goods were being produced very economically, and these goods had come to dominate world markets. In addition, British technology had become so advanced and complicated that few engineers or skilled technicians outside England understood it. Moreover, the technology of steam power had grown much more expensive. It involved large investments in the iron and coal industries and, after 1830, required the existence of railroads. All these factors slowed the spread of machine-powered industry (**Map 20.2**).

Nevertheless, western European nations possessed a number of advantages that helped them respond to their challenges. Most had a rich tradition of putting-out enterprise, which endowed them with experienced merchant capitalists and skilled urban artisans. While British inventors and entrepreneurs had to discover and implement new technologies on their own, other nations could simply "borrow" the new methods developed in Great Britain. European countries also had a third asset that many non-Western areas lacked in the nineteenth century: they had strong, independent governments that did not fall under foreign political control. These governments would use the power of the state to promote industry and catch up with Britain.

Agents of Industrialization

Western European success in adopting British methods took place despite the best efforts of the British to prevent it. The British realized the great value of their technical discoveries and tried to keep their secrets to themselves. Until 1825, it was illegal for artisans and skilled mechanics to leave Britain; until 1843, the export of textile machinery and other equipment was forbidden. Many talented,

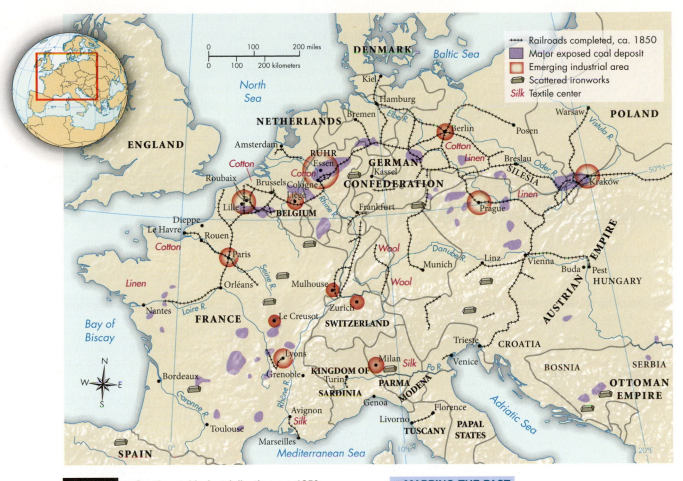

MAP 20.2 ■ Continental Industrialization, ca. 1850

Although continental countries were beginning to make progress by 1850, they still lagged far behind Great Britain. For example, continental railroad building was still in an early stage, whereas the British rail system was essentially complete (see Map 20.1). Coal played a critical role in nineteenth-century industrialization both as a power source for steam engines and as a raw material for making iron and steel.

> MAPPING THE PAST

ANALYZING THE MAP: Locate the major exposed (that is, known) coal deposits in 1850. Which countries and areas appear rich in coal resources, and which appear poor? Is there a difference between northern and southern Europe?

CONNECTIONS: What is the relationship between known coal deposits and emerging industrial areas in continental Europe? In Great Britain (see Map 20.1)?

ambitious workers slipped out of the country illegally, however, and introduced the new methods abroad.

Thus British technicians and skilled workers were a powerful force in the spread of early industrialization. A second agent of industrialization consisted of talented entrepreneurs such as Fritz Harkort (1793–1880), a pioneer in the German machinery industry. Serving in England as a Prussian army officer during the Napoleonic Wars, Harkort was impressed with what he saw. Once the wars were over, he set up shop building steam engines in the Ruhr Valley, on the western border with France.

Lacking skilled laborers, Harkort turned to Britain for experienced, though expensive, mechanics. Getting materials was also difficult. In spite of all these problems, Harkort succeeded in building and selling engines. His ambitious efforts over sixteen years also resulted in large financial losses for himself and his partners.

How did countries outside Britain respond to the challenge of industrialization?

How did work and daily life evolve during the Industrial Revolution?

What were the social consequences of industrialization?

✓ LearningCurve
Check what you know.

His career illustrates both the great efforts of a few important business leaders to duplicate the British achievement and the difficulty of the task.

Entrepreneurs like Harkort were obviously exceptional. Most continental businesses adopted factory technology slowly, and handicraft methods lived on. Indeed, continental industrialization usually brought substantial but uneven expansion of handicraft industry in both rural and urban areas for a time. Artisan production of luxury items, for example, grew in France as the rising income of the international middle class created increased foreign demand.

Government Support and Corporate Banking

tariff protection

▶ A government's way of supporting and aiding its own economy by laying high taxes on imported goods from other countries, as when the French responded to cheaper British goods flooding their country by imposing high tariffs on some imported products.

Just as the British government provided crucial support for the growth of industrialization, so did national governments in other parts of Europe. After 1815, western European states adopted a set of largely successful policies similar to those in Britain. Tariff protection was one such support.

After 1815, continental governments also bore the cost of building roads, canals, and railroads to improve transportation. Belgium led the way in the 1830s and 1840s. Built rapidly as a unified network, Belgium's state-owned railroads stimulated the development of heavy industry and made the country an early industrial leader. The Prussian government guaranteed that the state treasury would pay the interest and principal on railroad bonds if the closely regulated private companies in Prussia were unable to do so. In France, the state shouldered all the expense of acquiring and laying roadbed, including bridges and tunnels. In short, governments helped pay for railroads, the all-important leading sector in continental industrialization.

Banks also played an important role in supporting development on the continent, more so than in Britain. Previously, almost all banks in Europe had been private. Because of the possibility of unlimited financial loss, the partners of private banks tended to be conservative and were content to deal with a few rich clients and a few big merchants. They generally avoided industrial investment as being too risky.

In the 1830s, two important Belgian banks pioneered in a new direction. They received permission from the growth-oriented government to establish themselves as corporations enjoying limited liability. That is, if the bank went bankrupt, stockholders could now lose only their original investments in the bank's common stock, and they could not be forced by the courts to pay for any additional losses out of other property they owned. Limited liability helped these Belgian banks attract investors. They mobilized impressive resources for investment in big companies, became industrial banks, and successfully promoted industrial development.

Similar corporate banks became important in France and the German lands in the 1850s and 1860s. Usually working in collaboration with governments, corporate banks established and developed many railroads and many companies working in heavy industry, which were also increasingly organized as limited liability corporations.

The combined efforts of governments, skilled workers, entrepreneurs, and industrial banks meshed successfully after 1850. As a result, rail networks were completed in western and much of central Europe, and the leading continental countries mastered the industrial technologies that had first been developed by the British. In the early 1870s, Britain was still Europe's most industrial nation, but a select handful of nations had closed the gap. Western European countries—

CHAPTER LOCATOR | What were the origins of the Industrial Revolution in Britain?

CHAPTER 20

626 THE REVOLUTION IN ENERGY AND INDUSTRY

along with the United States—thus became technological innovators in their own right and enjoyed sustained economic growth that made them the wealthiest nations in the world.

The Situation Outside Europe

The Industrial Revolution did not have a transformative impact beyond Europe prior to the 1860s, with the exception of the United States and Japan, both early adopters of British practices. In many countries, national governments and pioneering entrepreneurs did make efforts to adopt the technologies and methods of production that had proved so successful in Britain, but they fell short of transitioning to an industrial economy. In Russia, for example, the imperial government brought steamships to the Volga River and a railroad to the capital, St. Petersburg, in the first decades of the nineteenth century. By midcentury, ambitious entrepreneurs had established steam-powered cotton factories using imported British machines. However, these advances did not lead to overall industrialization of the country. Instead, Russia confirmed its role as provider of raw materials, especially timber and grain, to the hungry West.

Egypt similarly began an ambitious program of modernization in the first decades of the nineteenth century, which included the use of imported British technology and experts in textile manufacture and other industries. These industries, however, could not compete with lower-priced European imports. Like Russia, Egypt fell back on agricultural exports, like sugar and cotton, to European markets.

Such examples of faltering efforts at industrialization could be found in many other regions of the Middle East, Asia, and Latin America. Where European governments maintained direct or indirect political control, they acted to monopolize colonial markets as both sources of raw materials and consumers for their own products rather than encouraging the spread of industrialization. Such regions could not respond to low-cost imports by raising tariffs, as the United States and western European nations had done, because they were controlled by imperial powers that did not allow them to do so. In India, millions of poor textile workers lost their livelihood because they could not compete with industrially produced British cottons.

Latin American countries were distracted from economic concerns by the early-nineteenth-century wars of independence. By the mid-nineteenth century, they had adopted steam power for sugar and coffee processing, but as elsewhere these developments led to increased reliance on agricultural crops for export, not a rise in industrial production. As in India, the arrival of cheap British cottons destroyed the pre-existing textile industry that had employed many Latin American men and women. The rise of industrialization in Britain, western Europe, and the United States thus resulted in other regions of the world becoming increasingly economically dependent and, in turn, ever more vulnerable to political domination. Instead of industrializing, many territories underwent a process of deindustrialization due to imperialism and economic competition.

QUICK REVIEW <

How and why did the course of industrialization on the European continent differ from developments in Britain?

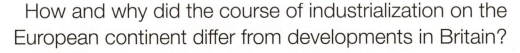

| How did countries outside Britain respond to the challenge of industrialization? | How did work and daily life evolve during the Industrial Revolution? | What were the social consequences of industrialization? | ✔ LearningCurve Check what you know. |

How did work and daily life evolve during the Industrial Revolution?

Workers at a Large Cotton Mill This 1833 engraving shows adult women operating power looms under the supervision of a male foreman, and it accurately reflects both the decline of family employment and the emergence of a gender-based division of labor in many British factories. The jungle of belts and shafts connecting the noisy looms to the giant steam engine on the ground floor created a constant din. (Time Life Pictures/Getty Images)

HAVING FIRST EMERGED IN THE BRITISH COUNTRYSIDE in the late eighteenth century, factories and industrial labor began migrating to cities by the early nineteenth century. As factories moved from rural to urban areas, their workforce evolved as well, from pauper children to families, to men and women uprooted from their traditional rural communities. For some people, the Industrial Revolution brought improvements, but living and working conditions for the poor stagnated or even deteriorated until around 1850, especially in overcrowded industrial cities.

Work in Early Factories

The first factories of the Industrial Revolution were cotton mills, which began functioning in the 1770s along fast-running rivers and streams and were often located in sparsely populated areas. Cottage workers, accustomed to the putting-out system, were reluctant to work in the new factories even when they received relatively good wages. In a factory, workers had to keep up with the machine and follow its relentless tempo. Moreover, they had to show up every day, on time, and work long, monotonous hours under the constant supervision of demanding overseers, and they were punished systematically if they broke the work rules.

Cottage workers were not used to that way of life. In the putting-out system, all members of the family worked hard and long, but in spurts, setting their own pace. Women and children could break up their long hours of spinning with other

CHAPTER LOCATOR | What were the origins of the Industrial Revolution in Britain?

tasks. On Saturday afternoon the head of the family delivered the week's work to the merchant manufacturer and got paid. Saturday night was a time of relaxation and drinking, especially for the men.

Also, early factories resembled English poorhouses, where destitute people went to live at public expense. Some poorhouses were industrial prisons, where the inmates had to work in order to receive food and lodging. The similarity between large brick factories and large stone poorhouses increased the cottage workers' fear of factories and their hatred of factory discipline. It was cottage workers' reluctance to work in factories that prompted the early cotton mill owners to turn to pauper children for their labor. Mill owners contracted with local officials to employ large numbers of such children, who had no say in the matter.

Working Families and Children

By the 1790s, the early pattern had begun to change. The use of pauper apprentices was in decline, and in 1802 it was forbidden by Parliament. Many more textile factories were being built, mainly in urban areas, where they could use steam power rather than waterpower and attract a workforce more easily than in the countryside. As a result, people came from near and far to work in the cities, both as factory workers and as porters, builders, and domestic servants. Collectively, these wage laborers came to be known as the "working class."

In some cases, workers were able to accommodate to the system by carrying over familiar working traditions. Some came to the mills and the mines as family units. The mill or mine owner bargained with the head of the family and paid him or her for the efforts of the whole family. In the cotton mills, children worked for their mothers or fathers, collecting scraps and "piecing" broken threads together. In the mines, children sorted coal and worked the ventilation equipment. Their mothers hauled coal in the tunnels below the surface, while their fathers hewed with pick and shovel at the face of the seam.

The preservation of the family as an economic unit in the factories helped people accommodate to the new surroundings during the early stages of industrialization. Parents disciplined their children and directed their upbringing. Adult workers were often complicit in the exploitation of their children. They were not particularly interested in limiting the minimum working age or the hours of children as long as family members worked side by side and they maintained control of their young. Only when technical changes threatened to place control in the hands of impersonal managers did adult workers protest against inhuman conditions in the name of their children.

Some enlightened employers and social reformers in Parliament argued that more humane standards were necessary, and they used widely circulated parliamentary reports to influence public opinion. For example, Robert Owen (1771–1858), a successful manufacturer in Scotland, testified in 1816 before an investigating committee on the basis of his experience. He argued that employing children under ten years of age as factory workers was "injurious to the children, and not beneficial to the proprietors."[3] Workers also provided graphic testimony at such hearings as reformers pressed Parliament to pass corrective laws.

These efforts resulted in a series of **Factory Acts** from 1802 to 1833 that progressively limited the workday of child laborers and set minimum hygiene and

Factory Acts
▶ English laws passed from 1802 to 1833 that limited the workday of child laborers and set minimum hygiene and safety requirements.

How did countries outside Britain respond to the challenge of industrialization?

How did work and daily life evolve during the Industrial Revolution?

What were the social consequences of industrialization?

☑ LearningCurve
Check what you know.

629

safety requirements. The 1833 act installed a system of full-time professional inspectors to enforce the provisions of previous acts. The Factory Acts constituted a major victory in preventing the exploitation of children, especially those without families to protect them at the worksite. One unintended drawback of restrictions on child labor, however, was that they broke the pattern of whole families working together in the factory because efficiency required standardized shifts for all workers. After 1833, the number of children employed in industry declined rapidly.

> **Key Provisions of the Factory Acts (1802–1833)**

- Children between ages nine and thirteen could work a maximum of eight hours per day
- Teenagers aged fourteen to eighteen could work up to twelve hours
- Children under nine were banned from employment

The New Sexual Division of Labor

With the restriction of child labor and the collapse of the family work pattern in the 1830s came a new sexual division of labor. By 1850, the man was emerging as the family's primary wage earner, while the married woman found only limited job opportunities. Generally denied good jobs at high wages in the growing urban economy, wives were expected to concentrate on their duties at home.

separate spheres
▶ A gender division of labor with the wife at home as mother and homemaker and the husband as wage earner.

This new pattern of **separate spheres** had several aspects. First, all studies agree that married women from the working classes were much less likely to work full-time for wages outside the house after the first child arrived. Second, when married women did work for wages outside the house, they usually came from the poorest families, where the husbands were poorly paid, sick, unemployed, or missing. Third, these poor married or widowed women were joined by legions of young unmarried women, who worked full-time but only in certain jobs, of which textile factory work, laundering, and domestic service were particularly important. Fourth, all women were generally confined to low-paying, dead-end jobs. Evolving gradually, but largely in place by 1850, the new sexual division of labor constituted a major development in the history of women and of the family.

Several factors combined to create this new sexual division of labor. First, the new and unfamiliar discipline of the clock and the machine was especially hard on married women of the laboring classes. Relentless factory discipline conflicted with child care in a way that labor on the farm or in the cottage had not.

Second, running a household in conditions of primitive urban poverty was an extremely demanding job in its own right. There were no supermarkets or public transportation. Shopping, washing clothes, and feeding the family constituted a never-ending challenge. Thus many women might well have accepted the emerging division of labor as the best available strategy for family survival in the industrializing society.[4]

Third, to a large degree the young, generally unmarried women who did work for wages outside the home were segregated from men and confined to certain "women's jobs" because the new sexual division of labor replicated long-standing patterns of gender segregation and inequality. In the preindustrial economy, a small sector of the labor market had always been defined as "women's work,"

CHAPTER LOCATOR | What were the origins of the Industrial Revolution in Britain?

CHAPTER 20

630 THE REVOLUTION IN ENERGY AND INDUSTRY

Child Laborer This illustration of a girl dragging a coal wagon was one of several that shocked the public and contributed to the Mines Act of 1842. (© The British Library Board B.S. Ref 18, vol. 17, 65)

especially tasks involving needlework, spinning, food preparation, and child care. This traditional sexual division of labor took on new overtones, however, in response to the factory system. The growth of factories and mines brought unheard-of opportunities for girls and boys to mix on the job, free of familial supervision. Such opportunities led to more unplanned pregnancies and fueled the illegitimacy explosion that had begun in the late eighteenth century and that gathered force until at least 1850. Thus segregation of jobs by gender was partly an effort by older people to control the sexuality of working-class youths.

Investigations into the British coal industry before 1842 provide a graphic example of this concern. The middle-class men leading the inquiry professed horror at the sight of girls and women working without shirts, which was a common practice because of the heat, and they quickly assumed the prevalence of licentious sex with the male miners, who also wore very little clothing. In fact, many girls and married women worked for related males in a family unit that provided considerable protection and restraint. Yet many witnesses from the working class also believed that the mines were inappropriate and dangerous places for women and girls. Some miners stressed particularly the danger of sexual aggression for girls working past puberty. The **Mines Act of 1842** prohibited underground work for all women and girls as well as for boys under the age of ten.

A final factor encouraging working-class women to withdraw from paid labor was the domestic ideals emanating from middle-class women, who had largely embraced the "separate spheres" ideology. Middle-class reformers published tracts and formed societies to urge poor women to devote more care and attention to their homes and families.

Mines Act of 1842
▶ English law prohibiting underground work for all women and girls as well as for boys under the age of ten.

QUICK REVIEW

How did work evolve during the Industrial Revolution?
How did daily life change for working people?

How did countries outside Britain respond to the challenge of industrialization?

How did work and daily life evolve during the Industrial Revolution?

What were the social consequences of industrialization?

☑ LearningCurve
Check what you know.

What were the social consequences of industrialization?

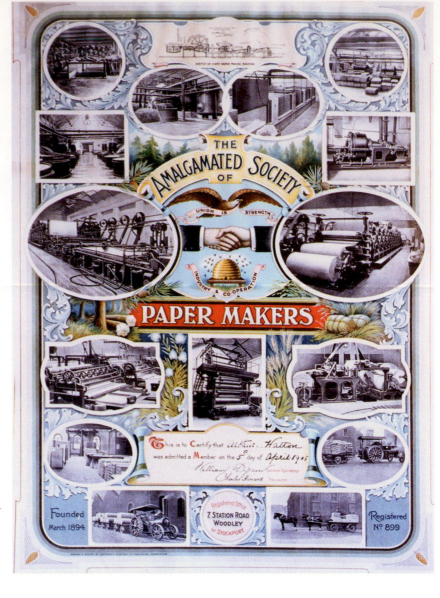

class-consciousness

▶ Awareness of belonging to a distinct social and economic class whose interests might conflict with those of other classes.

IN GREAT BRITAIN, INDUSTRIAL DEVELOPMENT LED to the creation of new social groups and intensified long-standing problems between capital and labor. A new class of factory owners and industrial capitalists arose. These men and women and their families strengthened the wealth and size of the middle class, which had previously been made up mainly of merchants and professional people. The demands of modern industry regularly brought the interests of the middle-class industrialists into conflict with those of the people who worked for them — the working class. Individuals experienced a growing sense of **class-consciousness**, or awareness of belonging to a distinct social and economic class whose interests might conflict with those of other classes. New questions about social relationships emerged. (See "Picturing the Past: Ford Maddox Brown, *Work*," page 633.) Meanwhile, enslaved labor in European colonies contributed to the industrialization process in multiple ways.

CHAPTER LOCATOR | What were the origins of the Industrial Revolution in Britain?

Ford Maddox Brown, *Work*

This midcentury painting provides a rich and realistic visual representation of the new concepts of social class that became common by 1850. (Birmingham Museums and Art Gallery/The Bridgeman Art Library)

> PICTURING THE PAST

ANALYZING THE IMAGE: Describe the different types of work shown. What different social classes are depicted, and what kinds of work (or leisure) are the members of the different social classes engaged in?

CONNECTIONS: What does this painting and Ford's title for it (*Work*) suggest about the artist's opinion of the work of common laborers?

The New Class of Factory Owners

Early industrialists operated in a highly competitive economic system. There were countless production problems, and success and large profits were by no means certain. Manufacturers therefore waged a constant battle to cut their production costs and stay afloat. Much of the profit had to go back into the business for new and better machinery.

Most early industrialists drew upon their families and friends for labor and capital, but they came from a variety of backgrounds. Many were from well-established families with rich networks of contacts and support. Others were of modest means, especially in the early days. Artisans and skilled workers of exceptional ability had unparalleled opportunities. Members of ethnic and religious groups who had been discriminated against jumped at the new chances and often helped each other.

As factories and firms grew larger, opportunities declined, at least in well-developed industries. It became considerably harder for a gifted but poor young

How did countries outside Britain respond to the challenge of industrialization?

How did work and daily life evolve during the Industrial Revolution?

What were the social consequences of industrialization?

✓ LearningCurve
Check what you know.

633

mechanic to start a small enterprise and end up as a wealthy manufacturer. In Britain by 1830 and in France and Germany by 1860, leading industrialists were more likely to have inherited their well-established enterprises, and they were financially much more secure than their struggling parents had been. They also had a greater sense of class-consciousness; they were fully aware that ongoing industrial development had widened the gap between themselves and their workers.

Just like working-class women, the wives and daughters of successful businessmen found fewer opportunities for active participation in Europe's increasingly complex business world. Rather than contributing as vital partners in a family-owned enterprise, as so many middle-class women had done, these women were increasingly valued for their ladylike gentility. By 1850, some influential women writers and most businessmen assumed that middle-class wives and daughters should avoid work in offices and factories. As we have seen, this ideology of "separate spheres" spread to working-class men and women as well.

Debates over Industrialization

Luddites

▶ Group of handicraft workers who attacked factories in northern England in 1811 and later, smashing the new machines that they believed were putting them out of work.

From the beginning, the British Industrial Revolution had its critics. Some handicraft workers—notably the **Luddites**, who attacked factories in northern England in 1811 and later—smashed the new machines, which they believed were putting them out of work. Doctors and reformers wrote of problems in the factories and new towns, while Malthus and Ricardo concluded that workers would earn only enough to stay alive.

This pessimistic view was accepted and reinforced by Friedrich Engels (1820–1895), the future revolutionary and colleague of Karl Marx (see Chapter 21, page 652). After studying conditions in northern England, this young son of a wealthy Prussian cotton manufacturer published in 1844 *The Condition of the Working Class in England*, a blistering indictment of the capitalist classes. The new poverty of industrial workers was worse than the old poverty of cottage workers and agricultural laborers, according to Engels. The culprit was industrial capitalism, with its relentless competition and constant technical change. Engels's extremely influential charge of capitalist exploitation and increasing worker poverty was embellished by Marx and later socialists (see Chapter 21, page 652).

And if the new class interpretation was more of a deceptive simplification than a fundamental truth for some critics, it appealed to many because it seemed to explain what was happening. Therefore, conflicting classes existed, in part, because many individuals came to believe they existed and developed an appropriate sense of class feeling—what we now call class-consciousness.

The Early British Labor Movement

Not everyone worked in large factories and coal mines during the Industrial Revolution. In 1850, more British people still worked on farms than in any other occupation, although rural communities were suffering from outward migration. The second-largest occupation was domestic service, with more than 1 million household servants, 90 percent of whom were women. Thus many old, familiar jobs outside industry lived on and provided alternatives to industrial labor. Within

CHAPTER LOCATOR | What were the origins of the Industrial Revolution in Britain?

industry itself, the pattern of artisans working with hand tools in small shops remained unchanged in many trades, even as others were revolutionized by technological change.

Working-class solidarity and class-consciousness developed both in small workshops and in large factories. A general strike of adult cotton spinners in Manchester in 1810 testifies to the growth of anticapitalist sentiment in Britain's northern factory districts in the first decades of the nineteenth century. Commenting in 1825 on a strike in the woolen center of Bradford and the support it had gathered from other regions, one paper claimed with pride that "it is all the workers of England against a few masters of Bradford."[5] Even in trades that did not undergo mechanization, unemployment and stagnant wages contributed to class awareness.

The classical liberal concept of economic freedom and laissez faire emerged in the late eighteenth century, and it continued to gather strength in the early nineteenth century in opposition to the rising tide of working-class anger. In 1799, Parliament passed the **Combination Acts**, which outlawed unions and strikes. In 1813 and 1814, Parliament repealed the old and often-disregarded law of 1563 regulating the wages of artisans and the conditions of apprenticeship. As a result of these and other measures, certain skilled artisan workers, such as bootmakers and high-quality tailors, found aggressive capitalists ignoring traditional work rules and trying to flood their trades with unorganized women workers and children to beat down wages.

The capitalist attack on artisan guilds and work rules was bitterly resented by many craftworkers, who subsequently played an important part in Great Britain and in other countries in gradually building a modern labor movement. The Combination Acts were widely disregarded by workers. Craftsmen continued to take collective action, and societies of skilled factory workers also organized unions in defiance of the law. Unions sought to control the number of skilled workers, to limit apprenticeship to members' own children, and to bargain with owners over wages. In the face of such widespread union activity, Parliament repealed the Combination Acts in 1824. Unions were subsequently tolerated, though they were not fully legal until 1867.

The next stage in the development of the British trade-union movement was the attempt to create a single large national union. This effort was led not so much by working people as by social reformers such as Robert Owen. Owen, a self-made cotton manufacturer, had pioneered in industrial relations by combining firm discipline with concern for the health, safety, and hours of his workers. In 1834, Owen was involved in the organization of one of the largest and most visionary of the early national unions, the Grand National Consolidated Trades Union.

When Owen's and other ambitious schemes collapsed, the British labor movement moved once again after 1851 in the direction of craft unions. These unions won real benefits for members by fairly conservative means and thus became an accepted part of the industrial scene.

British workers also engaged in direct political activity in defense of their own interests. After the collapse of Owen's national trade union, many working people went into the Chartist movement, which sought political democracy. The key Chartist demand—that all men be given the right to vote—became the great hope of millions of common people. Workers were also active in campaigns to limit

Combination Acts

▶ British laws passed in 1799 that outlawed unions and strikes, favoring capitalist business people over skilled artisans. Bitterly resented and widely disregarded by many craft guilds, the acts were repealed by Parliament in 1824.

How did countries outside Britain respond to the challenge of industrialization?

How did work and daily life evolve during the Industrial Revolution?

What were the social consequences of industrialization?

✓ LearningCurve
Check what you know.

635

the workday in factories to ten hours and to permit duty-free importation of wheat into Great Britain to secure cheap bread. Thus working people developed a sense of their own identity and played an active role in shaping the new industrial system.

The Impact of Slavery

Another mass labor force of the Industrial Revolution consisted of the millions of enslaved men, women, and children who toiled in European colonies in the Caribbean and in North and South America. Most historians agree that profits from colonial plantations and slave trading were a small portion of British national income in the eighteenth century and were probably more often invested in land than in industry. Nevertheless, the impact of slavery on Britain's economy was much broader than its direct profits alone. In the mid-eighteenth century, the need for items to exchange for colonial cotton, sugar, tobacco, and slaves stimulated demand for British manufactured goods in the Caribbean, North America, and West Africa. Britain's dominance in the slave trade also led to the development of finance and credit institutions that helped early industrialists obtain capital for their businesses. Investments in canals, roads, and railroads made possible by profits from colonial trade provided the necessary infrastructure to move raw materials and products of the factory system.

The British Parliament abolished the slave trade in 1807 and freed all slaves in British territories in 1833, but by 1850 most of the cotton processed by British mills was supplied by the labor of enslaved people in the southern United States. Thus the Industrial Revolution was deeply entangled with the Atlantic world and the misery of slavery.

> **QUICK REVIEW**

How did the changes brought about by the Industrial Revolution lead to new social classes, and how did people respond to the new structure?

CHAPTER LOCATOR | What were the origins of the Industrial Revolution in Britain?

636 CHAPTER 20
THE REVOLUTION IN ENERGY AND INDUSTRY

LOOKING BACK LOOKING AHEAD

One popular idea in the 1830s, first developed by a French economist, was that Britain's late-eighteenth-century "industrial revolution" paralleled the political events in France during the French Revolution. One revolution was economic, while the other was political; one was ongoing and successful, while the other had failed and come to a definite end in 1815, when Europe's conservative monarchs defeated Napoleon and restored the French kings of the Old Regime.

In fact, in 1815, the French Revolution, like the Industrial Revolution, was an unfinished revolution. Britain was in the midst of its economic transformation and the states of northwestern Europe had only begun industrialization, and after 1815, the political conflicts and ideologies of revolutionary France were still very much alive. Moreover, in 1815, the unfinished French Revolution carried the very real possibility of renewed political upheaval. This possibility, which conservatives feared and radicals longed for, would become dramatic reality in 1848, when political revolutions swept across Europe like a whirlwind.

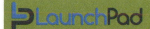

ONLINE DOCUMENT PROJECT

Josiah Wedgwood

How did observers of early industrialization imagine the relationship between workers and their work, and between workers and their employers?

You encountered Josiah Wedgwood's story on page 618. Keeping the question above in mind, explore different views on the impact of industrial production on individual workers in light of Wedgwood's approach to industrial labor. *See inside the front cover to learn more.*

How did countries outside Britain respond to the challenge of industrialization?	How did work and daily life evolve during the Industrial Revolution?	What were the social consequences of industrialization?	✔ LearningCurve Check what you know.

CHAPTER 20 STUDY GUIDE

 STEP 1

GET STARTED ONLINE

 **LearningCurve**

Now that you've read the chapter, make it stick by completing the LearningCurve activity.

STEP 2

EXPLAIN WHY IT MATTERS

Put your reading into practice. Identify each term below, and then explain why it matters in Western history.

TERM	WHO OR WHAT & WHEN	WHY IT MATTERS
Industrial Revolution (p. 614)		
spinning jenny (p. 615)		
water frame (p. 616)		
steam engines (p. 616)		
Rocket (p. 617)		
Crystal Palace (p. 620)		
iron law of wages (p. 621)		
tariff protection (p. 626)		
Factory Acts (p. 629)		
separate spheres (p. 630)		
Mines Act of 1842 (p. 631)		
class-consciousness (p. 632)		
Luddites (p. 634)		
Combination Acts (p. 635)		

 **STEP 3**

MOVE BEYOND THE BASICS

To demonstrate a more advanced understanding of the changes in work and home life brought on by the process of industrialization, complete the chart included below with descriptions of key aspects of work and home life for cottage and factory workers. How did the relationship between home and work life change as industrialization progressed? How did changes in work patterns reshape gender relations?

	Cottage industry	Factory work
Nature of work		
Work discipline and pace		
Work and gender		
Work and children		
Home life		
Identity/class-consciousness		

PUT IT ALL TOGETHER

Now, take a step back and try to explain the big picture. Remember to use specific examples from the chapter in your answers.

THE INDUSTRIAL REVOLUTION IN BRITAIN AND BEYOND

▶ How did British innovators solve the eighteenth-century energy crisis? How did their solution help transform the British economy?

▶ What role did government play in continental industrialization? How did continental governments work with private individuals and companies to promote economic development?

NEW PATTERNS OF WORKING AND LIVING

▶ How and why did the makeup of the industrial workforce change over the course of the first half of the nineteenth century?

▶ How did ideas about "women's work" change as a result of industrialization?

RELATIONS BETWEEN CAPITAL AND LABOR

▶ What role did workers play in shaping the development of the nineteenth-century industrial landscape?

▶ What is class-consciousness? How did industrialization help produce a new sense among workers of their own social identity?

MAKE CONNECTIONS

▶ How did the Agricultural Revolution of the seventeenth and eighteenth centuries make the Industrial Revolution possible?

▶ What connections can you make between industrialization and emergence of mass politics in the nineteenth century?

> ### IN YOUR OWN WORDS

Imagine that you must give an oral report to the class answering the following question: **How did the Industrial Revolution transform the society and economy of Europe?** What would be the most important points and why?

21

IDEOLOGIES AND UPHEAVALS

1815–1850

> **How did the forces unleashed by the French and Industrial Revolutions shape European politics in the first half of the nineteenth century?** Chapter 21 examines political and cultural developments in the first half of the nineteenth century. Attempts to manage the progressive forces associated with the French Revolution led first to a reassertion of conservative political control in continental Europe. The political and cultural innovations unleashed by the French Revolution and industrialization proved difficult to contain, however. In politics, powerful new ideologies — liberalism, nationalism, and socialism — emerged to oppose conservatism. In literature, art, and music, romanticism captured the intensity of the era. A successful revolution in Greece, liberal reform in Great Britain, and popular unrest in France gave voice to ordinary people's desire for political and social change. All these movements helped launch the great wave of revolutions that swept across Europe in 1848.

LearningCurve

After reading the chapter, use LearningCurve to retain what you've read.

Life in the Revolutionary Era. Between 1830 and 1848, crowds stormed public areas to force political change in many parts of Europe. Here French king Louis Phillipe leaves Versailles for the Paris City Hall to greet the people. (Châteaux de Versailles, France/Giraudon/The Bridgeman Art Library)

> How was peace restored and maintained after 1815?

> What new ideologies emerged to challenge conservatism?

> What were the characteristics of the romantic movement?

> How and where was conservatism challenged after 1815?

> What were the main causes and results of the revolutions of 1848?

How was peace restored and maintained after 1815?

Adjusting the Balance This French cartoon captures the essence of how the educated public thought about the balance-of-power diplomacy resulting in the Treaty of Vienna. The Englishman on the left uses his money to counterbalance the people that the Prussian and the fat Metternich are gaining in Saxony and Italy. Alexander I sits happily on his prize, Poland. (Bibliothèque nationale de France)

AFTER FINALLY DEFEATING NAPOLEON, the conservative, aristocratic monarchies of Russia, Prussia, Austria, and Great Britain—known as the Quadruple Alliance—reaffirmed their determination to hold France in line. Other international questions remained unresolved. Even before Napoleon's final defeat, the allies had agreed to meet to fashion a general peace accord in 1814 at the **Congress of Vienna**. By carefully managing the balance of power and embracing conservative restoration, they brokered an agreement that contributed to fifty years of peace in Europe (**Map 21.1**).

Congress of Vienna
▶ A meeting of the Quadruple Alliance (Russia, Prussia, Austria, and Great Britain), restoration France, and smaller European states to fashion a general peace settlement that began after the defeat of Napoleon's France in 1814.

The European Balance of Power

The allied powers were concerned first and foremost with the defeated enemy, France. Agreeing to the restoration of the Bourbon dynasty, the allies offered France lenient terms in the first Treaty of Paris, signed after Napoleon's abdication and exile to Elba. Thus the victorious powers avoided provoking a spirit of victimization and desire for revenge in the defeated country.

Representatives of the Quadruple Alliance (plus a representative of the restored Bourbon monarch of France) fashioned the peace at the Congress of Vienna from September 1814 to June 1815. One of the main tasks of the four allies was to raise a number of formidable barriers against renewed French aggression. The Low Countries—Belgium and Holland—were united under an enlarged Dutch monarchy capable of opposing France more effectively. Prussia received considerably more territory on France's eastern border to stand as the "sentinel on the Rhine" against France. In these ways, the Quadruple Alliance combined leniency toward France with strong defensive measures.

Self-interest and traditional ideas about the balance of power motivated allied moderation toward France. To Klemens von Metternich (MEH-tuhr-nihk) and Robert Castlereagh (KA-suhl-ray), the foreign ministers of Austria and Great Britain, respectively, as well as their French counterpart, Charles Talleyrand, the balance of power meant an international equilibrium of political and military forces that would discourage aggression by any combination of states or, worse, the domination of Europe by any single state.

The Great Powers—Austria, Britain, Prussia, Russia, and France—used the balance of power to settle their own dangerous disputes at the Congress of Vienna. The victors generally agreed that each of them should receive compensation in the form of territory for their successful struggle against the French. The compromises they reached in this context fell very much within the framework of balance-of-power ideology.

Unfortunately for France, Napoleon suddenly escaped from the island of Elba and reignited his wars of expansion for a brief time (see Chapter 19, page 599). Yet the second Treaty of Paris, concluded after Napoleon's final defeat at Waterloo in 1815, was still relatively moderate toward France. The members of the Quadruple Alliance did agree, however, to meet periodically to discuss their common

What new ideologies emerged to challenge conservatism?	What were the characteristics of the romantic movement?	How and where was conservatism challenged after 1815?	What were the main causes and results of the revolutions of 1848?	✔ LearningCurve Check what you know.

MAP 21.1 ■ Europe in 1815

In 1815, Europe contained many different states, but after the defeat of Napoleon, international politics was dominated by the five Great Powers: Russia, Prussia, Austria, Great Britain, and France. (The number rises to six if one includes the Ottoman Empire.)

> MAPPING THE PAST

ANALYZING THE MAP: Trace the political boundaries of each Great Power, and compare their geographical strengths and weaknesses. What territories did Prussia and Austria gain as a result of the war with Napoleon?

CONNECTIONS: How did Prussia's and Austria's territorial gains contribute to the balance of power established at the Congress of Vienna? What other factors enabled the Great Powers to achieve such a long-lasting peace?

interests and to consider appropriate measures for the maintenance of peace in Europe. This agreement marked the beginning of the European "Congress System," which lasted long into the nineteenth century and settled many international crises peacefully, through international conferences or "congresses" and balance-of-power diplomacy.

CHAPTER LOCATOR | **How was peace restored and maintained after 1815?**

- Belgium and Holland: United under an enlarged Dutch monarchy
- Prussia: Took part of Saxony, as well as territory on France's eastern border
- Austria: Gave up territories in Belgium and southern Germany, but took Venetia and Lombardy in northern Italy as well as former Polish possessions and new lands on the eastern coast of the Adriatic
- Russia: Acquired a small Polish kingdom
- Great Britain: Retained colonies and strategic outposts captured during the wars

Metternich and Conservatism

The political ideals of conservatism, often associated with Austrian foreign minister Prince Klemens von Metternich (1773–1859), dominated Great Power discussions at the Congress of Vienna. Austrian foreign minister from 1809 to 1848, the cosmopolitan and conservative Metternich had a pessimistic view of human nature, which he believed was ever prone to error, excess, and self-serving behavior. The disruptive events of the French Revolution and the Napoleonic Wars confirmed these views, and Metternich's conservatism would emerge as a powerful new political ideological force in response to the revolutionary age.

Metternich firmly believed that liberalism, as embodied in revolutionary America and France, bore the responsibility for the untold bloodshed and suffering caused by twenty-five years of war. Like Edmund Burke (see Chapter 19, page 591) and other conservatives, Metternich blamed liberal middle-class revolutionaries for stirring up the lower classes. Authoritarian governments, he concluded, were necessary to protect society from the baser elements of human behavior. Organized religion was another pillar of strong government; Metternich maintained that Christian morality was a vital bulwark against radical change.

Metternich defended his class and its rights and privileges with a clear conscience. The church and nobility were among Europe's most ancient and valuable institutions, and conservatives regarded tradition as the basic foundation of human society.

The threat of liberalism appeared doubly dangerous to Metternich because it generally went with aspirations for national independence. Liberals believed that each people, each national group, had a right to establish its own independent government and fulfill its own destiny. The idea of national self-determination under constitutional government was repellent to Metternich because it threatened to revolutionize central Europe and destroy the Austrian Empire.

After centuries of war, royal intermarriage, and territorial expansion, the vast Austrian Empire of the Habsburgs included many peoples within its borders (**Map 21.2**). The peoples of the Austrian Empire spoke at least eleven different languages, observed vastly different customs, and lived with a surprising variety of regional civic and political institutions. The multiethnic state Metternich served had strengths and weaknesses. A large population and vast territories gave the empire economic and military clout, but its potentially dissatisfied nationalities undermined political unity. In these circumstances, Metternich virtually had to

| What new ideologies emerged to challenge conservatism? | What were the characteristics of the romantic movement? | How and where was conservatism challenged after 1815? | What were the main causes and results of the revolutions of 1848? | ✓ **LearningCurve** Check what you know. |

645

MAP 21.2 ■ Peoples of the Habsburg Monarchy, 1815

The old dynastic state ruled by the Habsburg monarchy was a patchwork of nationalities and ethnic groups, in which territorial borders barely reflected the diversity of where different peoples actually lived. Note especially the widely scattered pockets of Germans and Hungarians. How do you think this ethnic diversity might have led to the rise of national independence movements in the Austrian Empire?

oppose liberalism and nationalism—if Austria was to remain intact and powerful, it could hardly accommodate ideologies that supported national self-determination.

On Austria's borders, Russia and, to a lesser extent, the Ottoman Empire supported and echoed Metternich's efforts to hold back liberalism and nationalism. These far-flung empires were both absolutist states with powerful armies and long traditions of expansion and conquest. Because of those conquests, both were also multinational empires with many peoples, languages, and religions. After 1815, both of these multinational absolutist states worked to preserve their respective traditional conservative orders. Only after 1840 did each in turn experience a profound crisis and embark on a program of fundamental reform and modernization, as we shall see in Chapter 23.

CHAPTER LOCATOR | **How was peace restored and maintained after 1815?**

Repressing the Revolutionary Spirit

Conservative political ideologies had important practical consequences. In September 1815 Austria, Prussia, and Russia formed the **Holy Alliance**. First proposed by Russia's Alexander I, the alliance worked to repress reformist and revolutionary movements and stifle desires for national independence across Europe.

The conservative restoration first brought its collective power to bear on southern Europe. In 1820, revolutionaries successfully forced the monarchs of Spain and the southern Italian Kingdom of the Two Sicilies to establish constitutional monarchies. Calling a conference at Troppau in Austria, Metternich and Alexander I proclaimed the principle of active intervention to maintain all autocratic regimes whenever they were threatened. Austrian forces then marched into Naples in 1821 and restored the autocratic power of Ferdinand I in the Two Sicilies. A French invasion of Spain in 1823 likewise returned power to the king there.

The conservative policies of Metternich and the Holy Alliance crushed reform not only in Austria and the Italian peninsula but also in the newly established German Confederation. The new confederation, a loose association of German-speaking states, replaced the roughly three hundred principalities, free cities, and dynastic states of the Holy Roman Empire with just thirty-eight German states, dominated by Prussia and Austria (see Map 21.1, page 644). Ambassadors from each state met in a Confederation Diet, or assembly. When liberal reformers and university students began to protest for the national unification of the German states, the Austrian and Prussian leadership used the diet to issue and enforce the infamous **Karlsbad Decrees** in 1819. These decrees required the German states to outlaw liberal political organizations, police their universities and newspapers, and establish a permanent committee with spies and informers to clamp down on liberal or radical reformers.

Limits to Conservative Power and Revolution in South America

In the following years, the members of the Holy Alliance continued to battle against liberal political change.[1] While Metternich's system proved quite effective in central Europe, at least until 1848, the monarchists failed to stop dynastic change in France in 1830 or prevent Belgium from winning independence from the Netherlands in 1831.

The most dramatic challenge to conservative power occurred not in Europe, but overseas in South America. In the 1820s, South American elites rose up and broke away from the Spanish crown and established a number of new republics based at first on liberal, Enlightenment ideals. The leaders of the revolutions were primarily wealthy Creoles, direct descendants of Spanish parents born in the Americas. The well-established and powerful Creoles—only about 5 percent of the population—resented the political and economic control of an even smaller elite minority of *peninsulares*, people born in Spain who lived in and ruled the colonies. The vast majority of the population, composed of "mestizos" and "mulattos" (people of ethnically mixed heritage), enslaved and freed Africans, and native indigenous peoples, languished at the bottom of the social pyramid.

Holy Alliance

▶ An alliance formed by the conservative rulers of Austria, Prussia, and Russia in September 1815 that became a symbol of the repression of liberal and revolutionary movements all over Europe.

Karlsbad Decrees

▶ Issued in 1819, these decrees were designed to uphold Metternich's conservatism, requiring the German states to root out subversive ideas and squelch any liberal organizations.

What new ideologies emerged to challenge conservatism?	What were the characteristics of the romantic movement?	How and where was conservatism challenged after 1815?	What were the main causes and results of the revolutions of 1848?	✓ LearningCurve Check what you know.

By the late 1700s, the Creoles had begun to question Spanish policy and even the necessity of further colonial rule. The spark for revolt came during the Napoleonic Wars, when the French occupation of Spain in 1808 weakened the power of the autocratic Spanish crown and the Napoleonic rhetoric of rights inspired revolutionaries. Yet the Creoles hesitated, worried that open revolt might upend the social pyramid or even lead to a slave revolution as in Haiti (see Chapter 19).

The South American revolutions thus began from below, with spontaneous uprisings by subordinated peoples of color. Creole leaders quickly emerged to take control of a struggle. In the north, Simón Bolívar—the Latin American equivalent of George Washington—defeated Spanish forces and established a short-lived "Gran Colombia," which lasted from 1819 to 1830. Bolívar dreamed of establishing a federation of South American states, modeled on the United States. To the south, José de San Martín, a liberal-minded military commander, successfully threw off Spanish control by 1825.

Dreams of South American federation and unity proved difficult to implement. By 1830, the large northern state established by Bolívar had fractured, and by 1840 the borders of the new nations looked much like the map of Latin America today. Most of the new states initially received liberal constitutions, but these quickly gave way to a new political system controlled by *caudillos* (caw-DEE-yohs), or strong men, sometimes labeled warlords. Often former Creoles, the caudillos ruled limited territories on the basis of military strength, family patronage, and populist politics. The South American revolutions had failed to establish lasting constitutional republics, but they did demonstrate the revolutionary potential of liberal ideals and the limits on conservative control.

> ## QUICK REVIEW

What steps did the Great Powers take to prevent the emergence of another Napoleon or a second French Revolution?

CHAPTER LOCATOR | How was peace restored and maintained after 1815?

What new ideologies emerged to challenge conservatism?

Mr. and Mrs. Karl Marx

Active in the revolution of 1848, Marx fled from Germany in 1849 and settled in London. There Marx and his young wife lived a respectable middle-class life while he wrote *Capital*, the weighty exposition of his socialist theories. Marx also worked to organize the working class. He earned a modest income as a journalist and received financial support from his coauthor and lifelong friend, Friedrich Engels. (Time Life Pictures/Getty Images)

IN THE YEARS FOLLOWING THE PEACE SETTLEMENT OF 1815, intellectuals and social observers sought to harness the radical ideas of the revolutionary age to new political movements. Often inspired by liberties championed during the French Revolution, radical thinkers developed and refined alternative ideologies and tried to convince society to act on them. In so doing, they helped articulate the basic political ideals that continue to shape Western society today.

Liberalism and the Middle Class

The principal ideas of **liberalism**—liberty and equality—were by no means defeated in 1815. Liberalism demanded representative government as opposed to autocratic monarchy, and equality before the law as opposed to legally separate classes. The idea of liberty also meant specific individual freedoms: freedom of the press, freedom of speech, freedom of assembly, freedom of worship, and freedom from arbitrary arrest. In Europe in 1815, only France with Louis XVIII's Constitutional Charter and Great Britain with its Parliament had realized any of the liberal program. Even in those countries, liberalism had only begun to succeed.

liberalism

▶ The principal ideas of this movement were equality and liberty; liberals demanded representative government and equality before the law as well as individual freedoms such as freedom of the press, freedom of speech, freedom of assembly, freedom of worship, and freedom from arbitrary arrest.

| **What new ideologies emerged to challenge conservatism?** | What were the characteristics of the romantic movement? | How and where was conservatism challenged after 1815? | What were the main causes and results of the revolutions of 1848? | ✓ LearningCurve Check what you know. |

Although conservatives still saw liberalism as a profound threat, it had gained a group of powerful adherents: the new upper classes made wealthy through growing industrialization and global commerce. Liberal economic principles, the doctrine of **laissez faire** (lay-zay FEHR), called for free trade (including relaxation of import/export duties), unrestricted private enterprise, and no government interference in the economy.

In the first half of the nineteenth century, liberal political ideals became closely associated with narrow class interests. Starting in the 1820s in Britain, business elites enthusiastically embraced laissez-faire policies because they proved immensely profitable, and they used liberal ideas to defend their right to do as they wished in their factories. Labor unions were outlawed because, these elites argued, unions restricted free competition and the individual's "right to work." Early-nineteenth-century liberals favored representative government, but they generally wanted property qualifications attached to the right to vote. In practice, this meant limiting the vote to very small numbers of well-to-do men.

As liberalism became increasingly identified with upper-class business interests, some opponents of conservatism felt that liberalism did not go nearly far enough. Inspired by memories of the French Revolution and the example of Jacksonian democracy in the young American republic, these republicans expanded liberal ideology to include universal voting rights, at least for males. Republicans were more radical than the liberals, and they were more willing than most liberals to endorse violent upheaval to achieve goals. As a result, liberals and radical republicans could join forces against conservatives only up to a point.

The Growing Appeal of Nationalism

Nationalism—an idea destined to have an enormous influence in the modern world—was another radical idea that gained popularity in the years after 1815. Early nationalists found inspiration in the vision of a people united by a common language, a common history and culture, and a common territory.

In the early nineteenth century, such national unity was more a dream than a reality as far as most ethnic groups or nationalities were concerned. Local dialects abounded, even in relatively cohesive countries like France. Moreover, a variety of ethnic groups shared the territory of most states. Over the course of the nineteenth century, nationalism nonetheless gathered force as a political philosophy. Advancing literacy rates, the establishment of a mass press, the growth of large state bureaucracies, compulsory education, and conscription armies all created a common culture that encouraged ordinary people to take pride in their national heritage.

In multiethnic states, however, nationalism also promoted disintegration. Recognizing the power of the "national idea," European nationalists—generally educated, middle-class liberals and intellectuals—sought to turn the cultural unity that they desired into political reality. They believed that every nation, like every citizen, had the right to exist in freedom and to develop its unique character and spirit, and they hoped to make the territory of each people coincide with well-defined borders in an independent nation-state.

This political goal made nationalism explosive, particularly in central and eastern Europe, where different peoples overlapped and intermingled. As dis-

---

laissez faire

▶ A doctrine of economic liberalism that calls for unrestricted private enterprise and no government interference in the economy.

nationalism

▶ The idea that each people had its own genius and specific identity that manifested itself especially in a common language and history, and often led to the desire for an independent political state.

CHAPTER LOCATOR | How was peace restored and maintained after 1815?

650   CHAPTER 21   IDEOLOGIES AND UPHEAVALS

cussed, the Austrian, Russian, and Ottoman central states refused to allow national minorities independence; that suppression fomented widespread discontent among nationalists who wanted freedom from oppressive imperial rule. In the many different principalities of the Italian peninsula and the German Confederation, to the contrary, nationalists yearned for national unification across what they saw as divisive and obsolete state borders.

Between 1815 and 1850, most people who believed in nationalism also believed in either liberalism or radical republicanism. A deep belief in the creativity and nobility of the people linked these two concepts. Liberals and especially democrats saw the people as the ultimate source of all government. Yet liberals and nationalists agreed that the benefits of self-government would be possible only if the people were united by common traditions that transcended local interests and even class differences. Thus the liberty of the individual and the love of a free nation overlapped greatly in the early nineteenth century.

Despite some confidence that a world system based on independent nations would promote global harmony, early nationalists eagerly emphasized the differences among peoples and developed a strong sense of "us" versus "them." To this "us-them" outlook, it was all too easy for nationalists to add two highly volatile ingredients: a sense of national mission and a sense of national superiority. As Europe entered an age of increased global interaction, these two underlying ideas would lead to aggression and conflict as powerful nation-states backed by patriotic citizens competed with each other on the international stage.

The Foundations of Modern Socialism

More radical than liberalism or nationalism was **socialism**. Early socialist thinkers were a diverse group with wide-ranging ideas. Yet they shared a sense that the political revolution in France, the growth of industrialization in Britain, and the rise of laissez faire had created a profound crisis. Modern capitalism, they believed, fomented a selfish individualism that encouraged inequality and split the community into isolated fragments. Society urgently required fundamental change to re-establish cooperation and a new sense of community.

Early socialists felt an intense desire to help the poor, and they preached that the rich and the poor should be more nearly equal economically. To this end, they believed that private property should be strictly regulated by the government, or abolished outright and replaced by state or community ownership. Economic planning, greater social equality, and state regulation of property were the key ideas of early socialism.

One influential group of early socialist advocates became known as the "utopian socialists" because their grand schemes for social improvement ultimately proved unworkable. The Frenchmen Count Henri de Saint-Simon (awn-REE duh san-see-MOHN) (1760–1825) and Charles Fourier (sharl FAWR-ee-ay) (1772–1837) and the British industrialist Robert Owen all founded movements intended to establish model communities that would usher in a new age of happiness and equality.

Saint-Simon optimistically proclaimed the tremendous possibilities of industrial development: "The golden age of the human species . . . is before us!"[2] The key to progress was proper social organization that required the "parasites"—the

socialism

▶ A backlash against the emergence of individualism and the fragmentation of industrial society, and a move toward cooperation and a sense of community; the key ideas were economic planning, greater social equality, and state regulation of property.

| What new ideologies emerged to challenge conservatism? | What were the characteristics of the romantic movement? | How and where was conservatism challenged after 1815? | What were the main causes and results of the revolutions of 1848? | ✓ LearningCurve Check what you know. |

651

court, the aristocracy, lawyers, and churchmen—to give way, once and for all, to the "doers"—the leading scientists, engineers, and industrialists. Saint-Simon also stressed in highly moralistic terms that every social institution ought to have as its main goal improved conditions for the poor.

After 1830, the utopian critique of capitalism became sharper. Charles Fourier envisaged a socialist utopia of mathematically precise, self-sufficient communities called "phalanxes." Fourier was also an early proponent of the total emancipation of women. Robert Owen, an early promoter of labor unions, likewise called for society to be reorganized into model industrial-agricultural communities. Saint-Simon, Fourier, and Owen all had followers who tried to put their ideas into practice. Though these attempts had basically collapsed by the 1850s, utopian socialist ideas remained an inspiration for future reformers and revolutionaries.

Some socialist thinkers embraced the even more radical ideas of anarchism. In his 1840 pamphlet *What Is Property?* Pierre-Joseph Proudhon (1809–1865), a self-educated printer, famously argued that "property is theft!" Property, he claimed, was profit that was stolen from the worker, the source of all wealth. Proudhon believed that states should be abolished and that society should be organized in loose associations of working people.

Other early socialists, like Louis Blanc (1811–1882), focused on more practical reforms. In his *Organization of Work* (1839), he urged workers to agitate for universal voting rights and to take control of the state peacefully. Blanc believed that the state should set up government-funded workshops and factories to guarantee full employment. The right to work had to become as sacred as any other right.

As industrialization advanced in European cities, working people began to embrace the socialist message. This happened first in France, where workers cherished the memory of the radical phase of the French Revolution. Developing a sense of class in the process of their protests, workers favored collective action and government intervention in economic life. Thus the aspirations of workers and radical theorists reinforced each other, and a genuine socialist movement emerged in Paris in the 1830s and 1840s.

The Birth of Marxist Socialism

In the 1840s, France was the center of socialism, but in the following decades the German intellectual Karl Marx (1818–1883) would weave the diffuse strands of socialist thought into a distinctly modern ideology. Marxist socialism—or **Marxism**—would have a lasting impact on political thought and practice.

The son of a Jewish lawyer who had converted to Lutheranism, the young Marx was a brilliant student. After earning a Ph.D. in philosophy at Humboldt University in Berlin in 1841, he turned to journalism, and his critical articles about the laboring poor caught the attention of the Prussian police. Forced to flee Prussia in 1843, Marx traveled around Europe, promoting socialism and avoiding the authorities. After the revolutions of 1848, Marx settled in London, where he spent the rest of his life as an advocate of working-class revolution. *Capital*, his magnum opus, appeared in 1867.

Marx was a dedicated scholar, and his work united sociology, economics, philosophy, and history in an impressive synthesis. From Scottish and English political economists like Adam Smith and David Ricardo, Marx learned to apply

Marxism

▶ An influential political program based on the socialist ideas of German radical Karl Marx, which called for a working-class revolution to overthrow capitalist society and establish a Communist state.

CHAPTER LOCATOR | How was peace restored and maintained after 1815?

652 CHAPTER 21 IDEOLOGIES AND UPHEAVALS

social-scientific analysis to economic problems. Deeply influenced by the utopian socialists, Marx championed ideals of social equality and community. Following German philosophies of idealism associated with Georg Hegel (1770–1831), Marx came to believe that history had patterns and purpose and moved forward in stages toward an ultimate goal.

Bringing these ideas together, Marx argued that class struggle over economic wealth was the great engine of human history. In his view, one class had always exploited the other, and with the advent of modern industry, society was split more clearly than ever before: between the upper class—the **bourgeoisie** (boor-JWAH-zee)—and the working class—the **proletariat**. The bourgeoisie, a tiny minority, owned the means of production and grew rich by exploiting the labor of workers. Over time, Marx argued, the proletariat would grow ever larger and ever poorer, and their increasing alienation would lead them to develop a sense of revolutionary class-consciousness. Then, just as the bourgeoisie had triumphed over the feudal aristocracy in the French Revolution, the proletariat would overthrow the bourgeoisie in a violent revolutionary cataclysm. The result would be the end of class struggle and the arrival of communism, a system of radical equality.

When Marx and Engels published *The Communist Manifesto* on the eve of the revolutions of 1848, their opening claim that "a spectre is haunting Europe—the spectre of Communism" was highly exaggerated. The Communist movement was in its infancy; scattered groups of socialists, anarchists, and labor leaders were hardly united around Marxist ideas. But by the time Marx died in 1883, Marxist socialism had profoundly reshaped left-wing radicalism in ways that would inspire revolutionaries around the world for the next one hundred years.

bourgeoisie
▶ The middle-class minority who owned the means of production and, according to Marx, exploited the working-class proletariat.

proletariat
▶ The industrial working class who, according to Marx, were unfairly exploited by the profit-seeking bourgeoisie.

QUICK REVIEW

What were the connections between liberalism and nationalism in the first half of the nineteenth century?

What new ideologies emerged to challenge conservatism?

What were the characteristics of the romantic movement?

How and where was conservatism challenged after 1815?

What were the main causes and results of the revolutions of 1848?

✓ LearningCurve
Check what you know.

What were the characteristics of the romantic movement?

Casper David Friedrich, *Two Men Contemplating the Moon* Casper David Friedrich's reverence for the mysterious powers of nature radiate from this masterpiece of romantic art. Completed in 1820, the painting shows two relatively small, anonymous figures mesmerized by the sublime beauty of the full moon. Viewers of the painting, positioned by the artist to look over the shoulders of the men, are likewise compelled to experience nature's wonder. In a subtle expression of the connection between romanticism and political reform, Friedrich has clothed the men in old-fashioned, traditional German dress, which radical students had adopted as a form of protest against the repressive conservatism of the post-Napoleonic era. (Galerie Neue Meister Dresden, Germany/© Staatliche Kunstsammlungen Dresden/ The Bridgeman Art Library)

romanticism
▶ An artistic movement, at its height from about 1790 to the 1840s, that was in part a revolt against classicism and the Enlightenment. It was characterized by a belief in emotional exuberance, unrestrained imagination, and spontaneity in both art and personal life.

THE EARLY NINETEENTH CENTURY BROUGHT CHANGES to literature and the other arts as well as political ideas. Followers of the new romantic movement, or romanticism, revolted against the emphasis on rationality, order, and restraint that characterized the Enlightenment and the controlled style of classicism.

The Tenets of Romanticism

Like other cultural movements, **romanticism** was characterized by intellectual diversity. Nonetheless, common parameters stand out. Artists inspired by romanticism repudiated the emphasis on reason associated with well-known Enlighten-

CHAPTER LOCATOR | How was peace restored and maintained after 1815?

ment philosophes (see Chapter 16, page 497). Romantics championed instead emotional exuberance, unrestrained imagination, and spontaneity in both art and personal life. Preoccupied with emotional excess, romantic works explored the awesome power of love and desire, and of hatred, guilt, and despair.

Where Enlightenment thinkers applied the scientific method to social issues and cast rosy predictions for future progress, romantics valued intuition and nostalgia for the past. Where Enlightenment thinkers embraced secularization, romantics sought the inspiration of religious ecstasy. Where the Enlightenment valued public life and civic affairs, romantics delved into the supernatural and turned inward, to the hidden recesses of the self.

Nowhere was the break with Enlightenment classicism more apparent than in romanticism's general conception of nature. Classicists were not particularly interested in nature. The romantics, in contrast, were enchanted by it. Nature could be awesome and tempestuous, a source of beauty or spiritual inspiration. Most romantics saw the growth of modern industry as an ugly, brutal attack on their beloved nature and on venerable traditions. They sought escape—in the unspoiled Lake District of northern England, in exotic North Africa, in an imaginary and idealized Middle Ages.

The study of history became a romantic obsession. History held the key to a universe now perceived to be organic and dynamic, not mechanical and static, as Enlightenment thinkers had believed. Professional historians influenced by romanticism, such as Jules Michelet, went beyond the standard accounts of great men or famous battles. Michelet's many books on the history of France consciously promoted the growth of national aspirations; by fanning the embers of memory, Michelet encouraged the French people to search the past for their special national destiny.

Romanticism was a lifestyle as well as an intellectual movement. Many early-nineteenth-century romantics lived lives of tremendous emotional intensity. Romantic artists typically led bohemian lives, wearing their hair long and uncombed in preference to donning powdered wigs, and rejecting the materialism of refined society. Great individualists, the romantics believed that the full development of one's unique human potential was the supreme purpose in life.

Literature

Romanticism found its distinctive voice in poetry, as the Enlightenment had in prose. Though romantic poetry had important forerunners in the German "Storm and Stress" movement of the 1770s and 1780s, its first great poets were English: William Blake, William Wordsworth, Samuel Taylor Coleridge, and Sir Walter Scott were all active by 1800, followed shortly by Lord Byron, Percy Bysshe Shelley, and John Keats.

William Wordsworth was deeply influenced by Rousseau and the spirit of the early French Revolution. Wordsworth settled in the rural Lake District of England with his sister, Dorothy, and Samuel Taylor Coleridge (1772–1834). In 1798, Wordsworth and Coleridge published their *Lyrical Ballads*, which abandoned flowery classical conventions for the language of ordinary speech and endowed simple subjects with the loftiest majesty. Wordsworth believed that

What new ideologies emerged to challenge conservatism?

What were the characteristics of the romantic movement?

How and where was conservatism challenged after 1815?

What were the main causes and results of the revolutions of 1848?

☑ LearningCurve
Check what you know.

655

INDIVIDUALS IN SOCIETY
Germaine de Staël

Rich, intellectual, passionate, and assertive, Germaine Necker de Staël (1766–1817) astonished contemporaries and still fascinates historians. She was strongly influenced by her parents, poor Swiss Protestants who soared to the top of prerevolutionary Parisian society. Her brilliant but rigid mother filled Germaine's head with knowledge, and each week the precocious child listened, wide-eyed and attentive, to illustrious writers and philosophers debating ideas at her mother's salon. At age twelve, she suffered a physical and mental breakdown. Only then was she allowed to have a playmate to romp about with on the family estate. Her adoring father was Jacques Necker, a banker who made an enormous fortune and became France's reform-minded minister of finance before the Revolution. Worshipping her father in adolescence, Germaine also came to love politics.

Accepting at nineteen an arranged marriage with Baron de Staël-Holstein, a womanizing Swedish diplomat bewitched by her dowry, Germaine began her life's work. She opened her own intellectual salon and began to write and publish. Her wit and exuberance attracted foreigners and liberal French aristocrats, one of whom became the first of many lovers as her marriage soured and she searched unsuccessfully for the happiness of her parents' union. Fleeing Paris in 1792 and returning after the Thermidorian reaction (see Chapter 19, page 596), she subsequently angered Napoleon by criticizing his dictatorial rule. In 1803, he permanently banished her from Paris.

Retiring again to her isolated estate in Switzerland and skillfully managing her inherited wealth, Staël fought insomnia with opium and boredom with parties that attracted luminaries from all over Europe. Always seeking stimulation for her restless mind, she traveled widely in Italy and Germany and drew upon these experiences in her novel *Corinne* (1807) and her study *On Germany* (1810). Both works summed up her romantic faith and enjoyed enormous success.

Staël urged creative individuals to abandon traditional rules and classical models. She encouraged them to embrace experimentation, emotion, and enthusiasm. Enthusiasm, which she had in abundance, was the key, the royal road to creativity, personal fulfillment, and human improvement. Thrilling to music, for example, she felt that only an enthusiastic person could really appreciate this gift of God, this wordless message that "unifies our dual nature and blends senses and spirit in a common rapture."*

Yet a profound sadness runs through her writing. This sadness, so characteristic of the romantic temperament, grew in part out of disappointments in love and prolonged

Germaine de Staël. (Château de Versailles, France/Giraudon/The Bridgeman Art Library)

exile. But it also grew out of the insoluble predicament of being an enormously gifted woman in an age of intense male sexism. Little wonder that uneasy male competitors and literary critics took delight in ridiculing and defaming

---

*Quoted in G. R. Besser, *Germaine de Staël Revisited* (New York: Twayne Publishers, 1994), p. 106. Enhanced by a feminist perspective, this fine study is highly recommended.

LaunchPad

ONLINE DOCUMENT PROJECT

How did the German landscape and the idea of enthusiasm figure into Staël's view of German romanticism? Examine excerpts from her work *On Germany* and key examples of German romantic paintings that echo Staël's ideas. Then complete a writing assignment based on the evidence and details from this chapter. *See inside the front cover to learn more.*

her as a neurotic and masculine woman, a mediocre and unnatural talent who had foolishly dared to enter the male world of serious thought and action. Even her supporters could not accept her for what she was. Poet Lord Byron recognized her genius and called her "the most eminent woman author of this, or perhaps of any century" but quickly added that "she should have been born a man."[†]

Buffeted and saddened by this scorn and condescension, Staël advocated equal rights for women throughout her life. Only with equal rights and duties — in education and careers, in love and marital relations — could a woman ever hope to realize her intellectual and emotional potential. Practicing what she preached as best she could, Germaine de Staël was a trailblazer in the struggle for women's rights.

QUESTIONS FOR ANALYSIS

1. In what ways did Germaine de Staël's life and thought reflect basic elements of the romantic movement?
2. Why did male critics often attack Staël? What do these criticisms tell us about gender relations in the early nineteenth century?

†Ibid., p. 139.

all natural things were sacred, and his poetry often expressed a mystical appreciation of nature.

In France under Napoleon, classicism remained strong and at first inhibited the growth of romanticism. An early French champion of the new movement, Germaine de Staël (duh STAHL) (1766–1817) urged the French to throw away their worn-out classical models. (See "Individuals in Society: Germaine de Staël," page 656.) Between 1820 and 1850, the romantic impulse broke through in the poetry and prose of Alphonse de Lamartine, Victor Hugo, and George Sand (pseudonym of the woman writer Armandine-Aurore-Lucile Dudevant). Of these, Victor Hugo (1802–1885) became the most well known.

Son of a Napoleonic general, Hugo achieved an amazing range of rhythm, language, and image in his lyric poetry. His powerful novels exemplified the romantic fascination with fantastic characters, exotic historical settings, and human emotions. The hero of Hugo's famous *The Hunchback of Notre Dame* (1831) is the great cathedral's deformed bell-ringer, a "human gargoyle" overlooking the teeming life of fifteenth-century Paris.

In central and eastern Europe, literary romanticism and early nationalism often reinforced one another. Well-educated romantics championed their own people's histories, cultures, and unique greatness. Like modern anthropologists, they studied peasant life and transcribed the folk songs, tales, and proverbs that the cosmopolitan Enlightenment had disdained. In the Slavic lands, romantics played a decisive role in converting spoken peasant languages into modern written languages. In the vast Austrian, Russian, and Ottoman Empires, with their many ethnic minorities, the combination of romanticism and nationalism was particularly potent.

Art and Music

Romantic concerns with nature, history, and the imagination extended well beyond literature into the realms of art and music. France's Eugène Delacroix (u-JHEHN deh-luh-KWAH) (1798–1863) painted dramatic, colorful scenes that stirred the emotions. The famous German painter Casper David Friedrich (1774–1840) preferred somber landscapes of ruined churches or remote arctic shipwrecks, which captured the divine presence in natural forces.

In England, the most notable romantic painters were Joseph M. W. Turner (1775–1851) and John Constable (1776–1837). Both were fascinated by nature, but their interpretations of it contrasted sharply, aptly symbolizing the tremendous emotional range of the romantic movement. Turner depicted nature's power and terror. Constable painted gentle landscapes in which human beings lived peacefully with their environment.

Musicians and composers likewise explored the romantic sensibility. Abandoning well-defined structures, the great romantic composers used a wide range of forms to create a thousand musical landscapes and evoke a host of powerful emotions. They transformed the small classical orchestra, tripling its size by adding wind instruments, percussion, and more brass and strings. The crashing chords evoking the surge of the masses in Chopin's "Revolutionary Etude," and the bottomless despair of the funeral march in Beethoven's Third Symphony — such were the modern orchestra's musical paintings that plumbed the depths of human feeling.

This range and intensity gave music and musicians much greater prestige than in the past. Music no longer simply complemented a church service or helped a nobleman digest his dinner. It became a sublime end in itself, most perfectly realizing the endless yearning of the soul.

> **QUICK REVIEW**

What aspects of Enlightenment thought were rejected by the romantics?

CHAPTER LOCATOR | How was peace restored and maintained after 1815?

| Delacroix, *Massacre at Chios* | The Greek struggle for freedom and independence won the enthusiastic support of liberals, nationalists, and romantics. The Ottoman Turks were portrayed as cruel oppressors who were holding back the course of history, as in this moving masterpiece by Delacroix. (Louvre, Paris, France/Giraudon/The Bridgeman Art Library) |

WHILE THE ROMANTICS ENACTED A REVOLUTION IN THE ARTS, liberal, national, and socialist forces battered against the conservative restoration of 1815. Political change could occur through gradual and peaceful reform or through violent insurrection, but everywhere it took the determination of ordinary people standing up to prerogatives of the powerful. Between 1815 and 1848, three important countries—Greece, Great Britain, and France—experienced variations on these basic themes.

National Liberation in Greece

In spite of centuries of foreign rule by the Ottoman Turks, the Greeks had survived as a people, united by their language and the Greek Orthodox religion. In the early nineteenth century, the general growth of national aspirations inspired

| What new ideologies emerged to challenge conservatism? | What were the characteristics of the romantic movement? | **How and where was conservatism challenged after 1815?** | What were the main causes and results of the revolutions of 1848? | ✓ LearningCurve Check what you know. |

Greek Independence, 1830

a desire for independence. This rising national movement led to the formation of secret societies and then to open revolt in 1821, led by Alexander Ypsilanti (ihp-suh-LAN-tee).

At first, the Great Powers opposed the revolution and refused to back Ypsilanti, primarily because they sought a stable Ottoman Empire as a bulwark against Russian interests in southeast Europe. Yet the Greek cause had powerful defenders. Educated Europeans and Americans cherished the culture of classical Greece; Russians admired the piety of their Orthodox brethren. Writers and artists, moved by the romantic impulse, responded enthusiastically to the Greek national struggle.

The Greeks battled the Ottomans while hoping for the support of European governments. In 1827, Great Britain, France, and Russia yielded to popular demands at home and directed Ottoman leaders to accept an armistice. When they refused, the navies of these three powers trapped the Ottoman fleet at Navarino and destroyed it. Russia then declared another of its periodic wars of expansion against the Ottomans. Great Britain, France, and Russia finally declared Greece independent in 1830 and installed a German prince as king of the new country in 1832. Despite this imposed regime, which left the Greek people restive, they had won their independence in a heroic war of liberation against a foreign empire.

Liberal Reform in Great Britain

Pressure from below also reshaped politics in Great Britain, but through a process of gradual reform rather than revolution. Eighteenth-century Britain had been remarkably stable. The landowning aristocracy dominated society, but that class was neither closed nor rigidly defined. Moreover, common people enjoyed limited civil rights. Yet the constitutional monarchy was hardly democratic. With only about 8 percent of the population allowed to vote, the British Parliament, easily manipulated by the king, remained in the hands of the upper classes.

In 1815, open conflict between the ruling class and laborers emerged when the aristocracy rammed far-reaching changes in the **Corn Laws** through Parliament. Britain had been unable to import cheap grain from eastern Europe during the war years, leading to high prices and large profits for the landed aristocracy. With the war over, grain (which the British generically called "corn") could be imported again, allowing the price of wheat and bread to go down and benefiting almost everyone — except aristocratic landlords. The new Corn Laws prohibited the importation of foreign grain unless the price at home rose to improbable levels.

The change in the Corn Laws, coming as it did at a time of widespread unemployment and postwar economic distress, triggered protests and demonstrations by urban laborers, who enjoyed the support of radical intellectuals. In 1817, the Tory government, controlled completely by the landed aristocracy, responded by temporarily suspending the traditional rights of peaceable assembly and habeas corpus, which gives a person under arrest the right to a trial. Two years later, Parliament passed the infamous Six Acts, which, among other things, placed controls on a heavily taxed press and practically eliminated all mass meetings. These acts followed an enormous but orderly protest, at Saint Peter's Fields in Manchester, which was savagely broken up by armed cavalry. Nicknamed the **Battle of Peterloo**, in scornful reference to the British victory at Waterloo, this incident demonstrated the government's determination to repress dissenters.

Corn Laws
▶ British laws governing the import and export of grain, which were revised in 1815 to prohibit the importation of foreign grain unless the price at home rose to improbable levels, thus benefiting the aristocracy but making food prices high for working people.

Battle of Peterloo
▶ The army's violent suppression of a protest that took place at Saint Peter's Fields in Manchester in reaction to the revision of the Corn Laws.

CHAPTER LOCATOR | How was peace restored and maintained after 1815?

In the 1820s, a less frightened Tory government moved in the direction of better urban administration, greater economic liberalism, civil equality for Catholics, and limited imports of foreign grain. These actions encouraged the middle classes to press on for reform of Parliament so they could have a larger say in government.

The Whig Party, though led like the Tories by great aristocrats, had by tradition been more responsive to middle-class commercial and manufacturing interests. In 1830, a Whig ministry introduced "an act to amend the representation of the people of England and Wales." After a series of setbacks, the Whigs' **Reform Bill of 1832** was propelled into law by a mighty surge of popular support.

Significantly, the bill moved British politics in a democratic direction and allowed the House of Commons to emerge as the all-important legislative body, at the expense of the aristocrat-dominated House of Lords. The new industrial areas of the country gained representation in the Commons, and many old "rotten boroughs"—electoral districts that had very few voters and that the landed aristocracy had bought and sold—were eliminated. The number of voters increased by about 50 percent, to include about 12 percent of adult men in Britain and Ireland. Comfortable middle-class groups in the urban population, as well as some substantial farmers who leased their land, received the vote.

The "People's Charter" of 1838 and the Chartist movement it inspired pressed British elites for yet more radical reform (see Chapter 20, page 634). Inspired by the economic distress of the working class in the 1830s and 1840s, the Chartists demanded universal male (but not female) suffrage. Hundreds of thousands of people signed gigantic petitions calling on Parliament to grant all men the right to vote, first in 1839, again in 1842, and yet again in 1848. Parliament rejected all three petitions. In the short run, the working poor failed with their Chartist demands, but they learned a valuable lesson in mass politics.

While calling for universal male suffrage, many working-class people joined with middle-class manufacturers in the Anti–Corn Law League, founded in Manchester in 1839. Mass participation made possible a popular crusade led by fighting liberals. When Ireland's potato

Reform Bill of 1832
▶ A major British political reform that increased the number of male voters by about 50 percent and gave political representation to new industrial areas.

The Anti–Corn Law Movement in Action

This contemporary illustration focuses on the Anti–Corn Law League's remarkable ability to mobilize a broad urban coalition that was dedicated to free trade and the end of tariffs on imported grain. (The Granger Collection, New York)

| What new ideologies emerged to challenge conservatism? | What were the characteristics of the romantic movement? | **How and where was conservatism challenged after 1815?** | What were the main causes and results of the revolutions of 1848? | ✓ LearningCurve Check what you know. |

crop failed in 1845 and famine prices for food seemed likely in England, Tory prime minister Robert Peel joined with the Whigs and a minority of his own party to repeal the Corn Laws in 1846 and allow free imports of grain. England escaped famine. Thereafter the liberal doctrine of free trade became almost sacred dogma in Great Britain.

The following year, the Tories passed a bill designed to help the working classes, but in a different way. The Ten Hours Act of 1847 limited the workday for women and young people in factories to ten hours. In competition with the middle class for the support of the working class, Tory legislators continued to support legislation regulating factory conditions. This competition between a still-powerful aristocracy and a strong middle class was a crucial factor in Great Britain's peaceful political evolution. The working classes could make temporary alliances with either competitor to better their own conditions.

Ireland and the Great Famine

The people of Ireland did not benefit from the political competition in Britain. In the mid-1800s, Ireland was an agricultural nation, and the great majority of the rural population (outside of the northern counties of Ulster, which were partly Presbyterian) were Irish Catholics. They typically rented their land from a tiny minority of Church of England Protestant landowners, who often resided in England. Trapped in an exploitative tenant system driven by a pernicious combination of religion and class, Irish peasants lived in abominable conditions. Wretched one-room mud cabins dotted the Irish countryside; the typical tenant farmer could afford neither shoes nor stockings.

Despite the terrible conditions, population growth sped upward, part of Europe's general growth trend begun in the early eighteenth century (see Chapter 17). Between 1780 and 1840, the Irish population doubled from 4 million to 8 million. Extensive cultivation of the humble potato was largely responsible for this rapid growth. A single acre of land planted with the nutritious potato could feed a family of six for a year, and the hardy tuber thrived on Ireland's boggy wastelands. About one-half of the Irish population subsisted on potatoes and little else.

As population and potato dependency grew, however, conditions became more precarious. From 1820 onward, deficiencies and diseases in the potato crop occurred with disturbing frequency. Then in 1845 and 1846, and again in 1848 and 1851, the potato crop failed in Ireland. Blight attacked the young plants, and leaves and tubers rotted. Unmitigated disaster—the **Great Famine**—followed, as already impoverished peasants experienced widespread sickness and starvation.

The British government, committed to rigid free-trade ideology, reacted slowly. Relief efforts were tragically inadequate. Moreover, the government continued to collect taxes, landlords demanded their rents, and tenants who could not pay were evicted and their homes destroyed.

The Great Famine shattered the pattern of Irish population growth. Fully 1 million emigrants fled the famine between 1845 and 1851, mostly to the United States and Canada, and up to 1.5 million people died. Alone among the countries of Europe, Ireland experienced a declining population in the second half of the nineteenth century.

Great Famine

▶ The result of four years of potato crop failure in the late 1840s in Ireland, a country that had grown dependent on potatoes as a dietary staple.

CHAPTER LOCATOR | How was peace restored and maintained after 1815?

662 CHAPTER 21 IDEOLOGIES AND UPHEAVALS

The Great Famine intensified anti-British feeling and promoted Irish nationalism: the bitter memory of starvation, exile, and British inaction burned deeply into the popular consciousness. Patriots of the later nineteenth and early twentieth centuries could call on powerful collective emotions in their campaigns for land reform, home rule, and eventually Irish independence.

The Revolution of 1830 in France

The Constitutional Charter granted by Louis XVIII in the Bourbon restoration of 1814 was basically a liberal constitution (see Chapter 19, page 599). The charter protected economic and social gains made by sections of the middle class and the peasantry in the French Revolution, permitted some intellectual and artistic freedom, and created a parliament with upper and lower houses.

However, the charter was hardly democratic. Only about 100,000 of the wealthiest males, out of a total population of 30 million, had the right to vote for the deputies who, with the king and his ministers, made the laws of the nation. Nonetheless, the "notable people" who did vote came from very different backgrounds. There were wealthy businessmen, war profiteers, successful professionals, ex-revolutionaries, large landowners from the old aristocracy and the middle class, Bourbons, and Bonapartists. The old aristocracy, with its pre-1789 mentality, was a minority within the voting population.

Louis's conservative successor, Charles X (r. 1824–1830), a true reactionary, wanted to re-establish the old order in France. Increasingly blocked by the opposition of the deputies, Charles's government turned in 1830 to military adventure in an effort to rally French nationalism and gain popular support. A long-standing economic and diplomatic dispute with Muslim Algeria, a vassal state of the Ottoman Empire, provided the opportunity.

In June 1830, a French force of thirty-seven thousand crossed the Mediterranean, landed to the west of Algiers, and took the capital city in three short weeks. Victory seemed complete, but in 1831, Algerians in the interior revolted and waged a fearsome war that lasted until 1847, when French armies finally subdued the country. The conquest of Algeria marked the rebirth of French colonial expansion.

Emboldened by the initial good news from Algeria, Charles repudiated the Constitutional Charter in an attempted coup in July 1830. The immediate reaction, encouraged by lawyers, liberal journalists, and middle-class businessmen, was an insurrection in the capital. Printers, other artisans, and small traders rioted in the streets of Paris, and three days of vicious street fighting brought down the government. Charles fled. Then the upper middle class, which had fomented the revolt, skillfully seated Charles's cousin, Louis Philippe, duke of Orléans, on the vacant throne.

Despite the abdication of Charles X, in France the political situation remained fundamentally unchanged. The new king, Louis Philippe (r. 1830–1848), did accept the Constitutional Charter of 1814 and adopted the red, white, and blue flag of the French Revolution. Beyond these symbolic actions, popular demands for reform went unanswered. The upper middle class had effected a change in dynasty that maintained the status quo and the narrowly liberal institutions of 1815. Republicans, democrats, social reformers, and the poor of Paris were bitterly disappointed. They had made a revolution, but it seemed for naught.

What new ideologies emerged to challenge conservatism?

What were the characteristics of the romantic movement?

How and where was conservatism challenged after 1815?

What were the main causes and results of the revolutions of 1848?

☑ LearningCurve
Check what you know.

663

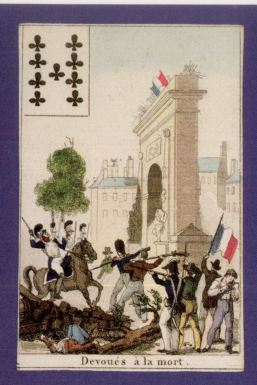

Devoués à la mort.

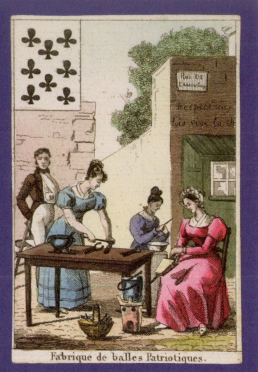

Fabrique de balles Patriotiques.

L'Amazône de 1830.

Secours au courage malheureux.

> **QUICK REVIEW**

What explains the relatively peaceful nature of political change in Great Britain in the first half of the nineteenth century?

CHAPTER LOCATOR | How was peace restored and maintained after 1815?

664 CHAPTER 21 IDEOLOGIES AND UPHEAVALS

What were the main causes and results of the revolutions of 1848?

Street fighting in Frankfurt, 1848 The striking similarities between the different national revolutions in 1848 suggest that Europeans lived through common experiences that shaped a generation. The first such experience was raising the barricades, fighting in the streets, and overthrowing rulers or forcing major concessions. Army commanders found deadly ways to respond to urban uprisings. First, they used cannon and field artillery to bombard and destroy the fighters behind their makeshift fortifications. Only then did obedient infantrymen attack and take the barricades in hand-to-hand combat, as Prussian soldiers did in Frankfurt. (The Granger Collection, New York)

IN THE LATE 1840s, Europe entered a period of tense economic and political crisis. Bad harvests across the continent caused widespread distress. Uneven industrial development failed to provide jobs or raise incomes, and revolts and insurrections rocked Europe.

Full-scale revolution broke out in France in February 1848, and its shock waves ripped across the continent. Only the most developed countries—Great Britain, Belgium, and the Netherlands—and the least developed—the Ottoman and Russian Empires—escaped untouched. Elsewhere governments toppled, as monarchs and ministers bowed or fled. National independence, liberal democratic constitutions, and social reform seemed at hand. Yet in the end, the revolutions failed.

What new ideologies emerged to challenge conservatism?

What were the characteristics of the romantic movement?

How and where was conservatism challenged after 1815?

What were the main causes and results of the revolutions of 1848?

☑ LearningCurve
Check what you know.

THE REVOLUTIONS OF 1848

■ 1848

January	Uprising in Naples, Italy
February	Revolution in Paris; proclamation of provisional republic
March	Revolt in Austrian Empire; Hungarian autonomy movement; uprisings in German cities
May	Frankfurt parliament convenes to write a constitution for a united Germany
June	Republican army defeats "June Days" workers' uprising in Paris; Austrian army crushes working-class revolt in Prague
September–November	Counter-revolutionary forces push back reformers in Prussia and the German states
December	Francis Joseph crowned Austrian emperor; Louis-Napoleon elected president in France

■ 1849

March	Frankfurt parliament completes draft constitution, elects Frederick William of Prussia emperor of a Lesser Germany, which he rejects
June	Russian troops subdue Hungarian autonomy movement; Prussian troops dissolve the remnants of the Frankfurt parliament

A Democratic Republic in France

For eighteen years, Louis Philippe's reign, labeled the "bourgeois monarchy" because it served the selfish interests of France's wealthy elites, had been characterized by stubborn inaction and complacency. Corrupt politicians refused to approve social legislation or consider electoral reform. The government's failures united a diverse group of opponents against the king. Bourgeois merchants, opposition deputies, and liberal intellectuals shared a sense of outrage with middle-class shopkeepers, skilled artisans, and unskilled working people. Widespread discontent eventually touched off a popular revolt in Paris. On the night of February 22, 1848, workers, joined by some students, began building barricades. Armed with guns and dug in behind their makeshift fortresses, the workers and students demanded a new government. On February 24, the French National Guard broke ranks and joined the revolutionaries. Louis Philippe refused to call in the army and abdicated in favor of his grandson. But the common people in arms would tolerate no more monarchy. This refusal led to the proclamation of a provisional republic, headed by a ten-man executive committee and certified by cries of approval from the revolutionary crowd.

The revolutionaries immediately set about drafting a democratic, republican constitution for France's Second Republic. Building such a republic meant giving the right to vote to every adult male, and this was quickly done. The provisional republican government further expressed sympathy for revolutionary freedoms by calling for liberty, fraternity, and equality; guaranteeing workplace reforms; freeing all slaves in French colonies; and abolishing the death penalty. (See "Picturing the Past: The Triumph of Democratic Republics," page 667.)

Yet there were profound differences within the revolutionary coalition. On the one hand, the moderate liberal republicans of the middle class viewed universal male suffrage as the ultimate concession to dangerous popular forces, and they strongly opposed any further radical social measures. On the other hand, radical republicans were committed to some kind of socialism. Hard-pressed urban artisans, who hated the unrestrained competition of cutthroat capitalism, advocated a combination of strong craft unions and worker-owned businesses.

Worsening depression and rising unemployment brought these conflicting goals to the fore in 1848. Louis Blanc (see page 651), who along with a worker named Albert represented the republican socialists in the provisional government, urged the creation of permanent government-sponsored cooperative workshops. Such workshops would be an alternative to capitalist employment and a decisive step toward a new, noncompetitive social order.

CHAPTER LOCATOR | How was peace restored and maintained after 1815?

The Triumph of Democratic Republics

This French illustration offers an opinion of the initial revolutionary breakthrough in 1848. The peoples of Europe, joined together around their respective national banners, are achieving republican freedom, which is symbolized by the statue, representing liberty, and the discarded crowns. The woman wearing pants at the base of the statue — very radical attire — represents feminist hopes for liberation. (Musée de la Ville, Paris/Giraudon/The Bridgeman Art Library)

> **PICTURING THE PAST**

ANALYZING THE IMAGE: How many different flags can you count or identify? How would you characterize the types of people marching and the mood of the crowd?
CONNECTIONS: What do the angels, the liberty statue, and the discarded crowns suggest about the artist's view of the events of 1848? Do you think this illustration was created before or after the collapse of the revolution in France? Why?

The moderate republicans, willing to provide only temporary relief, wanted no such thing. The resulting compromise set up national workshops — soon to become little more than a vast program of pick-and-shovel public works — and established a special commission under Blanc to "study the question." This satisfied no one. The national workshops were, however, better than nothing. An army of desperate poor from the French provinces and even from foreign countries streamed into Paris to sign up for the workshops. As the economic crisis worsened, the number enrolled in the workshops soared.

While the Paris workshops grew, the French people went to the election polls in late April. The result was a bitter loss for the republicans. Voting in most cases

| What new ideologies emerged to challenge conservatism? | What were the characteristics of the romantic movement? | How and where was conservatism challenged after 1815? | **What were the main causes and results of the revolutions of 1848?** | ✓ LearningCurve Check what you know. |

667

for the first time, the people of France elected to the new 900-person Constituent Assembly 500 monarchists and conservatives, only about 270 moderate republicans, and just 80 radicals or socialists.

The new government's executive committee dropped Blanc and thereafter included no representative of the Parisian working class. Fearing that their socialist hopes were about to be dashed, artisans and unskilled workers invaded the Constituent Assembly on May 15 and tried to proclaim a new revolutionary state. The government used the middle-class National Guard to squelch this uprising. As the workshops continued to fill and grow more radical, the fearful but powerful propertied classes in the Assembly took the offensive. On June 22, the government dissolved the workshops in Paris, giving the workers the choice of joining the army or going to workshops in the provinces.

A spontaneous and violent uprising followed. Barricades sprang up again in the narrow streets of Paris, and a terrible class war began. After three terrible "June Days" of street fighting and the death or injury of more than ten thousand people, the republican army under General Louis Cavaignac stood triumphant in a sea of working-class blood and hatred.

The revolution in France thus ended in spectacular failure. The February coalition of the middle and working classes had in four short months become locked in mortal combat. In place of a generous democratic republic, the Constituent Assembly completed a constitution featuring a strong executive. This allowed Louis Napoleon, nephew of Napoleon Bonaparte, to win a landslide victory in the election of December 1848. The appeal of his great name as well as the desire of the propertied classes for order at any cost had led to what would become a semi-authoritarian regime.

Revolution and Reaction in the Austrian Empire

The revolution in the Austrian Empire began in Hungary in March 1848, when nationalistic Hungarians demanded national autonomy, full civil liberties, and universal suffrage. When the monarchy in Vienna hesitated, Viennese students and workers took to the streets and raised barricades in defiance of the government, while peasant disturbances broke out in parts of the empire. The Habsburg emperor Ferdinand I (r. 1835–1848) capitulated and promised reforms and a liberal constitution. The old absolutist order seemed to be collapsing with unbelievable rapidity.

Yet the coalition of revolutionaries lacked stability. When the monarchy abolished serfdom, the newly free peasants lost interest in the political and social questions agitating the cities. Meanwhile, the coalition of urban revolutionaries broke down along class lines over the issue of socialist workshops and universal voting rights for men.

Conflicting national aspirations further weakened and ultimately destroyed the revolutionary coalition. In March, the Hungarian revolutionary leaders pushed through an extremely liberal, almost democratic, constitution. But the Hungarian revolutionaries also sought to transform the mosaic of provinces and peoples that was the kingdom of Hungary into a unified, centralized Hungarian nation. The minority groups that formed half of the population rejected such unification. Each

CHAPTER LOCATOR | How was peace restored and maintained after 1815?

group felt entitled to political autonomy and cultural independence. In a similar way, Czech nationalists based in Prague and other parts of Bohemia came into conflict with German nationalists. Thus desires for national autonomy within the Austrian Empire enabled the monarchy to play off one ethnic group against the other.

Finally, the conservative aristocratic forces rallied under the leadership of the archduchess Sophia, a Bavarian princess married to the emperor's brother. Deeply ashamed of the emperor's collapse, she insisted that Ferdinand, who had no heir, abdicate in favor of her son, Francis Joseph.[3] Powerful nobles organized around Sophia in a secret conspiracy to reverse and crush the revolution.

The first conservative breakthrough came when the army bombarded Prague and savagely crushed a working-class revolt there on June 17. Other Austrian officials and nobles led the minority nationalities of Hungary against the revolutionary government. At the end of October, the well-equipped, predominantly peasant troops of the regular Austrian army retook Vienna. The determination of the Austrian aristocracy and the loyalty of its army sealed the triumph of reaction and the defeat of revolution.

When Francis Joseph (r. 1848–1916) was crowned emperor of Austria in December 1848, only Hungary had yet to be brought under control. Another determined conservative, Nicholas I of Russia (r. 1825–1855), obligingly lent his iron hand. On June 6, 1849, Russian troops poured into Hungary and subdued the country after bitter fighting.

Prussia, the German Confederation, and the Frankfurt National Parliament

After Austria, Prussia was the largest and most influential kingdom in the German Confederation. Since the Napoleonic Wars, liberal German reformers had sought to transform absolutist Prussia into a constitutional monarchy, hoping it would then lead the thirty-eight states of the German Confederation into a unified nation-state. The agitation that followed the fall of Louis Philippe, on top of several years of crop failure and economic crises, encouraged liberals to press their demands. In March 1848, excited crowds in urban centers across the German Confederation called for liberal reforms and a national parliament, and many regional rulers quickly gave in to their demands.

When artisans and factory workers rioted in Berlin, the capital of Prussia, and joined temporarily with the middle-class liberals in the struggle against the monarchy, the Prussian king, Frederick William IV (r. 1840–1861), vacillated and then caved in. On March 21, he promised to grant Prussia a liberal constitution and to merge Prussia into a new national German state.

But urban workers wanted much more, and the Prussian aristocracy wanted much less than the moderate constitutional liberalism the king conceded. The workers issued a series of democratic and vaguely socialist demands that troubled their middle-class allies. An elected Prussian Constituent Assembly met in Berlin to write a constitution for the Prussian state, and a conservative clique gathered around the king to urge counter-revolution.

| What new ideologies emerged to challenge conservatism? | What were the characteristics of the romantic movement? | How and where was conservatism challenged after 1815? | **What were the main causes and results of the revolutions of 1848?** | ✔ LearningCurve Check what you know. |

669

At the same time, elections were held across the German Confederation for a national parliament, which convened in Frankfurt to write a federal constitution that would lead to national unification. In October 1848, the Frankfurt parliament turned to the question of national unification and borders. At first, the deputies proposed unification around a **Greater Germany** that would include the German-speaking lands of the Austrian Empire in a national state. This proposal foundered on Austrian determination to maintain its empire, and some parliamentarians advocated a Lesser Germany that would unify Prussia and other German states without Austria.

Despite Austrian intransigence, in March 1849, the national parliament finally completed its draft of a liberal constitution and elected Frederick William of Prussia emperor of a "lesser" German national state (minus Austria). By early 1849, however, reaction had rolled back liberal reforms across the German Confederation. Frederick William had already reasserted his royal authority and disbanded the Prussian Constituent Assembly, and he contemptuously refused to accept the "crown from the gutter" offered by the parliament in Frankfurt. Bogged down by their preoccupation with nationalist issues, the reluctant revolutionaries in Frankfurt had waited too long and acted too timidly. By May 1849, all but the most radical deputies had resigned from the parliament, and in June, Prussian troops dissolved the remnants of the parliament.

Greater Germany

▶ A liberal plan for German national unification that included the German-speaking parts of the Austrian Empire, put forth at the national parliament in 1848 but rejected by Austrian rulers.

> **QUICK REVIEW**

Why did the coalitions that led the revolutions of 1848 prove so fragile?

CHAPTER LOCATOR | How was peace restored and maintained after 1815?

670 CHAPTER 21 IDEOLOGIES AND UPHEAVALS

LOOKING BACK LOOKING AHEAD

Viewed from a broad historical perspective, Europe's economic and social foundations in 1750 remained agricultural and rural. Although Enlightenment thought was beginning to question the status quo, authoritarian absolutism dominated political life. One hundred years later, the unfinished effects of the Industrial and French Revolutions had brought fundamental changes to the social fabric of daily life and politics across Europe. The liberal ideals of representative government and legal equality realized briefly in revolutionary France inspired intellectuals and social reformers, who adopted ideologies of liberalism, nationalism, romanticism, and socialism to challenge the conservative order. The uneven spread of industrial technologies and factory organization into developed areas across Europe spurred the growth of an urban working class but did little to raise the living standards of most workers, peasants, and artisans. Living on the edge of subsistence, the laboring poor in rural and urban areas alike turned repeatedly to protest, riots, and violent insurrection in pursuit of economic and political rights.

In 1848, the poor joined middle- and upper-class reformers in a great wave of revolution that forced conservative monarchs across the continent to grant liberal and national concessions—at least for a moment. Divisions in the revolutionary coalition and the power of the autocratic state forced back the wave of reform, and the revolutions ended in failure. Yet protest on the barricades and debate in liberal parliaments had given a generation a wealth of experience with new forms of participatory politics, and the ideologies associated with the French Revolution would continue to invigorate reformers and revolutionaries after 1850. Nationalism, with its commitment to the nation-state and the imagined community of a great national family, would become a dominant political force, particularly as European empires extended their reach after 1875. At the same time, as agriculture and rural life gradually declined in economic importance, the consolidation of industrialization would raise living standards, sustain a growing urban society, and reshape family and class relationships.

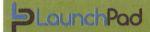

ONLINE DOCUMENT PROJECT

Germaine de Staël

How did the German landscape and the idea of enthusiasm figure into Staël's view of German romanticism?

You encountered Germaine de Staël's story on page 656. Keeping the question above in mind, examine excerpts from her work *On Germany* and key examples of German romantic paintings that echo Staël's ideas. Then complete a writing assignment based on the evidence and details from this chapter. *See inside the front cover to learn more.*

| What new ideologies emerged to challenge conservatism? | What were the characteristics of the romantic movement? | How and where was conservatism challenged after 1815? | What were the main causes and results of the revolutions of 1848? | ✔ **LearningCurve** Check what you know. |

CHAPTER 21 STUDY GUIDE

 **GET STARTED ONLINE**

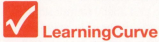 **LearningCurve**

Now that you've read the chapter, make it stick by completing the LearningCurve activity.

 **EXPLAIN WHY IT MATTERS**

Put your reading into practice. Identify each term below, and then explain why it matters in Western history.

TERM	WHO OR WHAT & WHEN	WHY IT MATTERS
Congress of Vienna (p. 642)		
Holy Alliance (p. 647)		
Karlsbad Decrees (p. 647)		
liberalism (p. 649)		
laissez faire (p. 650)		
nationalism (p. 650)		
socialism (p. 651)		
Marxism (p. 652)		
bourgeoisie (p. 653)		
proletariat (p. 653)		
romanticism (p. 654)		
Corn Laws (p. 660)		
Battle of Peterloo (p. 660)		
Reform Bill of 1832 (p. 661)		
Great Famine (p. 662)		
Greater Germany (p. 670)		

MOVE BEYOND THE BASICS

To demonstrate a more advanced understanding, complete the chart included below. Why did liberals tend to support nationalist movements and conservatives tend to resist them? How did the socialist understanding of nineteenth-century Europe differ from the liberal and conservative understandings?

Ideology	Key characteristics and beliefs
Liberalism	
Conservatism	
Nationalism	
Socialism	

STEP 4 **PUT IT ALL TOGETHER** Now, take a step back and try to explain the big picture. Remember to use specific examples from the chapter in your answers.

CONSERVATISM AND ITS OPPONENTS

▶ What were the goals of the participants in the Congress of Vienna? How did their experience of the French Revolution and the Napoleonic Wars shape their vision of postwar Europe?

▶ How did liberals tend to see the relationship between the individual and the marketplace? What about between "the people" and the nation? What policies and programs did liberals advance on the basis of these beliefs?

THE ROMANTIC MOVEMENT

▶ Compare and contrast romantic and Enlightenment views of nature and religion. What do the differences you note tell us about the essential characteristics of each movement?

▶ How did romantics see the individual? In their view, what was each person's supreme purpose in life?

MAKE CONNECTIONS

▶ How did memories of the French Revolution shape and inspire nineteenth-century political ideologies?

▶ Defend or refute the following statement: "The basic parameters of modern political debate emerged out of the ideological clashes of the first half of the nineteenth century."

REFORM AND REVOLUTION

▶ Compare and contrast Britain and France in 1830. How did Britain avoid the revolutionary upheaval that exploded in France in 1830?

▶ What explains the near simultaneous eruption of revolution across Europe in 1848, and why did all these revolutions fail?

> **IN YOUR OWN WORDS**

Imagine that you must give an oral report to the class answering the following question: **How did the forces unleashed by the French and Industrial Revolutions shape European politics in the first half of the nineteenth century?** What would be the most important points and why?

22
LIFE IN THE EMERGING URBAN SOCIETY

1840–1914

> **How and why did city life change between 1800 and 1900?** Chapter 22 examines social change in the nineteenth century. The urban society that emerged in this century had costs as well as benefits. Advances in public health and urban planning brought some relief to the squalid working-class slums. On the whole, living standards rose in the 1800s, but wages and living conditions varied greatly according to status, and many urban residents were still poor. Differences in income, education, and occupation divided people into socially stratified groups; rather than discuss "the" working class or "the" middle class, it is more accurate to speak of "working classes" and "middle classes" and consider the blurring boundaries between the two. Major changes in family life and gender roles accompanied this more diversified class system. Dramatic breakthroughs in science and technology further transformed urban society after 1880, and a new generation of artists, writers, and professional social scientists struggled to explain and portray the vast changes wrought by urbanization.

LearningCurve

After reading the chapter, use LearningCurve to retain what you've read.

Life in the Nineteenth-Century City. The excitement and variety of urban life sparkle in this depiction of a public entertainment gala in 1860, sponsored by London's Royal Dramatic College and held in the city's fabulous Crystal Palace. (© Fine Art Photographic Library/Corbis)

> How did urban life change in the nineteenth century?

> What were the characteristics of urban industrial society?

> How did urbanization affect family life and gender roles?

> How and why did intellectual life change in this period?

> How did urban life change in the nineteenth century?

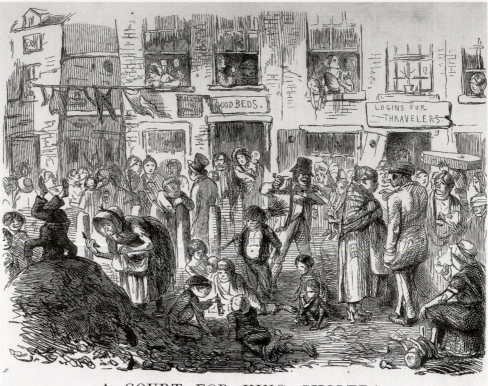

A COURT FOR KING CHOLERA.

King Cholera This 1852 drawing from *Punch* tells volumes about the unhealthy living conditions of the urban poor. In the foreground, children play with a dead rat and a woman scavenges a dung heap. Cheap rooming houses provide shelter for the frightfully overcrowded population. Such conditions and contaminated water spread deadly cholera epidemics throughout Europe in the 1800s. (© The British Library Board, P.P. 5270 vol 23, 139)

WHILE HISTORIANS MAY DEBATE whether the overall social impact of industrialization was generally positive or negative, there is little doubt that rapid urban growth worsened long-standing overcrowding, pollution, and unhealthy living conditions, and posed a frightening challenge for society. Only the full-scale efforts of government leaders, city planners, reformers, scientists, and reform-minded citizens would tame the ferocious savagery of the industrial city.

Industry and the Growth of Cities

The main causes of the poor quality of urban life—deadly overcrowding, pervasive poverty, and lack of medical knowledge—had existed for centuries. Packed together almost as tightly as possible, people in cities suffered and died from the spread of infectious disease in far greater numbers than their rural counterparts. In the larger towns, more people died each year than were born, on average, and urban populations maintained their numbers only because newcomers continually arrived from rural areas.

ca. 1840s–1890s
- Realism dominant in Western literature

1848
- First public health law in Britain

ca. 1850–1870
- Modernization of Paris

1850–1914
- Condition of working classes improves

1854
- Pasteur begins studying fermentation and in 1863 develops pasteurization

1854–1870
- Development of germ theory

1859
- Darwin publishes *On the Origin of Species by the Means of Natural Selection*

1869
- Mendeleev creates periodic table

1880–1913
- Second Industrial Revolution; birthrate steadily declines in Europe

1890s
- Electric streetcars introduced in Europe

The Industrial Revolution exacerbated these deplorable conditions. The steam engine freed industrialists from dependence on the energy of fast-flowing streams and rivers so that, by 1800, there was every incentive to build new factories in urban areas, which had many advantages. Cities had better shipping facilities than the countryside and thus better supplies of coal and raw materials. Cities had many hands wanting work. And it was a great advantage for a manufacturer to have other factories nearby to supply the business's needs and buy its products. Therefore, as industry grew, already overcrowded and unhealthy cities expanded rapidly.

Great Britain, the first country in the world to go through the early stages of the Industrial Revolution (see Chapter 20), was forced to face the acute challenges of a changing urban environment early on (**Map 22.1**). Except on the outskirts, early-nineteenth-century cities in Britain used every scrap of available

ONLINE DOCUMENT PROJECT

Capturing Life in the Modern City on Film

How did cities and individuals respond to the challenges brought on by rapid urbanization?

View video footage from the early twentieth century that documents new developments in city life—from mass transit to waste disposal—and then complete a writing assignment based on the evidence and details from this chapter. *See inside front cover to learn more.*

What were the characteristics of urban industrial society?	How did urbanization affect family life and gender roles?	How and why did intellectual life change in this period?	✓ LearningCurve Check what you know.

MAP 22.1 ■ **European Cities of 100,000 or More, 1800–1900**

There were more large cities in Great Britain in 1900 than in all of Europe in 1800.

> MAPPING THE PAST

ANALYZING THE MAP: Compare the spatial distribution of cities in 1800 with the distribution in 1900. Where in 1900 are large cities concentrated in clusters?

CONNECTIONS: In 1800, what common characteristics were shared by many large European cities? (For example, how many big cities were capitals or leading ports?) Were any common characteristics shared by the large cities in 1900? What does this suggest about the reasons behind this dramatic growth?

land to the fullest extent. Parks and open areas were almost nonexistent. Developers erected buildings on the smallest possible lots in order to pack the maximum number of people into a given space.

> The Rapid Pace of British Urbanization

- 1801: 1.5 million city dwellers (17 percent of total population)
- 1851: 6.3 million city dwellers (35 percent of total population)
- 1891: 15.6 million city dwellers (54 percent of total population)

CHAPTER LOCATOR | How did urban life change in the nineteenth century?

CHAPTER 22

678   LIFE IN THE EMERGING URBAN SOCIETY

These highly concentrated urban populations lived in extremely unsanitary and unhealthy conditions. Open drains and sewers flowed alongside or down the middle of unpaved streets. Toilet facilities were extremely primitive and inadequate. In parts of Manchester, as many as two hundred people shared a single outhouse. Such privies filled up rapidly, and since they were infrequently emptied, sewage often overflowed and seeped into cellar dwellings. By the 1840s there was among the better-off classes a growing, shocking "realization that," as one scholar put it, "millions of English men, women, and children were living in shit."[1]

The environmental costs of rapid urbanization and industrialization were enormous as well. Black soot from coal-fired factories and train engines fouled city air, and by 1850 the River Thames was little better than an open sewer.

Who or what bore responsibility for these awful conditions? The crucial factors included the tremendous pressure of more people and the total absence of public transportation. People simply had to jam themselves together to get to shops and factories on foot. In addition, government in Great Britain, both local and national, only slowly established sanitary facilities and adequate building codes.

Most responsible of all was the sad legacy of rural housing conditions in pre-industrial society combined with appalling ignorance of germs and basic hygiene. When ordinary people moved to the city, housing was far down on their list of priorities, and they generally took dirt for granted.

The Advent of the Public Health Movement

Toward the middle of the nineteenth century, people's fatalistic acceptance of their overcrowded, unsanitary surroundings began to give way to a growing interest in reform and improvement. Edwin Chadwick, one of the commissioners charged with the administration of relief to paupers under Britain's revised Poor Law of 1834, emerged as a powerful voice for reform. Chadwick found inspiration in the ideas of radical philosopher Jeremy Bentham (1748–1832), whose approach to social issues, called **utilitarianism**, had taught that public problems ought to be dealt with on a rational, scientific basis to advance the "greatest good for the greatest number." Applying these principles, Chadwick soon became convinced that disease and death actually caused poverty because a sick worker was an unemployed worker and orphaned children were poor children. Most important, Chadwick believed that government could help prevent disease by cleaning up the urban environment.

Chadwick collected detailed reports from local Poor Law officials on the "sanitary conditions of the laboring population" and published his hard-hitting findings in 1842. This mass of widely publicized evidence proved that disease was related to filthy environmental conditions, which were in turn caused largely by lack of drainage, sewers, and garbage collection. In 1848, Chadwick's report became the basis of Great Britain's first public health law, which created a national health board and gave cities broad authority to build modern sanitary systems.

The public health movement won dedicated supporters in the United States, France, and Germany from the late 1840s on. Governments accepted at least limited responsibility for the health of all citizens, and by the 1860s and 1870s, European cities were making real progress toward adequate water supplies and sewerage systems. Though pollution remained a serious problem, city dwellers

utilitarianism
▶ The idea of Jeremy Bentham that social policies should promote the "greatest good for the greatest number."

What were the characteristics of urban industrial society?	How did urbanization affect family life and gender roles?	How and why did intellectual life change in this period?	✓ LearningCurve Check what you know.

679

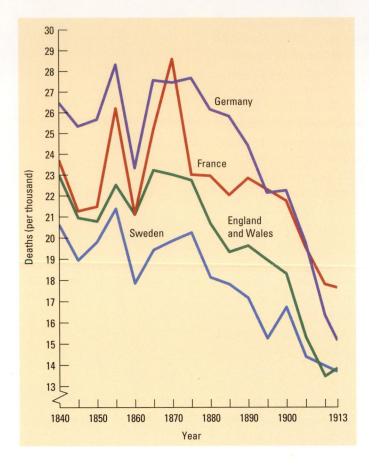

FIGURE 22.1 ■ The Decline of Death Rates in England and Wales, Germany, France, and Sweden, 1840–1913
A rising standard of living, improvements in public health, and better medical knowledge all contributed to the dramatic decline of death rates in the nineteenth century.

started to reap the reward of better health, and death rates began to decline (**Figure 22.1**).

The Bacterial Revolution

Although improved sanitation in cities promoted a better quality of life and some improvements in health care, effective control of communicable disease required a great leap forward in medical knowledge and biological theory. Early reformers, including Chadwick, were seriously handicapped by their adherence to the prevailing miasmatic theory of disease — the belief that people contracted disease when they inhaled the bad odors of decay and putrefying excrement.

The breakthrough in understanding how bad drinking water and filth actually made people sick arrived when the French chemist Louis Pasteur (pas-TUHR) (1822–1895) developed the **germ theory** of disease. Pasteur's experiments demonstrated that specific diseases were caused by specific living organisms — germs — and that those organisms could be controlled.

By 1870, the work of Pasteur and others had demonstrated the general connection between germs and disease. When, in the middle of the 1870s, German country doctor Robert Koch (kawkh) and his coworkers developed pure cultures of harmful bacteria and described their life cycles, the dam broke. Over the next twenty years, researchers identified the organisms responsible for disease after disease. These discoveries led to the development of a number of effective vaccines.

The achievements of the bacterial revolution coupled with the public health movement saved millions of lives, particularly after about 1880. Mortality rates began to decline dramatically in European countries (see Figure 22.1) as the awful death sentences of the past — diphtheria, typhoid, typhus, cholera, yellow fever — became vanishing diseases. City dwellers benefited especially from these developments. By 1910, a great silent revolution had occurred: the death rates for people of all ages in urban areas were generally no greater than those for people in rural areas, and sometimes they were lower.

Improvements in Urban Planning

In addition to public health improvements, more effective urban planning was a major key to a better quality of urban life in the nineteenth century. France took the lead in this area during the rule of Napoleon III (r. 1848–1870), who sought to

germ theory

▶ The idea that disease was caused by the spread of living organisms that could be controlled.

CHAPTER LOCATOR | **How did urban life change in the nineteenth century?**

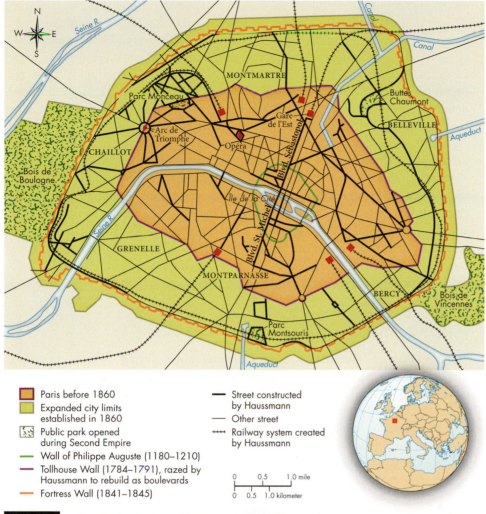

MAP 22.2 ■ The Modernization of Paris, ca. 1850–1870

The addition of broad boulevards, large parks, and grand train stations transformed Paris. The cutting of the new north-south axis — known as the Boulevard Saint-Michel — was one of Haussmann's most controversial projects. It razed much of Paris's medieval core and filled the Île de la Cité with massive government buildings.

promote the welfare of his subjects through government action. He believed that rebuilding much of Paris would provide employment, improve living conditions, limit the outbreak of cholera epidemics—and testify to the power and glory of his empire. In Baron Georges Haussmann (HOWS-muhn) (1809–1884), Napoleon III found an authoritarian planner capable of bulldozing both buildings and opposition. (**Map 22.2**).

The Paris of 1850 was a labyrinth of narrow, dark streets, the results of desperate overcrowding and a lack of effective planning. Residents faced terrible conditions and extremely high death rates. The entire metropolis had few open spaces and only two public parks.

For two decades Haussmann and his fellow planners proceeded on many interrelated fronts. They razed old buildings in order to cut broad, straight, tree-lined boulevards through the center of the city as well as in new quarters rising

| What were the characteristics of urban industrial society? | How did urbanization affect family life and gender roles? | How and why did intellectual life change in this period? | ☑ LearningCurve Check what you know. |

681

on the outskirts. These boulevards, designed in part to prevent the easy construction and defense of barricades by revolutionary crowds, permitted traffic to flow freely and afforded impressive vistas. Their creation also demolished some of the worst slums. New streets stimulated the construction of better housing, especially for the middle classes. Planners created small neighborhood parks and open spaces throughout the city and developed two very large parks suitable for all kinds of holiday activities. The city improved its sewers, and a system of aqueducts more than doubled the city's supply of clean, fresh water.

Rebuilding Paris provided a new model for urban planning and stimulated urban reform throughout Europe, particularly after 1870. In city after city, public authorities mounted a coordinated attack on many of the interrelated problems of the urban environment. As in Paris, improvements in public health through better water supply and waste disposal often went hand in hand with new boulevard construction (see Map 22.2, page 681). Zoning expropriation laws, which allowed a majority of the owners of land in a given quarter of the city to impose major street or sanitation improvements on a reluctant minority, were an important mechanism of this new urban reform movement.

Public Transportation

The development of mass public transportation often accompanied urban planning, further enhancing living conditions. In the 1870s many European cities authorized private companies to operate horse-drawn streetcars, which had been developed in the United States. Then in the 1890s the real revolution occurred: European countries adopted another American transit innovation: a streetcar that ran on the newly harnessed power of electricity.

Electric streetcars were cheaper, faster, more dependable, cleaner, and more comfortable than their horse-drawn counterparts. In 1886, the horse-drawn streetcars of Austria-Hungary, France, Germany, and Great Britain carried about 900 million riders per year. By 1910, electric streetcar systems in those four countries were carrying 6.7 billion riders.[2]

Mass transit helped greatly in the struggle for decent housing. The new boulevards and horse-drawn streetcars facilitated a middle-class move to better and more spacious housing in the 1860s and 1870s; after 1890, electric streetcars meant people of even modest means could access new, improved housing. Though still densely populated, cities expanded and became less congested. On the continent, many city governments in the early twentieth century built electric streetcar systems that provided transportation to new housing developments for the working classes beyond the city limits. Suburban commuting was born.

> **QUICK REVIEW**

Why were European cities approaching a crisis point by the middle of the nineteenth century?

CHAPTER LOCATOR | How did urban life change in the nineteenth century?

CHAPTER 22
682 LIFE IN THE EMERGING URBAN SOCIETY

The Labor Aristocracy This group of British foremen is attending the International Exhibition in Paris in 1862. Their "Sunday best" includes the silk top hats and long morning coats of the propertied classes, but they definitely remain workers, the proud leaders of laboring people. (© Victoria and Albert Museum, London.)

A

AS THE QUALITY OF URBAN LIFE IMPROVED ACROSS EUROPE, the class structure became more complex and diverse. Urban society featured many distinct social groups, all of which existed in a state of constant flux and competition. The gap between rich and poor remained enormous, but there were numerous gradations between the extremes.

The Distribution of Income

By 1850, at the latest, real wages — that is, wages received by workers adjusted for changes in the prices they paid — were rising for the mass of the population, and they continued to do so until 1914. The real wages of British workers, for example, almost doubled between 1850 and 1906. Ordinary people took a major step forward in the centuries-old battle against poverty, reinforcing efforts to improve many aspects of human existence.

Greater economic rewards for the average person did not eliminate hardship and poverty, however; nor did they make the wealth and income of the rich and the poor significantly more equal, as contemporary critics argued and economic

What were the characteristics of urban industrial society?	How did urbanization affect family life and gender roles?	How and why did intellectual life change in this period?	 LearningCurve Check what you know.

historians have clearly demonstrated. The aristocracy retained its position at the very top of the social ladder, followed closely by a new rich elite, composed mainly of the most successful business families from banking, industry, and large-scale commerce. In fact, the prominent families of the commercial elite tended to marry into the old aristocracy, to form a new upper class of at most 5 percent of the population.

Income inequality reflected social status. In almost every advanced country around 1900, the richest 5 percent of all households in the population received about a third of all national income, and the richest 20 percent of households received from 50 to 60 percent of it. As a result, the lower 80 percent received only 40 to 50 percent of all income—less than the two richest classes combined. Moreover, the bottom 30 percent of all households received 10 percent or less of all income.

The great gap between rich and poor endured, in part, because industrial and urban development made society more diverse and classes less unified. (See "Picturing the Past: Apartment Living in Paris.") Society had not split into two sharply defined opposing classes, as Karl Marx had predicted (see Chapter 21, page 652). Instead, the economic specialization that enabled society to produce goods more effectively had created a remarkable variety of new social groups. There developed an almost unlimited range of jobs, skills, and earnings; one group or subclass blended into another in a complex, confusing hierarchy. In this atmosphere of competition and hierarchy, neither the "middle

Apartment Living in Paris

This drawing shows a typical layout for a European city apartment building in about 1850. (Bibliothèque nationale de France)

> PICTURING THE PAST

ANALYZING THE IMAGE: Describe the inhabitants of each floor. How do the economic conditions of the tenants differ from le premier étage (the equivalent of the American second floor) to the garret apartments on the top floor?

CONNECTIONS: What does this drawing suggest about urban life in the nineteenth century? How might a sketch of a modern, urban American apartment building differ in terms of the types of people who reside in a single building?

CHAPTER LOCATOR | How did urban life change in the nineteenth century?

CHAPTER 22

684 LIFE IN THE EMERGING URBAN SOCIETY

class" nor the "working class" actually acted as a single unified force. Rather, the social and occupational hierarchy developed enormous variations, though the age-old pattern of great economic inequality remained firmly intact.

The People and Occupations of the Middle Classes

By the beginning of the twentieth century, the diversity and range within the urban middle class were striking. Indeed, it makes sense to replace the idea of a single "middle class" with a confederation of "middle classes" whose members engaged in occupations requiring mental, rather than physical, skill.

Below the wealthy top tier, the much larger, much less wealthy, and increasingly diversified middle class included moderately successful industrialists and merchants as well as professionals in law, business, and medicine. As industry and technology expanded in the nineteenth century, a growing demand developed for experts with specialized knowledge, and advanced education soared in importance among the middle classes.

Industrialization expanded and diversified the lower middle class. The number of independent, property-owning shopkeepers and small business people grew, and so did the number of white-collar employees. White-collar employees owned little property and often earned no more than better-paid skilled or semi-skilled workers. Yet white-collar workers were fiercely committed to the middle-class ideal of upward social mobility. The tie, the suit, the soft, clean hands that accompanied low-level retail and managerial work became important status symbols that set this group above those who earned a living through manual labor.

Middle-Class Culture and Values

Despite growing occupational diversity and conflicting interests, lifestyle preferences loosely united the European middle classes. Food, housing, clothes, and behavior all expressed middle-class values and testified to the superior social standing of this group over the working classes.

Unlike the working classes, the middle classes had the money to eat well, and they spent a substantial portion of their household budget on food and entertainment. They consumed meat in abundance: a well-off family might spend 10 percent of its annual income on meat and fully 25 percent on food and drink. The dinner party—a favored social occasion—boosted spending.

The employment of at least one full-time maid to cook and clean was the clearest sign that a family had crossed the cultural divide separating the working classes from what some contemporary observers called the "servant-keeping classes." The greater a family's income, the greater the number of servants it employed. Servants absorbed about another 25 percent of income at all levels of the middle class.

Well fed and well served, the middle classes were also well housed by 1900. And, just as the aristocracy had long divided the year between palatial country estates and lavish townhouses during "the season," so the upper middle class purchased country places or built beach houses for weekend and summer use.

What were the characteristics of urban industrial society? | How did urbanization affect family life and gender roles? | How and why did intellectual life change in this period? | ☑ LearningCurve Check what you know.

685

The middle classes paid great attention to outward appearances, especially their clothes. The factory, the sewing machine, and the department store had all helped reduce the cost and expand the variety of clothing. Private coaches and carriages, expensive items in the city, further testified to rising social status.

In addition to their material tastes, the middle classes generally agreed upon a strict code of behavior and morality, which stressed hard work, self-discipline, and personal achievement. Middle-class social reformers denounced drunkenness and gambling as vices and celebrated sexual purity and fidelity as virtues. Men and women who fell into crime or poverty were held responsible for their own circumstances. A stern sense of Christian morality, preached tirelessly by religious leaders, educators, and politicians, reaffirmed these values.

The People and Occupations of the Working Classes

At the beginning of the twentieth century, about four out of five people belonged to the working classes—that is, people whose livelihoods depended primarily on physical labor and who did not employ domestic servants. Many of them were still small landowning peasants and hired farm hands, and this was especially the case in eastern Europe. In western and central Europe, however, the typical worker had left the land. By 1900, less than 8 percent of the people in Great Britain worked in agriculture, and in rapidly industrializing Germany, only 25 percent were employed in agriculture and forestry.

The urban working classes were even less unified and homogeneous than the middle classes. First, economic development and increased specialization expanded the traditional range of working-class skills, earnings, and experiences. Meanwhile, the old sharp distinction between highly skilled artisans and unskilled manual workers gradually broke down. To be sure, highly skilled printers and masons as well as unskilled dockworkers and common laborers continued to exist. But between these extremes there appeared ever more semiskilled groups. In addition, skilled, semiskilled, and unskilled workers developed divergent lifestyles and cultural values. These differences undermined the class unity predicted by Marx.

Highly skilled workers—about 15 percent of the working classes—became known as the **labor aristocracy**. The most "aristocratic" of these highly skilled workers were construction bosses and factory foremen, who had risen from the ranks and were fiercely proud of their achievement. The labor aristocracy also included members of the traditional highly skilled handicraft trades that had not been mechanized or placed in factories, like cabinetmakers, jewelers, and printers.

While the labor aristocracy enjoyed its exalted position, maintaining that status was by no means certain. Gradually, as factory production eliminated more and more crafts, lower-paid, semiskilled factory workers replaced many skilled artisans. At the same time, industrialization opened new opportunities for new kinds of highly skilled workers, such as shipbuilders and railway locomotive engineers. Thus the labor elite remained in a state of flux, as individuals and whole crafts moved in and out of it.

To maintain this precarious standing, the upper working class adopted distinctive values and straitlaced, almost puritanical behavior. Like the middle classes, the labor aristocracy believed firmly in middle-class morality, frugality,

labor aristocracy

▶ The highly skilled workers, such as factory foremen and construction bosses, who made up about 15 percent of the working classes from about 1850 to 1914.

CHAPTER LOCATOR | How did urban life change in the nineteenth century?

686 CHAPTER 22
LIFE IN THE EMERGING URBAN SOCIETY

and economic improvement. Nonetheless, skilled workers viewed themselves not as aspirants to the middle class but as the pacesetters and natural leaders of all the working classes.

Below the labor aristocracy stood the enormously complex world of hard work, composed of both semiskilled and unskilled workers. Established construction workers stood near the top of the semiskilled hierarchy, often flirting with (or sliding back from) the labor elite. A large number of the semiskilled were factory workers, who earned highly variable but relatively good wages. These workers included substantial numbers of unmarried women, who began to play an increasingly important role in the industrial labor force.

Below the semiskilled workers, a larger group of unskilled workers included day laborers such as longshoremen, wagon-driving teamsters, and "helpers" of all kinds. Many of these people had real skills and performed valuable services, but they were unorganized and divided, united only by the common fate of meager earnings and poor living conditions. The same lack of unity characterized street vendors and market people—these self-employed members of the lower working classes competed savagely with each other and with established shopkeepers of the lower middle class.

One of the largest components of the unskilled group was domestic servants, whose numbers grew steadily in the nineteenth century. The great majority of domestic servants were women. Throughout Europe, many female domestics in the cities were recent migrants from rural areas. As in earlier times, domestic service meant hard work at low pay with limited personal independence and the danger of sexual exploitation. For the full-time general maid in a lower-middle-class family, an unending routine of babysitting, shopping, cooking, and cleaning defined a lengthy working day. In the wealthiest households, the serving girl was at the bottom of a rigid hierarchy of status-conscious butlers and housekeepers.

Nonetheless, domestic service had real attractions for young women from rural areas who had few specialized skills. Marriage prospects were better, or at least more varied, in the city than back home. And though wages were low, they were higher and more regular than in hard agricultural work. Finally, young girls and other migrants from the countryside were drawn to the city by its glamour, excitement, and diversity.

Many young domestics made the successful transition to working-class wife and mother. Yet with an unskilled or unemployed husband, a growing family, and limited household income, many working-class wives had to join the broad ranks of working women in the **sweated industries**. These industries expanded rapidly after 1850 and resembled the old putting-out and cottage industries of earlier times (see Chapter 17, page 526). The women normally worked at home and were paid by the piece, not by the hour. Women decorated dishes or embroidered linens, took in laundry for washing and ironing, or made clothing, especially after the advent of the sewing machine.

sweated industries
▶ Poorly paid handicraft production, often carried out by married women paid by the piece and working at home.

Working-Class Leisure and Religion

The urban working classes sought fun and recreation, and they found both. Across Europe, drinking remained unquestionably the favorite leisure-time activity of working people. Generally, however, heavy problem drinking declined in the

What were the characteristics of urban industrial society?   How did urbanization affect family life and gender roles?   How and why did intellectual life change in this period?   ☑ LearningCurve Check what you know.

687

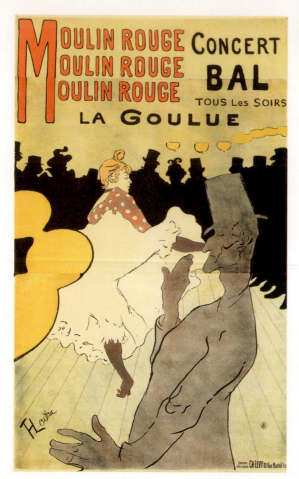

The most famous dance hall and cabaret in Paris was the Moulin Rouge. There La Goulue ("the Glutton"), portrayed on this poster, performed her provocative version of the cancan and reigned as the queen of Parisian sensuality. This is one of many colorful posters done by Henri de Toulouse-Lautrec (1864–1901), who combined stupendous creativity and dedicated debauchery in his short life. (Private Collection/Photo © Christie's Images/The Bridgeman Art Library)

late nineteenth century as it became less socially acceptable. This decline reflected in part the moral leadership of the labor aristocracy. At the same time, drinking became more publicly acceptable. Cafés and pubs became increasingly bright, friendly places. Working-class political activities, both moderate and radical, were also concentrated in taverns and pubs. Moreover, social drinking in public places by married couples and sweethearts became an accepted and widespread practice for the first time.

The two other leisure-time passions of working-class culture were sports and music halls. "Cruel sports," such as bullbaiting and cockfighting, had greatly declined throughout Europe by the late nineteenth century. Commercialized spectator sports filled their place. Working people gambled on sports events, and for many a working person, a desire to decipher racing forms provided a powerful incentive toward literacy. Music halls and vaudeville theaters were enormously popular throughout Europe.

In more serious moments, religion continued to provide working people with solace and meaning. The eighteenth-century vitality of popular religion in Catholic countries and the Protestant rejuvenation exemplified by German Pietism and English Methodism (see Chapter 18, page 567) carried over into the nineteenth century. Indeed, many historians see the early nineteenth century as an age of religious revival. Yet historians recognize that by the last few decades of the nineteenth century, a considerable decline in both church attendance and church donations had occurred in most European countries. And it seems clear that this decline was greater for the urban working classes than for their rural counterparts or for the middle classes.

Why did working-class church attendance decline? On one hand, the construction of churches failed to keep up with the rapid growth of urban population, especially in new working-class neighborhoods. On the other, throughout the nineteenth century, workers saw Catholic and Protestant churches as conservative institutions that defended status quo politics, hierarchical social order, and middle-class morality. As the working classes became more politically conscious, they tended to see established churches as allied with their political opponents. In addition, religion underwent a process historians call "feminization": in the working and middle classes alike, women were more pious and attended service more regularly than men. Urban workingmen in particular developed vaguely anti-church attitudes, even though they remained neutral or positive toward religion.

> **QUICK REVIEW**

What did the emergence of urban industrial society mean for rich and poor and those in between?

CHAPTER LOCATOR | How did urban life change in the nineteenth century?

Christmas and the Sentimental Pleasures of the Middle-Class Home Aptly portrayed in this sentimental painting by English genre artist Walter Dendy Sadler, the Victorian Christmas celebrated the family values and lifestyles of the middle classes at their most expressive. His clichéd portrait of a wealthy middle-class family holiday — with holly adorning the walls, mistletoe hanging above the fireplace, children singing carols with their parents, and contented grandparents sitting by a warm fire — captures the intimacy and love that increasingly bound together middle-class and working-class families alike during the nineteenth century. Titled *Home Sweet Home* and released for commercial reproduction and sale around 1900, prints of this image of domestic bliss no doubt adorned the walls of many middle-class parlors like the one shown in the painting. (Private Collection/Photo © Christie's Images/The Bridgeman Art Library)

WITH THE CONSOLIDATION CAUSED BY INDUSTRIALIZATION and urbanization, the growing middle classes created a distinctive middle-class lifestyle, which set them off from peasants, workers, and the aristocracy. New ideas about courtship and marriage, family and gender roles, homemaking and child rearing all expressed middle-class norms and values in ways that would have a profound impact on family life in the century to come. Changes in family life affected both men and women and all social classes, but to varying degrees. Leading a middle-class lifestyle was prohibitively expensive for workers and peasants, and middle-class family values at first had little relevance for their lives. Yet as the nineteenth century drew to a close, the middle-class lifestyle increasingly became the norm for all classes.

What were the characteristics of urban industrial society?

How did urbanization affect family life and gender roles?

How and why did intellectual life change in this period?

☑ LearningCurve
Check what you know.

Middle-Class Marriage and Courtship Rituals

companionate marriage

▶ Marriage based on romantic love and middle-class family values that became increasingly dominant in the second half of the nineteenth century.

Rather than marry for convenience, or for economic or social reasons, by the 1850s the middle-class couple was supposed to meet, fall in love, and join for life because of a shared emotional bond. Of course, economic considerations in marriage by no means disappeared. But an entire culture of romantic love now surrounded the middle-class couple. The growing popularity among all classes toward the end of the nineteenth century of what historians call **companionate marriage** underscores the way historical contexts influence human emotions and behaviors.

Strict rules for courtship and engagement enshrined in the concept of falling in love ensured that middle-class individuals would make an appropriate match. Young couples were seldom alone before they became engaged, and people rarely paired off with someone from an inappropriate class background. Premarital sex was taboo for women, though men might experiment, a double standard that expressed middle-class assumptions about sexual morality and especially women's virginity before marriage.

Engagement also followed a complicated set of rules and rituals. Secret engagements led to public announcements, and then the couple could appear together, though only with chaperones when in potentially delicate situations. They might walk arm in arm, but custom placed strict limits on physical intimacy.

Marriage had its own set of rules. Usually a middle-class man could marry only if he could support a wife, children, and a servant. He was supposed to be fairly prosperous and well established in his career. As a result, some middle-class men never married because they could not afford it. The system encouraged mixed-age marriages. A new husband was typically much older than his young wife, who usually had no career and entered marriage directly out of her parents' home or perhaps a girl's finishing school. She would have had little experience with the realities of adult life.

Since women generally were quite young when they married, the man was encouraged to see himself as the protector of a young and fragile creature. In short, the typical middle-class marriage was more similar to a child-parent relationship than a partnership of equals. The inequality of marriage was codified in European legal systems that, with rare exceptions, placed property ownership in the hands of the husband.

Middle- and Working-Class Sexuality

A double standard in sexual relations paralleled the gender inequalities built into middle-class standards of love and marriage. Middle-class moralists cast men as aggressively sexual creatures, while women were supposed to be pure and chaste and act as a brake on male desire. Contemporary science legitimized this double standard. According to late-nineteenth-century physicians, men were subject to raging biological drives, while respectable women were supposedly uninterested in sex by nature.

Middle-class moralists assumed that men would enter marriage with some sexual experience, though this was unthinkable for a middle-class woman. When middle-class men did seek premarital sex, middle-class women were off limits. Instead, bourgeois men took advantage of their class status and sought lower-class women, domestic servants, or prostitutes. If a young middle-class woman had experimented with or even was suspected of having had premarital sex, her chances for an acceptable marriage fell dramatically.

The sexual standards of the working classes stood in marked contrast to these norms early in the nineteenth century, but that changed over time. Premarital sex for both men and women was common and more acceptable among the working class. In the first half of the nineteenth century, among the lower classes, about one-third of the births in many large European cities occurred outside wedlock. The second half of the century saw the reversal of this high rate of illegitimacy: in western, northern, and central Europe, more babies were born to married mothers. Young, unmarried workers were probably engaging in just as much sexual activity as their parents and grandparents who had created the illegitimacy explosion of 1750 to 1850 (see Chapter 18, page 551). But in the later part of the nineteenth century, pregnancy for a young single woman, which a couple might see as the natural consequence of a serious relationship, led increasingly to marriage and the establishment of a two-parent household. This important development reflected the spread of middle-class ideals of family respectability among the working classes, as well as their gradual economic improvement. Romantic love held working-class families together, and marriage was less of an economic challenge. The urban working-class couple of the late nineteenth century thus became more stable, and that stability strengthened the family as an institution.

Prostitution

In the late nineteenth century, prostitution was legal in much of Europe. In streets, dance halls, and pubs across Europe, young working-class women used prostitution as a source of second income or as a way to weather a period of unemployment. Prostitutes generally serviced lower-class men, soldiers, and sailors, though middle- and upper-class men also paid for sexual encounters.

Prostitutes clearly transgressed middle-class ideals of feminine respectability, but among the working classes, prostitution was tolerated as more-or-less acceptable work of a temporary nature. Like domestic service, prostitution was a stage of life, not permanent employment. Having practiced it for a while in their twenties, many women went on to marry (or live with) men of their own class and establish homes and families.

As middle-class family values became increasingly prominent after the 1860s, prostitution generated great concern among social reformers. The prostitute served as the mirror image of the respectable middle-class woman. Moreover, authorities blamed prostitutes for spreading crime and disease, particularly syphilis.

As general concerns with public health gained publicity, state and city authorities across Europe subjected prostitutes to increased surveillance. The British Contagious Diseases Acts, in force between 1864 and 1886, exemplified the trend. Under these acts, special plainclothes policemen required women identified as "common prostitutes" to undergo biweekly medical exams. If they showed signs of venereal disease, they were interned in a "lock hospital" and forced to undergo treatment; when the outward signs of disease went away, they were released.

The Contagious Diseases Acts were controversial from the start. A determined middle-class feminist campaign against the policy, led by Josephine Butler

What were the characteristics of urban industrial society?

How did urbanization affect family life and gender roles?

How and why did intellectual life change in this period?

✓ LearningCurve
Check what you know.

691

and the Ladies National Association, loudly proclaimed that the acts physically abused poor women, violated their constitutional rights, and legitimized male vice. Under pressure, Parliament repealed the laws in 1886. Yet heavy-handed government regulation had devastated the informality of working-class prostitution. Now branded as "registered girls," prostitutes experienced new forms of public humiliation, and the trade was increasingly controlled by male pimps rather than by the women themselves. Prostitution had never been safe, but it had been accepted, at least among the working classes. Prostitutes were now stigmatized as social and sexual outsiders.

Separate Spheres and the Importance of Homemaking

After 1850, the work of wives became increasingly distinct and separate from that of their husbands in all classes. The preindustrial pattern among both peasants and cottage workers, in which husbands and wives both worked and shared basic household duties, became less common. In wealthier homes, this change was particularly dramatic. The good middle-class family man earned the wages to support the household; the public world of work, education, and politics was male space. Respectable middle-class women did not work outside the home and rarely even traveled alone in public. Thus many historians have stressed that the societal ideal in nineteenth-century Europe became a strict division of labor by gender within rigidly constructed **separate spheres**: the wife as mother and homemaker, the husband as wage earner and breadwinner.

For the middle classes, the single-family home, a symbol of middle-class status and a sanctuary from the callous outside world of competitive capitalism, was central to the notion of separate spheres. At the heart of the middle-class home stood the woman: notions of femininity, motherhood, and private life came together in the ideal of domestic space. Middle-class women were spared the manly burdens of the outside world, while lower-class servants ensured that they had free time to turn the private sphere into a domestic refuge of love and privacy.

By 1900, working-class families had adopted many middle-class values, but they did not have the means to fully realize the ideal of separate spheres. Women were the primary homemakers, and, as in the upper classes, men did little or no domestic labor. But many working-class women also made a monetary contribution to family income by taking in a boarder, doing piecework at home in the sweated industries (see page 686), or getting an outside job. Working women worked to create a homelike environment that at least resembled that of the middle class, but working men often preferred to spend time in the local pub with workmates rather than come home. Indeed, alcoholism and domestic violence afflicted many working-class families, even as they worked to build a relationship based on romantic love.

Feminist historians have often criticized the middle-class ideal of separate spheres because it restricted women's educational and employment opportunities. In recent years, however, some scholars have been rethinking gender roles within the long-term development of consumer behavior and household economies. In the era of industrialization, these scholars suggest, the "breadwinner-homemaker" household that developed from about 1850 onward was rational

separate spheres

▶ The nineteenth-century gendered division of labor and lifestyles that cast men as breadwinners and women as homemakers.

CHAPTER LOCATOR | How did urban life change in the nineteenth century?

692

CHAPTER 22
LIFE IN THE EMERGING URBAN SOCIETY

consumer behavior that improved the lives of all family members, especially in the working classes.[3]

According to this view, when husbands specialized in earning an adequate cash income—the "family wage" that labor unions demanded—and wives specialized in managing the home, the working-class wife could produce desirable goods that could not be bought in a market, such as improved health, better eating habits, and better behavior. For example, higher wages from the breadwinner could buy more raw food, but only the homemaker's careful selection, processing, and cooking would allow the family to benefit from increased spending on food. Running an urban household was a complicated, demanding, and valuable task. Working yet another job for wages outside the home had limited appeal for most married women unless the earnings were essential for family survival. The home-maker's managerial skills, however, enabled the working-class couple to maximize their personal well-being.

The woman's guidance of the household went hand in hand with the increased pride in the home and family and the emotional importance attached to them in working- and middle-class families alike. Domesticity and family ties were now central to the lives of millions of people of all classes.

Child Rearing

Another striking sign of deepening emotional ties within the family was a growing emphasis on the love and concern that mothers gave their infants. Early emotional bonding and a willingness to make real sacrifices for the welfare of the infant became increasingly important among the comfortable classes by the end of the eighteenth century, though the ordinary mother of modest means adopted new attitudes only as the nineteenth century progressed.

The surge of maternal feeling was shaped by and reflected in a wave of specialized books on child rearing and infant hygiene. Following expert advice, mothers increasingly breast-fed their infants rather than paying wet nurses to do so. Breast-feeding involved sacrifice—a temporary loss of freedom, if nothing else. Yet when there was no good alternative to mother's milk, it saved lives. Moreover, the practice of swaddling disappeared completely. Instead, ordinary mothers allowed their babies freedom of movement and delighted in their spontaneity.

The loving care lavished on infants was matched by greater concern for older children and adolescents. They, too, were wrapped in the strong emotional ties of a more intimate and protective family. For one thing, European women began to limit the number of children they bore in order to care adequately for those they had. By the end of the nineteenth century, the birthrate was declining across Europe (**Figure 22.2**), and it continued to do so until after World War II. The English-woman who married in the 1860s, for example, had an average of about six children; her daughter marrying in the 1890s

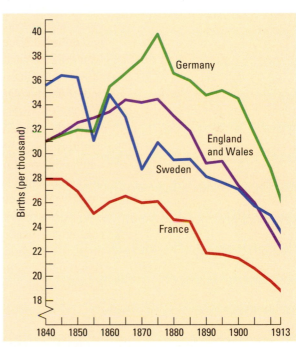

FIGURE 22.2 ■ The Decline of Birthrates in England and Wales, Germany, France, and Sweden, 1840–1913
Women had fewer babies for a variety of reasons, including the fact that their children were increasingly less likely to die before reaching adulthood. How does this compare with Figure 22.1 on page 680?

What were the characteristics of urban industrial society?

How did urbanization affect family life and gender roles?

How and why did intellectual life change in this period?

✓ LearningCurve
Check what you know.

693

had only four; and her granddaughter marrying in the 1920s had only two or possibly three.

The most important reason for this revolutionary reduction in family size, in which the comfortable and well-educated classes took the lead, was parents' desire to improve their economic and social position and that of their children. Children were no longer an economic asset in the late nineteenth century. By having fewer youngsters, parents could give those they had valuable advantages, from music lessons and summer vacations to long, expensive university educations and suitable dowries. Thus the growing tendency of couples in the late nineteenth century to use a variety of contraceptive methods reflected increased concern for children.

In middle-class households, parents expended considerable effort to ensure that they raised their children according to prevailing family values. Indeed, many parents, especially in the middle classes, probably became too concerned about their children, unwittingly subjecting them to an emotional pressure cooker of almost unbearable intensity. Professional family experts, including teachers, doctors, and reformers, produced a vast popular literature on child rearing that encouraged parents to focus on developing their children's self-control, self-fulfillment, and sense of Christian morality. Parents carefully monitored their children's sexual behavior, and masturbation—according to one expert "the most shameful and terrible of all vices"—was of particular concern.[4]

Attempts to repress the child's sexuality generated unhealthy tension, often made worse by the rigid division of gender roles within the family. At work all day, the father came home a stranger to his offspring; his world of business was far removed from the maternal world of spontaneous affection. Moreover, the father set demanding rules, often expecting the child to succeed where he himself had failed and making his love conditional on achievement. This kind of distance was the case among mothers as well as fathers in the wealthiest families. Domestic servants, nannies, and tutors did much of the work of child rearing; parents saw their children over dinner, or on special occasions like birthdays or holidays.

The children of the working classes probably had more avenues of escape from such tensions than did those of the middle classes. Unlike their middle-class counterparts, who remained economically dependent on their families until a long education was finished or a proper marriage secured, working-class boys and girls went to work when they reached adolescence. Earning wages on their own, they could bargain with their parents for greater independence within the household by the time they were sixteen or seventeen. If they were unsuccessful in these negotiations, they could and did leave home to live cheaply as paying lodgers in other working-class homes. Not until the twentieth century could middle-class youths be equally free to break away from the family when emotional ties became oppressive.

The Feminist Movement

The ideal of separate spheres and the rigid gender division of labor meant that middle-class women faced great obstacles when they needed—or wanted—to move into the man's world of paid employment outside the home. Married women were subordinated to their husbands by law and lacked many basic legal rights.

Facing discrimination in education and employment and suffering from a lack of legal rights, some women rebelled and began the long-continuing fight for equality of the sexes and the rights of women. Their struggle proceeded on two main paths. First, organizations founded by middle-class feminists campaigned for equal legal rights for women as well as access to higher education and professional employment. Middle-class feminists argued that unmarried women and middle-class widows with inadequate incomes simply had to have more opportunities to support themselves. Second, they also recognized that paid (as opposed to unpaid) work could relieve the monotony that some women found in their sheltered middle-class existence and add greater meaning to their lives. In the late

May.21.1914

First-Wave Feminists in Action

In May 1914 suffragette leader Emily Pankhurst was arrested by a police superintendent when she tried to present a petition to the King at Buckingham Palace. The British suffragettes often engaged in provocative public acts of civic disobedience in their campaign for women's right to vote. How do you account for the reaction of the male onlookers? (© Museum of London, UK/ Bridgeman Images)

What were the characteristics of urban industrial society?

How did urbanization affect family life and gender roles?

How and why did intellectual life change in this period?

☑ LearningCurve
Check what you know.

695

Why did a small number of women in the late nineteenth century brave great odds and embark on professional careers? And how did a few of them manage to reach their objectives? The career and personal reflections of Franziska Tiburtius (tigh-bur-TEE-uhs), a pioneer in German medicine, suggest that talent, determination, and economic necessity were critical ingredients to both the attempt and the success.*

Like many women of her time who studied and pursued professional careers, Franziska Tiburtius (1843–1927) was born into a property-owning family of modest means. The youngest of nine children growing up on a small estate in northeastern Germany, the sensitive child wilted under a harsh governess but flowered with a caring teacher and became an excellent student. Graduating at sixteen and needing to support herself, Tiburtius had few opportunities. A young woman from a "proper" background could work as a governess or teacher without losing her respectability and spoiling her matrimonial prospects, but that was about it. She tried both avenues. Working for six years as a governess in a noble family and no doubt learning that poverty was often one's fate in this genteel profession, she then turned to teaching. Called home from her studies in Britain in 1871 to care for her brother, who had contracted typhus as a field doctor in the Franco-Prussian War, she found her calling. She decided to become a medical doctor.

Supported by her family, Tiburtius's decision was truly audacious. In all Europe, only the University of Zurich accepted female students. Moreover, if it became known that she had studied medicine and failed, she would probably never get a job as a teacher. No parent would entrust a daughter to an emancipated radical who had carved up dead bodies. Although the male students at the university sometimes harassed the female ones with crude pranks, Tiburtius thrived. The revolution of the microscope and the discovery of microorganisms thrilled Zurich, and she was fascinated by her studies. She became close friends with a fellow female student from Germany, Emilie Lehmus, with whom she would form a lifelong partnership in medicine. She did her internship with families of cottage workers around Zurich and loved her work.

Graduating at age thirty-three in 1876, Tiburtius went to stay with her doctor brother in Berlin. Though well qualified to practice, she was blocked by pervasive discrimination. Not permitted to take the state medical exams, she could practice only as an unregulated (and unprofessional) "natural healer." But after persistent fighting with the bureaucrats, she was able to display her diploma and practice as "Franziska Tiburtius, M.D., University of Zurich."

*This portrait draws on Conradine Lück, *Frauen: Neun Lebensschicksale* (Reutlingen, Germany: Ensslin & Laiblin, n.d.), pp. 153–185.

Franziska Tiburtius, pioneering woman physician in Berlin. (The Granger Collection, New York)

Soon Tiburtius and Lehmus realized their dream and opened a clinic. Subsidized by a wealthy industrialist, they focused on treating women factory workers. The clinic filled a great need and was soon treating many patients. A room with beds for extremely sick women was later expanded into a second clinic.

Tiburtius and Lehmus became famous. For fifteen years, they were the only women doctors in all of Berlin and inspired a new generation of women. Though they added the wealthy to their thriving practice, they always concentrated on the poor, providing them with subsidized and up-to-date treatment. Talented, determined, and working with her partner, Tiburtius experienced fully the joys of personal achievement and useful service. Above all, Tiburtius overcame the tremendous barriers raised up against women seeking higher education and professional careers, providing an inspiring model for those who dared to follow.

QUESTIONS FOR ANALYSIS

1. Analyze Franziska Tiburtius's life. What lessons do you draw from it? How do you account for her bold action and success?
2. In what ways was Tiburtius's career related to improvements in health in urban society and to the expansion of the professions?

nineteenth century, these organizations scored some significant victories, such as the 1882 law giving English married women full property rights. More women gradually found professional and white-collar employment, especially after about 1880, in fields such as teaching, nursing, and social work.

Progress toward women's rights was slow and hard-won. In Britain, the women's **suffrage movement** mounted a militant struggle for the right to vote, particularly in the decade before World War I. "Suffragettes" marched in public demonstrations, heckled members of Parliament, and slashed paintings in London's National Gallery. Jailed for political activities, they went on highly publicized hunger strikes. Yet conservatives dismissed what they called "the shrieking sisterhood," and British women received the vote only in 1919.

In Germany before 1900, women were not admitted as fully registered students at a single university. Determined pioneers had to fight with tremendous fortitude to break through sexist barriers to advanced education and subsequent professional employment. (See "Individuals in Society: Franziska Tiburtius," page 696.) By 1913, the Federation of German Women's Association, an umbrella organization for regional feminist groups, had some 470,000 members. Their protests had a direct impact on the revised German Civil Code of 1906, which granted women substantial gains in family law and property rights.

Women inspired by utopian and especially Marxist socialism (see Chapter 21) blazed a second path. Often scorning the reform programs of middle-class feminists, socialist women leaders argued that the liberation of working-class women would come only with the liberation of the entire working class through revolution. In the meantime, they championed the cause of working women and won some practical improvements, especially in Germany, where the socialist movement was most effectively organized.

suffrage movement
► A militant movement for women's right to vote led by middle-class British women around 1900.

QUICK REVIEW

How did the middle classes define the ideal wife and mother in the second half of the nineteenth century? What about the working classes?

What were the characteristics of urban industrial society?

How did urbanization affect family life and gender roles?

How and why did intellectual life change in this period?

☑ LearningCurve
Check what you know.

697

How and why did intellectual life change in this period?

Madrid in 1900 This wistful painting of a Spanish square on a rainy day, by Enrique Martinez Cubells y Ruiz (1874–1917), offers a revealing commentary on how scientific discoveries transformed urban life. Coachmen wait atop their expensive hackney cabs for a wealthy clientele, while modern electric streetcars that carry the masses converge on the square from all directions. The development of electricity brought improved urban transportation and enabled the city to expand to the suburbs. (Museo Municipal, Madrid/The Bridgeman Art Library)

MAJOR CHANGES IN WESTERN SCIENCE and thought accompanied the emergence of urban society. Two aspects of these complex intellectual developments stand out as especially significant. First, scientific knowledge in many areas expanded rapidly. Second, between about the 1840s and the 1890s, European literature underwent a shift from soaring romanticism to tough-minded realism.

The Triumph of Science in Industry

As the pace of scientific advancements quickened and resulted in greater practical benefits, science exercised growing influence on human thought. The intellectual achievements of the Scientific Revolution (see Chapter 16) had resulted in

CHAPTER LOCATOR | How did urban life change in the nineteenth century?

few such benefits, and theoretical knowledge had also played a relatively small role in the Industrial Revolution in England (see Chapter 20). But breakthroughs in industrial technology in the late eighteenth century enormously stimulated basic scientific inquiry as researchers sought to explain theoretically how machines such as steam engines and blast furnaces actually worked. The result was an explosive growth of fundamental scientific discoveries from the 1830s onward. In contrast to earlier periods, these theoretical discoveries were increasingly transformed into material improvements for the general population.

A perfect example of the translation of better scientific knowledge into practical human benefits was the work of Louis Pasteur and his followers in biology and the medical sciences (see page 680). Another was the development of the branch of physics known as **thermodynamics**. Building on Isaac Newton's laws of mechanics and on studies of steam engines, thermodynamics investigated the relationship between heat and mechanical energy. By midcentury, physicists had formulated the fundamental laws of thermodynamics, which were then applied to mechanical engineering, chemical processes, and many other fields.

Chemistry and electricity were two other fields characterized by extremely rapid scientific progress. And in both fields, "science was put in the service of industry." Chemists devised ways of measuring the atomic weight of different elements, and in 1869 the Russian chemist Dmitri Mendeleev (mehn-duh-LAY-uhf) (1834–1907) codified the rules of chemistry in the periodic law and the periodic table. Chemistry was subdivided into many specialized branches, including organic chemistry—the study of the compounds of carbon. Applying theoretical insights gleaned from this new field, researchers in large German chemical companies discovered ways of transforming the coal tar that accumulated in coke ovens into synthetic dyes for the world of fashion. German production of synthetic dyes soared, and by 1900, German chemical companies controlled 90 percent of world production.

Electricity, a scientific curiosity in 1800, was totally transformed by a century of tremendous technological advancement. It became a commercial form of energy. And by 1890, the internal combustion engine fueled by petroleum was an emerging competitor to steam and electricity alike.

The successful application of scientific research in the fast-growing electrical and organic chemical industries between 1880 and 1913 provided a model for other industries. Systematic "R&D"—research and development—was born in the late nineteenth century. Above all, the burst of industrial creativity and technological innovation, often called the **Second Industrial Revolution**, promoted the strong economic growth in the last third of the nineteenth century that drove the urban reforms and the rising standard of living considered in this chapter.

The triumph of science and technology had three other significant consequences. First, though ordinary citizens continued to lack detailed scientific knowledge, everyday experience and innumerable articles in newspapers and magazines impressed the importance of science on the popular mind. Second, as science became more prominent in popular thinking, the philosophical implications of science formulated in the Enlightenment spread to broad sections of the population. Natural processes appeared to be determined by rigid laws, leaving little room for either divine intervention or human will. Yet scientific and technical advances had also fed the Enlightenment's optimistic faith in human progress.

thermodynamics
▶ A branch of physics built on Newton's laws of mechanics that investigated the relationship between heat and mechanical energy.

Second Industrial Revolution
▶ The burst of industrial creativity and technological innovation that promoted strong economic growth in the last third of the nineteenth century.

What were the characteristics of urban industrial society?   How did urbanization affect family life and gender roles?   **How and why did intellectual life change in this period?**   ☑ LearningCurve Check what you know.

699

Third, the methods of science acquired unrivaled prestige after 1850. For many, the union of careful experiment and abstract theory was the only reliable route to truth and objective reality.

Darwin and Natural Selection

Scientific research also progressed rapidly outside the world of industry and technology, sometimes putting forth direct challenges to traditional beliefs. In geology, for example, Charles Lyell (1797–1875) effectively discredited the long-standing view that the earth's surface had been formed by short-lived cataclysms, such as biblical floods and earthquakes. Instead, according to Lyell's principle of uniformitarianism, the same geological processes that are at work today slowly formed the earth's surface over an immensely long time. Similarly, the evolutionary view of biological development, first proposed by the Greek Anaximander in the sixth century B.C.E., re-emerged in a more modern form. Charles Darwin (1809–1882) was the most influential of all nineteenth-century evolutionary thinkers. Convinced by fossil evidence and by his friend Lyell that the earth and life on it were immensely ancient, Darwin came to doubt the general belief in a special divine creation of each species of animal. Instead, he concluded, all life had gradually evolved from a common ancestral origin in an unending "struggle for survival." After long hesitation, Darwin published his research, which immediately attracted wide attention.

Darwin's great originality lay in suggesting precisely how biological evolution might have occurred. His theory of **evolution** is summarized in the title of his work *On the Origin of Species by the Means of Natural Selection* (1859). Darwin argued that chance differences among the members of a given species help some survive while others die. Thus the variations that prove useful in the struggle for survival are selected naturally, and they gradually spread to the entire species through reproduction.

Some thinkers applied Darwin's theory of biological evolution to human affairs. English philosopher Herbert Spencer (1820–1903) saw the human race as driven forward to ever-greater specialization and progress by a brutal economic struggle that determined the "survival of the fittest." The poor were the ill-fated weak; the prosperous were the chosen strong. **Social Darwinism** gained adherents among nationalists, who viewed global competition between countries as a grand struggle for survival, as well as among imperialists, who used Social Darwinist ideas to justify the rule of the "advanced" West over their colonial subjects and territories.

The Modern University and the Social Sciences

By the 1880s, major universities across Europe had been modernized and professionalized. An increasingly diversified professoriate established many of the academic departments still at work in today's universities. In a striking development, faculty members devoted to the newly instituted human or social sciences took their place alongside the hard sciences. Using critical methods often borrowed from natural science, social scientists studied massive sets of numerical data that

evolution
▶ The idea, applied by thinkers in many fields, that stresses gradual change and continuous adjustment in the development of animal species.

Social Darwinism
▶ A body of thought drawn from the ideas of Charles Darwin that applied the theory of biological evolution to human affairs and saw the human race as driven by an unending economic struggle that would determine the survival of the fittest.

CHAPTER LOCATOR | How did urban life change in the nineteenth century?

CHAPTER 22
700 LIFE IN THE EMERGING URBAN SOCIETY

governments had begun to collect on everything from children to crime and from population to prostitution.

Sociology, the critical analysis of contemporary or historical social groups, emerged as a leading social science. Perhaps the most prominent and influential late-nineteenth-century sociologist was the German Max Weber (1864–1920). In his most famous book, *The Protestant Ethic and the "Spirit" of Capitalism* (1890), Weber argued that the rise of capitalism was directly linked to Protestantism in northern Europe. Pointing to the early and successful modernization of countries like the Netherlands and England, he concluded that Protestantism gave religious approval to hard work, saving, and investing—the foundations for capitalist development—because worldly success was a sign of God's approval. This argument seriously challenged the basic ideas of Marxism: ideas, for Weber, were just as important as economics or class struggle in the rise of capitalism.

In France, the prolific sociologist Émile Durkheim (1858–1917) earned an international reputation for his wide-ranging work. In his pioneering work of quantitative sociology, *Suicide* (1897), Durkheim concluded that ever-higher suicide rates were caused by widespread feelings of "anomie," or rootlessness. Because modern society had stripped life of all sense of tradition, purpose, and belonging, Durkheim believed, anomie was inescapable; only an entirely new moral order might offer some relief.

The new sociologists cast a bleak image of urban industrial society. While they acknowledged some benefits of rationalization and modernization, they bemoaned the accompanying loss of community and tradition. In some ways, their diagnosis of the modern individual as an isolated atom suffering from anomie and desperately seeking human connection was chillingly prescient: the powerful Communist and Fascist movements that swept through Europe after World War I seemed to win popular support precisely by offering ordinary people a renewed sense of belonging.

Realism in Art and Literature

In art and literature, the key themes of **realism** emerged in the 1840s and continued to dominate Western culture and style until the 1890s. Realist artists and writers believed that cultural works should depict life exactly as it was. Forsaking the personal, emotional viewpoint of the romantics for strict, supposedly scientific objectivity, the realists observed and recorded the world around them—often to expose the sordid reality of modern life.

Emphatically rejecting the romantic search for the exotic and the sublime, realism (or "naturalism," as it was often called) energetically pursued the typical and the commonplace. Beginning with a dissection of the middle classes, from which most of them sprang, many realists eventually focused on the working classes, especially the urban working classes, which had been neglected in imaginative literature before this time. The realists put a microscope to many unexplored and taboo subjects, including sex, labor strikes, violence, and alcoholism.

The realist movement started in France, where romanticism had never been completely dominant. Artists like Gustave Courbet, Jean-François Millet, and Honoré Daumier painted scenes of laboring workers and peasants in somber colors and simple compositions. Daumier's art championed the simple virtues of the urban working class and lampooned the greed and ill will of the rich bourgeoisie.

realism
▶ A literary movement that, in contrast to romanticism, stressed the depiction of life as it actually was.

| What were the characteristics of urban industrial society? | How did urbanization affect family life and gender roles? | **How and why did intellectual life change in this period?** | ☑ LearningCurve Check what you know. |

Realism in the Arts

Realist depictions of gritty everyday life challenged the romantic fascination with nature and the emotions, as well as the neoclassical focus on famous men and grand events. French painter Honoré Daumier's *The Third-Class Carriage*, completed in 1864, is a famous example of realism in the arts that portrays the effects of industrialization in the mid-nineteenth century. In muted colors, Daumier's painting captures the grinding poverty and weariness of the poor but also lends a sense of dignity to their humble lives. (Metropolitan Museum of Art, New York, USA/De Agostini Picture Library/The Bridgeman Art Library)

Literary realism also began in France, where Honoré de Balzac, Gustave Flaubert, and Émile Zola became internationally famous novelists. Balzac (1799–1850) spent thirty years writing a vastly ambitious panorama of postrevolutionary French life. Known collectively as *The Human Comedy*, this series of nearly one hundred stories, novels, and essays vividly portrays more than two thousand characters from virtually all sectors of French society.

Madame Bovary (1857), the masterpiece of Flaubert (floh-BEHR) (1821–1880), is far narrower in scope than Balzac's work but is still famous for its depth and accuracy of psychological insight. The novel tells the ordinary, even banal, story of a frustrated middle-class housewife who has an adulterous love affair and is betrayed by her lover. Without moralizing, Flaubert portrays the provincial middle class as petty, smug, and hypocritical.

Émile Zola (1840–1902) was most famous for his seamy, animalistic view of working-class life. But he also wrote gripping, carefully researched stories featuring the stock exchange, the big department store, and the army, as well as urban slums and bloody coal strikes. Like many later realists, Zola sympathized with socialism, a view evident in his novel *Germinal* (1885).

Realism quickly spread beyond France. In England, Mary Ann Evans (1819–1880), who wrote under the pen name George Eliot, brilliantly achieved a more deeply felt, less sensational kind of realism in her great novel *Middlemarch: A Study of Provincial Life* (1871–1872). The novels of Thomas Hardy (1840–1928) depict ordinary men and women frustrated and crushed by fate and bad luck. The greatest Russian realist, Count Leo Tolstoy (1828–1910), combined realism in description and character development with an atypical moralizing, especially in his later work. In *War and Peace* (1864–1869) Tolstoy developed his fatalistic theory of human history, which regards free will as an illusion and the achievements of even the greatest leaders as only the channeling of historical necessity. Yet Tolstoy's central message is one that most of the people discussed in this chapter would have readily accepted: human love, trust, and everyday family ties are life's enduring values.

 **LOOKING BACK LOOKING AHEAD** By the early twentieth century, the peoples of northwestern Europe had good reason to feel that the promise of the Industrial Revolution was being realized. The dark days of urban squalor and brutal working hours had given way after 1850 to a gradual rise in the standard of living for all classes. Scientific discoveries were combining with the applied technology of public health and industrial production to save lives and drive continued economic growth.

Moreover, social and economic advances seemed to be matched by progress in the political sphere. The years following the dramatic failure of the revolutions of 1848 saw the creation of unified nation-states in Italy and Germany, and after 1870 nationalism and the nation-state reigned in Europe. Although the rise of nationalism created tensions among the European countries, these tensions would not explode until 1914 and the outbreak of the First World War. Instead, the most aggressive and destructive aspects of European nationalism found their initial outlet in the final and most powerful surge of Western overseas expansion. Thus Europe, transformed by industrialization and nationalism, rushed after 1875 to seize territory and build new or greatly expanded authoritarian empires in Asia and Africa.

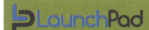

ONLINE DOCUMENT PROJECT

Capturing Life in the Modern City on Film

How did cities and individuals respond to the challenges brought on by rapid urbanization?

Keeping the question above in mind, go online and view video footage from the early twentieth century that documents new developments in city life—from mass transit to waste disposal. *See inside the front cover to learn more.*

| What were the characteristics of urban industrial society? | How did urbanization affect family life and gender roles? | How and why did intellectual life change in this period? | ✓ **LearningCurve** **Check what you know.** |

CHAPTER 22 STUDY GUIDE

 **GET STARTED ONLINE**

 **LearningCurve**
Now that you've read the chapter, make it stick by completing the LearningCurve activity.

 **EXPLAIN WHY IT MATTERS**

Put your reading into practice. Identify each term below, and then explain why it matters in Western history.

TERM	WHO OR WHAT & WHEN	WHY IT MATTERS
utilitarianism (p. 679)		
germ theory (p. 680)		
labor aristocracy (p. 686)		
sweated industries (p. 687)		
companionate marriage (p. 690)		
separate spheres (p. 692)		
suffrage movement (p. 697)		
thermodynamics (p. 699)		
Second Industrial Revolution (p. 699)		
evolution (p. 700)		
Social Darwinism (p. 700)		
realism (p. 701)		

 **MOVE BEYOND THE BASICS**

To demonstrate a more advanced understanding, fill in the chart included below with the members and values of the principal groups within the working and middle classes. What did the class and the labor aristocracy have in common? What were the primary sites of conflict between middle-class and working-class culture?

	Members	Values
Upper middle class		
Middle middle class		
Lower middle class		
Labor aristocracy		
Semiskilled workers		
Unskilled workers		

PUT IT ALL TOGETHER Now, take a step back and try to explain the big picture. Remember to use specific examples from the chapter in your answers.

A COURT FOR KING CHOLERA.

THE CITY

▶ Compare and contrast the eighteenth- and nineteenth-century cities. What role did industrialization play in producing the differences you note?

▶ How did government officials try to overcome the challenges of the nineteenth-century city? What role did advances in medicine and transportation play in alleviating the problems of the nineteenth-century city? What about new approaches to city planning?

SOCIETY AND THE FAMILY

▶ What explains the increasing diversity of the working classes in nineteenth-century Europe? What were the economic and political implications of this diversity?

▶ How did the ideal model of family relationships change over the course of the nineteenth century? How would you explain the transformation you describe?

SCIENCE AND THOUGHT

▶ In what ways did the scientific revolution of the nineteenth century differ from the scientific revolution of the sixteenth and seventeenth centuries? What was the relationship between science and industry in the second half of the nineteenth century?

▶ How did science influence late nineteenth-century trends in literature and art? Is it fair to describe science as the dominant intellectual influence in the second half of the nineteenth century?

MAKE CONNECTIONS

▶ Compare and contrast the typical Western city in 1700 and 1900. What similarities and differences do you note? How would you explain those differences?

▶ Compare and contrast the typical Western city in 1900 and 2000. What forces have played the most important role in shaping the city over the course of the last century?

> IN YOUR OWN WORDS

Imagine that you must give an oral report to the class answering the following question: **How and why did city life change between 1800 and 1900?** What would be the most important points, and why?

23

THE AGE OF NATIONALISM

1850–1914

> **How did nationalism shape the development of Western government and political life in the second half of the nineteenth century?** Chapter 23 examines the rise of nationalism and the nation-state in the nineteenth century. In the years that followed the revolutions of 1848, Western society progressively developed, for better or worse, an effective organizing principle capable of coping with the many-sided challenges of the unfinished industrial and political revolutions and the emerging urban society. That principle was nationalism — mass identification with the nation-state. Just as industrialization and urbanization had brought vast changes to class relations, family lifestyles, science, and culture, the triumph of nationalism remade territorial boundaries and forged new relations between the nation-state and its citizens.

LearningCurve

After reading the chapter, use LearningCurve to retain what you've read.

> What kind of state did Napoleon III build in France?

> How did conflict and war lead to the construction of strong nation-states?

> What steps did Russia and the Ottoman Turks take toward modernization?

> What general domestic political trends emerged after 1871?

> How did popular nationalism evolve?

> Why did the socialist movement grow, and how revolutionary was it?

Life in the Age of Nationalism. Conscripts in a small Italian village cheer a speech by a local dignitary as a soldier says good-bye to his family before joining the army in the field. (De Agostini Picture Library/A. Dagli Orti/The Bridgeman Art Library)

What kind of state did Napoleon III build in France?

Paris in the Second Empire The flash and glitter of unprecedented prosperity in the Second Empire come alive in this vibrant contemporary painting. Writers and intellectuals chat with elegant women and trade witticisms with financiers and government officials at the Café Tortoni, a favorite rendezvous for fashionable society. Horse-drawn omnibuses with open top decks mingle with cabs and private carriages on the broad new boulevard. (Musée de la Ville de Paris, Musée Carnavalet, Paris/Giraudon/The Bridgeman Art Library)

EARLY NATIONALISM WAS GENERALLY LIBERAL and idealistic and often democratic and radical. Yet nationalism can also flourish in authoritarian and dictatorial states. Napoleon Bonaparte's France had already combined national feeling with authoritarian rule. Napoleon's nephew, Louis Napoleon, revived and extended this merger.

France's Second Republic

Louis Napoleon Bonaparte won an overwhelming victory in the French presidential election of December 1848. This outcome occurred for several reasons. First, he had the great name of his uncle. Second, middle-class and peasant property owners feared the socialist challenge of urban workers and the chaos of the revolution of 1848, and they wanted a tough ruler to protect their property and provide stability. Third, Louis Napoleon enunciated a positive program for France in pamphlets widely circulated before the election.

Above all, Louis Napoleon promoted a vision of national unity and social progress. He believed that the government should represent the people and help them

CHAPTER LOCATOR | **What kind of state did Napoleon III build in France?** | How did conflict and war lead to the construction of strong nation-states?

CHAPTER 23
708 THE AGE OF NATIONALISM

1839–1876
– Western-style Tanzimat reforms in Ottoman Empire

1852–1870
– Reign of Napoleon III in France

1859–1870
– Unification of Italy

1861
– Freeing of Russian serfs

1861–1865
– U.S. Civil War

1866
– Austro-Prussian War

1870–1871
– Franco-Prussian War

1870–1878
– Kulturkampf, Bismarck's attack on the Catholic Church

1873
– Stock market crash spurs renewed anti-Semitism, beginning in central and eastern Europe

1880s
– Educational reforms in France create a secular public school system

1880s–1890s
– Widespread return to protectionism among European states

1883
– First social security laws to help workers in Germany

1890–1900
– Witte initiates second surge of Russian industrialization

1905
– Revolution in Russia

1906–1914
– Social reform in Great Britain

1908
– Young Turks seize power in Ottoman Empire

economically. But how, in the face of entrenched interest groups, could these tasks be accomplished? The answer, according to Louis Napoleon, was a strong, even authoritarian, national leader, like the first Napoleon, whose efforts to provide jobs and stimulate the economy would serve all people, rich and poor. This leader would be linked to each citizen by direct democracy, his sovereignty uncorrupted by politicians and legislative bodies.

Elected to a four-year term by an overwhelming majority, Louis Napoleon was required by the constitution to share power with the National Assembly, which was overwhelmingly conservative. With some misgivings, he signed conservative-sponsored bills that increased greatly the role of the Catholic Church in primary and secondary education and deprived many poor people of the right to vote. He took these steps in hopes that the Assembly would vote funds to pay his personal debts and change the constitution so he could run for a second term.

But in 1851, after the Assembly failed to cooperate with that last aim, Louis Napoleon began to conspire with key army officers. On December 2, 1851, he illegally dismissed the legislature and seized power in a coup d'état, using the army to crush all resistance. Restoring universal male suffrage and claiming to stand above political bickering, Louis Napoleon called on the French people, as the first Napoleon had done, to legalize his actions. They did: 92 percent voted to make him president for ten years. A year later, 97 percent in a plebiscite made him hereditary emperor.

| What steps did Russia and the Ottoman Turks take toward modernization? | What general domestic political trends emerged after 1871? | How did popular nationalism evolve? | Why did the socialist movement grow, and how revolutionary was it? | ☑ LearningCurve Check what you know. |

Napoleon III's Second Empire

Louis Napoleon—now proclaimed Emperor Napoleon III—experienced both success and failure between 1852 and 1870, when he fell from power. In the 1850s, his policies led to economic growth. His government promoted the new investment banks and massive railroad construction. It also fostered general economic expansion through an ambitious program of public works, which included rebuilding Paris. The profits of business owners soared, rising wages of workers outpaced inflation, and unemployment declined greatly.

Initially, Louis Napoleon's hope that economic progress would reduce social and political tensions was at least partially realized. Until the mid-1860s, he enjoyed support from France's most dissatisfied group, the urban workers. Government regulation of pawnshops and support for credit unions and better working-class housing were evidence of helpful reform in the 1850s. In the 1860s, Louis Napoleon granted workers the right to form unions and the right to strike.

At first, political power remained in the hands of the emperor. He alone chose his ministers, who had great freedom of action. At the same time, Louis Napoleon restricted but did not abolish the newly reformed Assembly. Members were elected by universal male suffrage every six years, and Louis Napoleon and his government took these elections very seriously.

In 1857 and again in 1863, Louis Napoleon's system resulted in overwhelming electoral victories for government-backed candidates. In the 1860s, however, this electoral system gradually disintegrated. A sincere nationalist, Napoleon had wanted to reorganize Europe on the principle of nationality and gain influence and territory for France and himself in the process. Instead, problems in Italy and the rising power of Prussia led to increasing criticism at home from his Catholic and nationalist supporters. With increasing effectiveness, the middle-class liberals who had always wanted a less authoritarian regime denounced his rule.

Napoleon was always sensitive to the public mood. Public opinion, he once said, always wins the last victory, and he responded to critics with progressive liberalization. He gave the Assembly greater powers and opposition candidates greater freedom; in 1870, he granted France a new constitution, which combined a basically parliamentary regime with a hereditary emperor as chief of state. Napoleon III's attempt to reconcile a strong national state with universal male suffrage moved in an increasingly democratic direction.

> **QUICK REVIEW**

How did Napoleon III seek to reconcile popular and conservative forces in an authoritarian nation-state?

CHAPTER LOCATOR | What kind of state did Napoleon III build in France? | How did conflict and war lead to the construction of strong nation-states?

710 CHAPTER 23
THE AGE OF NATIONALISM

How did conflict and war lead to the construction of strong nation-states?

Garibaldi and Victor Emmanuel II The historic meeting in Naples between the leader of Italy's revolutionary nationalists and the king of Sardinia sealed the unification of northern and southern Italy. With the sleeve of his red shirt showing, Garibaldi offers his hand — and his conquests — to the uniformed king and his moderate monarchical government. (Palazzo Pubblico, Siena, Italy/The Bridgeman Art Library)

LOUIS NAPOLEON PROVIDED THE OLD RULING CLASSES of Europe with a new model in politics. The question was, could this model be applied elsewhere? In Europe, the national unification of Italy and Germany offered a resounding answer. In the United States, nation building marked by sectional differences over slavery offered another.

Italy to 1850

Before 1850, Italy had never been united. The Italian peninsula was divided in the Middle Ages into competing city-states. A battleground for the Great Powers after 1494, Italy was reorganized in 1815 at the Congress of Vienna into a hodgepodge of different states (**Map 23.1**).

Between 1815 and 1848, the goal of a unified Italian nation captured the imaginations of many Italians. There were three basic approaches. First, the radical and idealistic patriot Giuseppe Mazzini called for a centralized democratic republic based on universal male suffrage and the will of the people. Second, Vincenzo Gioberti, a Catholic priest, called for a federation of existing states under the

What steps did Russia and the Ottoman Turks take toward modernization?	What general domestic political trends emerged after 1871?	How did popular nationalism evolve?	Why did the socialist movement grow, and how revolutionary was it?	☑ **LearningCurve** Check what you know.

711

MAP 23.1 ■ The Unification of Italy, 1859–1870

The leadership of Sardinia-Piedmont, nationalist fervor, and Garibaldi's attack on the Kingdom of the Two Sicilies were decisive factors in the unification of Italy.

presidency of a progressive pope. Many Italians, though, looked to the autocratic kingdom of Sardinia-Piedmont for leadership.

This third alternative was strengthened by the failures of 1848, when Austria smashed Mazzini's republicanism. Sardinia's king, Victor Emmanuel II, crowned in 1849, retained the liberal constitution granted by his father under duress the previous year. To some of the Italian middle classes, Sardinia appeared to be a liberal, progressive state ideally suited to drive Austria out of northern Italy and lead a united Italy. By contrast, Mazzini's brand of democratic republicanism seemed quixotic and too radical.

As for the papacy, the initial cautious support for unification by Pius IX (pontificate 1846–1878) had given way to hostility after he was temporarily driven from Rome during the upheavals of 1848. For a long generation, the papacy opposed not only national unification but also most modern trends.

CHAPTER LOCATOR | What kind of state did Napoleon III build in France? | **How did conflict and war lead to the construction of strong nation-states?**

Cavour and Garibaldi in Italy

Sardinia had the good fortune of being led by a brilliant statesman, Count Camillo Benso di Cavour (kuh-VOOR), from 1850 until his death in 1861. Cavour had limited and realistic national goals. Until 1859, he sought unity only for the states of northern and perhaps central Italy in a greatly expanded kingdom of Sardinia.

In the 1850s, Cavour worked to consolidate Sardinia as a liberal constitutional state capable of leading northern Italy. His program of building highways and railroads, expanding civil liberties, and opposing clerical privilege increased support for Sardinia throughout northern Italy. Yet Cavour realized that Sardinia could not drive Austria out of the north without the help of a powerful ally. Accordingly, he established a secret alliance with Napoleon III against Austria in July 1858.

Cavour then goaded Austria into attacking Sardinia in 1859, and Louis Napoleon came to Sardinia's defense. After the Franco-Sardinian victory, Napoleon did a sudden about-face. Worried by criticism from French Catholics for supporting the pope's declared enemy, he abandoned Cavour and made a compromise peace with the Austrians in July 1859. Sardinia would receive only Lombardy, the area around Milan, from Austria. The rest of Italy remained essentially unchanged. Cavour resigned in a rage.

Yet the skillful maneuvers of Cavour's allies in the moderate nationalist movement salvaged his plans for Italian unification. While the war against Austria raged in the north, pro-Sardinian nationalists in Tuscany and elsewhere in central Italy encouraged popular revolts that easily toppled their ruling princes. Using and controlling this popular enthusiasm, middle-class nationalist leaders in central Italy called for fusion with Sardinia. Returning to power in early 1860, Cavour gained Napoleon III's support by ceding Savoy and Nice to France. The people of central Italy then voted overwhelmingly to join a greatly enlarged kingdom of Sardinia under Victor Emmanuel (see Map 23.1, page 712).

For superpatriots such as Giuseppe Garibaldi (1807–1882), however, the job of unification was still only half done. The son of a poor sailor, Garibaldi personified the romantic, revolutionary nationalism and republicanism of Mazzini and 1848. Leading a corps of volunteers against Austria in 1859, Garibaldi emerged in 1860 as an independent force in Italian politics.

Partly to use him and partly to get rid of him, Cavour secretly supported Garibaldi's bold plan to "liberate" the Kingdom of the Two Sicilies. Landing in Sicily in May 1860, Garibaldi's guerrilla band of a thousand **Red Shirts** incited the peasantry to rise in rebellion against their landlords. Victorious in Sicily, Garibaldi and his men crossed to the mainland, marched toward Naples, and prepared to attack Rome and the pope. Cavour quickly sent Sardinian forces to occupy most of the Papal States (but not Rome) and to intercept Garibaldi.

Cavour realized that an attack on Rome would bring war with France, and he feared Garibaldi's radicalism and popular appeal. He immediately organized a plebiscite in which the people of the south voted to join the kingdom of Sardinia. When Garibaldi and Victor Emmanuel II rode together through Naples to cheering crowds, they symbolically sealed the union of north and south.

The new kingdom of Italy, which expanded to include Venice in 1866 and Rome in 1870, was a parliamentary monarchy under Victor Emmanuel II, neither radical nor fully democratic. Only a half million out of 22 million Italians had the right to vote, and the propertied classes and the common people remained

Red Shirts

▶ The guerrilla army of Giuseppe Garibaldi, who invaded Sicily in 1860 in an attempt to liberate it, winning the hearts of the Sicilian peasantry.

| What steps did Russia and the Ottoman Turks take toward modernization? | What general domestic political trends emerged after 1871? | How did popular nationalism evolve? | Why did the socialist movement grow, and how revolutionary was it? | ✔ LearningCurve Check what you know. |

divided. A great and growing social and cultural gap also separated the progressive, industrializing north from the stagnant, agrarian south. The new Italy was united on paper, but profound divisions remained.

Growing Austro-Prussian Rivalry

In the aftermath of 1848, the German states were locked in a political stalemate. Austria and Russia blocked Prussian king Frederick William IV's attempt in 1850 to unify Germany. After that, tension grew between Austria and Prussia as they struggled to dominate the German Confederation (see Chapter 21, page 669).

Economic differences exacerbated this rivalry. Austria had not been included in the German Customs Union, or *Zollverein* (TZOLE-fur-ayne), when it was founded in 1834 to stimulate trade and increase state revenues. By the end of 1853, Austria was the only state in the German Confederation outside the union.

Prussia had emerged from the upheavals of 1848 with a weak parliament, which was in the hands of the wealthy liberal middle class by 1859. These middle-class representatives wanted to establish—once and for all—that the parliament, not the king, held ultimate political power. Convinced that great political change and war were quite possible, Prussia's tough-minded William I (r. 1861–1888) and his top military advisers at the same time pushed to raise taxes and increase the defense budget in order to double the size of the army. The Prussian parliament rejected the military budget in 1862, and the liberals triumphed completely in new elections. King William then appointed Count Otto von Bismarck as Prussian prime minister and encouraged him to defy the parliament.

Bismarck and the Austro-Prussian War

Upon taking office, Otto von Bismarck (1815–1898) declared that William's government would rule without parliamentary consent. Bismarck had the Prussian bureaucracy go right on collecting taxes, even though the parliament refused to approve the budget. Bismarck also reorganized the army. And for four years, from 1862 to 1866, voters continued to express their opposition by sending large liberal majorities to the parliament.

Opposition at home spurred Bismarck to search for success abroad. Schleswig-Holstein—two provinces that belonged to Denmark but were members of the German Confederation (**Map 23.2**)—provided an opportunity. In 1864, when the Danish king tried, as he had in 1848, to bring these two provinces into a more centralized Danish state against the will of the German Confederation, Prussia enlisted Austria in a short and successful war against Denmark.

Bismarck, however, was convinced that Prussia had to control completely the northern, predominantly Protestant part of the confederation, which meant expelling Austria from German affairs. After the victory over Denmark, Bismarck's clever maneuvering left Prussia in a position to force Austria out by war.

The Austro-Prussian War of 1866 that followed lasted only seven weeks. Using railroads to mobilize troops quickly, the Prussian army won a decisive victory. Anticipating Prussia's future needs, Bismarck offered Austria generous peace terms. But the existing German Confederation was dissolved, and Austria agreed to withdraw from German affairs. Prussia conquered and annexed several small states north of the Main River and completely dominated the newly formed North

CHAPTER LOCATOR | What kind of state did Napoleon III build in France? | **How did conflict and war lead to the construction of strong nation-states?**

CHAPTER 23
714 THE AGE OF NATIONALISM

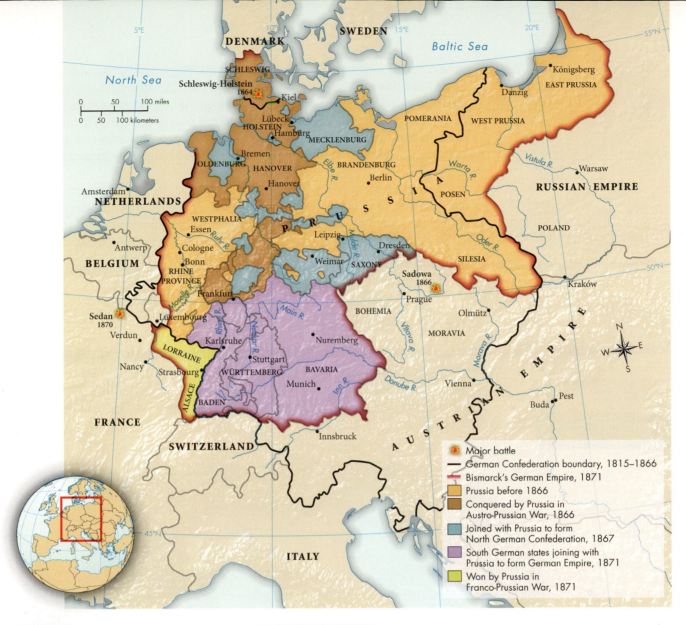

MAP 23.2 ■ The Unification of Germany, 1864–1871

This map shows how Prussia expanded and a new German Empire was created through the Austro-Prussian War of 1866 and the Franco-Prussian War of 1870–1871.

Map legend:
- Major battle
- German Confederation boundary, 1815–1866
- Bismarck's German Empire, 1871
- Prussia before 1866
- Conquered by Prussia in Austro-Prussian War, 1866
- Joined with Prussia to form North German Confederation, 1867
- South German states joining with Prussia to form German Empire, 1871
- Won by Prussia in Franco-Prussian War, 1871

> MAPPING THE PAST

ANALYZING THE MAP: What losses did Austria experience in 1866? What territories did France lose as a result of the Franco-Prussian War?

CONNECTIONS: How was central Europe remade and the power of Prussia-Germany greatly increased as a result of the Austro-Prussian War and the Franco-Prussian War?

German Confederation. The mainly Catholic states of the south remained independent but allied with Prussia. Bismarck's fundamental goal of Prussian expansion was partially realized.

Taming the German Parliament

To consolidate Prussian control, Bismarck fashioned a federal constitution for the new North German Confederation. Each state retained its own local government, but the king of Prussia became president of the confederation, and the chancellor—

| What steps did Russia and the Ottoman Turks take toward modernization? | What general domestic political trends emerged after 1871? | How did popular nationalism evolve? | Why did the socialist movement grow, and how revolutionary was it? | ✓ LearningCurve Check what you know. |

Bismarck—was responsible only to the president. The federal government—William I and Bismarck—controlled the army and foreign affairs. There was also a legislature with members of the lower house elected by universal male suffrage. With this radical innovation, Bismarck opened the door to popular participation and the possibility of going over the head of the middle class directly to the people. All the while, however, ultimate power rested in the hands of the Prussian king and army.

In Prussia itself, Bismarck held out an olive branch to the parliamentary opposition. Marshaling all his diplomatic skill, Bismarck asked the parliament to pass a special indemnity bill to approve after the fact all the government's spending between 1862 and 1866. With German unity in sight, most of the liberals eagerly cooperated. The constitutional struggle in Prussia ended, and the German middle class came to accept the monarchical authority that Bismarck represented.

The Franco-Prussian War

The final act in the drama of German unification followed quickly. Bismarck calculated that a patriotic war with France would drive the south German states into his arms. Taking advantage of a diplomatic issue—whether a distant relative of Prussia's William I might become king of Spain —Bismarck pressed France. By

Proclaiming the German Empire, January 1871

This commemorative painting by Anton von Werner testifies to the nationalistic intoxication in Germany after the victory over France at Sedan. William I of Prussia stands on a platform surrounded by princes and generals in the famous Hall of Mirrors in the palace of Versailles, while officers from all the units around a besieged Paris cheer and salute him with uplifted swords as emperor of a unified Germany. Bismarck, in white (center), stands between king and army. (akg-images)

CHAPTER LOCATOR | What kind of state did Napoleon III build in France?

How did conflict and war lead to the construction of strong nation-states?

1870, the French leaders of the Second Empire, goaded by Bismarck and alarmed by their powerful new neighbor, declared war to teach Prussia a lesson.

German forces under Prussian leadership decisively defeated the main French army at Sedan on September 1, 1870. Louis Napoleon himself was captured. Three days later, French patriots in Paris proclaimed yet another French republic and vowed to continue fighting. But after five months, in January 1871, a besieged and starving Paris surrendered, and France accepted Bismarck's harsh peace terms.

By this time, the south German states had agreed to join a new German Empire. With Bismarck by his side, William I was proclaimed emperor of Germany. As in the 1866 constitution, the king of Prussia and his ministers had ultimate power in the new German Empire, and the lower house of the legislature was elected by universal male suffrage.

The Franco-Prussian War released an enormous surge of patriotic feeling in the German Empire. The weakest of the Great Powers in 1862, Prussia with united Germany had become the most powerful state in Europe in less than a decade, and most Germans were enormously proud. Semi-authoritarian nationalism and a new conservatism, based on an alliance of the landed nobles and middle classes, had triumphed in Germany.

Slavery and Nation Building in the United States

The United States also experienced a process of bloody nation building. Nominally united, the country was divided by slavery from its birth, and economic development in the young republic carried free and slaveholding states in very different directions. By 1850, an industrializing, urbanizing North was building canals and railroads and attracting most of the European immigrants arriving in the nation. In sharp contrast, industry and cities developed more slowly in the South. Large landowners dominated the economy and society. These profit-minded slave owners used gangs of black slaves to establish a vast plantation economy across the Deep South, where cotton was king (**Map 23.3**). By 1850, the region produced 5 million bales a year, supplying textile mills in Europe and New England.

The rise of the cotton empire greatly expanded slave-based agriculture in the South, spurred exports, and played a key role in igniting rapid U.S. economic growth. The large profits flowing from cotton led influential Southerners to defend slavery. Because Northern whites viewed their free-labor system as more just, and economically and morally superior to slavery, North-South antagonisms intensified.

Tensions reached a climax after 1848 when the United States gained, through war with Mexico, a vast area stretching from west Texas to the Pacific Ocean. Debate over the extension of slavery in this new territory hardened attitudes on both sides. Abraham Lincoln's election as president in 1860 gave Southern secessionists the chance they had been waiting for. Determined to win independence, eleven states left the Union and formed the Confederate States of America.

The resulting Civil War (1861–1865) ended with the South decisively defeated and the Union preserved. In the aftermath of the war, certain dominant characteristics of American life and national culture took shape. Powerful business corporations

U.S. Secession, 1860–1861

| What steps did Russia and the Ottoman Turks take toward modernization? | What general domestic political trends emerged after 1871? | How did popular nationalism evolve? | Why did the socialist movement grow, and how revolutionary was it? | ☑ LearningCurve Check what you know. |

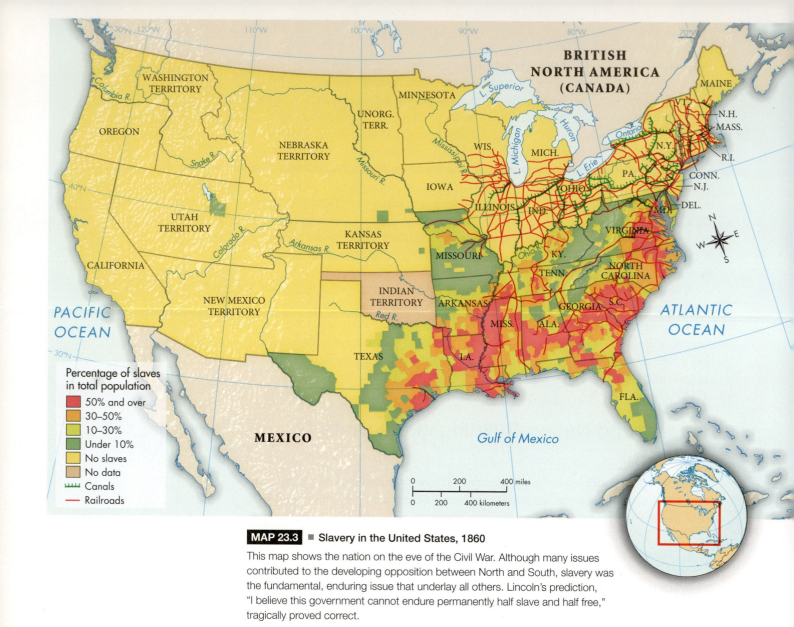

MAP 23.3 ■ Slavery in the United States, 1860

This map shows the nation on the eve of the Civil War. Although many issues contributed to the developing opposition between North and South, slavery was the fundamental, enduring issue that underlay all others. Lincoln's prediction, "I believe this government cannot endure permanently half slave and half free," tragically proved correct.

Percentage of slaves in total population
- 50% and over
- 30–50%
- 10–30%
- Under 10%
- No slaves
- No data
- Canals
- Railroads

Homestead Act

▶ An American law enacted during the Civil War that gave western land to settlers and reinforced the concept of free labor in a market economy.

emerged. The **Homestead Act** of 1862, which gave western land to settlers, and the Thirteenth Amendment of 1865, which ended slavery, reinforced the concept of free labor taking its chances in a market economy. Finally, the success of Lincoln and the North in holding the Union together seemed to confirm that the "manifest destiny" of the United States was to straddle a continent as a great world power. Thus a new American nationalism, grounded in economic and territorial expansion, grew out of a civil war.

> QUICK REVIEW

What are the similarities and difference among Italy, Germany, and the United States in their paths to strong nation-states?

CHAPTER LOCATOR | What kind of state did Napoleon III build in France? | How did conflict and war lead to the construction of strong nation-states?

Pasha Hilim Receiving Archduke Maximilian of Austria
As this painting suggests, Ottoman leaders became well versed in European languages and culture. They also mastered the game of power politics, playing one European state against another and securing the Ottoman Empire's survival. The black servants on the right may be slaves from Sudan. (Alfredo Dagli Orti/The Art Archive at Art Resource, NY)

IN THE EARLY NINETEENTH CENTURY, the governing elites in the Russian and Ottoman Empires strongly opposed representative government and national independence for ethnic minorities, concentrating on absolutist rule and competition with other Great Powers. For both states, however, relentless power politics led to serious trouble. Their leaders recognized that they had to embrace the process of modernization, defined narrowly as the economic, military, and social-political reforms that might enable a country to compete effectively with leading European nations.

The "Great Reforms" in Russia

In the 1850s, Russia was a poor agrarian society with a rapidly growing population. Almost 90 percent of the people lived off the land, and industrialization developed slowly. Bound to the lord from birth, the peasant serf was little more than a slave, and by the 1840s, serfdom had become a central moral and political issue for the government. The slow pace of modernization encouraged the growth of protest movements. Then a humiliating Russian defeat in the Crimean War underscored the need for modernizing reforms.

The **Crimean War** (1853–1856) grew out of the breakdown of the European balance of power established at the Congress of Vienna (see Chapter 21, page 642), general Great Power competition over the Middle East, and Russian desires

Crimean War
▶ A conflict fought between 1853 and 1856 over Russian desires to expand into Ottoman territory; Russia was defeated by France, Britain, and the Ottomans, a defeat that underscored the need for reform in the Russian empire.

What steps did Russia and the Ottoman Turks take toward modernization?
| What general domestic political trends emerged after 1871? | How did popular nationalism evolve? | Why did the socialist movement grow, and how revolutionary was it? | ✔ **LearningCurve** Check what you know. |

719

to expand into the European territories of the Ottoman Empire. An immediate Russian-French dispute over the protection of Christian shrines in Jerusalem sparked the conflict. By 1856, France and Great Britain, aided by the Ottoman Empire and Sardinia, had decisively defeated Russia.

The war convinced Russia's leaders that they had fallen behind the industrializing nations of western Europe. Thus, military disaster forced liberal-leaning Tsar Alexander II (r. 1855–1881) and his ministers along the path of rapid social change and modernization. In a bold move, Alexander II abolished serfdom in 1861. About 22 million emancipated peasants received citizenship rights and the chance to purchase, on average, about half of the land they cultivated. Yet they had to pay fairly high prices, and because the land was to be owned collectively, each peasant village was jointly responsible for the payments of all the families in the village. Collective ownership made it difficult for individual peasants to improve agricultural methods or leave their villages. Thus old patterns of behavior predominated, limiting the effects of reform.

Most of Alexander II's later reforms were also halfway measures. In 1864, the government established new elected local assemblies, the zemstvos. The zemstvos, however, remained subordinate to the traditional bureaucracy and the local nobility. In addition, changes to the legal system established independent courts and equality before the law. The government relaxed but did not remove censorship, and it somewhat liberalized policies toward Russian Jews.

Russian efforts to promote economic modernization proved more successful. Transportation and industry, both vital to the military, were transformed in two industrial surges. The first came after 1860, when the government encouraged and subsidized private railway companies. The railroads enabled Russia to export grain and thus earn money to finance further development. Industrial suburbs grew around Moscow and St. Petersburg, and a class of modern factory workers began to take shape.

Strengthened by industrial development, Russia began seizing territory in far eastern Siberia, on the border with China; in Central Asia, north of Afghanistan; and in the Islamic lands of the Caucasus. The rapid expansion of the Russian empire to the south and east excited ardent Russian nationalists and superpatriots, who became some of the government's most enthusiastic supporters.

In 1881, a member of the "People's Will," a small anarchist group, assassinated the tsar, and the era of reform came to an abrupt end. The new tsar, Alexander III (r. 1881–1894), was a determined reactionary. Nevertheless, from 1890 to 1900, economic modernization and industrialization surged ahead for the second time, led by finance minister Sergei Witte (suhr-GAY VIH-tuh).

Witte's greatest innovation was to use Westerners to catch up with the West. He encouraged foreigners to build factories in Russia. His efforts were especially successful in southern Russia. There, foreign entrepreneurs and engineers built an enormous and very modern steel and coal industry. In 1900, peasants still constituted the great majority of the population, but Russia was catching up with the more industrialized West.

The Russian Revolution of 1905

Catching up partly meant further territorial expansion because this was the age of Western imperialism. By 1903, Russia had established a sphere of influence in Chinese Manchuria and was eyeing northern Korea, which put Russia in conflict

CHAPTER LOCATOR | What kind of state did Napoleon III build in France? | How did conflict and war lead to the construction of strong nation-states?

with the goals of an equally imperialistic Japan. When Tsar Nicholas II (r. 1894–1917), who replaced his father in 1894, ignored their diplomatic protests, the Japanese launched a surprise attack in February 1904. After Japan scored repeated victories, Russia surrendered in September 1905.

Once again, military disaster abroad brought political upheaval at home. The business and professional classes had long wanted a liberal, representative government. Urban factory workers were organized in a radical and still-illegal labor movement. Peasants suffered from poverty and overpopulation. At the same time, the empire's minorities and subject nationalities called for self-rule. With the army pinned down in Manchuria, all these currents of discontent converged in the revolution of 1905.

On a Sunday in January 1905, a massive crowd of workers and their families converged peacefully on the Winter Palace in St. Petersburg to present a petition to Nicholas II. Suddenly troops opened fire, killing and wounding hundreds. The **Bloody Sunday** massacre turned many Russians against the tsar.

By the summer of 1905, strikes and political rallies, peasant uprisings, revolts among minority nationalities, and mutinies by troops were sweeping the country. The revolutionary surge culminated in October 1905 in a paralyzing general strike that forced the government to capitulate. The tsar then issued the **October Manifesto**, which granted full civil rights and promised a popularly elected **Duma** (or parliament) with real legislative power. The manifesto split the opposition. Frightened middle-class leaders embraced it, which helped the government repress the popular uprising and survive as a constitutional monarchy.

On the eve of the opening of the first Duma in May 1906, the government issued the new constitution, the Fundamental Laws. The tsar retained great powers. The Duma, elected indirectly by universal male suffrage with a largely appointive upper house, could debate and pass laws, but the tsar had an absolute veto. As in Bismarck's Germany, the tsar appointed his ministers, who did not need to command a majority in the Duma.

Cooperation between legislators and Nicholas II's ministers soon broke down, and after months of deadlock, the tsar dismissed the Duma. Thereupon he and his reactionary advisers unilaterally rewrote the electoral law, increasing greatly the weight of the conservative propertied classes. Thus, in 1914, on the eve of the First World War, Russia was partially modernized, a conservative constitutional monarchy with a peasant-based but industrializing economy.

Reform and Readjustment in the Ottoman Empire

By the early nineteenth century, the economic and political changes reshaping Europe were also at play in the Ottoman Empire, which stretched around the northeastern, eastern, and southern shores of the Mediterranean Sea.

Muhammad Ali, a ruthless and intelligent soldier-politician, ruled Egypt in the name of the Ottoman sultan from 1805 to 1848. His modernizing reforms (see Chapter 24) helped turn Egypt into the most powerful state in the eastern Mediterranean. In time, his growing strength directly challenged the Ottoman sultan and Istanbul's ruling elite. From 1831 to 1840, Egyptian troops under the leadership of Muhammad Ali's son Ibrahim occupied and governed the Ottoman province of Syria and Palestine, and threatened to depose the Ottoman sultan Mahmud II (r. 1808–1839).

This conflict forced the Ottomans to seek European support. Mahmud II's dynasty survived, but only because the European powers, led by Britain, allied

The Russian Revolution of 1905

Bloody Sunday
▶ A massacre of peaceful protesters at the Winter Palace in St. Petersburg in 1905, triggering a revolution that overturned absolute tsarist rule and made Russia into a conservative constitutional monarchy.

October Manifesto
▶ The result of a paralyzing general strike in October 1905, a Russian decree that granted full civil rights and promised a popularly elected Duma (parliament) with real legislative power.

Duma
▶ The Russian parliament that opened in 1906, elected indirectly by universal male suffrage but controlled after 1907 by the tsar and the conservative classes.

What steps did Russia and the Ottoman Turks take toward modernization?

What general domestic political trends emerged after 1871?

How did popular nationalism evolve?

Why did the socialist movement grow, and how revolutionary was it?

✓ LearningCurve
Check what you know.

721

Tanzimat

▶ A set of reforms designed to remake the Ottoman Empire on a western European model.

with the Ottomans to discipline Muhammad Ali. The European powers preferred a weak and dependent Ottoman Empire to a strong, economically independent state under a dynamic leader such as Muhammad Ali.

Faced with growing European military and economic competition, in 1839 liberal Ottoman statesmen launched an era of radical reforms known as the **Tanzimat**, or "Reorganization." The Tanzimat reforms were designed to modernize the empire and borrowed from western European models. The Imperial Rescript of 1856 marked a high point of reform. Articles in the decree called for equality before the law regardless of religious faith, a modernized administration and army, and private ownership of land. As part of the reform policy, and under pressure from the European powers, Ottoman leaders adopted free-trade policies. New commercial laws removed tariffs on foreign imports and permitted foreign merchants to operate freely throughout the empire.

The turn to nineteenth-century liberal capitalism had mixed effects. On one hand, with the growth of Western-style banking and insurance systems, elite Christian and Jewish businessmen in the empire prospered. Yet the bulk of the profits went to foreign investors rather than Ottoman subjects. More important, the elimination of traditional state-controlled monopolies sharply cut imperial revenues, forcing Ottoman rulers to borrow heavily from foreign lenders.

Intended to bring revolutionary modernization, the Tanzimat permitted partial recovery but fell short of its goals. The Ottoman initiatives did not curtail the appetite of Western imperialism, which secured a stranglehold on the imperial economy by issuing loans. The reforms also failed to halt the growth of nationalism among some Christian subjects in the Balkans, which resulted in crises and increased pressure from neighboring Austria and Russia, eager to gain access to the Balkans and the eastern Mediterranean.

Equality before the law for all citizens, regardless of religious affiliation, actually increased religious disputes, which were often encouraged and manipulated by the European powers eager to seize any pretext for intervention. This development embittered relations between religious conservatives and social liberals. Religious conservatives in both the Muslim and Greek Orthodox communities detested the religious reforms, which they viewed as an impious departure from tradition. These conservatives became dependable supporters of Sultan Abdülhamid II (ahb-dool-hah-MEED) (r. 1876–1909), who in 1876 halted the reform movement and turned away from European liberalism in his long and repressive reign.

Abdülhamid II's government failed to halt foreign efforts to fragment and ultimately take control over key Ottoman territories. By the 1890s, the government's failures had encouraged a powerful resurgence of the modernizing impulse under the banner of the Committee of Union and Progress (CUP), an umbrella organization that united multiethnic reformist groups from across the empire. These fervent patriots, unofficially called the **Young Turks**, seized power in a 1908 coup and forced the sultan to implement new reforms. The Young Turks helped prepare the way for the birth of modern secular Turkey after the defeat and collapse of the Ottoman Empire in World War I.

Young Turks

▶ Fervent patriots who seized power in a 1908 coup in the Ottoman Empire, forcing the conservative sultan to implement reforms.

> **QUICK REVIEW**

How did military defeats shape the course of modernization in both the Ottoman and Russian Empires?

CHAPTER LOCATOR | What kind of state did Napoleon III build in France? | How did conflict and war lead to the construction of strong nation-states?

CHAPTER 23

722 THE AGE OF NATIONALISM

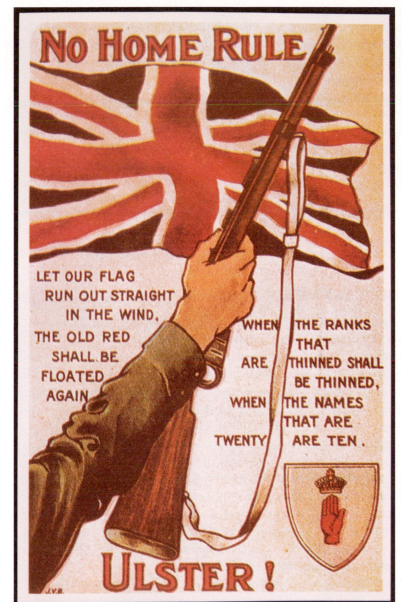

LET OUR FLAG RUN OUT STRAIGHT IN THE WIND, THE OLD RED SHALL BE FLOATED AGAIN

WHEN THE RANKS THAT ARE THINNED SHALL BE THINNED, WHEN THE NAMES THAT ARE TWENTY ARE TEN.

What general domestic political trends emerged after 1871?

"No Home Rule"

Posters like this one helped to incite pro-British, anti-Catholic sentiment in the northern Irish counties of Ulster before the First World War. The rifle raised defiantly and the accompanying rhyme are a thinly veiled threat of armed rebellion and civil war. (Photograph reproduced courtesy the Trustees of National Museums Northern Ireland. Photograph © Ulster Museum Belfast.)

THE DECADES AFTER 1870 brought dramatic change to the structures and ideas of European politics. Despite some major differences between countries, European domestic politics had a new common framework, the nation-state.

The common themes within that framework were the emergence of mass politics and growing popular loyalty toward the nation. Traditional elites hardly disappeared, but they were forced into new arrangements in order to exercise power, and a group of new, pragmatic politicians took leading roles. Powerful

What steps did Russia and the Ottoman Turks take toward modernization?

What general domestic political trends emerged after 1871?

How did popular nationalism evolve?

Why did the socialist movement grow, and how revolutionary was it?

LearningCurve
Check what you know.

bureaucracies emerged to govern growing populations and manage modern economies, and the growth of the state spurred a growth in the social responsibilities of government. The new responsive national state offered its citizens a variety of benefits, and for good reason many ordinary people felt increasing loyalty to their governments and their nations.

Building popular support for strong nation-states had a less positive side. Conservative and moderate leaders both found that workers who voted socialist would rally around the flag in a diplomatic crisis or cheer when colonial interests seized a distant territory. Therefore, after 1871, governing elites frequently used antiliberal militarist and imperialist policies in attempts to unite national populations and overcome or mask intractable domestic conflicts. In the end, the manipulation of foreign policy to manage domestic issues inflamed the international tensions that erupted in the cataclysms of World War I and the Russian Revolution.

The German Empire

Politics in Germany after 1871 reflected many of these general political developments. The new German Empire was a federal union of Prussia and twenty-four smaller states. Much of the everyday business of government was conducted by the separate states, but there was a strong national government with a chancellor and a popularly elected lower house called the **Reichstag** (RIKES-tahg). Although Bismarck repeatedly ignored the wishes of the parliamentary majority, he nonetheless preferred to win the support of the Reichstag to lend legitimacy to his policy goals. Until 1878, Bismarck relied mainly on the National Liberals, who supported legislation useful for economic growth and unification of the country.

Less wisely, the National Liberals backed Bismarck's attack on the Catholic Church, the so-called **Kulturkampf** (kool-TOOR-kahmpf), or "culture struggle." Kulturkampf initiatives aimed at making the Catholic Church subject to government control. However, only in Protestant Prussia did the Kulturkampf have even limited success because elsewhere Catholics generally voted for the Center Party, which blocked passage of laws hostile to the church.

In 1878, Bismarck abandoned his attack on the church and instead courted the Catholic Center Party, whose supporters included many Catholic small farmers in western and southern Germany. By revoking free-trade policy and enacting high tariffs on cheap foreign grain, he won over both the Catholic Center and the conservative Protestant Junkers, nobles with large landholdings.

Other governments followed Bismarck's lead, and the 1880s and 1890s saw a widespread return to protectionism in Europe. By raising tariffs, European governments offered an effective response to a major domestic economic problem—foreign competition—in a way that won greater popular loyalty. At the same time, the rise of protectionism exemplified the dangers of self-centered nationalism: new tariffs led to international name-calling and nasty trade wars.

After the failure of the Kulturkampf, Bismarck's government tried to stop the growth of the **German Social Democratic Party (SPD)**, Germany's Marxist, working-class political party that was established in the 1870s. In 1878, Bismarck pushed through the Reichstag the Anti-Socialist Laws, which banned Social Democratic associations, meetings, and publications. The Social Democratic Party was driven

Reichstag

▶ The popularly elected lower house of government of the new German Empire after 1871.

Kulturkampf

▶ Bismarck's attack on the Catholic Church within Germany from 1870 to 1878.

German Social Democratic Party (SPD)

▶ A German working-class political party founded in the 1870s, the SPD championed Marxism but in practice turned away from Marxist revolution and worked instead for social and workplace reforms in the German parliament.

CHAPTER LOCATOR | What kind of state did Napoleon III build in France? How did conflict and war lead to the construction of strong nation-states?

724 CHAPTER 23
THE AGE OF NATIONALISM

underground, but it maintained substantial influence, and Bismarck decided to try another tack.

In an attempt to win working-class support, Bismarck urged the Reichstag to enact a variety of state-supported social welfare measures. In 1883, he pushed through the Reichstag the first of several social security laws to help wage earners by providing national sickness insurance. An 1884 law created accident insurance; one from 1889 established old-age pensions and retirement benefits. Henceforth sick, injured, and retired workers could look forward to some regular benefits from the state. Bismarck's social security system did not wean workers from voting socialist, but it did give them a small stake in the system and it protected them from some of the uncertainties of the complex, modern industrial economy.

The great issues in German domestic politics were increasingly socialism and, specifically, the Social Democratic Party. In 1890, the new emperor, the young, idealistic, and unstable William II (r. 1888–1918), opposed Bismarck's attempt to renew the Anti-Socialist Laws. Eager to rule in his own right and to earn the support of the workers, William II forced Bismarck to resign. Afterward, German foreign policy changed profoundly and mostly for the worse, but the government did pass new laws to aid workers and legalize socialist political activity.

Yet William II was no more successful than Bismarck in getting workers to renounce socialism. Indeed, Social Democrats won more and more seats in the Reichstag, becoming Germany's largest single party in 1912. Though this electoral victory shocked aristocrats and their wealthy, conservative allies, who held exaggerated fears of an impending socialist upheaval, the revolutionary socialists had actually become less radical in Germany. In the years before World War I, the SPD broadened its base by adopting a more patriotic tone, allowing for greater military spending and imperialist expansion. German socialists abandoned revolutionary aims to concentrate instead on gradual social and political reform (see page 735).

Republican France

Although Napoleon III's reign made some progress in reducing antagonisms between classes, the Franco-Prussian War undid these efforts. The patriotic republicans who proclaimed the Third Republic in Paris after the military disaster at Sedan refused to admit defeat by the Germans. They defended Paris with great heroism for weeks, until they were starved into submission by German armies in January 1871.

When the next national elections sent a large majority of conservatives and monarchists to the National Assembly and France's new leaders decided they had no choice but to surrender Alsace (al-SAS) and Lorraine to Germany, Parisians exploded in patriotic frustration and proclaimed the Paris Commune in March 1871. Vaguely radical, the leaders of the Commune wanted to govern Paris without interference from the conservative French countryside. The National Assembly, led by Adolphe Thiers (TEE-ehr), ordered the French army into Paris and brutally crushed the Commune. Twenty thousand people died in the fighting.

Out of this tragedy, France slowly formed a new national unity, achieving considerable stability before 1914. How do we account for this? Luck played a part. Until 1875 the monarchists in the ostensibly republican National Assembly had a majority but could not agree on who should be king. In the meantime, Thiers's

| What steps did Russia and the Ottoman Turks take toward modernization? | **What general domestic political trends emerged after 1871?** | How did popular nationalism evolve? | Why did the socialist movement grow, and how revolutionary was it? | ☑ LearningCurve Check what you know. |

725

destruction of the radical Commune and his other firm measures showed the fearful provinces and the middle classes that the Third Republic could be politically moderate and socially conservative. France therefore reluctantly retained republican government.

Another stabilizing factor was the skill and determination of moderate republican leaders in the early years. By 1879 the great majority of members of both the upper and the lower houses of the National Assembly were republicans, and the Third Republic had firm foundations after almost a decade.

The moderate republicans sought to preserve their creation by winning the hearts and minds of the next generation. The Assembly legalized trade unions, and France worked to expand its colonial empire. More important, a series of laws between 1879 and 1886 greatly encouraged the state system of public, tax-supported schools and established free compulsory elementary education for both girls and boys. The expansion of public education served as a critical nation-building tool because the public schools emphasized and reinforced secular republican values.

Although the educational reforms of the 1880s disturbed French Catholics, many of them rallied to the republic in the 1890s. The election of the moderately liberal Pope Leo XIII (pontificate 1878–1903) eased tensions between church and state. Unfortunately, the **Dreyfus affair** changed all that.

In 1894, Alfred Dreyfus, a Jewish captain in the French army, was falsely accused and convicted of treason. His family never doubted his innocence and fought to reopen the case. In 1898 and 1899, the case split France apart. On one side was the army, which had manufactured evidence against Dreyfus; it was joined by anti-Semites and most of the Catholic establishment. On the other side stood civil libertarians and most of the more radical republicans.

Dreyfus was eventually declared innocent, but the battle revived republican animosity toward the Catholic Church. Between 1901 and 1905, the government severed all ties between the state and the church. Suddenly on their own financially, Catholic schools soon lost a third of their students, greatly increasing the state school system's reach and thus its power of indoctrination. In France, only the growing socialist movement, with its very different and thoroughly secular ideology, stood in opposition to republican nationalism.

Dreyfus affair
▶ A divisive case in which Alfred Dreyfus, a Jewish captain in the French army, was falsely accused and convicted of treason. The Catholic Church sided with the anti-Semites against Dreyfus; after Dreyfus was declared innocent, the French government severed all ties between the state and the church.

Great Britain and Ireland

Over the course of the nineteenth century, the right of British men to vote was gradually expanded, a trend that culminated in the establishment of near universal male suffrage in 1884. While the House of Commons drifted toward democracy, the House of Lords was content to slumber nobly. Between 1901 and 1910, however, the House of Lords tried to reassert itself. Acting as supreme court of the land, it ruled against labor unions in two important decisions. And after the Liberal Party came to power in 1906, the Lords vetoed several measures passed by the Commons, including the so-called **People's Budget**, which was designed to increase spending on social welfare services. The Lords finally capitulated when the king threatened to create enough new peers to pass the bill, and aristocratic conservatism yielded to popular democracy.

People's Budget
▶ A bill proposed after the Liberal Party came to power in Britain in 1906, it was designed to increase spending on social welfare services but was initially vetoed in the House of Lords.

CHAPTER LOCATOR | What kind of state did Napoleon III build in France? | How did conflict and war lead to the construction of strong nation-states?

CHAPTER 23
726 THE AGE OF NATIONALISM

- First Reform Act (1832): Vote granted to males of the wealthy middle class
- Second Reform Act (1867): Vote granted to all middle-class males and the best-paid workers
- Third Reform Act (1884): Vote granted to almost every adult male

Extensive social welfare measures, previously slow to come to Great Britain, were passed between 1906 and 1914. During those years the Liberal Party, led by David Lloyd George (1863–1945), enacted the People's Budget and substantially raised taxes on the rich. This income helped the government pay for national health insurance, unemployment benefits, old-age pensions, and a host of other social measures.

This record of accomplishment was only part of the story, however. On the eve of World War I, the unanswered question of Ireland brought Great Britain to the brink of civil war. The terrible Irish famine of the 1840s and early 1850s had fueled an Irish revolutionary movement. Thereafter, the English slowly granted concessions, and in 1913, Irish nationalists finally gained a home-rule bill for Ireland.

Thus Ireland was on the brink of achieving self-government. Yet to the same extent that the Catholic majority in the southern counties wanted home rule, the Protestants of the northern counties of Ulster came to oppose it. Motivated by the accumulated fears and hostilities of generations, the Ulster Protestants refused to submerge themselves in a majority-Catholic Ireland, just as Irish Catholics had refused to submit to a Protestant Britain.

By December 1913, the Ulsterites had raised one hundred thousand armed volunteers, and much of English public opinion supported their cause. In 1914, then, the Liberals in the House of Lords introduced a compromise home-rule bill that did not apply to the northern counties. This bill, which openly betrayed promises made to Irish nationalists, was rejected in the Commons, and in September the original home-rule bill passed but with its implementation delayed. The Irish question had been overtaken by the outbreak of World War I and final resolution was suspended for the duration of the hostilities.

Irish developments illustrated once again the power of national feeling and national movements in the nineteenth century. Moreover, they demonstrated that governments could not elicit greater loyalty unless they could capture and control national feeling. Though Great Britain had much going for it—power, parliamentary rule, prosperity—none of these availed in the face of the conflicting nationalisms created by Irish Catholics and Protestants.

The Austro-Hungarian Empire

The dilemma of conflicting nationalisms in Ireland helps one appreciate how desperate the situation in the Austro-Hungarian Empire had become by the early twentieth century as well. In 1848, Magyar nationalism had driven Hungarian

What steps did Russia and the Ottoman Turks take toward modernization?

What general domestic political trends emerged after 1871?

How did popular nationalism evolve?

Why did the socialist movement grow, and how revolutionary was it?

☑ LearningCurve
Check what you know.

patriots to declare an independent Hungarian republic, which Russian and Austrian armies savagely crushed in the summer of 1849 (see Chapter 21, page 645). Throughout the 1850s, Hungary was ruled as a conquered territory.

Then, in the wake of its defeat by Prussia in 1866 and loss of northern Italy, a weakened Austria agreed to a compromise and in 1867 established the so-called dual monarchy. The Austrian Empire was divided in two, and the Magyars gained virtual independence for Hungary. Henceforth each half of the empire dealt with its own ethnic minorities. The two states still shared the same monarch and common ministries for finance, defense, and foreign affairs.

In Austria, ethnic Germans were only one-third of the population, and many Germans saw their traditional dominance threatened by Czechs, Poles, and other Slavs. From 1900 to 1914, the legislature was so divided that ministries generally could not obtain a majority and ruled instead by decree. Efforts by both conservatives and socialists to defuse national antagonisms by stressing economic issues that cut across ethnic lines were largely unsuccessful.

In Hungary, the Magyar nobility in 1867 restored the constitution of 1848 and used it to dominate both the Magyar peasantry and the minority populations until 1914. While Magyar extremists campaigned loudly for total separation from Austria, the radical leaders of their subject nationalities dreamed of independence from Hungary. Unlike most major countries, which harnessed nationalism to strengthen the state after 1871, the Austro-Hungarian Empire was progressively weakened by it.

> ## QUICK REVIEW

What general trends or significant differences determined the way political nationalism unfolded in Europe in the late nineteenth century?

CHAPTER LOCATOR | What kind of state did Napoleon III build in France? | How did conflict and war lead to the construction of strong nation-states?

CHAPTER 23
728 THE AGE OF NATIONALISM

"The Expulsion of the Jews from Russia" So reads this postcard, correctly suggesting that Russian government officials often encouraged popular anti-Semitism and helped drive many Jews out of Russia in the late nineteenth century. The road signs indicate that these poor Jews are crossing into Germany, where they will find a grudging welcome and a meager meal at the Jolly Onion Inn. Other Jews from eastern Europe settled in France and Britain, thereby creating small but significant Jewish populations in both these countries for the first time since they had expelled most of their Jews in the Middle Ages. (Alliance Israelite Universelle, Paris/Archives Charmet/The Bridgeman Art Library)

IN THE FIRST TWO-THIRDS OF THE NINETEENTH CENTURY, liberal constitution-alists and radical republicans championed the national idea as a way to challenge authoritarian monarchs, liberate minority groups from imperial rule, and unify diverse territories into a single state. Yet in the decades after 1870—corresponding to the rise of the responsive national state—nationalist ideology evolved in a different direction. Nationalism became increasingly populist and began to appeal more to those on the right wing of the political spectrum than to those on the left. In these same years, the "us-them" outlook associated with nationalism gained force, bolstered by modern scientific racism.

Making National Citizens

As the nation-state extended voting rights and welfare benefits to more and more people, the question of national loyalty became more and more pressing: politicians and nationalist ideologues made forceful attempts to ensure the people's conformity to their laws, but how could they ensure that national governments would win their citizens' allegiance?

The issue was pressing. In Italy, only about 2 percent of the population spoke the language that would become official Italian. In Germany, regional and religious differences and strong traditions of local political autonomy undermined unity. In Great Britain, deep class differences still dampened national unity, and

| What steps did Russia and the Ottoman Turks take toward modernization? | What general domestic political trends emerged after 1871? | **How did popular nationalism evolve?** | Why did the socialist movement grow, and how revolutionary was it? | ☑ **LearningCurve** Check what you know. |

729

across central and eastern Europe, overlapping ethnic groups with distinct languages and cultures challenged the logic of nation building. Even in France, where national boundaries had been fairly stable for several centuries, only about 50 percent of the people spoke standard French.

Yet by the 1890s most ordinary people had accepted, if not embraced, the notion of national belonging. There were various reasons for nationalism's growing popularity. For one, modern nation-states imposed centralized institutions across their entire territories, which reached even the lowliest citizen. Universal military conscription, introduced in most of Europe after the Franco-Prussian War (Britain was an exception), exposed young male conscripts to patriotic values. Free compulsory education leveled out language differences and taught children about glorious national traditions.

Improved transportation and communication networks broke down regional differences and reinforced the national idea as well. The extension of railroad service into hinterlands and the improvement of local roads shattered rural isolation and boosted the growth of national markets for commercial agriculture. Literacy rates and compulsory schooling advanced rapidly in the late nineteenth century, and more and more people read about national history or the latest political events in growing numbers of newspapers, magazines, and books.

A diverse group of intellectuals, politicians, and ideologues of all stripes eagerly promoted national pride. Scholars uncovered the deep roots of national identity in ancient folk traditions; in shared language, customs, race, and religion; and in historic attachments to national territory. Such accounts, often based on flimsy historical evidence, were popularized in the classroom and the press. Few nationalist thinkers sympathized with French philosopher Ernest Renan, who suggested that national identity was based more on a people's current desire for a "common life" and an invented, heroic past than on actual historical experiences.

A variety of new symbols and rituals brought nationalism into the lives of ordinary people. Each nation had its own unique capital city, flag, military uniform, and national anthem. All citizens could participate in newly invented national holidays, such as Bastille Day in France, first held in 1880 to commemorate the French Revolution, or Sedan Day in Germany, instituted to celebrate Germany's victory over France in 1871. Royal weddings, coronations, jubilees, and funerals brought citizens into the streets to celebrate the nation's leaders. Public squares and parks received prominent commemorative statues and monuments.[1] (See "Picturing the Past: Building Nationalism," page 731.)

Nationalism and Racism

The ideal of national belonging had from the start created an "us-them" outlook (see Chapter 21, page 650); after 1871, new supposedly scientific understandings of racial difference added new layers of meaning to this dichotomy. Modern attempts to use race to categorize distinct groups of people had their roots in Enlightenment thought (see Chapter 16, page 504). Now a new group of intellectuals, including race theorists such as Count Arthur de Gobineau and Houston Stewart Chamberlain, claimed that their ideas about racial difference were scientific, based on hard biological "facts" about bloodlines and heredity. In his early book *On the Inequality of the Human Races* (1854), Gobineau divided humanity into the white, black, and yellow races based on geographical location and championed the white "Aryan

CHAPTER LOCATOR | What kind of state did Napoleon III build in France? | How did conflict and war lead to the construction of strong nation-states?

730 CHAPTER 23
THE AGE OF NATIONALISM

Building Nationalism

Nationalism was built through ideas and action but also in stone. The National Monument to Victor Emmanuel II in Rome and the Battle of the Nations Monument in Leipzig, Germany, are just two of the many buildings, monuments, and statues erected around 1900 to represent the glory of the nation-state and its people. Inaugurated in 1911 to commemorate the fiftieth anniversary of Italian unification and dedicated to Emmanuel II (unified Italy's first king), the massive neoclassical structure in Rome — nicknamed the "wedding cake" by local wits — features an equestrian statue of Emmanuel above a frieze of the Italian people and an imposing Roman-style colonnade crowned by two triumphal horse-drawn chariots. Inside is a museum dedicated to the history of the Italian military. The Leipzig monument, opened in 1913, pays homage to Prussian victory over Napoleon's armies on a nearby battlefield in 1813. Made of bulky, dark, and rough-hewn granite, this colossus is anchored by a large statue of the archangel Michael underneath an inscription reading "Gott Mit Uns" (God With Us). Teutonic knights with drawn swords stand watch around the memorial's crest; inside are somber statues of the Guards of the Dead and a "hall of fame" dedicated to the heroic qualities of the German people. (Monument to Victor Emmanuel II © Paul Thompson/Eye Ubiquitous/Corbis; Leipzig Monument: Ivan Vdovin/JAI/Corbis)

> PICTURING THE PAST

ANALYZING THE IMAGE: The insightful French sociologist Ernest Renan believed that nationalism depended more on an imagined and invented past than on what actually happened in a people's shared history. How do these two monuments reconstruct the past to engender nationalist pride? What values do the monuments and their decorations celebrate?

CONNECTIONS: Historians continue to ponder the immense popularity of nationalism around 1900 and indeed its ongoing resonance today. Can architecture help spread the popular appeal of the national idea? Are there similar structures in your own neighborhood or region? If so, when were they made and what do they represent? Do they continue to promote national values effectively?

race" for its supposedly superior qualities. Social Darwinist ideas about the "survival of the fittest," when applied to the "contest" between nations and races, drew on such ideas to further popularize stereotypes about inferior and superior races.

The close links between nationalism and scientific racism helped justify imperial expansion, as we shall see in the next chapter. Nationalist racism also

| What steps did Russia and the Ottoman Turks take toward modernization? | What general domestic political trends emerged after 1871? | **How did popular nationalism evolve?** | Why did the socialist movement grow, and how revolutionary was it? | ✓ LearningCurve Check what you know. |

x

fostered domestic persecution and exclusion. According to race theorists, the nation was supposed to be racially pure, and ethnic minorities were viewed as outsiders and targets for reform, repression, and relocation. For many nationalists, driven by ugly currents of race hatred, Jews were the ultimate outsiders, the stereotypical "inferior race" that posed the greatest challenge to national purity.

Jewish Emancipation and Modern Anti-Semitism

Changing political principles and the triumph of the nation-state had revolutionized Jewish life in western and central Europe. The decisive turning point came in 1848, when the Frankfurt Assembly endorsed full rights for German Jews. In 1871, the constitution of the new German Empire abolished all restrictions on Jewish marriage, choice of occupation, place of residence, and property ownership. However, even with this change, exclusion from government employment and discrimination in social relations remained. Nonetheless, by 1871, a majority of Jewish people in western and central Europe had improved their economic situation enough to enter the middle classes. Most Jewish people also identified strongly with their respective nation-states and, with good reason, saw themselves as patriotic citizens.

Vicious anti-Semitism reappeared with force in central and eastern Europe after the stock market crash of 1873. Drawing on long traditions of religious intolerance, ghetto exclusion, and periodic anti-Jewish riots and expulsions, this anti-Semitism also built on the exclusionary aspects of modern popular nationalism and the pseudoscience of race. Fanatic anti-Semites whipped up resentment against Jewish achievement and Jewish "financial control" and claimed that the Jewish race or "blood" (rather than the Jewish religion) posed a biological threat to Christian peoples. Such anti-Semitic beliefs were particularly popular among conservatives, extreme nationalists, and people who felt threatened by Jewish competition, such as small shopkeepers, officeworkers, and professionals.

Before 1914, anti-Semitism was most oppressive in eastern Europe, where Jews suffered from terrible poverty. In the western borderlands of the Russian empire, where 4 million of Europe's 7 million Jewish people lived in 1880 with few legal rights, officials used anti-Semitism to channel popular discontent away from the government and onto the Jewish minority. In 1881 to 1882, a wave of violent pogroms commenced in southern Russia. The police and the army stood aside for days while peasants looted and destroyed Jewish property, and official harassment continued in the following decades.

The growth of radical anti-Semitism spurred the emergence of **Zionism,** a Jewish political movement whose adherents believed that Christian Europeans would never overcome their anti-Semitic hatred. To escape the burdens of anti-Semitism, leading Zionists such as Theodor Herzl advocated the creation of a Jewish state in Palestine—a homeland where European Jews could settle and live free of social prejudice. (See "Individuals in Society: Theodor Herzl," page 733.)

Zionism

▶ A movement, started by Theodor Herzl, dedicated to building a Jewish national homeland in Palestine.

> **QUICK REVIEW**

What steps did European governments take to win the loyalty of their citizens in the second half of the nineteenth century?

INDIVIDUALS IN SOCIETY
Theodor Herzl

In September 1897, only days after his vision and energy had called into being the First Zionist Congress in Basel, Switzerland, Theodor Herzl (1860–1904) assessed the results in his diary: "If I were to sum up the Congress in a word — which I shall take care not to publish — it would be this: At Basel I founded the Jewish state. If I said this out loud today I would be greeted by universal laughter. In five years perhaps, and certainly in fifty years, everyone will perceive it."* Herzl's buoyant optimism, which so often carried him forward, was prophetic. Leading the Zionist movement until his death at age forty-four in 1904, Herzl guided the first historic steps toward modern Jewish political nationhood and the creation of Israel in 1948.

Theodor Herzl was born in Budapest, Hungary, into an upper-middle-class, German-speaking Jewish family. When he was eighteen, his family moved to Vienna, where he studied law. As a university student, he soaked up the liberal beliefs of most well-to-do Viennese Jews, which included assimilation of German culture. Wrestling with his nonreligious Jewishness and his strong pro-German feeling, Herzl embraced German nationalism and joined a German dueling fraternity. There he discovered that full acceptance required openly anti-Semitic attitudes and a repudiation of all things Jewish. Herzl resigned.

After receiving his law degree, Herzl embarked on a literary career. In 1889, he married into a wealthy Viennese Jewish family, but he and his socialite wife were mismatched and never happy together. Herzl achieved considerable success as both a journalist and a playwright. His witty comedies focused on the bourgeoisie, including Jewish millionaires trying to live like aristocrats. Accepting many German stereotypes, Herzl sometimes depicted eastern Jews as uneducated and grasping. But he believed that the Jewish shortcomings he perceived were the results of age-old persecution and would disappear through education and assimilation. Herzl also took a growing pride in Jewish steadfastness in the face of victimization and suffering.

The emergence of modern anti-Semitism (see page 732) shocked Herzl, as it did many acculturated Jewish Germans. Moving to Paris in 1891 as the correspondent for Vienna's leading liberal newspaper, Herzl studied contemporary politics and pondered recent historical developments. He came to a bold conclusion, published in 1896 as *The Jewish State: An Attempt at a Modern Solution to the Jewish Question*. According to Herzl, Jewish assimilation had failed, and attempts to combat anti-Semitism would never succeed. Only by building an independent Jewish state could the Jewish people flourish.

Theodor Herzl. (The Granger Collection, New York.)

Herzl developed his Zionism before the anti-Jewish agitation accompanying the Dreyfus affair, which only served to strengthen his faith in his analysis. Generally rebuffed by skeptical Jewish elites in western and central Europe, Herzl turned for support to youthful idealists and the poor Jewish masses. He became an inspiring man of action, rallying the delegates to the annual Zionist congresses, directing the growth of the worldwide Zionist organization, and working himself to death. Herzl also understood that national consciousness required powerful emotions and symbols, such as a Jewish flag. Flags build nations, he said, because people "live and die for a flag."

Putting the Zionist vision before non-Jews and world public opinion, Herzl believed in international diplomacy and political agreements. He traveled constantly to negotiate with European rulers and top officials, seeking their support in securing territory for a Jewish state, usually suggesting that it take form in Palestine, a territory in the Ottoman Empire. Aptly described by an admiring contemporary as "the first Jewish statesman since the destruction of Jerusalem," Herzl proved most successful in Britain. His work paved the way for the 1917 Balfour Declaration, which solemnly pledged British support for a "Jewish homeland" in Palestine.

QUESTIONS FOR ANALYSIS

1. Describe Theodor Herzl's background and early beliefs. Do you see a link between Herzl's early German nationalism and his later Zionism?
2. Why did Herzl believe an independent Jewish state with its own national flag was necessary?
3. How did Herzl work as a leader to turn his Zionist vision into a reality?

LaunchPad

ONLINE DOCUMENT PROJECT

What role did popular nationalism play in the emergence of modern anti-Semitism, and how did Herzl respond to the virulent anti-Semitism of this period? Examine examples of anti-Semitic nationalist writings and Herzl's argument for the creation of a Jewish state, and then complete a writing assignment based on the evidence and details from this chapter. *See inside the front cover to learn more.*

*Quotes are from Theodor Herzl, *The Diaries of Theodor Herzl*, trans. and ed. with an introduction by Marvin Lowenthal (New York: Grosset & Dunlap, 1962), pp. 224, 22, xxi.

Why did the socialist movement grow, and how revolutionary was it?

"Greetings from the May Day Festival" Workers participated enthusiastically in the annual one-day strike on May 1 in Stuttgart, Germany, to honor internationalist socialist solidarity, as this postcard suggests. Speeches, picnics, and parades were the order of the day, and workers celebrated their respectability and independent culture. Picture postcards like this one and the one on page 729 developed with railroads, mass travel, and high-speed printing. (akg-images)

NATIONALISM SERVED, FOR BETTER OR WORSE, as a new unifying principle. But what about socialism? Socialist parties, generally Marxist groups dedicated to international proletarian revolution, grew rapidly in these years. Did this mean that national states had failed to gain the support of workers?

CHAPTER LOCATOR | What kind of state did Napoleon III build in France? | How did conflict and war lead to the construction of strong nation-states?

The Socialist International

The growth of socialist parties after 1871 was phenomenal. By 1912, Germany's Social Democratic Party had millions of followers—mostly people from the working classes—and was the largest party in the Reichstag. Socialist parties grew in other countries as well, though nowhere else with such success.

Marxist socialist parties were eventually linked together in an international organization: the International Working Men's Association. Marx himself played an important role in founding the group, also known as the First International. In the following years, he battled successfully to control the organization and used its annual meetings as a means of spreading his doctrines. Marx enthusiastically endorsed the radical patriotism of the Paris Commune and its terrible struggle against the French state as a giant step toward socialist revolution. Marx's embrace of working-class violence frightened many of his early supporters, especially the more moderate British labor leaders. The First International collapsed.

Yet international proletarian solidarity remained an important objective for Marxists. In 1889, as the individual parties in different countries grew stronger, socialist leaders came together to form the Second International, which lasted until 1914. The International had a permanent executive, and every three years delegates from the different parties met to interpret Marxist doctrines and plan coordinated action. May 1 (May Day) was declared an annual international one-day strike, a day of marches and demonstrations.

Unions and Revisionism

Was socialism really radical and revolutionary in these years? On the whole, it was not. As socialist parties grew and attracted large numbers of members, they looked more and more toward gradual change and steady improvement for the working class and less and less toward revolution.

Workers themselves grew less inclined to follow radical programs for several reasons. As they gained the right to vote and to participate politically in the nation-state, workers focused their attention more on elections than on revolutions. As workers won real, tangible benefits, this furthered the process. And workers were not immune to patriotic education and indoctrination during military service. Nor were workers a unified social group. Perhaps most important of all, workers' standard of living rose gradually but substantially after 1850. The quality of life in urban areas improved dramatically as well. For all these reasons, workers became more moderate.

The growth of labor unions also reinforced this trend toward moderation. In the early stages of industrialization, unions were generally prohibited by law; they were considered subversive bodies to be hounded and crushed. From this sad position, workers struggled to escape.

Great Britain led the way in 1824 and 1825, when it granted unions the right to exist—though generally not the right to strike. After the collapse of Robert Owen's attempt to form one big national union in the 1830s (see Chapter 20, page 634), new and more practical kinds of unions appeared. Limited primarily to highly skilled workers, these "new model unions" concentrated on winning better wages and hours through collective bargaining and compromise. This approach

What steps did Russia and the Ottoman Turks take toward modernization?

What general domestic political trends emerged after 1871?

How did popular nationalism evolve?

Why did the socialist movement grow, and how revolutionary was it?

☑ LearningCurve
Check what you know.

735

helped pave the way to the full acceptance of unions in Britain in the 1870s, and after 1890, unions for unskilled workers developed.

German unions did not receive basic rights until 1869, and until the Anti-Socialist Laws were repealed in 1890, they were frequently harassed by the government as socialist fronts. As a result, in 1895, Germany had only about 270,000 union members in a male industrial workforce of nearly 8 million. Then, with almost all legal harassment eliminated, union membership skyrocketed, reaching roughly 3 million in 1912.

This great expansion both reflected and influenced the changing character of German unions. Increasingly, union activists focused on bread-and-butter issues — wages, hours, working conditions — rather than on fomenting socialist revolution. Genuine collective bargaining, long opposed by socialist intellectuals as a sellout, was officially recognized as desirable by the German Trade Union Congress in 1899.

The German trade unions and their leaders were in fact, if not in name, thoroughgoing revisionists. **Revisionism** was an effort by various socialists to update Marx's doctrines to reflect the realities of the time. Thus, the socialist Eduard Bernstein (1850–1932) argued in 1899 in his *Evolutionary Socialism* that many of Marx's predictions had been proved false. Therefore, Bernstein argued, socialists should reform their doctrines and tactics. They should combine with other progressive forces to win continued evolutionary gains for workers through legislation, unions, and further economic development.[2]

Moderation found followers elsewhere. In France, the socialist leader Jean Jaurès (1859–1914) formally repudiated revisionism in order to establish a unified socialist party, but he remained at heart a gradualist and optimistic secular humanist. Questions of revolution or revisionism also divided Russian Marxists.

By the early twentieth century, socialist parties had clear-cut national characteristics. Russians and socialists in the Austro-Hungarian Empire tended to be the most radical. The German party talked revolution and practiced reformism; it was greatly influenced by its enormous trade-union movement. The French party talked revolution and tried to practice it, unrestrained by a trade-union movement that was both very weak and very radical. In Britain, the socialist but non-Marxist Labour Party, reflecting the well-established union movement, was formally committed to gradual reform. In Spain and Italy, Marxist socialism was very weak. There anarchism, seeking to smash the state rather than the bourgeoisie, dominated radical thought and action.

In short, socialist policies and doctrines varied from country to country. Socialism itself was to a large extent "nationalized" behind the façade of international unity. This helps explain why, when war came in 1914, almost all socialist leaders and most workers supported their national governments and turned away from international solidarity.

revisionism

▶ An effort by moderate socialists to update Marxist doctrines to reflect the realities of the time.

> **QUICK REVIEW**

How and why did the reception of socialism by the working classes vary by nation?

CHAPTER LOCATOR | What kind of state did Napoleon III build in France? | How did conflict and war lead to the construction of strong nation-states?

LOOKING BACK LOOKING AHEAD

In 1900, the triumph of the national state in Europe seemed almost complete. Responsive and capable of tackling many practical problems, the European nation-state of 1900 was in part the realization of ideologues and patriots like Mazzini and the middle-class liberals active in the unsuccessful revolutions of 1848. Whereas early nationalists had envisioned a Europe of free peoples and international peace, the nationalists of 1900 had been nurtured in the traditional competition between European states and the wars of unification in the 1850s and 1860s. This new generation of nationalists reveled in the strength of their unity, and the nation-state became a system of power.

Thus, after 1870, at the same time the responsive nation-state improved city life and brought social benefits to ordinary people, Europe's leading countries also projected power throughout the world. In Asia and Africa, the European powers seized territory, fought brutal colonial wars, and built authoritarian empires. Moreover, in Europe itself, the universal faith in nationalism promoted a bitter, almost Darwinian competition between states. Thus European nationalism threatened the very progress and unity it had helped to build. In 1914, the power of unified nation-states would turn on itself, unleashing the First World War.

ONLINE DOCUMENT PROJECT

Theodor Herzl

What role did popular nationalism play in the emergence of modern anti-Semitism, and how did Herzl respond to the virulent anti-Semitism of this period?

You encountered Herzl's story on page 733. Keeping the question above in mind, examine examples of anti-Semitic nationalist writings and Herzl's argument for the creation of a Jewish state. *See inside the front cover to learn more.*

What steps did Russia and the Ottoman Turks take toward modernization?

What general domestic political trends emerged after 1871?

How did popular nationalism evolve?

Why did the socialist movement grow, and how revolutionary was it?

✓ LearningCurve
Check what you know.

737

CHAPTER 23 STUDY GUIDE

STEP 1

GET STARTED ONLINE

LearningCurve

Now that you've read the chapter, make it stick by completing the LearningCurve activity.

STEP 2

EXPLAIN WHY IT MATTERS

Put your reading into practice. Identify each term below, and then explain why it matters in Western history.

TERM	WHO OR WHAT & WHEN	WHY IT MATTERS
Red Shirts (p. 713)		
Homestead Act (p. 718)		
Crimean War (p. 719)		
Bloody Sunday (p. 721)		
October Manifesto (p. 721)		
Duma (p. 721)		
Tanzimat (p. 722)		
Young Turks (p. 722)		
Reichstag (p. 724)		
Kulturkampf (p. 724)		
Dreyfus affair (p. 726)		
People's Budget (p. 726)		
Zionism (p. 732)		
revisionism (p. 736)		

STEP 3

MOVE BEYOND THE BASICS

To demonstrate a more advanced understanding, fill in the chart below by describing the key participants, events, and the role of ideology in the unification of Italy and Germany. How did conflicting visions of the nation shape the unification process and new government in each country?

	Key participants	Key events	Role of ideology
Italy			
Germany			

STEP 4 **PUT IT ALL TOGETHER** Now, take a step back and try to explain the big picture. Remember to use specific examples from the chapter in your answers.

NATION BUILDING AND MODERNIZATION

▶ How did Napoleon III use the memory of the French Revolution to promote national unity and legitimize his own authority?

▶ How successful were the modernization efforts of the Russian and Ottoman empires?

THE RESPONSIVE NATIONAL STATE

▶ Compare and contrast the relationship between the people and the government in France and Britain in the late nineteenth century.

▶ Compare and contrast the domestic politics of Germany and Austria-Hungary in the late nineteenth century.

MARXISM AND THE SOCIALIST MOVEMENT

▶ What was the relationship between nationalism and socialism in the late nineteenth century? How did European governments respond to the challenge of international socialism?

▶ Why did most workers reject radical socialism? What does this tell us about working-class values and ambitions in the late nineteenth century?

MAKE CONNECTIONS

▶ What role did Enlightenment thought and romanticism play in shaping nineteenth-century nationalism?

▶ In your opinion, is nationalism as potent a force now as it was in the decades before World War I? Why or why not?

> IN YOUR OWN WORDS

Imagine that you must give an oral report to the class answering the following question: **How did nationalism shape the development of Western government and political life in the second half of the nineteenth century?** What would be the most important points and why?

24

THE WEST AND THE WORLD

1815–1914

> **How and why did the relationship between the West and the rest of the world change over the course of the nineteenth century?** Chapter 24 examines Western expansion in the century prior to World War I. While industrialization and nationalism were transforming urban and rural life throughout Europe, Western society itself was reshaping the world. At the peak of its power and pride, the West entered the third and most dynamic phase of the aggressive expansion that had begun with the Crusades and continued with the rise of seaborne colonial empires. At the same time, millions of Europeans emigrated abroad, primarily to North and South America but also to Australia, North and South Africa, and Asiatic Russia.

LearningCurve

After reading the chapter, use LearningCurve to retain what you've read.

Life on the Imperial Frontier. Colonialism entangled the lives of Europeans, natives, and immigrants, as seen in this 1886 painting of the city of Durban in the British colony of South Africa, the site of a minor gold rush. (Photo © Tarker/The Bridgeman Art Library)

> What were some of the global consequences of European industrialization?

> How was massive migration an integral part of Western expansion?

> How did Western imperialism change after 1880?

> What was the general pattern of non-Western responses to Western expansion?

What were some of the global consequences of European industrialization?

Britain and China at War Britain capitalized on its overwhelming naval superiority in its war against China, as shown in this British painting celebrating a dramatic moment in a crucial 1841 battle near Guangzhou. Having received a direct hit from a steam-powered British ironclad, a Chinese sailing ship explodes into a wall of flame. The Chinese lost eleven ships and five hundred men in the two-hour engagement; the British suffered only minor damage. (© National Maritime Museum, London/The Image Works)

OVER THE COURSE OF THE NINETEENTH CENTURY, the economic system created by the Industrial Revolution expanded across the face of the earth. Some of this extension into non-Western areas was peaceful and beneficial. If peaceful methods failed, however, Europeans used their superior military power to force non-Western nations to open their doors to Western economic interests.

The Rise of Global Inequality

Those regions of the world that industrialized in the nineteenth century (mainly Europe and North America) increased their wealth and power enormously in comparison to those that did not. A gap between the core industrializing regions and the soon-to-be colonized or semi-colonized regions outside the European–North American core (mainly in Africa, Asia, the Middle East, and Latin America) emerged and widened throughout the nineteenth century. Moreover, this pattern of uneven global development became institutionalized, or built into the structure of the world economy.

In recent years, historical economists have charted the long-term evolution of this gap, and **Figure 24.1** summarizes the findings of one important study. Three main points stand out. First, in 1750, the average standard of living was no higher in Europe as a whole than in the rest of the world. Second, it was industrialization

1805–1848 – Muhammad Ali modernizes Egypt	**1884–1885** – Berlin Conference
1839–1842 – First Opium War; Treaty of Nanking	**1885** – Russian expansion reaches borders of Afghanistan
1853 – Perry "opens" Japan for trade	**1898** – United States takes over Philippines; hundred days of reform in China; Battle of Omdurman
1856–1860 – Second Opium War	**1899** – Kipling writes "The White Man's Burden"
1857–1858 – Britain crushes Great Rebellion in India	**1899–1902** – South African War
1863–1879 – Reign of Ismail in Egypt	**1902** – Conrad publishes *Heart of Darkness*; Hobson publishes *Imperialism*
1867 – Meiji Restoration in Japan	**1912** – Western-style republic replaces China's Qing Dynasty
1869 – Suez Canal opens	**1914** – Panama Canal opens
1880–1900 – Most of Africa falls under European rule	

that opened the gaps in average wealth and well-being among countries and regions. Third, income per person stagnated in the colonized world before 1913, in striking contrast to the industrializing regions.

The rise of these enormous income disparities has generated a great deal of debate. One school of interpretation stresses that the West used science, technology, capitalist organization, and even its rational worldview to create massive wealth, and then used that wealth and power to its advantage. Another school argues that the West used its political and economic power to steal much of the world's riches, continuing in the nineteenth and twentieth centuries the rapacious colonialism born of the era of expansion. Because these issues are complex and there are few simple answers, it is helpful to consider them in the context of world trade in the nineteenth century.

The World Market

Commerce between nations has always stimulated economic development. In the nineteenth century, Europe directed an enormous increase in international commerce. Great Britain took the lead in cultivating export markets for its booming industrial output, as British manufacturers looked first to Europe and then around the world.

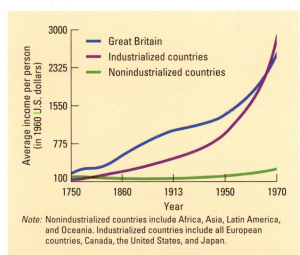

Note: Nonindustrialized countries include Africa, Asia, Latin America, and Oceania. Industrialized countries include all European countries, Canada, the United States, and Japan.

FIGURE 24.1 ■ The Growth of Average Income per Person in Industrialized Countries, Nonindustrialized Countries, and Great Britain, 1750–1970
Growth is given in 1960 U.S. dollars and prices.

How was massive migration an integral part of Western expansion?	How did Western imperialism change after 1880?	What was the general pattern of non-Western responses to Western expansion?	☑ LearningCurve Check what you know.

Take the case of cotton textiles. By 1820, Britain was exporting 50 percent of its production. Europe bought 50 percent of these cotton textile exports, while India bought only 6 percent and had its own well-established textile industry. Then as European nations and the United States erected protective tariff barriers to promote domestic industry, British cotton textile manufacturers looked to markets in non-Western areas. By 1850, India was buying 25 percent and Europe only 16 percent of a much larger volume of production. As a British colony, India could not raise tariffs to protect its indigenous cotton textile industry, which consequently collapsed.

In addition to its dominance in the export market, Britain was also the world's largest importer of agricultural products, raw materials, and manufactured goods. Under free-trade policies, open access to Britain's market stimulated the development of mines and plantations in many non-Western areas.

International trade grew as transportation systems improved. European investors funded much of the railroad construction undertaken in Latin America, Asia, and Africa, which connected seaports with resource-rich inland cities and regions, as opposed to linking and developing cities and regions within a given country. Thus railroads dovetailed effectively with Western economic interests, facilitating the inflow and sale of Western manufactured goods and the export and the development of local raw materials.

The power of steam revolutionized transportation by sea as well as by land. Steam power began to supplant sails on the oceans of the world in the late 1860s. The time needed to cross the Atlantic dropped from three weeks in 1870 to about ten days in 1900, and the opening of the Suez and Panama Canals (in 1869 and 1914, respectively) shortened transport time to other areas of the globe considerably.

The revolution in land and sea transportation encouraged European entrepreneurs to open up and exploit vast new territories around the world. Improved transportation enabled Asia, Africa, and Latin America to ship not only familiar agricultural products but also new raw materials for industry, such as jute, rubber, cotton, and coconut oil. The export of raw materials supplied by these "primary producers" to Western manufacturers boosted economic growth in core countries but did little to establish independent industry in the nonindustrialized periphery.

New communications systems were used to direct the flow of goods across global networks. Transoceanic telegraph cables, firmly in place by the 1880s, enabled rapid communications among the financial centers of the world. The same communications network conveyed world commodity prices instantaneously.

As their economies grew, Europeans began to make massive foreign investments beginning about 1840. By the outbreak of World War I in 1914, Europeans had invested more than $40 billion abroad (**Map 24.1**). The great gap between rich and poor within Europe meant that the wealthy and moderately well-to-do could and did send great sums abroad in search of interest and dividends.

About three-quarters of total European investment went to other European countries, or to settler colonies or **neo-Europes**—regions that already had significant populations of ethnic Europeans, including the United States, Canada, Australia, New Zealand, Latin America, and Siberia. Europe found its most profitable opportunities for investment in construction of the railroads, ports, and utilities that were necessary to settle and develop the lands in places such as Australia and the Americas. By lending money to construct foreign railroads, Europeans

neo-Europes

▶ Settler colonies with established populations of Europeans, such as North America, Australia, New Zealand, and Latin America, where Europe found outlets for population growth and its most profitable investment opportunities in the nineteenth century.

CHAPTER LOCATOR | What were some of the global consequences of European industrialization?

744 CHAPTER 24
THE WEST AND THE WORLD

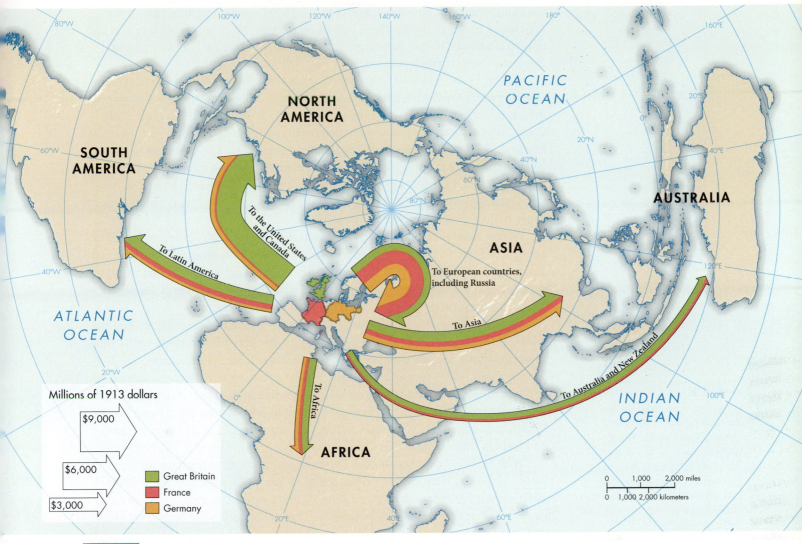

MAP 24.1 ■ European Investment to 1914

Foreign investment grew rapidly after 1850, and Britain, France, and Germany were the major investing nations. As this map suggests, most European investment was not directed to the African and Asian areas seized in the new imperialism after 1880.

enabled white settlers to buy European rails and locomotives and to develop sources of cheap food and raw materials.

The extension of Western economic power and the construction of neo-Europes were disastrous for indigenous peoples. Native Americans and Australian aborigines especially were decimated by the diseases, liquor, and weapons of an aggressively expanding Western society.

The Opening of China

For centuries China had sent more goods and inventions to Europe than it had received, and such was still the case in the early nineteenth century. Trade with Europe was carefully regulated by the Chinese imperial government—ruled by

How was massive migration an integral part of Western expansion?	How did Western imperialism change after 1880?	What was the general pattern of non-Western responses to Western expansion?	☑ LearningCurve Check what you know.

the Qing (ching), or Manchu, Dynasty in the 1800s — which required all foreign merchants to live in the southern port of Guangzhou (Canton) and to buy and sell only to licensed Chinese merchants. Practices considered harmful to Chinese interests were strictly forbidden.

By the 1820s, however, British merchants were flexing their muscles. Moreover, in opium the British found a means to break China's self-imposed isolation. British merchants smuggled opium grown legally in British-occupied India into China, where its use and sale were illegal. Huge profits and growing addiction led to a rapid increase in sales. By 1836, the British merchants in Guangzhou aggressively demanded the creation of an independent British colony in China and "safe and unrestricted liberty" in their Chinese trade. They pressured the British government to take decisive action and enlisted the support of British manufacturers eager to gain access to Chinese markets.

At the same time, the Qing government decided that the opium trade had to be stamped out. In 1839, it sent special envoy Lin Zexu to Guangzhou to deal with the crisis. Lin Zexu punished Chinese who purchased opium and seized the opium supplies of the British merchants, who then withdrew to Hong Kong. He sent a famous letter justifying his policy to Queen Victoria in London.

The British merchants appealed to their allies in London for support, and the British government responded. It also wanted free, unregulated trade with China, as well as the establishment of diplomatic relations on the European model. Taking advantage of its control of the seas, Britain occupied several coastal cities and in the first of two **Opium Wars** forced China to give in to British demands. In the Treaty of Nanking in 1842, China was required to cede the island of Hong Kong to Britain, pay an indemnity of $100 million, and open up four large cities to unlimited foreign trade with low tariffs.

With Britain's new power over Chinese commerce, the opium trade flourished, and Hong Kong developed rapidly as an Anglo-Chinese enclave. But disputes over trade between China and the Western powers continued. Finally, the second Opium War (1856–1860) culminated in the occupation of Beijing by British and French troops. Another round of one-sided treaties gave European merchants and missionaries greater privileges and protection and forced the Chinese to accept trade and investment on unfavorable terms in several more cities.

Japan and the United States

European traders and missionaries first arrived in Japan in the sixteenth century. In 1640, the government decided to expel all foreigners and seal off the country from all European influences in order to preserve traditional Japanese culture and society. When American and British whaling ships began to appear off Japanese coasts almost two hundred years later, the policy of exclusion was still in effect.

After several unsuccessful American attempts to establish commercial relations with Japan, Commodore Matthew Perry steamed into Edo (now Tokyo) Bay in 1853. Relying on **gunboat diplomacy** by threatening to attack, Perry demanded diplomatic negotiations with the emperor. Japan entered a grave crisis. Some Japanese military leaders urged resistance, but senior officials realized how defenseless their cities were against naval bombardment. Shocked and humiliated, they

Opium Wars
▶ Two mid-nineteenth-century conflicts between China and Great Britain over the British trade in opium, which was designed to "open" China to European free trade. In defeat, China gave European traders and missionaries increased protection and concessions.

gunboat diplomacy
▶ The use or threat of military force to coerce a government into economic or political agreements.

CHAPTER LOCATOR | **What were some of the global consequences of European industrialization?**

reluctantly signed a treaty with the United States that opened two ports and permitted trade. Over the next five years, more treaties spelled out the rights and privileges of the Western nations and their merchants in Japan. Japan was "opened."

Western Penetration of Egypt

Egypt's experience illustrates not only the explosive power of the expanding European economy and society but also their seductive appeal. European involvement in Egypt also led to a new model of formal political control, which European powers applied widely in Africa and Asia after 1882.

Since 525 B.C E., Egypt had been ruled by a succession of foreigners, most recently by the Ottoman sultans. In 1798, French armies under young General Napoleon Bonaparte invaded the Egyptian part of the Ottoman Empire and occupied the territory for three years. Into the power vacuum left by the French withdrawal stepped an Albanian-born, Turkish-speaking general, Muhammad Ali (1769–1849).

First appointed governor of Egypt in 1805 by the Ottoman sultan, Muhammad Ali set out to build his own state on the strength of a large, powerful army organized along European lines. He drafted the peasant masses of Egypt, and he hired French and Italian army officers to train both these raw recruits and their Turkish officers in modern military methods. He also reformed the government, cultivated new lands, and improved communication networks.

Muhammad Ali's modernization program attracted large numbers of Europeans, who served not only as army officers but also as engineers, doctors, government officials, and police officers. Others turned to trade, finance, and shipping.

To pay for his ambitious plans, Muhammad Ali encouraged the development of commercial agriculture. This development had profound implications. Egyptian peasants were poor but largely self-sufficient, growing food for their own consumption on state-owned lands allotted to them by tradition. Faced with the possibility of export agriculture, high-ranking officials and members of Muhammad Ali's family began carving large private landholdings out of the state domain. These new landlords made the peasants their tenants and forced them to grow cash crops such as cotton and rice geared to European markets.

These trends continued under Muhammad Ali's grandson Ismail (ihs-MAH-eel). Educated at France's leading military academy, Ismail was a westernizing autocrat. The large irrigation networks he promoted boosted cotton production and exports to Europe, and with his support a French company completed the Suez Canal in 1869. Young Egyptians educated in Europe spread new skills; Cairo acquired

The Suez Canal, 1869

How was massive migration an integral part of Western expansion?

How did Western imperialism change after 1880?

What was the general pattern of non-Western responses to Western expansion?

☑ LearningCurve
Check what you know.

modern boulevards and Western hotels. As Ismail proudly declared, "My country is no longer in Africa, we now form part of Europe."[1]

Ismail's projects were enormously expensive, however, and by 1876, Egypt owed foreign bondholders a colossal debt that it could not pay. France and Great Britain intervened and forced Ismail to appoint French and British commissioners to oversee Egyptian finances to ensure payment of the Egyptian debt in full. This momentous decision marked a sharp break with the past. Throughout most of the nineteenth century, Europeans had used military might and political force primarily to make sure that non-Western lands would accept European trade and investment. Now Europeans were going to effectively rule Egypt.

Foreign financial control evoked a violent nationalistic reaction among Egyptian religious leaders, young intellectuals, and army officers. Continuing diplomatic pressure on the government, which forced Ismail to abdicate in favor of his weak son, Tewfiq (r. 1879–1892), resulted in bloody anti-European riots in Alexandria in 1882. Further upheaval resulted in the arrival of a British expeditionary force and the occupation of all of Egypt.

The British said that their occupation was temporary, but British armies remained in Egypt until 1956. They maintained the façade of Egypt as an autonomous province of the Ottoman Empire, but the Egyptian government was a mere puppet. British rule did result in tax reforms and somewhat better conditions for peasants, while foreign bondholders received their interest and Egyptian nationalists nursed their injured pride.

British rule in Egypt provided a new model for European expansion in densely populated lands. Such expansion was based on military force, political domination, and a self-justifying ideology of beneficial reform. This model predominated until 1914. Thus did Europe's Industrial Revolution lead to tremendous political as well as economic expansion throughout the world after 1880.

> **QUICK REVIEW**

Why did global inequality intensify over the course of the nineteenth century?

CHAPTER LOCATOR | What were some of the global consequences of European industrialization?

748   CHAPTER 24
THE WEST AND THE WORLD

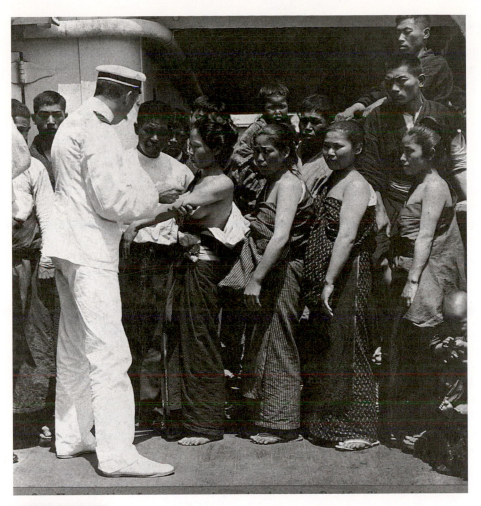

Vaccinating Migrants Bound for Hawaii, 1904 First Chinese, then Japanese, and finally Koreans and Filipinos went across the Pacific in large numbers to labor in Hawaii on American-owned sugar plantations in the late nineteenth century. The native Hawaiians had been decimated by disease, creating a severe labor shortage for Hawaii's plantation economy. (© Corbis)

A POIGNANT HUMAN DRAMA accompanied economic expansion: millions of people pulled up stakes and left their ancestral lands in the course of history's greatest migration. It was, in part, because of this **global mass migration** that the West's impact on the world in the nineteenth century was so powerful and many-sided.

A note on vocabulary may be in order here: *migration* refers to general human movement; *emigrants* (or *emigration*) refers to people leaving one country for another; *immigrants* (or *immigration*) refers to people entering one country from another. People emigrate from and immigrate to.

global mass migration
▶ The mass movement of people from Europe in the nineteenth century; one reason that the West's impact on the world was so powerful and many-sided.

| How was massive migration an integral part of Western expansion? | How did Western imperialism change after 1880? | What was the general pattern of non-Western responses to Western expansion? | ☑ LearningCurve Check what you know. |

The Pressure of Population

In the early eighteenth century, European population growth entered its third and decisive stage, which continued unabated until the early twentieth century. During the hundred years before 1900 the population of Europe (including Asiatic Russia) more than doubled, from approximately 188 million to roughly 432 million.

These figures actually understate Europe's population explosion, for between 1815 and 1932, more than 60 million people left Europe. The growing number of Europeans provided further impetus for Western expansion, and it drove more and more people to emigrate. These emigrants went primarily to the rapidly growing neo-Europes—North and South America, Australia, New Zealand, and Siberia.

Before looking at the people who emigrated, consider these three facts. First, the number of men and women who left Europe increased rapidly at the end of the nineteenth century and leading up to World War I. As **Figure 24.2** shows, more than 11 million left in the first decade of the twentieth century, over five times the number departing in the 1850s. Thus, large-scale emigration was a defining characteristic of European society at the turn of the century.

Second, different countries had very different patterns of migration. People left Britain and Ireland in large numbers from the 1840s on. This outflow reflected not only rural poverty but also the movement of skilled industrial technicians and the preferences shown to British migrants in the overseas British Empire. German emigration was quite different. It grew irregularly after about 1830, reaching a first peak in the early 1850s and another in the early 1880s. Thereafter it declined rapidly, for at that point Germany's rapid industrialization provided adequate jobs at home. This pattern contrasted sharply with that of Italy. More and more Italians left the country right up to 1914, reflecting severe problems in Italian villages and relatively slow industrial growth.

Third, although the United States did absorb the largest overall number of European emigrants, fewer than half of all these emigrants went to the United States. Asiatic Russia, Canada, Argentina, Brazil, Australia, and New Zealand also attracted large numbers, as **Figure 24.3** shows. Moreover, immigrants accounted for a larger proportion of the total population in Argentina, Brazil, and Canada than in the United

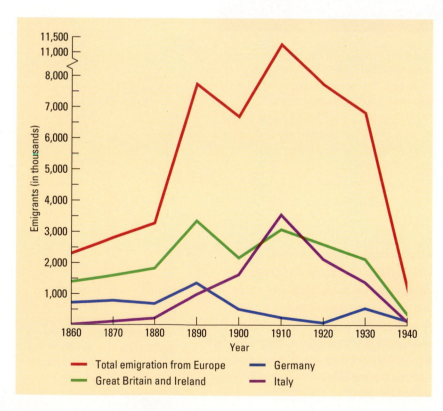

FIGURE 24.2 ■ Emigration from Europe by Decade, 1860–1940
Emigration from Europe grew quickly until the outbreak of World War I in 1914, after which it declined rapidly.

CHAPTER LOCATOR | What were some of the global consequences of European industrialization?

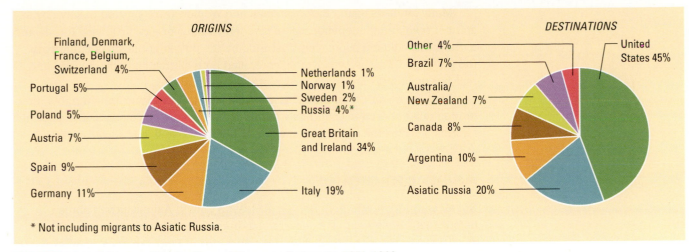

ORIGINS

Finland, Denmark, France, Belgium, Switzerland 4%
Portugal 5%
Poland 5%
Austria 7%
Spain 9%
Germany 11%
Netherlands 1%
Norway 1%
Sweden 2%
Russia 4%*
Great Britain and Ireland 34%
Italy 19%

* Not including migrants to Asiatic Russia.

DESTINATIONS

Other 4%
Brazil 7%
Australia/ New Zealand 7%
Canada 8%
Argentina 10%
Asiatic Russia 20%
United States 45%

FIGURE 24.3 ■ Origins and Destinations of European Emigrants, 1851–1960
European emigrants came from many countries; almost half of them went to the United States.

States. The common American assumption that European emigration meant immigration to the United States is quite inaccurate.

European Emigration

What kind of people left Europe, and what were their reasons for doing so? The European emigrant was generally a small farmer or skilled artisan trying hard to stay ahead of poverty. These small peasant landowners and village craftsmen typically left Europe because of the lack of available land and the growing availability of cheap factory-made goods, which threatened their traditional livelihoods.

Immigrants brought great benefits to the countries that received them, in large part because the vast majority were young, typically unmarried, and ready to work hard in the new land. Many Europeans moved but remained within Europe, settling temporarily or permanently in another European country. A substantial number of Europeans were actually migrants as opposed to immigrants who settled in new lands—that is, they returned home after some time abroad.

The likelihood of repatriation varied greatly by nationality. People who emigrated from the Balkans, for instance, were much more likely to return to their countries than people from Ireland or eastern European Jews. For those who returned, the possibility of buying land in the old country was of central importance. In Ireland, large, often-absentee landowners owned most land; little was up for sale. In Russia, most Jews faced discrimination and were forced to live in the Pale of Settlement (see Chapter 16, page 511). Therefore, when Irish farmers and Russian Jewish artisans emigrated in search of opportunity, or, for Jews, to escape pogroms (see Chapter 23, page 732), it was basically a once-and-for-all departure.

Ties of family and friendship played a crucial role in the emigration process. Many people from a given province or village settled together in rural enclaves or tightly knit urban neighborhoods thousands of miles away. Very often a strong individual—a businessman, a religious leader, a family member—would blaze the way and others would follow, forming a "migration chain."

How was massive migration an integral part of Western expansion?

How did Western imperialism change after 1880?

What was the general pattern of non-Western responses to Western expansion?

✓ LearningCurve
Check what you know.

Many landless young European men and women were spurred to leave by a spirit of revolt and independence. In Sweden and in Norway, in Jewish Russia and in Italy, these young people felt frustrated by the power of the small minority in the privileged classes, which often controlled both church and government, and resisted demands for change and greater opportunity.

Thus for many, emigration was a radical way to gain basic human rights. Emigration rates slowed in countries where the people won basic political and social reforms, such as the right to vote, equality before the law, and social security.

Asian Emigration

Not all emigration was from Europe. At least 3 million Asians moved abroad before 1920. Most went as indentured laborers to work under incredibly difficult conditions on the plantations or in the gold mines of Latin America, southern Asia, Africa, California, Hawaii, and Australia. White estate owners very often used Asian immigrants to fill labor shortages caused by the suppression of the slave trade.

Emigration from Asia would undoubtedly have grown to much greater proportions if planters and mine owners in search of cheap labor had been able to hire as many Asian workers as they wished. But they could not. Many Asians fled the plantations and gold mines as soon as possible, seeking greater opportunities in trade and towns. There they came into conflict with local populations, whether in Malaya, southern Africa, or areas settled by Europeans. When that took place in neo-Europes, European settlers demanded a halt to Asian immigration. By the 1880s, the American and Australian governments had instituted exclusionary acts—discriminatory laws designed to keep Asians from entering the country.

In fact, the explosion of mass mobility in the late nineteenth century, combined with the growing appeal of nationalism and scientific racism (see Chapter 23, page 730), encouraged a variety of attempts to control immigration flows and seal off national borders. National governments established strict rules for granting citizenship and asylum to foreigners. Passports and customs posts monitored movement across increasingly tight national boundaries. Such attempts were often inspired by **nativism**, beliefs that led to policies giving preferential treatment to established inhabitants above immigrants.

nativism
▶ Policies and beliefs, often influenced by nationalism, scientific racism, and mass migration, that give preferential treatment to established inhabitants over immigrants.

A crucial factor in the migrations before 1914 was, therefore, immigration policies that offered preferred status to "acceptable" racial and ethnic groups in the open lands of possible permanent settlement. This, too, was part of Western dominance. Largely successful in monopolizing the best overseas opportunities, Europeans and people of European ancestry reaped the main benefits from the mass migration. By 1913, people in Australia, Canada, and the United States had joined the British in having the highest average incomes in the world, while incomes in Asia and Africa lagged far behind.

> **QUICK REVIEW**

What characterized the typical European emigrant in the late nineteenth century?

CHAPTER LOCATOR | What were some of the global consequences of European industrialization?

How did Western imperialism change after 1880?

Tools for Empire Building Western technological advances aided Western political ambitions in Africa and Asia. The Maxim machine gun shown above, right was highly mobile and could lay down a continuous barrage that would decimate charging enemies, as in the slaughter of Muslim soldiers at the Battle of Omdurman in the Sudan. Quinine (above, left) was also very important to empire building. First taken around 1850 in order to prevent the contraction of deadly malaria, quinine enabled European soldiers and officials to move safely into the African interior and overwhelm native peoples. (gun: Lordprice Collection/Alamy; quinine: Wellcome Library, London)

THE EXPANSION OF WESTERN SOCIETY reached its apex between about 1880 and 1914. In those years, the leading European nations rushed to create or enlarge vast political empires. This political empire building contrasted sharply with the economic penetration of non-Western territories between 1816 and 1880, which had left a China or a Japan "opened" but politically independent. Because this renewed imperial push came after a long pause in European expansionism, contemporaries termed it the **new imperialism**.

The new imperialism had momentous consequences. By the early 1900s, almost 84 percent of the globe was dominated by European nations. The new imperialism created new tensions among competing European states and led to wars and threats of war with non-European powers. Aimed primarily at Africa and Asia, the new imperialism put millions of black, brown, and yellow peoples directly under the rule of whites.

new imperialism
▶ The late-nineteenth-century drive by European countries to create vast political empires abroad.

How was massive migration an integral part of Western expansion?

How did Western imperialism change after 1880?

What was the general pattern of non-Western responses to Western expansion?

☑ LearningCurve
Check what you know.

The European Presence in Africa Before 1880

Prior to 1880, European nations controlled only 10 percent of Africa. The French had begun conquering Algeria in 1830, and by 1880 substantial numbers of French, Italian, and Spanish colonists had settled among the overwhelming Arab majority there.

At the southern tip of the African continent, Britain had taken possession of the Dutch settlements in and around Cape Town during the wars with Napoleon I. This takeover of the Cape Colony had led disgruntled Dutch cattle ranchers and farmers in 1835 to make their so-called Great Trek into the interior. After 1853, the Boers, or **Afrikaners** (a-frih-KAH-nuhrz), as the descendants of the Dutch in the Cape Colony were beginning to call themselves, proclaimed their independence and defended it against British armies. By 1880, Afrikaner and British settlers, who detested each other and lived in separate areas, had wrested control of much of South Africa from the Zulu, Xhosa, and other African peoples.

In addition to the French in the north and the British and Afrikaners in the south, European trading posts and forts dotted the coast of West Africa, and the Portuguese maintained a loose hold on their old possessions in Angola and Mozambique. Elsewhere, over the great mass of the continent, Europeans did not rule.

After 1880, the situation changed drastically. In a spectacular manifestation of the new imperialism, European countries jockeyed for territory in Africa, breaking sharply with previous patterns of colonization and diplomacy.

Afrikaners

▶ Descendants of the Dutch settlers in the Cape Colony in southern Africa.

The Scramble for Africa After 1880

Between 1880 and 1900, Britain, France, Belgium, Germany, and Italy scrambled for African possessions (**Map 24.2**). By 1900, nearly the whole continent had been carved up and placed under European rule: only Ethiopia, which fought off Italian invaders, and Liberia, which had been settled by freed slaves from the United States, remained independent.

The Dutch-settler republics also succumbed to imperialism, but the final outcome was different. The British, led by Cecil Rhodes (1853–1902) in the Cape Colony, leapfrogged over the two Afrikaner states—the Orange Free State and the Transvaal—in the early 1890s and established protectorates over Bechuanaland (bech-WAH-nuh-land; now Botswana) and Rhodesia (now Zimbabwe and Zambia). English-speaking capitalists like Rhodes developed fabulously rich gold mines in the Transvaal, and the British eventually conquered their white rivals in the bloody South African War, or Boer War (1899–1902). In 1910, the Afrikaner territories were united with the old Cape Colony and the eastern province of Natal in a new Union of South Africa, established as a largely "self-governing" colony. Gradually, though, the defeated Afrikaners used their numerical superiority over the British settlers to take political power, as even the most educated nonwhites lost the right to vote, except in the Cape Colony. (See "Individuals in Society: Cecil Rhodes," page 756.)

In the complex story of the European seizure of Africa, certain events and individuals stand out. Of enormous importance was the British occupation of Egypt in 1882, which established the new model of formal political control (see page 747). King Leopold II of Belgium (r. 1865–1909), an energetic, strong-willed

CHAPTER LOCATOR | What were some of the global consequences of European industrialization?

754 CHAPTER 24
THE WEST AND THE WORLD

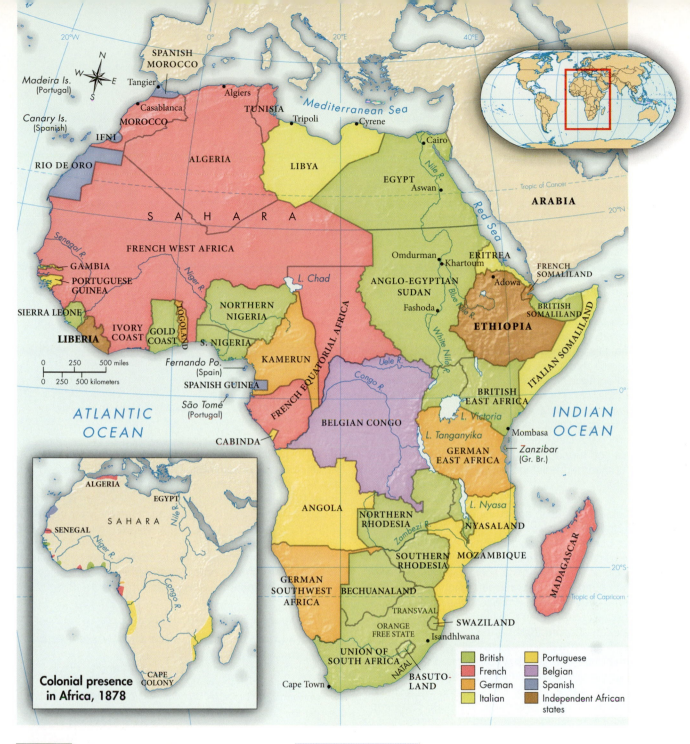

Legend

British	Portuguese
French	Belgian
German	Spanish
Italian	Independent African states

Colonial presence in Africa, 1878

MAP 24.2 ■ The Partition of Africa

The European powers carved up Africa after 1880 and built vast political empires. European states also seized territory in Asia in the nineteenth century, although some Asian states and peoples managed to maintain their political independence (see Map 24.3, page 759). Compare the patterns of European imperialism in Africa and Asia, using this map and Map 24.3.

> **MAPPING THE PAST**

ANALYZING THE MAP: What European countries were leading imperialist states in both Africa and Asia, and what lands did they hold? What countries in Africa and Asia maintained their independence? What did the United States and Japan have in common in Africa and Asia?

CONNECTIONS: The late nineteenth century was the high point of European imperialism. What were the motives behind the rush for land and empire in Africa and Asia?

How was massive migration an integral part of Western expansion?

How did Western imperialism change after 1880?

What was the general pattern of non-Western responses to Western expansion?

✓ LearningCurve
Check what you know.

Cecil Rhodes, after crushing the last African revolt in Rhodesia in 1896. (Brown Brothers)

Cecil Rhodes epitomized the dynamism and the ruthlessness of the new imperialism. He built a corporate monopoly, claimed vast tracts in Africa, and established the famous Rhodes scholarships to develop colonial (and American) leaders who would love and strengthen the British Empire. But to Africans, he left a bitter legacy.

Rhodes came from a large middle-class family and at seventeen went to southern Africa to seek his fortune. He soon turned to diamonds, newly discovered at Kimberley, picked good business partners, and was wealthy by 1876. But Rhodes, often called a dreamer, wanted more. He entered Oxford University, where he studied while returning periodically to Africa. His musings crystallized in a Social Darwinist belief in progress through racial competition and territorial expansion. "I contend," he wrote, "that we [English] are the finest race in the world and the more of the world we inhabit the better it is for the human race."*

Rhodes's belief in British expansion never wavered. In 1880, he formed the De Beers Mining Company, and by 1888, his firm had monopolized southern Africa's diamond production and earned fabulous profits. Rhodes also entered the Cape Colony's legislature and became the colony's all-powerful prime minister from 1890 to 1896.

His main objective was to annex the Afrikaner republics and impose British rule on as much land as possible beyond their northern borders. Working through a state-approved private company financed in part by De Beers, Rhodes's agents forced and cajoled African kings to accept British "protection," and then put down rebellions with machine guns. Britain thus obtained a great swath of empire on the cheap.

But Rhodes, like many high achievers obsessed with power and personal aggrandizement, went too far. He backed, and then in 1896 declined to call back, a failed invasion of the Transvaal, which was designed to topple the Dutch-speaking republic. Repudiated by top British leaders who had encouraged his plan, Rhodes had to resign as prime minister. In declining health, he continued to agitate against the Afrikaner republics. He died at age forty-nine as the South African War (1899–1902) ended.

In accounting for Rhodes's remarkable but flawed achievements, both sympathetic and critical biographers stress his imposing physical size, enormous energy, and charismatic personality. His ideas were commonplace, but he believed in them passionately, and he could persuade and inspire others to follow his lead. Rhodes the idealist was nonetheless a born negotiator, a crafty deal maker who believed that everyone could be had for a price. According to his most insightful biographer, Rhodes's homosexuality — discreet, partially repressed, but undeniable — was also "a major component of his magnetism and his success."† Never comfortable with women, he loved male companionship. He drew together a "band of brothers," both gay and straight, who shared in his pursuit of power.

Rhodes cared nothing for the rights of Africans and blacks. Both a visionary and an opportunist, he looked forward to an eventual reconciliation of Afrikaners and British in a united white front. Therefore, as prime minister of the Cape Colony, he broke with the colony's liberal tradition and supported Afrikaner demands to reduce drastically the number of black voters and limit black freedoms. This helped lay the foundation for the Union of South Africa's brutal policy of racial segregation known as *apartheid* after 1948.

QUESTIONS FOR ANALYSIS

1. In what ways did Rhodes's career epitomize the new imperialism in Africa?
2. How did Rhodes relate to Afrikaners and to black Africans? How do you account for the differences and the similarities?

ONLINE DOCUMENT PROJECT

What does the life of Cecil Rhodes suggest about the "great man" theory of history that was popular during this period? Examine a variety of perspectives on Rhodes's legacy. Then complete a writing assignment based on the evidence and details from this chapter. *See inside the front cover to learn more.*

*Robert I. Rotberg, *The Founder: Cecil Rhodes and the Pursuit of Power* (New York: Oxford University Press, 1988), p. 150.
†Ibid., p. 408.

monarch of a tiny country with a lust for distant territory, also played an important role.

By 1876, Leopold's expansionism focused on central Africa. He formed a financial syndicate under his personal control to send Henry M. Stanley to the Congo basin. Stanley established trading stations, signed unfair treaties with African chiefs, and planted the Belgian flag. Leopold's actions alarmed the French, who quickly took steps to establish a French protectorate on the north bank of the Congo River.

Leopold's intrusion into the Congo area called attention to the possibilities of African colonization, and by 1882, Europe had caught "African fever." To lay down some basic rules for this new and dangerous global competition, Jules Ferry of France and Otto von Bismarck of Germany arranged an international conference on Africa in Berlin in 1884 and 1885. The **Berlin Conference** established the principle that European claims to African territory had to rest on "effective occupation" (a strong presence on the ground) to be recognized by other states. The conference recognized Leopold's personal rule over a neutral Congo Free State and agreed to work to stop slavery and the slave trade in Africa.

The Berlin Conference coincided with Germany's sudden emergence as an imperial power. Prior to about 1880, Bismarck, like many other European leaders at the time, had seen little value in colonies. In 1884 and 1885, as political agitation for expansion increased, Bismarck did an abrupt about-face, and Germany established protectorates over a number of small African kingdoms and tribes. In acquiring colonies, Bismarck cooperated against the British with France's Jules Ferry, an ardent republican who also embraced imperialism. With Bismarck's tacit approval, the French took control of parts of West and Central Africa.

Meanwhile, the British began enlarging their own West African enclaves and impatiently pushed northward from the Cape Colony and westward from Zanzibar. Their thrust southward from Egypt was blocked in Sudan by fiercely independent Muslims who massacred a British force at Khartoum in 1885.

A decade later, another British force, under General Horatio H. Kitchener, moved cautiously and more successfully up the Nile River, building a railroad to supply arms and reinforcements as it went. Finally, in 1898, these British troops met their foe at Omdurman (ahm-duhr-MAHN) (see Map 24.2, page 755), where Sudanese Muslim troops charged time and time again, only to be cut down by the recently invented Maxim machine gun. In the end, about 10,000 Muslim soldiers lay dead, while only 28 Britons had been killed and 145 wounded.[2]

Berlin Conference
► A meeting of European leaders held in 1884 and 1885 in order to lay down some basic rules for imperialist competition in sub-Saharan Africa.

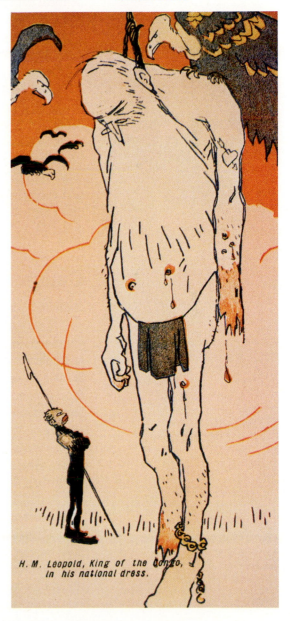

H. M. Leopold, King of the Congo, in his national dress.

European Imperialism at Its Worst

This 1908 English cartoon, "Leopold, King of the Congo, in his national dress," focuses on the barbaric practice of cutting off the hands and feet of Africans who refused to gather as much rubber as Leopold's company demanded. In 1908, an international human rights campaign forced the Belgian king to cede his personal fief to the Belgian state. (The Granger Collection, New York)

| How was massive migration an integral part of Western expansion? | **How did Western imperialism change after 1880?** | What was the general pattern of non-Western responses to Western expansion? | ✓ LearningCurve Check what you know. |

Continuing up the Nile after the Battle of Omdurman, Kitchener's armies found that a small French force had already occupied the village of Fashoda (fuh-SHOH-duh). The result was a serious diplomatic crisis and the threat of war between two Great Powers. Wracked by the Dreyfus affair (see Chapter 23, page 725) and unwilling to fight, France eventually backed down and withdrew its forces, allowing the British to take over.

Imperialism in Asia

Although their sudden division of Africa was more spectacular, Europeans also exerted political control over much of Asia. Here the Dutch were a major player. In 1815, the Dutch ruled little more than the island of Java in the East Indies. Thereafter they gradually brought almost all of the Malay Archipelago under their political authority, though they had to share some of the spoils with Britain and Germany. In the critical decade of the 1880s, the French, under the leadership of Ferry, took Indochina. India, Japan, and China also experienced a profound imperialist impact (**Map 24.3**).

Two other great imperialist powers, Russia and the United States, also acquired territories in Asia. Russians conquered Muslim areas to the south in the Caucasus and in Central Asia, reaching the border of Afghanistan in 1885. Russia also proceeded to nibble greedily on China's outlying provinces, especially in the 1890s.

The great conquest by the United States was the Philippines, which was taken from Spain in 1898 through the Spanish-American War. When it quickly became clear that the United States had no intention of granting the independence it had promised, Philippine patriots rose in revolt and were suppressed only after long, bitter fighting. Thus another great Western power joined the imperialist ranks in Asia.

Causes of the New Imperialism

Many factors contributed to the late-nineteenth-century rush for empire, which was in turn one aspect of Western society's generalized expansion in the age of industry and nationalism. Economic motives played an important role in the extension of political empires, especially in the British Empire. By the late 1870s, France, Germany, and the United States were industrializing rapidly behind rising tariff barriers. Great Britain was losing its early economic lead and facing increasingly tough competition in foreign markets. In this new economic climate, the seizure of Asian and African territory by continental powers in the 1880s raised alarms. Fearing that France and Germany would seal off their empires with high tariffs, which would result in the permanent loss of future economic opportunities, the British followed suit and began their own push to expand empire.

Actually, the overall economic gains of the new imperialism proved quite limited before 1914. The new colonies were simply too poor to buy much, and they offered few immediately profitable investments. Nonetheless, even the poorest, most barren desert was jealously prized. Colonies became important for political and diplomatic reasons. Each leading country saw overseas possessions as crucial to national security and military power.

Along with economic motives, many people were convinced that colonies were essential to great nations. "There has never been a great power without

MAP 24.3 ■ Asia in 1914

India remained under British rule, while China precariously preserved its political independence. The Dutch Empire in modern-day Indonesia was old, but French control of Indochina was a product of the new imperialism. Russia continued to expand to the south and also to the east.

great colonies," wrote one French publicist. Such statements reflected the growing intensity of European nationalism but also reflect Social Darwinian theories of brutal competition among races (see Chapter 23, page 730). As one prominent English economist argued, the "strongest nation has always been conquering the weaker . . . and the strongest tend to be best."[3] Thus European nations, which saw themselves as racially distinct parts of the dominant white race, had to seize colonies to show they were strong and virile. Moreover, since victory of the fittest in the struggle for survival was nature's inescapable law, the conquest of "inferior" peoples was just. Social Darwinism and pseudoscientific racial doctrines fostered imperialist expansion.

So did the industrial world's unprecedented technological and military superiority. Three aspects were particularly important. First, the rapidly firing Maxim machine gun was an ultimate weapon in many unequal battles. Second, newly

| How was massive migration an integral part of Western expansion? | **How did Western imperialism change after 1880?** | What was the general pattern of non-Western responses to Western expansion? | ☑ LearningCurve Check what you know. |

discovered quinine proved effective in controlling malaria, which had previously decimated whites in the tropics. Third, the combination of the steamship and the international telegraph permitted Western powers to quickly concentrate their firepower in a given area when it was needed. Never before — and never again after 1914 — would the technological gap between the West and non-Western regions of the world be so great.

Social tensions and domestic political conflicts also contributed mightily to overseas expansion. In Germany and Russia, and in other countries to a lesser extent, conservative political leaders manipulated colonial issues to divert popular attention from the class struggle at home and to create a false sense of national unity. Thus imperial propagandists relentlessly stressed that colonies benefited workers as well as capitalists. Government leaders and their allies in the tabloid press successfully encouraged the masses to savor foreign triumphs and to glory in the supposed increase in national prestige. In short, conservative leaders defined imperialism as a national necessity, which they used to justify the status quo and their hold on power.

Finally, certain special-interest groups in each country were powerful agents of expansion. White settlers in the colonial areas demanded more land and greater state protection. Missionaries and humanitarians wanted to spread religion and stop the slave trade within Africa. Shipping companies wanted lucrative subsidies to protect rapidly growing global trade. Military men and colonial officials foresaw rapid advancement and highly paid positions in growing empires. The actions of such groups pushed the course of empire forward.

A "Civilizing Mission"

To satisfy their consciences and answer their critics, imperialists promoted the idea that Westerners could and should civilize more primitive nonwhite peoples. According to this view, Westerners shouldered the responsibility for governing and converting the supposed savages under their charge and strove to remake them on superior European models. Africans and Asians would eventually receive the benefits of industrialization and urbanization, Western education, Christianity, advanced medicine, and finally higher standards of living. In time, they might be ready for self-government and Western democracy. In 1899, the British writer Rudyard Kipling (1865–1936) summarized such ideas in his poem "The White Man's Burden."

white man's burden

▶ The idea that Europeans could and should civilize more primitive nonwhite peoples and that imperialism would eventually provide nonwhites with modern achievements and higher standards of living.

Many Americans accepted the ideology of the **white man's burden**. It was an important factor in the decision to rule, rather than liberate, the Philippines after the Spanish-American War. Another argument was that imperial government protected natives from tribal warfare as well as from cruder forms of exploitation by white settlers and business people.

Peace and stability under European control also facilitated the spread of Christianity. Catholic and Protestant missionaries competed with Islam south of the Sahara, seeking converts and building schools to spread the Gospel. Many Africans' first real contact with whites was in mission schools. Some peoples, such as the Ibo in Nigeria, became highly Christianized.

Such occasional successes in black Africa contrasted with the general failure of missionary efforts in India, China, and the Islamic world. There Christians often preached in vain to peoples with ancient, complex religious beliefs.

CHAPTER LOCATOR | What were some of the global consequences of European industrialization?

Orientalism

Even though many Westerners shared a sense of superiority over non-Western peoples, they were often fascinated by foreign cultures and societies. In the late 1970s, the influential literary scholar Edward Said (Sie-EED) (1935–2003) coined the term **Orientalism** to describe this fascination and the stereotypical and often racist Western understandings of non-Westerners that dominated nineteenth-century Western thought.

As Said demonstrated, it was almost impossible for people in the West to look at or understand non-Westerners without falling into some sort of Orientalist stereotype. Politicians, scholarly experts, writers, artists, and ordinary people readily adopted "us versus them" views of foreign peoples. As part of this view of the non-West as radically "other," Westerners imagined the Orient as a place of mystery and romance, populated with exotic, dark-skinned peoples. (See "Picturing the Past: Orientalism in Art and Everyday Life," page 762.)

Such views swept through North American and European scholarship, arts, and literature in the late nineteenth century. The emergence of ethnography and anthropology as academic disciplines in the 1880s was part of the process. Inspired by a new culture of collecting, scholars and adventurers went into the field, where they studied supposedly primitive cultures and acquired artifacts from non-Western peoples. The results of their work were reported in scientific publications, and intriguing objects filled the display cases of new public museums of ethnography and natural history. In a slew of novels published around 1900, authors portrayed romance and high adventure in the colonies and so contributed to the Orientalist worldview. Artists followed suit, and dramatic paintings of ferocious Arab warriors, Eastern slave markets, and the sultan's harem adorned museum walls and wealthy middle-class parlors. Scholars, authors, and artists were not necessarily racists or imperialists, but they found it difficult to escape Orientalist stereotypes. In the end they helped spread the notions of Western superiority and justified colonial expansion.

Orientalism
▶ A term coined by literary scholar Edward Said to describe the way Westerners misunderstood and described colonial subjects and cultures.

> Orientalist Dualities

West	Non-West
Modern	Primitive
White	Colored
Christian	Pagan or Islamic

Critics of Imperialism

The expansion of empire aroused sharp, even bitter, critics. A forceful attack was delivered in 1902, after the unpopular South African War, by radical English economist J. A. Hobson (1858–1940) in his *Imperialism*. Hobson contended that the rush to acquire colonies was due to the economic needs of unregulated capitalism, and that it only produced profits for unscrupulous special-interest groups. Moreover, Hobson argued that the quest for empire diverted popular attention away from domestic reform and the need to reduce the great gap between rich and poor.

Like Hobson, Marxist critics offered a thorough analysis and critique of Western imperialism, placing it in the context of class conflict. Socialist arguments, however, were not broadly persuasive. Most people then (and now) were sold on the idea that imperialism was economically profitable for the homeland, and the masses developed a broad and genuine enthusiasm for empire.

Hobson and many other critics struck home, however, with their moral condemnation of whites imperiously ruling nonwhites. They rebelled against crude Social Darwinian thought. Kipling and his kind were lampooned as racist bullies whose rule rested on brutality, racial contempt, and the Maxim machine gun.

| How was massive migration an integral part of Western expansion? | **How did Western imperialism change after 1880?** | What was the general pattern of non-Western responses to Western expansion? | ✓ **LearningCurve** Check what you know. |

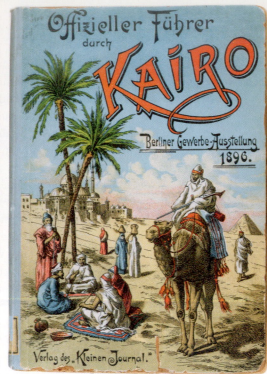

Orientalism in Art and Everyday Life

Stereotyped Western impressions of Arabs and the Islamic world became increasingly popular in the West in the nineteenth century. This wave of Orientalism found expression in high art, as in the renowned painting *Women of Algiers in Their Apartment* (1834), by French painter Eugène Delacroix. Delacroix portrays three women and their African servant at rest in a harem, the segregated, women-only living quarters for the wives of elite Muslim men (Islamic law allows a man to have several wives). Orientalist ideas also made their way into the fabric of everyday life, when ordinary people visited museum exhibits, read newspaper articles, or purchased popular colonial products like cigarettes, coffee, and chocolate. This "Official Guide" to an exhibition on Cairo held in Berlin offers an exotic look at foreign lands. Note the veiled women in the center and the pyramid and desert mosque in the background. (Travel Guide: Private Collection/Archives Charmet/The Bridgeman Art Library; Women of Algiers: Louvre, Paris/Giraudon/The Bridgeman Art Library)

Critics charged Europeans with applying a degrading double standard and failing to live up to their own noble ideals. At home, Europeans had won or were winning representative government, individual liberties, and a certain equality of opportunity. In their empires, Europeans imposed military dictatorships; forced Africans and Asians to work involuntarily, almost like slaves; and subjected them to shameless discrimination. Only by renouncing imperialism, its critics insisted, and giving captive peoples the freedoms Western society had struggled for since the French Revolution would Europeans be worthy of their traditions. These critics provided colonial peoples with a Western ideology of liberation.

> ### QUICK REVIEW

Why did the leaders of European nations come to believe that it was imperative that they control as much of Africa as possible?

CHAPTER LOCATOR | What were some of the global consequences of European industrialization?

ÉVÉNEMENTS DE CHINE

Massacre dans l'église de Moukden en Mandchourie

What was the general pattern of non-Western responses to Western expansion?

Demonizing the Boxer Rebellion

The Sunday supplement to *Le Petit Parisien*, a popular French newspaper, ran a series of gruesome front-page pictures of ferocious Boxers burning buildings, murdering priests, and slaughtering Chinese Christians. In this 1910 illustration, Boxer rebels invade a church in Mukden, Manchuria, and massacre the Christian worshippers. Whipping up European outrage about native atrocities was a prelude to harsh reprisals by the Western powers. (Mary Evans Picture Library)

TO AFRICANS AND ASIANS, Western expansion represented a profoundly disruptive assault. Everywhere it threatened traditional ruling classes, local economies, and long-standing ways of life. Christian missionaries and European secular ideologies challenged established beliefs and values. Non-Western peoples experienced a crisis of identity, one made all the more painful by the power and arrogance of the white intruders.

The Pattern of Response

Generally, the initial response of African and Asian rulers to aggressive Western expansion was to try to drive the unwelcome foreigners away. In almost all cases, however, the superior military technology of the industrialized West prevailed. Beaten in battle, many Africans and Asians concentrated on preserving their

How was massive migration an integral part of Western expansion?

How did Western imperialism change after 1880?

What was the general pattern of non-Western responses to Western expansion?

✓ LearningCurve
Check what you know.

763

cultural traditions at all costs. Others found themselves forced to reconsider their initial hostility. Some (such as Ismail of Egypt) concluded that the West was indeed superior in some ways and that it was therefore necessary to copy some European achievements. Thus it is possible to think of responses to the Western impact as a spectrum, with "traditionalists" at one end, "westernizers" or "modernizers" at the other, and many shades of opinion in between. Both before and after European domination, the struggle among these groups was often intense. With time, however, the modernizers tended to gain the upper hand.

When the power of both the traditionalists and the modernizers was thoroughly shattered by superior force, some Asians and Africans accepted imperial rule. At times, the European ruling elite received considerable support from both traditionalists (local chiefs, landowners, religious leaders) and modernizers (Western-educated professional classes and civil servants).

Nevertheless, imperial rule was in many ways an imposing edifice built on sand. Support for European rule among subjugated peoples was shallow and weak. Colonized lands were primarily peasant societies, and much of the burden of colonization fell on small farmers who fought tenaciously for some measure of autonomy. When colonists demanded extra taxes or crops, peasants played dumb and hid the extent of their harvest; when colonists asked for increased labor, peasants dragged their feet. Moreover, native people followed with greater or lesser enthusiasm the few determined personalities who came to oppose the Europeans openly. Such leaders always arose, both when Europeans ruled directly and when they manipulated native governments, for at least two basic reasons.

First, the nonconformists—the eventual anti-imperialist leaders—developed a burning desire for human dignity, economic emancipation, and political independence, all incompatible with foreign rule. Second, and somewhat ironically, potential leaders found in the Western world the ideologies underlying and justifying their protest. They discovered liberalism, with its credos of civil liberties and political self-determination. They echoed the demands of anti-imperialists in Europe and America that the West live up to its own ideals. Above all, they found themselves attracted to nationalism, which asserted that every people had the right to control its own destiny. After 1917, anti-imperialist revolt would find another European-made weapon in Lenin's version of Marxist socialism. The history of imperialism in India, Japan, and China exemplifies these broad trends.

Empire in India

India was the jewel of the British Empire, and no colonial area experienced a more profound British impact. Arriving in India on the heels of the Portuguese in the seventeenth century, the British East India Company had conquered the last independent native state by 1848. The last "traditional" response to European rule—an attempt by the indigenous ruling classes to drive the invaders out by military force—was broken in India in 1857 and 1858. Those were the years of the **Great Rebellion**, an insurrection by Muslim and Hindu mercenaries in the British army that spread throughout northern and central India before it was finally crushed. Britain then ruled India directly until Indian independence was gained in 1947.

India was ruled by the British Parliament in London and administered by a tiny, all-white civil service in India. The white elite, backed by white officers and

Great Rebellion

▶ The 1857 and 1858 insurrection by Muslim and Hindu mercenaries in the British army that spread throughout northern and central India before finally being crushed.

CHAPTER LOCATOR | What were some of the global consequences of European industrialization?

native troops, was competent and generally well disposed toward the welfare of the Indian peasant masses. Yet it practiced strict job discrimination and social segregation, and most of its members quite frankly considered Indian peoples to be racially inferior.

British women played an important part in the imperial enterprise, especially after the opening of the Suez Canal in 1869 made it much easier for civil servants and businessmen to bring their wives and children with them to India. These British families tended to live in their own separate communities, where they occupied large houses staffed with a multitude of servants. It was the wife's responsibility to manage this complex household.

A small minority of British women—many of them feminists, social reformers, or missionaries, both married and single—sought to go further and shoulder what one historian has called the "white women's burden" in India.[4] These women tried especially to improve the lives of Indian women, both Hindu and Muslim, promoting education and legislation to move them closer to the better conditions they believed Western women had attained. Their greatest success was educating some elite Hindu women who took up the cause of reform.

With British men and women sharing a sense of mission as well as strong feelings of racial and cultural superiority, the British acted energetically and introduced many desirable changes to India. Realizing that they needed well-educated Indians to serve as skilled subordinates in both the government and the army, the British established a modern system of secondary education, with all instruction in English. Thus some Indians gained excellent opportunities for economic and social advancement. High-caste Hindus, particularly quick to respond, emerged as skillful intermediaries between the British rulers and the Indian people, and soon they formed a new elite profoundly influenced by Western thought and culture. This new native elite joined British officials and businessmen to promote modern economic development, a second result of British rule. Unfortunately, the lot of the Indian masses improved little, for the profits from the increase in production went to native and British elites.

Finally, with a well-educated, English-speaking Indian bureaucracy and steps toward economic development, the British created a unified, powerful state. They placed under the same system of law and administration the different Hindu and Muslim peoples and the vanquished kingdoms of the entire subcontinent— groups that had fought each other for centuries and had been repeatedly conquered by Muslim and Mongol invaders.

Despite these achievements, the decisive reaction to European rule was the rise of nationalism among the Indian elite. No matter how anglicized and necessary a member of the educated classes became, he or she could never become the white ruler's social equal. For Indian nationalists, racial discrimination flagrantly contradicted the cherished Western concepts of human rights and equality that they had learned about in Western schools. Moreover, it was based on dictatorship, no matter how benign.

By 1885, when educated Indians came together to found the predominantly Hindu Indian National Congress, demands were increasing for the equality and self-government that Britain had already granted white-settler colonies, such as Canada and Australia. By 1907, emboldened in part by Japan's success (see the next section), a radical faction in the Indian National Congress called for Indian independence.

The Great Rebellion, 1857–1858

How was massive migration an integral part of Western expansion?

How did Western imperialism change after 1880?

What was the general pattern of non-Western responses to Western expansion?

☑ LearningCurve
Check what you know.

The Example of Japan

When Commodore Matthew Perry arrived in Tokyo in 1853, Japan was a complex feudal society. At the top stood a figurehead emperor, but real power was in the hands of a hereditary military governor, the shogun, who ruled with the help of a warrior nobility known as samurai. The intensely proud samurai were humiliated by the sudden American intrusion and the unequal treaties with Western countries that followed.

When foreign diplomats and merchants began to settle in Yokohama, radical samurai reacted with a wave of antiforeign terrorism and antigovernment assassinations that lasted from 1858 to 1863. In response, an allied fleet of American, British, Dutch, and French warships demolished key forts, further weakening the power and prestige of the shogun's government. Then in 1867, a coalition led by patriotic samurai seized control of the government and restored the political power of the emperor in the **Meiji Restoration**.

The immediate goal of the new government was to meet the foreign threat. Yet how was this to be accomplished? In a remarkable about-face, the leaders of Meiji Japan dropped their antiforeign attacks. Convinced that Western civilization was indeed superior in its military and industrial aspects, they initiated a series of measures to reform Japan along modern lines. In the broadest sense, the Meiji leaders tried to harness Western industrialization and political reform to protect their country and catch up with Europe.

In 1871, the new leaders abolished the old feudal structure of aristocratic, decentralized government and formed a strong unified state. They declared social equality; decreed freedom of travel; and created a free, competitive, government-stimulated economy. Japan began to build railroads and modern factories. The new generation adopted many principles of a free, liberal society, and, as in Europe, the resulting freedom resulted in a tremendously creative release of human energy.

Yet the overriding concern of Japan's political leadership was always to maintain a powerful state and a strong military. State leaders created a powerful modern navy and completely reorganized the army along European lines. In addition, Japan skillfully adapted the West's science and technology, particularly in industry, medicine, and education, and many Japanese studied abroad. The government paid large salaries to attract foreign experts, who were replaced by trained Japanese as soon as possible.

By 1890, when the new state was firmly established, the wholesale borrowing of the early restoration had given way to a more selective emphasis on those things foreign that were in keeping with Japanese tradition. Following the model of the German Empire, Japan established an authoritarian constitution and rejected democracy.

Japan also successfully copied the imperialism of Western society. Expansion proved that Japan was strong and cemented the nation together in a great mission. Having "opened" Korea with its own gunboat diplomacy in 1876, Japan decisively defeated China in a war over Korea in 1894 and 1895 and took Formosa (modern-day Taiwan). In the next years, Japan competed with European powers for influence and territory in China, particularly in Manchuria, where Japanese and Russian imperialism collided. In 1904, Japan attacked Russia without warning. After a bloody but victorious war, Japan emerged with a valuable foothold in

Meiji Restoration

▶ The restoration of the Japanese emperor to power in 1867, leading to the subsequent modernization of Japan.

CHAPTER LOCATOR | What were some of the global consequences of European industrialization?

China, Russia's former protectorate over Port Arthur (see Map 24.3, page 755). By 1910, with the annexation of Korea, Japan had become a major imperialist power.

Japan became the first non-Western country to use an ancient love of country to transform itself and thereby meet the many-sided challenge of Western expansion. Japan's achievement fascinated many Chinese and Vietnamese nationalists and provided patriots throughout Asia and Africa with an inspiring example of national recovery and liberation.

Toward Revolution in China

In 1860, the two-hundred-year-old Qing Dynasty in China appeared on the verge of collapse. Yet the government drew on its traditional strengths and made a surprising comeback that lasted more than thirty years.

Two factors were crucial in this reversal. First, the traditional ruling groups temporarily produced new and effective leadership. Loyal scholar-statesmen and generals quelled disturbances such as the great Tai Ping rebellion. The remarkable empress dowager Tzu Hsi (tsoo shee) governed in the name of her young son, combining shrewd insight with vigorous action to revitalize the bureaucracy.

Second, destructive foreign aggression lessened, for the Europeans had obtained their primary goal of establishing commercial and diplomatic relations. Indeed, some Europeans in the Chinese government contributed to the dynasty's recovery. Such efforts dovetailed with the dynasty's efforts to adopt some aspects of Western government and technology while maintaining traditional Chinese values and beliefs.

The parallel movement toward domestic reform and limited cooperation with the West collapsed under the blows of Japanese imperialism. The Sino-Japanese War of 1894 to 1895 and the subsequent harsh peace treaty revealed China's helplessness in the face of aggression, triggering a rush by foreign western powers for concessions and protectorates. Probably only the jealousy each nation felt toward its imperialist competitors saved China from partition. In any event, the tempo of foreign encroachment greatly accelerated after 1894.

China's precarious position after the war with Japan led to a renewed drive for fundamental reforms. In 1898, modernizers convinced the young emperor to launch a desperate **hundred days of reform** in an attempt to meet the foreign

Japan's Modernized Army

A set of woodblock prints depicting the new sights of Tokyo included this illustration of a military parade ground. The soldiers' brightly colored Western-style uniforms undoubtedly helped make this a sight worth seeing. (The Granger Collection, New York)

hundred days of reform
▶ A series of Western-style reforms launched in 1898 by the Chinese government in an attempt to meet the foreign challenge.

How was massive migration an integral part of Western expansion?

How did Western imperialism change after 1880?

What was the general pattern of non-Western responses to Western expansion?

✓ LearningCurve
Check what you know.

challenge. More radical reformers, such as the revolutionary Sun Yatsen (1866–1925), sought to overthrow the dynasty altogether and establish a republic.

The efforts at radical reform by the young emperor and his allies threatened the Qing establishment and the empress dowager Tzu Hsi, who had dominated the court for a quarter of a century. In a palace coup, she and her supporters imprisoned the emperor, rejected the reform movement, and put reactionary officials in charge.

A violent antiforeign reaction swept the country, encouraged by the Qing court and led by a secret society that foreigners called the Boxers. The conservative, patriotic Boxers blamed China's ills on foreigners. In the agony of defeat and unwanted reforms, the Boxers and other secret societies struck out at their enemies. In northeastern China, more than two hundred foreign missionaries and several thousand Chinese Christians were killed, prompting threats and demands from Western governments. The empress dowager answered by declaring war, hoping that the Boxers might relieve the foreign pressure on the government.

The imperialist response was swift and harsh. Western armies defeated the Boxers and occupied and plundered Beijing. In 1901, China was forced to accept a long list of penalties, including a heavy financial indemnity payable over forty years.

The years after this heavy defeat were ever more troubled. Anarchy and foreign influence spread as the power and prestige of the Qing Dynasty declined still further. Finally, in 1912, a spontaneous uprising toppled the Qing Dynasty. A loose coalition of revolutionaries proclaimed a Western-style republic and called for an elected parliament. The transformation of China under the impact of expanding Western society entered a new phase, and the end was not in sight.

> **QUICK REVIEW**

How and why did a nationalist independence movement develop in India?

CHAPTER LOCATOR | What were some of the global consequences of European industrialization?

CHAPTER 24
768 THE WEST AND THE WORLD

LOOKING BACK LOOKING AHEAD

In the early twentieth century, educated Europeans had good reason to believe that they were living in an age of progress. The ongoing triumphs of industry and science and the steady improvements in the standard of living beginning about 1850 were undeniable. There had also been progress in the political realm. The bitter class conflicts that culminated in the bloody civil strife of 1848 had given way in most European countries to stable nation-states with elected legislative bodies. Moreover, there had been no general European war since 1815. Only the brief, limited wars connected with German and Italian unification at midcentury had broken the peace in the European heartland.

In the global arena, peace was much more elusive. In the name of imperialism, Europeans (and North Americans) used war and the threat of war to open markets and punish foreign governments around the world. These foreign campaigns resonated with European citizens and stimulated popular nationalism. Thus imperialism and nationalism reinforced and strengthened each other in Europe, especially after 1875.

This was a dangerous development. Easy imperialist victories over weak states and poorly armed non-Western peoples encouraged excessive pride and led Europeans to underestimate the fragility of their accomplishments as well as the murderous power of their weaponry. Imperialism also made nationalism more aggressive and militaristic. At the same time that European imperialism was dividing the world, the leading European states were also dividing themselves into two opposing military alliances. Thus when the two armed camps stumbled into war in 1914, there would be a superabundance of nationalistic fervor, patriotic sacrifice, and military destruction.

ONLINE DOCUMENT PROJECT
Cecil Rhodes

What does the life of Cecil Rhodes suggest about the "great man" theory of history that was popular during this period?

You encountered Cecil Rhodes's story on page 756. Keeping the question above in mind, examine a variety of perspectives on Rhodes's legacy. *See inside the front cover to learn more.*

How was massive migration an integral part of Western expansion?

How did Western imperialism change after 1880?

What was the general pattern of non-Western responses to Western expansion?

✔ LearningCurve
Check what you know.

CHAPTER 24 STUDY GUIDE

STEP 1 GET STARTED ONLINE

LearningCurve

Now that you've read the chapter, make it stick by completing the LearningCurve activity.

STEP 2 EXPLAIN WHY IT MATTERS

Put your reading into practice. Identify each term below, and then explain why it matters in Western history.

TERM	WHO OR WHAT & WHEN	WHY IT MATTERS
neo-Europes (p. 744)		
Opium Wars (p. 746)		
gunboat diplomacy (p. 746)		
global mass migration (p. 749)		
nativism (p. 752)		
new imperialism (p. 753)		
Afrikaners (p. 754)		
Berlin Conference (p. 757)		
white man's burden (p. 760)		
Orientalism (p. 761)		
Great Rebellion (p. 764)		
Meiji Restoration (p. 766)		
hundred days of reform (p. 767)		

STEP 3 MOVE BEYOND THE BASICS

To demonstrate a more advanced understanding, fill in the chart included below with descriptions of the causes, motives, and characteristics of Western expansion before and after 1880.

	Causes and motives	Key characteristics
Western expansion before 1880		
Western expansion after 1880		

STEP 4 PUT IT ALL TOGETHER

Now, take a step back and try to explain the big picture. Remember to use specific examples from the chapter in your answers.

INDUSTRIALIZATION AND THE WORLD ECONOMY

▶ How did the West come to dominate the world economy?

▶ Compare and contrast Western economic penetration and domination of China, Japan, and Egypt.

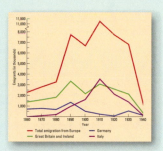

GLOBAL MIGRATION

▶ What other factors, including population pressure, contributed to European migration in the nineteenth century?

▶ Compare and contrast European and Asian migration during the nineteenth century.

WESTERN IMPERIALISM

▶ What role did Western domestic politics play in Western imperialism after 1880? How did European governments use the acquisition of colonies to their political advantage?

▶ How did non-Westerners use Western ideas and culture to resist imperialism?

MAKE CONNECTIONS

▶ Compare and contrast European overseas expansion in the sixteenth and nineteenth centuries.

▶ Compare and contrast the role of the West in the world economy in 1900 and 2000.

> IN YOUR OWN WORDS

Imagine that you must give an oral report to the class answering the following question: **How and why did the relationship between the West and the rest of the world change over the course of the nineteenth century?** What would be the most important points and why?

25

WAR AND REVOLUTION

1914–1919

> ### > What were the most significant causes and consequences of World War I? Chapter 25 examines World War I and the Russian Revolution. When the First World War began in August 1914, both peoples and governments confidently expected a short war and thought that European society would be able to go on as before. These expectations were totally mistaken. The First World War was long, indecisive, and tremendously destructive. Grand states collapsed: the Russian, Austro-Hungarian, and Ottoman Empires passed into history. The trauma of war contributed to the rise of extremist politics — in the Russian Revolution of 1917, the Bolsheviks established a radical Communist regime, and totalitarian Fascist movements gained popularity across Europe in the postwar decades. Explaining the war's causes and consequences remains one of the great challenges for historians of modern Europe.

LearningCurve
After reading the chapter, use LearningCurve to
retain what you've read.

Life in World War I. This painting by British artist Paul Nash portrays a supply road on the western front. Nash's somber palette, tiny figures, and Cubist-influenced landscape capture the devastation and anonymous violence of total war. (© Imperial War Museum, London, U.K./The Bridgeman Art Library)

> What caused the outbreak of the First World War?

> How did the First World War differ from previous wars?

> In what ways did the war transform life on the home front?

> Why did world war lead to revolution in Russia, and what was its outcome?

> In what ways was the Allied peace settlement flawed?

> What caused the outbreak of the First World War?

German Militarism The German emperor William II reviews his troops with the Italian king Victor Emmanuel in front of the royal palace in Potsdam in 1902. Aggressive militarism and popular nationalism helped pave the road to war. (SV-Bilderdienst/The Image Works)

WORLD WAR I HAD NO SINGLE MOST IMPORTANT CAUSE. Growing competition over colonies and world markets, a belligerent arms race, and a series of diplomatic crises sharpened international tensions. On the home front, new forms of populist nationalism strengthened people's unquestioning belief in "my country right or wrong," while ongoing domestic conflicts encouraged governments to pursue aggressive foreign policies in attempts to bolster national unity. All helped pave the road to war.

Growing International Conflict

The First World War began, in part, because European statesmen failed to resolve the diplomatic problems created by Germany's rise to Great Power status. After 1871, Bismarck declared that Germany was a "satisfied" power. Within Europe, he stated, Germany had no territorial ambitions and wanted only peace.

CHAPTER LOCATOR | **What caused the outbreak of the First World War?**

1914–1918
– World War I

June 28, 1914
– Serbian nationalist assassinates Archduke Francis Ferdinand

August 1914
– War begins

September 1914
– Battle of the Marne; German victories on the eastern front

October 1914
– Ottoman Empire joins the Central Powers

1915
– Italy joins the Triple Entente; German submarine sinks the *Lusitania*; Germany halts unrestricted submarine warfare

1915–1918
– Armenian genocide; German armies occupy large parts of east-central Europe

1916
– Battles of Verdun and the Somme

1916–1918
– Antiwar movement spreads throughout Europe; Arab rebellion against Ottoman Empire

1917
– Germany resumes unrestricted submarine warfare

March 1917
– February Revolution in Russia

April 1917
– United States enters the war

October–November 1917
– Battle of Caporetto

November 1917
– Bolshevik Revolution in Russia; Balfour Declaration on Jewish homeland in Palestine

1918
– Treaty of Brest-Litovsk; revolution in Germany

1918–1920
– Civil war in Russia

1919
– Treaty of Versailles; Allies invade Turkey

1923
– Treaty of Lausanne recognizes Turkish independence

But how was peace to be preserved? Bismarck's first concern was to keep France—bitter over its defeat in the Franco-Prussian War and the consequent loss of Alsace and Lorraine—diplomatically isolated and without allies. His second concern was the threat to peace posed by the enormous multinational empires of Austria-Hungary and Russia, particularly in southeastern Europe, where the waning strength of the Ottoman Empire had created a threatening power vacuum in the disputed border territories of the Balkans.

Bismarck's accomplishments in foreign policy were great, but they were only temporary. From 1871 to the late 1880s, he maintained German leadership in international affairs, and he signed a series of defensive alliances with Austria-Hungary and Russia designed to isolate France. In 1890, however, the new emperor William II dismissed Bismarck and this carefully planned alliance system began to unravel. Germany refused to renew a nonaggression pact with Russia, the center-piece of Bismarck's system, in spite of Russian willingness to do so. This fateful move prompted the establishment of a Franco-Prussian military alliance in 1894. As a result, continental Europe was divided into two rival blocs. The **Triple Alliance** of Austria, Germany, and Italy faced an increasingly hostile Dual Alliance of Russia and France, and the German general staff began secret preparations for a war on two fronts (**Map 25.1**).

Triple Alliance
▶ The alliance of Austria, Germany, and Italy. Italy left the alliance when war broke out in 1914 on the grounds that Austria had launched a war of aggression.

How did the First World War differ from previous wars?	In what ways did the war transform life on the home front?	Why did world war lead to revolution in Russia, and what was its outcome?	In what ways was the Allied peace settlement flawed?	✓ LearningCurve Check what you know.

MAP 25.1 ■ European Alliances at the Outbreak of World War I, 1914

At the start of World War I, Europe was divided into two hostile alliances: the Triple Entente of Britain, France, and Russia, and the Triple Alliance of Germany, Austria-Hungary, and Italy. Italy joined the Entente in 1915.

As rivalries deepened on the continent, Great Britain's foreign policy became increasingly crucial. After 1891, Britain was the only uncommitted Great Power. Many Germans and some Britons felt that the advanced, racially related Germanic and Anglo-Saxon peoples were natural allies. However, the good relations that had prevailed between Prussia and Great Britain since the mid-eighteenth century gave way to a bitter Anglo-German rivalry.

There were several reasons for this development. Commercial rivalry in world markets between Germany and Great Britain increased sharply in the 1890s, as Germany became a great industrial power. Germany's ambitious pursuit of colonies further threatened British interests. Above all, Germany's decision in 1900 to expand significantly its battle fleet posed a challenge to Britain's long-standing naval supremacy. In response to German expansion, British leaders prudently shored up their exposed global position with alliances and agreements. Of partic-

CHAPTER LOCATOR | **What caused the outbreak of the First World War?**

ular concern to the Germans was the Anglo-French Entente of 1904, which settled all outstanding colonial disputes between Britain and France.

Alarmed by Britain's closer ties to France, Germany's leaders decided to test the strength of their alliance. In 1905, William II declared that Morocco—where France had colonial interests—was an independent, sovereign state and demanded that Germany receive the same trading rights as France. William II insisted on an international conference to settle the Moroccan question to Germany's benefit. But his crude bullying only brought France and Britain closer together, and Germany left the conference empty-handed.

The result of the First Moroccan Crisis in 1905 was something of a diplomatic revolution. Britain, France, Russia, and even the United States began to see Germany as a potential threat. At the same time, German leaders began to see sinister plots to encircle Germany and block its development as a world power. In 1907, Russia agreed to settle its quarrels with Great Britain in Persia and Central Asia and signed the Anglo-Russian Agreement. This agreement laid the foundation of the **Triple Entente** (ahn-TAHNT), an alliance among Britain, Russia, and France.

Germany's decision to expand its navy with a large, enormously expensive fleet of big-gun battleships heightened international tensions. German patriots saw a large navy as the legitimate right of a great world power and as a source of national pride. But British leaders saw the German buildup as a military challenge.

The leading nations of Europe were now divided into two hostile camps. Britain, France, and Russia—the Triple Entente—were in direct opposition to the German-led Triple Alliance. This unfortunate treaty system only confirmed the failure of all European leaders to incorporate Bismarck's mighty empire permanently and peacefully into the international system. By 1914, many believed that war was inevitable (see Map 25.1, page 776).

Triple Entente
▶ The alliance of Great Britain, France, and Russia prior to and during the First World War.

The Mood of 1914

Diplomatic rivalries and international crises played key roles in the rush to war, but a complete understanding of the war's origins requires an account of the attitudes and convictions of Europeans around 1914.[1] Widespread militarism and nationalism encouraged leaders and citizens alike to see international relations as an arena for the testing of national power, with war if necessary.

Germany was especially famous for militarism, but military institutions played a prominent role in affairs of state and in the lives of ordinary people across Europe. In a period marked by diplomatic tensions, politicians relied on generals and military experts to help shape public policy. All the Great Powers built up their armed forces and designed mobilization plans to rush men and weapons to the field of battle. Universal conscription in most European nations exposed hundreds of thousands of young men each year to military culture and discipline.

The continent had not experienced a major conflict since the Franco-Prussian War (1870–1871), so Europeans vastly underestimated the destructive potential of modern weapons. Encouraged by the patriotic national press, many believed that war was glorious, manly, and heroic. If they expected another conflict, they thought

How did the First World War differ from previous wars?	In what ways did the war transform life on the home front?	Why did world war lead to revolution in Russia, and what was its outcome?	In what ways was the Allied peace settlement flawed?	✓ LearningCurve Check what you know.

it would be over quickly. Leading politicians and intellectuals likewise portrayed war as a test of strength that would lead to national unity and renewal. Such ideas permeated European society.

Support for military values was closely linked to a growing sense of popular nationalism, the notion that one's country was superior to all others. Nationalism drove the spiraling arms race and the struggle over colonies. Broad popular commitment to national interests above all else weakened groups that thought in terms of international communities and consequences. Inspired by nationalist beliefs, much of the population was ready for war.

Political leaders had long used foreign adventurism and diplomatic posturing to distract the people from domestic conflicts. Determined to hold onto power and frightened by rising popular movements, ruling classes across Europe were willing to gamble on diplomatic brinksmanship and even war to postpone dealing with intractable social and political conflicts. Victory promised to preserve the privileged positions of elites and rally the masses behind the national cause. The patriotic nationalism bolstered by the outbreak of war did bring unity in the short run, but the wealthy governing classes underestimated the risk of war to themselves. They had forgotten that great wars and great social revolutions very often go hand in hand.

The Outbreak of War

On June 28, 1914, Archduke Francis Ferdinand, heir to the Austro-Hungarian throne, was assassinated by Serbian revolutionaries during a state visit to the Bosnian capital of Sarajevo (sar-uh-YAY-voh). After a series of failed attempts to bomb the archduke's motorcade, Gavrilo Princip, a fanatical member of the radical group the Black Hand, shot the archduke and his wife, Sophie, in their automobile.

Princip's deed led Europe into world war. In the early years of the twentieth century, war in the Balkans seemed inevitable. The reason was simple: between 1900 and 1914, the Western powers had successfully forced the Ottoman rulers to give up their European territories. Serbs, Bulgarians, Albanians, and others now sought to establish independent nation-states, and the ethnic nationalism inspired by these changing state boundaries was destroying the Ottoman Empire and threatening Austria-Hungary (**Map 25.2**). The only questions were what kinds of wars would result and where they would lead.

By the early twentieth century, nationalism in southeastern Europe was on the rise. Independent Serbia was eager to build a state that would include all ethnic Serbs. To block Serbian expansion, Austria in 1908 annexed the territories of Bosnia and Herzegovina (hehrt-suh-goh-VEE-nuh), a region with a significant Serbian population. Serbians expressed rage but could do nothing without support from Russia, their traditional ally.

The tensions in the Balkans soon erupted into regional warfare. In the First Balkan War (1912), Serbia joined Greece and Bulgaria to attack the Ottoman Empire and then quarreled with Bulgaria over the spoils of victory. In the Second Balkan War (1913), Bulgaria attacked its former allies. Austria intervened and forced Serbia to give up Albania. After centuries, nationalism had finally destroyed the Otto-

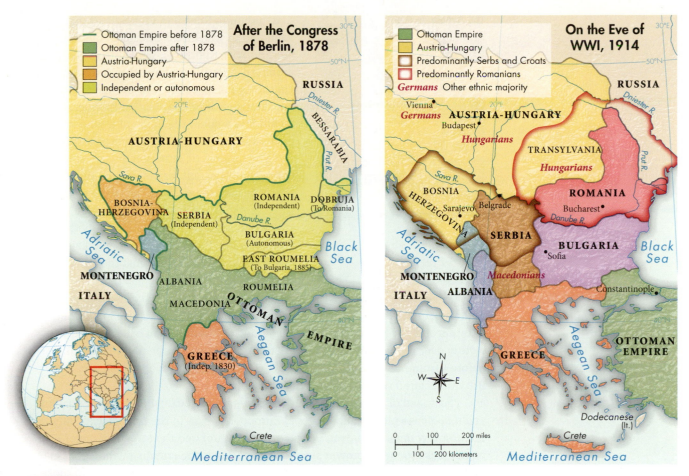

MAP 25.2 ■ The Balkans, 1878–1914

After the Congress of Berlin in 1878, the Ottoman Empire suffered large territorial losses but remained a power in the Balkans. By 1914, Ottoman control had given way to ethnic population groups that flowed across political boundaries, and growing Serbian national aspirations threatened Austria-Hungary.

man Empire in Europe. Encouraged by their success against the Ottomans, Balkan nationalists increased their demands for freedom from Austria-Hungary.

Within this complex context, the assassination of Archduke Francis Ferdinand instigated a five-week period of intense diplomatic activity that culminated in world war. The leaders of Austria-Hungary concluded that Serbia was implicated and, on July 23, Austria-Hungary gave Serbia an unconditional ultimatum that would violate Serbian sovereignty. When Serbia replied moderately but evasively, Austria mobilized its armies and declared war on Serbia on July 28.

From the beginning of the crisis, Germany pushed Austria-Hungary to confront Serbia and thus bore much responsibility for turning a little war into a world war. Emperor William II and his chancellor Theobald von Bethmann-Hollweg realized that war between Austria and Russia was likely because Russia would not stand by and watch the Austrians crush the Serbs. Yet Bethmann-Hollweg hoped

How did the First World War differ from previous wars?	In what ways did the war transform life on the home front?	Why did world war lead to revolution in Russia, and what was its outcome?	In what ways was the Allied peace settlement flawed?	✓ LearningCurve Check what you know.

The Schlieffen Plan

Planned German offensive

Neutral nations

NETHERLANDS

GERMANY

Brussels

BELGIUM

LUX.

Reims

Paris

• Metz

Rhine R.

Seine R.

Marne R.

FRANCE

0   100   200 mi.
0   100   200 km.

SWITZ.

Schlieffen Plan

▶ Failed German plan calling for a lightning attack through neutral Belgium and a quick defeat of France before turning on Russia.

that, although Russia (and its ally France) would go to war, Great Britain would remain neutral. With that hope, the German chancellor promised Austria-Hungary, that Germany would "faithfully stand by" its ally in case of war. This encouraged the prowar faction in Vienna to take a hard line against the Serbs at a time when moderation might still have limited the crisis.

The diplomatic situation quickly spiraled out of control as military plans and timetables began to dictate policy. Because the complicated mobilization plans of the Russian general staff assumed a two-front war with both Austria and Germany, Russia could not mobilize against one without mobilizing against the other. Therefore, on July 29, Tsar Nicholas II ordered full mobilization, which in effect declared war on both the empire and Germany. The German general staff had also long thought in terms of a two-front war. Their misguided **Schlieffen Plan** called for a quick victory over France after a lightning attack on Paris through neutral Belgium before turning on Russia. On August 3, German armies invaded Belgium. Great Britain declared war on Germany the following day.

The speed of the so-called July Crisis created shock, panic, and excitement, and a bellicose public helped propel Europe into war. In the final days of July and the first few days of August, massive crowds thronged the streets of major European cities. Shouting prowar slogans, the enthusiastic crowds pushed politicians and military leaders toward confrontation. Events proceeded rapidly, and those who opposed the war could do little to prevent its arrival. In a little over a month, a limited Austrian-Serbian war had become a European-wide conflict, and the First World War had begun.

> **QUICK REVIEW**

How did the alliance system limit the ability of the European powers to diffuse tensions and resolve conflicts?

CHAPTER LOCATOR | What caused the outbreak of the First World War?

780   CHAPTER 25
WAR AND REVOLUTION

How did the First World War differ from previous wars?

Writing Home from the Front

Cramped within the tight network of trenches on the western front, a British soldier writes a letter home while his compatriots rest before the next engagement. The post was typically the only connection between soldiers and their relatives, and over 28 billion pieces of mail passed between home and front on all sides during the war. (© Imperial War Museum (CO 2533))

WHEN THE GERMANS INVADED BELGIUM IN AUGUST 1914, they and everyone else thought that the war would be short and relatively painless. On the western front in France and the eastern front in Russia, the belligerent armies bogged down in a new and extremely costly kind of war, termed **total war** by German general Erich Ludendorff. At the front, total war meant lengthy, deadly battles fought with all the destructive weapons a highly industrialized society could produce. At home, national economies were geared toward the war effort. The struggle expanded outside Europe, and the Middle East, Africa, East Asia, and the United States were all brought into the maelstrom of total war.

total war

▶ A war in which distinctions between the soldiers on the battlefield and civilians at home are blurred, and where the government plans and controls economic and social life in order to provide the armies at the front with supplies and weapons.

Stalemate and Slaughter on the Western Front

In the face of the German invasion, the Belgian army slowed the German advance and then fell back in good order to join a rapidly landed British army corps near the Franco-Belgian border. At the same time, Russian armies attacked eastern Germany, forcing the Germans to transfer much-needed troops to the east.

How did the First World War differ from previous wars?	In what ways did the war transform life on the home front?	Why did world war lead to revolution in Russia, and what was its outcome?	In what ways was the Allied peace settlement flawed?	☑ LearningCurve Check what you know.

Instead of quickly capturing Paris per the Schlieffen Plan, by the end of August German soldiers were advancing slowly along an enormous front.

On September 6 the French attacked a gap in the German line at the Battle of the Marne. For three days, France threw everything into the attack. Finally, the Germans fell back. France had been saved (**Map 25.3**). With the armies stalled, both sides dug in. By November 1914, an unbroken line of four hundred miles of defensive trenches extended from the Belgian coast through northern France and on to the Swiss frontier. The cost in lives of **trench warfare** was staggering. For ordinary soldiers, conditions in the trenches were atrocious. Recently invented weapons, the products of an industrial age, made battle impersonal, traumatic, and extremely deadly. The machine gun, hand grenades, poison gas, flamethrowers, long-range artillery, the airplane, and the tank all favored the defense, increased casualty rates, and revolutionized the practice of war.

The leading generals of the combatant nations struggled to understand trench warfare. For four years, they repeated the same mistakes, mounting massive offensives designed to achieve decisive breakthroughs, failing again and again. In 1916, the unsuccessful German campaign against Verdun cost some 700,000 lives on both sides and ended with the combatants in their original positions. In hard-fought battles on all fronts, millions of young men were wounded or died for no real gain.

The Battle of the Somme, a great British offensive undertaken in the summer of 1916 in northern France, exemplified the horrors of trench warfare. The battle began with a weeklong heavy artillery bombardment on the German line, intended to cut the barbed wire fortifications, decimate the enemy trenches, and prevent the Germans from making an effective defense. On July 1, the British went "over the top," climbing out of the trenches and moving into no-man's land toward the German lines.

During the bombardment, the Germans had fled to their dugouts—underground shelters dug deep into the trenches. As the British soldiers neared the German lines and the shelling stopped, the Germans emerged from their bunkers, set up their machine guns, and mowed down the approaching troops. In many places, the wire had not been cut by the bombardment, so the attackers, held in place by the wire, made easy targets. About 20,000 British men were killed and 40,000 more were wounded on just the first day. The battle lasted until November, and in the end the British did push the Germans back—a whole seven miles. Some 420,000 British, 200,000 French, and 600,000 Germans were killed or wounded defending an insignificant piece of land.

The anonymous, almost unreal qualities of high-tech warfare made its way into the art and literature of the time. In each combatant nation, artists and writers sought to portray the nightmarish quality of total war. Paintings by artists like Paul Nash, whose painting *Men in Road* opens this chapter, or the poems of the famous British "trench poets," may do more to capture the experience of the war than contemporary photos or the dry accounts of historians.

The Widening War

On the eastern front, the slaughter did not immediately degenerate into trench warfare, and the fighting was dominated by Germany. The Germans repulsed the initial Russian attacks, counterattacked, and by 1915 the eastern front had

trench warfare

▶ A type of fighting used in World War I behind rows of trenches, mines, and barbed wire; the cost in lives was staggering and the gains in territory minimal.

The Battle of the Somme, 1916

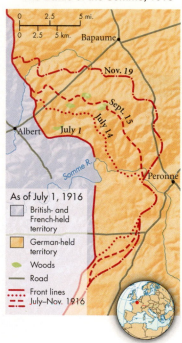

Triple Entente and allies
Central Powers and allies
Greatest extent of territory gained by Germany-Austria
German submarine war zone
Neutral nations
Farthest advance by Central Powers on date marked
Farthest advance by Entente Powers on date marked
British naval blockade
Major battle

0   200   400 miles
0   200   400 kilometers

NORWAY
SWEDEN
FINLAND
North Sea
Petrograd (St. Petersburg)
Helsinki
DENMARK
Jutland 1916
ESTONIA
Riga
LATVIA
Baltic Sea
COURLAND
Moscow
Farthest Russian advance, 1914
LITHUANIA
Vilnius
RUSSIA
Kiel
Aug. 1914
E. PRUSSIA
Masurian Lakes 1914
BELARUS
GREAT BRITAIN
NETHERLANDS
GERMANY
Berlin
Tannenberg 1914
Armistice line, December 1917
Lusitania 1915
London
Elbe R.
Vistula R.
KINGDOM OF POLAND (Russia)
Warsaw
Brest-Litovsk
March 1918
Treaty of Brest-Litovsk, March 1918
BELGIUM
1914
Rhine R.
LUXEMBOURG
Kiev
Dnieper R.
Armistice line, November 1918
ALSACE-LORRAINE
GALICIA
May 1915
Farthest German military advance
Western front
Seine R.
SWITZERLAND
Vienna
AUSTRIA-HUNGARY
FRANCE
Bordeaux
Garonne R.
Loire R.
Aug. 1917
Mar.
Po R.
Caporetto 1917
Budapest
TRANSYLVANIA
Black Sea
March 1918
Caspian Sea
Italian front
ROMANIA
Bucharest
Danube R.
Rhône R.
Adriatic Sea
Sarajevo
SERBIA
MONTENEGRO
BULGARIA
SPAIN
Corsica
ITALY
Elba
Rome
1917–1918
Constantinople
Nov. 1917
PERSIA
Balearic Is.
Sardinia
ALBANIA
1916
1915
Dardanelles
OTTOMAN EMPIRE
Mar.
Ebro R.
Middle Eastern front
IRAQ
Al Kut 1915 1916 1917
Balkan front
GREECE
Gallipoli 1915
Oct. 1918
Baghdad
Basra
ALGERIA (Fr.)
Tunis
TUNISIA (Fr.)
Sicily
Malta
Crete
Mediterranean Sea
Cyprus
SYRIA
Damascus
LIBYA (It.)
EGYPT (Gr. Br.)
Red Sea
Al Aqabah 1917

N W E S

MAP 25.3 ■ **World War I in Europe and the Middle East, 1914–1918**

Trench warfare on the western front was concentrated in Belgium and northern France (inset), while the war in the east encompassed an enormous territory.

The Western Front

NETHERLANDS
Dover
Ostend
FLANDERS
Ghent
Antwerp
Ruhr R.
Ypres
Calais
Brussels
Schelde R.
Louvain
Liège
Cologne
English Channel
BELGIUM
Rhine R.
Armistice line, November 1918
Arras
Somme R.
ARDENNES
Meuse R.
Coblenz
Amiens
St. Quentin
Somme
Sedan
LUX.
GERMANY
Compiègne
Belleau Wood
Reims
Aisne R.
ARGONNE FOREST
LORRAINE
Mosel R.
Marne I
Marne R.
Verdun
St. Mihiel
Saar R.
Paris
Seine R.
Marne II
Château-Thierry
Châlons-sur-Marne
Nancy
Strasbourg
FRANCE
Epinal
ALSACE
Mulhouse
Basel
SWITZ.

0   25   50 miles
0   25   50 kilometers

Germany, 1914
Greatest extent of territory gained by Germany, Sept. 1914
Front at beginning of 1915
German offensive, Summer 1918
Major battle

stabilized in Germany's favor. A staggering 2.5 million Russian soldiers had been killed, wounded, or captured. German armies occupied huge swaths of the Russian empire in central Europe. Yet Russia continued to fight, marking another failure of the Schlieffen Plan.

To govern these occupied territories, the Germans installed a vast military bureaucracy. Anti-Slavic prejudice dominated the mind-set of the occupiers, who viewed the local Slavs as savages and ethnic "mongrels." About one-third of the civilian population was killed or became refugees under this brutal occupation. In the long run, the German state hoped to turn these territories into German possessions, a chilling forerunner of Nazi policies in World War II.[2]

The changing tides of war brought neutral countries into the war (see Map 25.3, page 783). Italy, a member of the Triple Alliance since 1882, had declared its neutrality in 1914 on the grounds that Austria had launched a war of aggression. Then in May 1915, Italy switched sides to join the Triple Entente in return for promises of Austrian territory. The war along the Italian-Austrian front cost some 600,000 Italian lives.

In October 1914, the Ottoman Empire joined Austria and Germany, by then known as the Central Powers. The following September, Bulgaria followed suit in order to settle old scores with Serbia. The Balkans, with the exception of Greece, were occupied by the Central Powers.

The entry of the Ottomans carried the war into the Middle East. Heavy fighting between the Ottomans and the Russians enveloped the Armenians, who lived on both sides of the border. When in 1915 some Armenians welcomed Russian armies as liberators, the Ottoman government, with German support, ordered a mass deportation of its Armenian citizens from their homeland. In this early example of modern ethnic cleansing, about 1 million Armenians died from murder, starvation, and disease.

In 1915, at the Battle of Gallipoli, British forces tried and failed to take the Dardanelles and Constantinople from the Ottoman Turks. The ten-month-long battle cost the Ottomans 300,000 and the British 265,000 men killed, wounded, or missing.

The British were more successful at inciting the Arabs to revolt against their Ottoman rulers. They bargained with the foremost Arab leader, Hussein ibn-Ali (1856–1931). Controlling much of the Ottoman Empire's territory along the Red Sea, an area known as the Hejaz (see Map 25.5, page 803), Hussein managed in 1915 to win vague British commitments for an independent Arab kingdom. In 1916, Hussein rebelled against the Turks, proclaiming himself king of the Arabs. Hussein was aided by the British officer T. E. Lawrence, who in 1917 helped lead Arab soldiers in a successful guerrilla war against the Turks on the Arabian peninsula.

The British enjoyed similar victories in the Ottoman province of Iraq. British troops occupied Basra in 1914 and captured Baghdad in 1917. In September 1918, British armies and their Arab allies rolled into Syria. This offensive culminated in the entry of Hussein's son Faisal (FIE-suhl) into Damascus. Arab patriots in Syria and Iraq now

The Armenian Genocide, 1915–1918

CHAPTER LOCATOR | What caused the outbreak of the First World War?

expected a large, unified Arab nation-state to rise from the dust of the Ottoman collapse—though they would later be disappointed by the Western powers (see page 801).

The war spread to East Asia and colonial Africa as well. Japan declared war on Germany in 1914, seized Germany's Pacific and East Asian colonies, and used the opportunity to expand its influence in China. In Africa, colonial subjects of the British and French generally supported the Allied powers and helped local British and French commanders take over German colonies. More than a million Africans and Asians served in the various armies of the warring powers. Large numbers of troops came from the British Commonwealth, a voluntary association of former British colonies.

After three years of refusing to play a fighting role, the United States was finally drawn into the expanding conflict. American intervention grew out of the war at sea and general sympathy for the Triple Entente. At the beginning of the war, Britain and France established a naval blockade to strangle the Central Powers. In early 1915, Germany retaliated with attacks on supply ships from a new weapon, the submarine.

In May 1915, a German submarine sank the British passenger liner *Lusitania*, claiming more than 1,000 lives, among them 139 U.S. citizens. President Woodrow Wilson protested vigorously. To avoid almost-certain war with the United States, Germany halted its submarine warfare for almost two years.

Early in 1917, the German military command—hoping that improved submarines could starve Britain into submission before the United States could come to its rescue—resumed unrestricted submarine warfare. This gamble failed, and the United States declared war on Germany in April of that year. Eventually the United States tipped the balance in favor of the British, French, and their allies.

QUICK REVIEW

Why did the fighting on the Western Front result in so many casualties and so little military gain?

| How did the First World War differ from previous wars? | In what ways did the war transform life on the home front? | Why did world war lead to revolution in Russia, and what was its outcome? | In what ways was the Allied peace settlement flawed? | ☑ LearningCurve Check what you know. |

In what ways did the war transform life on the home front?

Women Factory Workers Building a Truck, London, 1917

Millions of men on all sides were drafted to fight in the war, creating a serious labor shortage. When women left home to fill jobs formerly reserved for men, they challenged traditional gender roles. (© Hulton-Deutsch Collection/Corbis)

THE WAR'S IMPACT ON CIVILIANS was no less massive than it was on the men crouched in the trenches. Total war encouraged the growth of state bureaucracies, transformed the lives of ordinary women and men, and by the end inspired mass antiwar protest movements.

Mobilizing for Total War

In August 1914, many people greeted the outbreak of hostilities enthusiastically. Yet by mid-October, generals and politicians had begun to realize that victory would require more than patriotism. Heavy casualties and the stalemate meant each combatant country experienced a desperate need for men and weapons. To keep the war machine moving, national leaders aggressively intervened in society and the economy.

New government ministries mobilized soldiers and armaments, established rationing programs, and provided care for war widows and wounded veterans. Censorship offices controlled news about the course of the war. Government planning boards temporarily abandoned free-market capitalism and set mandatory production goals and limits on wages and prices.

Germany went furthest in developing a planned economy to wage total war. As soon as war began, the Jewish industrialist Walter Rathenau convinced the government to set up the War Raw Materials Board to ration and distribute raw

CHAPTER LOCATOR | What caused the outbreak of the First World War?

CHAPTER 25
WAR AND REVOLUTION

786

materials. Under Rathenau's direction, every useful material was inventoried and rationed. Food was rationed in accordance with physical need.

Following the Battles of Verdun and the Somme in 1916, German military leaders forced the Reichstag to accept the Auxiliary Service Law, which required all males between seventeen and sixty to work only at jobs considered critical to the war effort. Women also worked in war factories, mines, and steel mills. While war production increased, people lived on little more than one thousand calories a day.

After 1917, Germany's leaders ruled by decree. Generals Paul von Hindenburg and Erich Ludendorff drove Chancellor Bethmann-Hollweg from office. With the support of the newly formed ultraconservative Fatherland Party, the generals established a military dictatorship. Hindenburg called for the ultimate mobilization for total war. Germany could win, he said, only "if all the treasures of our soil that agriculture and industry can produce are used exclusively for the conduct of War."[3] Thus, in Germany, total war led to the establishment of history's first "totalitarian" society, a model for future National Socialists, or Nazis.

Only Germany was directly ruled by a military government, yet leaders in all the belligerent nations took power from parliaments, suspended civil liberties, and ignored democratic procedures. After 1915, the British Ministry of Munitions organized private industry to produce for the war, allocated labor, set wage and price rates, and settled labor disputes. In France, a weakened parliament met without public oversight, and the courts jailed pacifists who dared criticize the state. Once the United States entered the war, new federal agencies regulated industry, labor relations, and agricultural production, while the Espionage and Sedition Acts weakened civil liberties.

The Social Impact

The social changes wrought by total war were no less profound than the economic impacts, though again there were important national variations. National conscription sent millions of men to the front, exposing many to foreign lands for the first time in their lives. The insatiable needs of the military created a tremendous demand for workers, making jobs readily available. This situation brought momentous changes.

The need for workers meant greater power and prestige for labor unions. Unions cooperated with war governments in return for real participation in important decisions. The entry of labor leaders and unions into policymaking councils paralleled the entry of socialist leaders into war governments. Both reflected a new government openness to the needs of those at the bottom of society.

The role of women changed dramatically. Women moved into skilled industrial jobs long considered men's work. Women became highly visible in public — as munitions workers, bank tellers, and mail carriers, and even as police officers, firefighters, and farm laborers. Women also served as auxiliaries and nurses at the front. (See "Individuals in Society: Vera Brittain," page 788.)

The war expanded the range of women's activities and helped change attitudes about proper gender roles, but the long-term results were mixed. At the war's end, millions of demobilized soldiers demanded their jobs back, and governments forced women out of the workplace. Thus, women's employment gains

| How did the First World War differ from previous wars? | **In what ways did the war transform life on the home front?** | Why did world war lead to revolution in Russia, and what was its outcome? | In what ways was the Allied peace settlement flawed? | ☑ LearningCurve Check what you know. |

787

Although the Great War upended millions of lives, it struck Europe's young people with the greatest force. For Vera Brittain (1893–1970), as for so many in her generation, the war became life's defining experience, which she captured forever in her famous autobiography, *Testament of Youth* (1933).

Brittain grew up in a wealthy business family in northern England, bristling at small-town conventions and discrimination against women. Very close to her brother Edward, two years her junior, Brittain read voraciously and dreamed of being a successful writer. Finishing boarding school and overcoming her father's objections, she prepared for Oxford's rigorous entry exams and won a scholarship to its women's college. Brittain also fell in love with Roland Leighton, an equally brilliant student from a literary family and her brother's best friend. All three, along with two other close friends, Victor Richardson and Geoffrey Thurlow, confidently prepared to enter Oxford in late 1914.

When war suddenly loomed in July 1914, Brittain shared with millions of Europeans a surge of patriotic support for her government, a prowar enthusiasm she later downplayed in her published writings. She wrote in her diary that her "great fear" was that England would declare its neutrality and commit the "grossest treachery" toward France.* She supported Leighton's decision to enlist, agreeing with his glamorous view of war as "very ennobling and very beautiful." Later, exchanging anxious letters with Leighton in France in 1915, Brittain began to see the conflict in personal, human terms. She wondered if any victory or defeat could be worth her fiancé's life.

Struggling to quell her doubts, Brittain redoubled her commitment to England's cause and volunteered as an army nurse. For the next three years, she served with distinction in military hospitals in London, Malta, and northern France, repeatedly torn between the vision of noble sacrifice and the reality of human tragedy. Having lost sexual inhibitions while caring for mangled male bodies, she longed to consummate her love with Leighton. Awaiting his return on leave on Christmas Day in 1915, she was greeted instead with a telegram: he had been killed two days before.

Leighton's death was the first of several devastating blows that eventually overwhelmed Brittain's idealistic patriotism. In 1917, Thurlow and then Richardson died from gruesome wounds. In early 1918, as the last great German offensive covered the floors of her war-zone hospital with maimed and dying German prisoners, the bone-weary Brittain felt a common humanity and saw only more victims. A few weeks later her brother Edward — her last hope — died in action.

Vera Brittain was marked forever by her wartime experiences. (Vera Brittain fonds, William Ready Division of Archives and Research Collections, McMaster University Library)

When the war ended, she was, she said, a "complete automaton," with her "deepest emotions paralyzed if not dead."

Returning to Oxford and finishing her studies, Brittain gradually recovered. She formed a deep, restorative friendship with another talented woman writer, Winifred Holtby; published novels and articles; and became a leader in the feminist campaign for gender equality. She also married and had children. But her wartime memories were always with her. Finally, Brittain succeeded in coming to grips with them in *Testament of Youth*, her powerful antiwar autobiography. The unflinching narrative spoke to the experiences of an entire generation and became a runaway bestseller. Above all, Brittain captured the contradictory character of the war, in which millions of young people found excitement, courage, and common purpose but succeeded only in destroying their lives with their superhuman efforts and futile sacrifices. Becoming increasingly committed to pacifism, Brittain opposed England's entry into World War II.

QUESTIONS FOR ANALYSIS

1. What were Brittain's initial feelings toward the war? How and why did they change as the conflict continued?
2. Why did Brittain volunteer as a nurse, as many women did? How might wartime nursing have influenced women of her generation?
3. In portraying the contradictory character of World War I for Europe's youth, was Brittain describing the character of all modern warfare?

LaunchPad

ONLINE DOCUMENT PROJECT

What role did wartime propaganda play in encouraging women like Vera Brittain to get involved in the war effort? Analyze a variety of propaganda posters calling for women to serve as military nurses. Then complete a writing assignment based on the evidence and details from this chapter. *See inside the front cover to learn more.*

*Quoted in the excellent study P. Berry and M. Bostridge, *Vera Brittain: A Life* (London: Virago Press, 2001), p. 59; additional quotations are from pp. 80 and 136.

were mostly temporary. As a result of women's many-sided war effort, the United States, Britain, Germany, Poland, and other countries granted women the right to vote immediately after the war, but women's rights movements faded in the 1920s and 1930s.

To some extent, the war promoted greater social equality, blurring class distinctions and lessening the gap between rich and poor. This blurring was most apparent in Great Britain, where the bottom third of the population generally lived better than they ever had because the poorest gained most from the severe shortage of labor. Elsewhere, greater equality was reflected in full employment, distribution of scarce rations according to physical needs, and a sharing of hardships. In general, despite some war profiteering, European society became more uniform and egalitarian.

Growing Political Tensions

During the first two years of war, patriotic nationalism and belief in a just cause united peoples behind their national leaders. Each government used rigorous censorship and crude propaganda to bolster popular support. (See "Picturing the Past: Wartime Propaganda Posters," page 790.) Patriotic posters and slogans, slanted news, and biased editorials inflamed national hatreds, helped control public opinion, and encouraged soldiers to keep fighting.

Political and social tensions re-emerged, however, and by the spring of 1916 ordinary people were beginning to crack under the strain of total war. Strikes and protest marches over war-related burdens and shortages flared up on every home front. On May 1, 1916, several thousand demonstrators in Berlin heard the radical socialist leader Karl Liebknecht (1871–1919) attack the costs of the war effort. In France, Georges Clemenceau (zhorzh kleh-muhn-SOH) (1841–1929) established a virtual dictatorship, arrested strikers, and jailed without trial journalists and politicians who dared to suggest a compromise peace with Germany.

In April 1916, Irish republican nationalists renewed their rebellion against British rule. During the great Easter Rising, armed republican militias took over parts of Dublin and proclaimed an independent Irish Republic. After a week of bitter fighting, British troops crushed the rebels and executed their leaders. Though the republicans were defeated, the Rising set the stage for the success of the nationalist Sinn Fein Party and a full-scale civil war for Irish independence in the early 1920s.

On all sides, soldiers' morale began to decline. Numerous French units refused to fight after the disastrous French offensive of May 1917. Facing defeat, wretched conditions at the front, and growing hopelessness, Russian soldiers deserted in droves, providing fuel for the Russian Revolution of 1917. In the massive battles of 1916 and 1917, the British armies had been "bled dry." Only the promised arrival of fresh troops from the United States stiffened the resolve of the allies.

The strains were even worse for the Central Powers. In October 1916, a young socialist assassinated the chief minister of Austria-Hungary. In spite of absolute censorship, political dissatisfaction and conflicts among nationalities grew. By April 1917, the Austro-Hungarian people and army were exhausted. Another winter of war would bring revolution and disintegration.

Germans likewise suffered immensely. The British naval blockade greatly limited food imports, and the resulting scarcity had horrific results: some 750,000

How did the First World War differ from previous wars?

In what ways did the war transform life on the home front?

Why did world war lead to revolution in Russia, and what was its outcome?

In what ways was the Allied peace settlement flawed?

✔ LearningCurve
Check what you know.

789

Wartime Propaganda Posters

This famous French propaganda poster from 1918 (left) proclaims "They shall not pass" and expresses the French determination to hold back the German invaders at any cost. The American recruitment poster from 1917 (right) encourages "fighting men" to "join the Navy." (French poster: Private Collection/© Galerie Bilderwelt/The Bridgeman Art Library; Join the Navy: Private Collection/© Galerie Bilderwelt/The Bridgeman Art Library)

> PICTURING THE PAST

ANALYZING THE IMAGE: How would you describe the soldier and sailor pictured on these posters? What messages about the war do the posters convey?

CONNECTIONS: The "They shall not pass" poster was created after France had been at war for four years, while the naval recruitment poster came out before American troops were actively engaged overseas. How might the country of origin and the date of publication have affected the messages conveyed?

German civilians starved to death. For the rest, heavy rationing of everyday goods undermined morale. A growing minority of moderate socialists in the Reichstag gave voice to popular discontent when they called for a compromise "peace without annexations or reparations."

Such a peace was unthinkable for the Fatherland Party. Yet Germany's rulers faced growing unrest, strikes, and political defections. Thus Germany, like its ally Austria-Hungary (and its enemy France), was beginning to crack in 1917. Yet it was Russia that collapsed first and saved the Central Powers—for a time.

> ## QUICK REVIEW

What significant changes did World War I bring to the lives of European civilians?

CHAPTER LOCATOR | What caused the outbreak of the First World War?

Lenin Rallies Soldiers Lenin, known for his fiery speeches, addresses Red Army soldiers in Moscow in the midst of the Russian civil war, in May 1920. Leon Trotsky, the leader of the Red Army, stands on the podium stairs to the right. (Time Life Pictures/Getty Images)

THE RUSSIAN REVOLUTION OF 1917 grew out of the crisis of the First World War and was one of modern history's most momentous events. For some, the revolution was Marx's socialist vision come true; for others, it was the triumph of a Communist dictatorship. To all, it presented a radically new prototype of state and society.

The Fall of Imperial Russia

Like its allies and enemies, Russia had embraced war with patriotic enthusiasm in 1914. Enthusiasm for the war soon waned, however, as better-equipped German armies inflicted terrible losses. Russia's battered peasant army nonetheless continued to fight, and Russia moved toward full mobilization on the home front. The government set up special committees to coordinate defense, industry, transportation, and agriculture. These efforts improved the military situation, but overall Russia mobilized less effectively than the other combatants.

| How did the First World War differ from previous wars? | In what ways did the war transform life on the home front? | **Why did world war lead to revolution in Russia, and what was its outcome?** | In what ways was the Allied peace settlement flawed? | ☑ LearningCurve Check what you know. |

One problem was weak leadership. A kindly but narrow-minded aristocrat, Tsar Nicholas II (r. 1894 – 1917) distrusted the publicly elected Duma and resisted popular involvement in government, relying instead on the old bureaucracy. In September 1915, parties ranging from conservative to moderate socialist formed the Progressive bloc, which called for a completely new government responsible to the Duma instead of the tsar. In answer, Nicholas temporarily adjourned the Duma. The tsar then announced that he was traveling to the front in order to lead Russia's armies, leaving the government in the hands of his wife, Tsarina Alexandra.

His departure was a fatal turning point. In his absence, Tsarina Alexandra arbitrarily dismissed loyal political advisers. She turned to her court favorite, the disreputable and unpopular Rasputin, an uneducated Siberian preacher. In a desperate attempt to right the situation, three members of the high aristocracy murdered Rasputin in December 1916. The ensuing scandal further undermined support for the tsarist government.

Imperial Russia had entered a terminal crisis. Tens of thousands of soldiers deserted. By early 1917, the cities were wracked by shortages, and the economy was breaking down. In March, violent street demonstrations broke out in Petrograd (formerly St. Petersburg), spread to the factories, and then engulfed the city. From the front, the tsar ordered the army to open fire on the protesters, but the soldiers refused to shoot and joined the revolutionary crowd instead. The Duma declared a provisional government on March 12, 1917. Three days later, Nicholas abdicated.

The Provisional Government

February Revolution

▶ Unplanned uprisings accompanied by violent street demonstrations begun in March 1917 (old Russian calendar February) in Petrograd, Russia, that led to the abdication of the tsar and the establishment of a provisional government.

The **February Revolution,** then, was the result of an unplanned uprising of hungry, angry people in the capital, but it was eagerly accepted throughout the country. (The name of the revolution matches the Russian calendar, which used a different dating system.) After generations of autocracy, the provisional government established equality before the law; freedom of religion, speech, and assembly; and the right of unions to organize and strike.

Yet both liberals and moderate socialist leaders rejected these broad political reforms. Though the Russian people were sick of fighting, the new leaders would not take Russia out of the war. A new government formed in May 1917 included the socialist Alexander Kerensky, who became prime minister in July. For the patriotic Kerensky, as for other moderate socialists, the continuation of war was still a national duty. Human suffering and war-weariness grew, testing the limited strength of the provisional government.

Petrograd Soviet

▶ A huge, fluctuating mass meeting of two to three thousand workers, soldiers, and socialist intellectuals modeled on the revolutionary soviets of 1905.

From its first day, the provisional government had to share power with a formidable rival—the **Petrograd Soviet** (or council) of Workers' and Soldiers' Deputies. The Petrograd Soviet comprised two to three thousand workers, soldiers, and socialist intellectuals. Seeing itself as a true grassroots product of revolutionary democracy, the Soviet acted as a parallel government. It issued its own radical orders, weakening the authority of the provisional government.

The most famous edict of the Petrograd Soviet was Army Order No. 1, issued in May 1917, which stripped officers of their authority and placed power in the hands of elected committees of common soldiers. The order led to a collapse of army discipline.

In July 1917, the provisional government ordered a poorly considered summer offensive against the Germans. The campaign was a miserable failure, and desertions mounted. By the summer of 1917, Russia was descending into anarchy. It was an unparalleled opportunity for the most radical and talented of Russia's many revolutionary leaders, Vladimir Ilyich Lenin (1870–1924).

Lenin and the Bolshevik Revolution

A pragmatic and flexible thinker, Lenin updated Marx's revolutionary philosophy to address existing conditions in Russia. Three interrelated concepts were central for Lenin. First, he stressed that only violent revolution could destroy capitalism. Second, Lenin argued that, under certain conditions, a Communist revolution was possible even in a predominantly agrarian country like Russia. Peasants, who were numerous, poor, and exploited, could take the place of Marx's traditional working class in the coming revolutionary conflict.

Third, Lenin believed that the possibility of revolution was determined more by human leadership than by historical laws. He called for a highly disciplined workers' party strictly controlled by a small, dedicated elite of intellectuals and professional revolutionaries. This elite would not stop until revolution brought it to power.

Other Russian Marxists challenged Lenin's ideas. At meetings of the Russian Social Democratic Labor Party in London in 1903, matters came to a head. Lenin demanded a small, disciplined, elitist party dedicated to Communist revolution, while his opponents wanted a more democratic, reformist party with mass membership. The Russian Marxists split into two rival factions. Lenin called his camp the **Bolsheviks**.

Unlike other socialists, Lenin had not rallied around the national flag in 1914. Observing events from neutral Switzerland, where he lived in exile, Lenin viewed the war as a product of imperialist rivalries and an opportunity for socialist revolution. After the February Revolution of 1917, the German government provided Lenin with safe passage across Germany and back into Russia. The Germans hoped Lenin would undermine the sagging war effort of the provisional government. They were not disappointed.

Arriving in Petrograd on April 3, Lenin attacked at once. He rejected all cooperation with the provisional government. His slogans were radical in the extreme: "All power to the soviets"; "All land to the peasants"; "Stop the war now." Lenin was a superb tactician. His promises of "Peace, Land, and Bread" spoke to the expectations of suffering soldiers, peasants, and workers and earned the Bolsheviks substantial popular support. The moment for revolution was at hand.

KEY EVENTS OF THE RUSSIAN REVOLUTION

August 1914	Russia enters World War I
1916–1917	Tsarist government in crisis
March 1917	February Revolution; establishment of provisional government; tsar abdicates
April 1917	Lenin returns from exile
July 1917	Bolshevik attempt to seize power fails
October 1917	Bolsheviks gain a majority in the Petrograd Soviet
November 6–7, 1917	Bolsheviks seize power; Lenin named head of new Communist government
March 1918	Treaty of Brest-Litovsk; Trotsky becomes head of the Red Army
1918–1920	Civil war
1920	Civil war ends; Lenin and Bolshevik-Communists take control of Russia

Bolsheviks
► Lenin's radical, revolutionary arm of the Russian party of Marxist socialism, which successfully installed a dictatorial socialist regime in Russia.

| How did the First World War differ from previous wars? | In what ways did the war transform life on the home front? | **Why did world war lead to revolution in Russia, and what was its outcome?** | In what ways was the Allied peace settlement flawed? | ✓ LearningCurve Check what you know. |

793

The Radicalization of the Russian Army Russian soldiers inspired by the Bolshevik cause carry banners with Marxist slogans calling for revolution and democracy, around July 1917. One reads "All Power to the Proletariat," a telling response to the provisional government's failure to pull Russia out of the war. Sick of defeat and wretched conditions at the front, the tsar's troops welcomed Lenin's promises of "Peace, Land, and Bread" and were enthusiastic participants in the Russian Revolution. (Hulton Archive/Getty Images)

Trotsky and the Seizure of Power

Throughout the summer, the Bolsheviks greatly increased their popular support, and in October the Bolsheviks gained a fragile majority in the Petrograd Soviet. Now Lenin's supporter Leon Trotsky (1879–1940) brilliantly executed the Bolshevik seizure of power. Painting a vivid but untruthful picture of German and counter-revolutionary plots, Trotsky convinced the Petrograd Soviet to form a special military-revolutionary committee in October and make him its leader. Thus military power in the capital passed into Bolshevik hands. On the night of November 6, militants from Trotsky's committee joined with trusted Bolshevik soldiers to seize government buildings in Petrograd and arrest members of the provisional government. Then they went on to the Congress of Soviets, where a Bolshevik majority declared that all power had passed to the soviets and named Lenin head of the new government.

The Bolsheviks came to power for three key reasons. First, by late 1917, democracy had given way to anarchy: power was there for those who would

CHAPTER LOCATOR | What caused the outbreak of the First World War?

take it. Second, in Lenin and Trotsky, the Bolsheviks had an utterly determined and superior leadership, which both the tsarist and the provisional governments lacked. Third, Bolshevik policies appealed to ordinary Russians. Exhausted by war and weary of tsarist autocracy, they were eager for radical changes.

Dictatorship and Civil War

The Bolsheviks' truly monumental accomplishment was not taking power, but keeping it. Over the next four years, they conquered the chaos they had helped create and began to build a Communist society.

The Bolsheviks promised that a freely elected Constituent Assembly would draw up a new constitution. But free elections in November produced a stunning setback: the Bolsheviks won only 23 percent of the elected delegates. The Socialist Revolutionary Party—the peasants' party—had a clear plurality with about 40 percent of the vote. After the Constituent Assembly met for one day, however, Bolshevik soldiers acting under Lenin's orders disbanded it. By January 1918, Lenin had moved to establish a one-party state.

Lenin acknowledged that Russia had effectively lost the war with Germany and that the only realistic goal was peace at any price. That price was very high. Germany demanded that the Soviet government give up all its western territories.

At first, Lenin's fellow Bolsheviks refused to accept such great territorial losses. But when German armies resumed their unopposed march into Russia in February 1918, Lenin had his way. A third of old Russia's population was sliced away by the **Treaty of Brest-Litovsk**, signed with Germany in March 1918. With peace, Lenin escaped the disaster of continued war and could pursue his goal of absolute power within Russia.

The peace treaty and the abolition of the Constituent Assembly inspired armed opposition to the Bolshevik regime. The officers of the old army organized the so-called White opposition to the Bolsheviks in southern Russia, Ukraine, Siberia, and the area west of Petrograd. The Whites came from many social groups and were united only by their hatred of communism and the Bolsheviks—the Reds.

By the summer of 1918, Russia was in a full-fledged civil war, and by the end of the year White armies were on the attack. In October 1919, they closed in on central Russia from three sides, and it appeared they might triumph. They did not.

Lenin and the Red Army beat back the counter-revolutionary White armies for several reasons. Most important, the Bolsheviks had quickly developed a better army. Once again, Trotsky's leadership was decisive. Trotsky re-established strict discipline and the draft. Soldiers deserting or disobeying an order were summarily shot. Moreover, Trotsky made effective use of former tsarist army officers, who were actively recruited and given unprecedented powers over their troops. Trotsky's disciplined and effective fighting force repeatedly defeated the Whites in the field.

Ironically, foreign military intervention helped the Bolsheviks. For a variety of reasons, but primarily to stop the spread of communism, the Western Allies sent troops to support the White armies. Yet their efforts were limited and halfhearted. By 1919, with the Great War over, Westerners were sick of war, and few politicians wanted to get involved in a new military crusade. Allied intervention failed to offer effective aid, though it did permit the Bolsheviks to appeal to the patriotic nationalism of ethnic Russians.

Treaty of Brest-Litovsk

▶ Peace treaty signed in March 1918 between the Central Powers and Russia that ended Russian participation in World War I and ceded Russian territories containing a third of the Russian empire's population to the Central Powers.

- ▨ Ceded after Treaty of Brest-Litovsk, 1918
- ▧ Bolshevik territory, 1919
- ▧ Occupied by Allies, 1919
- → White Army forces
- — Boundary of U.S.S.R., 1921

The Russian Civil War, 1918–1920

How did the First World War differ from previous wars?

In what ways did the war transform life on the home front?

Why did world war lead to revolution in Russia, and what was its outcome?

In what ways was the Allied peace settlement flawed?

☑ LearningCurve
Check what you know.

Other conditions favored a Bolshevik victory as well. Strategically, the Reds controlled central Russia and the crucial cities of Moscow and Petrograd. The Whites attacked from the fringes and lacked coordination. Moreover, the poorly defined political program of the Whites was incapable of uniting the Bolsheviks' enemies. And while the Bolsheviks promised ethnic minorities in Russian-controlled territories substantial autonomy, the nationalist Whites sought to preserve the tsarist empire.

The Bolsheviks mobilized the home front for the war by establishing a system of centralized controls called **War Communism**. The leadership nationalized banks and industries and outlawed private enterprise. Bolshevik commissars introduced rationing, seized grain from peasants to feed the cities, and maintained strict workplace discipline.

Revolutionary terror also contributed to the Communist victory. Lenin and the Bolsheviks set up a fearsome secret police known as the Cheka. During the civil war, the Cheka imprisoned and executed without trial tens of thousands of supposed "class enemies." The tsar and his family were executed in July 1918. The "Red Terror" of 1918 to 1920 helped establish the secret police as a central tool of the new Communist government.

By the spring of 1920, the White armies were almost completely defeated, and the Bolsheviks had retaken much of the territory ceded to Germany under the Treaty of Brest-Litovsk. The Red Army reconquered Belarus and Ukraine, both of which had briefly gained independence. The Bolsheviks then moved westward into Polish territory, but they were halted on the outskirts of Warsaw in August 1920. This defeat halted Bolshevik attempts to spread communism further into Europe, though in 1921 the Red Army overran the independent national governments of the Caucasus. The Russian civil war was over, and the Bolsheviks had won.

War Communism

▶ The application of centralized state control during the Russian civil war, in which the Bolsheviks seized grain from peasants, introduced rationing, nationalized all banks and industry, and required everyone to work.

> **QUICK REVIEW**

How were the Bolsheviks able to gain and hold power in Russia?

CHAPTER LOCATOR | What caused the outbreak of the First World War?

Prince Faisal at the Versailles Peace Conference, 1919 Standing in front, Faisal is supported by his allies and black slave. Nur-as-Said, an officer in the Ottoman army who joined the Arab revolt, is second from the left, and the British officer T. E. Lawrence — popularly known as Lawrence of Arabia — is fourth from the left in back. Faisal failed to win political independence for the Arabs, as the British backed away from the vague promises they had made during the war. (© Imperial War Museum (Q 55581))

EVEN AS CIVIL WAR RAGED IN RUSSIA and chaos engulfed much of central and eastern Europe, the war in the west came to an end in November 1918. Early in 1919, the victorious Western Allies came together in Paris, where they worked out terms for peace. The resulting settlement turned out to be a disappointment for peoples and politicians alike. Rather than lasting peace, the immediate post-war years brought economic crisis and violent political conflict.

The End of the War

In early 1918, facing the arrival of fresh American troops, the German leadership launched a last-ditch, all-out attack on France: the great Spring Offensive of 1918. German armies came within thirty-five miles of Paris but never broke through.

| How did the First World War differ from previous wars? | In what ways did the war transform life on the home front? | Why did world war lead to revolution in Russia, and what was its outcome? | **In what ways was the Allied peace settlement flawed?** | ☑ LearningCurve Check what you know. |

797

They were stopped in July at the second Battle of the Marne, where 140,000 American soldiers saw action. The late but massive American intervention tipped the scales in favor of Allied victory.

By September, British, French, and American armies were advancing steadily on all fronts. Not wanting to shoulder the blame, Hindenburg and Ludendorff insisted that moderate politicians should take responsibility for the defeat. On October 4, the German emperor formed a new, more liberal civilian government to sue for peace.

As negotiations over an armistice dragged on, frustrated Germans rose up in revolt. On November 3, sailors in Kiel mutinied, and throughout northern Germany soldiers and workers established revolutionary councils. The same day, Austria-Hungary surrendered to the Allies and began breaking apart. Revolution erupted in Germany. With army discipline collapsing, William II abdicated and fled to Holland. Socialist leaders in Berlin proclaimed a German republic on November 9 and agreed to surrender. The armistice went into effect on November 11, 1918. The war was over.

Revolution in Austria-Hungary and Germany

Military defeat brought turmoil and revolution to Austria-Hungary and Germany, as it had to Russia. The independent states of Austria, Hungary, and Czechoslovakia, and a larger Romania, were carved out of the territory of the former Austro-Hungarian Empire (**Map 25.4**). A greatly expanded Serbian monarchy gained control of the western Balkans and took the name Yugoslavia.

In late 1918, Germany likewise experienced a dramatic revolution that resembled the Russian Revolution of March 1917. In Germany, however, moderates from the Social Democratic Party and their liberal allies held on to power and established the Weimar Republic—a democratic government that would lead Germany for the next fifteen years.

There were several reasons for the German outcome. The great majority of the Marxist politicians in the Social Democratic Party were moderates, not revolutionaries. They were also German nationalists, appalled by the prospect of civil war and revolutionary terror. Of crucial importance was the fact that the moderate Social Democrats quickly came to terms with the army and big business, which helped prevent total national collapse.

Yet the triumph of the Social Democrats brought violent chaos to Germany in 1918 to 1919. The new republic was attacked from both sides of the political spectrum. Radical Communists tried unsuccessfully to seize control of the government in the Spartacist Uprising in Berlin in January 1919. In Bavaria, a short-lived Bolshevik-style republic was violently overthrown on government orders. Nationwide strikes by leftist workers and a short-lived, right-wing military takeover—the Kapp Putsch—were repressed by the central government.

By the summer of 1920, the situation in Germany had calmed down, but the new republican government faced deep discontent. Communists and radical socialists blamed the Social Democrats for the violent suppression of radical unrest. Right-wing nationalists, including the new Nazi Party, despised the government from the start. They spread the myth that the German army had never actually lost the war—instead, the nation was "stabbed in the back" by socialists and pacifists at home.

CHAPTER LOCATOR | What caused the outbreak of the First World War?

798 CHAPTER 25
WAR AND REVOLUTION

Map Labels

NORWAY
Oslo
SWEDEN
Stockholm
FINLAND
Helsinki
Petrograd (St. Petersburg)
Tallinn
ESTONIA
LATVIA
Riga
Moscow
North Sea
Baltic Sea
DENMARK
Copenhagen
LITHUANIA
Vilnius
SOVIET UNION
IRELAND
Elbe R.
Danzig
EAST PRUSSIA
POLISH CORRIDOR
GREAT BRITAIN
London
NETHERLANDS
Amsterdam
GERMANY
Berlin
POLAND
Warsaw
Vistula R.
Kiev
Weimar
Dnieper R.
ATLANTIC OCEAN
Brussels
BELGIUM
RHINELAND
Cologne
Rhine R.
Frankfurt
Versailles
Paris
LUX.
SAAR
LORRAINE
Strasbourg
ALSACE
Prague
CZECHOSLOVAKIA
GALICIA
Dniester R.
Loire R.
FRANCE
Bern
Vienna
Geneva
SWITZ.
Garonne R.
S. TYROL
AUSTRIA
HUNGARY
Budapest
BESSARABIA
Locarno
Milan
Trieste
ROMANIA
Rhône R.
Po R.
Venice
Zagreb
CROATIA
Belgrade
Bucharest
Danube R.
Genoa
Rapallo
YUGOSLAVIA
Black Sea
Elba
ITALY
Sarajevo
SERBIA
BULGARIA
PORTUGAL
SPAIN
Corsica
Sofia
Constantinople
Rome
MONTENEGRO (To Yugoslavia 1921)
Naples
ALBANIA
Sardinia
GREECE
TURKEY
Izmir
Mediterranean Sea
Sicily
Athens
Crete

Legend
— Boundaries of German, Russian, and Austro-Hungarian Empires in 1914
■ New and reconstituted nations
■ Demilitarized or Allied occupation zone

0   100   200 miles
0 100 200 kilometers

MAP 25.4 ■ Territorial Changes After World War I

World War I brought tremendous changes to eastern Europe. New nations and new boundaries were established, and a dangerous power vacuum was created by the relatively weak states established between Germany and Soviet Russia.

> **MAPPING THE PAST**

ANALYZING THE MAP: What territory did Germany lose, and to whom? Why was Austria referred to as a head without a body in the 1920s? What new independent states were formed from the old Russian empire?

CONNECTIONS: How were the principles of national self-determination applied to the redrawing of Europe after the war, and why didn't this theory work in practice?

| How did the First World War differ from previous wars? | In what ways did the war transform life on the home front? | Why did world war lead to revolution in Russia, and what was its outcome? | **In what ways was the Allied peace settlement flawed?** | ✓ LearningCurve Check what you know. |

799

The Treaty of Versailles

In January 1919, international delegates met in Paris to hammer out a peace accord. The conference produced several treaties, including the **Treaty of Versailles**, which laid out the terms of the postwar settlement with Germany. The peace negotiations inspired great expectations. A young British diplomat later wrote that the victors "were journeying to Paris . . . to found a new order in Europe. We were preparing not Peace only, but Eternal Peace."[4]

This idealism was greatly strengthened by U.S. president Wilson's January 1918 peace proposal, the **Fourteen Points**. The plan called for open diplomacy; a reduction in armaments; freedom of commerce and trade; and the establishment of a **League of Nations**, an international body designed to provide a place for peaceful resolution of international problems. Perhaps most important, Wilson demanded that peace be based on the principle of **national self-determination**, meaning that peoples should be able to choose their own national governments through democratic majority-rule elections. Despite the general optimism inspired by these ideas, the conference and the treaty itself quickly generated disagreement.

The "Big Three" — the United States, Great Britain, and France — controlled the conference. Germany, Austria-Hungary, and Russia were excluded. Italy took part, but its role was quite limited. Representatives from the Middle East, Africa, and East Asia attended as well, but their concerns were largely ignored.

Almost immediately, the Big Three began to quarrel. Wilson insisted that discussion of the League of Nations come first, for he passionately believed that only a permanent international organization could avert future wars. Wilson had his way — the delegates agreed to create the League, though the details would be worked out later and the final structure was too weak to achieve its grand purpose.

The question of what to do with Germany dominated discussions among the Big Three. Prime Minister Georges Clemenceau of France wanted revenge, economic retribution, and lasting security for his country. This, he believed, required the creation of a buffer state between France and Germany, the permanent demilitarization of Germany, and vast reparation payments. Lloyd George, Britain's prime minister, supported Clemenceau but was less harsh. Wilson disagreed. By April, the conference was deadlocked, and Wilson packed his bags to go home.

In the end, Clemenceau, agreed to a compromise. He gave up the French demand for a Rhineland buffer state in return for French military occupation of the region for fifteen years and a formal defensive alliance with the United States and Great Britain. The Allies moved quickly to finish the settlement, believing that further adjustments would be possible within the dual framework of a strong Western alliance and the League of Nations.

The various agreements signed at Versailles redrew the map of Europe. The new independent nations carved out of the Austro-Hungarian and Russian Empires included Poland, Czechoslovakia, Finland, the Baltic States, and Yugoslavia. The Ottoman Empire was also split apart, its territories placed under the control of the victors.

The Treaty of Versailles, signed by the Allies and Germany, was key to the settlement. Germany's African and Asian colonies were given to France, Britain, and Japan as League of Nations mandates or administered territories, though Germany's losses within Europe were relatively minor, thanks to Wilson. Germany

- Alsace-Lorraine was returned to France.
- Ethnic Polish territories seized by Prussia during the eighteenth-century partition of Poland were returned to a new independent Polish state.
- Predominantly German Danzig was also placed within the Polish border but as a self-governing city under League of Nations protection.

had to limit its army to one hundred thousand men, agree to build no military fortifications in the Rhineland, and accept temporary French occupation of that region.

More harshly, in Article 231, the famous **war guilt clause**, the Allies declared that Germany (with Austria) was entirely responsible for the war and thus had to pay reparations equal to all civilian damages caused by the fighting. When presented with these terms, the new German government protested vigorously but to no avail. On June 28, 1919, representatives of the German Social Democrats signed the treaty.

The rapidly concluded Versailles treaties were far from perfect, but within the context of war-shattered Europe they were a beginning. Germany had been punished but not dismembered. A new world organization complemented a defensive alliance of Britain, France, and the United States. The remaining serious problems, the Allies hoped, could be worked out in the future.

Yet the great hopes of early 1919 had turned to ashes by the end of the year. The Western alliance had collapsed, and a plan for permanent peace had given way to a fragile truce. There were several reasons for this turn of events. The U.S. Senate rejected American membership in the League of Nations and refused to ratify treaties forming a defensive alliance with France and Great Britain. Using U.S. actions as an excuse, Great Britain too refused to ratify its defensive alliance with France. Betrayed by its allies, France stood alone.

A second cause for the failure of the peace was that the principle of national self-determination was good in theory but flawed in practice. In Europe, the borders of new states cut through a jumble of ethnic and religious groups that often despised each other. The new central European nations would prove to be economically weak and politically unstable. In the colonies, desires for self-determination were simply ignored, leading to problems, particularly in the Middle East.

war guilt clause
▶ An article in the Treaty of Versailles that declared that Germany (with Austria) was solely responsible for the war and had to pay reparations equal to all civilian damages caused by the fighting.

The Peace Settlement in the Middle East

The British government had encouraged the wartime Arab revolt against the Ottoman Turks (see page 782) and had even made vague promises of an independent Arab kingdom. However, when the fighting stopped, the British and the French chose instead to honor their own secret wartime agreements to divide and rule the Ottoman lands. Most important was the Sykes-Picot Agreement of 1916. In the secret accord, Britain and France agreed that former Ottoman territories would be administered by the European powers under what was later termed

How did the First World War differ from previous wars?	In what ways did the war transform life on the home front?	Why did world war lead to revolution in Russia, and what was its outcome?	**In what ways was the Allied peace settlement flawed?**	✔ LearningCurve Check what you know.

the **mandate system**. France would receive a mandate to govern modern-day Lebanon and Syria and much of southern Turkey, and Britain would control Palestine (including territories that would become the modern state of Israel in 1948), Transjordan, and Iraq. When Britain and France set about implementing their agreements after the armistice, Arab nationalists reacted with understandable surprise and resentment.

British plans for the former Ottoman lands that would become Palestine further angered Arab nationalists. The **Balfour Declaration** of November 1917 announced that Britain favored a "National Home for the Jewish People" in Palestine. The declaration enraged Arabs.

In 1914, Jews accounted for about 11 percent of the population in the three Ottoman districts that would form Palestine; the rest of the population was predominantly Arab. Both groups understood that the Balfour Declaration's National Home for the Jewish People implied the establishment of some kind of Jewish state that would violate majority rule.

Though Arab leaders attended the Versailles Peace Conference, their efforts to secure autonomy in the Middle East came to nothing. Only the kingdom of Hejaz was granted independence (**Map 25.5**). In response, Arab nationalists came together in Damascus as the General Syrian Congress in 1919 and unsuccessfully called again for political independence.

The Western reaction was swift and decisive. The French attacked Syria, taking Damascus in July 1920. Meanwhile, the British put down an uprising in Iraq and established control there. Brushing aside Arab opposition, the British in Palestine formally incorporated the Balfour Declaration and its commitment to a Jewish national home.

The Allies sought to impose even harsher terms on the defeated Turks than on the "liberated" Arabs. A treaty forced on the Ottoman sultan dismembered the Turkish heartland. Great Britain and France occupied parts of modern-day Turkey, and Italy and Greece claimed shares. There was a sizable Greek minority in western Turkey, and Greek nationalists wanted to build a modern Greek empire. In 1919, Greek armies carried by British ships landed on the Turkish coast at Smyrna (SMUHR-nuh) and advanced unopposed into the interior, while French troops moved in from the south. Turkey seemed finished.

Turkey survived the postwar invasions. Led by Mustafa Kemal (1881–1938), the Turks gradually mounted a successful resistance. The Greeks and British sued for peace. Signed in 1923, the Treaty of Lausanne (loh-ZAN) recognized the territorial integrity of Turkey and abolished the capitulations that the European powers had imposed over the centuries to give their citizens special privileges in the Ottoman Empire.

Kemal believed that Turkey should modernize and secularize along Western lines. He established a republic, was elected president, and created a one-party political system. His most radical reforms pertained to religion and culture. Profoundly influenced by the example of western Europe, Kemal set out to limit the place of religion and religious leaders in daily affairs. He decreed a separation of church and state, promulgated law codes inspired by European models, and established a secular public school system. Women received rights that they never had before. By the time of his death in 1938, Kemal had implemented much of his revolutionary program and moved Turkey much closer to Europe.

CHAPTER LOCATOR | What caused the outbreak of the First World War?

802 CHAPTER 25 WAR AND REVOLUTION

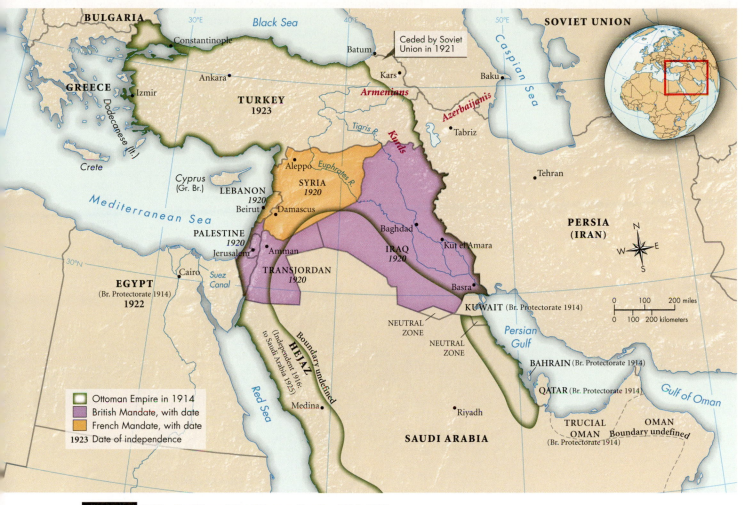

MAP 25.5 ■ The Partition of the Ottoman Empire, 1914–1923

By 1914, the Ottoman Turks had been pushed out of the Balkans, and their Arab provinces were on the edge of revolt. That revolt, in alliance with the British, erupted during the First World War and contributed greatly to the Ottoman defeat. Refusing to grant independence to the Arabs, the Allies established League of Nations mandates and replaced Ottoman rulers in Syria, Iraq, Transjordan, and Palestine.

The Human Costs of the War

World War I broke empires, inspired revolutions, and changed national borders on a worldwide scale. It also had immense human costs. Estimates vary, but total deaths on the battlefield numbered about 8 million soldiers (**Figure 25.1**). Between 7 and 10 million civilians died because of the war and war-related hardships, and another 20 million people died in the worldwide influenza epidemic that followed the war in 1918.

The victims of the First World War included millions of widows and orphans and huge numbers of emotionally scarred and disabled veterans. Countless soldiers suffered from what is now termed post-traumatic stress disorder. In addition,

| How did the First World War differ from previous wars? | In what ways did the war transform life on the home front? | Why did world war lead to revolution in Russia, and what was its outcome? | **In what ways was the Allied peace settlement flawed?** | ✓ LearningCurve Check what you know. |

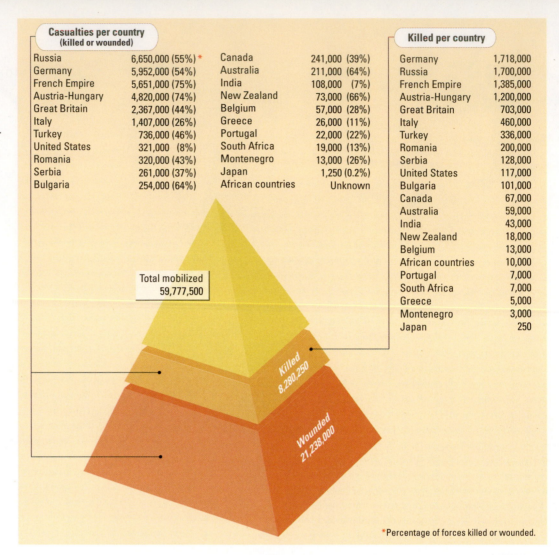

FIGURE 25.1 ◼
Casualties of World War I

The losses of World War I were the highest ever for a war in Europe. These numbers are approximate because of problems with record keeping caused by the destructive nature of total war.

Casualties per country (killed or wounded)			
Russia	6,650,000 (55%) *	Canada	241,000 (39%)
Germany	5,952,000 (54%)	Australia	211,000 (64%)
French Empire	5,651,000 (75%)	India	108,000 (7%)
Austria-Hungary	4,820,000 (74%)	New Zealand	73,000 (66%)
Great Britain	2,367,000 (44%)	Belgium	57,000 (28%)
Italy	1,407,000 (26%)	Greece	26,000 (11%)
Turkey	736,000 (46%)	Portugal	22,000 (22%)
United States	321,000 (8%)	South Africa	19,000 (13%)
Romania	320,000 (43%)	Montenegro	13,000 (26%)
Serbia	261,000 (37%)	Japan	1,250 (0.2%)
Bulgaria	254,000 (64%)	African countries	Unknown

Killed per country	
Germany	1,718,000
Russia	1,700,000
French Empire	1,385,000
Austria-Hungary	1,200,000
Great Britain	703,000
Italy	460,000
Turkey	336,000
Romania	200,000
Serbia	128,000
United States	117,000
Bulgaria	101,000
Canada	67,000
Australia	59,000
India	43,000
New Zealand	18,000
Belgium	13,000
African countries	10,000
Portugal	7,000
South Africa	7,000
Greece	5,000
Montenegro	3,000
Japan	250

Total mobilized
59,777,500

Killed
8,280,250

Wounded
21,238,000

*Percentage of forces killed or wounded.

some 10 million soldiers came home physically disfigured or mutilated. Governments tried to take care of the disabled and the survivor families, but there was never enough money to fund pensions and job-training programs adequately, and employers rarely wanted disabled workers. Crippled veterans were often forced to beg on the streets, a common sight for the next decade.

The German case is illustrative. Nearly 10 percent of German civilians were direct victims of the war, and the new German government struggled to take care of them. Fully one-third of the federal budget of the Weimar Republic was tied up in war-related pensions and benefits. With the onset of the Great Depression in 1929, benefits were cut, leaving bitter veterans vulnerable to Nazi propagandists. The human cost of the war thus had another steep price: across Europe, newly formed radical right-wing parties, including the German Nazis and the Italian Fascists, successfully manipulated popular feelings of loss and resentment to undermine fragile parliamentary governments.

> **QUICK REVIEW**

Why did consensus between the victorious Allies break down so quickly after the war?

CHAPTER LOCATOR | What caused the outbreak of the First World War?

LOOKING BACK LOOKING AHEAD

World War I broke peoples and nations. The trials of total war increased the power of the centralized state and brought down the Austro-Hungarian, Ottoman, and Russian Empires. The brutal violence shocked and horrified observers around the world; ordinary citizens were left to mourn their losses.

Despite high hopes for Wilson's Fourteen Points, the Treaty of Versailles hardly brought lasting peace. The war's disruptions encouraged radical political conflict in the 1920s and 1930s and the rise of totalitarian regimes across Europe, which led to the even more extreme violence of the Second World War. Indeed, some historians believe that the years from 1914 to 1945 might most accurately be labeled a modern Thirty Years' War because the problems unleashed in August 1914 were only really resolved in the 1950s. For all of Europe, World War I was a revolutionary conflict of gigantic proportions with lasting traumatic effects.

ONLINE DOCUMENT PROJECT

Vera Brittain

What role did wartime propaganda play in encouraging women like Vera Brittain to get involved in the war effort?

You encountered Vera Brittain's story on page 788. Keeping the question above in mind, analyze a variety of propaganda posters calling for women to serve as military nurses. *See inside the front cover to learn more.*

| How did the First World War differ from previous wars? | In what ways did the war transform life on the home front? | Why did world war lead to revolution in Russia, and what was its outcome? | In what ways was the Allied peace settlement flawed? | ✔ LearningCurve Check what you know. |

CHAPTER 25 STUDY GUIDE

 STEP 1

GET STARTED ONLINE

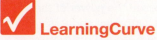 **LearningCurve**

Now that you've read the chapter, make it stick by completing the LearningCurve activity.

STEP 2

EXPLAIN WHY IT MATTERS

Put your reading into practice. Identify each term below, and then explain why it matters in Western history.

TERM	WHO OR WHAT & WHEN	WHY IT MATTERS
Triple Alliance (p. 775)		
Triple Entente (p. 777)		
Schlieffen Plan (p. 780)		
total war (p. 781)		
trench warfare (p. 782)		
February Revolution (p. 792)		
Petrograd Soviet (p. 792)		
Bolsheviks (p. 793)		
Treaty of Brest-Litovsk (p. 795)		
War Communism (p. 796)		
Treaty of Versailles (p. 800)		
Fourteen Points (p. 800)		
League of Nations (p. 800)		
national self-determination (p. 800)		
war guilt clause (p. 801)		
mandate system (p. 802)		
Balfour Declaration (p. 802)		

STEP 3

MOVE BEYOND THE BASICS

To demonstrate a more advanced understanding, fill in the chart included below with descriptions of the military, political, social, and economic impact of total war. Why were European leaders so quick to recognize the political and economic implications of total war but so slow to recognize its military implications?

	Military	Political	Social	Economic
Impact of total war				

PUT IT ALL TOGETHER

Now, take a step back and try to explain the big picture. Remember to use specific examples from the chapter in your answers.

WORLD WAR I

▶ How would you explain the enthusiasm many Europeans had for war on the eve of the First World War?

▶ How did industrialization change the nature of warfare?

THE RUSSIAN REVOLUTION

▶ How did the war undermine the tsarist regime in Russia and how did the tsar himself contribute to the collapse of his government?

▶ Compare and contrast the wartime revolutionary movements in Russia and Germany.

MAKE CONNECTIONS

▶ How did the destruction of World War I compare to the human and material costs of the Thirty Years' War and/or the Napoleonic wars?

   ▶ Defend or refute the following statement. "Given the events of 1918 and 1919, the outbreak of the Second World War was inevitable."

THE PEACE SETTLEMENT

▶ Compare and contrast the peace settlements that followed the Napoleonic wars and World War I.

▶ Who was excluded from the negotiations that led to the Treaty of Versailles and what were the long-term consequences of these exclusions?

> ### IN YOUR OWN WORDS

Imagine that you must give an oral report to the class answering the following question: **What were the most significant causes and consequences of World War I?** What would be the most important points and why?

26

THE AGE OF ANXIETY

1880–1940

> **Why were anxiety and uncertainty such prominent components of early-twentieth-century thought and culture?** Chapter 26 examines science, culture, and politics in the Age of Anxiety. Late-nineteenth-century thinkers called attention to the pessimism, uncertainty, and irrationalism that seemed to accompany modern life. By 1900, radical developments in philosophy and the sciences had substantiated and popularized such ideas. The modernist movement had begun its sweep through literature, music, and the arts. A growing consumer society and, in the twentieth century, the new media of radio and film transformed the habits of everyday life and leisure.

Even as modern science, art, and culture challenged received wisdom of all kinds, international relations spiraled into crisis. Despite some progress in the mid-1920s, political stability remained short-lived, and the Great Depression that began in 1929 cast millions into poverty and shocked the status quo. Democratic liberalism was besieged by the rise of authoritarian and Fascist governments, and another world conflict seemed imminent.

**LearningCurve**

After reading the chapter, use LearningCurve to retain what you've read.

> How did intellectual developments reflect the general crisis in Western thought?

> How did modernism revolutionize Western culture?

> How did consumer society change everyday life?

> What obstacles to lasting peace did European leaders face?

> What were the causes and consequences of the Great Depression?

Life in the Age of Anxiety. Dadaist George Grosz's *Inside and Outside* illustrates the class conflict wrought by the economic crises of the 1920s. Wealthy elites celebrate "inside," while "outside" a disabled veteran begs in vain. (akg-images. Art © Estate of George Grosz/Licensed by VAGA, New York, NY. www.vagarights.com)

How did intellectual developments reflect the general crisis in Western thought?

En amerikansk tecknares bekymmer för framtiden.

Dä professorn äntligen efter årslånga experiment lyckades sönderdela en atom.

Unlocking the Power of the Atom Many of the fanciful visions of science fiction came true in the twentieth century, although not exactly as first imagined. This 1927 Swedish reprint of a drawing by American cartoonist Robert Fuller satirizes a pair of professors who have split the atom and unwittingly destroyed their building and neighborhood in the process. In the Second World War, professors indeed harnessed the atom in bombs and decimated faraway cities and foreign civilians. (Mary Evans Picture Library/The Image Works)

THE DECADES SURROUNDING THE FIRST WORLD WAR—from the 1880s to the 1930s—brought intense cultural and intellectual experimentation. As people grappled with the costs of the First World War and the difficulty of postwar recovery, philosophers and scientists questioned and even abandoned many of the cherished values and beliefs that had guided Western society since the eighteenth-century Enlightenment and the nineteenth-century triumph of industry and science.

CHAPTER LOCATOR | **How did intellectual developments reflect the general crisis in Western thought?**

1919
- Treaty of Versailles; Freudian psychology gains popularity; Keynes publishes *The Economic Consequences of the Peace*; Rutherford splits the atom; Bauhaus school founded

1920s
- Existentialism, Dadaism, and surrealism gain prominence

1922
- Eliot publishes *The Waste Land*; Joyce publishes *Ulysses*; Woolf publishes *Jacob's Room*; Wittgenstein writes on logical positivism

1923
- French and Belgian armies occupy the Ruhr

1924
- Dawes Plan

1925
- Berg's opera *Wozzeck* first performed; Kafka publishes *The Trial*

1926
- Germany joins the League of Nations

1927
- Heisenberg formulates the "uncertainty principle"

1928
- Kellogg-Briand Pact

1929
- Faulkner publishes *The Sound and the Fury*

1929–1939
- Great Depression

1933
- The National Socialist Party takes power in Germany

1935
- Release of Riefenstahl's documentary film *Triumph of the Will*

1936
- Formation of Popular Front in France

Modern Philosophy

Before 1914, most people still believed in Enlightenment ideals of progress, reason, and individual rights. Supporters of these philosophies had some cause for optimism. Women and workers were gradually gaining support in their struggles for political and social recognition, and the rising standard of living, the taming of the city, and the growth of state-supported social programs suggested that life was indeed improving.

Nevertheless, in the late nineteenth century, a small group of serious thinkers mounted a determined attack on these optimistic beliefs. The German philosopher Friedrich Nietzsche (NEE-chuh) (1844–1900) was particularly influential. In the first of his *Untimely Meditations* (1873), he argued that ever since classical Athens, the West had overemphasized rationality and stifled the authentic passions and animal instincts that drive human activity and true creativity.

Nietzsche believed that reason, progress, and respectability were outworn social and psychological constructs that suffocated self-realization and excellence. Though he was the son of a Lutheran minister, Nietzsche rejected religion. In his 1887 book, *On the Genealogy of Morals*, he claimed that Christianity embodied a "slave morality" that glorified weakness, envy, and mediocrity. In one of his most famous lines, an apparent madman proclaims that "God is dead," metaphorically murdered by lackadaisical modern Christians who no longer really believed in him.

Nietzsche warned that Western society was entering a period of nihilism— the philosophical idea that human life is entirely without meaning, truth, or purpose. According to Nietzsche, the only hope for the individual was to accept the

| How did modernism revolutionize Western culture? | How did consumer society change everyday life? | What obstacles to lasting peace did European leaders face? | What were the causes and consequences of the Great Depression? | ✓ LearningCurve Check what you know. |

meaninglessness of human existence and then make that very meaninglessness a source of self-defined personal integrity and hence liberation. In this way, at least a few superior individuals could free themselves from the humdrum thinking of the masses and become true heroes.

Little read during his active years, Nietzsche's works attracted growing attention in the early twentieth century. Artists and writers experimented with his ideas, which were fundamental to the rise of the philosophy of existentialism in the 1920s. Subsequent generations remade Nietzsche to suit their own needs, and his influence remains enormous to this day.

The growing dissatisfaction with established ideas before 1914 was apparent in other important thinkers as well. In the 1890s, French philosophy professor Henri Bergson (1859–1941), for one, argued that immediate experience and intuition were as important as rational and scientific thinking for understanding reality. According to Bergson, a religious experience or mystical poem was often more accessible to human comprehension than a scientific law or a mathematical equation.

The First World War accelerated the revolt against established certainties in philosophy, but that revolt went in two very different directions. In English-speaking countries, the main development was the acceptance of logical positivism in university circles. In the continental countries, the primary development in philosophy was existentialism.

Adherents of **logical positivism** argued that what we know about human life must be based on rational facts and direct observation. They concluded that theology and most traditional philosophy was meaningless because ideas about God, eternal truth, and ethics were impossible to prove using logic. This outlook is often associated with the Austrian philosopher Ludwig Wittgenstein (VIHT-guhn-shtine) (1889–1951), who later immigrated to England where he trained numerous disciples.

In his *Tractatus Logico-Philosophicus* (*Essay on Logical Philosophy*), published in 1922, Wittgenstein argued that philosophy is only the logical clarification of thoughts and that therefore it should concentrate on the study of language, which expresses thoughts. In his view, the great philosophical issues of the ages—God, freedom, morality, and so on—were quite literally senseless because neither science nor mathematics could demonstrate their validity. Logical positivism, which has remained dominant in England and the United States to this day, drastically reduced the scope of philosophical inquiry and offered little solace to ordinary people.

On the continent, others looked for answers in **existentialism**. This new philosophy loosely united highly diverse and even contradictory thinkers in a search for usable moral values in a world of anxiety and uncertainty. Modern existentialism had many nineteenth-century forerunners, including Nietzsche, the Danish religious philosopher Søren Kierkegaard (1813–1855), and the Russian novelist Fyodor Dostoyevsky (1821–1881). The philosophy gained recognition in Germany in the 1920s through the efforts of philosophers Martin Heidegger (1889–1976) and Karl Jaspers (1883–1969). These writers placed great emphasis on the loneliness and meaninglessness of human existence in a godless world and the individual's need to come to terms with the fear caused by this situation.

Most existential thinkers in the twentieth century were atheists. They did not believe that a supreme being had established humanity's fundamental nature and given life its meaning. In the words of French existentialist Jean-Paul Sartre (ZHAWN-pawl SAHR-truh) (1905–1980), "existence precedes essence." By that, Sartre meant that there are no God-given, timeless truths outside or independent

logical positivism
▶ A philosophy that sees meaning in only those beliefs that can be empirically proven and that therefore rejects most of the concerns of traditional philosophy, from the existence of God to the meaning of happiness, as nonsense.

existentialism
▶ A philosophy that stresses the meaninglessness of existence and the importance of the individual in searching for moral values in an uncertain world.

of individual existence. Only after they are born do people struggle to define their essence, entirely on their own. According to thinkers like Sartre and his life-long intellectual partner Simone de Beauvoir (1908–1986), human beings are terribly alone, for there is no God to help them. They are left to confront the inevitable arrival of death and so are hounded by despair.

At the same time, existentialists recognized that human beings must act in the world. Because life is meaningless, existentialists believe that individuals are forced to create their own meaning and define themselves through their actions. To live authentically, individuals must become "engaged" and choose their own actions in full awareness of their inescapable responsibility for their own behavior. Existentialism thus had a powerful ethical component. It placed great stress on individual responsibility and choice, on "being in the world" in the right way.

The Revival of Christianity

Though philosophers such as Nietzsche, Wittgenstein, and Sartre all argued that religion had little to teach people in the modern age, the decades after the First World War witnessed a tenacious revival of Christian thought. Christianity—and religion in general—had been on the defensive in intellectual circles since the Enlightenment. In the years before 1914, some theologians, especially Protestant ones, had felt the need to interpret Christian doctrine and the Bible so that they did not seem to contradict science, evolution, and common sense. Indeed, some modern theologians were embarrassed by the miraculous, unscientific aspects of Christianity and rejected them.

Especially after World War I, a number of thinkers and theologians began to revitalize the fundamental beliefs of Christianity. Sometimes called Christian existentialists because they shared the loneliness and despair of atheistic existentialists, they stressed human beings' sinful nature, their need for faith, and the mystery of God's forgiveness. The revival of Christian belief after World War I was fed by the rediscovery of the work of the nineteenth-century Danish theologian Søren Kierkegaard (KIHR-kuh-gahrd). Kierkegaard believed it was impossible for ordinary individuals to prove the existence of God, but he rejected the notion that Christianity was an empty practice. In his classic *Sickness unto Death* (1849), Kierkegaard suggested that people must take a "leap of faith" and accept the existence of an objectively unknowable but nonetheless awesome and majestic God.

In the 1920s, the Swiss Protestant theologian Karl Barth (1886–1968) propounded similar ideas. In brilliant and influential writings, Barth argued that human beings were imperfect, sinful creatures whose reason and will are hopelessly flawed. Religious truth is therefore made known to human beings only through God's grace, not through reason. People have to accept God's word and the supernatural revelation of Jesus Christ with awe, trust, and obedience, not reason or logic.

Among Catholics, the leading existential Christian was the French philosopher Gabriel Marcel (1889–1973). Marcel found in the Catholic Church an answer to what he called the postwar "broken world." Catholicism and religious belief provided the hope, humanity, honesty, and piety for which he hungered. Marcel and his countryman Jacques Maritain (1882–1973) denounced anti-Semitism and supported closer ties with non-Catholics.

| How did modernism revolutionize Western culture? | How did consumer society change everyday life? | What obstacles to lasting peace did European leaders face? | What were the causes and consequences of the Great Depression? | ☑ LearningCurve Check what you know. |

813

After 1914, religion became much more meaningful to intellectuals than it had been before the war. Between about 1920 and 1950, poets T. S. Eliot and W. H. Auden, novelists Evelyn Waugh and Aldous Huxley, historian Arnold Toynbee, writer C. S. Lewis, psychoanalyst Karl Stern, and physicist Max Planck were all either converted to a faith or became attracted to religion for the first time. Religion was one meaningful answer to uncertainty and anxiety and the horrific costs of world war.

The New Physics

By the late nineteenth century, science was one of the main pillars supporting Western society's optimistic and rationalist worldview. To progressive minds, unchanging natural laws seemed to determine physical processes and permit useful solutions to more and more problems. All this was challenged by the new physics.

An important first step came at the end of the nineteenth century with the discovery that atoms were not like hard, permanent little billiard balls. They were actually composed of many far-smaller particles, such as electrons and protons. Polish-born physicist Marie Curie (1867–1934) and her French husband, Pierre, discovered that radium constantly emits subatomic particles and thus does not have a constant atomic weight. Building on this and other work in radiation, German physicist Max Planck (1858–1947) showed in 1900 that subatomic energy is emitted in uneven little spurts, which Planck called "quanta." Planck's discovery called into question the old sharp distinction between matter and energy: the implication was that matter and energy might be different forms of the same thing.

In 1905, the German-Jewish genius Albert Einstein (1879–1955) went further than the Curies and Planck in undermining Newtonian physics. His **theory of special relativity** postulated that time and space are relative to the viewpoint of the observer and that only the speed of light is constant for all frames of reference in the universe. In explaining his idea, Einstein used analogies involving moving trains. For example, if a woman in the middle of a moving car got up and walked forward to the door, she had gone, relative to the train, a half car length. But relative to an observer on the embankment, she had gone farther. To Einstein, this meant that time and distance were not natural universals but depended on the position and motion of the observer.

The 1920s saw breakthrough after breakthrough in physics. In 1919, Ernest Rutherford (1871–1937) showed that the atom could be split. By 1944, seven subatomic particles had been identified, the most important of which was the neutron. Physicists realized that the neutron's capacity to shatter the nucleus of another atom could lead to chain reactions of shattered atoms that would release unbelievable force. This discovery was fundamental to the subsequent development of the nuclear bomb.

Although few nonscientists truly understood the revolution in physics, its implications, as presented by newspapers and popular writers, were disturbing to millions of men and women in the 1920s and 1930s. As unsettling as Einstein's ideas was a notion popularized by German physicist Werner Heisenberg (VER-nuhr HIE-zuhn-buhrg) (1901–1976). In 1927, Heisenberg formulated the "uncertainty principle," which postulates that nature itself is ultimately unknowable

theory of special relativity

▶ Albert Einstein's theory that time and space are relative to the observer and that only the speed of light remains constant.

CHAPTER LOCATOR | How did intellectual developments reflect the general crisis in Western thought?

814 CHAPTER 26
THE AGE OF ANXIETY

and unpredictable. He suggested that the universe lacked any absolute objective reality. Everything was "relative," that is, dependent on the observer's frame of reference. Such ideas fascinated ordinary people, who found the unstable, relativistic world described by the new physicists strange and troubling. Like modern philosophy, physics no longer provided comforting truths about natural laws or optimistic answers about humanity's place in an understandable world.

Freudian Psychology

With physics presenting an uncertain universe so unrelated to ordinary human experience, questions regarding the power and potential of the rational human mind assumed special significance. The findings and speculations of Sigmund Freud were particularly influential yet also deeply disturbing.

Most scientists assumed that the conscious mind processed sense experiences in a rational and logical way. Human behavior in turn was the result of rational calculation—of "thinking." Beginning in the late 1880s, Freud developed a very different view of the human psyche. Basing his insights on the analysis of dreams and of hysteria, Freud concluded that human behavior was basically irrational, governed by the unconscious, a sort of mental reservoir that contained vital instinctual drives and powerful memories. Though the unconscious profoundly influenced people's behavior, it was unknowable to the conscious mind, leaving people unaware of the source or meaning of their actions.

Freud's Couch

As part of his "talking cure," Austrian neurologist Sigmund Freud invited neurotic patients to lie back on a couch and speak about their dreams and innermost thoughts. This photo shows Freud's famous couch in his office in Vienna. His theories about the unconscious and instinctual motivation of human behavior cast doubt on Enlightenment ideals of rationalism and progress.
(© Peter Aprahamian/CORBIS)

| How did modernism revolutionize Western culture? | How did consumer society change everyday life? | What obstacles to lasting peace did European leaders face? | What were the causes and consequences of the Great Depression? | ✓ LearningCurve Check what you know. |

815

id, ego, and superego
▶ Freudian terms to describe the three parts of the self and the basis of human behavior, which Freud saw as basically irrational.

Freud described three structures of the self—the **id**, the **ego**, and the **super-ego**—that were basically at war with one another. The primitive, irrational id was entirely unconscious. The source of sexual, aggressive, and pleasure-seeking instincts, the id sought immediate fulfillment of all desires and was totally amoral. Keeping the id in check was the superego, the conscience or internalized voice of parental or social control. For Freud, the superego was also irrational. Overly strict and puritanical, it was constantly in conflict with the pleasure-seeking id. The third component was the ego, the rational self that was mostly conscious and worked to negotiate between the demands of the id and the superego.

For Freud, the healthy individual possessed a strong ego that effectively balanced the id and superego. Neurosis, or mental illness, resulted when the three structures were out of balance. Freud's "talking cure"—in which neurotic patients lay back on a couch and shared their innermost thoughts with the psychoanalyst—was an attempt to resolve such unconscious tensions and restore the rational ego to its predominant role.

Yet Freud, like Nietzsche, believed that the mechanisms of rational thinking and traditional moral values could be too strong. In his book *Civilization and Its Discontents* (1930), Freud argued that civilization was possible only when individuals renounced their irrational instincts in order to live peaceably in groups. Such renunciation made communal life possible, but it left basic instincts unfulfilled and so led to widespread unhappiness. Freud gloomily concluded that Western civilization was itself inescapably neurotic.

> **QUICK REVIEW**

How did breakthroughs in physics in the early twentieth century reinforce the anxieties reflected in modern philosophy?

CHAPTER LOCATOR | How did intellectual developments reflect the general crisis in Western thought?

816 CHAPTER 26 THE AGE OF ANXIETY

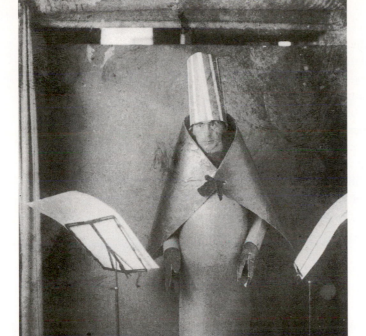

The Shock of the Avant-Garde

Dadaist Hugo Ball recites his nonsense poem "Karawane" at the notorious Cabaret Voltaire in Zurich, Switzerland, in 1916. Avant-garde artists such as Ball consciously used their work to overturn familiar artistic conventions and challenge the assumptions of the European middle classes. (Apic/Getty Images)

LIKE THE SCIENTISTS AND INTELLECTUALS who were part of this increasingly unsettled modern culture, creative artists rejected old forms and old values. **Modernism** in architecture, art, literature, and music meant constant experimentation and a search for new kinds of expression.

Architecture and Design

Already in the late nineteenth century, architects inspired by modernism had begun to transform the physical framework of urban society. The United States, with its rapid urban growth and lack of rigid building traditions, pioneered the new architecture. In the 1890s, the Chicago School of architects, led by Louis H. Sullivan (1856–1924), used inexpensive steel, reinforced concrete, and electric elevators to build skyscrapers and office buildings lacking almost any exterior ornamentation. In the first decade of the twentieth century, Sullivan's student Frank Lloyd Wright (1867–1959) built a series of radically modern houses featuring low lines, open interiors, and mass-produced building materials.

modernism

▶ A label given to the artistic and cultural movements of the late nineteenth and early twentieth centuries, which were typified by radical experimentation that challenged traditional forms of artistic expression.

How did modernism revolutionize Western culture?	How did consumer society change everyday life?	What obstacles to lasting peace did European leaders face?	What were the causes and consequences of the Great Depression?	✓ LearningCurve Check what you know.

functionalism

▶ The principle that buildings, like industrial products, should serve as well as possible the purpose for which they were made, without excessive ornamentation.

Bauhaus

▶ A German interdisciplinary school of fine and applied arts that brought together many leading modern architects, designers, and theatrical innovators.

Promoters of modern architecture argued that buildings and living spaces in general should be ordered according to a new principle: **functionalism**. Buildings, like industrial products, should be "functional"—that is, they should serve, as well as possible, the purpose for which they were made. According to the Franco-Swiss architect Le Corbusier (luh cowr-booz-YAY) (1887–1965), one of the great champions of modernism, "a house is a machine for living in."[1]

In Europe, architectural leadership centered in German-speaking countries until Hitler took power in 1933. In 1919, twenty-eight-year-old Walter Gropius (1883–1969) merged the schools of fine and applied arts at Weimar into a single interdisciplinary school, the **Bauhaus**. The Bauhaus brought together many leading modern architects, designers, and theatrical innovators. Working as an effective, inspired team, they combined the study of fine art with the study of applied art in the crafts of printing, weaving, and furniture making. Throughout the 1920s, the Bauhaus, with its stress on functionalism and quality design for everyday goods, attracted students from all over the world.

New Artistic Movements

In the decades surrounding the First World War, the visual arts also experienced radical change and experimentation. For the last several centuries, artists had tried to produce accurate representations of reality. Now a new artistic avant-garde emerged to challenge that practice. Modern painting and sculpture became increasingly abstract as artists turned their backs on figurative representation and began to break down form into its constituent parts: lines, shapes, and colors.

One of the earliest modernist movements was impressionism, which blossomed in Paris in the 1870s. French artists such as Claude Monet (1840–1926) and Edgar Degas (1834–1917) and the American Mary Cassatt (1844–1926), who settled in Paris in 1875, tried to portray their sensory "impressions" in their work. Monet's colorful and atmospheric paintings of farmland haystacks and Degas's many pastel drawings of ballerinas exemplify the way impressionists moved toward abstraction. Capturing a fleeting moment of color and light, in often blurry and quickly painted images, was far more important than making a heavily detailed, precise rendering of an actual object.

In the next decades, an astonishing array of new artistic movements emerged one after another. Postimpressionists and expressionists, such as Vincent van Gogh (1853–1890), built on impressionist motifs of color and light but added a deep psychological element to their pictures, reflecting the attempt to search within the self and reveal (or "express") deep inner feelings on the canvas.

After 1900, avant-garde artists increasingly challenged the art world status quo. In Paris, in 1907, painter Pablo Picasso (1881–1973), along with other artists, established cubism—a highly analytical approach to art concentrated on a complex geometry of zigzagging lines and sharply angled, overlapping planes that exemplified the ongoing trend toward abstract, nonrepresentational art. In 1909, Italian Filippo Tommaso Marinetti (1876–1944) announced the founding of futurism. According to Marinetti, traditional culture could not deal with the advances of modern technology and the way these had changed human consciousness. Marinetti embraced the future and cast away the past, calling for radically new art forms that would express the modern condition.

CHAPTER LOCATOR | How did intellectual developments reflect the general crisis in Western thought?

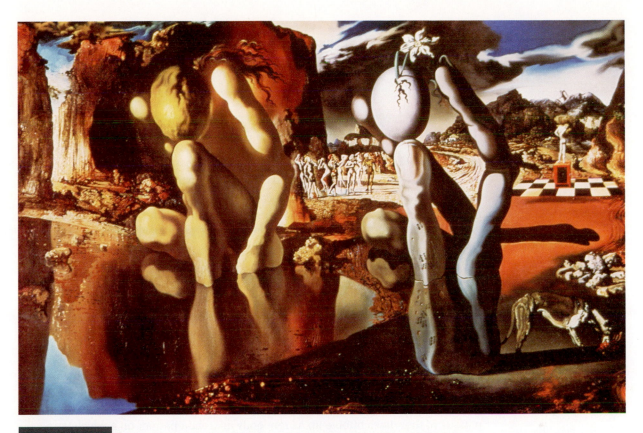

Salvador Dalí, *Metamorphosis of Narcissus* Dalí was a leader of the surrealist art movement, which emerged in the late 1920s. Surrealists were deeply influenced by the theories of Sigmund Freud and used strange and evocative symbols to capture the inner workings of dreams and the unconscious in their work. In this 1937 painting, Dalí plays with the Greek myth of Narcissus, who fell in love with his own reflection and drowned in a pool. What mysterious significance, if any, lies behind this surreal reordering of everyday reality? (The Granger Collection, New York. © Salvador Dalí, Fundacío Gala-Salvador Dalí, Artists Rights Society (ARS), New York 2013)

The shock of World War I encouraged further radicalization. In 1916, a group of artists and intellectuals in exile in Zurich, Switzerland, championed a new movement they called **Dadaism**, which attacked all the familiar standards of art and delighted in outrageous behavior. The war had shown once and for all that life was meaningless, the Dadaists argued, so art should be meaningless as well. Dadaists tried to shock their audiences with what they called "anti-art," works and public performances that were insulting and entirely nonsensical. After the war, Dadaism became an international movement, spreading to Paris, New York, and particularly Berlin in the early 1920s.

During the mid-1920s, some Dadaists were attracted to surrealism. Surrealists such as Salvador Dalí (1904–1989) were deeply influenced by Freudian psychology and portrayed images of the unconscious in their art. They painted fantastic worlds of wild dreams and uncomfortable symbols.

Many modern artists sincerely believed that art had a radical mission. By calling attention to the bankruptcy of mainstream society, they believed, art had the

Dadaism

▶ An artistic movement of the 1920s and 1930s that attacked all accepted standards of art and behavior and delighted in outrageous conduct.

How did modernism revolutionize Western culture?   How did consumer society change everyday life?   What obstacles to lasting peace did European leaders face?   What were the causes and consequences of the Great Depression?

☑ LearningCurve
Check what you know.

power to change the world. The sometimes-nonsensical manifestos written by members of the Dadaist, futurist, and surrealist movements were meant to spread their ideas, challenge conventional assumptions of all kinds, and foment radical social change.

Twentieth-Century Literature

In the decades that followed the First World War, Western literature was deeply influenced by the general intellectual climate of pessimism and alienation and the turn toward radical experimentation sweeping through the other arts. The great nineteenth-century novelists had typically written as all-knowing narrators, describing realistic characters and their relationships to an understandable, if sometimes harsh, society (see Chapter 22, page 701). Modernist writers now developed new techniques to express new realities. In the twentieth century, many authors adopted the limited, often confused viewpoint of a single individual. Like Freud, they focused their attention on the complexity and irrationality of the human mind. French novelist Marcel Proust (1871–1922), in his semi-autobiographical *Remembrance of Things Past* (1913–1927), recalled bittersweet memories of childhood and youthful love and tried to discover their innermost meaning.

Some novelists used the **stream-of-consciousness technique,** relying on internal monologues to explore the human psyche. The English author Virginia Woolf (1882–1941) portrayed characters whose ideas and emotions from different periods of their lives bubble up as randomly as from a patient on a psychoanalyst's couch. William Faulkner (1897–1962), one of America's greatest novelists, used the same technique in *The Sound and the Fury* (1929), with much of its intense drama confusedly seen through the eyes of a man who is mentally challenged.

The most famous and perhaps most experimental stream-of-consciousness novel is *Ulysses* (1922) by Irish novelist James Joyce (1882–1941). Into an account of a single day in the life of an ordinary man, Joyce weaves an extended ironic parallel between the aimless wanderings of his hero through the streets and pubs of Dublin and the adventures of Homer's hero Ulysses on his way home from Troy. Abandoning any sense of a conventional plot; breaking rules of grammar; and blending foreign words, puns, bits of knowledge, and scraps of memory together in bewildering confusion, *Ulysses* is intended to mirror modern life: a gigantic riddle impossible to unravel.

As creative writers turned their attention from society to the individual and from realism to psychological relativity, they rejected the idea of progress. With its biblical references, images of a ruined and wasted natural world, and general human incomprehension, T. S. Eliot's (1888–1965) poem *The Waste Land* (1922) expressed the widespread despair that followed the First World War. The Czech writer Franz Kafka (1883–1924) likewise portrayed an incomprehensible, alienating world. Kafka's novels *The Trial* (1925) and *The Castle* (1926) are stories about helpless individuals crushed by inexplicably hostile forces, as is his famous novella *The Metamorphosis* (1915), in which the main character turns into a giant insect. In these and many other works, authors between the wars used new literary techniques and dark imagery to capture the anxiety of the age.

stream-of-consciousness technique
▶ A literary technique, found in works by Virginia Woolf, James Joyce, and others, that uses interior monologue — a character's thoughts and feelings as they occur — to explore the human psyche.

CHAPTER LOCATOR | How did intellectual developments reflect the general crisis in Western thought?

Modern Music

Developments in modern music paralleled those in painting and fiction. Composers and performers expressed the emotional intensity and shock of the age in radically experimental forms. The ballet *The Rite of Spring* by Russian composer Igor Stravinsky (1882–1971), for example, practically caused a riot when it was first performed in Paris in 1913. The combination of pulsating rhythms and dissonant sounds from the orchestra pit with earthy representations of lovemaking by the strangely dressed dancers on the stage shocked audiences accustomed to traditional ballet.

After the First World War, when irrationality and violence had seemed to pervade human experience, modernism flourished in opera and ballet. One of the most powerful examples was the opera *Wozzeck*, by Alban Berg (1885–1935), first performed in Berlin in 1925. Blending a half-sung, half-spoken kind of dialogue with harsh, atonal music, *Wozzeck* is a gruesome tale of a soldier driven by Kafka-like inner terrors and vague suspicions of infidelity to murder his mistress.

Some composers turned their backs on long-established musical conventions. Just as abstract painters arranged lines and color but did not draw identifiable objects, so modern composers arranged sounds without creating recognizable harmonies. Led by Viennese composer Arnold Schönberg (SHUHN-buhrg) (1874–1951), they abandoned traditional harmony and tonality. Accustomed to the harmonies of classical and romantic music, audiences generally resisted atonal music. Only after the Second World War did it begin to win acceptance.

QUICK REVIEW

What alternatives to the traditional arts emerged in the late nineteenth and early twentieth centuries and how did they reflect the larger society?

| How did modernism revolutionize Western culture? | How did consumer society change everyday life? | What obstacles to lasting peace did European leaders face? | What were the causes and consequences of the Great Depression? | ✔ LearningCurve Check what you know. |

821

How did consumer society change everyday life?

FUNDAMENTAL INNOVATIONS IN THE BASIC PROVISION and consumption of goods and services accompanied the radical transformation of artistic and intellectual life. After the First World War, modern business forms of credit, retail, and advertising helped sell increasing numbers of mass-produced goods to ever-larger numbers of people. With the arrival of cinema and radio, commercial entertainment increasingly dominated the leisure time of ordinary people.

Mass Culture

The emerging consumer society of the 1920s is a good example of the way technological developments can lead to widespread social change. The arrival of a highly industrialized manufacturing system dedicated to mass-producing inexpensive goods, the establishment of efficient transportation systems that could bring these goods to national markets, and the rise of professional advertising experts to sell them were all part of a revolution in the way consumer goods were made, marketed, and used.

Mass-produced goods had a profound impact on the lives of ordinary people. Housework and private life were increasingly organized around an array of modern appliances. The aggressive marketing of fashionable clothing and personal-care products encouraged a cult of youthful "sex appeal." The mass production and marketing of automobiles and the rise of tourist agencies opened roads to increased mobility and travel.

Commercialized mass entertainment likewise prospered and began to dominate the way people spent their leisure time. Movies and radio thrilled millions. Professional sporting events drew throngs of fans. Thriving print media brought readers an astounding variety of newspapers, inexpensive books, and glossy illustrated magazines. Flashy restaurants, theatrical revues, and nightclubs competed for evening customers.

CHAPTER LOCATOR | How did intellectual developments reflect the general crisis in Western thought?

CHAPTER 26
822 THE AGE OF ANXIETY

The Modern Girl: Image or Reality?

A young woman enjoys a drink at the Romanesque Café in Berlin in 1924. The independence of this modern girl, wearing fashionable clothes with a revealing hemline and lacking an escort, transgressed familiar gender roles and shocked and fascinated contemporaries. Images of the modern girl appeared in movies, illustrated magazines, and advertisements, such as this German poster selling "this winter's perfume." (Café: Bildarchiv Preussischer Kulturbesitz/Art Resource, NY; advertisement: Lordprice Collection/Alamy)

> **PICTURING THE PAST**

ANALYZING THE IMAGE: How did these portrayals of the modern girl challenge conventional gender roles? Do you think the woman in the Berlin café was influenced by advertisements for consumer products such as perfume and clothing?

CONNECTIONS: What role did the emergence of a modern consumer culture play in the way contemporaries understood the modern girl? Did consumer goods marketed to women open doors for liberating behavior, or did they set new standards that limited women's options?

The emergence of modern consumer culture both undermined and reinforced existing social differences. On one hand, consumerism helped democratize Western society. Since everyone with the means could purchase any good, mass culture helped break down old social barriers based on class, region, and religion. Yet it also reinforced social differences. Manufacturers soon realized they could profit by marketing goods to specific groups. Catholics, for example, could purchase their own popular literature and inexpensive devotional items, and young people eagerly bought the latest fashions marketed directly to them. The expense of many items meant that only the wealthy could purchase them.

The changes in women's lives were particularly striking. The new household items transformed how women performed housework. Advice literature of all kinds encouraged housewives to rush out and buy the latest appliances so they

How did modernism revolutionize Western culture?

How did consumer society change everyday life?

What obstacles to lasting peace did European leaders face?

What were the causes and consequences of the Great Depression?

☑ LearningCurve
Check what you know.

823

could "modernize" the home. Consumer culture brought growing public visibility to women, especially the young. Girls and young women worked behind the counters and shopped in the aisles of department stores, and they went out on the street alone in ways unthinkable in the nineteenth century. Contemporaries spoke repeatedly about the arrival of the **"modern girl,"** a surprisingly independent female who could vote and held a job, spent her salary on the latest fashions, applied makeup and smoked cigarettes, and used her sex appeal to charm any number of young men. (See "Picturing the Past: The Modern Girl: Image or Reality?" page 823.)

The modern girl was in some ways a stereotype, a product of marketing campaigns dedicated to selling goods to the masses. Few young women could afford to live up to this image, even if they did have jobs. Yet the changes associated with the First World War (see Chapter 25) and the emergence of consumer society did loosen traditional limits on women's behavior.

The emerging consumer culture generated a chorus of complaint. On the left, socialist writers worried that its appeal undermined working-class radicalism, creating passive consumers rather than active, class-conscious revolutionaries. On the right, conservatives complained that money spent on mass-produced goods sapped the livelihood of industrious artisans and undermined proud national traditions. Religious leaders protested that modern consumerism encouraged rampant individualism and warned that greedy materialism was replacing spirituality. Others bemoaned the supposedly loose morals of the modern girl and fretted over the decline of traditional family values.

The Appeal of Cinema

Nowhere was the influence of mass culture more evident than in the rapid growth of commercial entertainment, especially cinema and radio. Both became major industries in the interwar years, and an eager public enthusiastically embraced them, spending their hard-earned money and their leisure hours watching movies or listening to radio broadcasts. These mass media overshadowed and began to replace the traditional amusements of people in cities, and then in small towns and villages, thus changing familiar ways of life.

Cinema first emerged in the United States around 1880, driven in part by the inventions of Thomas Edison. By 1910, American directors and business people had set up "movie factories." Europeans were quick to follow. By 1914, small production companies had formed in Great Britain, France, Germany, and Italy, among others. World War I quickened the pace. National leaders realized that movies offered distraction to troops and citizens and served as an effective means of spreading propaganda.

In the 1920s, filmmaking became big business on an international scale, and motion pictures would remain the central entertainment of the masses until after the Second World War. People flocked to the gigantic movie palaces built across Europe in the mid-1920s. There, they viewed the latest features, which were reviewed by critics in newspapers and flashy illustrated magazines. Cinema audiences grew rapidly in the 1930s. In Great Britain, in the late 1930s, one in every four adults went to the movies twice a week, and two in five went at least once a week. Other countries had similar figures.

"modern girl"

▶ Somewhat stereotypical image of the modern and independent working woman popular in the 1920s.

CHAPTER LOCATOR | How did intellectual developments reflect the general crisis in Western thought?

As these numbers suggest, motion pictures could be powerful tools of indoctrination, especially in countries with dictatorial regimes. Lenin encouraged the development of Soviet filmmaking, believing that the new medium was essential to the social and ideological transformation of the country. In Nazi Germany, the filmmaker Leni Riefenstahl (REE-fuhn-shtahl) (1902–2003) directed a masterpiece of documentary propaganda, *Triumph of the Will*, based on the 1934 Nazi Party rally at Nuremberg. Riefenstahl's film combined stunning aerial photography with mass processions of young Nazi fanatics and images of joyful crowds welcoming Adolf Hitler.

The Arrival of Radio

Like film, radio became a full-blown mass medium in the 1920s. Experimental radio sets were first available in the 1880s. The work of Italian inventor Guglielmo Marconi (1874–1937) around 1900 and the development of the vacuum tube in 1904 made possible primitive transmissions of speech and music. But the first major public broadcasts of news and special events occurred only in 1920, in Great Britain and the United States.

Like the movies, radio was well suited for political propaganda and manipulation. Dictators such as Hitler and Italy's Benito Mussolini controlled the airwaves and could reach enormous national audiences with their dramatic speeches. In democratic countries, politicians such as American president Franklin Roosevelt and British prime minister Stanley Baldwin effectively used informal "fireside chats" to bolster their popularity.

QUICK REVIEW

How did accelerating industrialization contribute to twentieth-century consumer culture?

How did modernism revolutionize Western culture?

How did consumer society change everyday life?

What obstacles to lasting peace did European leaders face?

What were the causes and consequences of the Great Depression?

☑ LearningCurve
Check what you know.

What obstacles to lasting peace did European leaders face?

"German Women Protest the Colored Occupation on the Rhine"

In 1923, the French army occupied the industrial district of the Ruhr in Germany in an effort to force reparations payments. The occupying forces included colonial troops from West Africa, and Germans responded with a racist propaganda campaign that cast the West African soldiers as uncivilized savages. (Private Collection/© Galerie Bilderwelt/ Bridgeman Images)

AS ESTABLISHED PATTERNS OF THOUGHT AND CULTURE were further challenged and mangled by the ferocious impact of World War I, so too was the political fabric stretched and torn. The Versailles settlement had established a shaky truce, not a solid peace. After the war, leaders faced a gigantic task as they sought to create a stable international order within the general context of intellectual crisis, slow economic growth, and political turmoil.

Germany and the Western Powers

Germany was the key to lasting stability. Yet to Germans of all political parties, the Treaty of Versailles represented a harsh dictated peace, to be revised or repudiated as soon as possible. Germany still had the potential to become the strongest country in Europe but remained a source of uncertainty. Moreover, with ominous implications, France and Great Britain did not see eye to eye on Germany.

Immediately after the war, the French wanted to stress the harsh elements in the Treaty of Versailles. Most of the war in the west had been fought on French soil, and the expected costs of reconstruction, as well as of repaying war debts to the United States, were staggering. Thus French politicians believed that massive reparations from Germany were vital for economic recovery. After having

CHAPTER LOCATOR | How did intellectual developments reflect the general crisis in Western thought?

compromised with President Wilson, only to be betrayed by the failure of the U.S. Senate to ratify the treaty, many French leaders saw strict implementation of all provisions of the Treaty of Versailles as France's last best hope. Large reparation payments could hold Germany down indefinitely, ensuring French security.

The British soon felt differently. Before the war, Germany had been Great Britain's second-best market in the world; after the war a healthy, prosperous Germany appeared to be essential to the British economy. Many British people agreed with the analysis of the English economist John Maynard Keynes (1883–1946), who eloquently denounced the Treaty of Versailles in his book *The Economic Consequences of the Peace* (1919). According to Keynes, astronomical reparations and harsh economic measures would impoverish Germany, encourage Bolshevism, and increase economic hardship in all countries.

While French and British leaders drifted in different directions, the Allied commission created to determine German reparations completed its work. In April 1921, it announced that Germany had to pay the enormous sum of 132 billion German gold marks (U.S. $33 billion) in annual installments of 2.5 billion gold marks. Facing possible occupation of more of its territory, the young German republic—generally known as the Weimar Republic—made its first payment in 1921. Then in 1922, wracked by rapid inflation and political assassinations, and motivated by hostility and arrogance as well, the Weimar Republic announced its inability to pay more. It proposed a moratorium on reparations for three years, with the clear implication that thereafter reparations would be either drastically reduced or eliminated entirely.

The British were willing to accept a moratorium, but the French, led by their tough-minded prime minister, Raymond Poincaré (1860–1934), were not. If the Germans refused to pay reparations, France would use occupation to paralyze Germany and force it to accept the Treaty of Versailles. So, despite strong British protests, in early January 1923, French and Belgian armies moved out of the Rhineland and began to occupy the Ruhr district, the heartland of industrial Germany, creating the most serious international crisis of the 1920s.

Strengthened by a wave of German patriotism, the German government ordered the people of the Ruhr to stop working and offer passive resistance to the occupation. The French responded by sealing off the Ruhr and the Rhineland from the rest of Germany, letting in only enough food to prevent starvation.

By the summer of 1923, France and Germany were engaged in a great test of wills. French armies could not collect reparations from striking workers at gunpoint, but the occupation was paralyzing Germany and its economy. To support the striking workers and their employers, the German government began to print money to pay its bills, causing runaway inflation. Prices soared as German money rapidly lost all value. Catastrophic inflation cruelly mocked the old middle-class virtues of thrift, caution, and self-reliance as savings were wiped out. Many Germans felt betrayed. They hated and blamed the Western governments, their own government, big business, the Jews, the workers, and the Communists for their misfortune. Right-wing nationalists—including Adolf Hitler and the newly established National Socialist, or Nazi, Party—eagerly capitalized on the widespread discontent.

In August 1923, as the mark lost value and unrest spread throughout Germany, Gustav Stresemann (GOOS-tahf SHTRAY-zuh-mahn) (1878–1929) assumed leadership of the government. Stresemann tried compromise. He called off passive resistance in the Ruhr and in October agreed in principle to pay reparations, but he asked for a re-examination of Germany's ability to pay. Poincaré accepted. His

French Occupation of the Ruhr, 1923–1925

How did modernism revolutionize Western culture?

How did consumer society change everyday life?

What obstacles to lasting peace did European leaders face?

What were the causes and consequences of the Great Depression?

☑ LearningCurve
Check what you know.

hard line had become unpopular in France, and it was hated in Britain and the United States. (See "Individuals in Society: Gustav Stresemann," page 829.) In addition, power in both Germany and France was passing to more moderate leaders who realized that continued confrontation was a destructive, no-win situation. Thus, after five long years of hostility and tension, Germany and France both decided to try compromise. The British, and even the Americans, were willing to help. The first step was to reach an agreement on the reparations question.

Hope in Foreign Affairs

Dawes Plan

▶ War reparations agreement that reduced Germany's yearly payments, made payment dependent on economic prosperity, and granted large U.S. loans to promote recovery.

In 1924, an international committee of financial experts met to re-examine reparations from a broad perspective. The resulting **Dawes Plan** (1924) was accepted by France, Germany, and Britain. Germany's yearly reparations were reduced and linked to the level of German economic output. Germany would also receive large loans from the United States to promote economic recovery. In short, Germany would get private loans from the United States in order to pay reparations to France and Britain, thus enabling those countries to repay the large war debts they owed the United States.

This circular flow of international payments was complicated and risky, but for a while it worked. With continual inflows of American capital, the German republic experienced a shaky economic recovery. Thus, the Americans belatedly played a part in the general economic settlement that, though far from ideal, facilitated a worldwide recovery in the late 1920s.

A political settlement accompanied the economic accords. In 1925, the leaders of Europe signed a number of agreements at Locarno, Switzerland. Collectively, the agreements resolved many, but not all, of the most pressing international issues. The refusal to settle Germany's eastern borders angered the Poles, and though the "spirit of Locarno" lent some hope to those seeking international stability, political tensions deepened in central Europe.

> ### > The Locarno Agreements (1925)
>
> - Germany and France solemnly pledge to accept their common border.
> - Britain and Italy agree to fight either France or Germany if one invaded the other.
> - Germany agrees to settle boundary disputes with Poland and Czechoslovakia by peaceful means.
> - France reaffirms its pledge of military aid to Poland and Czechoslovakia if Germany attacks them.

Other developments suggested possibilities for international peace. In 1926, Germany joined the League of Nations, and in 1928, fifteen countries signed the Kellogg-Briand Pact, initiated by French Prime Minister Aristide Briand and U.S. Secretary of State Frank B. Kellogg. The signing states agreed to "renounce [war] as an instrument of international policy" and to settle international disputes peacefully. The pact made no provisions for action in case war actually occurred and could not prevent the arrival of the Second World War in 1939. In the late 1920s, however, it fostered a cautious optimism and encouraged the hope that the United States would accept its responsibilities as a great world power by contributing to European stability.

INDIVIDUALS IN SOCIETY
Gustav Stresemann

Foreign Minister Gustav Stresemann of Germany (right) leaves a meeting with Aristide Briand, his French counterpart. (© Bettman/Corbis)

German foreign minister Gustav Stresemann is a controversial historical figure. Hailed in the 1920s as a hero of peace, he was denounced as a traitor by radical German nationalists and Hitler's Nazis. After World War II, revisionist historians stressed Stresemann's persistent nationalism and cast doubt on his peaceful intentions. Weimar Germany's most renowned leader is a fascinating example of the restless quest for convincing historical interpretation.

Stresemann's origins were modest. His parents were Berlin innkeepers and beer retailers, and of their five children, only Gustav attended high school. Attracted first to literature and history, Stresemann later turned to economics, earned a doctoral degree, and quickly reached the top as a manager and director of German trade associations. A highly intelligent extrovert with a knack for negotiation, Stresemann became a deputy in the German Reichstag (parliament) in 1907 as a business-oriented liberal and nationalist. When World War I erupted, he believed, like most Germans, that Germany had acted defensively and was not at fault. A strident nationalist, he urged German annexation of conquered foreign territories. Germany's collapse in defeat and revolution devastated Stresemann. He seemed a prime candidate to join the hateful extremism of the far right.

Although Stresemann opposed the Treaty of Versailles as unjust and unrealistic, he turned toward the center instead of the far right. He accepted the new Weimar Republic and played a growing role in the Reichstag as the leader of his own small probusiness party. His hour came when French and Belgian troops occupied the Ruhr. Named chancellor in August 1923, he called off passive resistance and began talks with the French. His government also quelled Communist uprisings; put down rebellions in Bavaria, including Hitler's attempted coup; and ended runaway inflation with the introduction of a new currency. Stresemann fought to preserve German unity, and he succeeded.

Voted out as chancellor in November 1923, Stresemann remained as foreign minister in every German government until his death in 1929. Proclaiming a policy of peace and agreeing to pay reparations, he achieved his greatest triumph in the Locarno agreements of 1925 (see page 828). But these agreements did not lead the French to make any further concessions that might have disarmed Germany's extremists. Stresemann made little additional progress in achieving international reconciliation and true sovereignty for Germany. His premature death in office was a serious blow to German pragmatism, encouraging the turn to a more aggressive and nationalist foreign policy.

Stresemann was no fuzzy pacifist. Historians debunking his legend are right in seeing an enduring nationalism in his defense of German interests. But Stresemann, like his French counterpart Aristide Briand, was a statesman of goodwill who wanted peace through mutually advantageous compromise. A realist trained by business and politics in the art of the possible, Stresemann perceived that Germany had to be a satisfied and equal partner for peace to be secure. His unwillingness to guarantee Germany's eastern borders (see Map 25.4, page 799), which is often criticized as contributing to the coming of the Second World War, reflected his conviction that keeping some Germans under Polish and Czechoslovakian rule created a ticking time bomb in Europe. Stresemann was also convinced that war on Poland would almost certainly re-create the Allied coalition that had crushed Germany in 1918.* The mighty coalition that formed after Hitler's 1939 invasion of Poland proved this view prophetic.

QUESTIONS FOR ANALYSIS

1. What did Gustav Stresemann do to promote reconciliation in Europe? How did his policy toward France differ from that toward Poland and Czechoslovakia?
2. What is your interpretation of Stresemann? Does he arouse your sympathy or your suspicion and hostility? Why?

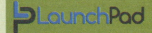

ONLINE DOCUMENT PROJECT

What were some of the challenges that leaders like Stresemann faced in building political consensus in Weimar Germany? Examine documents that illuminate the competing visions of major Weimar political parties during the 1920s. Then complete a writing assignment based on the evidence and details from this chapter. *See inside the front cover to learn more.*

*Robert Grathwol, "Stresemann: Reflections on His Foreign Policy," *Journal of Modern History* 45 (March 1973): 52–70.

Hope in Democratic Government

Domestic politics also offered reason to hope. During the occupation of the Ruhr and the great inflation, republican government in Germany had appeared on the verge of collapse. In 1923, Communists momentarily entered provincial governments, and in November, an obscure politician named Adolf Hitler leaped onto a table in a beer hall in Munich and proclaimed a "national socialist revolution." But the young republican government easily crushed Hitler's plot, and he was sentenced to prison. By the late 1920s, liberal democracy seemed to take root in Weimar Germany and the economy had stabilized.

Sharp political divisions remained, however. Throughout the 1920s, Hitler's Nazi Party attracted support from fanatical anti-Semites, ultranationalists, and disgruntled ex-servicemen. Many unrepentant nationalists and monarchists populated the right and the army. On the left, members of Germany's recently formed Communist Party were noisy and active. The Communists, directed from Moscow, reserved their greatest hatred for their cousins the Social Democrats, whom they accused of betraying the revolution. Though the working class was divided, a majority supported the nonrevolutionary Social Democrats.

The situation in France was similar to that in Germany. Communists and Socialists battled for workers' support. After 1924, the democratically elected government rested mainly in the hands of coalitions of moderates, with business interests well represented. France's great accomplishment was the rapid rebuilding of its war-torn northeastern region. The expense of this undertaking led, however, to a large deficit and substantial inflation.

Britain, too, faced challenges after 1920. The great problem was unemployment. In June 1921, 23 percent of the labor force was out of work, and throughout the 1920s, unemployment hovered around 12 percent, leading to a massive general strike in 1926. Yet the state provided unemployment benefits and supplemented the payments with subsidized housing, medical aid, and increased old-age pensions. These and other measures kept living standards from seriously declining, helped moderate class tensions, and pointed the way toward the welfare state Britain would establish after World War II.

Relative social harmony in Great Britain was accompanied by the rise of the Labour Party as a determined champion of the working class and of greater social equality. Committed to the kind of moderate revisionist socialism that had emerged before World War I (see Chapter 23, page 735), the Labour Party replaced the Liberal Party as the main opposition to the Conservatives. In 1924, and from 1929 to 1931, the Labour Party governed the country with the support of the smaller Liberal Party. Yet Labour moved toward socialism gradually and democratically, so as not to antagonize the middle classes.

> **QUICK REVIEW**

Why was the resolution of the question of reparations so important to the quest for political stability in the 1920s?

CHAPTER LOCATOR | How did intellectual developments reflect the general crisis in Western thought?

830 CHAPTER 26
THE AGE OF ANXIETY

Homelessness in London

The Great Depression of the 1930s disrupted the lives of millions across the United States and Europe. The frustration and agony of unemployment are evident in this common scene of homeless Londoners wrapping themselves in newspaper against the cold. (Mary Evans Picture Library/The Image Works)

THE FRAGILE OPTIMISM OF THE LATE 1920s was short-lived. Beginning in 1929, a massive economic downturn struck the entire world with ever-greater intensity. Recovery was slow and uneven, and contemporaries labeled the economic crisis the **Great Depression**.

The social and political consequences of the Great Depression were enormous. Mass unemployment and failing farms made insecurity and unemployment a reality for millions of people (**Map 26.1**). The prolonged economic collapse shattered the fragile political stability of the mid-1920s and encouraged the growth of extremists on both ends of the political spectrum.

Great Depression

▶ A worldwide economic depression from 1929 through 1939, unique in its severity and duration and with slow and uneven recovery.

The Economic Crisis

Though economic activity was already declining moderately in many countries by early 1929, the crash of the stock market in the United States in October of that year initiated a worldwide crisis. The American economy had prospered in the late 1920s, but there were large inequalities in income and a serious imbalance between actual business investment and stock market speculation. Thus, net investment—in factories, farms, equipment, and the like—actually fell from $3.5 billion in 1925 to $3.2 billion in 1929. In the same years, the value of shares traded on the exchanges soared from $27 billion to $87 billion. Such inflated prices should have raised serious concerns about economic solvency, but even experts failed to predict the looming collapse.

| How did modernism revolutionize Western culture? | How did consumer society change everyday life? | What obstacles to lasting peace did European leaders face? | **What were the causes and consequences of the Great Depression?** | ✓ LearningCurve Check what you know. |

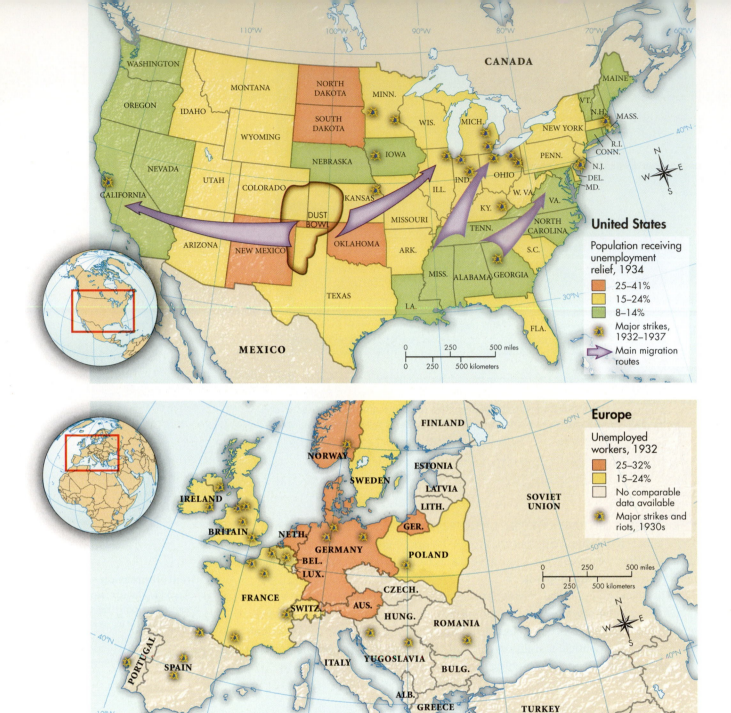

MAP 26.1 ■ The Great Depression in the United States and Europe, 1929–1939

These maps show that unemployment was high almost everywhere, but that national and regional differences were also substantial.

United States

Population receiving unemployment relief, 1934
- 25–41%
- 15–24%
- 8–14%
- ☀ Major strikes, 1932–1937
- ➤ Main migration routes

Europe

Unemployed workers, 1932
- 25–32%
- 15–24%
- No comparable data available
- ☀ Major strikes and riots, 1930s

> MAPPING THE PAST

ANALYZING THE MAP: Which European countries had the highest rate of unemployment? How do the rates of people on unemployment relief in the United States compare to the percentage of unemployed workers in Europe? In the United States, what were the main channels of migration?

CONNECTIONS: What tactics of reform and recovery did European nations use to combat the deprivations of the Great Depression?

This stock market "bubble" was built on borrowed money. Many wealthy investors, speculators, and people of modest means bought stocks "on margin," paying only a small fraction of the total purchase price and borrowing the remainder from their stockbrokers. When prices started falling in 1929, the hard-pressed margin buyers either had to put up more money, which was often impossible, or sell their shares to pay off their brokers. Thousands of people started selling all at once. The result was a financial panic. Countless investors and speculators were wiped out in a matter of days or weeks.

The consequences were swift and severe. Stripped of wealth and confidence, battered investors and their fellow citizens started buying fewer goods. Prices fell, production began to slow down, and unemployment began to rise. Soon the entire American economy was caught in a spiraling decline.

The financial panic triggered an international financial crisis. Throughout the 1920s, American bankers and investors had lent large amounts of capital to many countries. Once the panic broke, U.S. bankers began recalling the loans they had made to foreign businesses. It became very hard for European businesses to borrow money, and panicky Europeans began to withdraw their savings from banks. These banking problems eventually led to the crash of the largest bank in Austria in 1931 and then to general financial chaos. The recall of loans by American bankers also accelerated a collapse in world prices when businesses dumped industrial goods and agricultural commodities in a frantic attempt to get cash to pay their loans.

The financial crisis led to a general crisis of production: between 1929 and 1933, world output of goods fell by an estimated 38 percent. As this happened, each country turned inward and tried to manage the crisis alone. For example, country after country followed the example of the United States when, in 1930, it raised protective tariffs to their highest levels ever and tried to seal off shrinking national markets for domestic producers. Such actions further limited international trade. Within this context of fragmented and destructive economic nationalism, a recovery did not begin until 1933 and it was a halting one at that.

Although opinions differ, two factors probably best explain the relentless slide to the bottom from 1929 to early 1933. First, the international economy lacked leadership able to maintain stability when the crisis came. Neither Britain nor the United States—the world's economic leaders at the time—successfully stabilized the international economic system in 1929.

The second factor was poor national economic policy in almost every country. Governments generally cut their budgets when they should have raised spending and accepted large deficits in order to stimulate their economies. After World War II, this "counter-cyclical policy," advocated by John Maynard Keynes, became a well-established weapon against downturn and depression. But in the 1930s, Keynes's prescription was generally regarded with horror by orthodox economists who believed balanced budgets to be the key to economic growth.

Mass Unemployment

The lack of large-scale government spending contributed to the rise of mass unemployment. The financial crisis led to production cuts; as a result, workers lost their jobs and had little money to buy goods (see Map 26.1, page 832). Mass unemployment created great social problems. Poverty increased dramatically,

| How did modernism revolutionize Western culture? | How did consumer society change everyday life? | What obstacles to lasting peace did European leaders face? | **What were the causes and consequences of the Great Depression?** | ✓ LearningCurve Check what you know. |

833

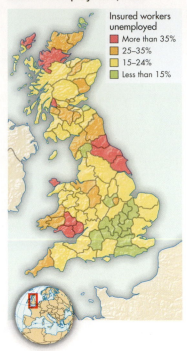

Insured workers
unemployed
■ More than 35%
■ 25–35%
☐ 15–24%
■ Less than 15%

although in most countries unemployed workers generally received some kind of meager unemployment benefits or public aid that prevented starvation. Millions of people lost their spirit, condemned to an apparently hopeless search for work. Homes and ways of life were disrupted in millions of personal tragedies. Young people postponed marriages, and birthrates fell sharply. There was an increase in suicide and mental illness. Poverty or the threat of poverty became a grinding reality. Only strong government action could deal with mass unemployment, a social powder keg preparing to explode.

The New Deal in the United States

The Great Depression and the government response to it marked a major turning point in American history. President Herbert Hoover (r. 1929–1933) and his administration initially reacted to the stock market crash and economic decline with limited action. When the full force of the financial crisis struck Europe in the summer of 1931 and boomeranged back to the United States, people's worst fears became reality. Banks failed; unemployment soared. Between 1929 and 1932, industrial production fell by about 50 percent.

In these dire circumstances, Franklin Delano Roosevelt (r. 1933–1945) won a landslide presidential victory in 1932 with promises of a "New Deal for the forgotten man." Roosevelt's goal was to reform capitalism in order to preserve it. Though Roosevelt rejected socialism and government ownership of industry, he advocated forceful government intervention in the economy and instituted a broad range of government-supported social programs designed to stimulate the economy and provide jobs.

The most ambitious attempt to control and plan the economy was the National Recovery Administration (NRA). Intended to reduce competition among industries by setting minimum prices and wages, the NRA broke with the cherished American tradition of free competition. Though participation was voluntary, the NRA aroused conflicts among business people, consumers, and bureaucrats and never worked well. The program was abandoned when declared unconstitutional by the Supreme Court in 1935.

Roosevelt and his advisers then attacked the key problem of mass unemployment. The federal government accepted the responsibility of employing as many people as financially possible. New agencies like the Works Progress Administration (WPA), set up in 1935, were created to undertake a vast range of projects. One-fifth of the entire U.S. labor force worked for the WPA at some point in the 1930s, constructing public buildings, bridges, and highways.

In 1935, the U.S. government also established a national social security system with old-age pensions and unemployment benefits. The National Labor Relations Act of 1935 gave union organizers the green light by declaring collective bargaining to be the policy of the United States. Union membership more than doubled from 4 million in 1935 to 9 million in 1940. In general, between 1935 and 1938, government rulings and social reforms chipped away at the privileges of the wealthy and tried to help ordinary people.

Programs like the WPA were part of the New Deal's fundamental commitment to use the federal government to provide relief welfare for all Americans. This commitment marked a profound shift from the traditional stress on family support and community responsibility. Embraced by a large majority in the 1930s, this shift in attitudes proved to be one of the New Deal's most enduring legacies.

CHAPTER LOCATOR | How did intellectual developments reflect the general crisis in Western thought?

OSLOFROKOSTEN
HVA DEN ER OG GIR

Despite undeniable accomplishments in social reform, the New Deal was only partly successful in responding to the Great Depression. At the height of the recovery in May 1937, 7 million workers were still unemployed. The economic situation then worsened seriously in the recession of 1937 and 1938, and unemployment had risen to a staggering 10 million when war broke out in Europe in September 1939. The New Deal never pulled the United States out of the depression; it took the Second World War to do that.

The Scandinavian Response to the Depression

Of all the Western democracies, the Scandinavian countries, under Social Democratic leadership, responded most successfully to the challenge of the Great Depression. Having grown steadily in the late nineteenth century, the Social Democrats became the largest political party in Sweden and then in Norway after the First World War. In the 1920s, they passed important social reform legislation that benefited both peasants and workers and developed a unique kind of socialism. Flexible and nonrevolutionary, this Scandinavian socialism grew out of a strong tradition of cooperative community action.

Sweden in particular pioneered in the use of large-scale deficits to finance public works and thereby maintain production and employment. In ways that paralleled some aspects of Roosevelt's New Deal, Scandinavian governments also increased social welfare benefits such as old-age pensions, unemployment insurance, subsidized housing, and maternity allowances. All this spending required a large bureaucracy and high taxes, first on the rich and then on practically everyone. Yet both private and cooperative enterprise thrived, as did democracy. Some observers saw Scandinavia's welfare socialism as an appealing middle way between sick capitalism and cruel communism or fascism.

Recovery and Reform in Britain and France

In Britain, both Labour and Conservative governments followed orthodox economic theory. The budget was balanced, spending was tightly controlled, and unemployed workers received barely enough to live. Still, the economy recovered

How did modernism revolutionize Western culture?

How did consumer society change everyday life?

What obstacles to lasting peace did European leaders face?

What were the causes and consequences of the Great Depression?

☑ LearningCurve
Check what you know.

considerably after 1932. By 1937, production was about 20 percent higher than in 1929. In fact, for Britain, the years after 1932 were actually somewhat better than the 1920s, the opposite of the situation in the United States and France.

This performance reflected the gradual reorientation of the British economy. After 1932, Britain concentrated increasingly on the national, rather than the international, market. The old export industries of the Industrial Revolution, such as textiles and coal, continued to decline, but new industries, such as automobiles and electrical appliances, grew in response to British home demand. Moreover, low interest rates encouraged a housing boom.

Because France was relatively less industrialized, the Great Depression came to it late. But once the depression hit France, it stayed. Economic stagnation both reflected and heightened an ongoing political crisis. As before 1914, the French parliament was made up of many political parties that could never cooperate for long.

The French had lost the underlying unity that had made government instability bearable before 1914, however. Fascist organizations agitated against parliamentary democracy and turned to Mussolini's Italy and Hitler's Germany for inspiration. At the same time, the Communist Party and many workers opposed to the existing system looked to Stalin's Russia for guidance. The vital center of moderate republicanism was weakened by attacks from both sides.

Frightened by the growing strength of the Fascists at home and abroad, the Communists, Socialists, and Radicals formed an alliance—the **Popular Front**—for the national elections of May 1936. Their clear victory reflected the trend toward polarization. The number of Communists in the parliament jumped dramatically from 10 to 72, while the Socialists, led by Léon Blum, became the strongest party in France, with 146 seats. The Radicals—who were actually quite moderate—slipped badly, and the conservatives lost ground to the far right.

In the next few months, Blum's Popular Front government made the first and only real attempt to deal with the social and economic problems of the 1930s in France. Inspired by Roosevelt's New Deal, it encouraged the union movement and launched a far-reaching program of social reform, complete with paid vacations and a forty-hour workweek. Supported by workers and the lower middle class, these measures were quickly sabotaged by rapid inflation and accusations of revolution from Fascists and frightened conservatives. Wealthy people sneaked their money out of the country, labor unrest grew, and France entered a severe financial crisis. Blum was forced to announce a "breathing spell" in social reform.

Political dissension in France was encouraged by the Spanish Civil War (1936–1939), during which authoritarian Fascist rebels overthrew the democratically elected republican government. French Communists demanded that the government support the Spanish republicans, while many French conservatives sided with the Spanish Fascists. Extremism grew, and France itself was within sight of civil war. Blum was forced to resign in June 1937, and the Popular Front quickly collapsed. An anxious and divided France drifted aimlessly once again, preoccupied by Hitler and German rearmament.

Popular Front

▶ A short-lived New Deal–inspired alliance in France led by Léon Blum that encouraged the union movement and launched a far-reaching program of social reform.

> **QUICK REVIEW**

Why were initial government efforts to respond to the Great Depression so ineffective?

CHAPTER LOCATOR | How did intellectual developments reflect the general crisis in Western thought?

LOOKING BACK LOOKING AHEAD

The decades before and especially after World War I brought intense intellectual and cultural innovation. At the same time, mass culture, embodied in cinema, radio, and an emerging consumer society, transformed everyday life. Yet the modern vision was often bleak and cold. Modern art and consumer society alike challenged traditional values, contributing to feelings of disorientation and pessimism that had begun late in the nineteenth century and were exacerbated by the searing events of the First World War. The situation was worsened by ongoing political and economic turmoil. The Treaty of Versailles had failed to create a lasting peace or resolve the question of Germany's role in Europe. The Great Depression revealed the fragility of the world economic system and cast millions out of work. In the end, perhaps, the era's intellectual achievements and the overall sense of crisis were closely related.

During the interwar years, many European nations—including Italy, Germany, Spain, Poland, Portugal, Austria, and Hungary—would fall one by one to authoritarian or Fascist dictatorships, succumbing to the temptations of totalitarianism. Liberal democracy was severely weakened. European stability was threatened by the radical programs of Soviet Communists on the left and Fascists on the right. And the world edged closer to the great conflict to come.

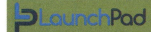

ONLINE DOCUMENT PROJECT

Gustav Stresemann

What were some of the challenges that leaders like Stresemann faced in building political consensus in Weimar Germany?

You encountered Gustav Stresemann's story on page 829. Keeping the question above in mind, examine documents that illuminate the competing visions of major Weimar political parties during the 1920s. *See inside the front cover to learn more.*

How did modernism revolutionize Western culture?	How did consumer society change everyday life?	What obstacles to lasting peace did European leaders face?	What were the causes and consequences of the Great Depression?	✔ **LearningCurve** Check what you know.

CHAPTER 26 STUDY GUIDE

STEP 1

GET STARTED ONLINE

LearningCurve

Now that you've read the chapter, make it stick by completing the LearningCurve activity.

STEP 2

EXPLAIN WHY IT MATTERS

Put your reading into practice. Identify each term below, and then explain why it matters in Western history.

TERM	WHO OR WHAT & WHEN	WHY IT MATTERS
logical positivism (p. 812)		
existentialism (p. 812)		
theory of special relativity (p. 814)		
id, ego, and superego (p. 816)		
modernism (p. 817)		
functionalism (p. 818)		
Bauhaus (p. 818)		
Dadaism (p. 819)		
stream-of-consciousness technique (p. 820)		
"modern girl" (p. 824)		
Dawes Plan (p. 828)		
Great Depression (p. 831)		
Popular Front (p. 836)		

STEP 3

MOVE BEYOND THE BASICS

To demonstrate a more advanced understanding, fill in the chart included below with descriptions of the work and ideas of key artistic and intellectual figures of the period. How did their work contribute to the intellectual and moral uncertainty of the early twentieth century?

Artist/intellectual	Key works or ideas	Overall contribution
Friedrich Nietzsche		
Ludwig Wittgenstein		
Jean-Paul Sartre		
Albert Einstein		
Sigmund Freud		
Virginia Woolf		
Pablo Picasso		
Igor Stravinsky		

PUT IT ALL TOGETHER

Now, take a step back and try to explain the big picture. Remember to use specific examples from the chapter in your answers.

MODERN SOCIETY AND CULTURE

▶ What is "modern" about modernism? How was modernism embodied in architecture, painting, and music in the early twentieth century?

▶ What shared experiences were made possible by cinema and radio? How did political leaders use these new forms of communication to promote their policies?

THE SEARCH FOR PEACE AND STABILITY

▶ What were the key sources of instability in the years following World War I, and how successful were Western leaders at responding to postwar challenges?

▶ What light does the breakdown of cooperation between governments in the 1930s shed on the policies and initiatives of the 1920s?

THE GREAT DEPRESSION

▶ How did the policies and problems of the 1920s contribute to both the onset of the Great Depression and the failure of Western nations to develop a coordinated response?

▶ Compare and contrast the response to the Great Depression in the United States, France, Britain, Germany, and the Scandinavian countries.

MAKE CONNECTIONS

▶ In your opinion, when did the modern age begin? Why did you choose the starting point you did?

▶ What trends and developments in the 1920s and 1930s decreased or increased the probability of a second world war?

> ## IN YOUR OWN WORDS

Imagine that you must give an oral report to the class answering the following question: **Why were anxiety and uncertainty such prominent components of early-twentieth-century thought and culture?** What would be the most important points and why?

27

DICTATORSHIPS AND THE SECOND WORLD WAR

1919–1945

> **How did totalitarian regimes attempt to remake European politics, culture, and society, and what impact did they have on World War II?**

Chapter 27 examines totalitarianism and World War II. In the age of anxiety, Communist and Fascist states undertook determined assaults on democratic government and individual rights across Europe. On the eve of the Second World War, popularly elected governments survived only in Great Britain, France, Czechoslovakia, the Low Countries, Scandinavia, and Switzerland. The human costs of totalitarianism were appalling. Millions died as Stalin forced communism on the Soviet Union in the 1930s. Attempts to build a "racially pure" New Order in Europe by Hitler's Nazi Germany led to the deaths of tens of millions more in World War II and the Holocaust, a scale of destruction far beyond that of World War I.

LearningCurve

After reading the chapter, use LearningCurve to retain what you've read.

Life at Auschwitz. This rough painting by an anonymous inmate of the Auschwitz-Birkenau Nazi concentration camp is preserved on the ceiling of a camp barracks. Prisoners labor on a drainage canal, while two carry a dead worker off the field. (De Agostini/Getty Images)

> How were Fascist and Communist totalitarian dictatorships similar and different?

> How did Stalin and the Communist Party build a totalitarian state in the Soviet Union?

> What kind of government did Mussolini establish in Italy?

> What policies did Nazi Germany pursue, and how did they lead to World War II?

> What explains the Allied victory in World War II?

> How were Fascist and Communist totalitarian dictatorships similar and different?

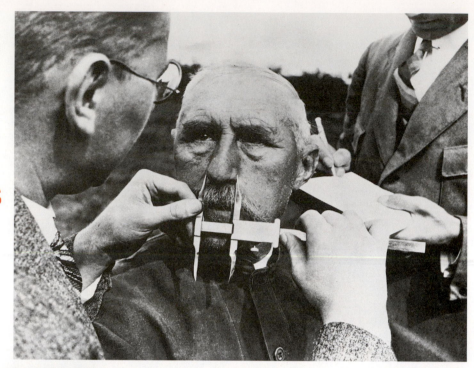

Eugenics in Nazi Germany

Nazi "race scientists" believed they could use the eugenic methods of social engineering to build a powerful Aryan race. In this photograph, published in a popular German magazine in 1933, a clinician measures a man's nose. Such pseudoscientific methods were used to determine an individual's supposed "racial value." (© Hulton-Deutsch Collection/Corbis)

BOTH CONSERVATIVE AND RADICAL DICTATORSHIPS took power in Europe in the 1920s and 1930s. Although these two types of dictatorship shared some characteristics, in essence they were quite different. Conservative authoritarian regimes, which had a long history in Europe, were limited in scope. Radical totalitarian dictatorships, based on the ideologies of communism and fascism, aimed at the radical reconstruction of society.

Conservative Authoritarianism and Radical Totalitarian Dictatorships

The traditional form of antidemocratic government in European history was conservative authoritarianism. Like Catherine the Great in Russia and Metternich in Austria, the leaders of such governments relied on obedient bureaucracies in their efforts to control society. Though political opponents were often jailed or exiled, these older authoritarian governments were limited in both power and objectives. They had neither the ability nor the desire to control many aspects of their subjects' lives. As long as the people did not try to change the system, they were typically allowed considerable personal independence. After the First World War,

1921
- New Economic Policy (NEP) in U.S.S.R.

1922
- Mussolini gains power in Italy

1924
- Mussolini seizes dictatorial powers

1924–1929
- Buildup of Nazi Party in Germany

1927
- Stalin comes to power in U.S.S.R.

1928
- Stalin's first five-year plan

1929
- Lateran Agreement; start of collectivization in Soviet Union

1929–1939
- Great Depression

1931
- Japan invades Manchuria

1932–1933
- Famine in Ukraine

1933
- Hitler appointed chancellor in Germany; Reichstag passes the Enabling Act, granting Hitler absolute dictatorial power

1935
- Nuremberg Laws deprive Jews of all rights of citizenship

1936
- Start of great purges under Stalin; Spanish Civil War begins

1937
- Japanese army invades China

1938
- Kristallnacht marks beginning of more aggressive anti-Jewish policy in Germany

1939
- Germany occupies Czech lands and invades western Poland; Britain and France declare war on Germany, starting World War II; Soviet Union occupies eastern Poland

1940
- Germany defeats and occupies France; Battle of Britain begins

1941
- Germany invades U.S.S.R.; Japan attacks Pearl Harbor; United States enters war

1941–1945
- The Holocaust

1942–1943
- Battle of Stalingrad

1944
- Allied invasion at Normandy

1945
- Soviet and U.S. forces enter Germany; United States drops atomic bombs on Japan; World War II ends

authoritarianism revived, especially in eastern Europe. What emerged, however, were new kinds of radical dictatorship that went much further than conservative authoritarianism.

Some scholars use the term totalitarianism to describe these radical dictatorships, which made unprecedented "total claims" on the beliefs and behavior of their citizens. The totalitarian model emphasizes the characteristics that Fascist and Communist dictatorships had in common. One-party totalitarian states used violent political repression and intense propaganda to gain complete power. In addition, the state tried to dominate the economic, social, intellectual, and cultural aspects of people's lives.

Most historians agree that totalitarianism owed much to the experience of total war in 1914 to 1918 (see Chapter 25). World War I required state governments to limit individual liberties and intervene in the economy in order to achieve one supreme objective: victory. Totalitarian leaders were inspired by the example of the modern state at war and greatly expanded the power of the state in pursuit of social control.

totalitarianism
▶ A radical dictatorship that exercises "total claims" over the beliefs and behavior of its citizens by taking control of the economic, social, intellectual, and cultural aspects of society.

| How did Stalin and the Communist Party build a totalitarian state in the Soviet Union? | What kind of government did Mussolini establish in Italy? | What policies did Nazi Germany pursue, and how did they lead to World War II? | What explains the Allied victory in World War II? | ✓ LearningCurve Check what you know. |

Communist and Fascist dictatorships shared other characteristics. Both rejected parliamentary government and liberal values. Classical liberals (see Chapter 21, page 649) sought to limit the power of the state and protect the rights of the individual. Totalitarians, on the other hand, believed that individualism undermined equality and unity, and rejected democracy in favor of one-party political systems.

A charismatic leader typically dominated the totalitarian state—Stalin in the Soviet Union, Mussolini in Italy, Hitler in Germany. All three created political parties of a new kind, dedicated to promoting idealized visions of collective harmony. They used force and terror to intimidate and destroy political opponents and pursued policies of imperial expansion to exploit other lands. They censored the mass media and instituted propaganda campaigns to advance their goals. (See "Picturing the Past: The Appeal of Propaganda.") Finally, and perhaps most important, totalitarian governments engaged in massive projects of

The Appeal of Propaganda

Totalitarian leaders used extensive propaganda campaigns to enlist the support of the masses. Italian dictator Benito Mussolini repeatedly linked his regime to the glory of ancient Rome. Here he has donned the costume of a legionary to lead a parade in front of the Roman Coliseum (top). The Soviet dictator Stalin presented himself as the friend of all humankind. In this propaganda poster (bottom), titled "The Great Stalin is the Banner of Friendship Between the Peoples of the U.S.S.R.!," he receives flowers from a diverse group of Soviet citizens, including ethnic Russians and East and Central Asians. This idealized testament to peaceful coexistence within the Soviet empire masked the tensions aroused by Russian domination. (© Mussolini: Stefano Bianchetti/Corbis; Stalin poster: The Granger Collection, New York)

> PICTURING THE PAST

ANALYZING THE IMAGE: How do these images present the role of the dictatorial leader? How do they represent the relationship between the leader and the led?

CONNECTIONS: How might these idealized portrayals have helped build support for their respective regimes? Was there any truth behind the propaganda?

CHAPTER LOCATOR | **How were Fascist and Communist totalitarian dictatorships similar and different?**

state-controlled social engineering dedicated to replacing individualism with a unified "people" capable of exercising the collective will.

Communism and Fascism

Communism and fascism clearly shared a desire to revolutionize state and society, but there were important differences between them. Following Marx, Soviet Communists strove to create an international brotherhood of workers. In the Communist utopia to come, economic exploitation would disappear and society would be based on radical social equality (see Chapter 21). Under Stalin's rule, the state aggressively intervened in all walks of life to pursue this social leveling, attacking the upper and middle classes and nationalizing private property (see pages 847–849).

The Fascist vision of a new society was quite different. Leaders who embraced fascism, such as Mussolini and Hitler, claimed that they were striving to build a new community on a national—not an international—level. Extreme nationalists, and often racists, Fascists glorified war and the military. For them, the nation was the highest embodiment of the people, and the powerful leader was the materialization of the people's collective will.

Like Communists, Fascists promised to improve the lives of ordinary workers. Fascist governments intervened in the economy, but unlike Communist regimes they did not try to level class differences and nationalize private property. Instead, they presented a vision of a social community bound together by nationalism.

Communists and Fascists differed in another crucial respect: the question of race. Where Communists sought to build a new world around the destruction of class differences, Fascists typically sought to build a new national community grounded in racial homogeneity. Fascists embraced the doctrine of eugenics, a pseudoscience that maintained that the selective breeding of human beings could improve the general characteristics of a national population.

The clash between Communists and Fascists was in large part responsible for the horrific destruction and loss of life in the middle of the twentieth century. Explaining the nature of totalitarian dictatorships thus remains a crucial project for historians, even as they look more closely at the ideological differences between communism and fascism.

One important set of questions explores the way dictatorial regimes generated popular consensus. Neither Hitler nor Stalin ever achieved the total control each sought. Nor did they rule alone; modern dictators need the help of large state bureaucracies and the cooperation of large numbers of ordinary people. Which was more important for generating popular support: terror and coercion or material rewards? Under what circumstances did people resist or perpetrate totalitarian tyranny? These questions lead us toward what Holocaust survivor Primo Levi called the "gray zone" of moral compromise, which defined everyday life in totalitarian societies. (See "Individuals in Society: Primo Levi," page 869.)

fascism
▶ A movement characterized by extreme, often expansionist nationalism; antisocialism; a dynamic and violent leader; and glorification of war and the military.

eugenics
▶ A pseudoscientific doctrine that maintains that the selective breeding of human beings can improve the general characteristics of a national population. It helped inspire Nazi ideas about "race and space" and ultimately contributed to the Holocaust.

QUICK REVIEW <

What were the most important differences between traditional European antidemocratic governments and the radical dictatorships that emerged in the 1920s and 1930s?

| How did Stalin and the Communist Party build a totalitarian state in the Soviet Union? | What kind of government did Mussolini establish in Italy? | What policies did Nazi Germany pursue, and how did they lead to World War II? | What explains the Allied victory in World War II? | ✓ LearningCurve Check what you know. |

How did Stalin and the Communist Party build a totalitarian state in the Soviet Union?

Day Shift at Magnitogorsk Beginning in 1928, Stalin's government issued a series of ambitious five-year plans designed to industrialize the Soviet Union rapidly. The plans focused primarily on boosting heavy industry and included the building of a gigantic steel complex at Magnitogorsk in the Ural Mountains. Here, steelworkers review production goals at the Magnitogorsk foundry. (© Sovfoto)

A MASTER OF POLITICAL INFIGHTING, Joseph Stalin (1879–1953) cautiously consolidated his power and eliminated his enemies after Lenin's death in 1924. Then in 1928, as undisputed leader of the ruling Communist Party, Stalin launched the first **five-year plan**—the "revolution from above," as he termed it—the beginning of a radical attempt to transform Soviet society into a Communist state. The ultimate goal of this effort was to generate new attitudes, new loyalties, and a new socialist humanity. The means were constant propaganda, sacrifice by the people, harsh repression that included purges and executions, and rewards for those who followed the party line. Thus the Soviet Union in the 1930s became a totalitarian state.

five-year plan

▶ A plan launched by Stalin in 1928, and termed the "revolution from above," aimed at modernizing the Soviet Union and creating a new Communist society with new attitudes, new loyalties, and a new socialist humanity.

New Economic Policy (NEP)

▶ Lenin's 1921 policy to re-establish limited economic freedom in an attempt to rebuild agriculture and industry in the face of economic disintegration.

From Lenin to Stalin

By spring 1921, Lenin and the Bolsheviks had won the civil war, but they ruled a shattered and devastated land. In the face of economic disintegration, Lenin replaced War Communism with the **New Economic Policy (NEP)**, which

CHAPTER LOCATOR | How were Fascist and Communist totalitarian dictatorships similar and different?

re-established limited economic freedom in an attempt to rebuild agriculture and industry. Peasant producers were permitted to sell their surpluses in free markets, and private traders and small handicraft manufacturers were allowed to reappear. Heavy industry, railroads, and banks, however, remained wholly nationalized. The NEP brought rapid economic recovery, and by 1926 industrial output surpassed, and agricultural production almost equaled, prewar levels.

In 1924, as the economy recovered and the government partially relaxed its censorship and repression, Lenin died without a chosen successor, creating an intense struggle for power in the inner circles of the Communist Party. The principal contenders were Stalin and Trotsky. In the end, Stalin won, in large part because he was more effective at gaining the all-important support of the party. Having risen to general secretary of the party's Central Committee in 1922, he used his office to win friends and allies with jobs and promises.

Stalin's ascendancy had a momentous impact on the policy of the new Soviet state toward non-Russians. The Communists had inherited the vast multiethnic territories of the former Russian empire. Lenin initially argued that these ethnic groups should have the right to self-determination even if they claimed independence from the Soviet state. In 1922, reflecting such ideas, the Union of Soviet Socialist Republics (or U.S.S.R.) was organized as a federation of four Soviet republics: the Russian Soviet Federative Socialist Republic, Ukraine, Belorussia, and a Transcaucasian republic. The last was later split into Armenia, Azerbaijan, and Georgia, and five Central Asian republics were established in the 1920s and 1930s (**Map 27.1**).

In contrast to Lenin, Stalin argued for more centralized Russian control of these ethnic regions. His view would dominate state policy until the breakup of the Soviet Union in the early 1990s. The Soviet republics were granted some cultural independence but no real political autonomy. The Stalinists thus established a far-flung Communist empire on the imperial holdings of the former tsars.

Stalin achieved supreme power between 1922 and 1927. First he allied with Trotsky's personal enemies to crush his rival, and then he moved against all who might challenge his ascendancy, including former allies. Stalin's final triumph came at the party congress of December 1927, which condemned all "deviation from the general party line" that he had formulated.

The Five-Year Plans

The party congress of 1927, which ratified Stalin's consolidation of power, marked the end of the NEP; the following year marked the beginning of the era of socialist five-year plans. The first of these plans had staggering economic objectives. In just five years, total industrial output was to increase by 250 percent, with heavy industry, the preferred sector, growing even faster. Agricultural production was slated to increase by 150 percent, and one-fifth of the peasants in the Soviet Union were to give up their private plots and join collective farms.

Stalin unleashed his "second revolution" for a variety of interrelated reasons. There were, first of all, ideological considerations. Stalin and his militant supporters feared a gradual restoration of capitalism; wished to promote the working classes; and were eager to abolish the NEP's private traders, independent artisans, and property-owning peasants. Economic motivations were also important.

How did Stalin and the Communist Party build a totalitarian state in the Soviet Union? | What kind of government did Mussolini establish in Italy? | What policies did Nazi Germany pursue, and how did they lead to World War II? | What explains the Allied victory in World War II? | ✔ LearningCurve Check what you know.

847

MAP 27.1 ■ The Formation of the U.S.S.R.

When the Bolsheviks successfully overthrew the tsarist government and won the civil war that followed, they inherited the vast territories of the former Russian empire. Following policies instituted by Stalin, they established a Union of Soviet Socialist Republics (U.S.S.R.) that gave limited cultural independence but no real political autonomy to the various Soviet republics under Communist control.

A fragile economic recovery stalled in 1927 and 1928, and a new offensive seemed necessary to ensure industrial and agricultural growth and to help the U.S.S.R. to catch up with the West.

The independent peasantry remained a major problem as well. For centuries, the peasants had wanted to own the land, and finally they had it. Sooner or later, Stalinists reasoned, landowning peasants would embrace conservative capitalism and pose a threat to the regime. At the same time, the Communists—mainly urban dwellers—believed that the "class enemy" in the villages could be squeezed to provide the enormous sums needed for all-out industrialization. To resolve these issues, in 1929, Stalin ordered the **collectivization of agriculture**—the forced consolidation of individual peasant farms into large, state-controlled enterprises that served as agricultural factories.

collectivization of agriculture

▶ The forcible consolidation of individual peasant farms into large state-controlled enterprises in the Soviet Union under Stalin.

CHAPTER LOCATOR | How were Fascist and Communist totalitarian dictatorships similar and different?

The increasingly repressive measures instituted by the state first focused on the **kulaks**, the class of well-off peasants who had benefited the most from the NEP. The kulaks were held up as a great enemy of progress, and Stalin called for their "liquidation" and seizure of their land. Stripped of land and livestock, many starved or were deported to forced-labor camps for "re-education."

Forced collectivization led to disaster. Large numbers of peasants opposed to the change slaughtered their animals and burned their crops rather than turn them over to state commissars. Nor were the state-controlled collective farms more productive. The output of grain barely increased over the first five-year plan, and collectivized agriculture was unable to make any substantial financial contribution to Soviet industrial development in the first five-year plan.

Collectivization in the fertile farmlands of the Ukraine was more rapid and violent than in other Soviet territories. The drive against peasants snowballed into an assault on Ukrainians in general. In 1932, as collectivization and deportations continued, party leaders set levels of grain deliveries for the Ukrainian collectives at excessively high levels and refused to relax those quotas or allow food relief when Ukrainian Communist leaders reported that starvation was occurring. The result was a terrible man-made famine in Ukraine in 1932 and 1933, which claimed 3 to 3.5 million lives.

By the end of 1938, government representatives had moved 93 percent of peasant households onto collective farms, neutralizing them as a political threat. Nonetheless, peasant resistance had forced the supposedly all-powerful state to make modest concessions. Peasants secured the right to limit a family's labor on the state-run farms and to cultivate tiny family plots, which provided them with much of their food.

The rapid industrialization mandated by the five-year plans was more successful. Soviet industry produced about four times as much in 1937 as it had in 1928. No other major country had ever achieved such rapid industrial growth. Rapid industrialization had dramatic social consequences. An industrial labor force was created almost overnight as peasant men and women began working in the huge steel mills built across the country. The government could assign workers to any job anywhere in the country. When factory managers needed more hands, they called on their counterparts on the collective farms, who sent them millions of "unneeded" peasants over the years. Industrial growth led to urban development: more than 25 million people, mostly peasants, migrated to cities during the 1930s.

Life and Culture in Soviet Society

Daily life was difficult in Stalin's Soviet Union. The lack of housing was a particularly serious problem. Millions were moving into the cities, but the government built few new apartments. A relatively lucky family received one room for all its members and shared both a kitchen and a toilet with others living on the same floor. There were constant shortages of goods as well. Because consumption was reduced to pay for investment, there was little improvement in the average standard of living in the years before World War II.

Life was by no means hopeless, however. Idealism and ideology had real appeal for many Communists and ordinary citizens, who saw themselves heroically

kulaks

▶ The better-off peasants who were stripped of land and livestock under Stalin and were generally not permitted to join collective farms; many of them starved or were deported to forced-labor camps for "re-education."

| How did Stalin and the Communist Party build a totalitarian state in the Soviet Union? | What kind of government did Mussolini establish in Italy? | What policies did Nazi Germany pursue, and how did they lead to World War II? | What explains the Allied victory in World War II? | ✓ LearningCurve Check what you know. |

849

building the world's first socialist society. This optimistic belief in the future of the Soviet Union attracted many disillusioned Westerners to communism in the 1930s. On a more practical level, Soviet workers received important social benefits, such as old-age pensions, free medical services, free education, and day-care centers for children. Unemployment was almost unknown.

Communism also opened possibilities for personal advancement. Rapid industrialization required massive numbers of skilled workers, engineers, and plant managers. In the 1930s, the Stalinist state broke with the egalitarian policies of the 1920s, and began to offer high salaries and special privileges to its growing technical and managerial elite. This group joined with the political and artistic elites in a new upper class, whose members grew rich and powerful.

The radical transformation of Soviet society had a profound impact on women's lives. Marxists had traditionally believed that both capitalism and middle-class husbands exploited women, and the Russian Revolution of 1917 immediately proclaimed complete equality for women. In the 1920s, divorce and abortion were made easily available, and women were urged to work outside the home. After Stalin came to power, he reversed this trend. The government revoked many laws supporting women's emancipation in order to strengthen the traditional family and build up the state's population.

At the same time, women saw lasting changes in education. The Soviets opened higher education to women, who could now enter the ranks of the better-paid specialists in industry and science. Medicine practically became a woman's profession. By 1950, 75 percent of all doctors in the Soviet Union were female.

Alongside such advances, however, Soviet society demanded great sacrifices from women. The vast majority of women had to work outside the home. Peasant women continued to work on farms, and millions of women toiled in factories and in heavy construction. Men continued to dominate the very best jobs. Finally, rapid change and economic hardship led to many broken families, creating further physical and emotional strains for women.

Culture was thoroughly politicized for propaganda and indoctrination purposes. Party activists lectured workers in factories and peasants on collective farms, while newspapers, films, and radio broadcasts endlessly recounted socialist achievements and capitalist plots. In the 1930s, intellectuals were ordered by Stalin to become "engineers of human minds." Writers and artists who could effectively combine genuine creativity and political propaganda became the darlings of the regime.

Stalin seldom appeared in public, but his presence was everywhere—in portraits, statues, books, and quotations from his writings. Although the government persecuted those who practiced religion and turned churches into "museums of atheism," the state had both an earthly religion and a high priest—Marxism-Leninism and Joseph Stalin.

Stalinist Terror and the Great Purges

In the mid-1930s, the great offensive to build socialism and a new society culminated in ruthless police terror and a massive purging of the Communist Party. In late 1934, Stalin's number-two man, Sergei Kirov, was mysteriously killed. Stalin—who probably ordered Kirov's murder—blamed the assassination on "Fascist

CHAPTER LOCATOR | How were Fascist and Communist totalitarian dictatorships similar and different?

agents" within the party. He used the incident to launch a reign of terror that purged the Communist Party of supposed traitors and solidified his own control.

Murderous repression picked up steam over the next two years. It culminated in the "great purge" of 1936 to 1938, a series of spectacular public show trials in which false evidence, often gathered using torture, was used to incriminate party administrators and Red Army leaders. In August 1936, sixteen "Old Bolsheviks"—prominent leaders who had been in the party since the Russian Revolution—confessed to all manner of contrived plots against Stalin; all were executed. In 1937, the secret police arrested a mass of lesser party officials and newer members, using torture to extract confessions and precipitating more show trials. In addition to the party faithful, union officials, managers, intellectuals, army officers, and countless ordinary citizens were accused of counter-revolutionary activities. At least 6 million people were arrested, and probably 1 to 2 million of these were executed or never returned from prisons and forced-labor camps.

The purges seriously weakened the Soviet Union in economic, intellectual, and military terms. But they left Stalin in command of a vast new state apparatus, staffed by the 1.5 million new party members enlisted to replace the purge victims. Thus more than half of all Communist Party members in 1941 had joined since the purges, and they experienced rapid social advance. Often the children of workers, they had usually studied in the new technical schools, and they soon proved capable of managing the government and large-scale production. Despite their human costs, the great purges thus brought substantial practical rewards to this new generation of committed Communists. They would serve Stalin effectively until his death in 1953, and they would govern the Soviet Union until the early 1980s.

QUICK REVIEW <

Why did so many ordinary Soviet citizens support Stalin and his policies?

How did Stalin and the Communist Party build a totalitarian state in the Soviet Union?

What kind of government did Mussolini establish in Italy?

What policies did Nazi Germany pursue, and how did they lead to World War II?

What explains the Allied victory in World War II?

✓ LearningCurve
Check what you know.

What kind of government did Mussolini establish in Italy?

Fascist Youth on Parade Totalitarian governments in Italy and Nazi Germany established mass youth organizations to instill the values of national unity and train young soldiers for the state. These members of the Balila, Italy's Fascist youth organization, raise their rifles in salute at a mass rally in 1939. (© Hulton-Deutsch Collection/Corbis)

MUSSOLINI'S FASCIST MOVEMENT and his seizure of power in 1922 were important steps in the rise of dictatorships in Europe between the two world wars. Mussolini and his supporters were the first to call themselves "Fascists" — revolutionaries determined to create a new totalitarian state based on extreme nationalism and militarism.

The Seizure of Power

On the eve of World War I, the Italian parliament granted universal male suffrage, and Italy appeared to be moving toward democracy. But there were serious problems. Much of the population was still poor, and many peasants were more attached to their villages and local interests than to the national state. Moreover, the papacy, many devout Catholics, conservatives, and landowners remained strongly opposed to liberal institutions, and relations between church and state were often tense. Class differences were also extreme, leading to the development of a powerful revolutionary socialist movement.

World War I worsened the political situation. To win support for the war effort, the Italian government had promised territorial expansion as well as social and

CHAPTER LOCATOR | How were Fascist and Communist totalitarian dictatorships similar and different?

land reform, which it could not deliver. Instead, the Versailles treaty denied Italy any territorial gains, and soaring unemployment and inflation after the war created mass hardship. In response, radical workers and peasants began occupying factories and seizing land in 1920. These actions mobilized the property-owning classes. Moreover, after the war the pope lifted his ban on participation by Catholics in Italian politics, and a strong Catholic party quickly emerged. Thus, by 1921, revolutionary socialists, conservatives, Catholics, and property owners were all opposed—though for different reasons—to the liberal government.

Into these crosscurrents of unrest and fear stepped Benito Mussolini (1883–1945). Mussolini began his political career before World War I as a Socialist Party leader and radical newspaper editor. In 1914, he had urged that Italy join the Allies, a stand for which he was expelled from the Socialist Party. After the war, Mussolini began organizing bitter war veterans like himself into a band of Fascists—from the Italian word for "a union of forces."

At first, Mussolini's program was a radical combination of nationalist and socialist demands. As such, it competed directly with the well-organized Socialist Party and failed to get off the ground. When Mussolini saw that his violent verbal assaults on rival Socialists won him growing support from conservatives and the frightened middle classes, he shifted gears in 1920 and became a sworn enemy of socialism. Mussolini and his private militia of **Black Shirts** grew increasingly violent.

Fascism soon became a mass movement, one which Mussolini claimed would help the little people against the established interests. In 1922, in the midst of chaos largely created by his Black Shirt militias, Mussolini stepped forward as the savior of order and property. Striking a conservative, anticommunist note in his speeches and gaining the support of army leaders, Mussolini demanded the resignation of the existing government. In October 1922, a band of armed Fascists marched on Rome to threaten the king and force him to appoint Mussolini prime minister of Italy. The threat worked. Victor Emmanuel III (r. 1900–1946) asked Mussolini to take over the government and form a new cabinet. Thus, after widespread violence and a threat of armed uprising, Mussolini seized power using the legal framework of the Italian constitution.

Black Shirts
▶ Mussolini's private militia that destroyed socialist newspapers, union halls, and Socialist Party headquarters, eventually pushing Socialists out of the city governments of northern Italy.

The Regime in Action

Mussolini became prime minister in 1922, but he moved cautiously in his first two years in office to establish control of the government. Once in control, however, he moved rapidly to establish a one-party dictatorship. Starting in 1924, the government ruled by decree, abolished freedom of the press, and organized fixed elections. Mussolini arrested his political opponents, disbanded all independent labor unions, and put dedicated Fascists in control of Italy's schools.

Mussolini's Fascist Party drew support from broad sectors of the population, in large part because he was willing to compromise with the traditional elites that controlled the army, the economy, and the state. He left big business to regulate itself, and there was no land reform. Mussolini also drew increasing support from the Catholic Church. In the **Lateran Agreement** of 1929, he recognized the Vatican as an independent state, and he agreed to give the church significant financial support in return for the pope's support. Because he was forced to compromise

Lateran Agreement
▶ A 1929 agreement that recognized the Vatican as an independent state, with Mussolini agreeing to give the church heavy financial support in return for public support from the pope.

How did Stalin and the Communist Party build a totalitarian state in the Soviet Union?

What kind of government did Mussolini establish in Italy?

What policies did Nazi Germany pursue, and how did they lead to World War II?

What explains the Allied victory in World War II?

☑ LearningCurve
Check what you know.

Italy's Ethiopian Campaign,
1935–1936

with these conservative elites, Mussolini never established complete totalitarian control.

Mussolini's government nonetheless proceeded with attempts to bring fascism to Italy. The state engineered popular consent by staging massive rallies and sporting events, creating Fascist youth and women's movements, and providing new welfare benefits. Fascist propaganda promoted a "cult of the Duce" (leader), portraying Mussolini as a powerful strongman who embodied the best qualities of the Italian people. Like other Fascist regimes, his government was vehemently opposed to liberal feminism and promoted traditional gender roles. Mussolini also gained support by manipulating popular pride in the grand history of the ancient Roman Empire.

Mussolini matched his aggressive rhetoric with military action: Italian armies invaded the African nation of Ethiopia in October 1935. After surprising setbacks at the hands of the poorly armed Ethiopian army, the Italians won in 1936, and Mussolini could proudly declare that Italy again had its empire. Though it shocked international opinion, the war resulted in close ties between Italy and Nazi Germany.

Deeply influenced by Hitler's example (see page 862), Mussolini's government passed a series of anti-Jewish racial laws in 1938. Though the laws were unpopular, Jews were forced out of public schools and dismissed from professional careers. Nevertheless, extreme anti-Semitic persecution did not occur in Italy until late in World War II, when Italy was under Nazi control. Though Mussolini's repressive tactics were never as ruthless as those in Nazi Germany, his government did much to turn Italy into a totalitarian police state.

> **QUICK REVIEW**

What steps did Mussolini take to win the support of conservative groups in Italian society? Why was such support so important to him?

CHAPTER LOCATOR | How were Fascist and Communist totalitarian dictatorships similar and different?

Mothers in the Fatherland

Nazi ideologues promoted strictly defined gender roles for men and women, and the Nazi state implemented a variety of social programs to encourage "racially correct" women to stay home and raise "Aryan" children. This colorful poster portrays the joy of motherhood and calls for donations to the Mother and Child division of the National Socialist People's Welfare office. (akg-images)

What policies did Nazi Germany pursue, and how did they lead to World War II?

THE MOST FRIGHTENING DICTATORSHIP developed in Nazi Germany. Under Hitler, the Nazi dictatorship smashed or took over most independent organizations, established firm control over the German state and society, and violently persecuted the Jewish population and non-German peoples. Truly totalitarian in aspiration, the dynamism of Nazi Germany, based on racial aggression and territorial expansion, led to history's most destructive war.

The Roots of National Socialism

National Socialism grew out of many complex developments, of which the most influential were nationalism and racism. These two ideas captured the mind of the young Adolf Hitler (1889–1945), and he dominated Nazism until the end of World War II.

The son of an Austrian customs official, Hitler spent his childhood in small towns in Austria. After dropping out of school at age fourteen, Hitler moved to

National Socialism
▶ A movement and political party driven by extreme nationalism and racism, led by Adolf Hitler; its adherents ruled Germany from 1933 to 1945 and forced Europe into World War II.

| How did Stalin and the Communist Party build a totalitarian state in the Soviet Union? | What kind of government did Mussolini establish in Italy? | **What policies did Nazi Germany pursue, and how did they lead to World War II?** | What explains the Allied victory in World War II? | ✓ LearningCurve Check what you know. |

1919	Treaty of Versailles is signed
1922	Mussolini gains power in Italy
1927	Stalin takes full control in the Soviet Union
1931	Japan invades Manchuria
January 1933	Hitler appointed chancellor of Germany
October 1933	Germany withdraws from the League of Nations
March 1935	Hitler announces German rearmament
October 1935	Mussolini invades Ethiopia
March 1936	German armies move unopposed into the Rhineland
1936–1939	Civil war in Spain, culminating in taking of power by Fascist regime under Franco
October 1936	Rome-Berlin Axis created
1937	Japan invades China
March 1938	Germany annexes Austria
September 1938	Munich Conference: Britain and France agree to German seizure of the Sudetenland from Czechoslovakia
March 1939	Germany occupies the rest of Czechoslovakia; appeasement ends in Britain
August 1939	Nazi-Soviet pact signed
September 1, 1939	Germany invades Poland
September 3, 1939	Britain and France declare war on Germany

Vienna, where he was exposed to extreme Austro-German nationalists who advocated the union of Austria with Germany and the violent expulsion of "inferior" peoples as the means of maintaining German domination of the Austro-Hungarian Empire.

In Vienna, Hitler developed a belief in the crudest distortions of Social Darwinism (see Chapter 22, page 700), the superiority of Germanic races, and the inevitability of racial conflict. Exposure to poor eastern European Jews contributed to his anti-Semitic prejudice. Jews, Hitler now claimed, directed an international conspiracy of finance capitalism and Marxist socialism against German culture, German unity, and the German people.

Hitler was not alone. Racist anti-Semitism became wildly popular on the far right wing of European politics in the decades surrounding the First World War. Such irrational beliefs, rooted in centuries of Christian anti-Semitism, were given pseudoscientific legitimacy by nineteenth-century developments in biology and eugenics. These ideas came to define Hitler's worldview and would play an immense role in the ideology and actions of National Socialism.

Hitler greeted the outbreak of the First World War as a salvation. The struggle and discipline of war gave life meaning, and Hitler served on the western front. Germany's defeat shattered his world. Convinced that Jews and Marxists had "stabbed Germany in the back," he vowed to fight on.

In late 1919, Hitler joined a tiny extremist group in Munich called the German Workers' Party. By 1921, Hitler had gained control of this small but growing party, which had been renamed the National Socialist German Workers' Party, or Nazis for short. In late 1923 the Weimar Republic seemed on the verge of collapse, and Hitler, inspired by Mussolini's recent victory, organized an armed uprising in Munich—the so-called Beer Hall Putsch. Despite the failure of the poorly planned coup and Hitler's arrest, National Socialism had been born.

Hitler's Road to Power

At his trial, Hitler gained enormous publicity by denouncing the Weimar Republic. He used his brief prison term to dictate his book *Mein Kampf* (My Struggle), where he laid out his basic ideas on "racial purification" and territorial expansion that would define National Socialism.

In *Mein Kampf,* Hitler claimed that Germans were a "master race" that needed to defend its "pure blood" from groups he labeled "racial degenerates." The German race was destined to triumph and grow, and, according to Hitler, it

CHAPTER LOCATOR | How were Fascist and Communist totalitarian dictatorships similar and different?

needed *Lebensraum* (living space). This space could be found to Germany's east, which Hitler claimed was inhabited by the "subhuman" Slavs and Jews. The future dictator outlined a sweeping vision of war and conquest in which the German master race would colonize east and central Europe and ultimately replace the "subhumans" living there. He championed the idea of the leader-dictator, or *Führer* (FYOUR-uhr), who would lead the German nation to victory. These ideas— a deadly combination of race and space—would ultimately propel the world into the Second World War.

In the years of relative prosperity and stability between 1924 and 1929, Hitler built up the Nazi Party. The Nazis, however, still remained a small splinter group in 1928, when they received only 2.6 percent of the vote in the general elections and only twelve seats in the Reichstag, the German parliament.

The Great Depression of 1929 brought the ascent of National Socialism. Now Hitler promised German voters economic as well as political salvation. His appeals for "national rebirth" appealed to a broad spectrum of voters. Seized by panic as bankruptcies increased, unemployment soared, and the Communists made dramatic election gains, voters deserted conservative and moderate parties for the Nazis. In the election of 1930, the Nazis won 6.5 million votes and 107 seats, and in July 1932, they gained 14.5 million votes—38 percent of the total. They were now the largest party in the Reichstag.

The breakdown of democratic government helped the Nazis seize power. Chancellor Heinrich Brüning (BROU-nihng) tried to overcome the economic crisis by cutting back government spending and ruthlessly forcing down prices and wages. His conservative policies intensified Germany's economic collapse and undermined support for the country's republican leaders, adding to Hitler's appeal.

Division on the left also contributed to Nazi success. The Communists refused to cooperate with the Social Democrats. Failing to resolve their differences, these parties could not mount an effective opposition to the Nazi takeover.

Finally, Hitler excelled in backroom politics. In 1932, Hitler cleverly gained the support of the conservative politicians in power. They accepted Hitler's demand to be appointed chancellor in a coalition government, reasoning that he could be used and controlled. On January 30, 1933, Adolf Hitler, leader of the largest party in Germany, was appointed chancellor by President Hindenburg.

State and Society in Nazi Germany

Hitler moved rapidly and skillfully to establish an unshakable dictatorship that would pursue the Nazi program of race and space. To maintain appearances, Hitler called for new elections. In February 1933, in the midst of an electoral campaign plagued by violence—much of it caused by Nazi toughs—the Reichstag building was partly destroyed by fire. Hitler blamed the Communists and convinced Hindenburg to sign emergency acts that abolished freedom of speech and assembly as well as most personal liberties.

The façade of democratic government was soon torn asunder. When the Nazis won only 44 percent of the vote in the elections, Hitler outlawed the Communist Party and arrested its parliamentary representatives. Then on March 23, 1933, the

How did Stalin and the Communist Party build a totalitarian state in the Soviet Union?

What kind of government did Mussolini establish in Italy?

What policies did Nazi Germany pursue, and how did they lead to World War II?

What explains the Allied victory in World War II?

✔ LearningCurve
Check what you know.

857

Enabling Act

► An act pushed through the Reichstag by the Nazis that gave Hitler absolute dictatorial power for four years.

Nazis pushed through the Reichstag the **Enabling Act**, which gave Hitler dictatorial power for four years.

Germany became a one-party Nazi state. The new regime took over the government bureaucracy intact, installing Nazis in top positions. At the same time, it created a series of overlapping Nazi Party organizations responsible solely to Hitler. Once the Nazis were firmly in command, Hitler and the party turned their attention to constructing a National Socialist society defined by national unity and racial exclusion. First they eliminated political enemies. Communists, Social Democrats, and trade-union leaders were forced out of their jobs or arrested and taken to hastily built concentration camps.

Hitler then purged the Nazi Party itself of its more extremist elements. The Nazi storm troopers (the SA), the brown shirts who had fought Communists and beaten up Jews before the Nazis took power, now expected top positions in the army. Some SA radicals even talked of a "second revolution" that would sweep away capitalism. Now that he was in power, however, Hitler was eager to win the support of the traditional military and maintain social order. He decided that the leadership of the SA had to be eliminated. On the night of June 30, 1934, Hitler's elite personal guard—the SS—arrested and executed about one hundred SA leaders and other political enemies. Afterward, the SS grew rapidly. Under its methodical, ruthless leader Heinrich Himmler (1900–1945), the SS took over the political police and the concentration camp system.

Acting on its vision of racial purity, the party began a many-faceted campaign against those deemed incapable of making positive contributions to the "master race." The Nazis persecuted a number of supposedly undesirable groups. Jews headed the list, but Slavic peoples, Sinti and Roma (Gypsies), homosexuals, Jehovah's Witnesses, and people considered handicapped were also targets of ostracism and brutal repression.

In what some historians term the Nazi "racial state," barbarism and race hatred were institutionalized with the force of science and law.[1] New university academies, such as the German Society for Racial Research, wrote studies that measured and defined racial differences; prejudice was thus presented in the guise of enlightened science. The ethical breakdown was exemplified in a series of sterilization laws, which led to the forced sterilization of some four hundred thousand "undesirable" citizens.

From the beginning, German Jews were a special target of Nazi persecution. In 1935, the infamous Nuremberg Laws classified as Jewish anyone having three or more Jewish grandparents, outlawed marriage and sexual relations between Jews and those defined as German, and deprived Jews of all rights of citizenship. For the vast majority of German citizens not targeted by such laws, the creation of a demonized outsider group may well have contributed to feelings of national unity and support for the Hitler regime.

In late 1938, the assault on the Jews accelerated. During a well-organized wave of violence known as Kristallnacht (or the Night of Broken Glass), Nazi gangs smashed windows and looted over 7,000 Jewish-owned shops, destroyed many homes, burned down over 200 synagogues, and killed dozens of Jews. German Jews were then rounded up and made to pay for the damage. By 1939, some 300,000 of Germany's 500,000 Jews had emigrated, sacrificing almost all their property in order to escape this persecution. Some Germans privately opposed these outrages, but most went along or looked the other way.

CHAPTER LOCATOR | How were Fascist and Communist totalitarian dictatorships similar and different?

Popular Support for National Socialism

Why did millions of ordinary Germans back a brutally repressive regime? A combination of coercion and reward enlisted popular support for the racial state. Using the secret police and the growing concentration camp system in a reign of ruthless terror, the regime persecuted its political and "racial" enemies. Yet for the large majority of ordinary German citizens who were not Jews, Communists, or members of other targeted groups, Hitler's government brought new opportunities.

Hitler had promised the masses economic recovery, and he delivered. The Nazi state launched a large public works program to help pull Germany out of the depression. Work began on superhighways, offices, gigantic sports stadiums, and public housing, which created jobs and instilled pride in national recovery. By 1938, unemployment had fallen to 2 percent, and there was a shortage of workers. Between 1932 and 1938, the standard of living for the average worker increased moderately. Business profits rose sharply.

The persecution of Jews brought substantial benefits to ordinary Germans as well. As Jews were forced out of their jobs and compelled to sell their homes and businesses, Germans stepped in to take their place in a process known as Aryanization (named after the "Aryan master race" prized by the Nazis for their supposedly pure German blood).

Economic recovery was accompanied by a wave of social and cultural innovation intended to construct what Nazi propagandists called the *Volksgemeinschaft*—a "people's community" for racially pure Germans. The party set up mass organizations to spread Nazi ideology and enlist volunteers for the Nazi cause. Mass rallies, such as annual May Day celebrations and Nazi Party conventions in Nuremberg, brought together thousands of participants. Glowing reports on such events in the Nazi-controlled press brought the message home to millions more.

As the economy recovered, the government proudly touted a glittering array of inexpensive and enticing people's products. Items such as the Volkswagen (the "people's car") were intended to link individuals' desire for consumer goods to the collective ideology of the "people's community." Though such programs faltered as the state increasingly focused on rearmament for the approaching war, they suggested to all that the regime was working hard to improve German living standards.

Hitler's rule promoted economic growth and social stability, and Nazi propagandists continually played up the supposed accomplishments of the regime. The vision of a "people's community," national pride in recovery, and feelings of belonging created by acts of racial exclusion led many Germans to support the regime. Hitler himself remained popular with broad sections of the population well into the war.

Not all Germans supported Hitler, however, and a number of groups actively resisted him after 1933. But opponents of the Nazis were never unified. Moreover, the regime clamped down on dissidents: tens of thousands of political enemies were imprisoned, and thousands were executed. In 1938 and again during the war, a few high-ranking army officers, who feared the consequences of Hitler's reckless aggression, plotted against him, but their plans were unsuccessful.

How did Stalin and the Communist Party build a totalitarian state in the Soviet Union?

What kind of government did Mussolini establish in Italy?

What policies did Nazi Germany pursue, and how did they lead to World War II?

What explains the Allied victory in World War II?

☑ LearningCurve
Check what you know.

Aggression and Appeasement

At the same time that they built the "people's community," the Nazis aggressively pursued policies meant to achieve territorial expansion for the supposedly superior German race. At first, Hitler carefully camouflaged his expansionist goals because Germany was still militarily weak. Germany's withdrawal from the League of Nations in October 1933, however, indicated that Gustav Stresemann's policy of peaceful cooperation was dead (see Chapter 26, page 826). Then, in March 1935, Hitler declared that Germany would no longer abide by the disarmament clauses of the Treaty of Versailles. He established a military draft and began to build up the German army. France and Great Britain protested strongly and warned against future aggressive actions.

Any hope of a united front against Hitler quickly collapsed. Britain adopted a policy of **appeasement**, granting Hitler everything he could reasonably want (and more) to avoid war. British appeasement was motivated in large part by the pacifism of a population still horrified by the memory of the First World War. As in

appeasement

▶ The British policy toward Germany prior to World War II that aimed at granting Hitler whatever he wanted, including western Czechoslovakia, in order to avoid war.

"Peace for Our Time" British prime minister Neville Chamberlain speaks at the London airport after a meeting with Adolf Hitler in Munich in September 1938. In return for acceptance of the German annexation of the Czech Sudetenland, Hitler promised to halt foreign aggression, and Chamberlain famously announced that he had negotiated "peace for our time" with the Nazi leader. Less than a year later, Germany invaded Poland and Europe was at war. (Central Press/Getty Images)

CHAPTER LOCATOR | How were Fascist and Communist totalitarian dictatorships similar and different?

Germany, many powerful conservatives in Britain underestimated Hitler. They believed that Soviet communism was the real danger and that Hitler could be used to stop it.

When Hitler suddenly marched his armies into the demilitarized Rhineland in March 1936, violating the treaties of Versailles and Locarno (**Map 27.2**), Britain refused to act. France could do little without British support. Emboldened, Hitler moved ever more aggressively, enlisting powerful allies in international affairs. Italy and Germany established the so-called Rome-Berlin Axis in 1936. Japan, also under the rule of a Fascist dictatorship, joined the Axis alliance that same year. At the same time, Germany and Italy intervened in the Spanish Civil War (1936–1939), where their military aid helped General Francisco Franco's revolutionary Fascist movement defeat the democratically elected republican government.

MAP 27.2 ■ The Growth of Nazi Germany, 1933–1939

Until March 1939, Hitler's conquests brought ethnic Germans into the Nazi state; then he turned on the Slavic and Jewish peoples he had always hated. He stripped Czechoslovakia of its independence and prepared to attack Poland in September 1939.

| How did Stalin and the Communist Party build a totalitarian state in the Soviet Union? | What kind of government did Mussolini establish in Italy? | **What policies did Nazi Germany pursue, and how did they lead to World War II?** | What explains the Allied victory in World War II? | ✓ LearningCurve Check what you know. |

In late 1937 Hitler moved forward with plans to seize Austria and Czechoslovakia. By threatening Austria with invasion, Hitler forced the Austrian chancellor to put local Nazis in control of the government in March 1938. The next day, in the Anschluss (annexation), German armies moved in unopposed, and Austria became two provinces of Greater Germany (see Map 27.2).

Simultaneously, Hitler demanded that territories inhabited mostly by ethnic Germans in western Czechoslovakia—the Sudetenland—be ceded to Nazi Germany. Though Czechoslovakia was allied with France and the Soviet Union and prepared to defend itself, appeasement triumphed again. In negotiations, British Prime Minister Arthur Neville Chamberlain and the French agreed with Hitler that Germany should immediately take over the Sudetenland. Returning to London from the Munich Conference in September 1938, Chamberlain told cheering crowds that he had secured "peace with honor." Chamberlain's peace was short-lived. In March 1939 Hitler's armies invaded and occupied the rest of Czechoslovakia.

In August 1939, in an about-face that stunned the world, sworn enemies Hitler and Stalin signed a nonaggression pact that paved the road to war. Each dictator promised to remain neutral if the other became involved in open hostilities. An attached secret protocol ruthlessly divided Poland, the Baltic nations, Finland, and a part of Romania into German and Soviet spheres of influence. Stalin agreed to the pact because he remained distrustful of Western intentions and because Hitler offered immediate territorial gain.

For Hitler, everything was now set. On September 1, 1939, German armies and warplanes smashed into Poland from three sides. Two days later, Britain and France declared war on Germany. The Second World War had begun.

> ## QUICK REVIEW

What role did the ideas of "race" and "space" play in Hitler's ideology? How did they shape Nazi policies?

CHAPTER LOCATOR | How were Fascist and Communist totalitarian dictatorships similar and different?

862   CHAPTER 27
DICTATORSHIPS AND THE SECOND WORLD WAR

What explains the Allied victory in World War II?

German Bomber over Warsaw

Germany opened its September 1939 attack on Poland by subjecting the Polish capital to repeated bombardment. By the end of the war, both sides had engaged in massive air campaigns against civilian targets, taking the lives of hundreds of thousands of civilians and leading finally to the use of the atomic bomb against Japan in 1945. (INTERFOTO/Alamy)

HITLER'S ARMIES QUICKLY CONQUERED much of western and eastern Europe, establishing a vast empire of death and destruction based on Nazi ideas of race and space. At the same time, Japanese armies overran much of Southeast Asia and created their own racial empire. This reckless aggression brought together a coalition of powerful allies determined to halt the advance of fascism: Britain, the United States, and the Soviet Union. After years of slaughter, this "Grand Alliance" decisively defeated the Axis powers.

German Victories in Europe

Using planes, tanks, and trucks in the first example of a blitzkrieg, or "lightning war," Hitler's armies crushed Poland in four weeks. While the Soviet Union moved to occupy the eastern half of Poland and the independent Baltic states of Lithuania, Estonia, and Latvia, French and British armies prepared their defenses in the west.

In spring 1940 the Nazi lightning war struck again. After occupying Denmark, Norway, and Holland, the Germans broke into France through southern Belgium, split the Franco-British forces, and trapped the entire British army on the French

| How did Stalin and the Communist Party build a totalitarian state in the Soviet Union? | What kind of government did Mussolini establish in Italy? | What policies did Nazi Germany pursue, and how did they lead to World War II? | **What explains the Allied victory in World War II?** | ✓ LearningCurve Check what you know. |

beaches of Dunkirk. By heroic efforts, the British withdrew their troops. Soon after, France was taken by the Nazis. By July 1940 Hitler ruled practically all of continental Europe. Only the Balkans and Britain, the nation led by the uncompromising Winston Churchill (1874–1965), remained unconquered.

To prepare for an amphibious invasion of Britain, Germany sought to gain control of the air. In the Battle of Britain, which began in July 1940, up to a thousand German planes a day attacked British airfields and key factories. Losses were heavy on both sides. In September 1940, Hitler angrily turned from military objectives to indiscriminate bombing of British cities in an attempt to break British morale. British aircraft factories increased production, and the British people defiantly dug in. By October, Britain was beating Germany three to one in the air war, and the Battle of Britain was over. Stymied there, the Germans invaded and occupied Greece and the Balkans.

Hitler now allowed his lifetime obsession of creating a vast eastern European empire ruled by the master race to dictate policy. In June 1941, he broke his pact with Stalin and launched German armies into the Soviet Union (**Map 27.3**). By October, most of Ukraine had been conquered, Leningrad was practically surrounded, and Moscow was besieged. But the Soviets did not collapse, and when a severe winter struck German armies outfitted only in summer uniforms, the invaders were stopped. Nevertheless, Hitler and his allies ruled over a vast European empire. Hitler, the Nazi leadership, and the German army were positioned to greatly accelerate construction of their so-called New Order in Europe.

Europe Under Nazi Occupation

Hitler's **New Order** was based firmly on the guiding principle of National Socialism: racial imperialism. Occupied peoples were treated according to their place in the Nazi racial hierarchy.

In Holland, Norway, and Denmark, the Nazis established puppet governments; though many people hated the conquerors, the Nazis found willing collaborators. France was divided into two parts. The German army occupied the north, including Paris. The southeast remained nominally independent. There the aging First World War general Marshal Henri-Philippe Pétain formed a new French government—the Vichy (VIH-shee) regime—that adopted many aspects of National Socialist ideology and willingly placed French Jews in the hands of the Nazis.

In all conquered territories, the Nazis used a variety of techniques to enrich Germany and support the war effort. Occupied nations were forced to pay for the costs of the war and for the occupation itself. Nazi administrators stole goods and money from local Jews, set currency exchanges at favorable rates, and forced occupied peoples to accept worthless wartime scrip. Soldiers were encouraged to steal but also to purchase goods at cheap exchange rates and send them home. A flood of plunder thus reached Germany, helping maintain high living standards and preserving home-front morale well into the war.

In central and eastern Europe, the war and German rule were far more ruthless and deadly than in the west. From the start, the Nazi leadership had cast the war in the east as one of annihilation. With the support of military commanders, German policemen, and bureaucrats in the occupied territories, Nazi administrators and Himmler's elite SS corps now implemented a program of destruction and

New Order

▶ Hitler's program based on racial imperialism, which gave preferential treatment to the Nordic peoples; the French, an "inferior" Latin people, occupied a middle position; and Slavs and Jews were treated harshly as "subhumans."

Vichy France, 1940

Map legend:
- Occupied by Germany
- Annexed by Germany

CHAPTER LOCATOR | How were Fascist and Communist totalitarian dictatorships similar and different?

beaches of Dunkirk. By heroic efforts, the British withdrew their troops. Soon after, France was taken by the Nazis. By July 1940 Hitler ruled practically all of continental Europe. Only the Balkans and Britain, the nation led by the uncompromising Winston Churchill (1874–1965), remained unconquered.

Legend:
- Axis powers and their allies
- Occupied by Germany and its allies
- Allied powers and their allies
- Neutral nations
- Boundary of Greater Germany
- Major battle

Map labels and annotations:

Siege of Leningrad, Sept. 1941–Jan. 1944

Germans repulsed, Dec. 1941

Moscow, Oct. 1941–Jan. 1942

Russian front, spring 1944

SOVIET UNION

Siege of Stalingrad, Aug. 21, 1942–Jan. 31, 1943

Russian front, Nov. 1942

Kursk July–Aug. 1943

Dnieper Aug.–Dec. 1943

Russian front, Dec. 1941

Siege, Sept. 1939 Uprising, Aug.–Sept. 1944

Germany surrenders, May 8, 1945

Battle of Britain, fall 1940

Invasion of Normandy June 6, 1944

Battle of the Bulge Dec. 1944

Russian front, Feb. 1945

Western front Feb. 1945

Axis troops occupy Vichy France, Nov. 10 and 11, 1942

Italian front Feb. 1945

Rome (Liberated June 1944)

Monte Cassino May 1944

Salerno Sept. 1943

Allies invade Sicily and Italy, July–Sept. 1943

Axis troops evacuated, May 1943

Sicily July 1943

Battle for Crete, May 20–June 1, 1941

Joined Allies, Nov. 1942

El Alamein autumn 1942

Cities/Countries: NORWAY, SWEDEN, FINLAND, Helsinki, Leningrad, Oslo, Stockholm, ESTONIA, DENMARK, Copenhagen, Riga, LATVIA, LITHUANIA, BELARUS, Smolensk, Tula, NORTHERN IRELAND, IRELAND, GREAT BRITAIN, London, Dunkirk, NETHERLANDS, BELGIUM, Berlin, Posen, Warsaw, POLAND, Kiev, Stalingrad, Paris, FRANCE, GERMANY, Kraków, SLOVAKIA, Pinsk, UKRAINE, Vichy, VICHY FRANCE, SWITZERLAND, Vienna, HUNGARY, Budapest, Bologna, ROMANIA, Yalta, Bucharest, CROATIA, SERBIA, BULGARIA, Sofia, ITALY, Corsica, Sardinia, ALBANIA, GREECE, Athens, Ankara, TURKEY, SPAIN, Madrid, Lisbon, PORT., GIBRALTAR (Gr. Br.), SPANISH MOROCCO, Casablanca Nov. 1942, MOROCCO (Fr.), ALGERIA (Vichy France), TUNISIA (Fr.), Malta (Gr. Br.), Crete (Gr.), Cyprus (Gr. Br.), SYRIA (Fr. Mandate), LEBANON (Fr. Mandate), IRAQ (Br. Mandate), PALESTINE (Br. Mandate), TRANS-JORDAN (Br. Mandate), SAUDI ARABIA, Cairo, EGYPT, LIBYA (It.)

Seas/Oceans: North Sea, Baltic Sea, ATLANTIC OCEAN, Adriatic Sea, Black Sea, Mediterranean Sea

Rivers: Volga R., Don R., Dnieper R., Vistula R., Rhine R., Danube R., Po R., Ebro R., Nile R., Suez Canal

---

MAP 27.3 ■ World War II in Europe and Africa, 1939–1945

This map shows the extent of Hitler's empire before the Battle of Stalingrad in late 1942 and the subsequent advances of the Allies until Germany surrendered on May 8, 1945. Compare this map with Map 27.2 on page 861 to trace the rise and fall of the Nazi empire over time.

> MAPPING THE PAST

ANALYZING THE MAP: What was the first country conquered by Hitler (see Map 27.2, page 861)? Locate Germany's advance and retreat on the Russian front in December 1941, November 1942, spring 1944, and February 1945. How does this compare to the position of British and American forces on the battlefield at similar points in time?

CONNECTIONS: What implications might the battle lines in February 1945 have had for the postwar settlement in Europe?

How did Stalin and the Communist Party build a totalitarian state in the Soviet Union?

What kind of government did Mussolini establish in Italy?

What policies did Nazi Germany pursue, and how did they lead to World War II?

What explains the Allied victory in World War II?

✓ LearningCurve Check what you know.

Nazi Occupation of Poland and East-Central Europe, 1939–1942

— Boundary of Poland, 1938
■ Germany, 1938
■ Annexed by Germany, 1939
■ German civil administration, 1942
■ German military occupation, 1942
— Boundary of Greater Germany, 1942

annihilation to create a "mass settlement space" for racially pure Germans. Across the east, the Nazi armies destroyed cities and factories, stole crops and farm animals, and subjected conquered peoples to forced starvation and mass murder.

In response to such atrocities, small but determined underground resistance groups fought back. They were hardly unified. Communists and socialists often disagreed with more centrist or nationalist groups on long-term goals and short-term tactics. The resistance nonetheless presented a real challenge to the Nazi New Order. Poland, under German occupation longer than any other nation, had the most determined and well-organized resistance. Underground members of the Polish Home Army, led by the government in exile in London, passed intelligence about German operations to the Allies and committed sabotage. The famous French resistance undertook similar actions, as did groups in Italy, Greece, Russia, and the Netherlands.

The German response was swift and deadly. The Nazi army and the SS tortured captured resistance members and executed hostages in reprisal for attacks. Responding to actions undertaken by resistance groups, the German army murdered the male populations of Lidice (Czechoslovakia) and Oradour (France) and leveled the entire towns. Despite reprisals, Nazi occupiers were never able to eradicate popular resistance to their rule.

The Holocaust

Holocaust

▶ The systematic effort of the Nazi state to exterminate all European Jews and other groups deemed racially inferior during the Second World War.

The ultimate abomination of Nazi racism was the condemnation of all European Jews and other peoples considered racially inferior to extreme racial persecution and then annihilation in the **Holocaust**, a great spasm of racially inspired mass murder.

As already described, the Nazis began to use social, legal, and economic means to persecute Jews and other "undesirable" groups immediately after taking power. Between 1938 and 1940, persecution turned deadly in the Nazi euthanasia (mercy killing) campaign, an important step toward genocide. Just as Germany began the war, some 70,000 people with physical and mental disabilities deemed by Nazi administrators to be "unworthy lives" who might "pollute" the German race, were murdered in cold blood. The victims were mostly ethnic Germans, and the euthanasia campaign was stopped after church leaders and ordinary families spoke out. The staff involved took what they learned in implementing this program with them to the extermination camps the Nazis would soon build in the east (**Map 27.4**).

The German victory over Poland in 1939 brought some 3 million Jews under Nazi control. Jews in German-occupied territories were soon forced to move into urban districts termed "ghettos." In such ghettos, hundreds of thousands of Polish Jews lived in crowded and unsanitary conditions, without real work or adequate sustenance. Over 500,000 people died under these conditions.

The racial violence reached new extremes when Germany invaded the Soviet Union in 1941. Three military death squads known as Special Task Forces (*Einsatzgruppen*) and other military units moved systematically from town to town, shooting Jews and other target populations. In this way the German armed forces murdered some 2 million civilians.

| A "Transport" Arrives at Auschwitz | Upon arrival at Auschwitz in May 1944, Jews from Subcarpathian Rus, a rural district on the border of Czechoslovakia and Ukraine, undergo a "selection" managed by Nazi officers and prisoners in striped uniforms. Camp guards will send the fittest people to the barracks, where they will probably soon die from forced labor under the most atrocious conditions. The aged, ill, very young, or otherwise infirm will be murdered immediately in the Auschwitz gas chambers. The tower over the main gate to the camp, which today opens onto a vast museum complex, is visible in the background. (Yad Vashem [Public Domain] Panstwowe Museum Auschwitz-Birkenau w Oswiecimiu) |

In late 1941 Hitler and the Nazi leadership, in some still-debated combination, ordered the SS to implement the mass murder of all Jews in Europe. The Germans set up an industrialized killing machine to imprison and murder Jews and other so-called undesirables, and to exploit their labor before they died. In the occupied east, the surviving residents of the ghettos were loaded onto trains and taken to camps such as Auschwitz-Birkenau, where over 1 million people—the vast majority of them Jews—were murdered in gas chambers. Some few were put to work as expendable laborers. The Jews of Germany and then of occupied western and central Europe were likewise rounded up and sent to the camps. By 1945 the Nazis had killed about 6 million Jews and some 5 million other Europeans, including millions of ethnic Poles and Russian prisoners of war (POWs). (See "Individuals in Society: Primo Levi," page 869.)

| How did Stalin and the Communist Party build a totalitarian state in the Soviet Union? | What kind of government did Mussolini establish in Italy? | What policies did Nazi Germany pursue, and how did they lead to World War II? | **What explains the Allied victory in World War II?** | ✓ LearningCurve Check what you know. |

MAP 27.4 ■ The Holocaust, 1941–1945

The leadership of Nazi Germany established an extensive network of ghettos and concentration and extermination camps to persecute their political opponents and those people deemed "racially undesirable" by the regime. The death camps, where the Nazi SS systematically murdered millions of European Jews, Soviet prisoners of war, and others, were located primarily in Nazi-occupied territories in eastern Europe, but the conditions in the concentration camps within Germany's borders were almost as brutal.

Japanese Empire and the War in the Pacific

The racist war of annihilation in Europe was matched by racially inspired warfare in East Asia. In response to political divisions and economic crisis, a Fascist government had taken control of Japan in the 1930s. As in Germany and Italy, the Japanese government was highly nationalistic and militaristic, and it was deeply committed to imperial expansion. According to Japanese race theory, the Asian races were far superior to Western ones. In speeches, schools, and newspapers, ultranationalists eagerly voiced extreme anti-Western views. They glorified the

INDIVIDUALS IN SOCIETY
Primo Levi

Primo Levi, who never stopped thinking, writing, and speaking about the Holocaust. (Giani Giansanti/Sygma/Corbis)

Most Jews deported to Auschwitz-Birkenau were murdered soon after arriving, but the Nazis made some prisoners into slave laborers, and a few of them survived. Primo Levi (1919–1987), one of these laborers, lived to become one of the most influential witnesses to the Holocaust.

Like much of Italy's small Jewish community, Levi's family belonged to the urban professional classes. Levi graduated from the University of Turin with highest honors in chemistry in 1941. Growing discrimination against Italian Jews led him to join the antifascist resistance two years later. Captured, he was deported to Auschwitz with 650 Italian Jews in February 1944. Stone-faced SS men picked 96 men, Levi among them, and 29 women from this group to work in labor camps; the rest were gassed upon arrival.

Levi and his fellow prisoners were kicked, punched, stripped, branded with tattoos, crammed into huts, and worked unmercifully. Hoping for some prisoner solidarity, Levi found only a desperate struggle of each against all and enormous status differences among prisoners. Many bewildered newcomers, beaten and demoralized by their bosses — the most privileged prisoners — collapsed and died. Others struggled to secure their own privileges, however small, because food rations and working conditions were so abominable that prisoners who were not bosses usually perished in two to three months.

Sensitive and noncombative, Levi found himself sinking into oblivion. But instead of joining the mass of the "drowned," he became one of the "saved" — a complicated surprise with moral implications that he would ponder all his life. As Levi explained in *Survival in Auschwitz* (1947), the usual road to salvation in the camps was some kind of collaboration with German power. Savage German criminals were released from prison to become brutal camp guards; non-Jewish political prisoners competed for jobs entitling them to better conditions; and, especially troubling for Levi, a few Jews plotted and struggled to gain the power of life and death over other Jewish prisoners.

Though not one of these Jewish bosses, Levi believed that he, like almost all survivors, had entered the "gray zone" of moral compromise. "Nobody can know for how long and under what trials his soul can resist before yielding or breaking," Levi wrote. "The harsher the oppression, the more widespread among the oppressed is the willingness, with all its infinite nuances and motivations, to collaborate."* The camps held no saints, he believed: the Nazi system degraded its victims, forcing them to commit sometimes-bestial acts against their fellow prisoners in order to survive.

For Levi, salvation came from his education. Interviewed by a German technocrat for work in the camp's synthetic rubber program, Levi was chosen for this relatively easy labor because he spoke fluent German, including scientific terminology. Work in the warm camp laboratory offered Levi opportunities to pilfer equipment he could then trade to other prisoners for food and necessities. Levi also gained critical support from three prisoners who refused to do wicked and hateful acts. And he counted luck as essential for his survival: in the camp infirmary with scarlet fever in February 1945 as advancing Russian armies prepared to liberate the camp, Levi was not evacuated by the Nazis and shot to death like most Jewish prisoners.

After the war, Levi was haunted by the nightmare that the Holocaust would be ignored or forgotten. Ashamed that so many people whom he considered better than himself had perished, and wanting the world to understand the genocide in all its complexity so that people would never again tolerate such atrocities, he turned to writing about his experiences. Primo Levi, while revealing Nazi guilt, tirelessly grappled with his vision of individual choice and moral ambiguity in a hell designed to make the victims collaborate and persecute each other.

QUESTIONS FOR ANALYSIS

1. Describe Levi's experience at Auschwitz. How did camp prisoners treat each other? Why?
2. What does Levi mean by the "gray zone"?
3. Will a vivid historical memory of the Holocaust help to prevent future genocide?

▷LaunchPad

ONLINE DOCUMENT PROJECT

Why do so many Holocaust survivors like Levi struggle with the moral implications of their experiences in the camps? Watch personal testimonies of Holocaust survivors. Then complete a writing assignment based on the evidence and details from this chapter. *See inside the front cover to learn more.*

---

* Primo Levi, *The Drowned and the Saved* (New York: Vintage, 1989), pp. 43, 60. See also Levi, *Survival in Auschwitz: The Nazi Assault on Humanity* (London: Collier Books, 1961). These powerful testimonies are highly recommended.

warrior virtues of honor and sacrifice and proclaimed that Japan would liberate East Asia from Western colonialists.

Japan soon acted on its racial-imperial ambitions. In 1931, Japanese armies invaded and occupied Manchuria, a vast territory bordering northeastern China. In 1937, Japan brutally invaded China itself. Seeking to cement ties with the Fascist regimes of Europe, in 1940 the Japanese entered into a formal alliance with Italy and Germany, and in summer 1941, Japanese armies occupied southern portions of the French colony of Indochina (now Vietnam and Cambodia).

The goal was to establish what the Japanese called the Greater East Asia Co-Prosperity Sphere. Under the slogan "Asia for Asians," Japanese propagandists maintained that this expansion would free Asians from hated Western imperialists. By promising to create a mutually advantageous union for long-term development, the Japanese tapped currents of nationalist sentiment, and most local populations were glad to see the Westerners go.

But the Co-Prosperity Sphere was a sham. Real power remained in the hands of the Japanese. They exhibited great cruelty toward civilian populations and prisoners of war, and exploited local peoples for Japan's wartime needs. Nonetheless, the ability of the Japanese to defeat the Western colonial powers set a powerful example for national liberation groups in Asia, which would become important in the decolonization movement that followed World War II.

Japanese expansion from 1937 to 1941 evoked a sharp response from U.S. president Franklin Roosevelt, and Japan's leaders came to believe that war with the United States was inevitable. They decided to launch a surprise attack on the U.S. fleet based at Pearl Harbor in the Hawaiian Islands. On December 7, 1941, the Japanese sank or crippled every American battleship, but by chance all the American aircraft carriers were at sea and escaped unharmed. Pearl Harbor brought the Americans into the war in a spirit of anger and revenge.

As the Americans mobilized for war, Japanese expansion continued. By May 1942, Japan controlled a vast empire (**Map 27.5**) and was threatening Australia. The Americans pushed back and engaged the Japanese in a series of hard-fought naval battles. In July 1943, the Americans and their Australian allies opened a successful island-hopping campaign that slowly forced Japan out of its conquered territories. The war in the Pacific was extremely brutal and atrocities were committed on both sides. A product of spiraling violence, mutual hatred, and dehumanizing racial stereotypes, the fighting intensified as the United States moved toward Japan.[2]

The "Hinge of Fate"

While the Nazis and the Japanese built their savage empires, Great Britain, the United States, and the Soviet Union joined together in a military pact Churchill termed the Grand Alliance. Disagreements between the Soviets and the capitalist powers during the course of the war sowed mutual distrust, but there were broad areas of consensus. The Grand Alliance concurred on a policy of "Europe first." Only after Hitler was defeated would the Allies mount an all-out attack on Japan, the lesser threat. The Allies also agreed to concentrate on immediate military needs, postponing tough political questions about the eventual peace settlement that might have divided them. To further encourage mutual trust, the Allies

CHAPTER LOCATOR | How were Fascist and Communist totalitarian dictatorships similar and different?

CHAPTER 27
870 DICTATORSHIPS AND THE SECOND WORLD WAR

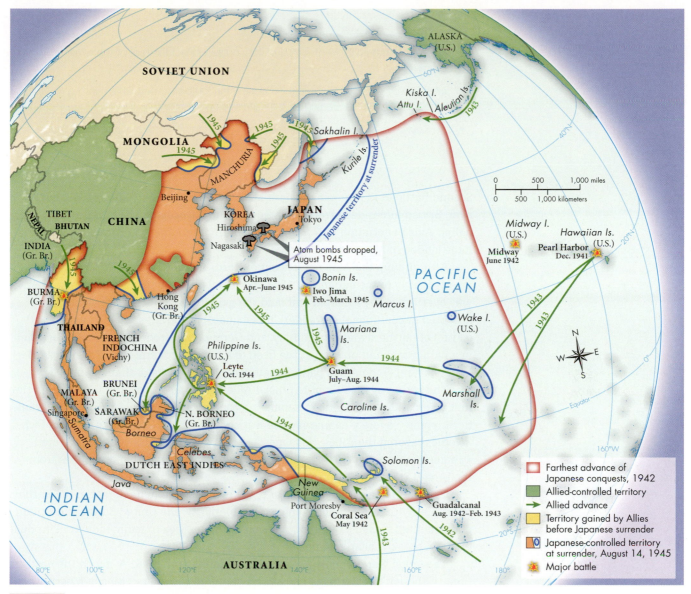

MAP 27.5 ■ World War II in the Pacific

In 1942, Japanese forces overran an enormous amount of territory, which the Allies slowly recaptured in a long, bitter struggle. As this map shows, Japan still held a large Asian empire in August 1945, when the unprecedented devastation of atomic warfare suddenly forced it to surrender.

adopted the principle of the unconditional surrender of Germany and Japan. This policy cemented the Grand Alliance because it denied Hitler any hope of dividing his foes. It also meant that Soviet and Anglo-American armies would almost certainly be forced to invade and occupy all of Germany, and that Japan would fight to the bitter end.

The combined might of the Allies forced back the Nazi armies on all fronts (see Map 27.3, page 865). Through early 1942, heavy fighting between British and Axis forces had resulted in significant German advances in North Africa. At the

How did Stalin and the Communist Party build a totalitarian state in the Soviet Union?

What kind of government did Mussolini establish in Italy?

What policies did Nazi Germany pursue, and how did they lead to World War II?

What explains the Allied victory in World War II?

✓ LearningCurve
Check what you know.

Second Battle of El Alamein (el al-uh-MAYN) in October–November 1942, however, British forces decisively defeated combined German and Italian armies and halted Axis penetration of North Africa. Shortly thereafter, an Anglo-American force landed in Morocco and Algeria.

After driving the Axis powers out of North Africa, U.S. and British forces invaded Sicily in the summer of 1943 and mainland Italy that autumn. Mussolini was overthrown by a coup d'état, and the new Italian government publicly accepted unconditional surrender. In response, Nazi armies invaded and seized control of northern and central Italy, and German paratroopers rescued Mussolini in a daring raid and put him at the head of a puppet government. Facing stiff German resistance, the Allies battled their way slowly up the Italian peninsula.

The spring of 1943 brought crucial Allied victories at sea and in the air. In the first years of the war, German submarines had successfully attacked North Atlantic shipping, severely hampering the British war effort. New antisubmarine technologies favored the Allies. Soon massive convoys of hundreds of ships were streaming across the Atlantic, bringing much-needed troops and supplies from the United States to Britain.

The German air force had never really recovered from its defeat in the Battle of Britain. With almost unchallenged air superiority, the United States and Britain now mounted massive bombing raids on German cities to maim industrial production and break civilian morale.

The worst German defeats came at the hands of the Red Army on the eastern front. Although the Germans had almost captured the major cities of Moscow and Leningrad in early winter 1941, they were forced back by determined Soviet counterattacks. The Germans mounted a second and initially successful invasion of the Soviet Union in the summer of 1942, but the campaign turned into a disaster. The downfall came at the Battle of Stalingrad, when in November 1942 the Soviets surrounded and systematically destroyed the entire German Sixth Army of 300,000 men. In summer 1943 the larger, better-equipped Soviet armies took the offensive and began to push the Germans back along the entire eastern front (see Map 27.3, page 865).

Allied Victory

The balance of power was now clearly in Allied hands, yet bitter fighting continued in Europe for almost two years. Germany, less fully mobilized for war in 1941 than Britain, stepped up its efforts. The German war industry put to work millions of prisoners of war and slave laborers from across occupied Europe.

CHAPTER LOCATOR | How were Fascist and Communist totalitarian dictatorships similar and different?

872 CHAPTER 27 DICTATORSHIPS AND THE SECOND WORLD WAR

Nuclear Wasteland at Hiroshima Only a handful of buildings remain standing in the ruins of Hiroshima in September 1945. Fearing the costs of a prolonged ground and naval campaign against the Japanese mainland, the United States dropped atomic bombs on Hiroshima and Nagasaki in August 1945. The bombings ended the war and opened the nuclear age. (AP Photo)

Between early 1942 and July 1944, German war production tripled despite heavy Anglo-American bombing.

German resistance against Hitler also failed to halt the fighting. An unsuccessful attempt by conservative army leaders to assassinate Hitler in July 1944 only brought increased repression. Closely disciplined by the regime, frightened by the prospect of unconditional surrender, and terrorized by Nazi propaganda that portrayed the advancing Russian armies as rapacious Slavic beasts, the Germans fought on with suicidal resolve.

On June 6, 1944, American and British forces under General Dwight Eisenhower landed on the beaches of Normandy, France. In a hundred dramatic days, more than 2 million men and almost half a million vehicles broke through the German lines and pushed inland. By spring of 1945 the Allies had finally forced the Germans out of the Italian peninsula. That April, Mussolini was captured in northern Italy by Communist partisans and executed.

How did Stalin and the Communist Party build a totalitarian state in the Soviet Union?

What kind of government did Mussolini establish in Italy?

What policies did Nazi Germany pursue, and how did they lead to World War II?

What explains the Allied victory in World War II?

☑ LearningCurve Check what you know.

873

The Soviets, who had been advancing steadily since July 1943, reached the outskirts of Warsaw by August 1944. Anticipating German defeat, the Polish underground Home Army ordered an uprising, so that the Poles might take the city on their own and establish independence from the Soviets. The Warsaw Uprising was a tragic miscalculation. Citing military pressure, the Red Army refused to enter the city. Stalin and Soviet leaders thus allowed the Germans to destroy the Polish insurgents, a cynical move that paved the way for the establishment of a postwar Communist regime. Only after the decimated Home Army surrendered did the Red Army continue its advance. Warsaw lay in ruins, and between 150,000 and 200,000 Poles—mostly civilians—had lost their lives.

Over the next six months, the Soviets moved southward into Romania, Hungary, and Yugoslavia. In January 1945 the Red Army crossed Poland into Germany, and on April 26 met American forces on the Elbe River. As Soviet forces fought their way into Berlin, Hitler committed suicide, and on May 8 the remaining German commanders capitulated.

The war in the Pacific also drew to a close. Despite repeated U.S. victories through the summer of 1945, Japanese troops had continued to fight. American commanders believed the invasion and conquest of Japan itself might cost 1 million American casualties and claim 10 to 20 million Japanese lives. In fact, Japan was almost helpless, its industry and cities largely destroyed by intense American bombing.

After much discussion at the upper levels of the U.S. government, American planes dropped atomic bombs on Hiroshima and Nagasaki in Japan on August 6 and 9, 1945. The mass bombing of cities and civilians, one of the terrible new practices of World War II, now ended in the final nightmare—unprecedented human destruction in a single blinding flash. On August 14, 1945, the Japanese announced their surrender. The Second World War, which had claimed the lives of more than 50 million soldiers and civilians, was over.

> **QUICK REVIEW**

How did Germany and Japan conquer enormous empires during World War II, and how did the Allies defeat them?

CHAPTER LOCATOR | How were Fascist and Communist totalitarian dictatorships similar and different?

LOOKING BACK LOOKING AHEAD

The first half of the twentieth century brought almost unimaginable violence and destruction. Shaken by the rapid cultural change and economic collapse that followed the tragedy of World War I, many Europeans embraced the radical politics of communism and fascism. Totalitarian dictators like Stalin and Hitler capitalized on the desire for social order, building dictatorial regimes that demanded total allegiance to an ideological vision. Even as these regimes rewarded supporters and promised ordinary people a new age, they violently repressed their enemies, real and imagined. The vision proved fatal: the great clash of ideologies that emerged in the 1920s and 1930s led to history's most deadly war.

Only the reluctant Grand Alliance of the liberal United States and Great Britain with the Communist Soviet Union was able to defeat the Axis powers. This alliance, however, did not long survive the end of the war. Trust quickly broke down. Europe would be divided into two hostile camps, and Cold War tensions between East and West would dominate European and world politics for the next fifty years.

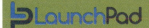

ONLINE DOCUMENT PROJECT
Primo Levi

Why do so many Holocaust survivors like Levi struggle with the moral implications of their experiences in the camps?

You encountered Primo Levi's story on page 869. Keeping the question above in mind, watch personal testimonies of Holocaust survivors. *See inside the front cover to learn more.*

How did Stalin and the Communist Party build a totalitarian state in the Soviet Union?

What kind of government did Mussolini establish in Italy?

What policies did Nazi Germany pursue, and how did they lead to World War II?

What explains the Allied victory in World War II?

✔ **LearningCurve**
Check what you know.

CHAPTER 27 STUDY GUIDE

STEP 1

GET STARTED ONLINE

LearningCurve

Now that you've read the chapter, make it stick by completing the LearningCurve activity.

STEP 2

EXPLAIN WHY IT MATTERS

Put your reading into practice. Identify each term below, and then explain why it matters in Western history.

TERM	WHO OR WHAT & WHEN	WHY IT MATTERS
totalitarianism (p. 843)		
fascism (p. 845)		
eugenics (p. 845)		
five-year plan (p. 846)		
New Economic Policy (NEP) (p. 846)		
collectivization of agriculture (p. 848)		
kulaks (p. 849)		
Black Shirts (p. 853)		
Lateran Agreement (p. 853)		
National Socialism (p. 855)		
Enabling Act (p. 858)		
appeasement (p. 860)		
New Order (p. 864)		
Holocaust (p. 866)		

STEP 3

MOVE BEYOND THE BASICS

To demonstrate a more advanced understanding, fill in the chart included below with descriptions of the ideologies and policies of the totalitarian governments of the Soviet Union, Italy, and Germany.

	Ideology	Social policy	Economic policy	Foreign policy
Soviet Union				
Italy				
Germany				

PUT IT ALL TOGETHER

Now, take a step back and try to explain the big picture. Remember to use specific examples from the chapter in your answers.

STALIN'S SOVIET UNION

▶ What hardships did Soviet citizens experience under Stalinism? Given these hardships, why were so many ordinary citizens enthusiastic about Stalinism?

▶ Could Stalin's economic and social policies have been implemented without a high degree of coercion? Why or why not?

FASCISM IN ITALY AND GERMANY

▶ In your opinion, was Italy under Mussolini a totalitarian state? Why or why not?

▶ Compare and contrast the efforts of Hitler and Stalin to gain the support of their respective populations. In this context, what did the two regimes have in common?

THE SECOND WORLD WAR

▶ What role did race play in the German and Japanese drive for territorial expansion? Is it fair to describe World War II, in Europe and in the Pacific, as a racial war?

▶ In your opinion, why did the Allies win the war? What role did industrial production play in the Allied victory? What other factors were important?

MAKE CONNECTIONS

▶ Defend or refute the following statement. "The first half of the twentieth century did not see two world wars, but rather a single war with a long truce in the middle."

▶ In your opinion, what are the most important lessons to be drawn from the events leading up to World War II?

> ## IN YOUR OWN WORDS

Imagine that you must give an oral report to the class answering the following question: **How did totalitarian regimes attempt to remake European politics, culture, and society, and what impact did they have on World War II?** What would be the most important points and why?

28

COLD WAR CONFLICT AND CONSENSUS

1945–1965

> **What new social, cultural, and political trends emerged in the decades following World War II?** Chapter 28 examines political, economic, and social developments in the two decades following the end of World War II. As Europeans struggled to recover from the devastation of war, the Allies worked to shape an effective peace accord. Disagreements between the Soviet Union and the Western allies quickly emerged and led to an apparently endless Cold War between the two new superpowers — the United States and the Soviet Union. This conflict split much of Europe into a Soviet-aligned Communist bloc and a U.S.-aligned capitalist bloc, and spurred military, economic, and technological competition. Conflict between the superpowers had an immense impact in the developing world, where independence movements won liberation from colonial powers. Such tensions notwithstanding, the postwar decades witnessed the construction of a relatively stable social and political consensus in both Communist and capitalist Europe. At the same time, changing class structures, new migration patterns, and new roles for women and youths had a profound impact on European society.

LearningCurve

After reading the chapter, use LearningCurve to retain what you've read.

> Why was World War II followed so quickly by the Cold War?

> What were the sources of postwar recovery and stability in western Europe?

> What was the pattern of postwar development in the Soviet bloc?

> What led to rapid decolonization after World War II?

> What kinds of societies emerged in Europe — East and West — after 1945?

Life in Eastern Europe. This relief sculpture, a revealing example of socialist realism from 1952 that portrays (from left to right) a mail carrier, a builder, industrial workers, and peasants, adorns the wall of the central post office in **Banská Bystrica**, a regional capital in present-day Slovakia (formerly part of Czechoslovakia). (Georgios Makkas/Alamy)

Why was World War II followed so quickly by the Cold War?

Displaced Persons in the Ruins of Berlin The end of the war in 1945 stopped the fighting but not the suffering. For the next two years, millions of displaced persons wandered across Europe searching for sustenance, lost family members, and a place to call home. (Fred Rampage/Getty Images)

IN 1945, HAVING WON THE WAR, the Allies faced the challenge of creating a lasting peace. Cooperation, however, proved difficult to sustain. Motivated by different goals and hounded by misunderstandings, Great Britain and the United States on one side found themselves at loggerheads with the Soviet Union (U.S.S.R.). By 1949, most of Europe was divided into East and West Blocs allied with the U.S.S.R. and the United States, respectively. For the next forty years, the competing superpowers engaged in the **Cold War**, a determined competition for political and military superiority around the world.

The Legacies of the Second World War

In the summer of 1945, Europe lay in ruins. Across the continent, the fighting had destroyed cities and landscapes and obliterated buildings, factories, farms, rail tracks, roads, and bridges. Many cities were completely devastated. The human costs of the Second World War are almost incalculable (**Map 28.1**). The death toll far exceeded the mortality figures for World War I. In total, about 50 million human beings perished in the conflict.

Cold War

▶ The rivalry between the Soviet Union and the United States that divided much of Europe into a Soviet-aligned Communist bloc and a U.S.-aligned capitalist bloc between 1945 and 1989.

CHAPTER LOCATOR | **Why was World War II followed so quickly by the Cold War?**

1945
- Yalta Conference; end of World War II in Europe; Potsdam Conference; Nuremberg trials begin

1945–1960s
- Decolonization of Asia and Africa

1945–1965
- United States takes lead in Big Science

1947
- Truman Doctrine; Marshall Plan

1948
- Founding of Israel

1948–1949
- Berlin airlift

1949
- Creation of East and West Germany; formation of NATO; establishment of COMECON

1950–1953
- Korean War

1953
- Death of Stalin

1955–1964
- Khrushchev in power; de-Stalinization of Soviet Union

1955
- Warsaw Pact founded

1956
- Suez crisis

1957
- Formation of Common Market; Pasternak publishes *Doctor Zhivago*

1961
- Building of Berlin Wall

1962
- Cuban missile crisis; Solzhenitsyn publishes *One Day in the Life of Ivan Denisovich*

1964
- Brezhnev replaces Khrushchev as Soviet leader

The destruction of war also left tens of millions homeless. These **displaced persons** (or DPs)—their numbers increased by concentration camp survivors, released prisoners of war, and hundreds of thousands of orphaned children— searched for food and shelter. From 1945 to 1947, the newly established United Nations Relief and Rehabilitation Administration (UNRRA) opened over 760 DP camps and spent $10 billion to house, feed, clothe, and repatriate the refugees.

When the fighting stopped, Germany and Austria had been divided into four occupation zones, each governed by one of the Allies—the United States, the Soviet Union, Great Britain, and France. The authorities in each zone worked to punish those guilty of Nazi atrocities. Across Europe, almost 100,000 Germans and Austrians were convicted of war crimes; many more were investigated or indicted. In Soviet-dominated central and eastern Europe—where the worst crimes had taken place—retribution was particularly intense.

In Germany and Austria, occupation authorities set up "denazification" procedures meant to eradicate National Socialist ideology from social and political institutions and identify and punish former Nazi Party members responsible for the worst crimes. At the Nuremberg trials (1945–1946), an international military tribunal organized by the four Allied powers tried the highest-ranking Nazi military and civilian leaders who had survived the war, charging them with war crimes and crimes against humanity. Twelve were sentenced to death and ten more to lengthy prison terms.

As the Cold War developed and the Soviets and the Western Allies drew increasingly apart, each carried out separate denazification programs in their own zones of occupation. In the Western zones, military courts at first actively

displaced persons
▶ Postwar refugees, including 13 million Germans, former Nazi prisoners and forced laborers, and orphaned children.

| What were the sources of postwar recovery and stability in western Europe? | What was the pattern of postwar development in the Soviet bloc? | What led to rapid decolonization after World War II? | What kinds of societies emerged in Europe — East and West — after 1945? | ✔ LearningCurve Check what you know. |

MAP 28.1 ■ The Aftermath of World War II in Europe, ca. 1945–1950

By 1945, millions of people displaced by war and territorial changes were on the move. The Soviet Union and Poland took land from Germany, which the Allies partitioned into occupation zones. Those zones subsequently formed the basis of the East and West German states. Austria was detached from Germany and similarly divided, but the Soviets subsequently permitted Austria to reunify as a neutral state.

> MAPPING THE PAST

ANALYZING THE MAP: Which groups fled west? Who went east? How would you characterize the general direction of most of these movements?

CONNECTIONS: What does the widespread movement of people at the end of the war suggest about the war? What does it suggest about the ensuing political climate?

prosecuted leading Nazis. But the huge numbers implicated in Nazi crimes, German opposition to the proceedings, and the need for stability in the looming Cold War made thorough denazification impractical. Except for the worst offenders, the Western authorities had quietly shelved denazification by 1948. The process was similar in the Soviet zone. At first, punishment was swift and harsh. As in the

CHAPTER LOCATOR | Why was World War II followed so quickly by the Cold War?

West, however, former Nazis who cooperated with the Soviet authorities could avoid prosecution. Thus, many former Nazis found leading positions in government and industry in both the Soviet and Western zones.

The Peace Settlement and Cold War Origins

The Allies began to quarrel almost as soon as the unifying threat of Nazi Germany disappeared, and the interests of the Communist Soviet Union and the capitalist Britain and United States increasingly diverged. The hostility between the Eastern and Western superpowers was the sad but logical outgrowth of military developments, wartime agreements, and long-standing political and ideological differences.

Once the United States entered the war in late 1941, the Allies had made military victory their highest priority, deferring discussion of postwar aims and the shape of the eventual peace settlement. By late 1943, however, negotiations about the postwar settlement could no longer be postponed. The conference that the "Big Three"—Stalin, Roosevelt, and Churchill—held in the Iranian capital of Teheran in November 1943 proved crucial for determining the shape of the postwar world.

At Teheran, the Big Three reaffirmed their determination to crush Germany, followed by tense discussions of Poland's postwar borders and a strategy to win the war. Stalin asked his allies to relieve his armies by opening a second front in German-occupied France. In the end, this was agreed to, though the date for the invasion was set later than the Soviet leader desired. This decision had momentous implications for the Cold War. While the delay in opening a second front fanned Stalin's distrust of the Allies, the agreement on a British-U.S. invasion of France also ensured that the American-British and Soviet armies would come together in defeated Germany along a north-south line, and that Soviet troops would play the predominant role in pushing the Germans out of eastern and central Europe. Thus the basic shape of postwar Europe was cast even as the fighting continued.

When the Big Three met again in February 1945 at Yalta, on the Black Sea in southern Russia, advancing Soviet armies had already occupied much of eastern Europe and the Balkans and were within a hundred miles of Berlin. The stalled American-British forces had yet to cross the Rhine into Germany. Moreover, the United States was far from defeating Japan. In

The Big Three

In 1945, a triumphant Winston Churchill, an ailing Franklin Roosevelt, and a determined Stalin met at Yalta in southern Russia to plan for peace. Cooperation soon gave way to bitter hostility, and the decisions made by these leaders transformed the map of Europe. (Franklin D. Roosevelt Presidential Library)

What were the sources of postwar recovery and stability in western Europe?	What was the pattern of postwar development in the Soviet bloc?	What led to rapid decolonization after World War II?	What kinds of societies emerged in Europe — East and West — after 1945?	✓ **LearningCurve** Check what you know.

short, the U.S.S.R.'s position on the ground was far stronger than that of the United States and Britain, which played to Stalin's advantage.

The Allies agreed at Yalta that each of the four victorious powers would occupy a separate zone of Germany and that the Germans would pay heavy reparations to the Soviet Union. At American insistence, Stalin agreed to declare war on Japan after Germany's defeat. As for Poland, the Big Three agreed that the U.S.S.R. would permanently incorporate the eastern Polish territories its army had occupied in 1939 and that Poland would be compensated with German lands to the west. They also agreed in an ambiguous compromise that the new governments in Soviet-occupied Europe would be freely elected but "friendly" to the Soviet Union.

The Yalta compromise over elections in these countries broke down almost immediately. Even before the conference, Communist parties were gaining control in Bulgaria and Poland. Elsewhere, the Soviets formed coalition governments but reserved key government posts for Moscow-trained Communists. At the Potsdam Conference of July 1945, the differences over elections in Soviet-occupied Europe surged to the fore. Roosevelt had died and had been succeeded by President Harry Truman (r. 1945–1953), who demanded immediate free elections throughout central and eastern Europe. Stalin refused.

Stalin, who had lived through two enormously destructive German invasions, was determined to establish a buffer zone of sympathetic states around the U.S.S.R. and at the same time expand the reach of communism and the Soviet state. He believed that only Communists could be dependable allies, and that free elections would result in independent and possibly hostile governments on his western border. With Soviet armies in central and eastern Europe, there was no way short of war for the United States to control the region's political future, and war was out of the question. The United States, for its part, pushed to maintain democratic capitalism and open access to free markets in western Europe. The Americans quickly showed that they, too, were determined to maintain predominance in their sphere of influence.

> Major Allied Conferences	
Where (When)	**What happened?**
Teheran (November 1943)	Allied war goals and strategy established.
Yalta (February 1945)	Basic outline of postwar peace established.
Potsdam (July 1945)	Agreement over elections in eastern Europe breaks down.

West Versus East

The Cold War took shape over the next five years, as both sides hardened their positions. After Japan's surrender in September 1945, Truman cut off aid to the ailing U.S.S.R. In October he declared that the United States would never recognize any government established by force against the will of its people. In March 1946, former British prime minister Churchill informed an American audience that an "iron curtain" had fallen across the continent, dividing Europe into two antagonistic camps (**Map 28.2**).

The Soviet Union was indeed consolidating its hold on central and eastern Europe, using political repression to establish Soviet-style, one-party Communist

CHAPTER LOCATOR | **Why was World War II followed so quickly by the Cold War?**

MAP 28.2 ■ Cold War Europe in the 1950s

The Cold War divided Europe into two hostile military alliances that formed to the east and west of an "iron curtain."

dictatorships. At the same time, bitter civil wars in Greece and China pitted Communist revolutionaries against authoritarian leaders backed by the United States.

By early 1947, it appeared to many Americans that the U.S.S.R. was determined to export communism by subversion throughout Europe and around the world. The United States responded with the **Truman Doctrine**, aimed at "containing" communism to areas already under Communist governments. The United States, President Truman promised, would use diplomatic, economic, and even military means to resist the expansion of communism anywhere on the globe. In the first examples of containment policies in action, Truman asked Congress to provide military aid to anticommunist forces in the Greek Civil War (1944–1949) and counter the threat of Soviet expansion in Turkey. With American support, both countries remained in the Western bloc. The American determination to enforce containment hardened when the Soviets exploded their own atomic bomb in 1949. By the early 1950s, the U.S. government was restructuring its military to meet the Soviet threat, pouring money into defense spending, and testing nuclear weapons that dwarfed the destructive power of atomic bombs.

Truman Doctrine

▶ America's policy geared to containing communism to those countries already under Soviet control.

What were the sources of postwar recovery and stability in western Europe?	What was the pattern of postwar development in the Soviet bloc?	What led to rapid decolonization after World War II?	What kinds of societies emerged in Europe — East and West — after 1945?	✓ **LearningCurve** Check what you know.

Military aid and a defense buildup were only one aspect of Truman's policy of containment. In 1947, western Europe was still on the verge of economic collapse. Recognizing that an economically and politically stable western Europe would be an effective block against the popular appeal of communism, U.S. secretary of state George C. Marshall offered Europe economic aid—the **Marshall Plan**—to help it rebuild.

The Marshall Plan was one of the most successful foreign aid programs in history. When it ended in 1951, the United States had given about $13 billion in aid (equivalent to over $200 billion in 2014 dollars) to fifteen western European nations, and Europe's economy was on the way to recovery. Marshall Plan funding was initially offered to East Bloc countries as well, but fearing Western interference in the Soviet sphere, they rejected the offer. In 1949, the Soviets established the **Council for Mutual Economic Assistance (COMECON)**, an economic organization of Communist states intended to rebuild the East Bloc independently of the West. Thus the generous aid of the Marshall Plan was limited to countries in the Western bloc, which further increased Cold War divisions.

In the late 1940s, Berlin, the capital city of Germany, was on the frontline of the Cold War. Like the rest of Germany and Austria, Berlin had been divided into four zones of occupation. In June 1948, the Western allies replaced the currency in the western zones of Germany and Berlin, an early move in plans to establish a separate West German state sympathetic to U.S. interests. The currency reform violated the peace settlement and raised Stalin's fears of the American presence in Europe. In addition, growing ties among Britain, France, Belgium, and the Netherlands convinced Stalin that a Western bloc was forming against the Soviet Union. In response, Stalin blocked all traffic through the Soviet zone of Germany to Berlin in an attempt to win concessions and perhaps reunify the city under Soviet control. Acting firmly, the Western allies coordinated around-the-clock flights of hundreds of planes over the Soviet roadblocks, supplying provisions to West Berliners and thwarting Soviet efforts to swallow up the western half of the city. After 324 days, the Berlin airlift succeeded, and the Soviets reopened the roads.

Success in breaking the Berlin blockade had several lasting results. First, it paved the way for the creation of two separate German states in 1949: the Federal Republic of Germany (West Germany), aligned with the United States, and the German Democratic Republic (East Germany), aligned with the U.S.S.R. The Berlin crisis also seemed to show that containment worked and thus strengthened U.S. resolve to maintain a strong European and U.S. military presence in western Europe. In 1949, the United States formed **NATO** (the North Atlantic Treaty Organization), an anti-Soviet military alliance of Western governments. In 1955, the Soviets countered by organizing the **Warsaw Pact**, a military alliance among the U.S.S.R. and its Communist satellites. In both political and military terms, most of Europe was divided into two hostile blocs.

The Cold War took shape in Europe, but it quickly spread around the globe, turning hot in East Asia. When Soviet-backed Communist North Korea invaded South Korea in 1950, President Truman swiftly sent U.S. troops. In the end, the Korean War was indecisive: the fragile truce agreed to in 1953 left Korea divided between a Communist north and a capitalist south. The war nonetheless showed that, though the superpowers might maintain a fragile peace in Europe, they were perfectly willing to engage in open conflict in non-Western territories.

By 1955, the Soviet-American confrontation had become an apparently permanent feature of world affairs. For the next thirty-five years, the superpowers would struggle to win political influence and territorial control and to achieve technological superiority. Cold War hostilities helped foster a nuclear arms race, a space race, and the computer revolution, all made possible by stunning advances in science and technology.

Big Science in the Nuclear Age

During the Second World War, most leading university scientists went to work on top-secret projects to help their governments fight the war. The development by British scientists of radar to detect enemy aircraft was a particularly important outcome of this new kind of sharply focused research. The air war also greatly stimulated the development of rocketry and jet aircraft. The most spectacular and deadly result of directed scientific research during the war was the atomic bomb.

The impressive results of this directed research inspired a new model for science—Big Science. By combining theoretical work with sophisticated engineering in a large bureaucratic organization, Big Science could tackle extremely difficult problems, from new and improved weapons for the military to better products for consumers. Big Science was extremely expensive, requiring large-scale financing from governments and large corporations.

After the war, scientists continued to contribute to advances in military technologies, and a large portion of all postwar scientific research supported the growing arms race. (See "Picturing the Past: A Soviet View of the Arms Race.") After 1945, roughly one-quarter of all men and women trained in science and engineering in the West—and perhaps more in the Soviet Union—were employed full-time in the production of weapons.

A Soviet View of the Arms Race

This propaganda poster from the 1950s reads, "We are a peaceful people, but our armored train stands in ready reserve." The reference to the armored train recalls the Bolshevik use of trains in combat against the White armies during the Russian civil war of the early 1920s. (© Sovfoto)

> **PICTURING THE PAST**

ANALYZING THE IMAGE: What does the "armored train" of the 1950s look like? How does the artist portray the Soviet people, and how does this supposedly peaceful image express Cold War hostility?

CONNECTIONS: Why might the Soviet citizens again need protection at this time, and why would the artist reference the Russian civil war? How did the emergence of Big Science contribute to the global confrontation between the superpowers?

| What were the sources of postwar recovery and stability in western Europe? | What was the pattern of postwar development in the Soviet bloc? | What led to rapid decolonization after World War II? | What kinds of societies emerged in Europe — East and West — after 1945? |  LearningCurve Check what you know. |

Sophisticated science, lavish government spending, and military needs came together in the space race of the 1960s. In 1957, the Soviets used long-range rockets developed in their nuclear weapons program to launch Sputnik, the first man-made satellite to orbit the earth. In 1961, they sent the world's first cosmonaut circling the globe. Embarrassed by Soviet triumphs, the United States made an all-out commitment to catch up with the Soviets. The U.S. National Aeronautics and Space Administration (NASA), founded in 1958, won a symbolic victory by landing a manned spacecraft on the moon in 1969.

Advanced nuclear weapons and the space race were made possible by the concurrent revolution in computer technology. The search for better weaponry in World War II boosted the development of sophisticated data-processing machines, and advances in computer technology continued in the decades following the war. By the 1960s, sophisticated computers were indispensable tools for a variety of military, commercial, and scientific uses.

Big Science had tangible benefits for ordinary people. During the postwar green revolution, directed agricultural research greatly increased the world's food supplies. Farming was industrialized and became more and more productive per acre. The application of scientific advances to industrial processes made consumer goods less expensive and more available to larger numbers of people. The transistor, for example, was used in computers but also in portable radios, kitchen appliances, and many other consumer products. In sum, in the nuclear age, Big Science created new sources of material well-being and entertainment as well as destruction.

> **QUICK REVIEW**

How did the agreements reached among the Allies at Tehran in 1943 shape the postwar world?

CHAPTER LOCATOR | Why was World War II followed so quickly by the Cold War?

CHAPTER 28
888 COLD WAR CONFLICT AND CONSENSUS

What were the sources of postwar recovery and stability in western Europe?

Life and Leisure in the Consumer Revolution

By the late 1950s, a rapidly expanding economy was making more consumer goods available to more people on both sides of the iron curtain, transforming the way they spent their leisure time. British teens listened to the latest rock 'n' roll hits on long-playing record albums. The *Six-Five Special* album featured recordings from the successful BBC television series of the same name. Consumer goods were not as readily available in the East, and the state controlled what goods were produced. Citizens of Communist Czechoslovakia could tune into state-censored television broadcasts on this Czech-made ten-inch tabletop receiver. (television: Martin Hajek/Visual Connection Archive; album: Science Museum/Science & Society Picture Library)

IN THE LATE 1940s, the outlook for Europe appeared bleak. In less than a generation, however, many western European countries constructed democratic political institutions and entered a period of unprecedented economic growth. As a consumer revolution brought improved living standards and a sense of prosperity to ever-larger numbers of people, politicians entered collective economic agreements and established the European Economic Community, the first steps toward broader European unity.

The Search for Political and Social Consensus

In the first years after the war, economic conditions in western Europe were terrible. Infrastructure of all kinds barely functioned, and runaway inflation and a thriving black market testified to severe shortages and hardships. In 1948, as

What were the sources of postwar recovery and stability in western Europe?	What was the pattern of postwar development in the Soviet bloc?	What led to rapid decolonization after World War II?	What kinds of societies emerged in Europe — East and West — after 1945?	✓ **LearningCurve** Check what you know.

economic miracle

▶ Term that contemporaries used to describe rapid economic growth, often based on the consumer sector, in post–World War II western Europe.

Marshall Plan dollars poured in, the battered economies of western Europe began to improve. The outbreak of the Korean War in 1950 further stimulated economic activity, and Europe entered a period of rapid economic progress that lasted into the late 1960s. Never before had the European economy grown so fast. By the late 1950s, contemporaries were talking about an **economic miracle** that had brought robust growth to most western European countries.

There were many reasons for this stunning economic performance. American aid got the process off to a fast start. Moreover, economic growth became a basic objective of all western European governments.

The postwar governments in western Europe thus embraced new political and economic policies that led to a remarkably lasting social consensus. They turned to liberal democracy and generally adopted Keynesian economics (see Chapter 26, page 826) in successful attempts to stimulate their economies. In addition, national leaders in the core European states applied a mixture of government planning and free-market capitalism to promote economic growth. They nationalized (or established government ownership of) significant sectors of the economy; used economic regulation to encourage growth; and established generous welfare provisions, paid for with high taxes, for all citizens. This consensual framework for good government lasted until the middle of the 1970s.

Across the West, newly formed Christian Democratic parties became important power brokers. Rooted in the Catholic parties of the prewar decades (see Chapter 23, page 724), the **Christian Democrats** offered voters tired of radical politics a center-right vision of reconciliation and recovery. Socialists and Communists, active in the resistance against Hitler, also increased their power and prestige, especially in France and Italy.

Christian Democrats

▶ Center-right political parties that rose to power in western Europe after the Second World War.

Across much of continental Europe, the centrist Christian Democrats defeated their left-wing competition. As they provided effective leadership for their respective countries, Christian Democrats drew inspiration from a common Christian and European heritage. They steadfastly rejected authoritarianism and narrow nationalism and placed their faith in democracy and liberalism. Steadfast cold warriors, their anticommunist rhetoric was unrelenting. Rejecting the class politics of the left, they championed a return to traditional family values, a vision with great appeal after a war that left many broken families and destitute households; the Christian Democrats often received a majority of women's votes.

Following their U.S. allies, Christian Democrats advocated free-market economics and promised voters prosperity. At the same time, they established education subsidies, family and housing allowances, public transportation, and public health insurance throughout continental Europe. When necessary, Christian Democratic leaders accepted the need for limited government planning.

Though Portugal, Spain, and Greece generally supported NATO and the United States in the Cold War, they proved exceptions to the rule of democratic transformation outside the Soviet bloc. In Portugal and Spain, nationalist authoritarian regimes had taken power in the 1930s. Portugal's authoritarian state was overthrown in a left-wing military coup only in 1974, while Spain's dictator Francisco Franco remained in power until his death in 1975. The authoritarian monarchy established in Greece when the civil war ended in 1949, bolstered by military support and kept in power in a series of army coups, was likewise replaced by democratic government only in 1975.

CHAPTER LOCATOR | Why was World War II followed so quickly by the Cold War?

By contrast, the Scandinavian countries and Great Britain took decisive turns to the left. Norway, Denmark, and especially Sweden earned a global reputation for long-term Social Democratic governance, generous state-sponsored welfare benefits, tolerant lifestyles, and independent attitudes toward Cold War conflicts. In Britain, the social-democratic Labour Party took power after the war and ambitiously established a "cradle-to-grave" welfare state. Many British industries were nationalized, including banks, iron and steel industries, and utilities and public transportation networks. The British government gave its citizens free medical services and hospital care, generous retirement pensions, and unemployment benefits, all subsidized by progressive taxation, with the wealthy paying significantly more than those earning much less.

Toward European Unity

Though there were important regional differences across much of western Europe, politicians and citizens supported policies that brought together limited state planning, strong economic growth, and democratic government, and this political and social consensus accompanied the first tentative steps on the long road toward a more unified Europe.

A number of new financial arrangements and institutions encouraged slow but steady moves toward European integration, as did cooperation with the United States. To receive Marshall Plan aid, the European states were required by the Americans to cooperate with one another, leading to the creation of the Organization for European Economic Cooperation and the Council of Europe in 1948, both of which promoted commerce and cooperation among European countries.

European federalists hoped that the Council of Europe would evolve into a European parliament with sovereign rights, but this did not happen. Britain, with its still-vast empire and its close relationship with the United States, consistently opposed conceding sovereignty to the council. On the continent, many prominent nationalists and Communists agreed with the British view.

Frustrated in political consolidation, European federalists turned to economics as a way of working toward genuine unity. Christian Democratic governments in West Germany, Italy, Belgium, the Netherlands, and Luxembourg founded the European Coal and Steel Community in 1951 (the British steadfastly refused to join). The founding states quickly attained their immediate economic goal—a single, transnational market for steel and coal without national tariffs or quotas. Close economic ties, advocates hoped, would eventually bind the six member nations so closely together that war among them would become unthinkable.

In 1957, the six countries of the Coal and Steel Community signed the Treaty of Rome, which created the European Economic Community, or **Common Market**. The first goal of the treaty was a gradual reduction of all tariffs among the six in order to create a single market. Other goals included the free movement of capital and labor and common economic policies and institutions. The Common Market encouraged trade among European states, promoted global exports, and helped build shared resources for the modernization of national industries. European integration thus meant not only increased transnational cooperation but also bolstered economic growth on the national level.

In the 1960s, hopes for rapid progress toward political as well as economic union were frustrated by a resurgence of nationalism. French president Charles

Common Market

▶ The European Economic Community, created by six western and central European countries in the West Bloc in 1957 as part of a larger search for European unity.

| What were the sources of postwar recovery and stability in western Europe? | What was the pattern of postwar development in the Soviet bloc? | What led to rapid decolonization after World War II? | What kinds of societies emerged in Europe — East and West — after 1945? | ☑ LearningCurve Check what you know. |

de Gaulle, re-elected to office in 1958, viewed the United States as the main threat to genuine French (and European) independence. He withdrew all French military forces from what he called an "American-controlled" NATO, developed France's own nuclear weapons, and vetoed the scheduled advent of majority rule within the Common Market. Thus, the 1950s and 1960s established a lasting pattern: Europeans would establish ever-closer economic ties, but the Common Market remained a union of independent, sovereign states.

The Consumer Revolution

In the late 1950s, western Europe's rapidly expanding economy led to a rising standard of living and remarkable growth in the number and availability of standardized consumer goods. Not only were more goods available, near full employment and high wages meant that more Europeans could buy more things than ever before. Shaken by war and eager to rebuild their homes and families, western Europeans eagerly embraced the new products of consumer society. They filled their houses and apartments with modern appliances, and they eagerly purchased the latest entertainment devices of the day: radios, record players, and televisions.

The purchase of consumer goods was greatly facilitated by the increased use of installment purchasing, which allowed people to buy on credit. With the expansion of social security safeguards reducing the need to accumulate savings for hard times and old age, ordinary people were increasingly willing to take on debt, and new banks and credit unions offered loans for consumer purchases on easy terms. The consumer market became an increasingly important component of general economic growth.

Visions of consumer abundance became a powerful weapon in an era of Cold War competition. Politicians in both East and West claimed that their respective systems could best provide citizens with ample consumer goods. In the competition over consumption, Western capitalism clearly surpassed Eastern planned economies in the production and distribution of inexpensive products. Western leaders boasted about the arrival of prosperity and promised new forms of social equality in which all citizens would have equal access to consumer goods—rather than relying on class leveling mandated by the state, as in the despised East Bloc.

> **QUICK REVIEW**

What domestic policies did most western European nations implement in the decade following World War II?

CHAPTER LOCATOR | Why was World War II followed so quickly by the Cold War?

What was the pattern of postwar development in the Soviet bloc?

May Day in Nowa Huta In 1951, marchers in a Soviet-planned steel town outside Kraków, Poland, carry posters of (from left to right) Marx, a Polish Communist leader, Lenin, and Engels. (Wiktor Pental/visavis.pl)

WHILE WESTERN EUROPE SURGED AHEAD ECONOMICALLY and increased its independent political power and while American influence gradually waned, East Bloc countries followed a different path. The Soviet Union first tightened its grip on peoples it had "liberated" during the Second World War and then refused to let go. Though limited reforms after Stalin's death in 1953 led to some economic improvement and limited gains in freedoms, postwar recovery in Communist central and eastern Europe proceeded along Soviet lines, and political and social developments there were strongly influenced by developments in the U.S.S.R.

Postwar Life in the East Bloc

The "Great Patriotic War of the Fatherland" had fostered Russian nationalism and a relaxation of dictatorial terror. It also had produced a rare but real unity between Soviet rulers and most citizens. However, even before the war ended, Stalin was moving the U.S.S.R. back toward rigid dictatorship. By early 1946, Stalin was argu-ing that war was inevitable as long as capitalism existed. Working to extend Com-munist influence around the globe, the Soviets established the Cominform, or Communist Information Bureau, an international organization dedicated to main-taining Russian control over Communist parties abroad, in western Europe and

What were the sources of postwar recovery and stability in western Europe?

What was the pattern of postwar development in the Soviet bloc?

What led to rapid decolonization after World War II?

What kinds of societies emerged in Europe — East and West — after 1945?

☑ LearningCurve
Check what you know.

893

the East Bloc. Stalin's new superpower foe, the United States, served as an excuse for re-establishing a harsh dictatorship in the U.S.S.R. itself. Rigid ideological indoctrination, attacks on religion, and the absence of civil liberties were soon facts of life for citizens of the Soviet empire. Millions of supposed political enemies were sent to prison, exile, or forced-labor camps.

In the satellite states of central and eastern Europe, national Communist parties remade state and society on the Soviet model. Though there were significant differences in these East Bloc countries, postwar developments followed a similar pattern. Popular Communist leaders who had led the resistance against Germany were ousted as Stalin sought to create obedient instruments. With Soviet backing, national Communist parties absorbed their Social Democratic rivals and established one-party dictatorships subservient to the Communist Party in Moscow.

Only Josip Broz Tito (TEE-toh) (1892–1980), the resistance leader and Communist chief of Yugoslavia, was able to proclaim political independence and successfully resist Soviet domination. Tito stood up to Stalin in 1948, and because there was no Russian army in Yugoslavia, he got away with it. Though Communist led, Yugoslavia remained outside the Soviet bloc. The country prospered as a multiethnic state until it began to break apart in 1991.

Within the East Bloc, the newly installed Communist governments moved quickly to restructure national economies along Soviet lines, introducing five-year plans to cope with the enormous task of economic reconstruction. Most industries and businesses were nationalized. These efforts transformed prewar patterns of everyday life, even as they laid the groundwork for industrial development later in the decade.

In their attempts to revive the economy, Communist planners gave top priority to heavy industry and the military, and neglected consumer goods and housing. In the 1950s, East Bloc leaders were generally suspicious of Western-style consumer culture. A glut of consumer goods, they believed, created waste, encouraged rampant individualism, and led to social inequality. Thus, for practical and ideological reasons, the provision of consumer goods lagged in the East Bloc, leading to complaints and widespread disillusionment with the constantly deferred promise of socialist prosperity.

For many people in the East Bloc, everyday life was hard throughout the 1950s. Socialist planned economies often led to production problems and persistent shortages of basic household items. Party leaders encouraged workers to perform almost superhuman labor to "build socialism," often for low pay and under poor conditions. In East Germany, popular discontent with this situation led to open revolt in June 1953. A strike by Berlin construction workers protesting poor wages and increased work quotas led to nationwide demonstrations that were put down with Soviet troops and tanks. At least fifty-five protesters were killed and about five thousand were arrested during the uprising.

Communist censors purged culture and art of independent voices in aggressive campaigns that imposed rigid anti-Western ideological conformity. In the 1950s and 1960s, the Communist states required artists and writers to conform to the dictates of **socialist realism**, which idealized the working classes and the Soviet Union. In short, the postwar East Bloc resembled the U.S.S.R. in the 1930s, although police terror was far less intense (see Chapter 27, page 850).

socialist realism

▶ Artistic movement that followed the dictates of Communist ideals, enforced by state control in the Soviet Union and East Bloc countries in the 1950s and 1960s.

CHAPTER LOCATOR | Why was World War II followed so quickly by the Cold War?

894   CHAPTER 28
COLD WAR CONFLICT AND CONSENSUS

Reform and De-Stalinization

In 1953, Stalin finally died. Even as his heirs struggled for power, they realized that reforms were necessary because of the widespread fear and hatred created by Stalin's political terrorism. The power of the secret police was curbed, and many forced-labor camps were gradually closed. Change was also necessary to spur economic growth, which had sputtered in the postwar years. Moreover, Stalin's belligerent foreign policy had led directly to a strong Western alliance, which took steps to isolate the Soviet Union.

The Soviet leadership was badly split on the question of just how much change could be permitted while still preserving the system. Conservatives wanted to move slowly. Reformers, led by Nikita Khrushchev (1894–1971), argued for major innovations. Khrushchev (kroush-CHAWF) emerged as the new Soviet premier in 1955.

To strengthen his position and that of his fellow reformers, Khrushchev launched a surprising attack on Stalin and his crimes at a closed session of the Twentieth Party Congress in 1956. Khrushchev told the delegates that Stalin had "supported the glorification of his own person with all conceivable methods" to build a propagandistic "cult of personality."[1] Moreover, Khrushchev claimed, Stalin had bungled the country's defense in World War II and unjustly imprisoned and tortured thousands of loyal Communists.

The U.S.S.R. now entered a period of genuine liberalization — or **de-Stalinization**, as it was called in the West. The party jealously maintained its monopoly on political power, but Khrushchev brought in new members. Calling for a relaxation of tensions with the West, the new premier announced a policy of "peaceful coexistence." In domestic policies, state planners shifted resources from heavy industry and the military toward consumer goods and agriculture, and relaxed Stalinist

de-Stalinization

▶ The liberalization of the post-Stalin Soviet Union led by reformer Nikita Khrushchev.

The Kitchen Debate

Khrushchev and Nixon discuss the merits of the American way during the famous kitchen debate. Leonid Brezhnev, the future leader of the Soviet Union (from 1964 to 1982), stands on the right, behind Nixon. (AP Photo)

| What were the sources of postwar recovery and stability in western Europe? | **What was the pattern of postwar development in the Soviet bloc?** | What led to rapid decolonization after World War II? | What kinds of societies emerged in Europe — East and West — after 1945? | ✓ LearningCurve Check what you know. |

workplace controls. Leaders in other Communist countries grudgingly adopted similar reforms, and the East Bloc's standard of living began to improve.

Khrushchev liked to boast that East Bloc living standards and access to consumer goods would soon surpass those of the West. Soviet and East Bloc reforms did spark a limited consumer revolution. Consumers' options were more modest than those in the West, but people in Communist countries also purchased automobiles, televisions, and other consumer goods in increasing numbers in the 1960s.

De-Stalinization created great ferment among writers and intellectuals who sought freedom from the constraints of socialist realism, such as Russian author Boris Pasternak (1890–1960), who published his great novel *Doctor Zhivago* in 1957. Appearing in the West but not in the Soviet Union until 1988, *Doctor Zhivago* is both a literary masterpiece and a powerful challenge to communism. Mainstream Communist critics denounced Pasternak, whose book was circulated in secret — but in an era of liberalization he was neither arrested nor shot. Other talented writers followed Pasternak's lead, and courageous editors let the sparks fly. Aleksandr Solzhenitsyn (sohl-zhuh-NEET-suhn) (1918–2008) created a sensation when his *One Day in the Life of Ivan Denisovich* was published in 1962. Solzhenitsyn's novel portrays, in grim detail, life in a Stalinist concentration camp, a life to which Solzhenitsyn himself had been unjustly condemned.

Foreign Policy and Domestic Rebellion

Khrushchev also de-Stalinized Soviet foreign policy. "Peaceful coexistence" with capitalism was possible, he argued, and war was not inevitable. Khrushchev negotiated with Western diplomats, agreeing in 1955, for example, to independence for a neutral Austria. As a result, Cold War tensions relaxed considerably between 1955 and 1957. At the same time, Khrushchev began wooing the new nations of Asia and Africa — even those that were not Communist — with promises of support and economic aid.

In the East Bloc states, Communist leaders responded in complex ways to de-Stalinization. In East Germany, the regime stubbornly resisted reform, but in Poland and Hungary, de-Stalinization stimulated rebelliousness. Poland took the lead in 1956, when extensive popular demonstrations brought a new government to power. By promising to remain loyal to the Warsaw Pact, the Polish Communists managed to win greater autonomy from Soviet control.

Hungary experienced an ultimately tragic revolution the same year. Led by students and workers, the people of Budapest installed Imre Nagy (IM-rey nadge), a liberal Communist reformer, as the new prime minister in October 1956. Though never renouncing communism, Nagy demanded open, multiparty elections, the relaxation of political repression, and other reforms.

At first, it seemed that the Soviets might negotiate, but the breathing space was short-lived. When Nagy announced that Hungary would leave the Warsaw Pact and asked the United Nations to protect the country's neutrality, the Soviets grew alarmed. On November 4, Soviet troops moved in on the capital city of Budapest and crushed the revolution. Fighting was bitter until the end, for the Hungarians hoped that the United Nations would come to their aid. This did not occur — in part because the Western powers were involved in the Suez crisis (see page 903) and were, in general, reluctant to confront the Soviets directly in Europe with military force. When a new, more conservative Communist regime executed Nagy and other protest leaders, many people in the East Bloc concluded that their best hope was to strive for internal reform without openly challenging Soviet control.

The outcome of the Hungarian uprising weakened support for Soviet-style communism in western Europe. At the same time, Western politicians saw that the U.S.S.R. would use military force to defend its control of the East Bloc and that only open war between East and West had the potential to overturn Communist rule there. This price was too high, and it seemed that Communist domination of the satellite states was there to stay.

The Limits of Reform

By late 1962, opposition to Khrushchev's reformist policies had gained momentum in party circles. Khrushchev's Communist colleagues began to see de-Stalinization as a dangerous threat to the authority of the party. Moreover, Khrushchev's policy toward the West was erratic and ultimately unsuccessful. In 1958, Khrushchev tightened border controls between East and West Berlin and ordered the Western allies to evacuate the city within six months. In response, the allies reaffirmed their unity in West Berlin, and Khrushchev backed down. Then, with Khrushchev's backing, the East German authorities built a wall between East and West Berlin in 1961, sealing off West Berlin, in clear violation of existing access agreements among the Great Powers. The recently elected U.S. president, John F. Kennedy (r. 1961–1963), privately hoping that the wall would lessen Cold War tensions by easing hostilities in Berlin, did little to prevent its construction.

Emboldened by American acceptance of the Berlin Wall and seeing a chance to change the balance of military power decisively, Premier Khrushchev secretly ordered missiles with nuclear warheads installed in Fidel Castro's Communist Cuba in 1962. When U.S. intelligence discovered missile sites under construction, Kennedy countered with a naval blockade of Cuba. After a tense diplomatic crisis, Khrushchev agreed to remove the Soviet missiles in return for American pledges not to disturb Castro's regime. In a secret agreement, Kennedy also promised to remove U.S. nuclear missiles from Turkey.

Khrushchev's influence declined rapidly after the Cuban missile crisis. In 1964, the reformist premier was displaced in a bloodless coup, and he spent the rest of his life under house arrest. Under his successor, Leonid Brezhnev (1906–1982), the U.S.S.R. began a period of limited re-Stalinization and economic stagnation. Soviet leaders, determined never to suffer Khrushchev's humiliation in the face of American nuclear superiority, launched a massive arms buildup. Yet Brezhnev proceeded cautiously in the mid-1960s and avoided direct confrontation with the United States.

Despite popular protests and changes in leadership, the U.S.S.R. and its satellite countries had achieved some stability by the late 1950s. East and West traded propaganda threats, but both sides basically accepted the division of Europe into spheres of influence. Violent conflicts now took place in the developing world, where decolonization was opening new paths for Cold War confrontation.

QUICK REVIEW <

How did the Soviet Union and Soviet rule over eastern Europe change after Stalin's death? What did not change?

What led to rapid decolonization after World War II?

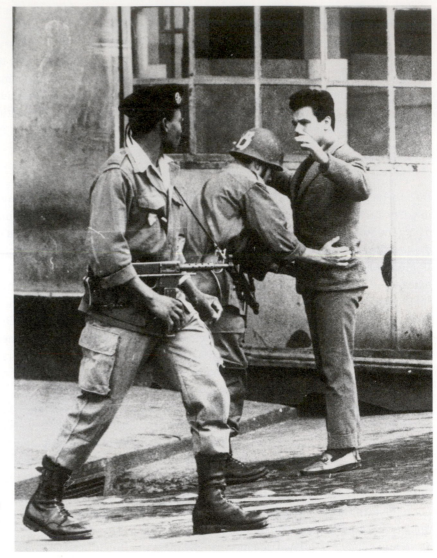

A French Checkpoint in Algeria, 1962

French soldiers search a civilian in Algiers, the capital of Algeria. Inspired by a potent mix of communism and Islamic radicalism, the Algerian National Liberation Front fought a lengthy and bloody struggle against the French colonial government that finally led to Algerian independence in 1962. (Agence France Presse/Getty Images)

decolonization

▶ The postwar reversal of Europe's overseas expansion caused by the rising demand of the colonized peoples themselves, the declining power of European nations, and the freedoms promised by U.S. and Soviet ideals.

IN THE POSTWAR ERA, Europe's long-standing overseas expansion was dramatically reversed. The retreat from imperial control—what Europeans called decolonization—remade the world map (**Map 28.3**). In some cases, decolonization proceeded relatively smoothly, with an orderly transition and little violence. In others, the European powers were determined to preserve colonial rule, and colonized peoples won independence only after long and bloody struggles.

The Cold War had a profound impact on decolonization. Independence movements often had to choose sides in the struggle between the superpowers. After independence was won, both the United States and the Soviet Union struggled to exert influence in the former colonies, where, in many cases, economic growth

CHAPTER LOCATOR | Why was World War II followed so quickly by the Cold War?

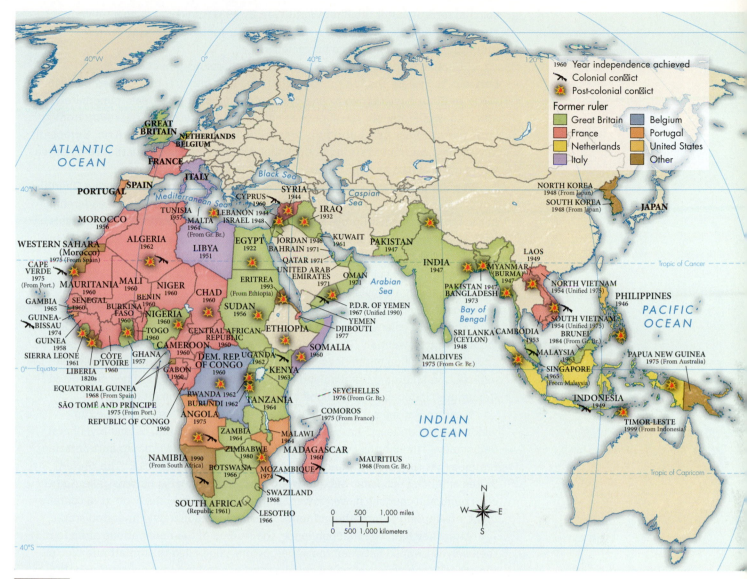

MAP 28.3 ■ Decolonization in Africa and Asia, 1947 to the Present

Divided primarily along religious lines into two states, British India led the way to political independence in 1947. Most African territories achieved statehood by the mid-1960s as European empires passed away, unlamented.

and political stability remained elusive. Liberation from colonial domination was a proud achievement that brought fundamental gains in human freedom but left lasting problems for the former colonized and colonizers alike.

Decolonization and the Global Cold War

The most basic cause of imperial collapse was the rising demand of non-Western peoples for national self-determination, racial equality, and personal dignity. This demand spread from intellectuals to ordinary people in nearly every

| What were the sources of postwar recovery and stability in western Europe? | What was the pattern of postwar development in the Soviet bloc? | **What led to rapid decolonization after World War II?** | What kinds of societies emerged in Europe — East and West — after 1945? | ☑ LearningCurve
Check what you know. |

colonial territory after the First World War. By 1939, the colonial powers were already on the defensive; the Second World War prepared the way for the eventual triumph of independence movements.

European empires had been based on an enormous power differential between the rulers and the ruled, a difference that had greatly declined by 1945. Western Europe was economically devastated and militarily weak immediately after the war. Moreover, the Japanese had driven Western imperial rulers from large parts of East Asia during the war in the Pacific. In Southeast Asia, European imperialists confronted strong anticolonial nationalist movements that re-emerged with new enthusiasm after the defeat of the Japanese.

Popular politicians, including China's Mao Zedong, India's Mohandas Gandhi, Egypt's Gamal Abdel Nasser, and many others, provided determined leadership in the struggle against European imperialism. A new generation of intellectuals, such as Jomo Kenyatta of Kenya and Aimé Césaire and Frantz Fanon, both from Martinique, wrote trenchant critiques of imperial power, often rooted in Marxist ideas. Anticolonial politicians and intellectuals alike helped inspire colonized peoples to resist and overturn imperial rule.

Around the globe, the Cold War had an inescapable impact on decolonization. Liberation from colonial rule had long been a central goal for proponents of Communist world revolution. The Soviets and, after 1949, the Communist Chinese advocated rebellion in the developing world and promised to help end colonial exploitation and bring freedom and equality in a socialist state. They supported Communist independence movements with economic and military aid.

Western Europe and particularly the United States offered a competing vision of independence, based on free-market economics and, ostensibly, liberal democracy—though the United States was often willing to prop up authoritarian regimes that supported staunch anticommunism. Like the U.S.S.R., the United States extended economic aid and weaponry to decolonizing nations. The Americans promoted cautious moves toward self-determination in the context of containment, attempting to limit the influence of communism in newly liberated states.

After they had won independence, the leaders of the new nations often found themselves trapped between the superpowers, compelled to support one bloc or the other. Many new leaders followed a third way, adopting a policy of **nonalignment**, that is, remaining neutral in the Cold War and playing both sides for what they could get.

nonalignment

▶ Policy of postcolonial governments to remain neutral in the Cold War and play both the United States and the Soviet Union for what they could get.

The Struggle for Power in Asia

The first major fight for independence that followed World War II, between the Netherlands and anticolonial insurgents in the Dutch East Indies (today's Indonesia), in many ways exemplified decolonization in the Cold War world. The Dutch had been involved in Indonesia since the early seventeenth century (see Chapter 14, page 436). During World War II, however, the Japanese had overrun the archipelago, encouraging hopes among the locals for independence from Western control. Following the Japanese defeat in 1945, the Dutch returned, hoping to pick up where they left off. But Dutch imperialists faced a determined group of rebels inspired by a powerful combination of nationalism, Marxism, and Islam. Four

CHAPTER LOCATOR | Why was World War II followed so quickly by the Cold War?

900
CHAPTER 28
COLD WAR CONFLICT AND CONSENSUS

years of deadly guerrilla war followed, and in 1949, the Netherlands reluctantly accepted Indonesian independence. The new Indonesian president became an effective advocate of nonalignment. He had close ties to the Indonesian Communist Party but received foreign aid from both the United States and the Soviet Union.

A similar combination of communism and anticolonialism inspired the independence movement in parts of French Indochina (now Vietnam, Cambodia, and Laos), though noncommunist nationalists were also involved. France tried its best to re-establish colonial rule after the Japanese occupation collapsed at the end of World War II. Despite substantial American aid, the French army fighting in Vietnam was defeated in 1954 by forces under the guerrilla leader Ho Chi Minh (hoe chee mihn) (1890–1969), who was supported by the U.S.S.R. and China. Vietnam was divided, a shaky truce established a Communist North and a pro-Western South Vietnam, which led to civil war and subsequent intervention by the United States. Cambodia and Laos also gained independence under noncommunist regimes, though Communist rebels remained active in both countries.

India played a key role in the decolonization process. Nationalist opposition to British rule coalesced after the First World War under the leadership of Mohandas Gandhi (1869–1948). In the 1920s and 1930s, Gandhi (GAHN-dee) built a mass movement preaching nonviolent "noncooperation" with the British. The Second World War interrupted progress toward Indian self-rule, but when the Labour Party came to power in Great Britain in 1945, it was ready to relinquish sovereignty. British socialists had long been critics of imperialism, and the heavy cost of governing India had become a large financial burden to the war-wracked country.

Britain withdrew peacefully, but conflict between India's Hindu and Muslim populations posed a lasting dilemma for South Asia. As independence neared, the Muslim minority grew increasingly anxious about their status in an India dominated by the Hindu majority. Muslim leaders called for partition—the division of India into separate Hindu and Muslim states—and the British agreed. When independence was made official on August 15, 1947, predominantly Muslim territories on India's eastern and western borders became Pakistan (the eastern section is today's Bangladesh). Seeking relief from ethnic conflict that erupted, some 10 million Muslim and Hindu refugees fled both ways across the new borders, an unprecedented population exchange that left mayhem and death in its wake. In just a few summer weeks, up to 1 million people (estimates vary widely) lost their lives. Then in January 1948, a radical Hindu nationalist who opposed partition assassinated Gandhi, and Jawaharlal Nehru became Indian prime minister.

In the early 1950s, Pakistan, an Islamic republic, developed close ties with the United States. Under the leadership of Nehru, India successfully maintained a policy of nonalignment. India became a liberal, if socialist-friendly, democratic state that dealt with both the United States and the U.S.S.R. Pakistan and India both joined the British Commonwealth, a voluntary and cooperative association of former British colonies.

Where Indian nationalism drew on Western parliamentary liberalism, Chinese nationalism developed and triumphed in the framework of Marxist-Leninist ideology. After the withdrawal of the occupying Japanese army in 1945, China erupted again in open civil war between the authoritarian Guomindang (Kuomintang, National People's Party), led by Jiang Jieshi (traditionally called Chiang Kai-shek;

| What were the sources of postwar recovery and stability in western Europe? | What was the pattern of postwar development in the Soviet bloc? | **What led to rapid decolonization after World War II?** | What kinds of societies emerged in Europe — East and West — after 1945? | ✓ LearningCurve Check what you know. |

901

A Refugee Camp During the Partition of India

A young Muslim man, facing an uncertain future, sits above a refugee camp established on the grounds of a medieval fortress in the northern Indian city of Dehli. In the camp, Muslim refugees wait to cross the border to the newly founded Pakistan. The chaos that accompanied the mass migration of Muslims and Hindus during the partition of India in the late summer and autumn of 1947 cost the lives of up to 1 million migrants and disrupted the livelihoods of millions more. (Margaret Bourke-White/Getty Images)

1887–1975), and the Chinese Communists, led by Mao Zedong (MA-OW zuh-DOUNG) and supported by a popular grassroots uprising. Winning the support of the peasantry by promising to expropriate the holdings of the big landowners, the tougher, better-organized Communists forced the Guomindang to withdraw to the island of Taiwan in 1949. Once in power, the Chinese Communists began building a new society that adapted Marxism to Chinese conditions. The new government promoted land reform, extended education and health-care programs to the peasantry, and introduced Soviet-style five-year plans that boosted industrial production. It also brought Stalinist-style repression to the Chinese people.

CHAPTER LOCATOR | Why was World War II followed so quickly by the Cold War?

Independence and Conflict in the Middle East

In some areas of the Middle East, the movement toward political independence went relatively smoothly. The French League of Nations mandates in Syria and Lebanon had collapsed during the Second World War, and Saudi Arabia and Transjordan had already achieved independence from Britain. But events in the British mandate of Palestine and in Egypt showed that decolonization in the Middle East could be a dangerous and difficult process.

As part of the peace accords that followed the First World War, the British government had advocated a Jewish homeland alongside the Arab population (see Chapter 25, page 801). This tenuous compromise unraveled after World War II. Neither Jews nor Arabs were happy with British rule, and violence and terrorism mounted on both sides. In 1947, the frustrated British decided to leave Palestine, and the United Nations voted in a nonbinding resolution to divide the territory into two states—one Arab and one Jewish. The Jews accepted the plan and founded the state of Israel in 1948.

The Palestinians and the surrounding Arab nations attacked the Jewish state as soon as it was proclaimed. The Israelis drove off the invaders and conquered more territory. Roughly nine hundred thousand Arab Palestinians fled or were expelled from their homes, creating a persistent refugee problem. The next fifty years saw four more wars between the Israelis and the Arab states and innumerable clashes between Israelis and Palestinians.

The Arab defeat in 1948 triggered a powerful nationalist revolution in Egypt in 1952, led by the young army officer Gamal Abdel Nasser (1918–1970). The revolutionaries drove out the pro-Western king, and in 1954 Nasser became president of an Egyptian republic. A crafty politician, Nasser advocated non-alignment and expertly played the superpowers against each other.

In July 1956, Nasser abruptly nationalized the foreign-owned Suez Canal Company. Infuriated, the British and the French, along with the Israelis, launched a military invasion. World reaction was outrage, and the United States feared that such a blatant show of imperialism would propel the Arab states into the Soviet bloc. The Americans joined with the Soviets to force the British, French, and Israelis to back down. Egyptian nationalism triumphed: Nasser got his canal, and Israel left the Sinai.

Israel, 1948

The Suez Crisis, 1956

| What were the sources of postwar recovery and stability in western Europe? | What was the pattern of postwar development in the Soviet bloc? | **What led to rapid decolonization after World War II?** | What kinds of societies emerged in Europe — East and West — after 1945? | ☑ LearningCurve Check what you know. |

Decolonization in Africa

In less than a decade, most of Africa won independence from European imperialism. In much of the continent south of the Sahara, decolonization proceeded relatively smoothly. Yet the new African states were quickly caught up in the struggles between the Cold War superpowers, and decolonization all too often left a lasting legacy of economic decline and political conflict (see Map 28.3, p. 899).

Starting in 1957, most of Britain's African colonies achieved independence with little or no bloodshed and then entered a very loose association with Britain as members of the British Commonwealth. There were exceptions to this relatively smooth transfer of power. In Kenya, British forces brutally crushed the nationalist Mau Mau rebellion in the early 1950s, but nonetheless recognized Kenyan independence in 1963. In South Africa, the white-dominated government left the Commonwealth in 1961 and declared an independent republic in order to preserve apartheid—an exploitative system of racial segregation enforced by law.

The decolonization of the Belgian Congo was one of the great tragedies of the Cold War. Belgian leaders maintained a system of apartheid there and dragged their feet in granting independence. These conditions sparked an anticolonial movement that grew increasingly aggressive in the late 1950s under the able leadership of Patrice Lumumba. In January 1960, the Belgians gave in and hastily announced that the Congo would be independent six months later, a schedule that was irresponsibly fast. Lumumba was chosen prime minister in democratic elections, but when the Belgians pulled out on schedule, the new government was entirely unprepared. Chaos broke out when the Congolese army attacked Belgian military officers who remained in the country.

With substantial financial investments in the Congo, the United States and western Europe worried that the new nation might fall into Soviet hands. To head off this perceived threat, U.S. leaders ordered the CIA to help implement a military coup against Lumumba, who was captured and then assassinated. The military set up a U.S.-backed dictatorship under the corrupt general Joseph Mobutu. Mobutu ruled until 1997 and became one of the world's wealthiest men, while the Congo remains one of the poorest, most violent, and most politically torn countries in the world.

Like the British, the French offered most of their African colonies the choice of a total break or independence within a kind of French commonwealth. All but one of the new states chose the latter option, largely because they identified with French culture and wanted aid from their former colonizer.

Things were more difficult in the French colony of Algeria, a large Muslim state on the Mediterranean Sea where some 1.2 million white European settlers, including some 800,000 French, had taken up permanent residency by the 1950s. Nicknamed *Pieds-Noirs* ("black feet"), many of these Europeans had raised families in Algeria for three or four generations, and they enforced a two-tiered system of citizenship, maintaining complete control of politics and the economy. When Algerian rebels, inspired by Islamic fundamentalism and Communist ideals, established the National Liberation Front (FLN) and revolted against French colonialism in the early 1950s, the Pieds-Noirs pressured the French government to help them. In response, France sent some 400,000 troops to crush the FLN and put down the revolt.

The resulting Algerian war lasted from 1954 to 1962. FLN radicals repeatedly attacked civilians while the French army engaged in systematic torture and the forced relocation of Muslim civilians who supported the insurgents. News reports turned French public opinion and indeed the government against the war, but efforts to open peace talks instigated a revolt by the Algerian French and threats of a coup d'état by the French army. In 1958, the immensely popular General Charles de Gaulle was reinstated as French prime minister as part of the movement to keep Algeria French. His appointment calmed the army, the Pieds-Noirs, and the French public. Yet de Gaulle pragmatically accepted Algerian self-determination and in 1962 ended the conflict.

By the mid-1960s, most African states had won independence. The colonial legacy, however, had long-term negative effects. African leaders may have expressed support for socialist or democratic principles in order to win aid from the superpowers; in practice, however, corrupt and authoritarian African leaders like Mobutu in the Congo often established lasting authoritarian dictatorships and enriched themselves at the expense of their populations.

Even after decolonization, western European countries managed to increase their economic and cultural ties with their former African colonies in the 1960s and 1970s. Above all, they used the lure of special trading privileges and provided heavy investment in French- and English-language education to enhance a powerful Western presence in the new African states. This situation led a variety of leaders and scholars to charge that western Europe (and the United States) had imposed a system of **neocolonialism** on the former colonies. According to this view, neocolonialism was a system designed to perpetuate Western economic domination and undermine the promise of political independence.

neocolonialism
▶ A postcolonial system that perpetuates Western economic exploitation in former colonial territories.

QUICK REVIEW

What role did the Cold War play in the colonial independence movements after the end of World War II?

What were the sources of postwar recovery and stability in western Europe?

What was the pattern of postwar development in the Soviet bloc?

What led to rapid decolonization after World War II?

What kinds of societies emerged in Europe — East and West — after 1945?

☑ LearningCurve
Check what you know.

What kinds of societies emerged in Europe — East and West — after 1945?

British Teddy Boys, 1953

These young men are dressed in the "Teddy boy" style with velvet collars, narrow ties, and peg trousers that combine British Edwardian and American fashions. Like other subcultures in the 1950s, the Teds used their appearance to express their youthful rebelliousness. Teddy boys quickly earned a reputation for street fighting, low-level criminal activity, and attacks on Britain's growing West Indian community. (Popperfoto/Getty Images)

EUROPEAN POLITICAL AND ECONOMIC RECOVERY after World War II was accompanied by remarkable social change. A changing class structure, new patterns of global migration, and new roles for women and youths had dramatic impacts on everyday life, on both sides of the iron curtain.

Changing Class Structures

The combination of rapid economic growth, growing prosperity and mass consumption, and the implementation of generous welfare policies went a long way toward creating a new society in Europe after the Second World War. Old class barriers relaxed, and class distinctions became fuzzier.

Changes in the structure of the middle class were particularly influential in this result. After 1945, a new breed of managers and experts—so-called white-collar workers—replaced property owners as the leaders of the middle class. Ability to serve the needs of a big organization largely replaced inherited property and family connections in determining an individual's social position in the middle and upper-middle classes. At the same time, the middle class grew massively and became harder to define.

There were several reasons for these developments. Rapid industrial and technological expansion and the consolidation of businesses created a powerful demand for technologists and managers in large corporations and government agencies. Moreover, the old propertied middle class lost control of many family-owned businesses. Numerous small businesses could no longer turn a profit, forcing their former owners to join the ranks of salaried employees.

Similar processes were at work in the Communist states of the East Bloc. The nationalization of industry, expropriation of property, and aggressive attempts to open employment opportunities to workers and equalize wage structures effectively reduced class differences. Communist Party members typically received better jobs and more pay than nonmembers, but by the 1960s the income differential between the top and bottom strata of East Bloc societies was far smaller than that in the West.

The structure of the lower classes also became more flexible and open. Continuing trends that began in the 1800s, large numbers of people left the countryside for the city, drastically reducing the number of European farmers. Meanwhile, the number of industrial workers in western Europe also began to fall as new jobs for white-collar and service employees grew rapidly. This change marked a significant transition in the world of labor. The welfare benefits extended by postwar governments also helped promote greater social equality because they raised lower-class living standards and were paid for in part by higher taxes on the wealthy. In general, European workers were better educated and more specialized than before, and the new workforce bore a greater resemblance to the growing middle class of salaried specialists than to traditional industrial workers.

Patterns of Postwar Migration

The 1950s and 1960s witnessed new waves of migration that had a significant impact on European society. Some postwar migration took place within countries. Many people left the countryside to seek better prospects in cities. In the poorer countries of Spain, Portugal, and Italy, millions moved to more developed regions of their own countries. The process was similar in the East Bloc, where the forced collectivization of agriculture and state subsidies for heavy industry opened opportunities in urban areas.

Many other Europeans moved across national borders seeking work. The general pattern was from south to north. Workers from less developed countries like Italy, Spain, and socialist Yugoslavia moved to the industrialized north, particularly to West Germany, which—having lost 5 million people during the war—was in desperate need of able-bodied workers. In the 1950s and 1960s, West Germany and other prosperous countries implemented **guest worker programs** designed to recruit much-needed labor for the booming economy. By the early 1970s, there were 2.8 million foreign workers in Germany and another 2.3 million in France, where they made up 11 percent of the workforce.

Most guest workers were young, unskilled single men who labored for low wages in entry-level jobs and sent much of their pay to their families at home.

guest worker programs
▶ Government-run programs in western Europe designed to recruit labor for the booming postwar economy.

What were the sources of postwar recovery and stability in western Europe?

What was the pattern of postwar development in the Soviet bloc?

What led to rapid decolonization after World War II?

What kinds of societies emerged in Europe — East and West — after 1945?

✓ LearningCurve
Check what you know.

(See "Individuals in Society: Armando Rodrigues," page 909.) According to government plans, these guest workers were supposed to return to their home countries after a specified period. Many built new lives, however, and chose to live permanently in their adoptive countries.

Europe was also changed by **postcolonial migration**, the movement of people from the former colonies and the developing world into prosperous Europe. In contrast to guest workers, who joined formal recruitment programs, postcolonial migrants could often claim citizenship rights from their former colonizers and moved spontaneously.

These new migration patterns had dramatic results. Immigrant labor helped fuel economic recovery. Growing ethnic diversity changed the face of Europe and enriched the cultural life of the continent. The new residents were not always welcome, however. Adaptation to European lifestyles could be difficult, and immigrants often lived in separate communities. They faced employment and housing discrimination, and the harsh anti-immigrant rhetoric and policies of xenophobic politicians. The tensions surrounding changed migration patterns would pose significant challenges to social integration in the decades to come.

postcolonial migration
▶ The postwar movement of people from former colonies and the developing world into Europe.

New Roles for Women

The postwar culmination of a one-hundred-year-long trend toward early marriage, early childbearing, and small family size in wealthy urban societies (see Chapter 22) had revolutionary implications for women. Above all, pregnancy and child care occupied a much smaller portion of a woman's life than in earlier times. By the early 1970s, about half of Western women were having their last baby by the age of twenty-six or twenty-seven, leaving the average mother with more than forty years of life in front of her.

Thus, in the postwar years, with motherhood no longer absorbing the energies of a lifetime, more and more married women looked for new roles in the world of work outside the family. Three major forces helped women searching for jobs in the changing post–World War II workplace. First, the economic boom created strong demand for labor. Second, the economy continued its gradual shift away from the old male-dominated heavy industries and toward the white-collar service industries in which some women already worked. Third, young women shared fully in a postwar education revolution, positioning them to take advantage of the growing need for officeworkers and well-trained professionals. Thus, more and more married women became full-time and part-time wage earners.

In the East Bloc, Communist leaders opened numerous jobs to women, who accounted for almost half of all employed persons. Many women made their way into previously male professions, including factory work but also medicine and engineering. In western Europe and North America, the percentage of married women in the workforce rose from a range of roughly 20 to 25 percent in 1950 to anywhere from 30 to 60 percent in the 1970s.

All was not easy for women entering paid employment. Married women workers faced widespread and long-established discrimination in pay, advancement, and occupational choice in comparison to men. Moreover, married working women in both East and West still carried most of the child-rearing and housekeeping responsibilities, leaving them with an exhausting "double burden."

Popping flashbulbs greeted Portuguese worker Armando Rodrigues when he stepped off a train in Cologne in September 1964. Celebrated in the national media as West Germany's 1 millionth guest worker, Rodrigues was met by government and business leaders — including the minister of labor — who presented him with a motorcycle and a bouquet of carnations.

In most respects, Rodrigues was hardly different from the many foreign workers recruited to work in West Germany and other northern European countries. Yet given his moment of fame, he is an apt symbol of a troubled labor program that helped turn Germany into a multiethnic society.

By the late 1950s, the new Federal Republic desperately needed able-bodied men to fill the low-paying jobs created by rapid economic expansion. The West German government signed labor agreements with several Mediterranean countries to meet this demand. Rodrigues and hundreds of thousands of other young men signed up for the employment program and then submitted to an arduous application process. Rodrigues traveled from his village to the regional Federal Labor Office, where he filled out forms and took written and medical exams. Months later, after he had received an initial one-year contract from a German employer, Rodrigues and twelve hundred other Portuguese and Spanish men boarded a special train reserved for foreign workers and embarked for West Germany.

For labor migrants, life was hard in West Germany. In the first years of the guest worker program, most recruits were men between the ages of twenty and forty who were either single or willing to leave their families at home. They typically filled low-level jobs in construction, mines, and factories, and they lived apart from West Germans in special barracks close to their workplaces, with six to eight workers in a room.

West Germans gave Rodrigues and his fellow migrants a mixed reception. Though they were a welcome source of inexpensive labor, the men who emigrated from what West Germans called "the southern lands" faced discrimination and prejudice. "Order, cleanliness, and punctuality seem like the natural qualities of a respectable person to us," wrote one official in 1966. "In the south, one does not learn or know this, so it is difficult [for a person from the south] to adjust here."*

According to official plans, the so-called guest workers were supposed to return home after a specified period of time. Rodrigues, for instance, went back to Portugal in the late 1970s. Resisting government pressure, millions of temporary "guests" raised families and became permanent West German residents, building substantial ethnic minorities in the Federal Republic. Because of strict naturalization laws, however, they could not become West German citizens.

Despite the hostility they faced, foreign workers established a lasting and powerful presence in West Germany, and they were a significant factor in the country's swift eco-

Armando Rodrigues received a standing ovation and a motorcycle when he got off the train in Cologne in 1964. (DPA/Landov)

nomic recovery. Nearly fifty years after Rodrigues arrived in Cologne, his motorcycle is on permanent display in the House of History Museum in Bonn. The exhibit is a remarkable testament both to the contribution of migrant labor to West German economic growth and to the ongoing struggle to come to terms with ethnic difference and integration in a democratic Germany.

QUESTIONS FOR ANALYSIS

1. How did Rodrigues's welcome at his 1964 reception differ from the general attitude toward guest workers in Germany at the time?
2. What were the long-term costs and benefits of West Germany's labor recruitment policies?

LaunchPad

ONLINE DOCUMENT PROJECT

What were the social and cultural consequences of the guest worker program in postwar Germany? Keeping the question above in mind, examine a variety of perspectives on the guest worker program. Then complete a writing assignment based on the evidence and details from this chapter. *See inside the front cover to learn more.*

*Quoted in Rita Chin, *The Guest Worker Question in Postwar Germany* (New York: Cambridge University Press, 2007), p. 43.

The injustices that married women encountered as wage earners contributed greatly to the movement for women's equality and emancipation that arose in the United States and western Europe in the 1960s. Sexism and discrimination in the workplace—and in the home—grew loathsome and evoked the sense of injustice that drives revolutions and reforms.

Youth Culture and the Generation Gap

The bulging cohort of so-called baby boomers born after World War II created a distinctive and very international youth culture, which brought remarkable changes to postwar youth roles and lifestyles. That youth culture was rooted in fashions and musical tastes that set them apart from their elders and fueled anxious comments about a growing "generation gap."

Youth styles in the United States often provided inspiration for movements in Europe, and American jazz and rock 'n' roll spread rapidly in western Europe. American musicians such as Elvis Presley, Bill Haley and His Comets, and Gene Vincent thrilled youths and worried parents, teachers, and politicians.

Youths played a key role in the consumer revolution. Marketing experts and manufacturers quickly recognized that the young people had money to spend due to postwar prosperity. An array of advertisements and products consciously targeted the youth market. As the baby boomers entered their late teens, they eagerly purchased trendy clothing and the latest pop music hits, as well as record players, transistor radios, magazines, hair products, and makeup, all marketed for the "young generation."

The postwar decades saw rapid growth in the number of universities and college students. In 1950, only 3 to 4 percent of western European youths went on to higher education; numbers in the United States were only slightly higher. Then, as government subsidies made education more affordable to ordinary people, enrollments skyrocketed. By 1960, at least three times more European students attended some kind of university than young people had before World War II, and the number continued to rise sharply until the 1970s.

The rapid expansion of higher education opened new opportunities for the middle and lower classes, but it also made for overcrowded classrooms. Many students felt that they were not getting the kind of education they needed for jobs in the modern world. At the same time, some reflective students feared that universities were doing nothing but turning out docile technocrats both to stock and to serve "the establishment." Thus it was no coincidence that students became leaders in a counterculture that attacked the ideals of the affluent society of the postwar world and shocked the West in the late 1960s.

> **QUICK REVIEW**

How did changes in social relations contribute to European stability on both sides of the iron curtain?

CHAPTER LOCATOR | Why was World War II followed so quickly by the Cold War?

LOOKING BACK LOOKING AHEAD

The division of Europe after World War II led to the emergence of a stable world system. In the West Bloc, economic growth, state provision of welfare benefits, and a strong alliance brought social and political consensus. In the East Bloc, a combination of political repression and partial reform likewise limited dissent and encouraged stability. During the height of the Cold War, Europe's former colonies won liberation in a process that was often flawed but that nonetheless resulted in political independence for millions of people. And large-scale transformations, including the rise of Big Science and rapid economic growth, opened new opportunities for women and immigrants and contributed to stability on both sides of the iron curtain.

By the early 1960s, Europeans had entered a remarkable age of affluence that almost eliminated real poverty on most of the continent. The following decades, however, would see substantial challenges to postwar consensus. Youth revolts and a determined feminist movement, an oil crisis and a deep economic recession, and political dissent and revolution in the East Bloc would shake and remake the foundations of Western society.

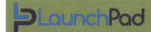

ONLINE DOCUMENT PROJECT

Armando Rodrigues

What were the social and cultural consequences of the guest worker program in postwar Germany?

You encountered Armando Rodrigues's story on page 909. Keeping the question above in mind, examine a variety of perspectives on the guest worker program. *See inside the front cover to learn more.*

What were the sources of postwar recovery and stability in western Europe?	What was the pattern of postwar development in the Soviet bloc?	What led to rapid decolonization after World War II?	What kinds of societies emerged in Europe — East and West — after 1945?	✓ LearningCurve Check what you know.

CHAPTER 28 STUDY GUIDE

STEP 1

GET STARTED ONLINE

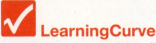

LearningCurve

Now that you've read the chapter, make it stick by completing the LearningCurve activity.

STEP 2

EXPLAIN WHY IT MATTERS

Put your reading into practice. Identify each term below, and then explain why it matters in Western history.

TERM	WHO OR WHAT & WHEN	WHY IT MATTERS
Cold War (p. 880)		
displaced persons (p. 881)		
Truman Doctrine (p. 885)		
Marshall Plan (p. 886)		
Council for Mutual Economic Assistance (COMECON) (p. 886)		
NATO (p. 886)		
Warsaw Pact (p. 886)		
economic miracle (p. 890)		
Christian Democrats (p. 890)		
Common Market (p. 891)		
socialist realism (p. 894)		
de-Stalinization (p. 895)		
decolonization (p. 898)		
nonalignment (p. 900)		
neocolonialism (p. 905)		
guest worker programs (p. 907)		
postcolonial migration (p. 908)		

STEP 3

MOVE BEYOND THE BASICS

To demonstrate a more advanced understanding, fill in the chart included below with descriptions of the key social, economic, and political developments in eastern and western Europe in the decades following World War II. In what ways did eastern and western Europe diverge and in what ways did they remain connected in the decades following World War II?

	Society	Economy	Politics
Eastern Europe			
Western Europe			

PUT IT ALL TOGETHER

Now, take a step back and try to explain the big picture. Remember to use specific examples from the chapter in your answers.

THE COLD WAR AND DECOLONIZATION

▶ Why did cooperation between the Western Allies and the Soviet Union break down so quickly once World War II was over?

▶ How did the Cold War shape decolonization?

ECONOMIC AND POLITICAL DEVELOPMENTS: EAST AND WEST

▶ What explains western Europe's "economic miracle" in the decade following World War II? What steps did the Soviet Union take to consolidate its hold on eastern Europe in the decades following World War II, and how did eastern Europeans respond to their new circumstances?

POSTWAR SOCIAL TRANSFORMATIONS

▶ How did the class structure of western and eastern Europe change after World War II?

▶ Compare and contrast the place of women and youths in European society before and after World War II.

MAKE CONNECTIONS

▶ How did the experience of the 1930s and World War II contribute to the drive toward European unity in the second half of the twentieth century?

▶ In your opinion, did western European governments make a mistake when they established robust social welfare systems in the postwar decades? Why or why not?

▶ IN YOUR OWN WORDS

Imagine that you must give an oral report to the class answering the following question: **What new social, cultural, and political trends emerged in the decades following World War II?** What would be the most important points and why?

29
CHALLENGING THE POSTWAR ORDER

1960–1991

> **How and why did protest movements challenge existing social, economic, and political institutions in both western Europe and the East Bloc?** Chapter 29 examines the challenges to the postwar social and political order that began in the 1960s and continued into the 1990s. As Europe entered the 1960s, the political and social systems forged in the postwar era appeared sound. By the late 1960s, however, this hard-won sense of stability had begun to disappear as popular protest movements in the East and the West arose to challenge dominant certainties. In the early 1970s, the astonishing postwar economic advance ground to a halt, with serious consequences. In western Europe, leaders and citizens alike grappled with the political implications of economic decline and the growth of global competition. In the East Bloc, leaders vacillated between central economic control and liberalization and left in place tight controls on social freedom, leading to stagnation, frustration, and ultimately to revolution.

 **LearningCurve**
After reading the chapter, use LearningCurve to retain what you've read.

> Why did the postwar consensus of the 1950s break down?

> What were the consequences of economic decline in the 1970s?

> What led to the decline of Soviet power in the East Bloc?

> Why did revolution sweep through the East Bloc in 1989?

Life in a Divided Europe. Watchtowers, armed guards, and minefields controlled the Communist eastern side of the Berlin Wall. In the West, to the contrary, ordinary folk turned what was an easily accessible wall into an ad hoc art gallery—this graffiti art appeared in the late 1980s. (© 2013 Artists Rights Society (ARS), New York/VC Bild-Kunst, Bonn)

> Why did the postwar consensus of the 1950s break down?

Student Rebellion in Paris These rock-throwing students in the Latin Quarter of Paris are trying to force education reforms and even topple de Gaulle's government. In May 1968, in a famous example of the protest movements that swept the world in the late 1960s, Parisian rioters clashed repeatedly with France's tough riot police in bloody street fighting. De Gaulle remained in power, but a major reform of French education did follow. (Bruno Barbey/Magnum Photos)

IN THE EARLY 1960s, politics and society in prosperous western Europe remained relatively stable. East Bloc governments, bolstered by modest economic growth and state-enforced political conformity and committed to providing generous welfare benefits for their citizens, maintained control. As the 1960s progressed, a youthful counterculture emerged in the West to critique the status quo. In the East Bloc, Khrushchev's limited reforms also inspired rebellions.

Cold War Tensions Thaw

In western Europe, the first two decades of postwar reconstruction had been overseen for the most part by center-right Christian Democrats (see Chapter 28, page 889). In the mid- to late 1960s, buoyed by the rapidly expanding economy, much of western Europe moved politically to the left. There were important exceptions to this general trend. Centrists remained in power in France until 1981. And in Spain, Portugal, and Greece, authoritarian regimes maintained control until the mid-1970s.

CHAPTER LOCATOR | Why did the postwar consensus of the 1950s break down?

916 CHAPTER 29 CHALLENGING THE POSTWAR ORDER

1961
– Building of Berlin Wall suggests permanence of the East Bloc

1962–1965
– Second Vatican Council

1963
– Wolf publishes *Divided Heaven*; Friedan publishes *The Feminine Mystique*

1964
– Civil Rights Act in the United States

1964–1973
– Peak of U.S. involvement in Vietnam War

1966
– Formation of National Organization for Women (NOW)

1968
– Soviet invasion of Czechoslovakia; "May Events" protests in France

1971
– Founding of Greenpeace

1973
– OPEC oil embargo

1975
– Helsinki Accords

1979
– Margaret Thatcher becomes British prime minister; founding of West German Green Party; Soviet invasion of Afghanistan

1985
– Mikhail Gorbachev named Soviet premier

1987
– United States and Soviet Union sign arms reduction treaty

1989
– Soviet withdrawal from Afghanistan

1989–1991
– Fall of communism in eastern Europe

December 1991
– Dissolution of the Soviet Union

Despite these exceptions, the general leftward drift encouraged a gradual relaxation of Cold War tensions. Though the Cold War continued to rage outside Europe, western European leaders took major steps to normalize relations with the East Bloc. German Chancellor Willy Brandt (1913–1992) took the lead. In December 1970, he flew to Poland for the signing of a historic treaty of reconciliation.

Brandt's treaty with Poland was part of his broader conciliatory foreign policy termed **Ostpolitik** (German for "Eastern policy"). Brandt aimed at nothing less than a comprehensive peace settlement for central Europe and the two postwar German states. Accordingly, the chancellor negotiated new treaties with the Soviet Union and Czechoslovakia, as well as Poland, that formally accepted existing state boundaries in return for a mutual renunciation of force or the threat of force. Using the imaginative formula of "two German states within one German nation," he broke decisively with past policy and entered into direct relations with East Germany.

Ostpolitik
▶ German for "Eastern policy"; West Germany's attempt in the 1970s to ease diplomatic tensions with East Germany, exemplifying the policies of détente.

> European Politics Shifts to the Left

Where? (When?)	What Happened?
Italy (1963)	Socialists enter the national government.
Britain (1964)	The Labour Party returns to power.
West Germany (1969)	Willy Brandt becomes the first postwar Social Democratic chancellor.

What were the consequences of economic decline in the 1970s?

What led to the decline of Soviet power in the East Bloc?

Why did revolution sweep through the East Bloc in 1989?

☑ LearningCurve
Check what you know.

détente

▶ The progressive relaxation of Cold War tensions that emerged in the early 1970s.

Brandt's Ostpolitik was part of a general relaxation of East-West tensions, termed **détente** (day-TAHNT), which began in the early 1970s. Though Cold War hostilities continued in the developing world, direct diplomatic relations between the United States and the Soviet Union grew less strained.

The move toward détente reached a high point when the United States, Canada, the Soviet Union, and all European nations (except isolationist Albania and tiny Andorra) met in Helsinki to sign the Final Act of the Conference on Security and Cooperation in Europe in 1975. Under what came to be called the Helsinki Accords, the thirty-five participating nations agreed that Europe's existing political frontiers could not be changed by force. They also accepted numerous provisions guaranteeing the civil rights and political freedoms of their citizens. The agreement was effective in diminishing Cold War conflict. Although Communist regimes would continue to curtail domestic freedoms and violate human rights guarantees, the accords encouraged East Bloc dissidents, who could now demand that their governments respect international declarations on human rights.

The shift to the left in western European politics also led to new domestic reforms. Building on the welfare systems established in the 1950s, politicians increased state spending on public services even further. By the early 1970s, state spending on such programs hovered around 40 percent of the gross domestic product in France, West Germany, and Great Britain, and even more in Scandinavia and the Netherlands. Center-right Christian Democrats generally supported increased spending on entitlements—as long as the economy prospered. The economic slowdown of the mid-1970s undermined support for the welfare state consensus (see page 925).

The Affluent Society

The 1960s were also a time of rapid social change across western Europe. A decade of economic growth and high wages meant that an expanding middle class could increasingly enjoy the benefits of the consumer revolution that began in the 1950s (see Chapter 28). However, what contemporaries called "the age of affluence" had clear limits. The living standards of workers and immigrants did not rise as fast as those of the educated middle classes, and the expanding economy did not always reach underdeveloped regions, such as southern Italy. Nonetheless the 1960s brought general prosperity to millions, and the construction of a full-blown consumer society had a profound impact on daily life.

The 1960s saw the blossoming of mass travel and tourism. With month-long paid vacations required by law in most western European countries and with widespread automobile ownership, travel to beaches and ski resorts came within the reach of the middle class and much of the working class. By the late 1960s, packaged tours with cheap group airfares and bargain hotel accommodations had made even distant lands easily accessible.

Consumerism also changed life at home. Household appliances that were still luxuries in the 1950s were now commonplace; televisions overtook radio as a popular form of domestic entertainment, while vacuum cleaners, refrigerators, and washing machines transformed women's housework. The establishment of U.S.-style self-service supermarkets across western Europe changed the way food was produced, purchased, and prepared, and threatened to force independent bakers, butchers, and neighborhood grocers out of business.

Many intellectuals and cultural critics worried that rampant consumerism created a bland conformity that wiped out regional and national traditions. Others complained that these changes threatened to Americanize Europe. Such worries were overstated. European nations preserved distinctive national cultures even during the consumer revolution, but social change nonetheless occurred. The moral authority of religious doctrine lost ground before the growing materialism of consumer society. In predominantly Protestant lands, church membership and regular attendance both declined significantly. Even in traditionally Catholic countries, outward signs of popular belief seemed to falter. At the **Second Vatican Council**, convened from 1962 to 1965, Catholic leaders agreed on a number of reforms meant to democratize and renew the church and broaden its appeal. These resolutions did little to halt the slide toward secularization, however.

The Counterculture Movement

One of the dramatic results of economic prosperity was the emergence of a youthful counterculture that came of age in the mid-1960s. The "sixties generation" angrily criticized the comforts of the affluent society and challenged the social and political status quo.

Simple demographics played an important role in the emergence of the counterculture. The two decades following World War II brought a dramatic increase in the number of births per year in Europe and North America. The children born during the postwar baby boom grew up in an era of political liberalism and unprecedented material abundance. Thus, when they came of age in the 1960s, they had the education to see problems like inequality and the lack of social justice, as well as the freedom from want to act on their concerns.

Second Vatican Council

▶ A meeting of Catholic leaders convened from 1962 to 1965 that initiated a number of reforms, including the replacement of Latin with local languages in church services, designed to democratize the church and renew its appeal.

What were the consequences of economic decline in the 1970s?

What led to the decline of Soviet power in the East Bloc?

Why did revolution sweep through the East Bloc in 1989?

☑ LearningCurve
Check what you know.

Counterculture movements in both Europe and the United States drew much inspiration from the American civil rights movement. In the late 1950s and early 1960s, African Americans effectively challenged institutionalized inequality, throwing off a deeply entrenched system of segregation and repression. If dedicated African Americans and their white supporters could succeed, student leaders reasoned, so could they. In 1964 and 1965, at the University of California–Berkeley, students consciously adapted the tactics of the civil rights movement, including demonstrations and sit-ins, to challenge limits on free speech and academic freedom at the university. Soon students across the United States and western Europe were engaged in active protests. The youth movement had come of age, and it mounted a determined challenge to the Western consensus.

Dreaming of economic justice and freer, more tolerant societies, student activists in western Europe and the United States embraced new forms of Marxism, creating a multidimensional and heterogeneous movement that came to be known as the **New Left**. In general, adherents of the various strands of the New Left advocated a more humanitarian style of socialism that could avoid the worst excesses of both capitalism and Soviet-style communism. New Left critics also attacked what they saw as the conformity of consumer society.

Much counterculture activity revolved around a lifestyle rebellion that seemed to have broad appeal. The 1960s brought frank discussion about sexuality, a new willingness to engage in premarital sex, and a growing acceptance of homosexuality. Sexual experimentation was facilitated by the development of the birth control pill, which eliminated the risk of unwanted pregnancy for millions of women. The popular music of the 1960s championed alternative lifestyles. Rock bands like the Beatles, the Rolling Stones, and many others sang songs about drugs and casual sex. Counterculture "scenes" developed in cities such as San Francisco, Paris, and West Berlin. Carnaby Street, the center of "swinging London" in the 1960s, was world famous for its clothing boutiques and record stores, revealing the inescapable connections between generational revolt and consumer culture.

The United States and Vietnam

The growth of the counterculture movement was also closely linked to the escalation of the Vietnam War. American involvement in Vietnam was a product of the Cold War policy of containment (see Chapter 28, page 884). After Vietnam won independence from France in 1954 and was divided into a Communist north and an anticommunist south, U.S. president Dwight D. Eisenhower (r. 1953–1961) provided the south with military aid to combat guerrilla insurgents who were supported by the Communist north. President John F. Kennedy (r. 1961–1963) later increased the number of American "military advisers" to 16,000, and in 1964, President Lyndon B. Johnson (r. 1963–1969) greatly expanded America's role in the Vietnam conflict, providing South Vietnam with massive military aid and eventually some 500,000 American troops. Though the United States bombed North Vietnam with ever-greater intensity, it did not invade the north or set up a naval blockade.

In the end, the American strategy of limited warfare backfired. The undeclared war in Vietnam, fought nightly on American television, eventually divided the nation. Initial public support was strong, but an antiwar movement quickly

New Left

▶ A 1960s counterculture movement that embraced updated forms of Marxism to challenge both Western capitalism and Soviet-style communism.

emerged on college campuses. In October 1965, student protesters joined forces with old-line socialists, New Left intellectuals, and pacifists in antiwar demonstrations in fifty American cities. The protests spread to western Europe. By 1967, a growing number of U.S. and European critics denounced the American presence in Vietnam.

Criticism reached a crescendo after the Vietcong staged the Tet Offensive in January 1968. The Communists' first comprehensive attack on major South Vietnamese cities failed militarily, but the Tet Offensive signaled that the war was not close to ending, as Washington had claimed. Within months of Tet, President Johnson announced that he would not stand for re-election and called for negotiations with North Vietnam.

President Richard M. Nixon (r. 1969–1974) sought to disengage America gradually from Vietnam once he took office. Nixon pursued a policy of "Vietnamization" designed to give the South Vietnamese responsibility for the war and reduce the U.S. presence. He suspended the draft and cut American forces in Vietnam from 550,000 to 24,000 in four years. In 1973, Nixon finally reached a peace agreement with North Vietnam and the Vietcong. Fighting declined markedly in South Vietnam, where the South Vietnamese army appeared to hold its own against the Vietcong.

In early 1974, however, North Vietnam launched a successful general invasion. The South Vietnamese were forced to accept a unified country under a Communist dictatorship, ending a conflict that had begun with the anticolonial struggle against the French at the end of World War II.

Student Revolts and 1968

While the Vietnam War raged, the counterculture became increasingly radical. In western European and North American cities, students and sympathetic followers organized massive antiwar demonstrations and then extended their protests to support colonial independence movements, demand an end to the nuclear arms race, and call for world peace and liberation from social conventions of all kinds.

Political activism erupted in 1968 in a series of protests and riots that circled the globe. One of the most famous and perhaps far-reaching of these revolts occurred in France in May 1968. The "May Events" began when a group of students, dismayed by conservative university policies and inspired by New Left ideals, occupied buildings at the University of Paris. Violent clashes with police followed. When police tried to clear the area around the university on the night of May 10, a pitched street battle took place.

The "May Events" might have been a typically short-lived student protest, but the demonstrations triggered a national revolt. By May 18, some 10 million workers were out on strike, and protesters occupied factories across France. For a brief moment, it seemed as if counterculture dreams of a revolution from below would come to pass. The French Fifth Republic was on the verge of collapse, and a shaken President de Gaulle surrounded Paris with troops.

In the end, however, the goals of the radical students did not correspond to the bread-and-butter demands of the striking workers. When the government promised workplace reforms, including immediate pay raises, the strikers returned to

| What were the consequences of economic decline in the 1970s? | What led to the decline of Soviet power in the East Bloc? | Why did revolution sweep through the East Bloc in 1989? | ✔ LearningCurve Check what you know. |

work. President de Gaulle dissolved the French parliament and called for new elections. His conservative party won almost 75 percent of the seats, showing that the majority of the French people supported neither general strikes nor student-led revolutions.

Counterculture protests generated a great deal of excitement and trained a generation of activists. In the end, however, the protests of the sixties generation resulted only in short-term, limited political change. Lifestyle rebellions involving sex, drugs, and rock music expanded the boundaries of acceptable personal behavior, but they hardly overturned the existing system.

The 1960s in the East Bloc

East Bloc economies clearly lagged behind those of the West, exposing the weaknesses of central planning. To address these problems, Communist governments implemented cautious forms of decentralization and limited market policies in the 1960s, with mixed results. At the same time, recognizing that the overwhelming emphasis on heavy industry was generating popular discontent, Communist planning commissions began to redirect resources to the consumer sector. Once again, results were mixed and varied from country to country. In general, ordinary people in the East Bloc grew increasingly tired of the shortages of basic consumer goods that seemed an endemic part of Communist society.

In the 1960s, Communist regimes also cautiously granted cultural freedoms. Cultural openness only went so far, however. The most outspoken dissidents were harassed and often forced to emigrate to the West; other critics contributed to the rise of an underground *samizdat* (SAH-meez-daht) literature. The label *samizdat*, a Russian term meaning "self-published," referred to books, periodicals, newspapers, and pamphlets published secretly and passed hand to hand by dissident readers because the works directly criticized communism. These unofficial net-

The East German Trabi

This small East German passenger car, produced between 1963 and 1990, was one of the best-known symbols of everyday life in East Germany. Though the cars were notorious for their poor engineering, the growing number of Trabis on East German streets nonetheless testified to the increased availability of consumer goods in the East Bloc in the 1960s and 1970s. (Visual Connection Archive)

The Invasion of Czechoslovakia Armed with Czechoslovakian flags, courageous Czechs in downtown Prague try to stop a Soviet tank and repel the invasion and occupation of their country by the Soviet Union and its eastern European allies. Realizing that military resistance would be suicidal, the Czechs capitulated to Soviet control. (AP Photo/Libor Hajsky/CTK)

works of communication kept critical thought alive and built contacts among dissidents, creating the foundation for the reform movements of the 1970s and 1980s.

The citizens of East Bloc countries sought political liberty as well, and the limits on reform were sharply revealed in Czechoslovakia during the 1968 "Prague Spring" (named for the country's capital city). In January 1968, reform elements in the Czechoslovak Communist Party gained a majority and voted out the long-time Stalinist leader in favor of Alexander Dubček (1921–1992). Dubček (DOOB-chehk) and his allies believed that they could reconcile genuine socialism with personal freedom and party democracy. They called for "socialism with a human face," relaxed state censorship, and replaced rigid bureaucratic planning with local

What were the consequences of economic decline in the 1970s?

What led to the decline of Soviet power in the East Bloc?

Why did revolution sweep through the East Bloc in 1989?

☑ LearningCurve
Check what you know.

decision making by trade unions, workers' councils, and consumers. The reform program proved enormously popular.

Remembering that the Hungarian revolution had revealed the difficulty of reforming communism from within (see Chapter 28, page 896), Dubček constantly proclaimed his loyalty to the Soviet Union and the Warsaw Pact. But his reforms threatened hard-line Communists, particularly in Poland and East Germany, where leaders knew full well that they lacked popular support. Moreover, Soviet leaders feared that a liberalized Czechoslovakia would eventually be drawn to neutrality or even to NATO. Thus the East Bloc leadership decided to end the Czechoslovak experiment, and five hundred thousand Soviet and East Bloc troops occupied Czechoslovakia in August 1968. The Czechoslovaks made no attempt to resist militarily, and the arrested leaders surrendered to Soviet demands. The reform program was abandoned.

Shortly after the invasion of Czechoslovakia, Soviet premier Leonid Brezhnev (1906–1982) announced that the Soviets would now follow the so-called **Brezhnev Doctrine**, under which the Soviet Union and its allies had the right to intervene militarily in any East Bloc country whenever they thought doing so was necessary to preserve Communist rule. The 1968 invasion of Czechoslovakia was the crucial event of the Brezhnev era: it demonstrated the determination of the Communist elite to maintain the status quo throughout the Soviet bloc. At the same time, the Soviet crackdown encouraged dissidents to change their focus from "reforming" Communist regimes from within to building a civil society that might bring internal freedoms independent of the regimes (see pages 936–938).

Brezhnev Doctrine

▶ Doctrine created by Leonid Brezhnev that held that the Soviet Union had the right to intervene in any East Bloc country when necessary to preserve Communist rule.

> **QUICK REVIEW**

What were the commonalities and differences between the counterculture in the West and anti-Soviet activism in the East?

CHAPTER LOCATOR | Why did the postwar consensus of the 1950s break down?

924   CHAPTER 29   CHALLENGING THE POSTWAR ORDER

What were the consequences of economic decline in the 1970s?

The Social Consequences of Thatcherism

As police watch in the background, picketers outside the largest coal mine in Britain hold up a poster reading "Save the Pits" during the miners' strike of 1984 to 1985. Prime Minister Margaret Thatcher broke the strike, weakening the power of Britain's trade unions and easing the turn to free-market economic reforms. Thatcher's neoliberal policies revived economic growth but cut state subsidies for welfare benefits and heavy industries, leading to lower living standards for many working-class Britons and, as this image attests, to popular protest. (Bride Lane Library/Popperfoto/Getty Images)

THE GREAT POSTWAR ECONOMIC BOOM came to a close in the early 1970s, opening a long period of economic stagnation, widespread unemployment, and social dislocation. By the end of the 1980s, the postwar social and political consensus based on prosperity, full employment, modest regulation, and generous welfare provisions had been deeply shaken.

Economic Crisis and Hardship

Starting in the early 1970s, the West entered into a long period of economic decline. One of the early causes of the downturn was the collapse of the international monetary system, which since 1945 had been based on the American dollar, valued in gold at $35 an ounce. In the postwar decades, the United States spent billions of dollars on foreign aid and foreign wars, weakening the value of American currency. In 1971, President Nixon attempted to reverse this trend by abruptly stopping the

What were the consequences of economic decline in the 1970s?	What led to the decline of Soviet power in the East Bloc?	Why did revolution sweep through the East Bloc in 1989?	✓ **LearningCurve** Check what you know.

exchange of U.S. currency for gold. The value of the dollar fell sharply, and inflation accelerated worldwide. Countries abandoned fixed rates of currency exchange, and great uncertainty replaced postwar predictability in international trade and finance.

Even more damaging to the global economy was the dramatic reversal in the price and availability of energy. The great postwar boom had been fueled in part by cheap oil from the Middle East. The fate of the developed world was thus increasingly linked to this turbulent region, where strains began to show in the late 1960s. In 1967, in the Six-Day War, Israel quickly defeated Egypt, Jordan, and Syria and occupied more of the former territories of Palestine, angering Arab leaders and exacerbating anti-Western feeling in the Arab states. Economics fed tension between Arab states and the West. Over the years, **OPEC**, the Arab-led Organization of Petroleum Exporting Countries, had watched the price of crude oil decline consistently compared with the rising price of Western manufactured goods. OPEC decided to reverse that trend by presenting a united front against Western oil companies.

The stage was thus already set for a revolution in energy prices when Egypt and Syria launched a surprise attack on Israel in October 1973, setting off the fourth Arab-Israeli war. With the help of U.S. weapons, Israel again achieved a quick victory. OPEC then declared an embargo on oil shipments to the United States and simultaneously raised oil prices. Within a year, crude oil prices quadrupled.

Coming on the heels of the upheaval in the international monetary system, the revolution in energy prices plunged the world into its worst economic decline since the 1930s. Unemployment rose, productivity and living standards declined, and inflation soared. Economists coined a new term—**stagflation**—to describe the combination of low growth and high inflation that drove the worldwide recession. By 1976, a modest recovery was in progress, but in 1979, a fundamentalist Islamic revolution overthrew the shah of Iran. When oil production in that country collapsed, the price of crude oil doubled again. Unemployment and inflation rose dramatically before another uneven recovery began in 1982.

The developing world was hit hard by slowed growth, and the global economic downturn widened the gap between rich and poor countries. Governments across South America, sub-Saharan Africa, and South Asia borrowed heavily from the United States and western Europe in attempts to restructure their economies, setting the stage for a serious international debt crisis. At the same time, the East Asian countries of Japan and then Singapore, South Korea, and Taiwan started exporting high-tech consumer goods to the West. Competition from these East Asian "tiger economies," whose labor costs were comparatively low, shifted manufacturing jobs away from the highly industrialized countries of northern Europe and North America.

Even though the world economy slowly began to recover in the 1980s, western Europe could no longer create enough jobs to replace those that were lost. By the end of the 1970s, the foundations of economic growth in the industrialized West had begun shifting to high-tech information industries and to services, including medicine, banking, and finance. Scholars spoke of the shift as the arrival of "the information age" or **postindustrial society**. In western Europe, heavy industry, such as steel, mining, automobile manufacture, and shipbuilding, lost ground. Factory closings led to the emergence of "rust belts"—formerly prosperous industrialized areas that were now ghost lands. By 1985, the unemployment rate in western Europe had risen to its highest level since the Great Depression.

OPEC
▶ The Arab-led Organization of Petroleum Exporting Countries.

stagflation
▶ Term coined in the early 1980s to describe the combination of low growth and high inflation that led to a worldwide recession.

postindustrial society
▶ A society that relies on high-tech and service-oriented jobs for economic growth rather than heavy industry and manufacturing jobs.

CHAPTER LOCATOR | Why did the postwar consensus of the 1950s break down?

The crisis struck countless ordinary people, upending lives and causing real hardships. Yet on the whole, the welfare system fashioned in the postwar era prevented mass suffering and degradation. The responsive, socially concerned national state undoubtedly contributed to the preservation of political stability and democracy in the face of economic difficulties that might have brought revolution and dictatorship in earlier times.

With the commitment of governments to supporting social needs, government spending in most European countries continued to rise sharply during the 1970s and early 1980s. Across western Europe, people were willing to see their governments increase spending, but they resisted higher taxes. This imbalance contributed to the rapid growth of budget deficits, national debts, and inflation. While this increased spending was generally popular, a powerful reaction against government's ever-increasing role had set in by the late 1970s that would transform governance in the 1980s.

The New Conservatism

The transition to a postindustrial society was led to a great extent by a new generation of conservative political leaders, who believed they had viable solutions for restructuring the relations between the state and the economy. During the thirty years following World War II, both Social Democrats and the more conservative Christian Democrats had usually agreed that economic growth and social stability were best achieved through full employment and high wages, some government regulation, and generous welfare provisions. In the late 1970s, however, with a weakened economy and increased global competition, this consensus began to unravel. Whether politics turned to the right, as in Great Britain, the United States, and West Germany, or to the left, as in France and Spain, leaders moved to cut government spending and regulation in attempts to improve economic performance.

The new conservatives of the 1980s followed a philosophy that came to be known as **neoliberalism** because of its roots in the free market, laissez-faire policies favored by eighteenth-century liberal economists (see Chapter 20, page 531). Neoliberal theorists argued that governments should limit support for social services including housing, education, and health insurance; cut business subsidies; and retreat from regulation of all kinds. Neoliberals also called for **privatization**— the sale of state-managed industries to private owners. Doing so, they argued, would both tighten government spending and lead to greater workplace efficiency. The main goal was to increase private profits, which neoliberals believed were the real engine of economic growth.

The effects of neoliberal policies are best illustrated by events in Great Britain. The broad shift toward greater conservatism, coupled with growing voter dissatisfaction with high taxes and runaway state budgets, helped elect Margaret Thatcher (1925–2013) prime minister in 1979. A member of the Conservative Party and a convinced neoliberal, Thatcher pushed through a series of controversial free-market policies that transformed Britain. Thatcher's government cut spending on health care, education, and public housing; reduced taxes; and privatized or sold off government-run enterprises. (See "Individuals in Society: Margaret Thatcher," page 928.)

neoliberalism
▶ Philosophy of 1980s conservatives who argued for decreased government spending on social services and privatization of state-run industries.

privatization
▶ The sale of state-managed industries such as transportation and communication networks to private owners, a key policy of neoliberalism meant to control government spending, increase private profits, and foster economic growth, which was implemented in western Europe in response to the economic crisis of the 1970s.

What were the consequences of economic decline in the 1970s?

What led to the decline of Soviet power in the East Bloc?

Why did revolution sweep through the East Bloc in 1989?

✔ LearningCurve
Check what you know.

INDIVIDUALS IN SOCIETY
Margaret Thatcher

Margaret Thatcher, the first woman elected to lead a major European state, was one of the late twentieth century's most significant leaders. The controversial "iron lady" attacked socialism, promoted capitalism, and changed the face of modern Britain.

Raised in a lower-middle-class family in a small city in southeastern England, Thatcher entered Oxford in 1943 to study chemistry. She soon discovered a passion for politics and was elected president of student conservatives. Four years after her graduation, she ran for Parliament in 1950 in a solidly Labour district to gain experience. Articulate and attractive, she won the attention of Denis Thatcher, a wealthy businessman who drove her to campaign appearances in his Jaguar. Married a year later, the new Mrs. Thatcher abandoned chemistry, went to law school, gave birth to twins, and became a tax attorney. In 1959, she returned to politics and won a seat in that year's Conservative triumph.

For the next fifteen years, Thatcher served in Parliament and held various ministerial posts when the Conservatives governed. In 1974, as the economy soured and the Conservatives lost two close elections, a rebellious Thatcher adroitly ran for the leadership of her party and won. Five years later, as the Labour government faced rampant inflation and crippling strikes, Thatcher promised to reduce union power, lower taxes, and promote free markets. Attracting swing votes from skilled workers, the Conservatives gained a majority, and she became prime minister.

A self-described "conviction politician," Thatcher rejected postwar Keynesian efforts to manage the economy, arguing that governments created inflation by printing too much money. Thus her government reduced the supply of money and credit and refused to retreat when interest rates and unemployment soared. Her popularity plummeted. But Thatcher remained in office, in part through an aggressive foreign policy. In 1982, the generals ruling Argentina suddenly seized the nearby Falkland Islands, home to 1,800 British citizens. A staunch nationalist, Thatcher dispatched a naval armada that recaptured the islands without a hitch. Britain admired Thatcher's determination and patriotism, and she was re-elected in 1983.

Thatcher's second term was the high point of her influence. Her commitment to privatization transformed British industry. More than fifty state-owned companies, ranging from the state telephone monopoly to the nationalized steel trust, were sold to private investors. Small investors were offered shares at bargain prices to promote "people's capitalism." Thatcher also curbed the power of British labor unions, most spectacularly in 1984, when the once-

Margaret Thatcher as prime minister.
(AP Photo/Staff/Caulkin)

mighty coal miners rejected more mine closings and doggedly struck for a year; Thatcher stood firm and beat them. This outcome had a profound psychological impact on the public, who blamed her for growing unemployment. Thatcher was also accused of mishandling a series of protest hunger strikes undertaken by the Irish Republican Army — in 1981 ten IRA members starved themselves to death in British prisons — but she refused to compromise with those she labeled criminals. As a result, the revolt in Northern Ireland entered one of its bloodiest phases.

Despite these problems, Thatcher was elected to a third term in 1987. Afterward, she became increasingly stubborn, overconfident, and uncaring. Working with her ideological soul mate, U.S. president Ronald Reagan, she opposed greater political and economic unity within the European Community. This, coupled with rising inflation, stubborn unemployment, and an unpopular effort to assert financial control over city governments, proved her undoing. In 1990, as in 1974, party stalwarts suddenly revolted and elected a new Conservative leader. The transformational changes of the Thatcher years nonetheless endured, consolidated by her Conservative successor, John Major, and largely accepted by the new Labour prime minister, the moderate Tony Blair, who served in office from 1997 to 2007.

QUESTIONS FOR ANALYSIS

1. Why did Margaret Thatcher want to change Britain, and how did she do it?
2. How did Thatcher's policies reflect the new conservatism of the 1970s and 1980s?

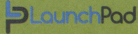

ONLINE DOCUMENT PROJECT

How did Thatcher's Conservative Party adapt its message to fit the values of the majority of British people? Keeping the question above in mind, explore Conservative Party campaign posters from the 1979 British general election. Then complete a writing assignment based on the evidence and details from this chapter. *See inside the front cover to learn more.*

Though she never eliminated all social programs, Thatcher's policies helped replace the interventionist ethos of the welfare state with a greater reliance on private enterprise and the free market. This transition involved significant human costs. In the first three years of her government, unemployment rates in Britain doubled to over 12 percent. The gap between rich and poor widened, and increasing poverty led to discontent and crime. Strikes and working-class protests sometimes led to violent riots. Thatcher successfully rallied support by leading a British victory over Argentina in the brief Falklands War (1982), but over time her position weakened. By 1990, Thatcher's popularity had fallen to record lows, and she was replaced by Conservative Party leader John Major.

In the United States, two-term president Ronald Reagan (r. 1981–1989) followed a similar path, though his success in cutting government was more limited. With widespread popular support and the agreement of most congressional Democrats as well as Republicans, Reagan pushed through major across-the-board cuts in income taxes in 1981. But Reagan and Congress failed to limit government spending, which increased as a percentage of national income in the course of his presidency. A massive military buildup was partly responsible, but spending on social programs also grew rapidly. As a result, the budget deficit soared, and U.S. government debt tripled in a decade.

West Germany also turned to the right. After more than a decade in power, the Social Democrats foundered, and in 1982, Christian Democrat Helmut Kohl (b. 1930) became the new chancellor. Like Thatcher, Kohl cut taxes and government spending. His policies led to increasing unemployment in heavy industry but also to solid economic growth. By the mid-1980s, West Germany was one of the most prosperous countries in the world.

The most striking temporary exception to the general drift to the right in European politics was François Mitterrand (1916–1996) of France. After his election as president in 1981, Mitterrand and his Socialist Party led France on a lurch to the left. Mitterrand launched a vast program of nationalization and public investment designed to spend the country out of economic stagnation. By 1983, this attempt had clearly failed, and Mitterrand's Socialist government made a dramatic about-face. The Socialists were compelled to reprivatize industries they had just nationalized. They imposed a wide variety of austerity measures and maintained those policies for the rest of the decade.

Despite persistent economic crises and high social costs, the developed nations of western Europe and North America were far more productive by 1990 than they had been in the early 1970s. Western Europe was at the center of the emerging global economy, and its citizens were far richer than those in Soviet bloc countries (see pages 935–936). Yet the collapse of the postwar consensus and the remaking of Europe in the transitional decades of the 1970s and 1980s helped generate new forms of protest and dissent across the political spectrum.

Challenges and Victories for Women

The 1970s marked the arrival of a diverse and widespread feminist movement devoted to securing genuine gender equality and promoting the general interests of women. Three basic reasons accounted for this dramatic development. First, ongoing changes in underlying patterns of motherhood and paid work created

What were the consequences of economic decline in the 1970s?	What led to the decline of Soviet power in the East Bloc?	Why did revolution sweep through the East Bloc in 1989?	✓ LearningCurve Check what you know.

novel conditions and new demands (see Chapter 28, page 908). Second, a vanguard of feminist intellectuals articulated a powerful critique of gender relations, which stimulated many women to rethink their assumptions and challenge the status quo. Third, taking a lesson from the civil rights movement in the United States and protests against the Vietnam War, dissatisfied women recognized that they had to band together if they were to influence politics and secure fundamental reforms.

Feminists could draw on a long heritage of protest, stretching back to the French Revolution and the women's movements of the late nineteenth century (see Chapters 19 and 22). They were also inspired by recent writings, such as the foundational book *The Second Sex* (1949) by the French writer and philosopher Simone de Beauvoir (1908–1986). Beauvoir analyzed the position of women within the framework of existential thought. She argued that women had almost always been trapped by particularly inflexible and limiting conditions. Only through courageous action and self-assertive creativity could a woman become a completely free person and escape the role of the inferior "other" that men had constructed for her gender.

The Second Sex inspired a generation of women intellectuals, and by the late 1960s and the 1970s, "second-wave feminism" had spread through North America and Europe. In the United States, writer and organizer Betty Friedan's (1921–2006) pathbreaking study *The Feminine Mystique* (1963) pointed the way. Friedan called attention to the stifling aspects of women's domestic life, devoted to the service of husbands and children. In 1966, Friedan helped found the National Organization for Women (NOW) to press for women's rights.

Many other women's organizations rose in Europe and North America. The diverse groups drew inspiration from Marx, Freud, or political liberalism, but in general feminists attacked patriarchy (the domination of society by men) and sexism (the inequalities faced by women simply because they were female). Advocates of women's rights pushed for new statutes governing the workplace: laws against discrimination, acts requiring equal pay for equal work, and measures such as maternal leave and affordable day care designed to help women combine careers and family responsibilities.

The movement also addressed gender and family questions, including the right to divorce (in some Catholic countries), legalized abortion, the needs of single mothers, and protection from rape and physical violence. In almost every country, the effort to decriminalize abortion served as a catalyst in mobilizing an effective, self-conscious women's movement—and, as in the United States, in creating opposition to it.

Italian Feminists

These women demonstrate in Rome in 1981 for the passage of legislation legalizing abortion, which the pope and the Catholic Church steadfastly opposed. The demonstrators raise their hands in a feminist salute during the peaceful march. (© Bettmann/Corbis)

CHAPTER LOCATOR | Why did the postwar consensus of the 1950s break down?

In countries that had long placed women in a subordinate position, the legal changes were little less than revolutionary. In Italy, for example, new laws abolished restrictions on divorce and abortion that had been strengthened by Mussolini and defended energetically by the Catholic Church in the postwar era. By 1988, divorce and abortion were common in Italy, which had the lowest birthrate in Europe. While the women's movement of the 1970s won new rights for women, subsequently it became more diffuse, a victim of both its successes and the resurgence of an antifeminist opposition.

The Rise of the Environmental Movement

By the 1970s, the destructive environmental costs of industrial development in western Europe and the East Bloc were everywhere apparent. The mighty Rhine River was an industrial sewer. The forests of southwestern Germany were dying from acid rain, a result of smokestack emissions. The coast of Brittany, in northwest France, was fouled by oil spills from massive tanker ships. Rapid industrialization in the East Bloc had been undertaken with little regard for environmental impact. Serious accidents at nuclear plants—at Three Mile Island in Pennsylvania (1979) and at Chernobyl in Soviet Ukraine (1986)—revealed nuclear power's potential to create human and environmental disaster (**Map 29.1**). These were just some examples of the environmental threats that inspired a growing environmental movement to challenge government and industry to clean up their acts.

Environmentalists had two main agendas. First, they worked to lessen the ill effects of unbridled industrial development on the natural environment. Second, they argued that local environmental problems often increased human poverty, inequality, and violence around the globe. Environmental groups pursued these goals in many ways. Some used the mass media to reach potential supporters; some worked closely with politicians and public officials to change government policies. Others took a more activist stance, organizing protests and demonstrations.

Environmental protesters also built new institutions, particularly in North America and western Europe. In 1971, Canadian activists established Greenpeace, a nongovernmental organization dedicated to environmental conservation and protection. Greenpeace quickly grew into an international organization, with strong support in Europe and the United States. In West Germany, in 1979, environmentalists founded the Green Party, a

MAP 29.1 ■ Pollution in Europe, ca. 1990
Despite attempts to remedy the negative consequences of the human impact on the environment, pollution remains a significant challenge for Europeans in the twenty-first century.

Nuclear power plants
Over 50   10–50   Under 10
Acid rain levels
High   Medium   Low
Severely polluted river
Oil tanker disaster, 1970s–1990s

Chernobyl nuclear accident April 26, 1986

| **What were the consequences of economic decline in the 1970s?** | What led to the decline of Soviet power in the East Bloc? | Why did revolution sweep through the East Bloc in 1989? | ✓ LearningCurve Check what you know. |

Green Party Representatives Enter Parliament

In 1983, members of the environmentally conscious West German Green Party won enough votes to send several representatives to the parliament for the first time, an important victory for the protest movements that emerged in the 1970s and 1980s. (bpk, Berlin/Art Resource, NY)

political party to fight for environmental causes. The West German Greens met with astounding success when they elected members to parliament in 1983, the first time in sixty years that a new political party had been seated in Germany. (See "Picturing the Past: Green Party Representatives Enter Parliament.") Their success was a model for like-minded activists in Europe and North America, and Green Party members were later elected to parliaments in Belgium, Italy, and Sweden. In the East Bloc, government planners increasingly recognized and tried to ameliorate environmental problems in the 1980s.

Separatism and Right-Wing Extremism

The 1970s also saw the rise of determined separatist movements across Europe. In Ireland, Spain, Belgium, and Switzerland—and in Yugoslavia and Czechoslovakia in the East Bloc—regional ethnic groups struggled for special rights, political autonomy, and even national independence. This separatism was most violent in

CHAPTER LOCATOR | Why did the postwar consensus of the 1950s break down?

932   CHAPTER 29
CHALLENGING THE POSTWAR ORDER

Spain and Northern Ireland, where well-established insurgent groups used terrorist attacks to win government concessions. In the ethnic Basque region of northern Spain, the ETA (short, in the Basque language, for Basque Homeland and Freedom) tried to use bombings and assassinations to force the government to grant independence. After the death in 1975 of Fascist dictator Francisco Franco, a new constitution granted the Basque region special autonomy, but it was not enough. The ETA stepped up its terrorist campaigns, killing over four hundred people in the 1980s.

The Provisional Irish Republican Army (IRA), a paramilitary organization in Northern Ireland, used similar tactics. Though Ireland had won autonomy in 1922, Great Britain retained control of six primarily Protestant counties in the north of the island. In the late 1960s, violence re-emerged as the IRA, hoping to unite these counties with Ireland, attacked British security forces. On Bloody Sunday in January 1972, British soldiers shot and killed thirteen demonstrators, who had been protesting anti-Catholic discrimination, in the town of Derry, and the violence escalated. For the next thirty years the IRA attacked soldiers and civilians in Northern Ireland and in Britain itself. Over two thousand British soldiers, civilians, and IRA members were killed during "the Troubles" before negotiations between the IRA and the British government opened in the late 1990s and a settlement was reached in 1998.

Mainstream European politicians also faced challenges from newly assertive political forces on the far right. Right-wing political parties such as the National Front in France, the Northern League in Italy, the Austrian Freedom Party, and the National Democratic Party in West Germany were founded or gained popularity in the 1970s and 1980s. New right-wing politicians promoted themselves as the champions of ordinary (white) workers, complaining that immigrants swelled welfare rolls and stole jobs from native-born Europeans. Though their programs at times veered close to open racism, they began to win seats in national parliaments in the 1980s.

QUICK REVIEW

What explains the move to the right in the 1970s?

| **What were the consequences of economic decline in the 1970s?** | What led to the decline of Soviet power in the East Bloc? | Why did revolution sweep through the East Bloc in 1989? | ✓ LearningCurve Check what you know. |

What led to the decline of Soviet power in the East Bloc?

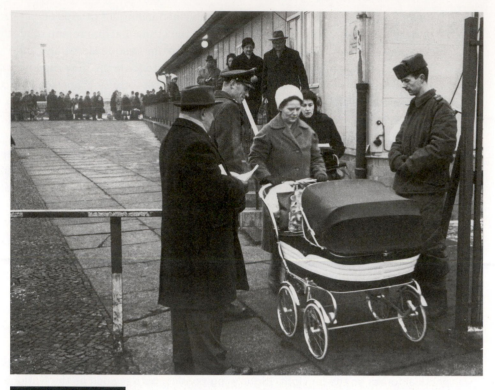

Crossing the Border Between East and West Berlin During the Christmas season of 1965, West Berliners were given special permission to visit relatives in the walled-off eastern part of the city. The limits on travel in the East Bloc were one of the most hated aspects of life under Communist rule. (bpk, Berlin/Art Resource, NY)

IN THE POSTWAR DECADES, the Communist states of the East Bloc had achieved a shaky social consensus based on a rising standard of living, an extensive welfare system, and political repression. When the Marxist utopia still had not arrived in the 1970s, Communist leaders told citizens that they had to be patient and accept the system as it was; in the long run, leaders claimed, "developed socialism" would prove better than capitalism. Such claims were an attempt to paper over serious tensions in Communist society. Everyday life could be difficult. Limits on personal and political freedoms encouraged the growth of determined reform movements, and a revival of Cold War tensions accompanied the turn to the right in the United States and western Europe in the 1980s.

When Mikhail Gorbachev burst on the scene in 1985, the new Soviet leader opened an era of reform that was as sweeping as it was unexpected. Although many believed that Gorbachev would soon fall from power, his reforms rapidly transformed Soviet culture and politics and drastically reduced Cold War tensions. But communism, which Gorbachev wanted so desperately to revitalize, continued to stagnate and decline.

CHAPTER LOCATOR | Why did the postwar consensus of the 1950s break down?

State and Society in the East Bloc

By the 1970s, many of the professed goals of communism had been achieved. Communist leaders in central and eastern Europe and the Soviet Union adopted the term **developed socialism** to describe the accomplishments of their societies. Agriculture had been thoroughly collectivized, industry and business had been nationalized, and only a small percentage of the economy remained in private hands in most East Bloc countries. The state had also done much to level class differences. Though some people—particularly party members—clearly had greater access to better opportunities and resources, the gap between rich and poor was far smaller than in the West. An extensive system of government-supported welfare benefits included free medical care, guaranteed employment, inexpensive public transportation, and large subsidies for rent and food.

Everyday life under developed socialism was defined by an uneasy mixture of outward conformity and private disengagement—or apathy. The Communist Party dominated public life. Party-led mass organizations for youth, women, workers, and sports groups staged huge rallies, colorful festivals, and new holidays that exposed citizens to the values of the socialist state. East Bloc citizens might grudgingly participate in party-sponsored public events, but at home, and in private, they often grumbled about and sidestepped the Communist authorities.

East Bloc living standards were well above those in the developing world, but well below those in the West. Centralized economic planning continued to lead to shortages, and people complained about the poor quality and lack of choice of the most basic goods. Though the secret police persecuted those who openly challenged the system and they generated mountains of files on ordinary people, they generally left alone those who demonstrated the required conformity.

Women in particular experienced the contradictions of the socialist system. Official state policy guaranteed equal rights for women and encouraged them to join the workforce in positions formerly reserved for men, while an extensive system of state-supported child care freed women to accept these employment opportunities and eased the work of parenting. Yet women rarely made it into the upper ranks of business or politics, and they faced the same double burden as those in the West. In addition, government control of the public sphere meant that the independent groups dedicated to feminist reform that emerged in the West in the 1970s never developed in the East Bloc or the Soviet Union.

Though everyday life was fairly comfortable in the East Bloc, a number of deeply rooted structural problems undermined popular support for Soviet-style communism. These fundamental problems would contribute to the re-emergence of civic dissent and ultimately to the revolutions of 1989. East Bloc countries—like those in the West—were hard hit by the energy crisis and stagflation of the 1970s. For a time, access to inexpensive oil from the Soviet Union, which had huge resources, helped prop up faltering economies, but this cushion began to fall apart in the 1980s. For a number of reasons, East Bloc leaders refused to make the economic reforms that might have made developed socialism more effective.

First, a move toward Western-style postindustrial society would have required fundamental changes to the Communist system. Communist East Bloc states were publicly committed to supporting the working classes, including coal miners, shipbuilders, and factory and construction workers. To pursue the neoliberal reforms undertaken in the West would have undermined popular support for

developed socialism
▶ A term used by Communist leaders to describe the socialist accomplishments of their societies, such as nationalized industry, collective agriculture, and extensive social welfare programs.

What were the consequences of economic decline in the 1970s?

What led to the decline of Soviet power in the East Bloc?

Why did revolution sweep through the East Bloc in 1989?

☑ LearningCurve
Check what you know.

935

the government among these basic constituencies, which were already tenuous at best.

Second, East Bloc regimes refused to cut spending on the welfare state because that was, after all, one of the proudest achievements of socialism. Third, the state continued to provide subsidies to heavy industries. High-tech industries failed to take off in Communist Europe, in part because the West maintained embargoes on technology exports. The industrial goods produced in the East Bloc became increasingly uncompetitive in the new global system. To stave off total collapse, governments borrowed massive amounts of hard currency from Western banks and governments, helping to convince ordinary people that communism was bankrupt, and setting up a cycle of indebtedness that helped bring down the entire system in 1989.

Economic decline was not the only reason people increasingly questioned one-party, Communist rule. The best career and educational opportunities were reserved for party members or handed out as political favors, leaving many talented people underemployed and resentful. Tight controls on travel continually called attention to the burdens of daily life in a repressive society. The one-party state had repeatedly quashed popular reform movements; retreated from economic liberalization; and jailed or exiled dissidents, even those who wished to reform communism from within. Though many East Bloc citizens still found the promise of Marxist egalitarian socialism appealing, they increasingly doubted the legitimacy of Soviet-style communism.

Dissent in Czechoslovakia and Poland

Stagnation in the East Bloc encouraged small numbers of dedicated people to try to change society from below. Developments in Czechoslovakia and Poland were the most striking and significant, and determined protest movements re-emerged in both countries in the mid-1970s.

In Czechoslovakia a small group of citizens, including future Czechoslovak president Václav Havel (VAH-slahf HAH-vuhl) (1936–2011), signed a manifesto in 1977 that came to be known as Charter 77. The group criticized the government for ignoring the human rights provision of the Helsinki Accords and called on Communist leaders to respect civil and political liberties. They also criticized censorship and argued for improved environmental policies. Despite immediate state repression, the group challenged passive acceptance of Communist authority and voiced public dissatisfaction with developed socialism.

In Poland the Communists had failed to dominate society to the extent seen elsewhere in the East Bloc. Most agricultural land remained in private hands, and the Catholic Church thrived. The Communists also failed to manage the economy effectively. The 1960s brought stagnation, and in 1970, Poland's working class rose again in angry protest. A new Communist leader came to power, and he wagered that massive inflows of Western capital and technology, especially from rich and now-friendly West Germany, could produce a Polish economic miracle. Instead, bureaucratic incompetence and the first oil shock in 1973 sent the economy into a nosedive. Workers, intellectuals, and the church became increasingly restive.

In August 1980, strikes broke out across Poland; at the gigantic Lenin Shipyards in Gdansk, sixteen thousand workers laid down their tools and occupied the plant. As other workers joined "in solidarity," the strikers advanced the ideals of civil society, including the right to form trade unions free from state control, freedom of speech, release of political prisoners, and economic reforms. After the strikers occupied the shipyard for eighteen days, the government gave in and accepted the workers' demands in the Gdansk Agreement. In a state in which the Communist Party claimed to rule on behalf of the proletariat, a working-class revolt had won an unprecedented, even revolutionary, victory.

Led by feisty Lenin Shipyards electrician and devout Catholic Lech Wałęsa (lehk vah-WEHN-suh) (b. 1943), the workers proceeded to organize a free and democratic trade union called **Solidarity**. Joined by intellectuals and supported by the Catholic Church, Solidarity became a national union with a full-time staff of 40,000 and 9.5 million members. Cultural and intellectual freedom blossomed in Poland, and Solidarity enjoyed tremendous public support. But Solidarity's leaders pursued a self-limiting revolution, meant only to defend the concessions won in the Gdansk Agreement. Solidarity thus practiced moderation, refusing to challenge directly the Communist monopoly on political power. At the same time, the ever-present threat of calling a nationwide strike gave them real leverage in ongoing negotiations with the Communist bosses.

Solidarity
▶ Independent Polish trade union that worked for workers' rights and political reform throughout the 1980s.

Lech Wałęsa and Solidarity

An inspiration for fellow workers at the Lenin Shipyards in the dramatic and successful strike against the Communist bosses in August 1980, Wałęsa played a key role in Solidarity before and after it was outlawed. Speaking here to old comrades at the Lenin Shipyards after Solidarity was again legalized in 1988, Wałęsa personified an enduring opposition to Communist rule in eastern Europe. (© Georges Merrillon/GAMMA)

What were the consequences of economic decline in the 1970s?

What led to the decline of Soviet power in the East Bloc?

Why did revolution sweep through the East Bloc in 1989?

☑ LearningCurve
Check what you know.

Solidarity's combination of strength and moderation postponed a showdown, as the Soviet Union played a waiting game of threats and pressure. After a confrontation in March 1981, Wałęsa settled for minor government concessions, and Solidarity dropped plans for a massive general strike. Criticism of Wałęsa's moderate leadership gradually grew, and Solidarity lost its cohesiveness. The worsening economic crisis also encouraged radical actions among disgruntled Solidarity members, and the Polish Communist leadership shrewdly denounced the union for promoting economic collapse and provoking a possible Soviet invasion. In December 1981, Wojciech Jaruzelski (VOY-chehk yahr-oo-ZEHL-skee), the general who headed Poland's Communist government, suddenly proclaimed martial law and arrested Solidarity's leaders.

Outlawed and driven underground, Solidarity survived in part because of the government's unwillingness (and probably its inability) to impose full-scale terror. Moreover, millions of Poles decided to continue acting as if they were free. Cultural and intellectual life remained extremely vigorous as the Polish economy continued to deteriorate. Thus popular support for outlawed Solidarity remained strong under martial law in the 1980s, preparing the way for the union's political rebirth toward the end of the decade.

The rise and survival of Solidarity showed that ordinary Poles would stubbornly struggle for greater political and religious liberty, cultural freedom, trade-union rights, patriotic nationalism, and a more humane socialism. Not least, Solidarity's challenge encouraged fresh thinking in the Soviet Union, ever the key to lasting change in the East Bloc.

From Détente Back to Cold War

The Soviets and the leaders of the Soviet satellite states also faced challenges from abroad as optimistic hopes for détente in international relations gradually faded in the late 1970s. Brezhnev's Soviet Union ignored the human rights provisions of the Helsinki agreement, and East-West political competition remained very much alive outside Europe. The Soviet invasion of Afghanistan in December 1979, designed to save an increasingly unpopular Marxist regime, alarmed the West. Many Americans feared that the oil-rich states of the Persian Gulf would be next, and once again they looked to the NATO alliance and military might to thwart Communist expansion.

President Jimmy Carter (r. 1977–1981) tried to lead NATO beyond verbal condemnation of the Soviet Union and urged economic sanctions against it, but only Great Britain among the European allies supported the American initiative. Some observers concluded that NATO had lost the will to act decisively in dealing with the Soviet bloc.

The Atlantic alliance endured, however, and the U.S. military buildup launched by Carter in his last years in office was greatly accelerated by President Reagan. Increasing defense spending enormously, the Reagan administration deployed short-range nuclear missiles in western Europe and built up the navy. The

The Soviet War in Afghanistan, 1979–1989

Afghanistan
Soviet Union
Soviet invasion
Controlled by Soviet forces

broad shift toward greater conservatism in the 1980s gave Reagan invaluable allies in western Europe, including Margret Thatcher of Great Britain and Germany's Helmut Kohl.

Gorbachev's Reforms in the Soviet Union

Cold War tensions aside, the Soviet Union's Communist elite seemed safe from any challenge from below in the early 1980s. A massive state bureaucracy stretched downward from the central ministries and state committees to provincial cities and from there to factories, neighborhoods, and villages. Organized opposition was impossible, and average people left politics to the bosses.

Although the state and party bureaucracy safeguarded the elite, it promoted widespread apathy and stagnation. When the ailing Brezhnev finally died in 1982, his successor, the long-time chief of the secret police, Yuri Andropov (1914–1984), tried to invigorate the system. Relatively little came of his efforts, but they combined with a sharply worsening economic situation to set the stage for the emergence in 1985 of Mikhail Gorbachev (b. 1931).

Gorbachev believed in communism but realized that the Soviet Union was failing to keep up with the West and was losing its superpower status. Thus Gorbachev tried to revitalize the Soviet system with fundamental reforms. An idealist who wanted to improve conditions for ordinary citizens, Gorbachev understood that the enormous expense of the Cold War arms race had had a disastrous impact on living conditions in the Soviet Union; improvement at home, he realized, required better relations with the West.

In his first year in office, Gorbachev attacked corruption and incompetence in the bureaucracy and consolidated his power. He worked out an ambitious reform program designed to transform and restructure the economy in order to provide for the real needs of the Soviet population. To accomplish this economic restructuring, or **perestroika** (pehr-uh-STROY-kuh), Gorbachev and his supporters permitted an easing of government price controls on some goods, more independence for state enterprises, and the creation of profit-seeking private cooperatives to provide personal services. These timid reforms initially produced a few improvements, but shortages grew as the economy stalled at an intermediate point between central planning and free-market mechanisms. By late 1988, widespread consumer dissatisfaction posed a serious threat to Gorbachev's leadership and the entire reform program.

Gorbachev's campaign for greater freedom of expression was much more successful. The newfound openness, or **glasnost** (GLAZ-nohst), of the government and the media marked an astonishing break with the past. Long-banned émigré writers sold millions of copies of their works in new editions, while denunciations of Stalin and his terror became standard fare in plays and movies. In another example of glasnost in action, the usually secretive Soviet government, after several days of hesitation, issued daily reports on the 1986 nuclear plant accident at Chernobyl, one of the worst environmental disasters in history.

Democratization was a third element of reform. Beginning as an attack on corruption in the Communist Party, it led to the first free elections in the Soviet Union since 1917. Gorbachev and the party remained in control, but a minority of

perestroika
▶ Economic restructuring and reform implemented by Premier Mikhail Gorbachev in the Soviet Union in 1985.

glasnost
▶ Soviet premier Mikhail Gorbachev's popular campaign for openness in government and the media.

What were the consequences of economic decline in the 1970s?

What led to the decline of Soviet power in the East Bloc?

Why did revolution sweep through the East Bloc in 1989?

☑ LearningCurve
Check what you know.

939

critical independents was elected in April 1989 to the Congress of People's Deputies. Millions of Soviets then watched the new congress for hours on television as Gorbachev and his ministers saw their proposals debated and even rejected. An active civil society was emerging—a new political culture at odds with the Communist Party's monopoly of power and control.

Democratization also ignited demands for greater political and cultural autonomy and even national independence among non-Russian minorities living in the fifteen Soviet republics. Once Gorbachev opened the doors to greater public expression and popular desires for democracy, tensions flared between central Soviet control and national separatist movements. Independence groups were particularly active in the Baltic Soviet socialist republics of Lithuania, Latvia, and Estonia; in western Ukraine; and in the Transcaucasian republics of Armenia, Azerbaijan, and Georgia.

Finally, Gorbachev brought reforms to the field of foreign affairs. He withdrew Soviet troops from Afghanistan in February 1989 and sought to reduce East-West tensions. Of enormous importance, the Soviet leader sought to halt the arms race with the United States and convinced President Reagan of his sincerity. In a Washington summit in December 1987, the two leaders agreed to eliminate all land-based intermediate-range missiles in Europe, setting the stage for more arms reductions. Gorbachev pledged to respect the political choices of the peoples of East Bloc countries, repudiating the Brezhnev Doctrine and giving encouragement to reform movements in Poland, Czechoslovakia, and Hungary.

> **QUICK REVIEW**

Why were Communist leaders in eastern Europe and the Soviet Union unable, or unwilling, to implement effective political and economic reforms?

CHAPTER LOCATOR | Why did the postwar consensus of the 1950s break down?

CHAPTER 29
940   CHALLENGING THE POSTWAR ORDER

Demonstrators During the Velvet Revolution Hundreds of thousands of Czechoslovakian citizens flooded the streets of Prague daily in peaceful protests after the police savagely beat student demonstrators in mid-November 1989. On the night of November 24, three hundred thousand people roared "Dubček" when Alexander Dubček, the aging reformer ousted in 1968 by the Soviets, stood on a balcony with Václav Havel, who had challenged the "bad government" of the Communist regime. Over the next several weeks, the Communists agreed to share power and then resigned from the government. (© Peter Turnley/CORBIS)

IN 1989, GORBACHEV'S PLAN TO REFORM COMMUNISM from within snowballed out of control. A series of largely peaceful revolutions swept across eastern Europe, overturning existing Communist regimes (**Map 29.2**). The revolutions of 1989 had momentous consequences. First, the peoples of the East Bloc gained political freedom. Second, West Germany absorbed its East German rival, and a reunified Germany emerged as the most influential country in Europe. Third, a complicated anticommunist revolution swept through the Soviet Union and the multinational empire broke into a large Russia and fourteen other independent states. The Cold War came to an end, and the United States suddenly stood as the world's only superpower.

| What were the consequences of economic decline in the 1970s? | What led to the decline of Soviet power in the East Bloc? | **Why did revolution sweep through the East Bloc in 1989?** | ✓ LearningCurve Check what you know. |

MAP 29.2 ■ Democratic Movements in Eastern Europe, 1989

Countries that had been satellites in the orbit of the Soviet Union began to set themselves free in 1989.

> MAPPING THE PAST

ANALYZING THE MAP: Why did the means by which communism was overthrown in the East Bloc vary from country to country? What accounts for the rapid spread of these democratic movements?

CONNECTIONS: How did Gorbachev's reforms in the Soviet Union contribute to the spread of democratic movements in eastern Europe, and how did his actions hasten the end of the Cold War?

The Collapse of Communism in the East Bloc

While the revolutions of 1989 appeared to erupt quite suddenly, long-standing, structural weaknesses in the Communist system had, in some ways, made revolt inevitable. East Bloc economies never really recovered from the economic catastrophe of the 1970s. State spending on outdated industries and extensive welfare systems led to massive indebtedness to Western banks and undermined economic growth, while limits on personal and political freedoms fueled a growing sense of injustice (see page 935).

Solidarity and the Polish people led the way to revolution. In 1988, widespread strikes, raging inflation, and the outlawed Solidarity's refusal to cooperate with the military government had brought Poland to the brink of economic collapse. Poland's Communist leaders offered to negotiate with Solidarity if the outlawed union's leaders could get the strikers back to work and resolve the political stalemate and the economic crisis. The subsequent agreement in April 1989 legalized Solidarity and declared that a large minority of representatives to the Polish parliament would be chosen by free elections that June. Still guaranteed a parliamentary majority and expecting to win many of the contested seats, the Communists believed that their rule was guaranteed for four years and that Solidarity would keep the workers in line.

Lacking access to the state-run media, Solidarity succeeded nonetheless in mobilizing the country and winning all but one of the contested seats in an overwhelming victory. Moreover, many angry voters crossed off the names of unopposed party candidates, so that the Communist Party failed to win the majority its leaders had anticipated. Solidarity members jubilantly entered the Polish parliament, and a dangerous stalemate quickly developed. But Lech Wałęsa, a gifted politician who always repudiated violence, adroitly obtained a majority by securing the allegiance of two minor pro-communist parties that had been part of the coalition government after World War II. In August 1989, Tadeusz Mazowiecki (Ta-DAY-ush MAH-zoe-vee-ETS-key) (1927–2013), the editor of one of Solidarity's weekly newspapers, was sworn in as Poland's new noncommunist prime minister.

In its first year and a half, the new Solidarity government cautiously introduced revolutionary political changes, moving slowly in order to avoid confrontation with the army or the Soviet Union. In economics, however, the Solidarity government was radical from the beginning. It applied economic shock therapy, an intense dose of neoliberal policy designed to make a clean break with state planning and move quickly to market mechanisms and private property.

Hungary followed Poland. In May 1988, in an effort to retain power by granting modest political concessions, the party replaced Hungary's Communist Party boss János Kádár (KAH-dahr) with a reform-minded Communist. But opposition

THE COLLAPSE OF COMMUNISM

1977	Charter 77 reform movement founded in Czechoslovakia
1980	Polish Solidarity movement formed
1981	Solidarity outlawed by Communist leaders
1982	Soviet premier Leonid Brezhnev dies
1985	Mikhail Gorbachev becomes Soviet premier and institutes perestroika and glasnost reforms
1988	Polish workers strike throughout country
■ 1989	
April	Solidarity legalized in Poland
August	Noncommunist prime minister elected in Poland
November	Berlin Wall opened
November–December	Velvet Revolution ends communism in Czechoslovakia
December	Communist dictator of Romania executed
■ 1990	
February	Communist Party defeated in Soviet elections
March	Free elections in Hungary
May	Boris Yeltsin elected leader of Russian Soviet Republic
October	Reunification of Germany
November	Paris Accord: arms reductions across Europe
■ 1991	
August	Communist hardliners kidnap Gorbachev and try to overthrow Soviet government
December	Soviet Union dissolved

What were the consequences of economic decline in the 1970s?

What led to the decline of Soviet power in the East Bloc?

Why did revolution sweep through the East Bloc in 1989?

☑ LearningCurve
Check what you know.

groups rejected piecemeal progress, and in the summer of 1989, the Hungarian Communist Party agreed to hold free elections the following March, believing, quite mistakenly, that they could defeat the opposition in the upcoming elections.

In an effort to strengthen their support at home, the Hungarians opened their border to East Germans and tore down the barbed wire curtain separating Hungary from Austria. Tens of thousands of dissatisfied East German "vacationers" then poured into Hungary, crossed into Austria as refugees, and continued on to immediate resettlement in West Germany.

The flight of East Germans fed the rapid growth of a homegrown, spontaneous protest movement in East Germany. In a desperate attempt to stabilize the situation, the East German government opened the Berlin Wall in November 1989, and people danced for joy atop that grim symbol of the prison state. A new, reformist government took power and scheduled free elections.

In Czechoslovakia, Communist rule began to dissolve peacefully in November to December 1989. This so-called **Velvet Revolution** grew out of popular demonstrations led by students and joined by intellectuals and a dissident playwright-turned-moral-revolutionary named Václav Havel (1936–2011). When the protesters took control of the streets, the Communist government resigned, leading to a power-sharing arrangement termed the "Government of National Understanding." As 1989 ended, the Czechoslovakian assembly elected Havel president.

In Romania, popular revolution turned violent and bloody. Faced with mass protests in December 1989, the Romanian dictator Nicolae Ceaușescu (chow-SHESS-koo) (1918–1989) ordered his ruthless security forces to quell unrest, sparking an armed uprising. After the dictator and his wife were captured and executed by a military court, Ceaușescu's forces were defeated. A coalition government emerged, although the legacy of Ceaușescu's long and oppressive rule left a very troubled country.

Velvet Revolution
▶ The term given to the relatively peaceful overthrow of communism in Czechoslovakia; the label came to signify the collapse of the East Bloc in general in 1989 to 1990.

German Unification and the End of the Cold War

The dissolution of communism in East Germany that began in 1989 reopened the "German question" and raised the threat of renewed Cold War conflict over Germany. In the end, East Germany was absorbed into an enlarged West Germany. Three factors were particularly important in this outcome. First, in the first week after the Berlin Wall was opened, almost 9 million East Germans—roughly half of the total population—poured across the border into West Germany. Almost all returned to their homes in the east, but the experience aroused long-dormant hopes of unity among ordinary citizens.

Second, West German chancellor Helmut Kohl and his closest advisers skillfully exploited the historic opportunity handed to them. In November 1989, Kohl presented a ten-point plan for step-by-step unification in cooperation with both East Germany and the international community. Kohl then promised the struggling citizens of East Germany an immediate economic bonanza—a generous though limited exchange of East German marks in savings accounts and pensions into much more valuable West German marks. This offer helped a well-financed conservative-liberal Alliance for Germany, established in East Germany with the support of Kohl's West German Christian Democrats, to win an overwhelming victory in the March 1990 elections. The Alliance for Germany quickly negotiated an economic and political union on favorable terms with Kohl.

Third, in the summer of 1990, the crucial international aspect of German unification was successfully resolved. Unification would once again make Germany the strongest state in central Europe and would directly affect the security of the Soviet Union. But Gorbachev swallowed hard and negotiated the best deal he could. In a historic agreement signed by Gorbachev and Kohl in July 1990, Kohl solemnly affirmed Germany's peaceful intentions, sweetening the deal by promising enormous loans to the hard-pressed Soviet Union. In October 1990, East Germany merged into West Germany, forming a single nation under the West German laws and constitution.

The peaceful reunification of Germany accelerated the pace of agreements to liquidate the Cold War. In November 1990, delegates from twenty-two European countries joined those from the United States and the Soviet Union in Paris and agreed to a scaling down of all their armed forces. The delegates also solemnly affirmed that all existing borders in Europe, including those of unified Germany and the emerging Baltic states, were legal and valid. The Paris Accord was, for all practical purposes, a general peace treaty bringing an end to both World War II and the Cold War.

The Reunification of Germany, 1990

The Disintegration of the Soviet Union

As 1990 began, the tough work of dismantling some forty-five years of Communist rule had started in all but two East Bloc states—tiny Albania and the vast Soviet Union. The great question now became whether the Soviet Union would follow its former satellites.

In February 1990, the Communist Party suffered a stunning defeat in local elections throughout the Soviet Union. As in East Bloc countries, democrats and anticommunists won clear majorities in the leading cities of the Russian Soviet Republic, the largest republic in the Soviet Union. Moreover, in Lithuania the people elected an uncompromising nationalist as president, and the newly chosen parliament soon after declared Lithuania an independent state.

Gorbachev responded by placing an economic embargo on Lithuania, but he refused to use the army to crush the separatist government. The result was a tense political stalemate that undermined popular support for Gorbachev. Separating himself further from Communist hardliners, Gorbachev asked Soviet citizens to ratify a new constitution that formally abolished the Communist Party's monopoly of political power and expanded the power of the Congress of People's Deputies. While retaining his post as party secretary, Gorbachev then convinced a majority of deputies to elect him president of the Soviet Union.

What were the consequences of economic decline in the 1970s?

What led to the decline of Soviet power in the East Bloc?

Why did revolution sweep through the East Bloc in 1989?

☑ LearningCurve
Check what you know.

945

Despite his victory, Gorbachev's power continued to erode, and his unwillingness to risk a universal suffrage election for the presidency strengthened his great rival, Boris Yeltsin (1931–2007). A radical reform Communist, Yeltsin embraced the democratic movement, and in May 1990 he was elected parliamentary leader of the Russian Soviet Republic. He boldly announced that Russia would put its interests first and declare its independence from the Soviet Union. Gorbachev tried to save the Soviet Union with a new treaty that would link the member republics in a looser, freely accepted confederation, but six of the fifteen Soviet republics rejected his plan.

Opposed by democrats and nationalists, Gorbachev was also challenged by the Communist old guard. In August 1991, a gang of hardliners kidnapped him and his family in the Caucasus and tried to seize the Soviet government. The attempted coup collapsed in the face of massive popular resistance that rallied around Yeltsin. The army supported Yeltsin, and Gorbachev was rescued and returned to power as head of the Soviet Union.

The leaders of the coup had wanted to preserve Communist power, state ownership, and the multinational Soviet Union; they succeeded in destroying all three. An anticommunist revolution swept Russia as Yeltsin and his supporters outlawed the Communist Party and confiscated its property. Yeltsin and his democratic allies declared Russia independent, withdrew from the Soviet Union, and changed the country's name from the Russian Soviet Republic to the Russian Federation. All the other Soviet republics also left. Gorbachev resigned on December 25, 1991, and the next day the Supreme Soviet dissolved itself, marking the end of the Soviet Union. The independent republics of the old Soviet Union then established a loose confederation, the Commonwealth of Independent States, which played only a minor role in the 1990s.

> **QUICK REVIEW**

What were the immediate and long-term consequences of the revolutions that swept through the East Bloc beginning in 1989?

CHAPTER LOCATOR | Why did the postwar consensus of the 1950s break down?

CHAPTER 29
946 CHALLENGING THE POSTWAR ORDER

LOOKING BACK LOOKING AHEAD

The unexpected collapse of Communist Europe capped three decades of turbulent historical change. In the 1960s, the counterculture challenged the status quo and steered western Europe to the left as reformists attempted (but failed) to liberalize East Bloc communism. In the 1970s, a global recession had devastating effects in the West and East Blocs alike. In the 1980s, conservative Western leaders pushed neoliberal plans to revive growth and meet growing global competition. In the East Bloc, structural problems and spontaneous revolt brought down communism, dissolved the Soviet Union, and ended the Cold War.

With the world economy on the road to recovery and new free-market systems in place across the former East Bloc, all of Europe would now have the opportunity to enter the information age. After forty years of Cold War division, the continent regained an underlying unity as faith in democratic government and market economics became the common European creed. In 1991, hopes for peaceful democratic progress were almost universal.

The post–Cold War years saw the realization of some of these hopes, but the new era brought its own problems and tragedies. New ethnic and nationalist tensions flared, leading to a disastrous civil war in the former Yugoslavia. The struggle to rebuild the shattered societies of the former East Bloc countries was far more difficult than the people living in them had hoped. Poor economic growth continued to complicate attempts to deal with the wide-open global economy. New conflicts with Islamic nations in the Middle East involved some European nations in war. The European Union expanded, but political disagreements, environmental issues, increased anxiety about non-Western immigrants, and a host of other problems undermined moves toward true European unity.

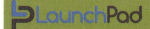

ONLINE DOCUMENT PROJECT

Margaret Thatcher

How did Thatcher's Conservative Party adapt its message to fit the values of the majority of British people?

You encountered Margaret Thatcher's story on page 928. Keeping the question above in mind, explore Conservative Party campaign posters from the 1979 British general election. *See inside the front cover to learn more.*

| What were the consequences of economic decline in the 1970s? | What led to the decline of Soviet power in the East Bloc? | Why did revolution sweep through the East Bloc in 1989? | ✓ **LearningCurve** Check what you know. |

CHAPTER 29 STUDY GUIDE

 **GET STARTED ONLINE**

 **LearningCurve**
Now that you've read the chapter, make it stick by completing the LearningCurve activity.

 EXPLAIN WHY IT MATTERS

Put your reading into practice. Identify each term below, and then explain why it matters in Western history.

TERM	WHO OR WHAT & WHEN	WHY IT MATTERS
Ostpolitik (p. 917)		
détente (p. 918)		
Second Vatican Council (p. 919)		
New Left (p. 920)		
Brezhnev Doctrine (p. 924)		
OPEC (p. 926)		
stagflation (p. 926)		
postindustrial society (p. 926)		
neoliberalism (p. 927)		
privatization (p. 927)		
developed socialism (p. 935)		
Solidarity (p. 937)		
perestroika (p. 939)		
glasnost (p. 939)		
Velvet Revolution (p. 944)		

 **MOVE BEYOND THE BASICS**

To demonstrate a more advanced understanding of the most important trends in late-twentieth-century western Europe, fill in the chart included below with descriptions of the social, economic, and political characteristics of western Europe in 1960 and 1980. How would you explain the differences you note between 1960 and 1980 in western Europe? What postwar trends continued into the 1980s and beyond?

	Society	Economy	Politics
Western Europe: 1960			
Western Europe: 1980			

STEP 4 **PUT IT ALL TOGETHER** Now, take a step back and try to explain the big picture. Remember to use specific examples from the chapter in your answers.

REFORM AND PROTEST IN THE 1960S

▶ What factors contributed to the emergence of the counterculture of the 1960s?

▶ Compare and contrast eastern Europe in the 1960s and the 1980s.

CRISIS AND CHANGE IN WESTERN EUROPE

▶ How did global developments and trends shape European life in the 1970s and 1980s?

▶ What were the most significant protest movements in western Europe in the 1960s and 1970s? Why?

REFORM AND REVOLUTION IN THE SOVIET UNION AND EASTERN EUROPE

▶ What were the sources of economic and social stagnation in eastern Europe in the 1970s and 1980s? How did Communist authorities respond to the challenges they faced?

▶ What do the revolutions of 1989 tell us about the nature of Soviet power and authority prior to 1989?

MAKE CONNECTIONS

▶ Defend or refute the following statement. "World War II came to an end not in 1945 when the Germans and the Japanese were defeated, but in 1989 when Soviet domination of eastern Europe collapsed."

▶ What similarities and differences do you see between the responses of European governments to the economic challenges of the 1970s and their responses to the global economic crisis that struck in 2008?

> **IN YOUR OWN WORDS**

Imagine that you must give an oral report to the class answering the following question: **How and why did protest movements challenge existing social, economic, and political institutions in both western Europe and the East Bloc?** What would be the most important points and why?

30

LIFE IN AN AGE OF GLOBALIZATION

1990 TO THE PRESENT

> **What opportunities and challenges are Europeans presented with at the dawn of the twenty-first century?** Chapter 30 examines the challenges and opportunities Europeans faced in the decades following the end of the Cold War. The revolutions of 1989 had opened a new chapter in European and world history and also opened many possibilities, but the new era also brought problems and tragedies. In addition, across the West and around the world, globalization, the digital revolution, and the ongoing flow of immigrants into western Europe had impacts both positive and negative. As Europeans faced serious tensions and complex changes in the twenty-first century, they also came together to form a strong new European Union that would prove a formidable economic competitor to the United States. Ties between western Europe and the United States began to loosen, but Europe and North America — as well as the rest of the world — confronted common challenges, challenges that would require innovation as well as creative cooperation.

LearningCurve

After reading the chapter, use LearningCurve to retain what you've read.

> How did life change in Russia and the former East Bloc countries after 1989?

> How did globalization affect European life and society?

> What are the main causes and effects of growing ethnic diversity in contemporary Europe?

> What challenges will Europeans face in the coming decades?

Life in a Globalizing World. Rapid globalization has had a profound impact on many aspects of society and culture. Here spectators view i-city, an interactive artwork in the Russian Pavilion at the 2012 Venice Biennale exhibition of contemporary art. (© Giulia Candussi/XianPix/Corbis)

How did life change in Russia and the former East Bloc countries after 1989?

Rich and Poor in Postcommunist Russia

A woman sells knitted scarves in front of a department store window in Moscow in September 2005. The collapse of the Soviet Union and the use of shock therapy to reform the Russian economy created new poverty as well as new wealth. (© ITAR-TASS/Sovfoto)

ESTABLISHING LIBERAL DEMOCRATIC GOVERNMENTS in the former East Bloc countries and the Soviet Union, now divided into fifteen republics with Russia at its core, would not prove easy. While Russia initially moved toward economic reform and political openness, it returned to its authoritarian traditions in the early 2000s, and conflict undermined Russia's relations with some former Soviet republics.

The transition to democracy in the countries of the former Communist East Bloc was also difficult. Some countries, such as Poland, the Czech Republic, Hungary, and the Baltic States, established relatively prosperous democracies and joined NATO and then the European Union. Others, such as Romania and Bulgaria, lagged behind. In multiethnic Yugoslavia, the collapse of communism and the onset of a disastrous civil war broke the country apart.

Economic Shock Therapy in Russia

Politics and economics were closely intertwined in Russia after the dissolution of the Soviet Union (see Chapter 29, page 945). President Boris Yeltsin (r. 1991–1999) wanted to create conditions that would prevent a return to communism and right

CHAPTER LOCATOR | How did life change in Russia and the former East Bloc countries after 1989?

1980s–1990s
– Emergence of globalization

1990s–2010s
– New waves of legal and illegal immigration to Europe

1991
– Maastricht Treaty

1991–2001
– Civil war in Yugoslavia

1992–1997
– Decline of Russian economy

1993
– Creation of the European Union

1999
– Protests against World Trade Organization (WTO) in Seattle

2000–2008
– Resurgence of Russian economy under Putin

2001
– September 11 terrorist attack on the United States; war in Afghanistan begins

2002
– Euro replaces national currencies in Eurozone

2003–2011
– Iraq War

2004
– Train bombings in Madrid by Islamic extremists

2005
– Young Muslims riot in France; subway bombing in London by Islamic extremists

2008
– Worldwide financial crisis begins

2009
– Ratification of Treaty of Lisbon; young Muslims riot in France

2011
– Start of Arab Spring

2012–2013
– Mass protests against government austerity plans in Greece and Spain

2013
– France legalizes same-sex marriage

the faltering economy. Following the example of Poland (see Chapter 29), Russian reformers opted in January 1992 for liberalization at breakneck speed.

To implement the plan, the Russians abolished price controls on 90 percent of all Russian goods. The government also launched rapid privatization—the sale of formerly state-owned industries and agricultural concerns to private investors. In an attempt to share the wealth that privatization was expected to generate, each citizen received a voucher to buy stock in these private companies, but ownership usually remained in the hands of the old bosses—the managers and government officials from the Communist era—undermining the reformers' goal of worker ownership.

President Yeltsin and his economic reformers believed that shock therapy would revive production and bring widespread prosperity. The results were quite different. Prices increased 250 percent on the very first day and kept on soaring, increasing by a factor of twenty-six in the course of 1992. At the same time, production fell a staggering 20 percent. Nor did the situation stabilize quickly. After 1995, inflation still raged, though at slower rates, and output continued to fall. The Russian economy crashed again in 1998 in the wake of Asia's financial crisis.

Rapid economic liberalization worked poorly in Russia for several reasons. Soviet industry had been highly monopolized. Production of many items had been concentrated in one or two gigantic factories or in interconnected combines. With

How did globalization affect European life and society?

What are the main causes and effects of growing ethnic diversity in contemporary Europe?

What challenges will Europeans face in the coming decades?

☑ LearningCurve
Check what you know.

953

privatization, these powerful state monopolies became powerful private monopolies that cut production and raised prices in order to maximize profits. Moreover, corporate managers and bureaucrats forced Yeltsin's government to hand out enormous subsidies to reinforce faltering firms and to avoid bankruptcies. New corporate leaders included criminals who intimidated would-be rivals in attempts to prevent the formation of competing businesses.

Runaway inflation and poorly executed privatization brought a profound social revolution to Russia. The new capitalist elite—the so-called Oligarchs— acquired great wealth and influence, while large numbers of people fell into abject poverty and the majority struggled to make ends meet. Managers, former Communist officials, and financiers who came out of the privatization process with large shares of the old state monopolies stood at the top. The new elite held more wealth than ever before, and the Oligarchs maintained control with corrupt business practices and rampant cronyism. Under these conditions, effective representative government failed to develop, and many Russians came to equate democracy with the corruption, poverty, and national decline they experienced throughout the 1990s. Yeltsin became increasingly unpopular; only the support of the Oligarchs kept him in power.

Russian Revival Under Vladimir Putin

This widespread disillusionment set the stage for the "managed democracy" of Vladimir Putin (POO-tihn) (b. 1952). First elected president as Yeltsin's chosen successor in 2000, Putin won re-election in a landslide in March 2004, and, after a four-year stint as prime minister, returned to the presidency in 2012. An officer in the secret police in the Communist era, Putin maintained relatively liberal economic policies but re-established semi-authoritarian political rule. Putin clamped down on the excesses of the Oligarchs, lowered corporate and business taxes, and re-established some government control over key industries.

This combination of autocratic politics and economic reform—aided greatly by high world prices for oil and natural gas, Russia's most important exports—led to a decade of strong economic growth. In 2008, however, the global financial crisis and a rapid drop in the price of oil caused a downturn, and the Russian stock market collapsed. The government initiated a $200 billion rescue plan, and the economy stabilized and returned to modest growth in 2010.

During his first two terms as president, Putin's domestic and foreign policies proved immensely popular with a majority of Russians. His housing, education, and health-care reforms significantly improved living standards. In foreign relations, Putin championed an assertive anti-Western Russian nationalism and regularly challenged U.S. and NATO foreign policy goals. In addition, the Russian president centralized power in the Kremlin, increased military spending, and expanded the secret police. Putin's carefully crafted manly image and his forceful international diplomacy soothed the country's injured pride and symbolized its national revival.

Putin and his United Russia Party moved decisively to limit political opposition. Though the Russian constitution guarantees freedom of the press, the government cracked down on the independent media. Using a variety of tactics, officials and pro-government businessmen influenced news reports and intimidated critical journalists.

Legend (top left):
— Boundary of the Soviet Union, 1991
BELARUS Member of the CIS, 1991

Inset map (top right):

Conflicts in the Caucasus

RUSSIAN FEDERATION

ABKHAZIA — Declared independence 1991; ongoing war with Russia — CHECHNYA · Grozny

Breakaway republic established 2008 — SOUTH OSSETIA — DAGESTAN

GEORGIA · Tblisi — AJARIA

TURKEY — ARMENIA — AZER.

☐ Ongoing conflict

MAP 30.1 ■ Russia and the Successor States, 1991–2010

After the failure of an attempt in August 1991 to depose Gorbachev, an anticommunist revolution swept the Soviet Union. The republics that formed the Soviet Union each declared their sovereignty and independence, with Russia, under President Boris Yeltsin, being the largest. Eleven of the fifteen republics then formed a loose confederation called the Commonwealth of Independent States, but the integrated economy of the Soviet Union dissolved into separate national economies, each with its own goals and policies. Conflict continues to simmer over these goals and policies, as evidenced by the ongoing civil war in Chechnya and the conflict between Russia and Georgia over South Ossetia.

Putin also took an aggressive and at times interventionist stance toward the Commonwealth of Independent States, a loose confederation of most of the former Soviet republics (**Map 30.1**). Since the breakup of the Soviet Union, Russian troops have repeatedly invaded Chechnya (CHEHCH-nyuh), a tiny Muslim republic with 1 million inhabitants on Russia's southern border that declared its independence in 1991. Despite nominal Russian control over Chechnya, the cost of the conflict has been high. Thousands on both sides have lost their lives, and both sides have committed serious human rights abuses. Moscow declared an end to military

---

| How did globalization affect European life and society? | What are the main causes and effects of growing ethnic diversity in contemporary Europe? | What challenges will Europeans face in the coming decades? | ☑ **LearningCurve** Check what you know. |

operations in April 2009, but Chechen insurgents, inspired by nationalism and Islamic radicalism, continued to fight.

Russia also intervened in the independent state of Georgia. Russian troops invaded Georgia in 2008 to support a separatist movement in South Ossetia (ah-SEE-shuh), which eventually established a breakaway independent republic recognized only by Russia and a handful of small states.

Putin stepped down when his term limits expired in 2008. His handpicked successor, Dimitri Medvedev (mehd-VEHD-yehf) (b. 1965), easily won election that year and then appointed Putin prime minister, leading observers to believe that the former president was still the dominant figure. This suspicion was confirmed when Putin won the presidential election of March 2012 with over 60 percent of the vote. Some fifteen thousand protesters marched through downtown Moscow to protest election fraud and the authoritarian aspects of Putin's rule, and demonstrations also accompanied the president's inauguration that May.

Coping with Change in the Former East Bloc

Developments in the former East Bloc paralleled those in Russia in important ways. The former satellites worked to replace state planning and socialism with market mechanisms and private property. Western-style electoral politics also took hold.

New leaders across the former East Bloc faced similar economic problems: how to restructure Communist economic systems and move state-owned businesses and property into private hands. Under Soviet-style communism, central planners determined production and distribution goals and often set wage and price controls; now former East Bloc countries would adopt market-based economic systems. In addition, industries, businesses, and farms, considered the "people's property" and managed by the state in the name of the entire population, would now be privatized.

The methods of restructuring and privatization varied from country to country. As noted earlier, Poland's new leaders turned to "shock therapy," the most rapid and comprehensive form of economic transformation, advocated by neoliberal Western institutions, including the International Monetary Fund and the World Bank. These radical moves at first brought high inflation and a rapid decline in living standards, which generated public protests and strikes. But because the plan had the West's approval, Poland received Western financial support that eased the pain of transition. By the end of the decade, the country had one of the strongest economies in the former East Bloc.

Other countries followed alternate paths. Czechoslovakia, Slovenia, and Estonia took more gradual approaches. Compared to Poland's approach, privatization in all three countries was slower, continued more practices from the Communist past, and caused less social disruption.

Economic growth in the former Communist countries was varied, but most observers agreed that Poland, the Czech Republic, and Hungary were the most successful. The reasons for these successes included considerable experience with limited market reforms before 1989, flexibility and lack of dogmatism in government policy, and an enthusiastic embrace of capitalism by a new entrepreneurial class.

Poland, the Czech Republic, and Hungary also did far better than Russia in creating new civic institutions, legal systems, and independent media outlets that reinforced political freedom and national revival. Lech Wałęsa in Poland and Václav Havel in Czechoslovakia were elected presidents of their countries and proved as remarkable in power as in opposition (see Chapter 29, page 942). After Czechoslovakia's Velvet Revolution in 1989, the Czechoslovak parliament accepted a "velvet divorce" in 1993, when Slovakian nationalists wanted to break off and form their own state, creating the separate Czech and Slovak Republics. Above all, the popular goal of adopting the liberal democratic values of western Europe reinforced political moderation and compromise. In 1999, Poland, Hungary, and the Czech Republic were accepted into NATO, and in 2004, they and Slovakia gained admission to the European Union (EU) (see page 961).

Romania and Bulgaria lagged behind in the postcommunist transition. Western traditions were much weaker there, and both countries were much poorer than their more successful neighbors. Romania and Bulgaria did make progress after 2000, however, and joined NATO in 2004 and the EU in 2007.

The social consequences of rebuilding the former East Bloc were similar to those in Russia, though people were generally spared the widespread shortages and misery that characterized Russia in the 1990s. Ordinary citizens and the elderly were once again the big losers, while the young and former Communist Party members were the big winners. Inequalities between richer and poorer regions also increased. Capital cities such as Warsaw, Prague, and Budapest concentrated wealth, power, and opportunity as never before, while provincial centers stagnated and old industrial areas declined. Crime, corruption, and gangsterism increased in both the streets and the executive suites.

Though few former East Bloc residents wanted to return to communism, some expressed longings for the stability of the old system. They missed the guaranteed jobs and generous social benefits provided by the Communist state, and they found the individualism and competitiveness of capitalism cold and difficult. Germans coined the term **Ostalgie**—a combination of the German words for "East" and "nostalgia"—to label this fondness for the lifestyles and culture of the vanished East Bloc.

At the same time, many East Bloc citizens had never fully accepted communism, primarily because they equated it with Russian imperialism and the loss of national independence. The joyous crowds that toppled Communist regimes in 1989 believed that they were liberating the nation as well as the individual. Thus, when communism died, nationalism re-emerged as a dominant force.

Ostalgie
▶ German term referring to nostalgia for the lifestyles and culture of the vanished East Bloc.

Tragedy in Yugoslavia

The great postcommunist tragedy was Yugoslavia, which, under Josip Broz Tito, had been a federation of republics under centralized Communist rule (see Chapter 28, page 893). After Tito's death in 1980, power passed increasingly to the sister republics, which encouraged a revival of centuries-old regional and ethnic conflicts that were exacerbated by charges of ethnically inspired massacres during World War II and a dramatic economic decline in the mid-1980s.

The revolutions of 1989 accelerated the breakup of Yugoslavia. In 1989, Serbian president Slobodan Milošević (SLOH-buh-dayn mee-LOH-sheh-veech) (1941–2006)

| How did globalization affect European life and society? | What are the main causes and effects of growing ethnic diversity in contemporary Europe? | What challenges will Europeans face in the coming decades? | ✔ LearningCurve Check what you know. |

severely limited self-rule in the Serbian province of Kosovo, where Albanian-speaking, primarily Islamic peoples constituted the overwhelming majority but which held a medieval battleground that he claimed was sacred to Serbian identity. In 1990, Milošević supported calls to grab land from other republics and unite all Serbs, regardless of where they lived, in a "greater Serbia." Milošević's moves strengthened the cause of national separatism in the federation, and in June 1991, Slovenia and Croatia declared their independence. Milošević ordered the federal army to invade both areas to assert Serbian control. The Serbs were quickly repulsed in Slovenia, but they managed to take about 30 percent of Croatia.

In 1992, the civil war spread to Bosnia-Herzegovina, which had also declared its independence. Serbs—about 30 percent of that region's population—refused to live under the more numerous Bosnian Muslims, or Bosniaks (**Map 30.2**). Yugoslavia had once been a tolerant and largely successful multiethnic state with different groups living side by side and often intermarrying. The new goal of the armed factions in the Bosnian civil war was **ethnic cleansing**, or genocide: the

ethnic cleansing

▶ The attempt to establish ethnically homogeneous territories by intimidation, forced deportation, and killing.

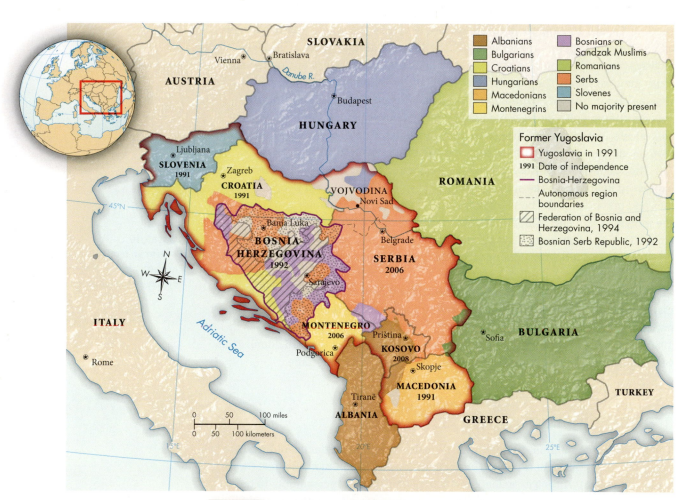

MAP 30.2 ■ The Breakup of Yugoslavia, 1991–2006

Yugoslavia had the most ethnically diverse population in eastern Europe. The republic of Croatia had substantial Serbian and Muslim minorities. Bosnia-Herzegovina had large Muslim, Serbian, and Croatian populations, none of which had a majority. In June 1991, Serbia's brutal effort to seize territory and unite all Serbs in a single state brought a tragic civil war.

CHAPTER LOCATOR | **How did life change in Russia and the former East Bloc countries after 1989?**

attempt to establish ethnically homogeneous territories by intimidation, forced deportation, and killing. Serbian armies and irregular militias attempted to "cleanse" the territory of its non-Serb residents, unleashing ruthless brutality, with murder, rape, destruction, and the herding of refugees into concentration camps. Before the fighting in Bosnia ended, some three hundred thousand people were dead, and millions had been forced to flee their homes.

The Western nations had difficulty formulating an effective, unified response to this appalling violence. The turning point came in July 1995 when Bosnian Serbs overran Srebrenica—a Muslim city previously declared a United Nations safe area. Serb forces killed about eight thousand of the city's Bosniak civilians, primarily men and boys. Public outrage prompted NATO to bomb Bosnian Serb military targets intensively, and the Croatian army drove all the Serbs from Croatia. In November 1995, U.S. President Bill Clinton helped the warring sides hammer out a complicated accord. Troops from NATO countries patrolled Bosnia to keep the peace; by 2013, only one thousand NATO troops remained, suggesting that the situation had significantly improved.

The Albanian Muslims of Kosovo, who hoped to establish self-rule, gained nothing from the Bosnian agreement. Frustrated Kosovar militants formed the **Kosovo Liberation Army (KLA)** and began to fight for independence. Serbian repression of the Kosovars increased, and in 1998, Serbian forces attacked both KLA guerrillas and unarmed villagers, displacing 250,000 people.

When Milošević refused to withdraw Serbian armies from Kosovo, NATO began bombing Serbia in March 1999. Serbian paramilitary forces responded by driving about 865,000 Albanian Kosovars into exile. NATO redoubled its destructive bombing campaign, which eventually forced Milošević to withdraw and allowed the Kosovars to regain their homeland. A United Nations and NATO peacekeeping force occupied Kosovo, ending ten years of Yugoslavian civil wars.

Kosovo Liberation Army (KLA)

▶ Military organization formed in 1998 by Kosovar militants who sought independence from Serbia.

QUICK REVIEW <

Which former East Bloc countries fared best after 1989? Which fared worst? Why?

How did globalization affect European life and society?	What are the main causes and effects of growing ethnic diversity in contemporary Europe?	What challenges will Europeans face in the coming decades?	✔ LearningCurve Check what you know.

How did globalization affect European life and society?

Antiglobalization Activism French protesters carry the figure of Ronald McDonald through the streets to protest the trial of José Bové, a prominent leader in campaigns against the human and environmental costs associated with globalization. Bové was accused of demolishing a McDonald's franchise in a small town in southern France. With its worldwide fast-food restaurants that pay little attention to local traditions, McDonald's has often been the target of antiglobalization protests. (Witt/Haley/Sipa)

globalization

▶ The emergence of a freer, more technologically connected global economy, accompanied by a worldwide exchange of cultural, political, and religious ideas.

CONTEMPORARY OBSERVERS OFTEN ASSERT that the world has entered a new era of **globalization**. Though the term is difficult to define, such assertions do not mean that there were never international connections before. Europe has long had close ties to other parts of the world. Yet new global relationships and increasing interdependence did emerge in the last decades of the twentieth century.

First, the growth of multinational corporations restructured national economies on a global scale. Second, an array of international governing bodies, such as the European Union, the United Nations, the World Trade Organization, and a number of nongovernmental organizations (or NGOs) increasingly set policies that challenged the autonomy of traditional nation-states. Finally, the expansion and ready availability of highly efficient computer and media technologies led to ever-faster exchanges of information and entertainment around the world. Taken together, these global transformations had a remarkable impact—both positive and negative—on Western society.

CHAPTER LOCATOR | How did life change in Russia and the former East Bloc countries after 1989?

The Global Economy

Though large business interests had long profited from systems of international trade and investment, multinational corporations grew and flourished in a world economy increasingly organized around policies of free-market neoliberalism, which relaxed barriers to international trade. Multinational corporations built global systems of production and distribution that generated unprecedented wealth and generally escaped the control of national regulators and politicians.

The development of sophisticated personal computer technologies and the Internet at the end of the twentieth century, coupled with the deregulation of national and international financial systems, further encouraged the growth of international trade. The ability to exchange information and capital rapidly meant that economic activity was no longer centered on national banks or stock exchanges but rather flowed quickly across international borders. Large cities like London, Moscow, New York, and Hong Kong became global centers of banking, trade, and financial services.

At the same time, the close connections between national economies also made the entire world vulnerable to economic panics and downturns. In 1997, a banking crisis in Thailand spread to Indonesia, South Korea, and Japan and then echoed around the world. The resulting slump in oil and gas prices hit Russia especially hard, leading to high inflation, bank failures, and the collapse of the Russian stock market. The crisis then spread to Latin America, plunging most countries there into a severe economic downturn. A decade later, a global recession triggered by a crisis in the U.S. housing market and financial system created the worst worldwide economic crisis since the Great Depression of the 1930s (see page 978).

The New European Union

Global economic pressures encouraged the expansion and consolidation of the European Common Market, which in 1993 was renamed the **European Union (EU)** (**Map 30.3**). The EU worked to add the free movement of European labor, capital, and services to the existing free trade in goods. In addition, member states sought to create a monetary union in which all EU countries would share a single currency. Membership in the monetary union required states to meet strict financial criteria defined in the 1991 **Maastricht Treaty**.

While western European elites and opinion makers generally supported the economic integration embodied in the Maastricht Treaty, support for the Maastricht Treaty was not universal. Many people resented the EU's ever-growing bureaucracy in Brussels, which imposed common standards on everything from cheese to day care, supposedly undermining national customs and local traditions. Moreover, increased unity meant yielding still more power to distant "Eurocrats" and political insiders, which limited national sovereignty and democratic control.

Above all, many citizens feared that the European Union was being created at their expense. Joining the monetary union required national governments to meet stringent fiscal standards, impose budget cuts, and contribute to the EU operating budget. The resulting reductions in health care and social benefits hit ordinary

European Union (EU)
▶ The economic, cultural, and political alliance of twenty-seven European nations.

Maastricht Treaty
▶ The basis for the formation of the European Union, which set financial and cultural standards for potential member states and defined criteria for membership in the monetary union.

How did globalization affect European life and society? | What are the main causes and effects of growing ethnic diversity in contemporary Europe? | What challenges will Europeans face in the coming decades? | ✓ LearningCurve Check what you know.

961

The European Union

- Original members, 1951
- New members, 1973
- New members, 1981
- New members, 1986
- German reunification, 1990
- New members, 1995
- New members, 2004
- New members, 2007
- New members, 2013
- Candidate countries, 2013
- € Eurozone countries, 2013

ICELAND
NORWAY
SWEDEN
FINLAND €
ESTONIA €
LATVIA
LITHUANIA
RUSSIA
North Sea
Baltic Sea
DENMARK
RUSSIAN FEDERATION
BELARUS
IRELAND UNITED KINGDOM €
NETHERLANDS €
BELGIUM €
GERMANY €
POLAND
ATLANTIC OCEAN
LUXEMBOURG €
CZECH REP.
SLOVAKIA €
UKRAINE
FRANCE €
SWITZ.
AUSTRIA €
HUNGARY
MOLDOVA
SLOVENIA €
CROATIA
ROMANIA
PORTUGAL €
SPAIN €
ITALY €
BOSNIA & HERZEGOVINA
SERBIA
Black Sea
KOSOVO
BULGARIA
MONTENEGRO
MACEDONIA
ALBANIA
TURKEY
Mediterranean Sea
GREECE €
MALTA €
CYPRUS €

MAP 30.3 ■ The European Union, 2013

No longer divided by ideological competition and the Cold War, much of today's Europe has banded together in a European Union that facilitates the open movement of people, jobs, and currency across borders.

> **MAPPING THE PAST**

ANALYZING THE MAP: Trace the expansion of membership from its initial founding as the European Economic Union to today. How would you characterize the most recent members? Whose membership is still pending?

CONNECTIONS: Which countries are and are not part of the Eurozone, and what does this suggest about how successful the European Union has been in adopting the euro?

citizens and did little to reduce high unemployment. When put to the public for a vote, ratification of the Maastricht Treaty was usually very close. Even after the treaty was ratified, battles over budgets, benefits, and high unemployment continued throughout the EU in the 1990s.

Then in 2002, the euro replaced the national currencies of all Eurozone countries. The establishment of the European monetary union built confidence in member nations and increased their willingness to accept new members. On May 1,

2004, the European Union began admitting its former East Bloc neighbors, and by 2007, the EU was home to 493 million citizens in twenty-seven countries.

This rapid expansion underscored the need to reform the EU's unwieldy governing structure. In June 2004, a special commission presented a new EU constitution that represented a significant step toward a more centralized federal system, though each state retained veto power over taxation, social policy, foreign affairs, and other sensitive areas. After many contentious referendum campaigns across the continent, the constitution failed to win the unanimous support required to take effect. Ultimately, nationalist fears about losing sovereignty and cultural identity outweighed the perceived benefits of a more unified Europe.

Though the constitution did not go into effect, the long postwar march toward greater European unity did not stop. In 2007, the rejected constitution was replaced with the Treaty of Lisbon. The new treaty kept many sections of the constitution but further streamlined the EU bureaucracy and reformed its political structure. When the Treaty of Lisbon went into effect on December 1, 2009, after ratification by all EU states, it capped a remarkable fifty-year effort to unify what had been a deeply divided and war-torn continent.

Supranational Organizations

Beyond the European Union, the trend toward globalization empowered a variety of other supranational organizations that had tremendous reach. National governments still played the leading role in defining and implementing policy, but they increasingly had to take the policies of institutions such as the United Nations and the World Trade Organization into consideration.

The United Nations (UN), established in 1945 after World War II, remains one of the most important players on the world stage. Representatives from all independent countries meet in the UN General Assembly in New York City to try to forge international agreements. While the smaller UN Security Council has broader powers, including the ability to impose sanctions to punish uncooperative states and even to endorse military action, its five permanent members—the United States, Russia, France, Great Britain, and China—each has the power to veto resolutions introduced in that body. The predominance of the United States and western European powers on the Security Council has led some critics to accuse the UN of implementing Western neocolonial policies (see Chapter 28, page 906). Others argue that UN policies should never take precedent over national needs, and UN resolutions are at times ignored or downplayed.

A trio of nonprofit international financial institutions has also gained power in a globalizing world. Initially founded to help rebuild war-torn Europe, the World Bank and the International Monetary Fund (IMF) now provide loans to the developing world. Their funding comes primarily from donations from the United States and western Europe, and they typically extend loans on the condition that recipient countries adopt neoliberal economic reforms.

The third economic supranational institution, the **World Trade Organization (WTO)**, is one of the most powerful supranational financial institutions. It sets trade and tariff agreements for over 150 member countries, thus helping to manage a large percentage of the world's import-export policies. Like the IMF and the World Bank, the WTO generally promotes neoliberal policies.

World Trade Organization (WTO)
▶ A powerful supranational financial institution that sets trade and tariff agreements for over 150 member countries and so helps manage a large percentage of the world's import-export policies. Like the IMF and the World Bank, the WTO promotes neoliberal policies around the world.

How did globalization affect European life and society?

What are the main causes and effects of growing ethnic diversity in contemporary Europe?

What challenges will Europeans face in the coming decades?

✓ LearningCurve
Check what you know.

nongovernmental organizations (NGOs)

▶ Independent organizations with specific agendas, such as humanitarian aid or environmental protection, that conduct international programs and activities.

The rise of these supranational institutions, which typically represent the shared interests of national governments, was paralleled by the emergence of a variety of **nongovernmental organizations (NGOs)**. Some NGOs act as lobbyists on specific issues, such as environmental protection or public health; others conduct international programs and activities in their chosen area of focus. Though financed by donations from governments and private citizens, NGOs' annual budgets can total hundreds of millions of dollars and their work can be quite extensive.

The Human Side of Globalization

Globalization transformed the lives of millions of people as the technological changes associated with postindustrial society (see Chapter 29) remade workplaces and lifestyles around the world. Widespread adoption of neoliberal free-trade policies and low labor costs in the developing world encouraged corporations to outsource labor-intensive manufacturing jobs to these regions. In the 1990s, China, with its low wages and rapidly growing industrial infrastructure, emerged as an economic powerhouse that supplied goods around the world—even as the West's industrial heartlands continued to decline.

The outsourcing of manufacturing jobs dramatically changed the nature of work in western Europe and North America. Fewer and fewer people worked in manufacturing, while more and more entered the service sector. The numbers varied country by country, yet across Europe the trend was clear: by 2005, only about one in three workers was still employed in the once-booming manufacturing sector.[1]

The deindustrialization of Europe established a multitiered society with winners and losers. At the top was a small, affluent group of experts, executives, and professionals—about one-quarter of the total population—who managed the new global enterprises. In the second, larger tier, the middle class struggled with stagnating incomes and a declining standard of living as once-well-paid industrial workers faced unemployment and cuts in both welfare and workplace benefits.

In the bottom tier—in some areas as much as a quarter of the population— a poorly paid underclass performed the unskilled jobs of a postindustrial economy or were chronically unemployed. In western Europe and North America, inclusion in this lowest segment of society was often linked to race, ethnicity, and a lack of educational opportunity.

Geographic contrasts further revealed the unequal aspects of globalization. Regions in Europe that had successfully shifted to a postindustrial economy enjoyed prosperity, while regions historically dependent on heavy industry lagged behind. In addition, a global north-south divide increasingly separated Europe and North America—both still affluent despite their economic problems—from the industrializing nations of Africa and Latin America. Though India, China, and other East Asian nations experienced solid growth, other industrializing nations struggled to overcome decades of underdevelopment.

The human costs of globalization resulted in new forms of global protest. Critics accused global corporations and financial groups of doing little to address problems caused by their activities, such as social inequality, pollution, and unfair labor practices. The Slow Food movement that began in Italy, for example, criti-

CHAPTER LOCATOR | How did life change in Russia and the former East Bloc countries after 1989?

964 CHAPTER 30
LIFE IN AN AGE OF GLOBALIZATION

cized American-style fast-food chains that proliferated in Europe and the world in the 1990s. Cooking with local products and traditional methods, followers argued, was healthier and kept jobs and profits in local neighborhoods.

The general tone of the antiglobalization movement was captured at the 1999 meeting of the WTO in Seattle, Washington. Tens of thousands of protesters from around the world, including environmentalists, consumer and antipoverty activists, and labor rights groups, marched in the streets and disrupted the meeting. Comparable demonstrations took place at later meetings of the WTO, the World Bank, and other supranational groups. As one angry participant put it, "The WTO seems to be on a crusade to increase private profit at the expense of all other considerations, including the well-being and quality of life of the mass of the world's people. . . . It seems to have a relentless drive to extend its power."[2]

Similar feelings inspired the Occupy movement, which began in the United States in 2011 and quickly spread to over eighty countries. Under the slogan "We are the 99 percent," thousands of people camped out in (or "occupied") public places to protest the rapidly growing social inequality that divided a tiny wealthy elite (the "1 percent") from the vast majority of ordinary people.

Life in the Digital Age

The growing sophistication of information technologies—a hallmark of the globalizing age—has had a profound and rapidly evolving effect on patterns of communications, commerce, and politics. Digitalization transformed familiar forms of communication in a few short decades. Many of these changes centered on the Internet, which began its rapid expansion around the globe in the late 1980s. In the first decade of the twenty-first century, the evolution of the cell phone into the smartphone, with its multimedia telecommunications features and more functions and power than the desktop computers of the previous decade, hastened the

How did globalization affect European life and society?

What are the main causes and effects of growing ethnic diversity in contemporary Europe?

What challenges will Europeans face in the coming decades?

☑ LearningCurve
Check what you know.

965

change. The growing popularity of Internet-based communication tools such as e-mail, text messaging, Facebook, Twitter, and other social media changed the way friends, families, and businesses kept in touch.

Entire industries were dramatically changed by the emergence of the Internet. With faster speeds and better online security came online shopping; people increasingly relied on the Internet to purchase goods, from clothes to computers to groceries. Online file sharing of books and popular music transformed the publishing and music industries, while massive online retailers undermined traditional distribution and retail systems.

The rapid growth of the Internet and social media raised complex questions related to personal privacy and politics. Governments and businesses can monitor personal Web use and use online tracking systems to amass an extraordinary amount of information on individuals and then use it to monitor political activities or target advertising. Privacy advocates worked with government regulators to shape laws that might preserve key elements of online privacy, and in general, rules were more stringent in Europe than in the United States. Conversely, citizens could use smartphones and social media sites to organize protest campaigns. Facebook and Twitter, for example, helped mobilize demonstrators in Egypt during the Arab Spring (see page 976) and allowed members of the Occupy movement to share news and shape strategy. A number of authoritarian states, from North Korea to Iran to Cuba, recognizing the disruptive powers of the Internet, strictly limited online access.

> **QUICK REVIEW**

What role did technology play in accelerating the process of globalization?

CHAPTER LOCATOR | How did life change in Russia and the former East Bloc countries after 1989?

What are the main causes and effects of growing ethnic diversity in contemporary Europe?

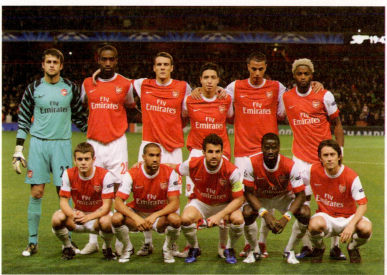

The Changing Face of London's Arsenal Football Club

Growing ethnic diversity is transforming many aspects of everyday life in contemporary Europe, including the ethnic makeup of European football (soccer) teams. In 1950, the Arsenal Football Club of northern London was composed entirely of white ethnic Britons (right). Today, its diverse roster includes players from around the globe (above). (1950 team: Bob Thomas/Hulton Archive/ Getty Images; 2010 team: AFP/Getty Images)

AS THE TWENTY-FIRST CENTURY OPENED and ongoing globalization transformed European society and politics, Europeans also saw the ethnic makeup of their communities change. On the one hand, Europe experienced a remarkable decline in birthrates that seemed to predict a shrinking and aging population in the future. On the other hand, the European Union attracted rapidly growing

How did globalization affect European life and society?

What are the main causes and effects of growing ethnic diversity in contemporary Europe?

What challenges will Europeans face in the coming decades?

☑ LearningCurve
Check what you know.

numbers of refugees and immigrants from the former Soviet Union, the Middle East, Africa, and Asia. The unexpected arrival of so many newcomers raised perplexing questions about ethnic diversity and the costs and benefits of multiculturalism.

The Prospect of Population Decline

Population is still growing rapidly in many poor countries but not in the world's industrialized nations. In 2000, families in developed countries had only 1.6 children on average; only in the United States did families have, almost exactly, the 2.1 children necessary to maintain a stable population.

If the current baby bust continues, the long-term consequences could be dramatic, though hardly predictable. At the least, Europe's population would decline and age. Social security taxes paid by the shrinking labor force would need to soar to meet the skyrocketing costs of pensions and health care for seniors—a recipe for generational conflict.

Why, in times of peace, were Europeans failing to reproduce? Research has shown that European women and men still wanted two or even three children—as their parents had wanted. But unlike their parents, young couples did not realize their ideal family size. Many women postponed the birth of their first child into their thirties in order to finish their education and establish careers. Then, finding that balancing a child and a career was more difficult than anticipated, new mothers tended to postpone and eventually forgo having a second child. In addition, European economic conditions since the mid-1970s played a role. High unemployment fell heavily on young people, especially after the recession of 2008, convincing youths to delay settling down and having children.

By 2005, some population experts believed that European women were no longer postponing having children. At the least, birthrates appeared to have stabilized. Moreover, the frightening implications of dramatic population decline had emerged as a major public issue. Opinion leaders, politicians, and the media started to press for more babies and more support for families with children.

Changing Immigration Flows

As European demographic vitality waned in the 1990s, a surge of migrants from Africa, Asia, and the former Soviet Bloc headed for western Europe. Some migrants entered the European Union legally, but increasing numbers were smuggled in. Large-scale immigration, both documented and undocumented, emerged as a critical and controversial issue.

Western Europe saw rising numbers of immigration in postcolonial population movements beginning in the 1950s, augmented by the influx of manual laborers in its boom years from about 1960 until about 1973 (see Chapter 28, page 907). A new and different surge of migration into western Europe began in the 1990s. The collapse of communism in the East Bloc and savage civil wars in Yugoslavia drove hundreds of thousands of refugees westward. Equally brutal conflicts outside Europe brought thousands more. Undocumented immigration into the European Union also exploded, rising from an estimated 50,000 people in 1993 to perhaps 500,000 a decade later, far exceeding the estimated 300,000 unauthorized foreigners entering the United States each year.

CHAPTER LOCATOR | How did life change in Russia and the former East Bloc countries after 1989?

Ethnic Diversity in Contemporary Europe

By 2010, immigration to Europe had profoundly changed the ethnic makeup of the continent. For centuries, the number of foreigners living in Europe had been relatively small. Now, permanently displaced ethnic groups, or **diasporas,** brought ethnic diversity to the continent.

> Immigrants as Percentage of National Population[3]

	1960	2006
Netherlands	1.0	10.0
Germany	1.2	12.3
France	4.7	11.0

The new immigrants were divided into two main groups. A small percentage of them were highly trained specialists who could find work in the upper ranks of education, business, and high-tech industries. The mass of immigrants, however, did not have access to high-quality education or language training, which limited their employment opportunities and made integration more difficult. They often lived in separate city districts marked by poor housing and crowded conditions, which set them apart from more established residents.

A variety of new cultural forms, ranging from sports and cuisine to music, the fine arts, and film, brought together native and foreign traditions and transformed European lifestyles. Food is a case in point. Recipes and cooks from former colonies in North Africa enlivened French cooking, while the döner kebab—the Turkish version of a gyro sandwich—became Germany's "native" fast food. Indian restaurants proliferated across Britain, and controversy raged when the British foreign minister announced in 2001 that chicken tikka masala—a spicy Indian stew— was Great Britain's new national dish.[4]

The **multiculturalism** and ethnic diversity associated with globalization have inspired numerous works in literature, film, and the fine arts. From rap to reggae, multiculturalism has also had a profound effect on popular music, a medium with a huge audience. Rai, which originated in the Bedouin culture of North Africa, exemplifies the new forms that emerged from cultural mixing. In the 1920s, rai traveled with Algerian immigrants to France. In its current form, it blends Arab and North African folk music, U.S. rap, and French and Spanish pop styles.

The growth of immigration and ethnic diversity created rich social and cultural interactions but also generated intense controversy and conflict in western Europe. The idea that cultural and ethnic diversity could be a force for vitality and creativity has run counter to deep-seated beliefs about national homogeneity. Some commentators have accused the newcomers of taking jobs from unemployed native Europeans and undermining national unity. Government welfare programs intended to support struggling immigrants have been criticized by some as a misuse of money, especially in times of economic downturn.

Immigration is a highly charged political issue. By the 1990s in France, some 70 percent of the population believed that there were "too many Arabs," and 30 percent supported right-wing politician Jean-Marie Le Pen's calls to rid France of its immigrants altogether. Le Pen's National Front and far-right political parties

How did globalization affect European life and society?

What are the main causes and effects of growing ethnic diversity in contemporary Europe?

What challenges will Europeans face in the coming decades?

☑ LearningCurve
Check what you know.

969

elsewhere, such as the Danish People's Party and Austria's Freedom Party, successfully exploited popular prejudice about what they called "foreign rabble" to make impressive gains in national elections. (See "Picturing the Past: National Front Campaign Poster," page 970.)

Europe and Its Muslim Citizens

General concerns with migration often fused with fears of Muslim migrants and Muslim residents who have grown up in Europe. Islam is now the largest minority religion in Europe. The EU's 15 to 20 million Muslims outnumber Catholics in Europe's mainly Protestant north, and they outnumber Protestants in Europe's Catholic south.[5]

Worries increased after the September 11, 2001, al-Qaeda attack on New York's World Trade Center (see page 974) and the subsequent war in Iraq. Terrorist attacks in Europe organized by Islamist extremists heightened anxieties. On a morning in March 2004 radical Moroccan Muslims living in Spain exploded bombs planted on trains bound for Madrid, killing 191 commuters and wounding 1,800 more. A year later, an attack on the London transit system carried out by British citizens of Pakistani descent killed over 50 people.

National Front Campaign Poster

This 2009 campaign poster calls on viewers to vote for the far-right French National Front in elections to the European Parliament. It portrays the familiar French image of Lady Liberty (see the image on page 591) with European Union stars circling her head. (Reuters/Handout)

> **PICTURING THE PAST**

ANALYZING THE IMAGE: How is Lady Liberty depicted? What mood is the illustrator trying to elicit in voters via this image?
CONNECTIONS: According to the National Front, which issue facing Europe today is a key contributor to Lady Liberty's distress? How effective do you think emotional appeals like this one are in garnering support for far-right parties across Europe?

CHAPTER LOCATOR | How did life change in Russia and the former East Bloc countries after 1989?

970   CHAPTER 30
LIFE IN AN AGE OF GLOBALIZATION

Terrorist Attack in Madrid In March 2004, radical Islamic terrorists set bombs on commuter trains in Madrid, killing almost two hundred people. The motivation of the perpetrators remains unclear, but the bombings were probably a response to Spanish involvement in the Iraq War. A similar bombing occurred in London the next year, exacerbating anti-Muslim feeling in Europe. (Reuters/ Pablo Torres/Guerrero/ El Pais)

The vast majority of Europe's Muslims clearly support democracy and reject violent extremism, but these spectacular attacks nonetheless sharpened the European debate on immigration. Security was not the only focus of concern; critics across the political spectrum warned that Europe's rapidly growing Muslim population posed a dire threat to the West's liberal tradition, which embraced freedom of thought; representative government; toleration; separation of church and state; and, more recently, equal rights for women and gays. Islamist extremists and radical clerics living in Europe, critics proclaimed, rejected these fundamental Western values.

Secular Europeans at times had a hard time understanding the depths of Muslim spirituality. French attempts to enforce a ban on wearing the hijab (the headscarf worn by many faithful Muslim women) in public schools expressed the tension between Western secularism and Islamic religiosity on a most personal level and evoked outrage and protests in the Muslim community. As busy

How did globalization affect European life and society?

What are the main causes and effects of growing ethnic diversity in contemporary Europe?

What challenges will Europeans face in the coming decades?

✓ LearningCurve
Check what you know.

971

INDIVIDUALS IN SOCIETY
Tariq Ramadan

Religious teacher, activist professor, and media star, Tariq Ramadan (b. 1962) is Europe's most famous Muslim intellectual. He is also a controversial figure, praised by many as a moderate bridge-builder and denounced by others as an Islamic militant in clever disguise.

Born in Switzerland of Egyptian ancestry, Ramadan is the grandson of Hassan al-Banna, the charismatic founder of the powerful Muslim Brotherhood. Al-Banna, who was assassinated in 1949, fought to reshape Arab nationalism within a framework of Islamic religious orthodoxy and anti-British terrorism. Tariq grew up in Geneva, where his father had sought refuge in 1954 after Egyptian president Gamal Abdel Nasser's anti-Islamic crackdown. He attended mainstream public schools, played soccer, and absorbed a wide-ranging Islamic heritage. For example, growing up fluent in French and Arabic, he learned English mainly from listening to Pakistani Muslims discuss issues with his father, who represented the Muslim Brotherhood and its ideology in Europe.

Ramadan studied philosophy and French literature as an undergraduate at the University of Geneva, and then earned a doctorate in Arabic and Islamic studies. Marrying a Swiss woman who converted to Islam, Ramadan moved his family to Cairo in 1991 to study Islamic law and philosophy. It proved to be a pivotal experience. Eagerly anticipating the return to his Muslim roots, Ramadan gradually realized that only in Europe did he feel truly at home. From this experience he concluded that Western Muslims should participate fully as active citizens and feel "at home" in their adopted countries. In developing this message, Ramadan left the classroom and became a publicly prominent intellectual, writing nonscholarly books and making audio recordings that sell tens of thousands of copies.

Slim and elegant in well-tailored suits and open collars, Ramadan is a brilliant speaker. His public lectures in French and English draw hundreds of Muslims and curious non-Muslims. He argues that Western Muslims have fundamental legal rights and can freely practice their religion, noting that they are often more secure than believers in the Muslim world, where governments are frequently repressive and arbitrary. According to Ramadan, Islamic teaching requires Western Muslims to obey Western laws, although in rare cases they may need to plead conscientious objection and disobey on religious grounds. Becoming full citizens and refusing to live as the foreign Other, Muslims should work with non-Muslims on matters of common concern, such as mutual respect, better schools, and economic justice.*

Ramadan is most effective with second- and third-generation Western Muslims who are also college graduates.

Tariq Ramadan. (Salvatore Di Nolfi/ Keystone)

He urges them to think for themselves and to distinguish the sacred revelation of Islam from the nonessential cultural aspects of Muslim life that their parents brought from Africa and Asia.

With growing fame has come growing controversy. In 2004, preparing to take up a professorship in the United States, he was denied an entry visa on the grounds that he had contributed to a Palestinian charity with ties to terrorists. Defenders disputed the facts and charged that his criticism of Israeli policies and the invasion of Iraq were the real reasons for the denial. Ramadan's critics also claim that he says different things to different groups: hard-edged criticism of the West found on recordings for Muslims belies the reasoned moderation of his books. Some critics argue that his recent condemnation of Western capitalism and globalization is an opportunistic attempt to win favor with European leftists and does not reflect his self-proclaimed Islamic passion for justice. Yet in 2010, the U.S. State Department lifted the ban that prevented Ramadan from entering the United States, and the scholar's reputation remains intact.[†] An innovative bridge-builder, he symbolizes the growing importance of Europe's Muslim citizens.

QUESTIONS FOR ANALYSIS

1. What is Ramadan's message to Western Muslims? How did he reach his conclusions?
2. Do you think Ramadan's ideas are realistic? Why?

*See, especially, Tariq Ramadan, *Western Muslims and the Future of Islam* (Oxford: Oxford University Press, 2004).

[†]See Ian Buruma, "Tariq Ramadan Has an Identity Issue," *New York Times Magazine*, February 4, 2007.

mosques came to outnumber dying churches in European cities, nationalist politicians exploited widespread doubts that immigrant populations from Muslim countries would ever assimilate into Western culture. Moreover, conservative intellectuals claimed, many so-called moderate Islamic teachers were really anti-Western radicals playing for time. (See "Individuals in Society: Tariq Ramadan," page 972.)

Admitting that Islamic extremism could pose a serious challenge, some observers focused instead on the problem of integration. Whereas the first generation of Muslim migrants had found jobs as unskilled workers in Europe's great postwar boom, they and their children had been hard hit after 1973 by the general economic downturn and the decline of manufacturing. Immigrants also suffered from a lack of educational opportunities. Provided for modestly by the welfare state and living in dilapidated housing projects, many second- and third-generation Muslim immigrants were outcasts in their adopted countries. To these observers, economics, inadequate job training, and discrimination had more influence on immigrant attitudes about their host communities than did religion and extremist teachings.

This argument was strengthened by widespread rioting in France in 2005 and again in 2009, which saw hundreds of Muslim youths go on a rampage. Almost always French by birth, language, and education, marauding groups labeled "Arabs" in press reports torched hundreds of automobiles night after night in Paris suburbs and other large cities. The rioters complained bitterly of high unemployment, systematic discrimination, and exclusion, and studies sparked by the rioting showed that religious ideology had almost no influence on their thinking.

QUICK REVIEW

What role has the issue of immigration played in recent European politics?

How did globalization affect European life and society?

What are the main causes and effects of growing ethnic diversity in contemporary Europe?

What challenges will Europeans face in the coming decades?

✓ LearningCurve
Check what you know.

What challenges will Europeans face in the coming decades?

Greeks Protest Against Cuts in Public Education In March 2013, teachers and students in Athens demonstrate against cuts in state support for public education, which threatened the integrity of the national school system and left many Greek schools without heat or food. Public protests against government austerity proposals set up to deal with the intractable economic crisis took place almost daily in hard-hit countries like Spain and Greece from fall 2012 to spring 2013. (Louisa Gouliamaki/Getty Images)

IN THE SECOND DECADE OF THE TWENTY-FIRST CENTURY, European societies faced a number of critical, interconnected challenges. The growing distance in international affairs between the United States and Europe revealed differences in social values and political goals, though both struggled to deal with turmoil in the Muslim world and Islamic terrorism. A persistent economic recession had a devastating impact on the lives of millions and undermined the unity of the Eurozone. Climate change and environmental degradation exposed the dangers of industrial development and the heavy dependence on fossil fuels for energy. At the same time, the relative wealth of European societies in the global context provoked serious thinking about European identity and Europe's humanitarian mission in the community of nations.

Growing Strains in U.S.-European Relations

In the fifty years after World War II, the United States and western Europe generally maintained close diplomatic relations. Though they were never in total agreement, they usually worked together to promote international consensus under

CHAPTER LOCATOR | How did life change in Russia and the former East Bloc countries after 1989?

U.S. guidance. Over time, however, the growing power of the European Union and the new unilateral thrust of Washington's foreign policy created strains in traditional transatlantic relations.

The growing gap between the United States and Europe had several causes. For one, the European Union was now the world's largest trading block, challenging the predominance of the United States. For another, under presidents George W. Bush (r. 2001–2009) and Barack Obama (r. 2009–), the United States often ignored international opinion in pursuit of its own interests. Citing the economic impact, Washington refused to ratify the Kyoto Protocol of 1997, which was intended to limit global warming and which had been agreed to by nearly two hundred countries. Nor did the United States join the International Criminal Court, a global tribunal meant to prosecute individuals accused of crimes against humanity, which nearly 140 states agreed to join.

A values gap between the United States and Europe contributed to cooler relations as well. Ever more secular Europeans had a hard time understanding the religiosity of many Americans. Relatively lax gun control laws and the use of capital punishment in the United States were viewed with dismay in Europe. Despite Obama's health-care reforms—which provoked controversy among Americans—U.S. reluctance to establish a single-payer, state-funded program surprised Europeans, who saw their own such programs as highly advantageous.

Hardball geopolitical issues relating to NATO further widened the gap. The dissolution of the Communist Warsaw Pact left NATO without its Cold War adversaries. Yet NATO continued to expand, primarily in the territories in the former East Bloc. NATO's expansion angered Russia's leaders, particularly when President Bush moved to deploy missile defense systems in Poland and the Czech Republic in 2008. Even within the alliance there were tensions. By 2009, with twenty-eight member states, it was difficult to shape unanimous support for NATO actions. As the EU expanded, some argued that Europe should determine its own military and defense policy without U.S. or NATO guidance.

American-led wars in Afghanistan and Iraq, undertaken in response to the September 11 terrorist attacks against the United States, further strained U.S.-European relations. On the morning of September 11, 2001, passenger planes hijacked by terrorists destroyed the World Trade Center towers in New York City and crashed into the Pentagon. Perpetrated by the radical Islamist group al-Qaeda, the attacks took the lives of more than three thousand people from many countries and put the personal safety of ordinary citizens at the top of the West's agenda.

Immediately after the September 11 attacks, the peoples and governments of Europe and the world joined Americans in heartfelt solidarity. Over time, however, tensions between Europe and the United States re-emerged and deepened markedly, particularly after President Bush declared a unilateral U.S. **war on terror**. The main acts in Bush's war on terror were a U.S.-led war in Afghanistan, which started in 2001, and another in Iraq, which lasted from 2003 to 2011. Both succeeded in quickly bringing down dictatorial regimes. At the same time, they fomented anti-Western sentiment in the Muslim world and failed to stop regional violence driven by ethnic and religious differences (see page 970).

The U.S. invasion of Iraq and subsequent events caused some European leaders, notably in France and Germany, to question the rationale for and indeed the very effectiveness of a "war" on terror. Military victory, even over rogue states,

war on terror
▶ American policy under President George W. Bush to fight global terrorism in all its forms.

How did globalization affect European life and society?

What are the main causes and effects of growing ethnic diversity in contemporary Europe?

What challenges will Europeans face in the coming decades?

☑ LearningCurve
Check what you know.

975

would hardly end terrorism because terrorist groups easily moved across national borders. Terrorism, they concluded, was better fought through police and intelligence measures.

American conduct of the war on terror also raised serious human rights concerns. The revelation of the harsh interrogation techniques used on prisoners held by American forces and abuse of prisoners in Iraq shocked many Europeans. U.S. willingness to engage in "extraordinary rendition"—secretly moving terrorism suspects to countries that allow coercive interrogation techniques—further caused concern.

The election of Barack Obama, America's first African American president, in 2008, and his re-election in 2012, brought improvement to U.S.-European foreign relations. Upon election, President Obama announced that he would halt deployment of missiles in central Europe and reduce nuclear arms, easing tensions with Russia. He took U.S. troops out of Iraq in 2011, promised to withdraw U.S. combat troops from Afghanistan in 2014, and quietly shelved the language of the "war on terror." In February 2013, the president's call for a free-trade agreement with the European Union, which would end tariffs and regulatory barriers to trade, raised hopes for closer economic and political cooperation in the future. Despite these changes, many Europeans continued to find U.S. willingness to undertake unilateral military action disturbing.[6] In the long run, though ties with the United States remained solid, European states increasingly responded independently to global affairs.

Turmoil in the Muslim World

Residents of North America and Europe expressed surprise and shock at the vehemence of the September 11 and other terrorist attacks, but radical Islamist hostility toward the West had a long history. Radical political Islam, a mixture of traditional religious beliefs and innovative social and political reform ideas, was at first a reaction against the foreign control and secularization represented by the mandate system established in the Middle East after World War I (see Chapter 25, page 801). Groups like the **Muslim Brotherhood**, founded in Egypt in 1928, called for national liberation from European control and a return to shari'a law (based on Muslim legal codes), and demanded land reform, extensive social welfare programs, and economic independence. By the 1960s, the Muslim Brotherhood had established chapters across the Middle East and North Africa, and a variety of other groups and leaders advocated similar ideas about the need for Islamic revival and national autonomy. The broad spectrum of Islamist ideas is difficult to summarize, but adherents tended to fall into two main groups: a moderate or centrist group that worked peacefully to reform society within existing institutions, and a much smaller, more militant radical minority willing to use violence to achieve its goals.

Decolonization and the Cold War sharpened anti-Western and particularly anti-U.S. sentiments among radical Islamists. As the western European powers loosened their ties to the Middle East, the Americans stepped in. Applying containment policy to limit the spread of communism, and eager to preserve steady supplies of oil, the United States supported secular, authoritarian regimes friendly to U.S. interests in Egypt, Saudi Arabia, Iran, and elsewhere.

Muslim Brotherhood

▶ Islamic social and political reform group founded in Egypt in 1928 that called for national liberation from European control and a return to shari'a law (based on Muslim legal codes), and demanded land reform, extensive social welfare programs, and economic independence.

U.S. policies in the Middle East at times produced "blowback," or unforeseen and unintended consequences. For example, the mujahideen, the Muslim guerrilla fighters in Afghanistan who successfully fought off the Soviet army there from 1979 to 1989 (see Chapter 29, page 938), were the recipients of substantial amounts of U.S. military aid and arms. Many of the mujahideen would go on to support the Taliban, a militant Islamist faction that came to rule Afghanistan in 1996. The Taliban established a strict Islamist state and provided a safe haven for the Saudi-born millionaire Osama bin Laden and the al-Qaeda terrorist network.

As a result of these policies, the United States, along with western Europe, became the main target for Islamist militants. During the 1990s, bin Laden and al-Qaeda mounted several terrorist attacks on U.S. installations, leading up to the horrific September 11 assault. After that attack, President Bush declared with some justification that the terrorists "hate our freedoms, our freedom of religion, our freedom of speech."[7] In public calls for jihad (or struggle) against the United States and the West, however, bin Laden offered a more pragmatic list of grievances, including U.S. support for Israel in the Israeli-Palestinian crisis, the sanctions on Iraq that followed the Persian Gulf War, and the presence of U.S. military bases in Saudi Arabia.

The Bush administration hoped that the invasions of Afghanistan and Iraq would end the terrorist attacks and bring peace and democracy to the Middle East, but both instead increased turmoil there. The military campaign in Afghanistan quickly achieved one of its goals, bringing down the Taliban, and the United States installed a friendly government. But U.S. troops failed to find bin Laden or disable al-Qaeda, and Taliban insurgents mounted a determined and lasting guerrilla war. Although U.S. commandos finally killed Osama bin Laden in Pakistan in May 2011, the apparently unwinnable war became increasingly unpopular in the United States and among NATO's European allies, and President Obama announced plans to withdraw American combat troops from Afghanistan by 2014.

With heavy fighting still under way in Afghanistan in late 2001, the Bush administration turned its attention to Saddam Hussein's Iraq, arguing that it was necessary to expand the war on terror to other hostile regimes in the Middle East. U.S. leaders effectively played on American fears of renewed terrorism and charged that Saddam Hussein was developing weapons of mass destruction. Many Americans shared the widespread doubts held by Europeans about the legality—and wisdom—of an American attack on Iraq, especially after UN inspectors found no weapons of mass destruction in the country. Though the UN failed to approve an invasion, in March 2003, the United States and Britain, with token support from a handful of other European states, invaded Iraq.

The U.S.-led invasion quickly overwhelmed the Iraqi army. Saddam's dictatorship collapsed in April, but America's subsequent efforts to establish a stable pro-American Iraq proved difficult. Poor postwar planning and management by administration officials was one factor. Another was sectarian conflict among Iraq's three largest population groups: non-Arab Kurds, Arab Sunni Muslims, and Arab Shi'ite Muslims. By 2006, deadly sectarian conflicts among these groups and against the United States and its Iraqi supporters had taken hold. Casualties in Iraq began to decline after President Bush sent additional troops to the country in 2007, and when President Obama took office in 2009, his administration moved forward with agreements to withdraw all U.S. forces in 2011. The shaky Iraqi government continues to struggle with ethnic divisions and terrorist violence, however.

Iraq, ca. 2010

Areas that are predominantly
- Sunni
- Shi'ite
- Mixed
- Kurdish

How did globalization affect European life and society?

What are the main causes and effects of growing ethnic diversity in contemporary Europe?

What challenges will Europeans face in the coming decades?

✓ LearningCurve
Check what you know.

Arab Spring

▶ A series of popular revolts in several countries in the Middle East and North Africa that sought an end to authoritarian, often Western-supported regimes.

In early 2011, an unexpected chain of events that came to be called the **Arab Spring** further destabilized the Middle East and North Africa. In a provincial town in Tunisia, a poor fruit vendor set himself on fire to protest official harassment. His death unleashed a series of spontaneous mass protests that forced Tunisia's authoritarian president to flee the country. Massive popular demonstrations in Egypt followed and forced the resignation of President Hosni Mubarak. An armed uprising in Libya, supported by NATO air strikes, brought down the dictatorial government of Muammar Gaddafi that October.

The demonstrations that opened the Arab Spring were not organized by radical Islamists but rather by young activists who sought greater political and social liberties from West-backed authoritarian regimes. This poorly organized group could hardly maintain control of the changes they unleashed, which opened power to multiple players: military leaders and old elites, liberal secularists, local chieftains representing ethnic or sectarian interests, and moderate and radical Islamists. In Egypt, for example, a democratically elected but unstable government backed by the Muslim Brotherhood was overthrown in a military coup in July 2013. In Libya on-going regional factionalism continued to undermine the ability of the new government to maintain control, and in Syria, the civil war that broke out in July 2011 dragged on into 2014 as Bashar Assad hurled his army at the rebels and Western powers disagreed about what to do. By spring 2014, the initial enthusiasm that greeted the Arab Spring was fading, and it was difficult to predict the ultimate outcome of these potentially transformative events.

The Global Recession and the Viability of the Eurozone

While chaos and change roiled the Muslim world, economic crisis sapped growth and political unity in Europe and North America. In 2008, the United States entered a deep recession caused by the burst of the housing boom, bank failures, and an overheated financial securities market. The U.S. government spent massive sums in attempts to recharge the economy and prop up failing companies and by 2014, the economy showed modest improvement. Yet as the housing market slowly recovered and unemployment slowly declined, the vast income inequality between a very wealthy and tiny elite and a far larger group of wage-earning Americans continued to trouble observers.

The recession quickly swept across Europe, where a housing bubble, high national deficits, and a weak bond market made the crisis particularly acute. In 2010, Spain, Portugal, and especially Greece were close to bankruptcy. Greek political leaders struggled to implement a painful neoliberal austerity plan—which meant raising taxes, privatizing state-owned businesses, reforming labor markets, and drastically reducing government spending on pensions and other popular social benefits. All these measures were required before Greece could receive financial aid from the IMF, the European Common Bank, and the European Union. In the summer of 2012, Greece was still flailing, prompting speculation that it might leave the Eurozone, followed, perhaps, by Portugal or even Spain and Italy.

This sudden "euro crisis" put the very existence of the Eurozone in question. Germany and France, the zone's two strongest economies, felt pressure to provide

CHAPTER LOCATOR | How did life change in Russia and the former East Bloc countries after 1989?

CHAPTER 30
978 LIFE IN AN AGE OF GLOBALIZATION

financial support to ensure the stability of far weaker countries, including Greece and Portugal, though they did so with strings attached. As with Greece, recipients were required to reduce deficits through austerity measures. Even so, the transfer of monies within the Eurozone angered the citizens of wealthier countries, who felt they were being asked to subsidize countries in financial difficulties of their own making.

If bailouts upset wealthy Europeans, deep cuts to benefits coupled with ongoing hardship from the recession infuriated the citizens of poorer countries. In Greece, unemployment hit a record 25 percent in 2012, and more than half of young adults lacked jobs.[8] As governments cut popular social programs, demonstrators took to the streets to protest declining living standards and the lack of work; in Athens, protests large and small were almost a daily occurrence in autumn 2012.

The euro crisis shook general faith in European unity, especially among conservatives. In Britain in January 2013, Conservative Party leader and prime minister David Cameron (r. 2010–) pledged to hold an "in/out" popular vote on Britain's membership in the EU within five years. On the far right, the crisis generated even stronger anti-EU sentiment and anti-immigrant extremism. By early 2014, Europe's mainstream leaders' commitment to the euro and the EU had stabilized the situation. Though weak economic growth and high unemployment remained troublesome, particularly in Greece and Spain, it appeared that the EU had overcome the worst of its economic woes and avoided political disintegration.

Dependence on Fossil Fuels

One of the most significant long-term challenges facing Europe and the world in the twenty-first century is the need for adequate energy resources. Maintaining standards of living in industrialized countries and modernizing the developing world requires extremely high levels of energy use, and current supplies are heavily dependent on fossil fuels: oil, coal, and natural gas. Scientists warned that such high levels of usage were unsustainable over the long run. Fossil fuel supplies will eventually run out, especially as the countries of the developing world—including giants such as India and China—increase their own rates of consumption.[9]

Struggles to control and profit from these shrinking resources often resulted in tense geopolitical conflicts, and military power is increasingly concentrated in oil-producing areas such as the Middle East, which holds about 65 percent of the world's oil reserves. One scholar labeled conflicts in the Persian Gulf and Central Asia "resource wars" because they are fought, in large part, to preserve the West's access to the region's energy supplies.[10]

The global struggle for ample energy has placed Russia, which in 2011 became the world's

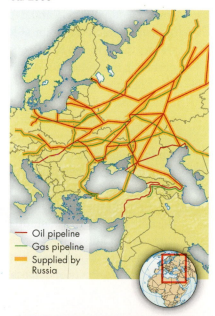

Primary Oil and Gas Pipelines to Europe, ca. 2005

— Oil pipeline
— Gas pipeline
— Supplied by Russia

How did globalization affect European life and society?

What are the main causes and effects of growing ethnic diversity in contemporary Europe?

What challenges will Europeans face in the coming decades?

☑ LearningCurve
Check what you know.

979

number-one oil producer (surpassing Saudi Arabia) and the number-two natural gas producer, in a powerful but strained position. The Russian invasions of Chechnya and Georgia were attempts to maintain political influence in these territories but also to preserve control of the region's rich energy resources.

Beyond military action, Russian leaders readily use their control over energy to assert political influence. The Russian corporation Gazprom sells Europe 28 percent of its natural gas, and the EU treads softly with Russia to maintain this supply. Russia has engaged in over fifty politically motivated disruptions of natural gas supply in the former Soviet republics, including one in January 2009 when Russia shut off supplies to Ukraine for three weeks, resulting in closed factories and no heat for hundreds of thousands of people.

Climate Change and Environmental Degradation

climate change

▶ Changes in long-standing weather patterns caused primarily by carbon dioxide emissions from the burning of fossil fuels.

Even setting aside the question of the supply of fossil fuels, their use has led to serious environmental problems. Burning oil and coal releases massive amounts of carbon dioxide (CO_2) into the atmosphere, the leading cause of **climate change**, or global warming. While the future effects of climate change are difficult to predict, climatologists generally agree that global warming is proceeding dramatically faster than previously predicted and that some climatic disruption is now unavoidable. Rising average temperatures were playing havoc with familiar weather patterns, melting glaciers and polar ice packs, and drying up freshwater resources around the world. Moreover, in the next fifty years, rising sea levels may well flood low-lying coastal areas.

Since the 1990s, the EU has spearheaded efforts to control energy consumption and contain climate change. EU leaders have imposed tight restrictions on CO_2 emissions, and Germany, the Netherlands, and Denmark have become world leaders in harnessing alternative energy sources such as solar and wind power.

Environmental degradation encompasses a number of problems beyond climate change. Overfishing and toxic waste threaten the world's oceans and freshwater lakes, which once seemed to be inexhaustible sources of food and drinking water. Deforestation, land degradation, soil erosion, and overfertilization; species extinction related to habitat loss; the accumulation of toxins in the air, land, and water; the disposal of poisonous nuclear waste—all will continue to pose serious problems in the twenty-first century.

Though North American and European governments, NGOs, and citizens have taken a number of steps to limit environmental degradation and regulate energy use, the overall effort to control energy consumption has been an especially difficult endeavor, underscoring the interconnectedness of the contemporary world. Industrializing countries such as India and China have had a difficult time balancing environmental concerns and the energy use necessary for economic growth.[11]

Can international agreements and good intentions make a difference? In December 2013, representatives of 189 nations met at the annual United Nations Climate Change Conference, in Warsaw, Poland. They set ambitious goals for the reduction of CO_2 emissions by 2020 and promised to help developing countries manage the effects of climate change. Such changes would require substantial

CHAPTER LOCATOR | How did life change in Russia and the former East Bloc countries after 1989?

980 CHAPTER 30 LIFE IN AN AGE OF GLOBALIZATION

Demonstrating for Peace Holding torches, some 3,500 people form the peace sign in Heroes Square in central Budapest, the capital of Hungary, in 2006. The rally marked the third anniversary of the U.S.-led invasion of Iraq. Millions long for peace, but history and current events suggest that bloody conflicts will continue. Yet Europeans have cause for cautious optimism: despite episodes of intense violence and suffering, since 1945 wars have been localized, cataclysmic catastrophes like World Wars I and II have been averted, and Europe has become a world leader in the push for human rights. (© Peter Kollanyi/epa/Corbis)

modifications in the planet's consumption of energy derived from fossil fuels, however, and the ultimate success of ambitious plans to limit the human impact on the environment remains uncertain.

Promoting Human Rights

Though regional differences persisted in the twenty-seven EU member states, Europeans entering the twenty-first century enjoyed some of the highest living standards in the world. The war in the former Yugoslavia as well as the memories of the horrors of World War II and the Holocaust cast in bold relief the ever-present reality of collective violence. For some Europeans, the realization that they had so much and so many others had so little kindled a desire to help. As

How did globalization affect European life and society?

What are the main causes and effects of growing ethnic diversity in contemporary Europe?

What challenges will Europeans face in the coming decades?

✓ LearningCurve
Check what you know.

981

a result, European intellectuals and opinion makers began to envision a new historic mission for Europe: the promotion of domestic peace and human rights around the world.

European leaders and humanitarians believed that more global agreements and new international institutions were needed to set moral standards and to regulate countries, leaders, armies, corporations, and individuals. In practice, this meant more curbs on the sovereign rights of the world's states, just as the states of the European Union had imposed increasingly strict standards of behavior on themselves in order to secure the rights and welfare of EU citizens.

Europeans also broadened definitions of individual rights. Having abolished the death penalty in the EU, they condemned its continued use in China, the United States, and other countries. At home, Europe expanded personal rights. The pace-setting Netherlands gave pensions and workers' rights to prostitutes and provided assisted suicide (euthanasia) for the terminally ill. By 2013, nine western European countries had legalized same-sex marriage and twelve others recognized alternative forms of civic union.

Europeans extended their broad-based concept of human rights to the world's poorer countries. Such efforts often included sharp criticism of globalization and unrestrained neoliberal capitalism. Advocating greater social equality and state-funded health care, European socialists embraced morality as a basis for the global expansion of human rights.

The record was not always perfect. Critics accused the European Union (and the United States) of selectively promoting human rights in their differential responses to the Arab Spring—the West was willing to act in some cases, as in Libya, but dragged its feet in others, as in Egypt and Syria. Attempts to extend rights to women, indigenous peoples, and immigrants remained controversial, but the general trend suggested that Europe's leaders and peoples alike took very seriously the ideals articulated in the 1948 UN Universal Declaration of Human Rights.

> **QUICK REVIEW**

What factors contributed to strains in U.S.-European relations in the decades following 1989?

CHAPTER LOCATOR | How did life change in Russia and the former East Bloc countries after 1989?

982   CHAPTER 30
LIFE IN AN AGE OF GLOBALIZATION

LOOKING BACK LOOKING AHEAD

The twenty-first century opened with changes and new challenges for the Western world. The collapse of the East Bloc brought more-representative government to central and eastern Europe but left millions struggling to adapt to a different way of life in market economies. High-tech information systems that quickened the pace of communications and the global reach of new supranational institutions made the world a smaller place, yet globalization left some struggling to maintain their livelihoods. New contacts between peoples, made possible by increased migration, revitalized European society but raised concerns about cultural differences and sometimes led to violent confrontations.

One thing is sure: despite the success of European democracy and liberalism, and despite the high living standards enjoyed by most Europeans, the challenges won't go away. The search for solutions to environmental degradation and conflicts between ethnic and religious groups, and the promotion of human rights around the globe, will clearly occupy European and world leaders for some time to come.

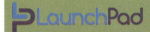

ONLINE DOCUMENT PROJECT
Contesting Globalization

What do the goals of major global organizations and antiglobal movements reveal about the experience of globalization in the twenty-first century?

Learn more about the goals of key global organizations and movements, from the World Trade Organization and its detractors to the Occupy movement. *See inside the front cover to learn more.*

| How did globalization affect European life and society? | What are the main causes and effects of growing ethnic diversity in contemporary Europe? | What challenges will Europeans face in the coming decades? | ✓ LearningCurve Check what you know. |

CHAPTER 30 STUDY GUIDE

STEP 1 GET STARTED ONLINE

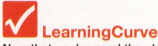 **LearningCurve**

Now that you've read the chapter, make it stick by completing the LearningCurve activity.

STEP 2 EXPLAIN WHY IT MATTERS

Put your reading into practice. Identify each term below, and then explain why it matters in Western history.

TERM	WHO OR WHAT & WHEN	WHY IT MATTERS
Ostalgie (p. 957)		
ethnic cleansing (p. 958)		
Kosovo Liberation Army (KLA) (p. 959)		
globalization (p. 960)		
European Union (EU) (p. 961)		
Maastricht Treaty (p. 961)		
World Trade Organization (WTO) (p. 963)		
nongovernmental organizations (NGOs) (p. 964)		
diasporas (p. 969)		
multiculturalism (p. 969)		
war on terror (p. 975)		
Muslim Brotherhood (p. 976)		
Arab Spring (p. 978)		
climate change (p. 980)		

STEP 3 MOVE BEYOND THE BASICS

To demonstrate a more advanced understanding, fill in the chart below with descriptions of European society, economics, politics, and culture in 1900, 1950, and 2000. What obstacles to European unity still remain?

	Society	Economics	Politics	Culture
1900				
1950				
2000				

PUT IT ALL TOGETHER

Now, take a step back and try to explain the big picture. Remember to use specific examples from the chapter in your answers.

RESHAPING RUSSIA AND THE FORMER EAST BLOC

▶ Compare and contrast the Russian/Soviet state in 1914, 1945, and 2014.

▶ How would you explain the pattern of post–Cold War development in Eastern Europe?

GLOBALIZATION AND EUROPEAN DIVERSITY

▶ How did new global connections change the economic relationship between Europe and the rest of the world?

▶ Fifty years from now, what current social and cultural conflicts and challenges do you think will remain for Europe's population?

CONFRONTING TWENTY-FIRST-CENTURY CHALLENGES

▶ What tensions and divisions within western Europe were revealed by the global recession that began in 2008?

▶ In your opinion, will the United States and the European Union move toward closer cooperation on global issues in the decades to come or will they drift further apart? Why?

MAKE CONNECTIONS

▶ What might a late nineteenth-century European find most surprising about the Europe of today? What developments might seem most unlikely from such a person's perspective?

▶ In your opinion, will western Europe be more or less unified in fifty years than it is today? Why?

> ## IN YOUR OWN WORDS

Imagine that you must give an oral report to the class answering the following question: **What opportunities and challenges are Europeans presented with at the dawn of the twenty-first century?** What would be the most important points and why?

ENDNOTES

Chapter 14

1. Thomas Benjamin, *The Atlantic World: Europeans, Africans, Indians and Their Shared History, 1400–1900* (Cambridge, U.K.: Cambridge University Press, 2009), p. 56.
2. G. V. Scammell, *The World Encompassed: The First European Maritime Empires, c. 800–1650* (Berkeley: University of California Press, 1981), pp. 101, 104.
3. Peter Hulme, *Colonial Encounters: Europe and the Native Caribbean, 1492–1797* (London: Methuen, 1986), pp. 22–31.
4. Benjamin, *The Atlantic World*, p. 141.
5. Ibid., pp. 35–59.
6. Quoted in L. B. Rout, Jr., *The African Experience in Spanish America* (New York: Cambridge University Press, 1976), p. 23.
7. Cited in Geoffrey Vaughn Scammell, *The First Imperial Age: European Overseas Expansion, c. 1400–1715* (London: Routledge, 2002), p. 432.
8. Herbert S. Klein, "Profits and the Causes of Mortality," in David Northrup, ed., *The Atlantic Slave Trade* (Lexington, Mass.: D. C. Heath and Co., 1994), p. 116.
9. Voyages: The Trans-Atlantic Slave Trade Database, http://www.slavevoyages.org/tast/assessment/estimates.faces.
10. Paul Freedman, *Images of the Medieval Peasant* (Stanford, Calif.: Stanford University Press, 1999).
11. C. Cotton, trans., *The Essays of Michel de Montaigne* (New York: A. L. Burt, 1893), pp. 207, 210.
12. Ibid., p. 523.

Chapter 15

1. H. Kamen, "The Economic and Social Consequences of the Thirty Years' War," *Past and Present* 39 (1968): 44–61.
2. John A. Lynn, "Recalculating French Army Growth," in *The Military Revolution Debate: Readings on the Military Transformation of Early Modern Europe*, ed. Clifford J. Rogers (Boulder, Colo.: Westview Press, 1995), p. 125.
3. Quoted in John A. Lynn, *Giant of the Grand Siècle: The French Army, 1610–1715* (Cambridge, U.K.: Cambridge University Press, 1997), p. 74.
4. J. H. Elliott, *Imperial Spain, 1469–1716* (New York: Mentor Books, 1963), pp. 306–308.
5. H. Rosenberg, *Bureaucracy, Aristocracy, and Autocracy: The Prussian Experience, 1660–1815* (Boston: Beacon Press, 1966), p. 40.
6. For a revisionist interpretation, see J. Wormald, "James VI and I: Two Kings or One?" *History* 62 (1983): 187–209.

Chapter 16

1. Quoted in Herbert Butterfield, *The Origins of Modern Science* (New York: Free Press, 1997), p. 47.
2. Ibid., p. 120.
3. Quoted in G. L. Mosse et al., eds., *Europe in Review* (Chicago: Rand McNally, 1964), p. 156.

Chapter 17

1. Richard J. Soderlund, "'Intended as a Terror to the Idle and Profligate': Embezzlement and the Origins of Policing in the Yorkshire Worsted Industry, c. 1750–1777," *Journal of Social History* 31 (Spring 1998): 658.
2. Jan de Vries, *The Industrious Revolution: Consumer Behavior and the Household Economy, 1650 to the Present* (Cambridge, U.K.: Cambridge University Press, 2008).
3. Jan de Vries, "The Industrial Revolution and the Industrious Revolution," *Journal of Economic History* 54, no. 2 (June 1994): 249–270; discusses the industrious revolution of the second half of the twentieth century.

4. Figures obtained from Voyages: The Trans-Atlantic Slave Trade Database, http://www.slavevoyages.org/tast/assessment/estimates .faces (accessed June 11, 2009).
5. Orlando Patterson, *Slavery and Social Death* (Cambridge, Mass.: Harvard University Press, 1982), p. 255.

Chapter 18

1. Peter Laslett, *Family Life and Illicit Love: Essays in Historical Sociology* (Cambridge, U.K.: Cambridge University Press, 1977).
2. Louis Crompton, *Homosexuality and Civilization* (Cambridge, Mass.: Belknap Press, 2003), p. 321.
3. Pier Paolo Viazzo, "Mortality, Fertility, and Family," in *Family Life in Early Modern Times, 1500–1789*, ed. David I. Kertzer and Marzio Barbagli (New Haven, Conn.: Yale University Press, 2001), p. 180.
4. Alysa Levene, "The Estimation of Mortality at the London Foundling Hospital, 1741–99," *Population Studies* 59, 1 (2005): 87–97.
5. Ibid., pp. 13, 16.
6. James Van Horn Melton, "The Theresian School Reform of 1774," in *Early Modern Europe*, ed. James B. Collins and Karen L. Taylor (Oxford, U.K.: Blackwell, 2006).
7. I. Woloch, *Eighteenth-Century Europe: Tradition and Progress, 1715–1789* (New York: W. W. Norton, 1982), pp. 220–221.
8. Neil McKendrik, John Brewer, and J. H. Plumb, *The Birth of a Consumer Society: The Commercialization of Eighteenth-Century England* (Bloomington: Indiana University Press, 1982).
9. Quoted in K. Pinson, *Pietism as a Factor in the Rise of German Nationalism* (New York: Columbia University Press, 1934), p. 13.

Chapter 19

1. Quoted in L. Gershoy, *The Era of the French Revolution, 1789–1799* (New York: Van Nostrand, 1957), p. 150.
2. T. Blanning, *The French Revolutionary Wars, 1787–1802* (London: Arnold, 1996), pp. 116–128.
3. D. Sutherland, *France, 1789–1815: Revolution and Counterrevolution* (New York: Oxford University Press, 1986), p. 420.

Chapter 20

1. N. F. R. Crafts, *British Economic Growth During the Industrial Revolution* (Oxford, U.K.: Oxford University Press, 1985), p. 32.
2. P. Bairoch, "International Industrialization Levels from 1750 to 1980," *Journal of European Economic History* 11 (Spring 1982): 269–333.
3. Quoted in E. R. Pike, *"Hard Times": Human Documents of the Industrial Revolution* (New York: Praeger, 1966), p. 109.
4. See especially J. Brenner and M. Rama, "Rethinking Women's Oppression," *New Left Review* 144 (March–April 1984): 33–71, and sources cited there.
5. Quoted in D. Geary, ed., *Labour and Socialist Movements in Europe Before 1914* (Oxford, U.K.: Berg, 1989), p. 29.

Chapter 21

1. Quoted in David Blackbourn, *The Long Nineteenth Century: A History of Germany, 1780–1918* (New York: Oxford University Press, 1998), p. 122.
2. Quoted in Frank E. Manuel and Fritzie P. Manuel, *Utopian Thought in the Western World* (Cambridge, Mass.: Harvard University Press, 1979), p. 589.
3. W. L. Langer, *Political and Social Upheaval, 1832–1852* (New York: Harper & Row, 1969), p. 361.

Chapter 22

1. S. Marcus, "Reading the Illegible," in *The Victorian City: Images and Realities*, ed. H. J. Dyos and Michael Wolff, vol. 1 (London: Routledge & Kegan Paul, 1973), p. 266.
2. J. McKay, *Tramways and Trolleys: The Rise of Urban Mass Transport in Europe* (Princeton, N.J.: Princeton University Press, 1976), p. 81.
3. See the pioneering work of J. de Vries, *The Industrious Revolution: Consumer Behavior and the Household Economy* (Cambridge, U.K.: Cambridge University Press, 2008), especially pp. 186–237.

4. Jonas Frykman and Orvar Löfgren, *Culture Builders: A Historical Anthropology of Middle-Class Life* (New Brunwick, N.J.: Rutgers University Press, 1987), p. 114.

Chapter 23

1. See Eric Hobsbawm, "Mass Producing Traditions: Europe, 1870–1914," in *The Invention of Tradition*, Eric Hobsbawm and Terrence Ranger, eds. (New York: Cambridge University Press, 1992), pp. 263–307.
2. Eduard Bernstein, *Evolutionary Socialism: A Criticism and Affirmation*, trans. Edith Harvey (New York: B. W. Huebsch, 1909), pp. x–xvi, quoted in J. H. Hexter et al., *The Traditions of the Western World* (Chicago, Ill.: Rand McNally, 1967), pp. 797–798.

Chapter 24

1. Quoted in Earl of Cromer, *Modern Egypt* (London, 1911), p. 48.
2. Quote from J. Ellis, *The Social History of the Machine Gun* (New York: Pantheon Books, 1975), pp. 86, 101. The numbers given for British casualties at the Battle of Omdurman vary; the total casualties quoted here come from an original British army report. See Lieutenant General H. M. L. Rundle, M.G., Chief of Staff, "Herewith Returns of Killed and Wounded of the Expeditionary Force at the Battle of Khartum, on September 2, 1898," Khartum, September 9, 1898, at North East Medals, http://www.britishmedals.us/kevin/other/lgomdurman.html.
3. Quoted in W. L. Langer, *The Diplomacy of Imperialism*, 2d ed. (New York: Alfred A. Knopf, 1951), p. 86.
4. A. Burton, "The White Women's Burden: British Feminists and 'The Indian Women,' 1865–1915," in *Western Women and Imperialism: Complicity and Resistance*, ed. N. Chauduri and M. Strobel (Bloomington: Indiana University Press, 1992), pp. 137–157.

Chapter 25

1. On the mood of 1914, see James Joll, *The Origins of the First World War* (New York: Longman, 1992), pp. 199–233.
2. Vejas Gabriel Liulevicius, *War Land on the Eastern Front: Culture, National Identity, and German Occupation in World War I* (New York: Cambridge University Press, 2000), pp. 54–89; quotation on p. 71.
3. Quoted in F. P. Chambers, *The War Behind the War, 1914–1918* (London: Faber & Faber, 1939), p. 168.
4. Quoted in H. Nicolson, *Peacemaking 1919* (New York: Grosset & Dunlap Universal Library, 1965), pp. 8, 31–32.

Chapter 26

1. C. E. Jeanneret-Gris (Le Corbusier), *Towards a New Architecture* (London: J. Rodker, 1931), p. 15.

Chapter 27

1. M. Burleigh and W. Wippermann, *The Racial State: Germany 1933–1945* (New York: Cambridge University Press, 1991).
2. J. Dower, *War Without Mercy: Race and Power in the Pacific War* (New York: Pantheon, 1986).

Chapter 28

1. Nikita Khrushchev, "On the Cult of Personality and Its Consequences" (1956), quoted in J. M. Brophy et al., *Perspectives from the Past* (New York: W. W. Norton, 2009), pp. 804–805.

Chapter 30

1. *Quarterly Labor Force Statistics, vol. 2004/4* (Paris: OECD Publications, 2004), p. 64.
2. Quoted in Geoffrey Lean, "Trade Wars—The Hidden Tentacles of the World's Most Secret Body," *The Independent*, July 18, 1999.
3. Mark Mazower, *Dark Continent: Europe's Twentieth Century* (New York: Vintage, 2000), p. 415; *United Nations International Migration Report 2006* (UN Department of Economic and Social Affairs), http://www.un.org/esa/populationpublications/2006_MigrationRep/report.htm.
4. L. Collingham, *Curry: A Tale of Cooks and Conquerors* (London: Oxford University Press, 2006), pp. 2, 9.

5. J. Klausen, *The Islamic Challenge: Politics and Religion in Western Europe* (New York: Oxford University Press, 2006), p. 16; Malise Ruthven, "The Big Muslim Problem!" *New York Review*, December 17, 2009, p. 62.

6. "Global Opinion of Obama Slips, International Policies Faulted," *Pew Research Global Attitudes Research Project*, June 13, 2012, http://www.pewglobal.org/2012/06/13/global-opinion-of-obama-slips-international-policies-faulted/.

7. Quoted in "Text: President Bush Addresses the Nation," September 20, 2001, *Washington Post Online*, http://www.washingtonpost.com/wpsrv/nation/specials/attacked/transcripts/bushaddress_092001.html.

8. Elena Becatoros, "Hit by Crisis, Greek Society in Free Fall," *Washington Times*, November 1, 2012, http://www.washingtontimes.com/news/2012/nov/1/hit-crisis-greek-society-free-fall/?page=all; "Eurozone Crisis—Spain in Numbers," *BBC News—Eurozone Crisis*, July 25, 2012, http://www.bbc.co.uk/news/world-europe-18338616.

9. Statistics in *BP Statistical Review of World Energy June 2012*, http://www.bp.com/statisticalreview.

10. M. T. Klare, *Resource Wars: The New Landscape of Global Conflict* (New York: Henry Holt, 2001), pp. 25–40.

11. Edward Wong, "Beijing Takes Steps to Fight Pollution as Problem Worsens," *New York Times*, January 31, 2013, p. A4.

INDEX

About the Authors

John P. McKay (Ph.D., University of California, Berkeley) is professor emeritus at the University of Illinois. He has written or edited numerous works, including the Herbert Baxter Adams Prize–winning book *Pioneers for Profit: Foreign Entrepreneurship and Russian Industrialization, 1885–1913*.

Clare Haru Crowston (Ph.D., Cornell University) teaches at the University of Illinois, where she is currently associate professor of history. She is the author of *Credit, Fashion, Sex: Economies of Regard in Old Regime France* and *Fabricating Women: The Seamstresses of Old Regime France, 1675–1791*, which won the Berkshire and Hagley Prizes. She edited two special issues of the *Journal of Women's History*, has published numerous journal articles and reviews, and is a past president of the Society for French Historical Studies.

Merry E. Wiesner-Hanks (Ph.D., University of Wisconsin–Madison) taught first at Augustana College in Illinois, and since 1985 at the University of Wisconsin–Milwaukee, where she is currently UWM Distinguished Professor in the department of history. She is the Senior Editor of the *Sixteenth Century Journal*, one of the editors of the *Journal of Global History*, and the author or editor of more than twenty books, including *The Marvelous Hairy Girls: The Gonzales Sisters and Their Worlds* and *Gender in History* (2nd ed.). She is the former Chief Reader for Advanced Placement World History.

Joe Perry (Ph.D., University of Illinois at Urbana-Champaign) is associate professor of modern German and European history at Georgia State University. He has published numerous articles and is author of *Christmas in Germany: A Cultural History*. His current research interests focus on issues of consumption, gender, and popular culture in West Germany and Western Europe after World War II.